UBIQUE.
WAR SERVICES OF ALL THE OFFICERS
OF
H. M.'S BENGAL ARMY,
EXHIBITING
THE RANK AND VARIOUS SERVICES
OF EVERY
OFFICER IN THE ARMY;
DISTINGUISHING THOSE
WHO HAVE RECEIVED MEDALS AND OTHER DISTINCTIONS
AND
WHO HAVE BEEN WOUNDED, AND IN WHAT ACTIONS,
WITH THEIR DATES OF COMMISSIONS;
AND SHOWING
THE LANGUAGES AND OTHER EXAMINATIONS THEY HAVE PASSED IN,
OR WHO HAVE BEEN MENTIONED IN DESPATCHES:
ALSO CONTAINING
THE ORDER OF THE VICTORIA CROSS, AND ROLLS OF OFFICERS
ENTITLED
TO COUNT LEAVE PASSED IN AND OUT OF INDIA AS SERVICE FOR PENSION;
ADDITIONAL SERVICE FOR LUCKNOW AND CAWNPORE;
THE ROLL OF ALL OFFICERS WHO COUNT PERIODS PASSED AT ADDISCOMBE AS SERVICE,
&c., &c., &c.

COMPILED

By CAPTAIN T. C. ANDERSON,

LATE 12TH REGIMENT, H. M.'S B. N. I., ADJUTANT GENERAL'S OFFICE, CALCUTTA;

Author of a Lecture on the Siege of Lucknow; On the Antiquity of Poetry; On the Principal Poets from Chaucer to Burns, in connection with the Italian School, from Dante to Alfieri; My Enthusiasm and other Poems; Little Fairy and other Poems; Readings in Natural History, Zoology and Instinct; The Natural and Antiquarian History and Psychological Study of Cats; Anthropophagy all the World over; Longevity all the World over, &c., &c., &c.

The Naval & Military Press Ltd

Published by

The Naval & Military Press Ltd
Unit 10 Ridgewood Industrial Park,
Uckfield, East Sussex,
TN22 5QE England

Tel: +44 (0) 1825 749494
Fax: +44 (0) 1825 765701

www.naval-military-press.com
www.nmarchive.com

In reprinting in facsimile from the original, any imperfections are inevitably reproduced and the quality may fall short of modern type and cartographic standards.

CONTENTS

Services 1-668

APPENDICES

Dates on which the Bengal Regiments were
  raised .... i-ii
The Army on the Bengal Establishment ..... iii-v
Regimental Battle Honours .... vi-xii
Roll of all Officers who have periods of Addiscombe
  Service .... xiii-xx
List of Officers attached to the Turkish
  Contingent .... xxi-xxiv
List of Officers entitled to reckon Service for
  Lucknow and Cawnpore xxv
Periods of Leave sanctioned for Wounds,
  & c .... xxvi-xxxiii
Order of the Bath .... xxxiv-xxxv
The Victoria Cross & Dates & Acts of
  Bravery .... xxxvi-xlv
Foreign Orders xlvi
Bengal Staff Corps .... xlvii-lxxiv

DEDICATION
BY
SPECIAL PERMISSION
TO
HIS EXCELLENCY
SIR HUGH ROSE, G.C.B.,

Knight of the Most Exalted Star of India, and Commander-in-Chief in India.

Sir,

In availing myself of the honor you have conferred upon me in sanctioning and accepting the dedication of my work "Ubique," I have to tender you my warmest thanks for the interest you have taken in it, which has resulted in creating a corresponding interest amongst the Officers composing that Army, whose glorious deeds during many hard fought campaigns, it has been my pleasing occupation to draw together in the more permanent shape of a single volume.

The order issued by your Excellency, calling upon Officers to send in to the office of the Adjutant-General of the Army a statement of their services, has enabled me to arrive at a much more accurate record than I could have produced had I availed myself of the only sources of information at my command. The warm interest your Excellency has evinced towards the Officers of the late Bengal Army, now amalgamated with the Forces of Her Most Gracious Majesty the Queen, led me to request you to accept of the dedication of my book, which I have now the honor of presenting to you, with the hope that any short-comings may be attributed more to the want of materials on my part than any desire to omit anything which might add to its value, either in the eyes of your Excellency, or in those of my comrades, whose services it records.

I have the honor to be,
Sir,
Your most obedient Servant,
THOMAS CARNEGY ANDERSON, *Captain,*
late 12th Regt. N. I., Adjutant General's Office.

PREFACE.

I AM aware that the Public is disinclined to read Prefaces, knowing before hand that a good book requires no introduction, whilst a bad one is put forth with verbose excuses and apologies for short-comings. I have, however, some things to explain, and having no other medium, must take advantage to say what I have, as briefly as possible, in the opening pages. I can safely assert that, although I may be blamed for short-comings in this Volume, I have striven hard to please every body; to collect accurate data, and to spare no labor in collating everything that could further the good end I had in view, *viz.*, the publication of a record of the brave and gallant deeds of the Officers of the old Bengal Army. In this Volume will be found the names of all Officers who were in the Service on the 1st of January 1861, the date on which the last number of the *Official* Army List was published in the Adjutant-General's Department. It was at this period that I had resolved on compiling "UBIQUE."

Those who may find their services unrecorded cannot blame me for the omission. I have, besides circulating over 1,200 copies of my Prospectus, advertised the work, and had it noticed in almost all the papers on this side of India, many remaining standing advertisements for several months. I have copied, or used, so far as was necessary, all the records in the Adjutant-General's Office, but so many Officers have not furnished their services, although called upon in General Orders to do so, that I have been left helpless. I have endeavored, as will be seen, to allow as many as possible to tell their own tale of duty done in their own language, and it was with the hope that all, or certainly a greater number, would have responded to my wishes, that I asked them for their own statements. It will be noticed that the records of the Officers of Artillery and Engineers are scanty; the services in one roll were prepared at Meerut and forwarded to the Adjutant-General's Office, but were despatched to the Secretary of State before I knew of their receipt, and I could procure no copy, there being non retained in Office, nor in the Secretariat Department. I have determined that, should I be sufficiently supported, to republish this Volume in England, in a more complete form, with certain illustrations, and a brief memoir, before January 1864; and I mention this here to invite co-operation on the part of those who have services to record. I trust the work will be much cheaper. I guarantee its present price shall not be exceeded, although it will, in every way, be materially improved and enlarged. There are some inaccuracies which are purely blameable to me. For them I would hope forgiveness, on the score of daily official work, and constant sickness in a very trying climate. Heart and soul I have given to my labors, and although, as I dismiss the work to those who have seconded my exertions by subscribing to it, I know I am the loser after two years' labor, I hope that as it is read, and seen by others, that all may turn out well. I had purposed writing a small introductory history, but as a writer in the *Cornhill Magazine* says of India, "there is a picture of it in every map," so may I conclude by adding, without my history, that there is in every Briton's mind a lively recollection and knowledge of what the brave Army of India is composed whenever they take up the history from Plassey to the Mutiny of 1857. Such deeds cannot die out of recollection, and require no recapitulation here. Wherever British Soldiers have trod, they have carried with them victory, and in the end have consolidated peace—a peace which speaks to us of difficulties overcome, based, not upon the strength of men only, but upon that religion which has conquered so much of the barbarous portions of the world, and been the pioneer of civilization wherever it has reached. To all those who have aided me with assistance I am deeply grateful, for one portion of my earliest longing since I entered the Service has now been fulfilled. I am equally sensible of the kindness of the Press, to which I owe more than I can express, especially so to the *Delhi Gazette*, the Editor of which has so frequently made my wants known to the Public in the columns he presides over.

T. C. ANDERSON.

January 1st, 1863.

ERRATA AND ADDENDA.

Page xvi., for 1 1 5 opposite the name of M. C. Sankey, read 1 10 2 (and vide G. G. O., p. 3 of '62).

Page xxix., in the list of H.'s insert the names of—

Hare, E., Surgeon-Major, 18

Harris, W. D., Brevet-Major, 3rd Europeans, 18

Page xxx., under the name of Mackenzie, insert that of Maclean, C. S., Lieutenant, 10th Native Infantry, 18

Page xxxii., for *Thompson, M.*, Lieutenant, 53rd Native Infantry, read *Thomson*, &c.

CASUALTIES IN THE ORDER OF THE BATH.

Sir W. Richards, Alexander Carnegy, Andrew Hervey, John Hoggan, Henry Foster, Robert Augustus Master, Sir R. C. Shakespear, Richard Baird Smith, C. Davidson, K. Young, and B. Henderson.

RETIREMENTS FROM THE STAFF CORPS, UNDER SIR CHARLES WOOD'S ORDER.

Major J. P. Briggs, Major G. B. Cookson, Captain H. A. Cockburn, Major E. S. Dennis, Sir H. Edwardes, Lieutenant C. J. Griffiths, Captain C. P. Hildebrand, Lieutenant R. S. Hill, Captain J. Keer, Major R. J. Meade, Major F. C. Maisey, Lieutenant A. B. Melville, Lieutenant H. P. Peacock, Major E. J. Simpson, Lieutenant M. G. Smith, Lieutenant W. Wroughton.

Page lxx., for *Thomson, R. L.*, read *Thompson, R. L.*

Page 6. Captain Alexander became Major, 11th December '61.

Page 8. Captain Alexander became Major in Staff Corps, 2nd March '62.

Page 11. For *Captain* H. C. Anderson, read *Brevet-Major*.

Page 19. Surgeon-Major Archer's Commission as such ante-dated to 10th February '62.

Page 20. Brevet-Captain C. Armstrong became a Brevet-Captain on the 22nd July '60.

Page 47. For *Brevet-Captain Beecher* read *Captain Becher*.

Page 70. For *Lieut.-Colonel* Boyd read *Lieut.*, &c.

Page 135. For since *resired* read *retired*.

Page 153. For *Ensign* E. R. Cox read *Lieut.*
Page 159. Captain C. Crossman (since retired).
Page 186. 4th line from bottom of 1st para., for *Takee* Forts read *Taku.*
Page 201. Captain Dunbar became Major in Staff Corps, 11th December '61. (He received a certificate of high proficiency in the Oordoo language· Has also passed an examination in Punjabee).
Page 255. Captain Godby's Ensigncy dates from 13th June '45, and his Lieutenantcy, 10th July '52. His Regiment was the 36*th* not the 35*th.*
Page 272. Add to Dr. Greenhow's services, " *and one year's extra service.*"
Page 284. After Captain W. C. Hamilton, add *P.*
Page 385. Add to Lieutenant C. S. Maclean's service, "was recommended by the late Major Shebbeare for the Victoria Cross."
Page 391. For *Captain* R. R. Mainwaring, read *Major :* date of Commission, 1st January '62.

SERVICES RECEIVED TOO LATE TO INSERT IN THE BODY OF THE BOOK.

For services of CAPTAIN W. R. E. ALEXANDER, at page 8, substitute the following :—

SERVICE.—Major W. R. E. ALEXANDER served with the Army of the Punjab in '48, '49, and present at the action of Goojerat. *Medal.* Served with the Army in Burmah, '52, '53 : present at relief of " Pegu," capture of Meaday, capture of stockade at " Thoma." *Medal.* Served with the Force under Brigadier Bird, in the Sonthal Campaign, in '55. Served again in quelling a fresh outbreak of the Sonthals in '56. Received the thanks of the Government of Bengal, Letter No. 2273, dated 23rd June '56, and the Honorable Court of Directors, *vide* their Despatch, dated 2nd January '57, No. 3 and para. 2, for services on this occasion. Served throughout the Mutiny of '57 and '58 ; escaped to Agra : present during the attack by Neemuch mutineers, on 5th July '57. Present also when Colonel Greathed's Column was attacked at Agra, on 10th October '57. Commanded the attacking party on 7th February '58, against a large force of rebels at Aununtram, in the Etawah District. Thanked by Governor-General, *vide* G. O. G. G., dated Allahabad, 21st February '58 ; by the Commander-in-Chief, *vide* Deputy Adjutant-General's letter, No. 92, dated Cawnpore, 19th February '58, published in above G. O. G. G., who requested Governor-General to take especial notice of the affair. Served with Mynpooree Moveable Column under Lieutenant-Colonel Riddell, till May '58, and afterwards employed in Etawah and Mynpooree Districts, till April '59, when ordered to Cawnpore, and from October to December '59 served with the Force under Brigadier Wheeler in Bundlecund. *Indian Mutiny Medal.* Raised and commanded " Alexander's Horse," from 19th October '57 to 19th July '60.

For CAPTAIN ALLGOOD'S services at page 9, substitute the following :—

SERVICE.—Captain ALLGOOD served during the Punjab Campaign, '48, 49: present at the 1st and 2nd sieges of Mooltan, including the attacks on the enemy's outposts, on the 9th and 12th September ; action of Sooroojkhoond, assault and capture of the city, and subsequent operations, resulting in the capitulation of the Fortress. *Medal and Clasp.* Accompanied the Mooltan Brigade as Deputy Assistant Quarter-Master-General to the North of Scinde, in '52, to coerce Meer Ali Moorad. Served during the Mutiny under Lord Clyde, as Deputy Assistant Quarter-Master-General and Officiating Assistant Quarter-Master-General. Present at the relief of Lucknow, including the storming of the Sekunder Bagh and Shah Nujeef, in

November '57. (*Horse wounded.*) Mentioned in the Despatch of His Excellency the Commander-in-Chief, and received the thanks of Government, 10th December '57. Present at the battle of Cawnpore, 6th December. Received the thanks of Government, 24th December '57. Present at the affair of Kala Nuddee, 2nd January '58 ; siege and capture of Lucknow, March '58; action of Bareilly, 5th May ; skirmish at Shahjehanpore, 19th May '58. *Medal and 2 Clasps.* Served in the Oude Campaign, '58, '59, as Officiating Assistant Quarter-Master-General. Present at the affair of Doundea Khera, 24th November ; Burjedia, 26th ; attack and capture of Fort Musjedia, 27th ; and affair on the Raptee, 31st December '58. Twice received the thanks of Government, 5th April '58 and 18th Jan. '59. Twice mentioned in the Despatches of His Excellency the Commander-in-Chief, 22nd March '58 and 7th January '59. Served during the China Campaign of '60 : present at the landing and occupation of Pehtang, 1st August ; and during the operations between the 12th and 21st, resulting in the capture of the Taku Forts ; action of Chan-kya-wan, 18th September ; Tongchow, 21st September. Advance on Pekin, 6th October, and subsequent occupation of the city. *Medal and 2 Clasps.*

CAPTAIN F. P. BAILEY, 6th Europeans.

(Page 24.)

SERVICE.—Captain F. P. BAILEY served with Generals Outram and Havelock during the Mutiny : present with the Irregulars during the defence, and after the relief by Lord Clyde, with Outram's Force at the Alum Bagh, and during the siege of Lucknow. Commanded part of Hale's Horse at Bunnee. *Medal and 2 Clasps.* Present at Busseerutgunge and Oonao.

LIEUTENANT C. F. BATTYE.

(Page 38, additional service.)

SERVICE.—Lieutenant C. F. BATTYE was present as Adjutant of the 22nd Punjab Native Infantry in the following actions against the Taipings :—Capture of stockades at Wongkadza, 4th April ; stockaded village at Chowpo, 17th April ; of stockades near Nahzeen, 29th April ; capture, by assault, of the walled town of Kading, 1st May ; of walled town of Tsingpoo, 12th May ; capture of walled and stockaded village of Nanjow, 17th May ; capture, by assault, of the walled town of Tsoling, 20th May ; repulse of attack made by the rebels on our advanced picquet at Nahzeean, 25th May '62.

LIEUTENANT W. B. BIRCH.

(Page 53) add :—

Honorably mentioned by Brigadier Staveley in his Despatches of 6th January '62.

LIEUTENANT H. C. CATTLEY.

(Page 117.)

SERVICE.—Lieutenant H. C. CATTLEY served in China. *Medal, Legion of Honor 5th Class, and V. C.* Mentioned in Despatches.

CAPTAIN W. D. COUCHMAN.

(Page 152.)

SERVICE.—Captain W. D. COUCHMAN served during the Central India Campaign, and was present at the capture of Neembherah, and during the defence of the Fort at Neemuch, besieged by the rebels. Served in the Oude Campaign of '58, '59. *Medal.* Mentioned in the Despatch of the Commander-in-Chief of Bombay.

MAJOR R. W. H. FANSHAWE.

(Page 218.)

SERVICE.—Major R. W. H. FANSHAWE served as a Volunteer with a Detachment from Agra under Major Montgomery, and defeated a large body of rebels near Agra. *Medal*, and the thanks of Government.

CAPTAIN F. C. INNES.

(Page 330.)

SERVICE.—Captain INNES served as Orderly Officer to Brigadier Showers throughout the siege of Delhi. Present at nearly all the engagements before the walls of Delhi. *Medal and Clasp.*

LIEUTENANT H. S. MARSHALL.

(Page 396.)

SERVICE.—Lieutenant H. S. MARSHALL accompanied the expedition against the rebels in the Cossyah and Jyntia Hills with a Wing of the 20th Native Infantry. Present at the capture of the stockade at Ooksal, 11th March '62.

ASSISTANT-SURGEON R. PARKER.

(Page 463.)

SERVICE.—Assistant-Surgeon PARKER served at the siege and capture of Delhi. *Medal and Clasp.*

SERVICES

OF ALL THE

OFFICERS OF THE BENGAL ARMY.

LIEUTENANT-GENERAL SIR HUGH HENRY ROSE, G.C.B., Knight of the Exalted Star of India, Colonel of the 45th (Nottinghamshire) Regiment of Foot, and Commander-in-Chief in India.

Ensign, 8 June 20—Lieut., 24 Oct. 21—Captain, 22 July 24—Major, 30 Dec. 26—Lieut.-Colonel, 17 Sept. 39—Colonel, 11 Nov. 51—Major-Genl., 12 Dec. 54—Lieut.-Genl., 28 Feb. 60—Colonel, 45th Foot, 20 July 58.

SERVICE.—General Sir HUGH ROSE, G.C.B., served the Syrian Campaign of 1840-41. *(Medal, C.B., Cross of St. John of Jerusalem of Prussia, and Sword of Honor from the Sultan.)* Served the Eastern Campaign of 1854-55 as the Queen's Commissioner at the Head Quarters of the French Army, and was wounded before Sebastopol. *(Medal and Clasps, Major-General, K.C.B., Commander of the Legion of Honor, and Third Class of the Medjidie.)* Commanded the Central India Field Force throughout the Mutiny of 1857-58, including the relief of Saugor, capture of Kotghur, Shahghur, and Chundehree, siege and capture of Jhansi and Calpee, and various other engagements, terminating in the storm and capture of Gwalior, and restoration of the Maharajah Scindia to his Capital. *(G.C.B., and promoted to Lieut.-General, " in consideration of his eminent services.")* Medal and Clasp, and subsequently Knight of the Exalted Star of India.

BENGAL ARMY.

A

MAJOR-GENERAL A. ABBOTT, C.B., Bengal Artillery.

2nd Lieut., 16 April 19—Lieut., 7 Aug. 21—Bt.-Captain, 16 April 34—Captain, 10 May 35—Bt.-Major, 4 Oct. 42—Lieut.-Colonel, 3 July 45—Colonel, Regtl., 14 Nov. 58 and 28 Nov 54—Major-Genl., 13 April 60.

SERVICE.—Major-General ABBOTT served at the siege and capture of Bhurtpore, 1825-26. *Medal*. Served in Affghanistan, 1839-40-41-42. Present at the capture of Ghuznee. Defence of Jellallabad, under Sir R. Sale *(wounded.)* Re-occupation of Cabul under Sir G. Pollock. *Medals* for Ghuznee, Jellallabad and Cabul, and C.B.

LIEUTENANT-COLONEL H. E. S. ABBOTT, P., late 73rd Native Infantry.

Ensign, 8 Dec. 31—Lieut., 23 May 36—Capt., 24 Jan. 45—Major, 11 Nov. 54—Colonel, 22 Aug. 58.

SERVICE.—Commanded 2nd Fusiliers at Delhi. *Medal and Clasp.*

COLONEL J. ABBOTT, Bengal Artillery.

2nd Lieut., 6 June 23—Lieut., 28 Sept. 27—Bt.-Captain, 6 June 38—Captain, 4 Aug. 41—Bt.-Major, 7 June 49—Major, 6 Mar. 54—Lieut.-Colonel, 4 July 57—Bt.-Colonel, 28 Nov. 57—Colonel, 18 Feb. 61.

SERVICE.—Colonel ABBOTT was present at the siege and capture of Bhurtpore, 1826. *Medal*. Served in Affghanistan in 1839.

LIEUTENANT-COLONEL P. ABBOTT, late 72nd Native Infantry.

Ensign, 23 Dec. 25—Lieut., 16 May 27—Captain, 1 Dec. 36—Bt.-Major, 9 Nov. 46—Major, 10 May 53—Bt.-Lieut.-Colonel, 20 June 54—Lieut.-Colonel, 28 Aug. 57—Bt.-Colonel, 20 June 57.

(Since dead).

(3)

ASSISTANT-SURGEON R. T. ABBOTT, M.D., Bengal Medical Establishment.

Asst.-Surgeon, 10 Dec. 56.

SERVICE.—Assistant Surgeon R. T. ABBOTT accompanied Captain Osborne, Political Agent to the Governor-General at Rewah, through Boghailcund and Bundlecund, in 1858-59. Was present in the action of Khoorree Kurarayah with a Detachment of General Whitlock's Column on the 2nd January 1859. Was present with the Column under command of Brigadier Faddy, R. A., at the attack of the rebels at Kewtee, on 5th March 1859. Received the thanks of Government and General Whitlock, Commanding Saugor Field Division.

BREVET-COLONEL S. A. ABBOTT, P., late 51st Native Infantry, H. A. D. C. to the G. G.

Ensign, 12 June 28—Lieut., 18 Feb. 38—Bt.-Captain, 12 June 43—Captain, 2 Aug. 50—Bt.-Major, 3 Aug. 50—Lieut.-Colonel, 28 Nov. 54—Colonel, 25 Jan. 61.

SERVICE.—Bt.-Colonel ABBOTT served during the Sutlej Campaign. Present at the Battles of Moodkee and Ferozeshuhur; *dangerously wounded. Medal and Clasp.*

MAJOR R. R. ADAMS, P., late 12th Native Infantry.

Ensign, 26 Sept. 40—Lieut., 16 Sept. 42—Captain, 3 Sept. 53—Major, 18 Feb. 61.

SERVICE.—Served as Interpreter to H. M.'s 50th Foot, with the Gwalior Army, 1843. Present at Punniar. *Bronze Star.* Served with the 12th Native Infantry, with the Army of the Sutlej, in 1846. Served as Brigade Major to Punjab Irregular Force, under Brigadier Chamberlain, in an expedition on the Kohat Frontier, in 1855. Present at the affair with the Raabia Khel on that occasion. Mentioned in Brigadier C.'s Despatch. Served as Staff Officer to Punjab Irregular Force, in the expedition to Mecranzaie and the Koorum Valley, from October to December 1856. Served with Nicholson's Force while operating against the Sealkote rebels, from 11th to 21st July 1857, as

(4)

Assistant Commissioner. Present at the actions of Trimmoo Ghaut on the 12th and 16th July 1857, and commanded in the latter action a Detachment of Punjab Infantry. *Medal.* Mentioned in General Nicholson's Despatch.

LIEUTENANT D. ADAMSON, late 28th Native Infantry.

Ensign, 5 Jan. 59—Lieut., 9 Nov. 60.

CAPTAIN H. C. ADLAM, P. H., 5th (late 42nd) Native Infantry.

Ensign, 13 Jan. 39—Lieut., 16 July 42—Captain, 9 Aug. 54.

SERVICE.—Served throughout the operations of the Candahar Force under General Nott, during the years 1840-42, including the advance of Ghuznee and Cabul; also the storming of Istaliff. *Medal.* Served with the Ghilzies and commanded the Escort (2 flank Companies) of the Governor-General, at the battle of Maharajpore, 29th December 1843. *Bronze Star.* Present with the 42nd at the battle of Sobraon. *Medal.*

ASSISTANT-SURGEON W. H. ADLEY,† Bengal Medical Establishment.

Asst.-Surgeon, 2 Sept. 50.

SERVICE.—Assistant-Surgeon ADLEY was present at the fight at Pung Pao, between the Garrison of Fort Shubkuddur, under Lieut.-Colonel Colin Campbell, K.C.B., May 1852. With the Force under Brigadier Boileau, in the Boorie Pass, November 1853. Present at the affairs at Michnee, under Brigadier Cotton, August and September 1854. Operations against the Bussy Khel Affreedies under Lieut.-Colonel Craigie, C.B., 1855.

MAJOR WM. AGNEW, P. H., late 29th Native Infantry.

Ensign, 11 Jan. 39—Lieut., 16 July 42—Captain, 9 March 55—Major, 18 Feb. 61.

SERVICE.—Served with his Regiment during the Punjab Campaign in 1848-49. Employed against the rebels north of Jullundur. Present at the first attack of Captain Williams on Ram Singh's position at Dullah. *Medal.* Has passed a successful examination in Assamese and Bengali.

GENERAL J. A'HMUTY, Bengal Artillery.
2nd Lieut., 7 Sept. 91—Lieut., 6 Sept. 99—Captain, 16 May 07—Major, 15 Feb. 18—Lieut.-Colonel, 14 Jan. 21—Colonel, 29 Aug. 24—Major-General, 28 June 38—Lieut.-General, 11 Nov. 51.

SERVICE.—General A'HMUTY served during Lord Lake's Campaign. Present at the battles of Delhi and Deig, and siege and capture of Bhurtpore. *Medal.*

CAPTAIN F. R. AIKMAN, V.C., P. H., late 4th Native Infantry.
Ensign, 18 Jan. 45—Lieut., 7 July 48—Captain, 26 April 58.

SERVICE.—Captain AIKMAN served during the Sutlej Campaign. Present at the battle of Sobraon. *Medal.* Served during the Punjab Campaign, 1848-49, under Brigadier-General Wheeler. Present at the siege of Delhi, 1857; and other engagements during the Mutiny. *Medal and Clasp and Victoria Cross.* (*Vide* V. C. Roll.)

SURGEON M. AINGER,† F.R.C.S., Bengal Medical Establishment.
Asst.-Surgeon, 15 May 46—Surgeon, 23 Sept. 59.

LIEUTENANT R. AISLABIE, P. H., Bengal Artillery.
Lieut., 28 Sept. 57.

LIEUTENANT W. B. AISLABIE, General List.
Ensign, 20 Dec. 59—Lieut., 1 Jan. 62.

ASSISTANT-SURGEON J. E. T. AITCHISON,† M.D., Bengal Medical Establishment.
Asst.-Surgeon, 27 Jan. 58.

SURGEON T. AITCHISON,† Bengal Medical Establishment.
Asst.-Surgeon, 26 June 47—Surgeon, 25 May 61.

SERVICE.—Surgeon AITCHISON served during the Punjab Campaign, 1848-49. Present at the siege of Mooltan, action of Sooroojkhund and battle of Goojerat. *Medal and 2 Clasps.*

CAPTAIN R. H. M. AITKEN, P., late 13th Native Infantry.

Ensign, 2 Sept. 47—Lieut., 15 Nov. 53—Captain, 18 Feb. 61.

SERVICE.—Served with the 13th Native Infantry during the Punjab Campaign in 1848-49. Present at the passage of the Chenab and battle of Goojerat, and the pursuit of the Sikhs and Affghans. *Medal and Clasp.* Served as Interpreter and Quarter Master of the 13th Native Infantry in the Sontal Campaign. Present in several petty skirmishes. Served in the 13th Native Infantry and Cawnpore Levy during the Indian Mutiny of 1857-58. Present at the Mutiny, Lucknow, 30th May; defeat of Mutineers, 31st May; action of Chinhut, 30th June; defence of Residency, from 30th June to 22nd November 1857. Present in four sorties, and commanded two. Present during the fighting at Cawnpore, from 28th November to 5th December; battle of Cawnpore, 6th December 1857. Field service in Futtehpore District during Oude Campaign of 1858. Mentioned three times in Despatches of General Inglis's G. O., 12th December 1857; and in Despatch, G. O., 22nd December 1857. Mentioned in Sortie Despatches of Major Apthorp, Major Lowe, Captain Hardinge, and Lieutenant Aitken, G. O., 28th December 1857. Mentioned in Engineering Despatch of Captain Anderson, G. O., 15th December 1857. Received the thanks of the Government, G. G. O., 8th December 1857. *Medal and Defence Clasp, and recommended for Brevet-Majority on promotion to Regimental Captain,* and one year's extra service.

CAPTAIN F. ALEXANDER, P., Bengal Artillery.

2nd Lieut., 11 Dec. 41—Lieut., 3 July 45—Captain, 8 June 56.

SERVICE.—Captain ALEXANDER served with the expedition under Sir C. Napier into Boogtie Hills, Scinde, as Adjutant, Artillery Division. Served during the Punjab Campaign, 1848-49. Present in all the siege operations before Mooltan, up to date of capture, and at the battle of Goojerat. *Medal and 2 Clasps.*

LIEUTENANT F. H. ALEXANDER,† 6th (late 43rd) Native Infantry.

Ensign, 11 Dec. 58—Lieut., 18 Sept. 60.

(7)

LIEUTENANT F. J. ALEXANDER, Invalid Establishment.
Cornet, 26 July 37—Lieut., 10 July 44—Invalided, 17 Feb. 49.

LIEUTENANT G. ALEXANDER, P. H., late 35th Native Infantry.
Ensign, 1 Jan. 52—Lieut., 30 Nov. 54.

LIEUTENANT J. ALEXANDER, Bengal Artillery.
2nd Lieut., 14 June 50—Lieut., 7 Sept. 57.

SERVICE.—Lieutenant ALEXANDER served during the defence of the Lucknow Residency from 30th June to 22nd November 1857. *Wounded in two places.* Served with Sir J. Outram's Force at the Alum Bagh. Present at the final storm and capture of Lucknow, under Lord Clyde, March 1858. *Medal and 2 Clasps.*

MAJOR-GENERAL J. ALEXANDER, C.B., Bengal Artillery.
2nd Lieut., 16 June 20—Lieut., 6 April 24—Bt.-Captain, 16 June 35—Captain, 21 Dec. 36—Bt.-Major, 23 Dec. 42—Major, 1 July 47—Bt.-Lieut.-Colonel, 30 April 44—Lieut.-Colonel, 25 Feb. 53—Bt.-Colonel, 20 June 54—Colonel, 18 Feb. 61—Major-General, 18 May 56.

SERVICE.—Major-General ALEXANDER, C.B., served at the siege and capture of Bhurtpore, 1825-26. *Medal.* Capture of Beana and Weir, 1825-26. Commanded the Artillery with the Force under Major-General Pollock, C.B., at the forcing of the Khyber Pass, 5th April 1842; action of Tazeen and capture of Cabul, 15th September 1842. *Medal* and *Brevet-Majority.* Present at the battle of Maharajpore, 1843. *Bronze Star* and *Brevet-Lieutenant-Colonel.* Served during the Sutlej Campaign. Present at the actions of Buddiwal, Alliwal and Sobraon, 1846. *Medal and Clasp and C.B.*

LIEUTENANT J. E. ALEXANDER, Bengal Artillery.
Lieut., 8 June 60.

(8)

LIEUTENANT J. H. ALEXANDER, Bengal Artillery.
Lieut., 27 Aug. 60.

CAPTAIN R. ALEXANDER,† late 2nd Bengal European Light Cavalry.
Cornet, 20 Dec. 48—Lieut., 10 Aug. 50—Captain, 23 Nov. 56.
SERVICE.—Captain ALEXANDER served at the siege and capture of Lucknow, March 1858, and during the subsequent operations in Oude. *Medal and Clasp.*

CAPTAIN W. R. E. ALEXANDER, P. H., late 53rd Native Infantry.
Ensign, 2 March 42—Lieut., 1 Oct. 43—Captain, 24 April 55.
SERVICE.—Captain ALEXANDER served during the Punjab Campaign, 1848-49. *Medal.* Served during the Burmese War. *Medal.*

LIEUTENANT W. S. ALEXANDER, Bengal Artillery.
Lieut., 27 Aug. 58.

LIEUTENANT G. B. P. ALCOCK,† late 24th Native Infantry.
Ensign, 11 Dec. 57—Lieut., 13 June 59.

CAPTAIN H. J. ALLAN,† late 9th Native Infantry.
Ensign, 19 March 45—Lieut., 15 Nov. 53—Bt.-Captain, 19 March 60.

SURGEON J. ALLAN,† F.R.C.S., Bengal Medical Establishment.
Asst.-Surgeon, 3 July 44—Surgeon, 16 Sept. 57.

CAPTAIN A. ALLEN, P. H., late 55th Native Infantry.
Ensign, 10 June 42—Lieut., 28 June 43—Captain, 15 Nov. 54.
Captain ALLEN served during the Sutlej Campaign, 1845-46. Present at the battle of Sobraon. *Medal.*

CAPTAIN A. S. ALLEN, P. C. H., late 34th Native Infantry.
Ensign, 23 Feb. 42—Lieut., 24 June 47—Bt.-Captain, 23 Feb. 57—Captain, 19 May 58.

LIEUTENANT F. ALLEN, P. H., 5th (late 42nd) Native Infantry.
Ensign, 20 Sept. 52—Lieut., 9 Aug. 54.
SERVICE.—Served throughout the Sontal Campaign under General Lloyd, 1855-56.

ASSISTANT-SURGEON F. F. ALLEN,† Bengal Medical Establishment.
Asst.-Surgeon, 20 Nov. 48.
SERVICE.—Assistant-Surgeon ALLEN served in 1851 in Medical Charge of a Field Force employed against the Hill Fort of Kureecha in Bundlecund. Served during the siege of Delhi in 1857 in Medical Charge of 4th Irregular Cavalry and in the Hospital of the 2nd Bengal Fusiliers. Present at the assault and capture of the place on the 14th September 1857. Proceeded in September 1857 in Medical Charge of 2nd Bengal Fusiliers with Brigadier Showers's Column. Present at the taking of Forts Bewaree, Kandund, and Shujjar. Served in the Oude Campaign of 1858-59 with Brigadier Barker's Column. In Medical Charge of the Sirmoor Rifle Regiment. *Medal and Clasp*.

ASSISTANT-SURGEON J. B. ALLEN,† Bengal Medical Establishment.
Asst.-Surgeon, 25 July 51.
SERVICE.—Assistant-Surgeon ALLEN served under Major Rattray, being in Medical Charge of a Detachment of Her Majesty's 84th Regiment. *India Medal*.

ASSISTANT-SURGEON W. E. ALLEN,† Bengal Medical Establishment.
Asst.-Surgeon, 10 Feb. 59.

LIEUTENANT G. ALLGOOD, P. H., late 49th Native Infantry.
Ensign, 20 Dec. 46—Lieut., 14 Sept. 58—Bt.-Captain, 20 Dec. 61.
SERVICE.—Lieutenant ALLGOOD served at the siege and capture of Mooltan under General Whish. *Medal and Clasp*. During the

Mutiny Campaign of 1857-58, and in China, 1860. 2 *Medals and Clasps.* Mentioned in Despatches.

ASSISTANT-SURGEON J. W. R. AMESBURY, Bengal Medical Establishment.

Asst.-Surgeon, 20 Jan. 51 —Bt.-Surgeon, 14 Aug. 60.

SERVICE.—Assistant-Surgeon AMESBURY served in Burmah in 1852-53. *Medal.* Commanded a Troop of 3rd Oude Irregular Cavalry in all the engagements with the rebels in and near Allahabad, from the 6th June 1857. *(Horse shot under him).* For his services was made Acting A. D. C. to General Neill, and thanked by that Officer in Garrison Orders. Raised and horsed the Volunteer Cavalry that was made over to General Havelock by General Neill, and was instrumental in saving the lives of 15 Europeans at Bawanee, on the lines of rail towards Sohunda. Served in Medical Charge of the Bengal Yeomanry Cavalry. Present at the action of the 2nd March 1858, at the attack of Belwar Fort, battle of Amorah 5th March, and action of Thelga 17th April 1858. Mentioned in Regimental Despatches. Present at the action of Amorah, 25th April 1858. Mentioned in the Despatches of Brigadier Rowcroft, 18th April 1858. Present at the capture of Fort Nuggur, and attack on the rebels at Doburcah. Thanked in Regimental Orders, 10th May 1858. *Medal.*

ASSISTANT-SURGEON S. C. AMESBURY,† Bengal Medical Establishment.

Asst.-Surgeon, 14 Jan. 55.

LIEUTENANT J. H. ANAND, P. H., Bengal Artillery.

Lieut., 27 Aug. 58.

LIEUTENANT A. C. ANDERSON, P. H., General List.

Ensign, 16 June 59—Lieut., 21 Oct. 60.

LIEUTENANT A. D. ANDERSON, Bengal Artillery.

Lieut., 8 June 60.

(11)

LIEUTENANT A. D. ANDERSON, late 61st Native Infantry.
Ensign, 4 Sept. 58—Lieut., 15 July 59.

LIEUTENANT E. A. ANDERSON, Bengal Artillery.
Lieut., 11 Dec. 58.

BREVET-CAPTAIN F. C. ANDERSON, P., late 71st Native Infantry.
Ensign, 13 Dec. 45—Lieut., 18 March 50—Bt.-Captain, 13 Dec. 61.

SERVICE.—Served with the Force under Brigadier Wheeler in the Punjab, 1848-49. *Medal.* Served during the Mutiny Campaign of 1857-58. *Medal.*

SURGEON-MAJOR F. ANDERSON,† M.D., Bengal Medical Establishment.
Asst.-Surgeon, 15 Jan. 37—Surgeon, 13 Aug. 50—Surgeon-Major, 13 Jan. 60.

SERVICE.—Surgeon-Major F. ANDERSON served during the Sutlej Campaign, 1845-46. Present at the battles of Moodkee, Ferozeshuhur, and Sobraon. *Medal and 2 Clasps.*

CAPTAIN H. C. ANDERSON, P., late 54th Native Infantry.
Ensign, 2 Sept. 42—Lieut., 7 March 47—Captain, 11 May 57—Bt.-Major, 20 July 58.

SERVICE.—Captain ANDERSON served during the Sutlej Campaign. Present at the battle of Ferozeshuhur. *Medal.* Served also during the Mutiny Campaign, 1857-58. *Medal and Brevet-Major.*

DEPUTY INSPECTOR-GENERAL OF HOSPITALS JAMES ANDERSON, M.D., Bengal Medical Establishment.
Asst.-Surgeon, 18 April 33—Surgeon, 17 April 48—Supdg.-Surgeon, 11 June 59.

SERVICE.—Dr. J. ANDERSON served in Medical Charge of the Troops n service against the Coles, 1837-38. Services noticed in Regimental

Orders of the Ramgurh Light Infantry Battalion. Served with the 36th Native Infantry, and in Medical Charge of the 5th and 10th Light Field Batteries, throughout the Punjab Campaign. Present at the battles of Ramnuggur, Sadoolapore, Chillianwallah, and Goojerat. *Medal and 2 Clasps.*

LIEUTENANT-GENERAL J. ANDERSON, late 61st Native Infantry.

Ensign, 6 Feb. 02—Lieut., 28 March 04—Captain, 1 Aug. 18—Major 14 July 25—Lieut.-Colonel, 30 June 30—Colonel, 7 June 42—Major-General, 20 June 54—Lieut.-General, 5 Dec. 55.

SERVICE.—Lieutenant-General ANDERSON was present at the storm and capture of Kaomonah, 1807, and served during the Nepal War. *Medal.*

CAPTAIN P. C. ANDERSON, P. H., Bengal Artillery.

2nd Lieut., 14 June 50—1st Lieut., 9 Dec. 50—2nd Captain, 12 Sept. 59.

SERVICE.—Captain P. C. ANDERSON served during the war in Burmah, 1852-53. Present at the operations in the vicinity, and capture of Rangoon. *Medal.*

CAPTAIN R. E. ANDERSON,† late 3rd Europeans.

Ensign, 11 June 47—Lieut., 1 Feb. 50—Captain, 1 March 61.

SERVICE.—Served throughout the Campaign in the Punjab, 1848-49. Present at the passage of the Chenab, and the actions of Chillianwallah and Goojerat. *Medal and 2 Clasps.* Served throughout the Indian Mutinies of 1857-58. Accompanied the Khakee Ressalah in every expedition, till the end of August 1857. Present with his Regiment at the battle of Agra, having joined Greathed's Column after the fall of Delhi, and served with it at Allyghur *en route* to Agra, with Colonel Cotton's Column at Futtehpore Sikree and the Agra Column towards Gwalior, June 1858. Accompanied Showers's Column, and present at the action of Dorosa (14th January 1859) against Tantia Topee; also commanded 200 men of the 3rd Europeans under Major Hennessy in the Agra District, December 1858. *Medal.*

(13)

MAJOR R. P. ANDERSON, P. C., late 25th Native Infantry.
Ensign, 28 Dec. 42—Lieut., 13th Jan. 49—Captain, 23 Nov. 56—Bt.-Major, 24 Mar. 58.

SERVICE.—Major ANDERSON served during the Punjab Campaign. Present at the actions of Ramnuggur, Sadoolapore, Chillianwallah, Goojerat, and the passage of the Chenab. *Medal and* 2 *Clasps.* Previous to the siege of Lucknow volunteered and proceeded with a party of Sikhs (under Captain Forbes) to escort European fugitives (from Seetapore in Oude) into Lucknow. Volunteered and joined a party of 200 of H. M.'s 32nd Volunteers, with two guns and Sikh Cavalry, and charged the Lucknow Police Battalion, which broke into open mutiny on the 12th June 1857. Commanded a most exposed and dangerous outpost during the entire siege of Lucknow, from the 30th June till 22nd November 1857. Worked for three-quarters of an hour under a fire of musketry and round shot (the enemy only 40 yards off), and succeeded in extricating W. Capper, Esq., of the B. C. S., who had been buried under the ruins of the verandah of the outpost. Held a sand-bag breast-work (4½ feet high), which connected his post with the Cawnpore Battery, with six men of H. M.'s 32nd Regiment, from the commencement of the siege till the arrival of the relief under Generals Outram and Havelock. The enemy had eleven guns in position, firing day and night at this outpost. The farthest of these guns was 100 yards, the nearest only 40 yards. Amongst these was a Company's 8-inch howitzer (taken at Chinhut), a 24 and an 18-pounder. At the commencement of the siege there was one 18-pounder and one 9-pounder behind this breast-work, but they had to be withdrawn, as they were completely commanded by the enemy's riflemen in the adjacent houses. On the identical spot on which this 4½ feet breastwork stood, General Outram (after the relief arrived) constructed an 18-feet thick battery, and placed in it two 18 and three 9-pounders, with two 8-inch mortars in rear of them. The men of H. M.'s 32nd were relieved regularly every week. Major Anderson was not. Proceeded as a guide and led the right assault in a sortie on the "Garden Guns," under General Sir R. Napier, 1st October 1857. Present at Cawnpore on its re-occupation. Proceeded as Commissariat Officer with the Highland Brigade under General Sir Hope Grant, in the pursuit of the Gwalior rebels and capture of their guns at Serai Ghaut. Made a forced march at night, whilst the enemy were retreating towards Bithoor and Serai Ghaut, in charge of a convoy of Commissariat stores escorted by Sikh horsemen, and brought all in safe, within the rear guard of General Hope Grant's Force, that had marched in advance, in time to issue supplies to the troops the following day. Slightly wounded in the head and face, and knocked down in the sortie on the " Garden Guns." Slightly wounded in the foot by a piece of a shell during the siege. *Medal and Clasp*, with "Defence of Lucknow." Promoted by *Brevet to Major*, for services at Lucknow. Permitted to count *one year additional* service for Lucknow. Thanked most cordially by the Commissary General of India (Colonel Ramsay) for his services in the Allahabad Commissariat for eighteen months, during the last Burmese war. Specially mentioned in the Lucknow Despatch by General Inglis, as having satisfactorily commanded a dangerous outpost during the entire siege; and the outpost is prominently mentioned as the one where a desperate attempt at escalade was repulsed. *(Vide Despatch of General Inglis.)* Thanked, with others, by the Governor-General of India and the Commander-in-Chief, for services at Lucknow, mentioned in the Despatch of General Hope Grant, when with the Highland Brigade at Serai Ghaut.

ASSISTANT-SURGEON T. ANDERSON,† M.D., Bengal Medical Establishment.

Asst.-Surgeon, 20 May 54.

CAPTAIN T. C. ANDERSON,† late 12th Native Infantry, Adjutant-General's Office.

Ensign, 27 Aug. 49—Lieut., 31 Dec. 54—Captain, 3 Oct. 58.

SERVICE.—Captain ANDERSON accompanied the Mooltan Special Field Force under Brigadier W. H. Hewitt to Subzul Kot, in Scinde, in January and February 1852, to coerce Meer Ali Moorad. Captain ANDERSON served for thirteen months prior to entering the service as a "Special Constable" during the "Chartist Riots," for which he received the thanks of the Queen.

LIEUTENANT W. C. ANDERSON, late 22nd Native Infantry.

Ensign, 13 Dec. 56—Lieut., 17 Nov. 57.

SERVICE.—Served during the Mutinies, 1857-58-59, and with Havelock's Columns in the Alum Bagh Garrison, till relieved by Lord Clyde, in November 1857. Present at the final relief of Lucknow Garrison, and at the relief of Cawnpore, and defeat of Gwalior Contingent, at the action of Kallah Nuddee, near Khoda Gunge, 1st January 1858. Did duty with the Squadron of 18th Punjab Cavalry. Present at the action of Meran Gunge, February 1858. Served throughout the siege of Lucknow with the Division under General Outram, and at the action of Koorsee, in March 1858, under General Grant. Served throughout the Rohilcund Campaign under the command of the Commander-in-Chief. Served throughout the 2nd Oude Campaign, 1858-59, with Wetherall's Column. Present at the taking of the three Oude forts with Grant's Column, at the passage of the Gogra, at Fyzabad, and defeat of the rebels. Present with the same Column in several other minor actions. Took part in the action near Chunda. Present at the action near the banks of the Raptee, when the rebels under the Nana were defeated and driven across the river into Nepal. Accompanied the 1st Punjab Cavalry with the Column under the command of Brigadier Horsford into Nepal, and present at the action of Sitka Ghaut. Left in command of a wing, 1st Punjab Cavalry, on the banks of the Raptee, and accompanied Vaughan's Rifles on several expeditions. *Medal and 2 Clasps.* Served in the China Campaign. Present in the actions of Singho 12th August 1860, Chunkee Awan 18th September, and Tonghou 21st September 1861: Occupation of Pekin, 7th October 1860. *Medal and 2 Clasps.* Mentioned by General Grant, *vide* G. O. G. G., 1st March 1861.

(16)

COLONEL R. C. ANDREE, late 69th Native Infantry.

Ensign, 5 Nov. 1800—Lieut., 10 May 02—Captain, 16 Dec. 14—Major, 1 May 24—Lieut.-Colonel, 27 Jan. 26—Colonel, 20 June 36—Major-General, 23 Nov. 41—Lieut.-General, 11 Nov. 51.

SERVICE.—Lieutenant-General ANDREE was present at the engagements of Allygurh, Coel, Chundree *(wounded)*, Peckolabad, and Deig. *Medal.*

LIEUTENANT A. ANDREW, P. H., late 27th Native Infantry.

Ensign, 4 March 58—Lieut., 21 Aug. 58.

LIEUTENANT D. C. ANDREW, General List.

Ensign, 9 Dec. 59—Lieut., 7 Mar. 60.

CAPTAIN C. ANDREWS,† late 72nd Native Infantry.

Ensign, 27 Aug. 42—Captain, 11 April 45—Lieut., 1 July 57.

SERVICE.—Served at the siege and surrender of Mooltan and action of Goojerat. *Medal and Clasp.* Served throughout the field operations in Bundlecund under Brigadier Wheeler, in 1859, with Ross's Camel Corps.

SURGEON-MAJOR C. G. ANDREWS,† Bengal Medical Establishment.

Asst.-Surgeon, 15 Sept. 38—Surgeon, 13 Jan. 60.

SERVICE.—Surgeon-Major ANDREWS served with the 67th Native Infantry throughout the war in Burmah in 1852 and 1853. Mentioned in the Despatch of Sir John Cheape, K.C.B. G. O. G. G., 25th April 1853. Was with the 1st and 2nd expeditions to Donabiew, and Field Surgeon in that under Sir John Cheape. Present with the 30th Regiment at the mutiny at Nusseerabad, in May 1857. Burmah *Medal.*

CAPTAIN J. R. B. ANDREWS, Invalid Establishment.

Ensign, 1 Jan. 26—Lieut., 18 Feb. 28—Captain, 1 Jan. 41—Invalided—2 Oct. 46.

(17)

MAJOR F. ANGELO, Invalid Establishment.
Cornet, 10 Jan. 20—Lieut., 14 Aug. 22—Captain, 6 Aug. 31—Major, 26 July 41—Invalided, 28 Sept. 51.

CAPTAIN J. A. ANGELO, P. H., Bengal Artillery.
2nd Lieut., 9 June 43—Lieut., 26 Sept. 45—Captain, 27 April 58.

SERVICE.—Captain ANGELO served during the Sutlej Campaign. Present at the battle of Sobraon. *Medal and Clasp.* Served during the Punjab Campaign, 1848-49. Present at the actions of Sadoolapore, Chillianwallah, and Goojerat. *Medal and 2 Clasps.*

LIEUTENANT J. ANGELO, P., 8th (late 59th) Native Infantry.
Ensign, 7 Feb. 50—Lieut., 8 May 53.

SERVICE.—Served as Extra A. D. C. (as a Volunteer) to Major-General Thackwell, during the Punjab Campaign of 1848-49. Present at Ramnuggur, Sadoolapore, and Chillianwallah. *Medal and Clasp.* Mentioned in Despatch for gallant conduct at Sadoolapore, the skirmish at Phalia and Chillianwallah. Served against the mutineers in 1857-58. Present at the action of Trimmoo Ghaut, in the Punjab, and Nudjufghur, near Delhi, July 1857: at the siege and assault of Delhi, September 1857, as D. A. C. G. to Punjab Moveable Column under General Nicholson. Accompanied Showers's Column in the Jhujjur and Mewat Districts in the same capacity. Present at several skirmishes on the lower bank of the Jumna, near Calpee, in April and May 1858; at the action of Ooraya Ghaut, in May 1858; and action against the rebel Feroze Shah, in December 1858. *Medal and Clasp.* Mentioned in Brigadier Herbert's Despatch in G. O. G. G., 12th January 1859.

LIEUTENANT R. F. ANGELO, P., late 41st Native Infantry.
Ensign, 4 Jan. 55—Lieut., 23 Nov. 56.

C

LIEUTENANT G. ANGUS, General List.
Ensign, 20 Oct. 59—Lieut., 1 Jan. 61.

CAPTAIN J. A. ANGUS, P. H., late 9th Native Infantry.
Ensign, 15 July 41—Lieut., 14 Dec. 44—Captain, 7 Dec. 55.

BREVET-CAPTAIN R. M. S. ANNESLEY, P., 10th (late 65th) Native Infantry.
Ensign, 9 Dec. 42—Lieut., 11 March 47—Bt.-Captain, 9 Dec. 57.

SERVICE.—Proceeded in political charge of a force against rebels under Tantia Topee, in 1858.

LIEUTENANT C. O. W. APPERLEY, General List.
Ensign, 4 Jan. 60—Lieut., 1 Jan. 62.

LIEUTENANT-COLONEL W. W. APPERLEY, late 3rd Bengal European Light Cavalry.
Cornet, 14 April 21—Lieut., 13 May 25—Bt.-Captain, 14 April 39—Captain, 1 March 43—Bt.-Major, 11 Nov. 51—Major, 28 Nov. 54—Bt.-Lieut.-Colonel, 1 May 58.

SERVICE.—Major and Brevet-Lieutenant-Colonel APPERLEY served at the siege and capture of Bhurtpore. *Medal.*

LIEUTENANT B. V. ARBUCKLE, Bengal Artillery.
Lieut., 27 Aug. 58.

SERVICE.—Lieutenant ARBUCKLE served with the force under Brigadier-General Chamberlain against the Mahsood Wuzeerees in 1860.

(19)

2ND CAPTAIN C. V. ARBUCKLE, P. H., Bengal Artillery.
2nd Lieut., 14 June 50—Lieut., 1 Feb. 57—2nd Captain, 31 May 60.
SERVICE.—Captain ARBUCKLE served during the Burmese War, 1852. During the Crimean Campaign, in 1855, as A. D. C. to Lieutenant-General Cannon, and on the Staff of H. H. Omer Pasha. Present at the siege and bombardment of Sebastopol. *Medal and Clasp.*

LIEUTENANT G. A. P. ARBUTHNOT, 4th Bengal European Cavalry.
Cornet, 25 June 58—Lieut., 24 Aug. 58.

CAPTAIN THE HON'BLE C. J. D. ARBUTHNOTT, Invalid Establishment, Commanding at Chunar.
Cornet, 29 June 44—Lieut., 20 April 49—Captain, 5 Nov. 59—Invalided, 1 Sept. 53.
SERVICE.—Captain ARBUTHNOTT served during the Sutlej Campaign, 1845-46. Present at the actions of Moodkee (*horse shot under him*), Ferozeshuhur, Alliwal, and Sobraon. *Medal and 3 Clasps.* Served during the Mutiny in Shahabad, 1858-59. Present at the affair of Karesath (*charger wounded*). Capture of Jugdespore, and pursuit of the rebels to and from the Soane. Present at the skirmishes of Mujowlee and Mukoolaon. Served under Colonel Seymour at Doomraon, who drove the last party of rebels out of the district. *Medal.* Mentioned in the Despatch of Brigadier Douglas, C.B., 27th October 1858. Brought to the notice of H. E. the Commander-in-Chief in the Despatch of Brigadier Douglas, C. B., 27th October 1858, also on the 31st October 1858. Received the thanks of the Lieutenant-Governor of Bengal, 27th October 1858. Promoted to the rank of Captain on the Invalid Establishment for "valuable active service," 5th November 1859.

SURGEON-MAJOR C. ARCHER, M.D., Bengal Medical Establishment.
Asst.-Surgeon, 10 Feb. 42—Surgeon, 24 Feb. 46—Surg -Major, 13 June 62.

CAPTAIN A. T. ARMSTRONG, P., late 72nd Native Infantry.

Ensign, 3 Jan. 45—Lieut., 20 Jan. 49—Captain, 24 Aug. 58.

SERVICE.—Captain ARMSTRONG served during the Punjab Campaign, 1848-49. Present at the siege and surrender of Mooltan, and action of Goojerat. *Medal and Clasp.*

LIEUTENANT AND BREVET-CAPTAIN C. ARMSTRONG, P., late 10th Native Infantry.

Ensign, 22 July 45—Lieut., 29 July 49—Bt.-Captain, 22 July 1861.

SERVICE.—Bt.-Captain ARMSTRONG served as a Volunteer at the attack on the Redan, 18th June 1855, in the Crimea. *Medal and Clasp.* Served with the 2nd Battalion Rifle Brigade under Major-General Wyndham at Cawnpore, 26th, 27th, 28th, 29th November 1857. *Severely wounded, right leg amputated. Medal.* (Received a 1st Class Certificate, Royal School of Musketry, Hythe.)

LIEUTENANT C. E. ARMSTRONG, P. H., Bengal Artillery.

Lieut., 26 May 58.

LIEUTENANT F. M. ARMSTRONG,† late 4th Europeans.

Ensign, 20 Jan. 51—Lieut., 23 Nov. 56.

LIEUTENANT G. C. H. ARMSTRONG, P. H., late 59th Native Infantry.

Ensign, 20 Jan. 55—Lieut., 23 July 57.

LIEUTENANT R. G. ARMSTRONG, P. H., late 27th Native Infantry.

Ensign, 14 Dec. 53—Lieut., 16 Jan. 56.

SERVICE.—Served in the Regiment of Ferozepore in June 1857, with the advanced Column under Command of the late Major Renaurd, 1st Madras Fusiliers, which advanced from Allahabad towards Cawnpore for the relief of the latter station, and was afterwards joined by the Force under Command of the late Major-General Sir Henry Havelock, K.C.B. Present at the affair of Belindah and re-capture of Futtehpore, detached from the force and employed on outpost duty between Allahabad and Cawnpore during the whole of 1857. *Medal.*

LIEUTENANT G. ATKINS,† late 21st Native Infantry.

Ensign, 20 Dec. 56—Lieut., 30 April 58.

LIEUTENANT R. ATKINS,† late 48th Native Infantry.

Ensign, 4 Feb. 58—Lieut., 7 June 58.

SERVICE.—Lieutenant ATKINS served with the Suraon Field Force under Brigadier Barclay, 1858-59. Served on the Nepaul Frontier, 1859-60.

LIEUTENANT W. ATKINS, General List.

Ensign, 4 June 60—Lieut., 1 Jan. 62.

SURGEON A. R. ATKINSON,† M.D., Bengal Medical Establishment.

Asst.-Surgeon, 11 Aug. 46—Surgeon, 1 Jan. 60.

SERVICE.—Surgeon ATKINSON served with the late 11th Light Cavalry during the siege of Mooltan. Served with H. M.'s 29th Regiment of Foot at the battle of Goojerat. Served with the 1st Punjab Cavalry at the forcing of the Kohat Pass under Sir C. Napier. *Medal and Clasp*.

LIEUTENANT-COLONEL F. D. ATKINSON, P. C., late 2nd Europeans.

2nd Lieut., 11 June 33—Lieut., 3 Oct. 40—Captain, 12 July 47—Major, 16 Dec. 59—Lieut.-Colonel in Staff Corps, 18 Feb. 61.

SERVICE.—Major ATKINSON served against the Hill Tribes in Scinde under Sir C. Napier.

SURGEON R. J. ATKINSON,† Bengal Medical Establishment

Asst.-Surgeon, 24 Jan. 45—Surgeon, 2 Sept. 58.

CAPTAIN E. ATLAY, P. H., Bengal Artillery.

2nd Lieut., 30 Jan. 42—Lieut., 3 July 45—Bt.-Captain, 30 Jan. 57—Captain, 30 May 57.

SERVICE.—Captain ATLAY served during the Punjab Campaign. Present at the actions of Moodkee, Ferozeshuhur *(wounded,)* and Sobraon. *Medal and 2 Clasps.* Accompanied the expedition to Kangra, 1846. Served during the Punjab Campaign, 1848-49, under Brigadier-General Wheeler. *Medal.*

CAPTAIN W. W. AUBERT, P. H., Invalid Establishment.

Ensign, 28 July 39—Lieut., 13 Oct. 41—Captain, 29 June 53—Invalided, 11 Dec. 57.

SERVICE.—Captain AUBERT served during the Sutlej Campaign. Present at the battle of Sobraon. *(Slightly wounded.)* *Medal.*

CAPTAIN J. R. AULDJO,† late 36th Native Infantry.

Ensign, 28 Feb. 44—Lieut., 22 June 47—Bt.-Captain, 28 Feb. 59— Captain, 25 Sept. 60.

SERVICE—Lieutenant AULDJO served during the Sutlej Campaign, 1845-46. Present at the battle of Alliwal. *Medal.* Served during the Punjab Campaign, 1848-49. Present at the affair of Ramnuggur and battles of Sadoolapore, Chillianwallah, and Goojerat. *Medal and 2 Clasps.*

BREVET-MAJOR A. G. AUSTEN,† Bengal Artillery.

2nd Lieut., 11 June 41—Lieut., 2 Feb. 44—Captain, 31 July 54— Bt.-Major, 20 July 58.

SERVICE.—Major AUSTEN served during the Sutlej Campaign. Present at the battles of Ferozeshuhur, Alliwal, and Sobraon. *Medal and 2 Clasps.* Served the Mutiny Campaign. *Medal. Brevet-Major.*

(23)

B

CAPTAIN H. P. BABBAGE, P. C., late 55th Native Infantry.

Ensign, 10 June 43—Lieut., 28 Jan. 46—Bt.-Captain, 10 June 58.

SERVICE.—Captain BABBAGE served with the Army of the Sutlej in 1846, commanded a detachment of the 1st Assam Light Infantry, employed in February 1848 against the Hill Tribe of " Abors." *(Passed examination in Bengalee.)*

LIEUTENANT C. W. BABBINGTON, General List.

Ensign, 4 May 60—Lieut., 1 Jan. 62.

MAJOR B. E. BACON, P., late 50th Native Infantry.

Ensign, 22 June 38—Lieut., 16 July 42—Bt.-Captain, 22 June 53—Captain, 9 Aug. 54—Major in Staff Corps, 18 Feb. 61.

SERVICE.—Captain BACON served at the battle of Punniar. *Bronze Star.* Served throughout the Punjab Campaign. Present at the battles of Sadoolapore, Chillianwallah, and Goojerat. *Medal.*

CAPTAIN C. B. G. BACON, P., late 3rd Europeans.

Ensign, 24 May 41—Lieut., 24 May 43—Bt.-Captain, 24 May 56—Captain, 1 June 56.

SERVICE.—Captain BACON served during the Mutinies till March 1858, and was present at the actions near Agra against the Neemuch mutineers on 5th July 1857, against the Mhow and Indore Insurgents 10th October 1857, and in the engagement at Maun Singh's Garden near Allygurh 24th August 1857. *Medal.*

CAPTAIN F. K. BACON, late 22nd Native Infantry.

Ensign, 19 March 45—Lieut., 29 July 53—Bt.-Captain, 19 March 60—Captain, 1 Jan. 62.

SERVICE.—Captain BACON served throughout the Punjab Campaign, 1848-49. *Medal.*

LIEUTENANT W. F. BADGLEY, P. H., late 20th Native Infantry.

Ensign, 4 April 57—Lieut., 18 May 58.

SERVICE.—Lieutenant BADGLEY served with H. M.'s 88th Regiment at the siege and relief of Cawnpore, December 1857; and in the Central India Field Force under Sir Hugh Rose, K.C.B. Served with H. M.'s 53rd during the operations in Oude, from April to November 1858. Served with the Oude Military Police on the Nepaul Frontier in June and July 1859. *Medal and Clasp.*

LIEUTENANT A. H. BAGGE, Bengal Engineers.

Lieut., 27 Aug. 58.

LIEUTENANT I. BAGGS, Veteran Establishment.

Lieut., 2 Feb. 52.

CAPTAIN AND BREVET-MAJOR A. BAGOT, P. H., late 15th Native Infantry.

Ensign, 18 Sept. 40—Lieut., 16 July 42—Captain, 23 July 54—Major, 24 July 54.

SERVICE.—Brevet-Major BAGOT served as A. D. C. to the Commander-in-Chief at the battle of Maharajpore. *Bronze Star.* Served throughout the Sutlej Campaign. Present at the actions of Moodkee, Ferozeshuhur, and Sobraon. *Medal and 2 Clasps.* Served during the Punjab Campaign, 1848-49. Present at the Passage of the Chenab, and battles of Chillianwallah and Goojerat. *Medal and 2 Clasps.*

LIEUTENANT J. S. BAGSHAW, late 5th Europeans.

Ensign, 4 Dec. 57—Lieut., 1 April 59.

SERVICE.—Lieutenant BAGSHAW served with the Army of Lucknow 1858. Present at the storm and capture of the City with H. M.'s 53rd Regiment, and throughout the subsequent operations in Oude. *Medal and Clasp.*

CAPTAIN F. P. BAILEY, P. H., late 6th Europeans.

Ensign, 9 Feb. 44—Lieut., 16 May 49—Captain, 23 Nov. 56.

(25)

2ND CAPTAIN G. BAILLIE, P. H., Invalid Establishment.

2nd Lieut., 14 June 45—Lieut., 5 May 49—2nd Captain, 27 Aug. 58.

SERVICE.—Captain BAILLIE served with the expedition to Kangra, 1846, under Brigadier Wheeler, C.B. *Medal.*

ASSISTANT-SURGEON G. O. BAILLIE,† M.D., Bengal Medical Establishment.

Asst.-Surg., 14 May 53.

SERVICE.—Assistant-Surgeon BAILLIE served in Burmah in 1853-54, also during the operations in 1854 in the Tharawaddy District, against the Rebel Chief Moung Goung Gyee, and in Medical Charge of the Field Force under command of Major Phillpott.

SURGEON H. BAILLIE,† F.R.C.S., Bengal Medical Establishment.

Asst.-Surg., 20 April 46—Surgeon, 2 Aug. 59.

CAPTAIN J. BAILLIE, P., late 26th Native Infantry.

Ensign, 25 Feb. 43—Lieut., 1 Dec. 46—Bt.-Captain, 25 Feb. 58—Captain, 11 Aug. 58.

SERVICE.—Captain BAILLIE served throughout the Sutlej Campaign 1845-46. Present at the actions of Moodkee, Ferozeshuhur, and Sobraon. *Medal and Clasp.*

LIEUTENANT J. C. P. BAILLIE, P., late 35th Native Infantry.

Ensign, 20 Dec. 52—Lieut., 23 Nov. 56.

SERVICE.—Lieutenant BAILLIE served throughout the Campaign 1857-58-59. Orderly Officer to Brigadier General Nicholson in the engagement with the Sealkote Mutineers at Trimmoo Ghaut, near Goordaspore, 12th July 1857. Served with Brigadier Seaton's Column at the action of Ghungeree, Puttialee, and re-occupation of Mynpoorie, December 1857. At Kankur, Rohilcund border, April 1858. With the Soraon Field Force at taking of Forts Dehain and Tirrowl, July 1858. With Brigadier Kelly's Force during the operations in the Terai. Present at the actions of Ruthunpore, 25th March 1859. In the attack on the rebel's position, Lower Nepaul Range, 28th March 1859. *(Wounded severely.)* Trimmoo Ghaut, 12th July 1857. Wounded severely with Brigadier Kelly's Force, Nepaul Frontier. *Medal.* Mentioned in Despatch of Brigadier Kelly, Commanding Field Force, Nepaul Frontier, 1859. *(Passed examination in Punjabee.)*

ASSISTANT-SURGEON N. B. BAILLIE, Bengal Medical Establishment.

Asst.-Surg., 8 April 56.

SERVICE.—Assistant-Surgeon BAILLIE served with the Bengal Foot Artillery at the siege and occupation of Delhi from August to September 1857. Served throughout the Campaign of Rohilcund and Oude in charge of Cureton's Mooltanee Cavalry. Present at the actions of Bhogwalla on 17th April 1858, Nungena on 21st April, Moradabad 26th April, Bareilly 6th May, Shahjehanpore 11th May, Mahumdee 25th May, Bunnai 28th May, Bunkagaon 8th October, Pusgaon 19th October, Russoolpore 25th October, Mehtowlee 9th November, and Biswa 1st December 1858. *Medal and Clasp.*

CAPTAIN C. BAILY, P. H., late 17th Native Infantry.

Ensign, 14 June 45—Lieut., 15 Nov. 53—Bt.-Captain, 14 June 60.

SERVICE.—Captain BAILY served with the Army of the Sutlej in 1846. Served with the 19th Punjab Infantry in the late expedition to China, 1860. *Medal.*

LIEUTENANT F. T. BAINBRIDGE, P. H., late 64th Native Infantry.

Ensign, 20 Jan. 52—Lieut., 23 Nov. 56.

SERVICE.—Lieutenant BAINBRIDGE served with the 88th Connaught Rangers in the Allahabad and Cawnpore Districts, November and December 1857. Served with the 3rd Battalion Rifle Brigade as Interpreter in Oude, 1858. Present at the siege and capture of Lucknow, 16th March 1858. *Medal and Clasp.* Served with the 3rd Sikh Infantry from May 1859, on the Goruckpore and Nepaul Frontiers up to the end of 1859, and final dispersion of the rebels in the Nepaul Terai.

(27)

CAPTAIN A. F. BAIRD, P., late 18th Native Infantry.
Ensign, 17 Feb. 41—Lieut., 1 Mar. 46—Captain, 15 Jan. 55.

MAJOR F. M. BAKER, P. H., late 65th Native Infantry.
Ensign, 6 July 36—Lieut., 14 April 39—Captain, 11 March 47—Major, 15 July 57.

LIEUTENANT G. A. A. BAKER,† late 60th Native Infantry.
Ensign, 8 June 54—Lieut., 24 Jan. 57.

SERVICE.—Lieutenant BAKER took part in the Campaign of 1857 and 1858. Accompanied a detachment 2nd Bengal Fusiliers in pursuit of the Jullundur Mutineers along the foot of the Hills in June. Rode with Mr. Forsyth, C.S., Deputy Commissioner at Umballah, 30 miles, to head the mutineers and save a district tehseel, in which was a large amount of treasure. Succeeded and gave such information to the troops on the River Jumna, as caused the effectual guarding of the fords and the dispersion of the rebels. At the siege and assault of Delhi, September 14th 1857. Present in Command of a Troop of Hodson's Horse, at Humayoon's Tomb, when Major Hodson was endeavoring to capture the King of Delhi. Received command of a squadron, was the first to receive the King, and held the rear until Major Hodson had safely conveyed his prisoner into Delhi. With a squadron of Hodson's Horse under Lieutenant Hugh Gough, formed part of a pursuing Column under Brigadier Greathed. Present at the actions of Boolundshuhur, September 28th; Allyghur, October 6th; and pursuit at Akarabad, October 7th 1857. Detached from the Column with a troop to hold Allyghur, in conjunction with two companies under Lieutenant Sheriff. Joined the Agra Garrison, and in Command of Agra Volunteer Cavalry, a Convalescent Division of 9th Lancers, and troop of Hodson's Horse. Served with Brigadier Cotton and Colonel Riddell's Columns. Present at the taking of Futtehpore-Seekree, October 28th. Joined Sir Thomas Seaton's Column, and Head Quarters of his Regiment at Allyghur, December 11th 1857. Present at the actions of Gungeree, Puttialee, and Mynpoorie, December 1857. Joined the Army under the Commander-in-Chief at Futtehghur. Was detached to meet and take Command of the Agra Convoy of ladies and invalids and escort to Cawnpore. On detached duty at Radun Ghat on the Ganges, guarding 20 miles of river bank, and watching the Nana. Joined his Regiment at the "Alum Bagh" before Lucknow on the 24th February 1858. Was present at the action of Jellallabad, February 25th, under Sir James Outram at the final siege of Lucknow. Accompanied the 2nd Brigade Cavalry under Brigadier Campbell in its march round Lucknow. Present at the affair with fanatics near Moosa Bagh: reins severed. Honorably mentioned by Brigadier Hagart, H. M.'s 7th Hussars. With the Column under Sir Hope Grant in Oude District, from June 12th to August 18th 1858. Present at the action of Nawabgunge. Honorably mentioned by Colonel Daly and Sir Hope Grant in his Despatch. *Medal and 2 Clasps.* Volunteered for, and served during the China Campaign in 1860. Present at the descent on Pehtang, August 1st; action of Sinho, August 12th; capture of the Taku Forts, August 21st, with the advance on Pekin. Present at the actions of Hoosug-Woo, September 18th, and Chunkiehwan, September 21st (*wounded and charger wounded.*) Mentioned in Lieutenant Randall's Despatch on both occasions. *Medal and Clasp.*

LIEUTENANT T. N. BAKER,† late 31st Native Infantry.

Ensign, 20 Sept. 49—Lieut., 23 Nov. 56.

SERVICE.—Lieutenant BAKER served during the Sonthal Campaign in 1855.

COLONEL W. E. BAKER, Bengal Engineers.

2nd Lieut., 15 Dec. 26—Lieut., 28 Sept. 27—Captain, 31 March 40—Bt.-Major, 19 June 46—Major, 15 Jan. 51—Bt.-Lieut.-Colonel, 20 June 54—Lieut.-Colonel, 21 Aug. 54—Colonel, 10 March 57.

SERVICE.—Colonel BAKER served during the Sutlej Campaign, 1845-46. Present at the action of Sobraon. *Medal;* and promoted to the rank of Brevet-Major.

CAPTAIN W. J. BAKER, P., late 60th Native Infantry.

Ensign, 10 June 42—Lieut., 24 Nov. 45—Captain, 24 Jan. 57.

(29)

CAPTAIN G. V. BALDERSTON,† late 23rd Native Infantry.

Ensign, 21 April 44—Lieut., 6 March 53—Bt.-Captain, 21 April 59—Captain, 7 July 61.

SERVICE.—Captain BALDERSTON served with the Force employed against the Afreedees in the Kohat Pass, February 1850.

INSPECTOR-GENERAL OF HOSPITALS JOHN BALDOUR,† Bengal Medical Establishment.

Asst.-Surgeon, 18 Dec. 36—Surgeon, 15 May 50—Surgeon-Major, 13 Jan. 60.

SERVICE.—Proceeded with the 67th Native Infantry from Kyook Phyoo to Rangoon in May 1852, and continued with the Regiment till appointed Field Surgeon, 8th September 1852. Present at the relief of Pegu in December 1852. Name mentioned in Despatches by General Godwin, in G. O. C. C., 18th January 1853. *Medal.*

LIEUTENANT J. H. BALDWIN, late 68th Native Infantry.

Ensign, 20 Dec. 38—Lieut., 3 Sept. 59.

CAPTAIN P. BALDWIN, P. C., late 2nd Bengal Fusiliers.

2nd Lieut., 10 July 43—Lieut., 8 Jan. 47—Captain, 1 May 58.

SERVICE.—Captain BALDWIN served with the Force under Sir Charles Napier against the Hill Tribes in Upper Scinde, 1845. Served in the Punjab Campaign in 1848-49. Present at the action of Ramnuggur and battles of Chillianwallah and Goojerat. *Medal and 2 Clasps.* Accompanied as Deputy Commissioner of Jubbulpore several parties of Troops sent out against the mutineers of the 52nd Native Infantry and rebels during 1857. Mentioned in the Despatch of Colonel Miller, 10th July 1858. *Medal.* Accompanied the Force under General Mitchell from 6th to 20th November as Deputy Commissioner of Baitool, in pursuit of Tantia Topee.

BREVET-MAJOR J. H. BALMAIN,† late 4th Bengal European Cavalry.

Cornet, 21 April 42—Lieut., 16 Oct. 46—Captain, 9 Oct. 56—Brevet-Major, 20 July 58.

SERVICE.—Brevet-Major BALMAIN served with the Army in Scinde, 1843. *Medal.* Sutlej Campaign 1846. With a Force against the Jâts, in the Googaira District, in 1857. With the Column under Brigadier Franks in Oude, and at the siege and capture of Lucknow, by Lord Clyde, March 1858. Served in the Rohilcund Campaign 1858. With the Soraon Field Force under Brigadier Berkley. Present at the capture of the Forts of Dugshai, Turoul, and Bhyspore 1858. Present at the action of Bareilly, 5th May 1858. *Medal and Clasp.* Promoted to the rank of Brevet-Major for services in the Mutiny 1858.

CAPTAIN A. H. BAMFIELD, P. H., late 56th Native Infantry.

Ensign, 9 June 48—Lieut., 1 Oct. 50—Captain, 27 June 57.

SERVICE.—Captain BAMFIELD served with the Army of the Punjab in 1848-49. Present at the actions of Chillianwallah and Goojerat, and subsequent pursuit of the Sikhs and Affghans to Peshawur by the Force under Major-General Sir W. Gilbert. *Medal and 2 Clasps.* Accompanied an Expeditionary Force, which proceeded from Rawul Pindee in September 1853, against the Boree Khel Tribe, in the Kohat Hills, under Command of Colonel S. B. Boileau, 22nd Foot.

ASSISTANT-SURGEON R. BANBURY,† Bengal Medical Establishment.

Asst.-Surgeon, 4 Aug. 57.

SERVICE.—Assistant-Surgeon BANBURY served with the Turkish Contingent Force in Turkey, in the Crimea, from its formation to its disbandment in 1855-56. Served with Detachment I. N. Brigade in the Shahabad district in 1858. Appointed to the Medical Charge of Field Hospital at Sasseram, December 12th 1858. Served with the Regiment of Loodianah, 16th N. I. In China, 1860-61. *Turkish Medal—Mutiny Medal.*

(31)

SURGEON G. BANISTER, F.R.C.S., Bengal Medical Establishment.

Asst.-Surgeon, 12 Jan. 45—Surgeon, 16 Jan. 58.

SERVICE.—Surgeon BANISTER served with the 18th Native Infantry throughout the Mutiny, from May 1857 to July 1859. Present during the siege and capture of Delhi, and the operations of Rewaree, Jujjur, and Kanound, with the Force under Brigadier Showers, and subsequently during the subjection of the Mewattees, and final Campaign in Oude, ending in the action and capture of guns at Sonai Ghaut on the Raptee. *Medal and Clasp.*

CAPTAIN R. T. H. BARBER, P. H., 9th Native Infantry.

Ensign, 18 Jan. 45—Lieut., 30 April 48—Captain, 31 Dec. 55.

SERVICE.—Captain BARBER served with the Army of the Sutlej in 1846. Present at the action of Sobraon. Wounded slightly. (*Contusion*). *Medal and Clasp.* Served in the Sonthal Campaign.

BREVET-MAJOR C. H. BARCHARD, C.B., P. H., late 20th Native Infantry.

Ensign, 12 Jan. 45—Lieut., 3 Sept. 49—Captain, 10 May 57—Major, 19 Jan. 58.

SERVICE.—Brevet-Major BARCHARD served during the Punjab Campaign 1848-49. Present at the actions of Chillianwallah and Goojerat. *Medal and Clasp.* Present at the operations in the Boori Pass, under Brigadier Boileau, in 1853. Operations against the Bussy Khel Afreedees, under Lieutenant-Colonel Craigie, C.B., March 1855. Served on Sir A. Wilson's Staff from May 1857 till March 1858. Present at the actions with the insurgents on the Hindun, 30th and 31st May 1858. Badle-ke-serai, 8th June 1859. Served throughout the siege, assault, and capture of Delhi, from June to September 1857. Present at the operations and capture of Lucknow, March 1858. *Medal and 2 Clasps. Brevet-Major and C.B.*

CAPTAIN J. D'O. BARING,† late 55th Native Infantry.

Ensign, 1 July 40—Lieut., 12 Nov. 42—Captain, 15 June 48.

SERVICE.—Captain BARING served during the Sutlej Campaign 1845-46.

CAPTAIN R. BARING, P. H., late 1st Bengal European Cavalry, A. D. C. to the G. G.
Cornet, 25 July 51—Lieut., 20 Sept. 54—Captain, 9 Jan. 58.

LIEUTENANT J. G. BARLOW, late 54th Native Infantry.
Ensign, 6 March 57—Lieut., 18 May 58.

CAPTAIN *Sir* M. BARLOW, *Bart.*,† late 4th Bengal European Cavalry.
Cornet, 6 May 54—Lieut., 18 July 55—Captain, 9 May 60.

CAPTAIN W. J. P. BARLOW, P. H., late 63rd Native Infantry.
Ensign, 22 July 45—Lieut., 16 Oct. 48—Captain, 23 Nov. 56.

ASSISTANT-SURGEON G. BARNARD,† Bengal Medical Establishment.
Asst.-Surgeon, 25 Nov. 53.

LIEUTENANT C. H. BARNES, P. H., Bengal Artillery.
Lieut., 24 Aug. 57.

LIEUTENANT C. ST. J. B. BARNETT, P. H., late 19th Native Infantry.
Ensign, 4 Nov. 57—Lieut., 12 Dec. 59.

LIEUTENANT-COLONEL W. BARR, Bengal Artillery.
2nd Lieut., 11 Dec. 29—Lieut., 1 Aug. 38—Bt.-Captain, 11 Dec. 44—Captain, 9 Aug. 47—Bt.-Major, 28 Nov. 54—Major, 18 Aug. 58—Lieut.-Colonel, 27 Aug. 58.

SERVICE.—Lieutenant-Colonel BARR served at the forcing of the Khyber Pass, July 1839, and advance on Cabul, with Lieutenant-Colonel Wade and Shahzada Timoor. *Medal.* Served during the Sutlej Campaign, 1845-46. Present at the actions of Buddiwal, Alliwal, and Sobraon. *Medal and Clasp.*

(33)

MAJOR J. BARRETT,† late 37th Native Infantry.
Ensign, 30 Sept. 26—Lieut., 8 Oct. 39—Brevet-Captain, 30th Sept. 41—Captain, 26 April 49—Brevet-Major, 20 June 54—Major, 26 Jan. 61.

LIEUTENANT W. BARRON, P. H., Bengal Artillery.
Lieut., 11 Dec. 58.

COLONEL J. A BARSTOW, late 58th Native Infantry.
Ensign, 30 July 12—Lieut., 1 June 17—Bt.-Captain, 13 Aug. 29—Captain, 31 March 31—Major, 1 Jan. 45—Lieut.-Colonel, 17 May 51—Bt.-Colonel, 28 Nov. 54.
SERVICE.—Colonel BARSTOW served during the Nepal War, 1814-15-16, and at the siege and capture of Bhurtpore. *Medal.* Served in Affghanistan in 1839. *Wounded. Medal.*

LIEUTENANT J. BARTLEMAN,† late 23rd Native Infantry.
Ensign, 20 Oct. 53—Lieut., 31 May 57.
SERVICE.—Lieutenant BARTLEMAN served with H. M.'s 86th Regiment in the Campaign in Central India, 1857-58. Present at the siege and capture of Chundehree. Siege and capture of Jhansie. Action of Koonch. Operations before and taking of Calpee. Served with the 2nd Sikh Police Corps against the rebels in Jugdespore District, from August to November 1858. *Medal and Clasp.* Served with the 8th Punjab Infantry (now 24th Native Infantry) in the Campaign in China, 1860. Present at the action of Sinho; capture of the entrenched Camp at Tong-Ko. Capture of the Taku Forts. Occupation of Tientsing and capture of Pekin. *Medal and 2 Clasps.*

LIEUTENANT W. F. BARTLEMAN, late 39th Native Infantry.
Ensign, 16 Sept. 57—Lieut., 18 May 58.
SERVICE.—Served with H. M.'s 13th Light Infantry with the Sarun Field Force under Brigadier Rowcroft during the late Mutiny in 1858.

E

Present at the actions of Almorah, 17th and 25th April 1858; and at the capture of the Fort of Nuggur. *Medal.*

CAPTAIN H. T. BARTLETT, P. C., late 21st Native Infantry.

Ensign, 21 April 41—Lieut., 23 June 43—Captain, 13 April 55.

Passed examination in Punjabee.

LIEUTENANT N. BARTON,† late 52nd Native Infantry.

Ensign, 10 June 48—Lieut., 24 June 54.

SERVICE.—Lieutenant BARTON served during the Punjab Campaign, 1848-49. *Medal.*

MAJOR N. D. BARTON, P., late 3rd Bengal European Cavalry.

Cornet, 1 May 22—Lieut., 1 May 24—Bt.-Captain, 1 May 37—Captain, 30 Oct. 37—Bt.-Major, 11 Nov. 51—Major, 24 Dec. 55—Bt.-Lieut.-Colonel, 18 March 56.

BREVET-LIEUTENANT-COLONEL C. A. BARWELL, P., late 71st Native Infantry.

Ensign, 20 June 43—Lieut., 1 April 47—Captain, 30 June 57—Bt.-Major, 24 March 58—Bt.-Lieut.-Colonel, 26 April 59.

SERVICE.—Brevet-Lieutenant-Colonel BARWELL served with the Force under Brigadier Wheeler in the Punjab, 1848-49. *Medal.* Was officiating Major of Brigade at Lucknow at the time of the outbreak, May 1857. Continued to serve in that capacity until the final relief of the Lucknow Garrison in November 1857. Also as Fort Adjutant from the commencement of the siege of the Residency. Mentioned in the Despatch of Sir John Inglis, K.C.B. Received the thanks of Government; promoted to the rank of *Brevet-Major. Medal and Clasp, and one year's service.* Served as Brigade Major to the 6th Brigade in the Field; and present at the battle of Cawnpore, in that capacity, on the 6th December 1857. Thanked in Despatch on the subject. Served as

(35)

Brigade-Major to a Force ordered to march through the Etawah and Mynpoorie Districts to Futtehghur under Brigadier Walpole, C.B. Served as Deputy Assistant Adjutant General of the 3rd division of the Army at the siege and capture of Lucknow. Mentioned in the Despatch of Brigadier-General Walpole to the Commander-in-Chief. *Clasp.* Served as Deputy Assistant Adjutant General to a Force ordered to march through Oude to Rohilcund; present at the attack on Fort Kooyd and action of Allygunge. Thanked on both occasions in the Despatches. Served as Deputy Assistant Adjutant General of the whole Force that entered Rohilcund. Present at the re-occupation of Shahjehanpore and battle of Bareilly, 5th May 1858. Thanked by Lord Clyde in his Despatch on the subject. Served as Deputy Assistant Adjutant General of the Rohilcund and Kumaon Divisions, in the action on the Sardah, 15th January 1859. *Wounded slightly.* Thanked by Brigadier General Sir R. Walpole, K.C.B., and brought to the notice of the Commander-in-Chief, in Despatch. Promoted to the rank of Brevet-Lieutenant-Colonel.

LIEUTENANT W. B. BARWELL, P. H., late 18th Native Infantry.

Ensign, 4 Feb. 55—Lieut., 6 June 57.

SERVICE.—Lieutenant BARWELL was present with Head Quarters on the mutiny of the Regiment, 31st May 1857. Served with the Force under Colonel McCausland in defence of the Kumaon Hills in 1857 and 1858. Present at the actions of Kuldwanee, 18th September and 28th October 1857; Charpoorah, 10th February; Sittargunge, 25th February; and Russoolpoor, 5th July 1858. Commanded a Squadron of the Rohilcund Horse, (now 16th Bengal Cavalry,) at the action of Maila Ghaut, under Major-General Walpole, K.C.B., in 1858. Commanded a Squadron of the Rohilcund Horse, with the Column under Colonel Smyth on the banks of the Sardar River, 1859. Commanded a Squadron of the Rohilcund Horse with the Column under Lieutenant-Colonel Williamson on the Nepaul Frontier. *Medal.* Mentioned in a Despatch of Colonel McCausland at the action of Charpoorah on the 10th February 1858.

(36)

CAPTAIN C. B. BASDEN, P. H., late 61st Native Infantry

Ensign, 25 Dec. 40—Lieut., 16 July 42—Captain, 6 July 53.

SERVICE.—Captain BASDEN served in Bundlecund from November 1843 to March 1845. Served with a Column under Major Forbes at the capture of the Fort of Geguahut, in Bundlecund, in 1844. Present at the mutiny of the late 61st Native Infantry on 7th June 1861. Received a sabre wound in the right arm. Served with a Column under Major Olphert's Artillery in 1857. Joined the Army of Delhi on 21st September 1857. Served in Command of the 5th Punjab Cavalry and Frontier of Dehra Ismael Khan on the 13th March 1860, when 3,000 Mahsood Wuzeerees, who threatened the city of Tâk, were repulsed, leaving 200 dead on the field. *Medal.*

LIEUTENANT G. H. BASEVI, P. H., late 27th Native Infantry.

Ensign, 9 June 48—Lieut., 11 Nov. 56.

SERVICE.—Captain BASEVI served with the Kohat Force at the attack on the Kothul on the 12th and 25th November 1853, as Assistant Field Engineer. (Has furnished Certificates of qualification in Surveying and Civil Engineering.)

CAPTAIN C. BATCHELOR, P. H., late 3rd Bengal European Cavalry.

Cornet, 10 June 46—Lieut., 20 July 49—Captain, 7 Nov. 57.

LIEUTENANT C. E. BATES, P. H., late 36th Native Infantry.

Ensign, 20 April 56—Lieut., 23 Nov. 56.

SERVICE.—Lieutenant BATES served in India in 1857, and was severely and dangerously wounded on the occasion of the Mutiny at Jullundur, 7th June 1857. Right arm disabled. *Medal.* Served with No. 2 Column, Bundlecund Field Force, during the operations in 1859. Served throughout the China Expedition of 1860. Present at the batttle of Sinho, taking of Tonko, capture of the Taku Forts, and surrender of Pekin.

Medal and 2 Clasps. 1st class Certificate as Instructor of Musketry from Hythe.

ASSISTANT-SURGEON R. S. BATESON, P. H., Bengal Medical Establishment.

Asst.-Surgeon, 20 Feb. 56.

SERVICE.—Assistant-Surgeon BATESON served with the 3rd Bengal European Regiment throughout the Indian Mutinies, 1857-58-59; present at the actions near Agra, 5th July and 10th October 1857. Present at the affair at Oorge during the operations at Shereghut Ghaut, May 1858. Served with the Agra Column towards Gwalior, June 1858. Served with Brigadier Showers's Column. Present at the action of Dowsa, 14th January 1859, against Tantia Topee. *Medal.*

VETERINARY-SURGEON H. BATH, Bengal Veterinary Establishment.

Vety.-Surgeon, 12 April 58.

SERVICE.—Veterinary-Surgeon BATH served with the Osmanlii Irregular Cavalry in Turkey, under Generals Beatson and Smith, during the Eastern Campaign of 1855-56.

SURGEON-MAJOR S. H. BATSON,† Bengal Medical Establishment.

Asst.-Surgeon, 22 April 36—Surgeon, 31 Dec. 49—Surg.-Major, 13 Jan. 60.

SERVICE.—Surgeon-Major BATSON served with the 36th Native Infantry during the whole Sutlej Campaign. Present at the battle of Alliwal. Brought in the wounded after the action, and deserters of Buddiwal. *Medal.* Volunteered to carry expresses from Delhi to Meerut on the 11th May 1857. Appointed Field Surgeon to the Army Head Quarters, Delhi Field Force; afterwards appointed to the Medical charge of the Field Depôt Hospital at Selimghur, Delhi, with temporary charge of the Superintending Surgeon's duties in addition. *Medal and Clasp.*

(38)

VETERINARY-SURGEON E. J. BATT, Bengal Artillery.
 Vety.-Surgeon, 20 Nov. 59.

LIEUTENANT A. BATTYE, P. H., late 19th Native Infantry.
 Ensign, 6 Jan. 57—Lieut., 22 Jan. 58.
 SERVICE.—Lieutenant BATTYE served with the 101st Royal Bengal Fusiliers (1st Bengal Fusiliers) in Oude 1858. Present at the siege and capture of Lucknow, March 1858. At the action of Uttereah, 13th April 1858. At the action of Bhumore Ghaut, 18th September 1858. At the action of Kintoor, 6th October 1858. *Medal and Clasp.*

LIEUTENANT C. F. BATTYE, P. H., 4th (late 33rd) Native Infantry.
 Ensign, 2 Sept. 55—Lieut., 21 July 57.
 SERVICE.—Served with the Field Force under General Douglas in the Behar and Ghazeepore Districts, 1858. *Medal.* With the China Expeditionary Force, 1860-61. *Medal.*

CAPTAIN G. M. BATTYE, P., late 1st Fusiliers.
 Ensign, 20 Aug. 45—Lieut., 23 Jan. 50—Captain, 2 Aug. 58.
 SERVICE.—Captain BATTYE served with the 1st Fusiliers throughout the war in Burmah in 1852-53-54. *Medal.* Has furnished a Certificate of qualification in Engineering.

CAPTAIN H. D. BATTYE, P. H., late 56th Native Infantry.
 Ensign, 7 Jan. 50—Lieut., 21 June 54—Captain, 27 June 57.

(39)

LIEUTENANT W. BATTYE, P. H., late 65th Native Infantry.
Ensign, 4 April 54—Lieut., 23 Nov. 56.
SERVICE.—Lieutenant BATTYE served against the rebels in the Azimghur District during the Mutiny. Received the thanks of Government whilst serving with the Goorkah Force, for aiding Mr. Venables in the capture and death of a noted rebel at Azimghur. Served in China in 1858.

LIEUTENANT W. BATTYE, late 6th Europeans.
Ensign, 6 Jan. 59—Lieut., 2 Aug. 59.

BREVET-CAPTAIN B. H. BAUGH, P., late 34th Native Infantry.
Ensign, 10 July 42—Lieut., 21 Nov. 48—Bt.-Captain, 10 July 57.
SERVICE.—Captain BAUGH served in the 26th Native Infantry with the Army of the Sutlej in 1846. Present at the actions of Moodkee, Ferozeshuhur, and Sobraon. *Medal and 2 Clasps*. Was severely wounded in several places by a mutineer of the late 34th Native Infantry at Barrackpore in 1857. *Wound Pension.*

CAPTAIN AND BREVET-MAJOR F. W. BAUGH,† late 26th Native Infantry.
Ensign, 13 Jan. 39—Lieut., 3 Nov. 41—Captain, 18 June 50—Bt.-Major, 24 March 58.
SERVICE.—Captain and Brevet-Major BAUGH served with Major-General Sir G. Pollock's, G.C.B., Force in Affghanistan in 1842; with the Army of the Sutlej in 1846; in the Burmah Campaign in 1853, and in the Indian Mutiny 1857-58. Present at the actions of forcing the Khyber Pass, Mamoo Khail, Jugdulluck, Tazeen, and Istaliff in 1842; Moodkee, Ferozeshuhur, and Sobraon in 1845-46; against the rebel Burmese, near Prome, in 1853; and the action of Chinpoorah in 1858. *4 Medals and 2 Clasps*. Mentioned in the Despatch of Colonel J. K. McCausland, Commanding in Kumaon, 1st March 1858. Received the thanks of Government and of the Secretary of State for India, 30th November

1858. Promoted to the rank of Brevet-Major for services in the Indian Mutiny.

ENSIGN W. BAX, General List.
Ensign, 4 Sept. 60.

ENSIGN J. BAXTER (unattached.)
Ensign, 20 Sept. 57.

SERVICE.—Ensign BAXTER served under Sir C. Campbell against the Momunds and Hill Tribes north of Peshawur, November and December 1851 to April 1852. Served throughout the Delhi Campaign, 1857; present at the battles of Ghazee-ood-din-nuggur, 30th and 31st May; Badle-ke-serai, 8th June; attack on the Eegah, 17th June; repulse of an attack by the enemy, in rear of the camp, 19th June; battle of Nudjufghur, 25th and 26th August 1857; and minor engagements during the siege. *(Wounded.)* Ensign's Commission. Present at the siege, storm and capture of Lucknow by Lord Clyde, March 1858. Present with General Walpole's Column at the attack on Fort Rooyah, 13th, and action of Allygunge, 20th April 1858. Battle and capture of Bareilly, 5th May 1858, and subsequent affairs at Shahjehanpore, 15th and 18th May 1858. Present at the capture of Fort Bunnee, 23rd, and destruction of the Fort of Mohumdee, 24th May 1858. At the attack and destruction of the Fort of Shahabad, 1st June 1858, under Colonel Taylor, C.B. *Medal and 2 Clasps.*

LIEUTENANT C. A. BAYLAY,† Bengal Artillery.
Lieut., 27 April 58.

LIEUTENANT H. J. BAYLIS, General List.
Ensign, 19 Jan. 60—Lieut., 1 Jan. 62.

LIEUTENANT R. BAZETT, Bengal Artillery.
Lieut., 10 June 59.

(41)

LIEUTENANT-COLONEL J. P. BEADLE, Bengal Engineers.

2nd Lieut., 11 Dec. 40—Lieut., 5 April 44—Captain, 1 May 55—Lieut.-Colonel, 13 March 61.

SERVICE.—Lieutenant-Colonel BEADLE served during the Sutlej Campaign, and was present at Busseah on the day of the battle of Sobraon, and proceeded with the Army to Lahore. *Medal.*

LIEUTENANT R. BEADON, P. H., late 4th Bengal European Cavalry.

Cornet, 20 Nov. 56—Lieut., 16 April 58.

SERVICE.—Lieutenant BEADON served during the Mutinies, 1857-58. Present at the siege of Lucknow. Present at the skirmish at Tigree, near Jounpore, when two of the enemy's guns were captured; at the capture of Azimghur, and subsequent pursuit; at Sanilwar he captured one of the enemy's guns (a 9-pounder) complete. Mentioned by Brigadier Douglas in his Despatch and thanked by Government, 11th May 1858. Engaged with the enemy in the Jugdespore jungles, under General Lugard, May and June 1858. Mentioned in General Lugard's Despatch, 27th May 1858. Commanded a Squadron of the 3rd Sikh Cavalry under Colonel Walters, to guard the left bank of the Soane, and to co-operate with the other Columns engaged in the attack on the rebel's position in the Jugdespore jungles. Engaged with the enemy on several occasions. Mentioned in Colonel Walter's Despatch, 30th July 1858. Formed part of the pursuing Cavalry under Sir H. Havelock, on the flight of the rebels from Jugdespore. Present at a sharp engagement at the village of Nonadee. Received the personal congratulations of Sir H. Havelock on the field, and for the five days following accompanied Sir H. Havelock in unceasing pursuit of the rebels, until they were driven across the trunk road to the foot of the Kymon Hills. Employed in watching the ghâts on the left side of the Soane, returned with Colonel Walker's Column from Tilloltoo, in pursuit of the rebels, and took part in the conference with the Rebel Chiefs at Jugdespore, 25th November 1858. *Medal and Clasp.* Served in China in 1860. Present at the taking of the Taku Forts, Chunkeandan, and taking of Pekin. *Medal and Clasps.*

F

(42)

LIEUTENANT H. BEAL, General List.
Ensign, 8 May 60—Lieut., 1 Jan. 62.

SURGEON-MAJOR A. BEALE, Bengal Medical Establishment.
Asst.-Surgeon, 8 Feb. 40—Surgeon, 1 Dec. 53—Surgeon-Major, 8 Feb. 60.
SERVICE.—Surgeon-Major BEALE served in Bundlecund in 1842. During the Sutlej Campaign 1845-46. Present at the action of Ferozeshuhur. *Medal.*

CAPTAIN J. W. F. BEAN, P. H., late 13th Native Infantry.
Ensign, 21 June 43—Lieut., 30 June 48—Captain, 4 Sept. 57.
SERVICE.—Captain BEAN served with the Army of the Punjab in 1848-49. Present at the passage of the Chenab and battle of Goojerat. *Medal and Clasp.*

CAPTAIN A. B. BEATSON,† late 56th Native Infantry.
Ensign, 27 Sept. 40—Lieut., 20 Nov. 45—Bt.-Captain, 27 Sept. 55—Captain, 29 August 1861.
SERVICE.—Captain BEATSON served during the Sutlej Campaign, 1845-46. *Medal.* Present at the capture of Kote Kangra. Served with the 1st European Bengal Fusiliers before Delhi in 1857. Present at the storm and capture of that city, 16th September 1857. *Medal and Clasp.*

SURGEON J. F. BEATSON,† M.D., A.B., Bengal Medical Establishment.
Asst.-Surgeon, 16 June 43—Surgeon, 27 June 57.
SERVICE.—Surgeon BEATSON served during the Sutlej Campaign. Present at the defence of Ferozepore, and at Ferozeshuhur. *Medal.* Served during the Punjab Campaign 1848-49. *Medal.*

(43)

MAJOR T. F. B. BEATSON, late 4th Bengal European Cavalry.

Cornet, 27 June 26—Lieut., 29 Aug. 32—Bt.-Captain, 27 June 41—Captain, 14 Oct. 44—Bt.-Major, 20 June 54—Major, 23 July 58.

ASSISTANT-SURGEON W. B. BEATSON,† M.D., Bengal Medical Establishment.

Asst.-Surgeon, 30 June 52.

SERVICE.—Assistant-Surgeon BEATSON, M.D., served with the Field Hospital of the Burmah Force in 1853, from 1st February to the beginning of November. *Medal and Clasp.*

COLONEL W. F. BEATSON, late 4th Europeans.

Ensign, 13 July 20—Lieut., 11 July 23—Captain, 26 Jan. 37—Bt.-Major, 9 Nov. 46—Major, 18 July 48—Lieut.-Colonel, 15 Nov. 53—Bt.-Colonel, 28 Nov. 54.

SERVICE.—Colonel William Ferguson BEATSON entered the Bengal Army in 1820. Being on furlough, he, with the sanction of the British Government, served with the British Legion in Spain in 1835-36, first as Major, and afterwards as Lieutenant-Colonel Commanding a Regiment, at the head of which he was *severely wounded.* For services in Spain, received the Cross of San Fernando from the Queen of Spain, and Her Britannic Majesty's permission to wear it, 12th September 1837. Returned to India in 1837, and received the thanks of the Government of India for capture of Jignee in Bundlecund in 1840, and of Chirgong in 1841. In February 1844, received the thanks of the Governor-General's Agent of Scindia's Dominions, for recovering for the Gwalior Government forts and strongholds in Kuchwahagar. In March 1844, received the thanks of Government for the volunteering of the Bundlecund Legion for Scinde, which volunteering the Governor-General declared placed the Government of India under great obligation. In March 1846, was mentioned in Sir Charles Napier's Despatch, regarding the Campaign in the Boogtee Hills, which service called forth the approbation of Government. In July 1846, the conduct of the Bundlecund Legion while in Scinde,

(44)

of which he was Commandant, and was praised in General Orders by Governor-General Viscount Hardinge. In July 1848, received the approbation of the Government of India for taking Jagheer and Fort of Rymow from the Rohillas. In November 1850, re-captured Rymow from the Arabs. In February 1851, took the Fort of Dharoor, one of the strongest in the Deccan. In March 1851, the following General Order was issued by the Resident at Hyderabad:—" Brigadier Beatson having tendered his resignation of the Command of the Nizam's Cavalry from date of his embarkation for England, the Resident begs to express his entire approval of this Officer's conduct, during the time he has exercised the important Command of the Cavalry Division." " Brigadier Beatson has not only maintained, but improved, the interior economy and arrangement of the Cavalry Division; and the value of his active Military services in the field has been amply attested to, and rendered subject of record in the several instances of Kamgaon, Rymow, Arnee, and Dharoor." Proceeded to Turkey on special service, 1st May 1854, with rank as Colonel on the Staff in the British Army, and received the rank of Lieutenant-General in the Turkish Army, on his arrival at Constantinople. For his services on the Danube, he received *Gold Medal from the Sultan* (*the ' Nishan-Iftihar.'*) In 1854 was with the Heavy Brigade at Balaklava and Inkermann. Mentioned in General Scarlett's Despatch regarding the charge at Balaklava, and received *the British and Turkish Silver Medals for the Crimea, the former with three Clasps*. Was given the local rank of Major-General in Her Majesty's Army in Turkey, 1st November 1854, and organized 4,000 Bashee Bazouks. Returned to India on the breaking out of the Mutiny in 1857; raised, organized, and took two Regiments of Cavalry into the field. *Medal.* For services with one of the Regiments of this Brigade, the 18th Royal Irish and Bombay Artillery, received the thanks of Sir Hugh Rose, in Despatch, February 24th 1859, of which an extract is here given:—" Sir Hugh Rose has recently made known to the Commander-in-Chief of the Bombay Army the satisfaction he derived from the manner in which you discharged your duties whilst under his Command; and he avails himself of this opportunity for conveying to you his best thanks for the zeal and energy with which you carried out his instructions. He is perfectly aware of your readiness

(45)

to encounter any hardship or fatigue for the good of the service."*—
Extract of a letter from the Assistant Quarter Master General, with Sir Hugh Rose, dated 24th February 1859. Has received a Cross of the First Class of the National and Military Order of San Fernando of Spain.

CORNET W. A. S. DEV. BEAUCLERK, General List, Cavalry.

Cornet, 12 March 60.

LIEUTENANT R. BEAVAN, General List.

Ensign, 4 May 60—Lieut., 1 Jan. 62.

LIEUTENANT R. C. BEAVAN,† late 62nd Native Infantry.

Ensign, 4 Nov. 58—Lieut., 1 Mar. 59.

MAJOR-GENERAL A. M. BECHER, C.B., late 61st Native Infantry, H. A. D. C. to G. G.

Ensign, 20 Oct. 33—Lieut., 16 July 39—Captain, 11 April 45—Bt.-Major, 3 April 46—Bt.-Lieut.-Colonel, 7 June 49—Bt.-Colonel, 28 Nov. 54—Major-General, 29 April 61.

SERVICE.—Major-General BECHER served in Affghanistan in 1839. Present at the storm and capture of Ghuznee. *Medal*. Served throughout the Sutlej Campaign, including the actions of Moodkee, Ferozeshuhur, and Sobraon. *Medal, 2 Clasps, and Brevet-Majority*. Served during the Punjab Campaign, 1848-49. Present at the siege and surrender of Mooltan and battle of Goojerat. *Medal, Clasp, and Brevet-Lieutenant-Colonel*.

---

* Colonel Beatson has the proud satisfaction of knowing, that his having refused to submit quietly to the arbitrary acts of a despotic Ambassador, caused by the false reports of Levantine Consuls, and to the unparallelled injustice of a War Minister, prevented his being a K.C.B. long ago, which distinction one of the most chivalrous and high-minded Officers in the British Army declared his services entitled him to; the same cause prevented his getting the 2nd Class of the Medjidié, which every Officer who served in the late war must acknowledge was most unjustly withheld from Colonel Beatson after his services on the Danube, in Turkey, and in the Crimea; while it was given to some who never were under fire in either. This has been inserted at Colonel Beatson's request.

CORNET A. W. R. BECHER, General List, Cavalry.
Cornet, 20 Dec. 59.

LIEUTENANT G. A. B. BECHER, General List.
Ensign, 4 Aug. 59—Lieut., 21 June 61.

LIEUTENANT H. G. BECHER, late 73rd Native Infantry.
Ensign, 6 Jan. 59—Lieut., 12 Dec. 59.

LIEUTENANT-COLONEL J. R. BECHER, C.B., P. H., Bengal Engineers.
2nd Lieut., 6 March 38—Lieut., 3 April 42—Bt.-Captain, 6 March 53—Captain, 1 August 54—Bt.-Major, 2 August 54—Lieut.-Colonel, 18 Feb. 61.

SERVICE.—Lieutenant-Colonel BECHER, C.B., served in Affghainstan in 1842. Present at the forcing of the Khyber Pass by Sir G. Pollock. *Medal.* Served during the Sutlej Campaign. Present at the battle of Sobraon. *(Severely wounded.) Medal.* Employed as Civil Officer in 1857 against the Mutineers on the Huzara Frontier. *Medal and C.B.*

LIEUTENANT S. E. BECHER, General List.
Ensign, 7 July 60—Lieut., 1 Jan. 62.

MAJOR S. H. BECHER, P. H., late 61st Native Infantry.
Ensign, 11 June 34—Lieut., 3 Oct. 40—Captain, 1 Dec. 46—Bt.-Major, 29 August 59—Major in Staff Corps, 18 Feb. 61.

CAPTAIN S. J. BECHER, late 11th Native Infantry.
Ensign, 14 June 34—Lieut., 30 July 39—Captain, 13 May 48.

LIEUTENANT S. BECKETT, P. H., late 25th Native Infantry.
Ensign, 13 June 57—Lieut., 18 May 58.

SERVICE.—Lieutenant BECKETT served in the Oude Campaign of 1858-59, with the 1st Sikh Infantry. Present at the crossing of the Gogra

(47)

(in Oude) under Sir J. H. Grant, K.C.B., in November 1858; at the skirmish near Bunkussia Fort in December 1858, and the action near Jerwah Pass, Trans-Raptee, in March 1859. *Wounded dangerously* in abdomen and *severely* in left arm on the latter occasion. *Mutiny Medal.* Mentioned in the Despatch of Lieutenant-Colonel Gordon, Commanding 1st Sikh Infantry and Outpost at Jerwah, 26th April 1861.

LIEUTENANT W. H. BECKETT, T. C., P. H., General List.

Ensign, 20 Feb. 59—Lieut., 3 April 60. (Passed an examination in Civil Engineering.)

LIEUTENANT E. BEDDY, P. H., late 53rd Native Infantry.

Ensign, 20 Feb. 57—Lieut., 18 May 58.

BREVET-CAPTAIN D. W. BEECHER, P. H., 2nd Bengal Fusiliers.

2nd Lieut., 27 July 46—Lieut., 15 Nov. 49—Bt.-Captain, 27 July 61—Captain, 1 Jan. 62.

SERVICE.—Captain BEECHER served with the Army of the Punjab 1848-49. Present at Ramnuggur and the Passage of the Chenab; actions of Chillianwallah and Goojerat, and subsequent pursuit of the Sikhs and Affghans under Sir W. Gilbert. *Medal and 2 Clasps*. Commanded a Detachment 8th Irregular Cavalry, on the occasion of the repulse of the rebels from Huldwaine on 18th September 1857. Mentioned in the Despatch of Major H. Maxwell, who commanded on the above occasion. *Medal.*

ENSIGN R. D. BEETSON, General List

Ensign, 28 Aug. 60.

ASSISTANT-SURGEON H. W. BELLEW, P. C. H., Bengal Medical Establishment.

Asst.-Surgeon, 14 Nov. 55.

ASSISTANT-SURGEON P. F. BELLEW,† Bengal Medical Establishment.
Asst.-Surgeon, 6 Sept. 54.

LIEUTENANT W. F. BELLI, P. H., late 40th Native Infantry.
Ensign, 11 June 53—Lieut., 20 Jan. 57.
SERVICE.—Lieutenant BELLI served against the Insurgent Sonthals in 1855, under Major General Lloyd, C.B. *(Since dead.)*

ASSISTANT-SURGEON C. E. W. BENSLEY,† M.D., Bengal Medical Establishment.
Asst.-Surgeon, 4 Aug. 56.
SERVICE.—Served with various forces during the Indian Mutiny of 1857-58.

ASSISTANT-SURGEON E. C. BENSLEY,† Bengal Medical Establishment.
Asst.-Surgeon, 10 Feb. 59.

LIEUTENANT C. E. BENTHAL,† General List, Cavalry.
Lieut., 12 July 59.

LIEUTENANT C. H. BERGMAN, late 60th Native Infantry.
Ensign, 15 July 58—Lieut., 17 Mar. 59.

LIEUTENANT H. L. C. BERNARD, P. H., late 4th Europeans.
Ensign, 11 Dec. 49—Lieut., 10 Sept. 55.
SERVICE.—Lieutenant BERNARD served with the 3rd Native Infantry with the Force under Colonel Mackeson, C.B., in Huzara, and the Hussunzaie Campaign, 1852-53. Present at the affairs of the Black Mountain and taking of the Fort. As Adjutant Officiating 2nd Sikh Infantry, served in the pursuit of the 55th Native Infantry Mutineers to the borders of Raghan under Major Becher, C.B., and in the subsequent

(49)

operations in the district during July and August 1857. As Adjutant, Huzara Goorkha Battalion, served throughout the Mahsood Wuzeeree Campaign with the Tank Field Force under Brigadier General N. Chamberlain, C.B., in 1860. Present at the repulse of the attack on the British Camp at Paloseen, 23rd April 1860. At the storming of the heights of Burrurah, 4th May 1860, and in the subsequent operations leading to the occupation of Raneegorum and burning of Mookeen.

LIEUTENANT F. A. BERTIE, P. H., late 74th Native Infantry.

Ensign, 26 Mar. 57—Lieut., 18 May 58.

SERVICE.—Lieutenant BERTIE served during the Mutiny, 1857-58-59. Served in Brigadier Rowcroft's Column, including the actions of the 2nd March 1858 at the attack of Belwah Fort, in Oude. The general actions of 5th March and 25th April 1858 at Amorah. Capture of Fort Nuggur, 29th April. Action at Amorah, 8th June 1858. Hurriah, 18th June. Attack and capture of Hurriah; actions of Bawnpore, Dumooriergunge, and Toolsipore, in the Trans-Gogra Campaign. *Medal.*

ASSISTANT-SURGEON A. V. BEST,† M.D., Bengal Medical Establishment.

Asst.-Surg., 29 Jan. 57.

LIEUT. THE HON'BLE F. B. BEST, late 2nd European Bengal Fusiliers.

2nd Lieut., 7 Feb. 49.—Lieut., 24 Nov. 53.

SERVICE.—Lieutenant BEST served under General Wyndham during the siege of Cawnpore, and under Lord Clyde at the expulsion of the rebels from Cawnpore and the Kali Nuddee. *Medal.*

CAPTAIN H. N. BEST, P., late 5th Bengal European Cavalry.

Cornet, 20 Dec. 45—Lieut., 8 May 49—Captain, 23 Nov. 56.

SERVICE.—Captain BEST served during the Punjab Campaign 1848-49. *Medal.* Present at the siege of Delhi in 1857 and at the battle of Bolundshuhur. *(Severely wounded.) Medal and Clasp.*

(50)

LIEUTENANT E. M. BETHUNE, 12th (late 70th) Native Infantry.
Ensign, 20 Feb. 59—Lieut., 22 April 61.

ENSIGN J. H. BESWEY (unattached.)
Ensign, 10 Feb. 60.

LIEUTENANT F. C. BEWSHER, P. H., 7th (late 47th) Native Infantry.
Ensign, 20 Jan. 57—Lieut., 30 April 58.
SERVICE.—Lieutenant BEWSHER served with the 49th Native Infantry in China from November 1858 to April 1860. Present at Shek-tsing.

VETERINARY-SURGEON I. BICKNELL, 1st Brigade Bengal Horse Artillery.
Vety.-Surgeon, 10 May 28.
SERVICE.—Veterinary-Surgeon BICKNELL served during the Affghanistan Campaign 1839, including the siege and capture of Ghuznee. *Medal.* Served with the Governor-General's Body Guard during the Sutlej Campaign 1845-46. Present at the battles of Moodkee, Alliwal, and Sobraon. *Medal and 2 Clasps.*

LIEUTENANT J. BIDDULPH, late 5th Bengal European Cavalry.
Ensign, 20 Jan. 58—Lieut., 18 May 58.
SERVICE.—Lieutenant BIDDULPH served with the 6th Dragoon Guards during the Campaign of 1858, with the force under Lord Clyde. Present at the action of Buxar Ghat. Served in the Trans-Gogra Campaign. Present at the actions of Churda Mujeedia and Bankee. *Medal.*

LIEUTENANT J. A. M. BIGGS, P. H., late 10th Native Infantry.
Ensign, 20 Jan. 48—Lieut., 8 Feb. 51.

CAPTAIN H. BINGHAM (unattached.)
Captain, 3 Jan. 59.
(*Since dead.*)

CAPTAIN W. H. BINNY, P. H., late 9th Native Infantry.
Ensign, 10 June 43—Lieut., 4 March 48—Bt.-Captain, 10 June 58—Captain, 4 Feb. 61.

SERVICE.—Captain BINNY served with the late 9th Native Infantry when it formed a portion of the Army of the Sutlej in 1846. Present during the operations undertaken against the Hill tribes in the Peshawur District 1855. Commanded the Banda Military Police Battalion at the relief of Kirwee in December 1858, and subsequent operations against the rebels in the Banda District and adjoining Native States.

LIEUTENANT H. H. BIRCH, P. H., late 27th Native Infantry.
Ensign, 4 Aug. 58—Lieut., 4 June 60.

SERVICE.—Lieutenant BIRCH served as a Volunteer throughout the defence of the Lucknow Residency in 1857, with the Oude Field Force at the Alum Bagh in 1857-58, and at the capture of Lucknow in 1858. *Medal and 2 Clasps.*

CAPTAIN R. C. BIRCH, P., late 1st European Bengal Fusiliers.
2nd Lieut., 14 Jan. 46—Lieut., 1 March 50—Captain, 17 March 60.

SERVICE.—Captain BIRCH served with the Burmah Field Force in 1852-53-54. Present at the relief of the Garrison of Pegu and the subsequent operations against the besieging Force in 1852. Present throughout the operations of the Martaban Column under General Steele. *Medal.* Accompanied the Force under Captain Hall, which operated against the rebel Rajah of Porahat and the insurgent Poles, in the capacity of Assistant Commissioner in charge of the Singbhoom Division. Present at the capture of Porahat in November, at the defeat of a large body of the insurgents on the 25th December 1857. Present at the affair at Mograh in the Colehan on the 14th January 1858. *Wounded severely*. Directed the operations of the Police Corps under Lieutenant Reeves and the Naval Brigade under Lieutenant Windus, B. N., which ended in the surrender of the ex-Rajah of Porahat in February 1859. Honorably mentioned by the Governor-General in his Minute, published at the close of the disturbances consequent on the mutiny of the Sepoys of the Bengal Army. *India Medal.*

LIEUTENANT R. G. BIRCH, late 1st Bengal European Cavalry.

Cornet, 20 Nov. 56—Lieut., 13 Jan. 57.

SERVICE.—Lieutenant BIRCH served with the Volunteer Cavalry, Oude Field Force, under Sir J. Outram, in 1857. *Severely wounded* at the first relief of Lucknow. *Medal and Clasp.*

MAJOR-GENERAL *Sir* R. J. H. BIRCH, K.C.B.

Ensign, 7 Jan. 21—Lieut., 11 July 23—Bt.-Captain, 7 Jan. 36—Captain, 20 March 36—Bt.-Major, 30 April 44—Major, 31 Oct. 49—Bt.-Lieut.-Colonel, 3 April 46—Lieut.-Colonel, 10 Dec. 54—Bt.-Colonel, 20 June 54—Major-General, 4 May 58.

SERVICE.—Major-General BIRCH served at Maharajpore. *Bronze Star and Brevet-Majority*. Throughout the Sutlej Campaign, including the actions of Moodkee, Ferozeshuhur, and Sobraon. *Medal*, 2 *Clasps and Brevet-Lieutenant-Colonel*. Served during the Punjab Campaign, 1848-49. Present at the actions of Chillianwallah and Goojerat. *Medal, Clasp, and C.B.*

MAJOR W. BIRCH, P., late 6th Bengal Fusiliers.

Ensign, 31 Jan. 37—Lieut., 15 Jan. 41—Captain, 1 March 51—Major, 22 Jan. 59.

SERVICE.—Served during the Mutiny Campaign 1857-58. *Medal and Clasp.*

LIEUTENANT W. B. BIRCH,† 1st (late 21st) Native Infantry.

Ensign, 30 July 58—Lieut., 23 Dec. 58.

SERVICE.—Lieutenant BIRCH served in the following operations against the Taipsing rebels: at the attack and capture of Stockades at

Wong-ka-Dya 4th April, Chowpoo 17th April, and Nahzeean 29th April. At the capture of the walled Towns of Kahding 1st May, Chingpoo 12th May, Nagow 17th May, and Isoling 20th May 1862.

LIEUTENANT A. N. BIRD, General List.

Ensign, 8 May 60—Lieut., 1 Jan. 62.

MAJOR H L. BIRD, late 48th Native Infantry.

Ensign, 13 Jan. 35—Lieut., 30 June 38—Captain, 12 May 45—Bt.-Major, 28 Nov. 54—Major, 25 May 61.

SERVICE.—Major BIRD served with the Army of the Indus 1838-39-40. Served with the Army of the Sutlej in 1846. At the defence of the Residency of Lucknow 1859. Present at the Battle of "Tuctoo," Quetta, in the Shawl Valley, storm and capture of Ghuznee, battle of Alliwal, battle of Cawnpore. 3 *Medals and* 1 *Clasp*. Slightly wounded at the battle of Alliwal in the leg and cheek.

CAPTAIN J. W. L. BIRD, P. H., late 11th Native Infantry.

Ensign, 23 Sept. 38—Lieut., 3 Oct. 40—Captain, 13 Oct. 51.

SERVICE.—Captain BIRD served during the Sutlej Campaign. *Medal.* Present at the capture of Kote Kangra, 1846.

COLONEL L. S. BIRD, late 23rd Native Infantry.

Ensign, 8 June 08—Lieut., 16 Dec. 14—Bt.-Captain, 4 June 23—Captain, 5 April 25—Bt.-Major, 28 June 38—Major, 18 June 40—Bt.-Lieut.-Colonel, 3 April 46—Lieut.-Colonel, 12 Sept. 46—Bt.-Colonel, 20 June 54—Colonel, 17 April 56.

SERVICE.—Major-General BIRD, 23rd Native Infantry, served at the capture of the Island of Mauritius, 1810; with the Column under the command of Sir David Ochterlony during the Nepal Campaign, 1816; and the Force under Brigadier Nation in Oude, 1816-17. *India Medal.* During the Pindaree war, 1817-18-19; Bundlecund 1821; in Hurrianah 1824-25; against the Coles 1832-33, and throughout the Campaign on the Sutlej, including the battles of Moodkee, Ferozeshuhur, Buddiwal, and Alliwal. *Medal, 2 Clasps, and Brevet-Lieutenant-Colonel.* Commanded the Sonthal Brigade during the insurrection of 1855-56.

ASSISTANT-SURGEON R. BIRD,† M.D., Bengal Medical Establishment.
Asst.-Surgeon, 4 Aug. 55—Bt.-Surgeon, 7 Sept. 58.

ENSIGN T. BIRD (unattached.)
Ensign, 16 Aug. 58.

SERVICE.—Ensign BIRD served in the Gwalior Campaign, 1842-43. Present at the battle of Punniar, 29th December 1842. *Bronze Star.* Served in the Sutlej Campaign of 1845-46. Present at the battle of Moodkee, 18th December 1845; Ferozeshuhur, 21st and 22nd December 1845; and Sobraon, 10th February 1846. *Medal and 2 Clasps.* Served in the Punjab Campaign of 1848-49. Present at Ramnuggur; battles of Chillianwallah and Goojerat. *Medal and 2 Clasps.* Served in the Indian Campaign of 1858-59. Present at the siege and capture of Lucknow, attack on Fort Rooya, action at Allygunge, capture of Bareilly, action of Pusgaon, Russoolpore, capture of Fort Mittowlee, actions of Biswa and Mehindee.

LIEUTENANT D. DE LA G. BIRKETT, late 3rd Europeans.
Ensign, 13 Dec. 56—Lieut., 30 April 58.

SERVICE.—Lieutenant BIRKETT served with the 3rd Europeans throughout the Mutinies, with the Agra Column to Allyghur from August to October 1857, with Colonel Cotton's Column towards Delhi in October 1857, and the Agra Column towards Gwalior June 1858, and some minor operations. Present at the action of Sussea near Agra, 5th July 1857; at the action near Maun Singh's Garden, Allyghur, on the 24th August 1857; at the battle of Agra on the 11th October 1857; and at the affair at Futtehpore Seekree in 1857. *Slightly wounded*, 5th July 1857. *Medal.*

LIEUTENANT J. BIRNEY, Bengal Engineers.
Lieut., 27 April 58.

LIEUTENANT W. R. BIRNEY, late 26th Native Infantry.
Ensign, 20 June 58—Lieut., 11 Aug. 58.

(55)

MAJOR-GENERAL D. BIRRELL.

Ensign, 30 Aug. 18—Lieut., 20 Oct. 18—Captain, 26 April 27—Bt.-Major, 23 Nov. 41—Major, 10 Nov. 43—Bt.-Lieut.-Colonel, 3 April 46—Lieut.-Colonel, 1 March 50—Bt.-Colonel, 20 June 54—Colonel, 20 July 59—Major-General, 25 April 58.

SERVICE.—Major-General BIRRELL served during the Burmese war, 1825-26, and with the army of the Indus in Affghanistan, 1839-40. Present at the assault and capture of Ghuznee. *Medal.* And the operations in the Wuzeeree Valley. *3rd Class Dooranee Order.* Served in the Sutlej Campaign. Present at the battles of Ferozeshuhur *(horse killed under him)* and Sobraon. *Medal, Clasp, and Brevet-Lieutenant-Colonel.*

CORNET W. W. BISCOE, P. H., General List, Cavalry.

Cornet, 4 Feb. 60.

LIEUTENANT G. A. BISHOP, P. H., late 2nd Bengal Fusiliers.

2nd Lieut., 12 June 52—Lieut., 2 July 56.

SERVICE.—Lieutenant BISHOP served with his Regiment in Burmah in 1853, with the expedition against the Rebel Chief "Moung Yong Gye." Acted as Interpreter to a Detachment of the 5th Fusiliers in the neighborhood of Arrah during the early part of 1857. Served with Her Majesty's 64th Regiment at the besiege of Cawnpore by the Gwalior Contingent, and at their subsequent defeat by Sir Colin Campbell on the 6th December 1857. Was present with the 64th on the 28th November during a charge on a battery of the enemy's guns, when a great many Officers were left killed, and being carried away from the vicinity of the guns, the only body rescued was that of Brigadier Wilson, Commanding. Was present at the battle of Kala-Nuddee under Sir Colin Campbell. *Medal.* Has furnished certificates of qualification in surveying.

LIEUTENANT ST. G. M. BISHOP, P. H., 11th Goorkha Light Infantry.

Ensign, 12 Dec. 57—Lieut., 8 Nov. 58.

SERVICE.—Lieutenant BISHOP served with H. M.'s 19th Regiment in Behar and Tirhoot, 1858.

(56)

LIEUTENANT-COLONEL G. W. BISHOP, late 23rd Native Infantry.

Ensign, 26 April 26—Lieut., 20 Nov. 28—Bt.-Captain, 26 April 41—Captain, 28 May 43—Major, 10 July 52—Lieut.-Colonel, 31 May 57.

CAPTAIN H. P. BISHOP, P. H., Bengal Artillery.

2nd Lieut., 13 June 45—Lieut., 30 June 48—2nd Captain, 27 Aug. 58—Captain, 18 Feb. 61—Bt.-Major, 28 Aug. 58.

SERVICE.—Captain (Brevet-Major) BISHOP was present at the siege and render of Mooltan 1848-49, and battle of Goojerat. *Medal and 2 Clasps.* Served during the Mutiny Campaign 1857-58. *Medal and Brevet-Major.*

CAPTAIN W. D. BISHOP, P., late 30th Native Infantry.

Ensign, 31 Aug. 40—Lieut., 3 Nov. 43—Bt.-Captain, 31 Aug. 55—Captain, 8 April 56.

SERVICE.—Captain BISHOP served with the Force under General Pollock. Present at the forcing of the Khyber Pass. *Medal.* Served during the Sutlej Campaign, 1845-46. During the Punjab Campaign, 1848-49. Present at the actions of Chillianwallah and Goojerat. *Medal.*

CAPTAIN G. A. BLACK, P., late 69th Native Infantry.

Ensign, 8 Jan. 42—Lieut., 24 Jan. 45—Captain, 23 Nov. 56.

SERVICE.—Captain BLACK served under Sir C. Napier in Scinde against the Hill Tribes in 1845. Was present at the battles of Chillianwallah and Goojerat, 1849. *Medal and 2 Clasps.*

CAPTAIN S. BLACK, P. H., 37th Native Infantry.

Ensign, 29 Dec. 44—Lieut., 13 April 48—Captain, 20 March 57.

SERVICE.—Captain BLACK served with the 37th Native Infantry at Lahore in 1848-49. *Medal.* Served in 1857 with the Force under Colonel Paton in suppression of the rebellion in the Googaira and adjoining districts. *Medal.*

(57)

COLONEL R. BLACKALL, late 13th Native Infantry.

Ensign, 27 March 06—Lieut., 4 Nov. 07—Bt.-Captain, 27 March 21—Captain, 11 July 23—Major, 21 June 30—Lieut.-Colonel, 22 April 36—Bt.-Colonel, 9 Nov. 46—Colonel, 18 July 48—Major-General, 20 June 54.

SERVICE.—General BLACKALL served at Hattrass, Pindaree War, 1817-18, and during the Cole Campaign, 1832-33.

CAPTAIN A. BLACKWOOD, P., late 59th Native Infantry.

Ensign, 15 Feb. 40—Lieut., 23 Dec. 44—Bt.-Captain, 15 Feb. 55—Captain, 5 Apl. 55.

SERVICE.—Captain BLACKWOOD served during the Sutlej Campaign, 1846. Present at the battle of Sobraon. *Medal.*

LIEUTENANT C. D. BLACKWOOD, General List.

Ensign, 4 Sept. 60—Lieut., 1 Jan. 62.

LIEUTENANT G. F. BLACKWOOD,† Bengal Artillery.

Lieut., 27 Aug. 58.

MAJOR T. C. BLAGRAVE,† late 26th Native Infantry.

Ensign, 3 Jan. 36—Lieut., 3 Oct. 40—Captain, 1 Apl. 50—Major, 11 Aug. 58.

SERVICE.—Major BLAGRAVE served during the Sutlej Campaign, 1846. Present at the battle of Sobraon. *Medal.* (*Since retired.*)

LIEUTENANT H. F. BLAIR,† Bengal Engineers.

Lieut., 27 Aug. 58.

SERVICE.—Lieutenant BLAIR served at Mooltan on the Brigadier's Staff, during the mutiny of the 62nd and 69th Native Infantry in 1857.

H

(58)

CAPTAIN C. R. BLAIR, late 2nd European Bengal Fusiliers.

2nd Lieut., 27 July 46—Lieut., 1 March 52—Bt.-Captain, 27 July 61.

SERVICE.—Captain BLAIR served during the Punjab Campaign, 1848-49. Present at Ramnuggur; passage of the Chenab; battles of Chillianwallah and Goojerat; and pursuit of the Sikhs and Affghans to Peshawur under General Gilbert. *Medal and Clasp.*

CAPTAIN E. R. BLAIR,† late 51st Native Infantry.

Ensign, 10 July 42—Lieut., 24 Jan. 45—Captain, 27 June 57.

SERVICE.—Captain BLAIR served at the action of Punniar. *Bronze Star.* Served during the Punjab Campaign, 1848-49. Present at the siege and surrender of Mooltan, and battle of Goojerat. *Medal and Clasp.* Served with the Auxiliary Force under Colonel McCausland, '58. Present at the action of Chapoorah, 10th February '58. Commanded part of the 22nd Punjab Regiment at the action of Mohumdee.

LIEUTENANT J. J. BLAIR, P. H., 31st Native Infantry.

Ensign, 13 Dec. 56—Lieut., 30 April 58.

SERVICE.—Lieutenant BLAIR served with the Meerut Volunteer Cavalry during the months of June, July, and August '57 in the Delhi and Meerut districts. Also with the 7th Punjab Infantry in Brigadier Seaton's Column from November '57 to February '58. Present at the actions of Gungeeree, 14th December '57; Putualu, 17th December '57; Mynpoorie, 27th December '57; and Bowgong, 7th April '58. Served in Mayne's Horse with General Michel's Force in pursuit of Tantia Topee and the Rao Sahib during the months of September, October, and November '58. Present at the affair at Koorai, 25th October '58. Served with General Napier's, Colonel Riche's, and Captain Roome's flying Columns from January to September '59 in the Seronge jungles, and those on the Saugor Frontier. Present at the affairs of Richwa, 16th May '59; Goonapoorie, 23rd June '59, and several minor ones. Mentioned in a Despatch by Captain F. Roome, Commanding Basoda Field Force, 24th June '59. *Mutiny Medal.*

(59)

LIEUTENANT R. BLAIR, P. H., late 32nd Native Infantry.

Ensign, 7 Aug. 55—Lieut., 16 July 57.

SERVICE.—Lieutenant BLAIR served with the late 32nd Native Infantry in the expedition against the Sonthals in '56, and during the mutiny in '57. Served in the Bundlecund Campaign against the rebels in '59 with Alexander's Horse in Brigadier Wheeler's Force. Attached with a Squadron of Alexander's Horse to No. 4 Column under Command of Colonel Oakes. *Medal.*

LIEUTENANT W. A. BLANE, Bengal Artillery.

Lieut., 8 June 60.

MAJOR J. H. BLANSHARD, Invalid Establishment.

Ensign, 11 May 24—Lieut., 13 May 25—Bt.-Captain, 11 May 39—Captain, 14 Oct. 41—Bt.-Major, 11 Nov. 51—Major, 19 Jan. 55—Invalided, 31 Dec. 55.

SERVICE.—Major BLANSHARD served at the siege of Bhurtpore. *Medal.* Throughout the Sutlej Campaign, 1845-46. Present at the battle of Sobraon. *Medal and Clasp.*

LIEUTENANT L. BLATHWAYT,† late 54th Native Infantry.

Ensign, 11 Aug. 57—Lieut., 6 June 58.

SERVICE.—Lieutenant BLATHWAYT served with the Army in India under Lord Clyde in 1858-59. Present at the siege and capture of Lucknow in March 1858, and at the taking of Bareilly and the relief of Shahjehanpore in the same year. Served in the Oude Campaign of 1858-59. *Medal and Clasp.* Served with the China Expeditionary Force. *Medal.* Also served in the following operations, against the Taiping Rebels, at the capture of stockades at Wong-ka-Dya, 4th April; stockaded village of Chowpoo, 17th April ; and stockades near Nezeean, 29th April; at the capture of the walled towns of Kahding, 1st May; Tsingpoo, 12th May ; Tsoling, 20th May; stockaded village of Manchioo, 17th May; and repulse of the rebels at Nezeean, 20th May 1862.

(60)

CAPTAIN J. BLEAYMIRE, late 2nd European Bengal Fusiliers.

2nd Lieut., 11 Dec. 40—Lieut., 12 Nov. 42—Captain, 15 Nov. 49.

SERVICE.—Served in Scinde against the Mountain Tribes in 1845. With the Indus Field Force under Sir C. Napier, 1846. In the Punjab Campaign of 1848-49, including the affairs of Ramnuggur; passage of the Chenab; and actions of Chillianwallah, (*severely wounded*), and Goojerat. *Medal and 2 Clasps.* With the Army under General Gilbert in pursuit of the Seikhs and Affghans to Peshawur. In Burmah, 1853. Present at the operations against the Rebel Chief " Moung-Goung-Gee."

CAPTAIN G. C. BLOOMFIELD, P. H., late 45th Native Infantry.

Ensign, 27 Jan. 42—Lieut., 10 June 46—Captain, 10 June 53.

SERVICE.—Captain BLOOMFIELD served throughout the Sutlej Campaign, 1845-46. Present at the battles of Moodkee, Ferozeshuhur, and Sobraon. *Medal and Clasps.* Served during the Punjab Campaign, 1848-49. Present at the actions of Chillianwallah and Goojerat. *Medal and Clasps.*

BREVET-LIEUTENANT-COLONEL BLUNT, C.B., P. H., Bengal Artillery.

2nd Lieut., 11 June 42—Lieut., 3 July 45—Bt.-Captain, 11 June 57—Captain, 7 Sept. 57—Bt.-Major, 24 March 58—Bt.-Lieut.-Colonel, 24 March 58.

SERVICE.—Captain (Bt.-Lieut.-Colonel) BLUNT, C.B., was present at the battles of Ferozeshuhur and Sobraon, 1845-46. *Medal and Clasp.* Served the Mutiny Campaign. *Medal, C.B., and Brevets of Major and Lieutenant-Colonel.*

CAPTAIN A. BLUNT, P. H., late 13th Native Infantry.

Ensign, 9 Dec. 48—Lieut., 28 Nov. 54—Captain in Staff Corps, 18 Feb. 61.

LIEUTENANT J. H. BLUNT, late 49th Native Infantry.

Ensign, 4 Oct. 57—Lieut., 11 Oct. 59.

SERVICE.—Lieutenant BLUNT served with the 23rd R. W. Fusiliers in the Oude Campaign, 1857-58. Present at the taking of Futtehgurh, the affair on the Ramgunga under Brigadier Walpole, and siege and capture of Lucknow under Lord Clyde. Served in the Campaign on the Gogra, 1858-59, under Colonel Pratt, C.B. *Medal and Clasp.*

CAPTAIN H. M. BODDAM, P. H., Bengal Artillery.

2nd Lieut., 9 June 43—Lieut., 3 July 45—Captain, 27 March 58.

LIEUTENANT W. W. BODDAM,† late 16th Native Infantry.

Ensign, 12 Dec. 51—Lieut., 22 Oct. 55.

COLONEL SIR A. BOGLE, KT., 5th (late 42nd) Native Infantry.

Ensign, 13 March 23—Lieut., 13 May 25—Captain, 14 Aug. 32— Major, 4 Oct. 44—Lieut.-Colonel, 17 Feb. 51—Bt.-Colonel, 28 Feb. 54.

SERVICE.—Colonel BOGLE served in the first Burmese War. Present at the taking of the Fort of Rungpore in Assam, and of the stockades of Duffa and Beessa, in the Now-Dheeing, in 1825. *Medal.* At the defeat of the Dewanghiri (Bootan) Rajah, and capture of his stockade at Sooban Kottah, in 1836. Served in the 2nd Burmese War. Present at the taking of Martaban and Rangoon, April 1852. *Severely wounded. Medal.* At the recapture of Beeling stockade, April 1853.

BREVET-MAJOR A. H. BOGLE, P. H., Bengal Artillery.

2nd Lieut., 8 Dec. 48—Lieut., 28 April 53—2nd Capt., 27 Aug. 58— Bt.-Major, 24 July 60.

ASSISTANT-SURGEON A. L. BOGLE,† M.D., Bengal Medical Establishment.

Asst.-Surgeon, 20 Oct. 47.

(62)

MAJOR-GENERAL A. H. E. BOILEAU, Bengal Engineers.

2nd Lieut., 17 June 24—Lieut., 7 Feb. 27—Captain, 20 May 39—Bt.-Major, 19 Aug. 47—Lieut.-Colonel, 1 May 49—Colonel, 28 Nov. 54—Regimentally, 8 June 56.

SERVICE.—Major-General A. H. E. BOILEAU served throughout the siege of Bhurtpore, and commanded two Companies of Sappers and Miners during the storming of that fortress. *Medal.*
(*Since dead.*)

BREVET-COLONEL F. B. BOILEAU, Bengal Artillery.

2nd Lieut., 6 June 23—Lieut., 28 Sept. 27—Bt.-Captain, 6 June 38—Captain, 12 August 41—Bt.-Major, 19 June 46—Major, 10 March 54—Lieut.-Colonel, 10 July 57—Bt.-Colonel, 20 June 57.

SERVICE.—Lieutenant-Colonel (Brevet-Colonel) BOILEAU was present at the siege and capture of Bhurtpore, 1825-26. *Medal.* Capture of Biona and Weir, 1825-26. Served throughout the Sutlej Campaign. Present at the affair of Buddiwal and Battle of Alliwal, 1845-46. *Medal and Brevet-Major.*

LIEUTENANT F. W. BOILEAU, P., late 16th Native Infantry.

Ensign, 20 March 55—Lieut., 23 Nov. 56.

SERVICE.—Lieutenant BOILEAU commanded a Detachment of Rajah Jawahir Sing's Contingent, under General VanCortland, in Hurrianah, from Lahore, 18th July 1857. At Ferozepore took charge of 2 guns of General VanCortland's Force. Present at the action of Hissar, 19th August 1857. Served under Brigadier Troup in 1858. Present at the action of Biswah. Served with the Saugor Field Force under General Whitlock, 1859. Commanded Squadron of 2nd Sikh Cavalry at the action of Kewtee in Bundlecund, under Brigadier Faddy, March 1859. Served under Brigadier Wheeler, 1859; under Colonel Shubrick, in the Sohagpore District, 1860. *Wounded. Wounded dangerously* with sabre cut in the face, at Hissar, also in the hand, 19th August 1857. *Wounded* at Kewtee, 4th March 1859. (Pistol shot in knee.) *Medal.* Mentioned in the Despatch of Lieutenant Mildway, 19th August 1857, and in that of Brigadier Faddy, March 1859. Received the thanks of the Governor-

(63)

General. Services especially recognized by the Commander-in-Chief, and received the thanks of the Governor-General, 1859.

CAPTAIN (BT.-MAJOR) G. W. BOILEAU, P. H., late 34th Native Infantry.

Ensign, 10 Dec. 39—Lieut., 23 June 42—Captain, 5 Aug. 54—Bt.-Major, 20 July 58.

SERVICE.—Brevet-Major BOILEAU served at the assault and capture of the Fort of Betive, in Oude, 1850. Pursuit and death of the Sultan. Fuze Ally, Oude, March 1857. Present at the action of Benares, 6th July; Azimghur, 19th July; Guggah, 13th August; Mundree, 20th September; and Atrowlea, October and November 1857. Served in the Oude Campaign, 1858-59. Present at the assault and capture of the Fort of Birwa, and subsequent operations of Sir G. Barker's Column. Received the thanks of Government. *Medal and Brevet-Majority. (Since retired).*

CAPTAIN N. E. BOILEAU, P. C., late 27th Native Infantry.

Ensign, 5 July 43—Lieut., 3 May 47—Captain, 26 May 58.

SERVICE.—Captain BOILEAU served throughout the Sutlej Campaign 1845-46. Present at the battle of Ferozeshuhur. *Medal.* Served with the Arracan Battalion in the Burmese Campaign, 1852-53. *Medal and Clasp.*

LIEUTENANT T. B. BOILEAU, P. H., late 4th Bengal Europeans.

Ensign, 28 Dec. 53—Lieut., 23 Nov. 56.

BREVET-MAJOR T. T. BOILEAU, P. H., late 2nd Bengal European Cavalry.

Cornet, 27 July 41—Lieut., 8 May 49—Captain, 13 April 55—Bt.-Major, 24 March 58.

SERVICE.—Major BOILEAU served during the Punjab Campaign, 1848-49. *Medal.* Formed one of the Garrison of Lucknow from June to November 1857, and was brought to the favorable notice of the Governor-General in the Despatch of Sir J. Inglis, K.C.B., 25th September 1857, and thanked by the Governor-General, 8th December 1857. *(Medal and Defence Clasp, and 1 year's extra service for Lucknow.)*

(64)

BREVET-MAJOR H. F. M. BOISRAGON, P. H., late 1st Bengal European Fusiliers.

2nd Lieut., 14 June 45—Lieut., 13 Oct. 46—Captain, 23 Nov. 56—Bt.- Major, 19 Jan. 58.

SERVICE.—Captain (Brevet-Major) BOISRAGON served in the Burmese War of 1852-53-54-55. Present at the relief of the Garrison of Pegu, 14th December 1852; Commanded a Field Force in the Tharrawaddy District, Burmah, against the Rebel Chief Mong Gouneggie, in which operation several of his strongholds were destroyed, and a quantity of stores and supplies were captured of various descriptions. (*Medal and Clasp.*) Served in the Campaign in Hindustan of 1857-58. Commanded a Wing of the Kumaon Goorkha Battalion at the siege, storm and capture of Delhi, 14th September 1857. (*Dangerously wounded.*) *Medal and Clasp.*) Commanded a Force in the Seharunpore District ; and on the 10th January 1858, encountered and beat back across the Ganges, at Hurdwar, upwards of 1,000 of the enemy, with 4 guns, destroying a quantity of them, and capturing arms and munitions of war. Received the thanks of the Governor-General in Council for the defeat of mutineers at Hurdwar, on the 10th January 1858, by the Troops under his command. Also the thanks of the Chief Commissioner of the Punjab for the organization of a large body of men for the Oude Police Force. Also the thanks of the Chief Commissioner of Oude for raising Cavalry and Infantry for the Oude Police Force. Was promoted to the rank of Brevet-Major for services before Delhi.

CAPTAIN T. W. R. BOISRAGON, P., late 69th Native Infantry.

Staff Corps—Ensign, 2 Sept. 46—Lieut., 15 Aug. 50—Captain, Staff Corps, 18 Feb. 61.

SERVICE.—Captain BOISRAGON served in the Saharunpore and Mozuffernuggur Districts during the Mutiny and Rebellion in 1857-58. Commanded the Troops engaged at " Sedhowlie," " Nookur," " Gungah," &c., and commanded the Infantry Detachment at the engagement at Hurdwar, January 10th 1857. *Medal.* Mentioned in Despatch of Captain H. Boisragon, who commanded the Troops at the engagement at Hurdwar. Appointed by Sir Hugh Rose, K.C.B., to the important

(65)

Command of the 30th Native Infantry, in consideration of useful and gallant service in the Field.

LIEUTENANT A. W. BOLTON, P., late 50th Native Infantry.

Ensign, 20 June 48—Lieut., 27 Oct. 50.

SERVICE.—Lieutenant BOLTON served during the Sonthal Insurrection, 1855-56. Present with Brigadier-General Frank's Division at the engagements of Chandah and Humeerpore on the 19th, and Sultanpore 23rd February 1858. Present at the siege and capture of Lucknow. *Medal and Clasp.*

CAPTAIN J. C. BONAMY, P., 3rd (late 32nd) Native Infantry.

Ensign, 1 Jan, 44—Lieut., 16 Aug. 49—Captain, 21 Nov. 57.

ASSISTANT-SURGEON E. BONAVIA,† M.D., Bengal Medical Establishment.

Asst.-Surgeon, 4 Aug. 57.

SERVICE.—Assistant-Surgeon BONAVIA served in the Lucknow Field Hospital throughout the operations at the capture of Lucknow in March 1858. Served with the Oude Military Police during the Trans-Gogra Campaign in December 1858. *Medal and Clasp.*

LIEUTENANT E. E. B. BOND, P. H., late 57th Native Infantry.

Ensign, 13 June 52—Lieut., 1 Jan. 54.

SERVICE.—Lieutenant BOND served with the Guides throughout the siege, assault, and capture of Delhi. Commanded a Detachment of Infantry the day of the assault: severely wounded. *Medal and Clasp.* Mentioned in the Despatch of Sir H. Grant, who commanded the Cavalry Division at the capture of Delhi, 1859. Served with the Force under Sir S. Cotton, K.C.B , in Eusufzaie in 1858. Served in the Expedition under Brigadier-General N. B. Chamberlain, C.B., against the Mahsood Wuzeerees. Present at the repulse of the night attack on Camp Palooseen and at the forcing of the Burrarah Pass, May 1860.

I

LIEUTENANT J. BONHAM, P. H., Bengal Artillery.
2nd Lieut., 14 June 50—Lieut., 1 Sept. 57.

LIEUTENANT-COLONEL J. BONTEIN, late 37th Native Infantry.
Ensign, 17 Aug. 26—Lieut., 7 Feb. 37—Bt.-Captain, 17 Aug. 41—Captain, 27 June 46—Bt.-Major, 20 June 54—Major, 20 March 57—Lieut.-Colonel, 26 Jan. 61.
(Since dead.)

LIEUTENANT C. M. BOSWELL, P. H., late 23rd Native Infantry.
Ensign, 13 June 57—Lieut., 18 May 58.

CAPTAIN A. C. BOSWELL,† Invalid Establishment.
Ensign, 1 March 34—Lieut., 14 April 37—Captain, 1 March 49—Invalided, 1 Nov. 50.

LIEUTENANT J. J. BOSWELL, late 69th Native Infantry.
Ensign, 10 Aug. 52—Lieut., 23 Nov. 56.
SERVICE.—Lieutenant BOSWELL served with General Nicholson's moveable Column against the Sealkôt Mutineers in 1857. Present at the affair of Trimmoo Serai against the above. *Medal.*

MAJOR N. C. BOSWELL, late 2nd Native Infantry.
Ensign, 12 June 40—Lieut., 26 March 24—Captain, 17 Feb. 51—Major, 1 Jan. 62.
SERVICE.—Major BOSWELL served with the Force under General Nott in Affghanistan, 1842. *Medal.* Present at the action of Maharajpore. *Bronze Star.* Served throughout the Sutlej Campaign, 1845-46, including the actions of Moodkee and Ferozeshuhur. *Medal and Clasp.* Present at the capture of Kôt Kangra.

RIDING-MASTER J. BOUCHER.
Riding-Master, 28 Mar. 52.

(67)

CORNET J. BOULDERSON, General List.
   Cornet, 20 Nov. 60.

LIEUTENANT S. BOULDERSON, 5th Bengal European Cavalry.
   Cornet, 20 Nov. 56—Lieut., 23 Jan. 57.

LIEUTENANT S. S. BOULDERSON, P. C. H., late 37th Native Infantry.
   Ensign, 11 Dec. 46—Lieut., 30 June 49.

2ND CAPTAIN R. DE BOURBEL, Bengal Engineers.
   2nd Lieut., 14 June 50—Lieut., 23 Jan. 55—2nd Captain, 27 Aug. 58.

BT.-LIEUT.-COLONEL G. BOURCHIER, C.B., P., Bengal Artillery.
   2nd Lieut., 11 Dec. 38—Lieut., 17 Aug. 41—Captain, 3 Mar. 53—Bt.-Major, 19 Jan. 58.
   SERVICE.—Captain (Brevet-Lieutenant.-Colonel) BOURCHIER, C.B., was present at the battle of Punniar, 1843. *Bronze Star.* Served during the Mutiny, 1857. Present with Nicholson's Column at the defeat of the Sealkôt Mutineers, 12th and 16th July, at Trimmoo Ghat on the Rooee, Siege and Capture of Delhi. *Brevet-Majority.* With Greathed's Column, at the actions of Boolundshuhur, 28th September, and Agra, 10th October. Present with Lord Clyde's Force at the relief of Lucknow, 16th November 1857. Defeat of the Gwalior Contingent, 6th December 1857. Promoted to the rank of *Lieutenant-Colonel. Medal and 2 Clasps, and C.B.*

ASSISTANT-SURGEON S. G. BOUSFIELD,† Bengal Medical Establishment.
   Asst.-Surgeon, 10 Nov. 48.

MAJOR P. A. P. BOUVERIE, P. H., late 35th Native Infantry.
   Ensign, 12 June 40—Lieut., 29 Oct. 41—Captain, 10 July 54—Bt.-Major, 11 July 54.
   SERVICE.—Major BOUVERIE served at the forcing of the Khyber Pass, and in the different operations leading to the re-occupation of Cabul.

Medal. Served at Maharajpore. *Bronze Star.* Throughout the Sutlej Campaign, 1845-46. Present at the actions of Moodkee, where he commanded the Governor-General's Body-Guard and brought it off the field, (horse shot under him), Ferozeshuhur, Alliwal, and Sobraon. *Medal and 3 Clasps.*

ASSISTANT-SURGEON J. C. BOW,† M.D., Bengal Medical Establishment.

Asst.-Surgeon, 20 Apl. 48.

SERVICE.—Assistant-Surgeon Bow served with the 2nd Bengal Fusiliers throughout the Punjab Campaign, 1848-49. Present at the action of Ramnuggur, passage of the Chenab, and battles of Chillianwallah and Goojerat. Served at Ramnuggur; assisted in the Hospital of the 14th Dragoons. Accompanied the Force under Sir Walter Gilbert in pursuit of the Sikhs and Affghans. From Bar to Peshawur, six marches, left in charge of all the sick of the Columns. *Medal and 2 Clasps.*

SURGEON-MAJOR J. BOWHILL,† M.D., Bengal Medical Establishment.

Asst.-Surgeon, 4 June 40—Surgeon, 31 March 54—Surgeon-Major, 4 June 60.

SERVICE.—Surgeon-Major BOWHILL served at the siege and capture of Delhi with the 2nd Fusiliers and Bourchier's Battery from July till 23rd September '57. With Bourchier's Battery at the action of Boolundshuhur, 30th September '57. At Agra, 10th October '57. Served during other operations of Greathed's and Grant's Column, October '57. At the relief of Lucknow by the army under Sir Colin Campbell, November '57. Served with the 3rd Brigade Horse Artillery at the action of Cawnpore, 6th December '57. With Walpole's Column through Etawah and Mynpoory on Futtehghur, January '58. With Sir J. Grant's Column in all the operations left bank of Ganges and terminating in capture of Meeagunge, March. With His Excellency Sir C. Campbell at the siege and capture of Lucknow, March '58. With Walpole's Column at Rooeya, Alligunge, and other affairs, 15th and 28th April. With the Army under the Commander-in-Chief at Bareilly, 5th May '58. With Brigadier Troup's Force at the actions of Moodipore and Russoolpore, 21st and 25th

October '58. At the capture of the Fort of Mittowlee, 10th November '58, and at other operations terminating in the affair at Mendee and Biswah, 18th November '58. *Medal and 3 Clasps.*

BREVET-MAJOR C. N. BOWIE, P. H., Bengal Artillery.

2nd Lieut., 10 Dec. 41—Lieut., 3 July 45—Captain, 21 Jan. 56—Bt.-Major, 22 Jan. 56.

SERVICE.—Brevet-Major BOWIE served during the Sutlej Campaign, 1845-46. Present at the battles of Moodkee, Ferozeshuhur, and Sobraon. *(Wounded). Medal and 2 Clasps.* Taken prisoner by Rajah Shere Singh and released at the conclusion of the Punjab Campaign.

LIEUTENANT H. BOWLES, Invalid Establishment.

Ensign, 29 Feb. 44—Lieut., 11 April 51—Invalided, 24 Oct. 51.

MAJOR A. BOYD, late 2nd European Bengal Fusiliers.

2nd Lieut., 21 Jan. 35—Lieut., 27 Dec. 41—Captain, 15 Aug. 47—Bt.-Major, 19 Jan. 58—Major, 1 Jan. 62.

SERVICE.—Major BOYD served in the 5th Native Infantry with the Army of the Indus in Scinde in 1838-39. Served with the 2nd Europeans under Sir C. Napier, against the Hill tribes in Scinde, 1844-45. Served in the 2nd Bengal European Regiment with the Army of the Punjab in 1848-49. Present at Ramnuggur, passage of the Chenab, and actions of Chillianwallah and Goojerat. *(Wounded slightly).* Present at the pursuit and surrender of the Sikh Army to Sir Walter R. Gilbert, G.C.B., and subsequent pursuit of the Affghans to the Khyber Pass. *Medal and 2 Clasps.* Commanded 4 Companies of the European Bengal Fusiliers in the operations in Burmah against the Rebel Chief Moung-Goung-Gee, 1854-55. Commanded the 2nd Bengal Fusiliers at the battle of Badlee-ka-Serai, 8th June 1857, and during all the operations before Delhi, storm and capture of the city on 14th September 1857. *Medal and Clasp.* Mentioned in the Despatch of Brigadier Jones, C.B., 17th September '57, and Major-General Sir H. Barnard, K.C.B., 12th June '57. Promoted to the rank of *Brevet-Major*, 19th January '58. Commanded a Column in the Delhi District, '59.

(70)

LIEUT.-COLONEL B. BOYD,† Her Majesty's 68th Native Infantry.

Ensign, 20 Jan. 35—Lieut., 13 Nov. 36—Captain, 20 May 46—Major, 20 Apl. 55—Lieut.-Colonel, 15 May 59.

SERVICE.—Lieut.-Colonel BOYD served with the expedition against the Bheels in Malwa in 1836. Served with the Army of the Sutlej in 1846. Present at the action of Sobraon. *Medal.* Served during the Burmese Campaign of 1852-53. *Medal.* Served in Bundlecund in 1858, with Purma Sing, in co-operation with General Whitlock's Column.

LIEUT.-COLONEL and BT.-COLONEL H. BOYD, late 59th Native Infantry.

Ensign, 17 Jan. 24—Lieut., 27 Mar. 26—Bt.-Captain, 17 Jan. 39— Captain, 5 Nov. 41—Major, 20 Sept. 49—Lieut.-Colonel, 28 Nov. 54—Bt.-Colonel, 28 Nov. 57.

SERVICE.—Brevet-Colonel BOYD served in Arracan, 1824-25. Present at the siege of Bhurtpore, 1826. *Medal.*

COLONEL M. BOYD, late 53rd Native Infantry.

Ensign, 3 Mar. 97—Lieut., 30 Oct. 97—Captain, 18 Oct. 07—Major, 21 May 16—Lieut.-Colonel, 11 June 22—Colonel, 13 May 25—Major-General, 28 June 38—Lieut.-General, 11 Nov. 51—General, 9 Apl. 56.

SERVICE.—General BOYD served during Lord Lake's Campaign, including the battle of Delhi and taking of Agra. *India Medal.*

LIEUTENANT M. O. BOYD, General List.

Ensign, 4 April 60—Lieut., 1 Jan. 62.

LIEUTENANT P. BOYD.

Ensign, 16 June 59—Lieut., 4 Feb. 61.

LIEUTENANT R. E. BOYLE, P. H., late 46th Native Infantry.

Ensign, 10 Dec. 54—Lieut., 14 July 57.

SERVICE.—Lieutenant BOYLE served in the pursuit of the Sealkôt Mutineers, July '57. Served with Brigadier Showers's Column in the

(71)

districts west of Delhi, '57. Present at the occupation of Rewaree, Jhujjur, and Kanound. Served with the Bundlecund Field Force. Engaged at Geree Patoree, 7th November '59. Commanded No. 3 Bundlecund Flying Column, December '59 to March '60. Received the thanks of the Governor-General's Agent, Central India, for "valuable services," 29th May '60. *Medal.*

CAPTAIN R. D'O. C. BRACKEN, P. H., late 52nd Native Infantry.

Ensign, 26 April 47—Lieut., 20 May 53—Captain, 4 Feb. 61.

SERVICE.—Captain BRACKEN served at the first and second siege operations of Mooltan, 1848-49. Present at the surrender of Mooltan and battle of Goojerat. *Medal and Clasps.* Present with a Detachment, 2nd Sikh Infantry (as Commanding) at the repulse of Insurgents at Murree. Present with the Force under Major General Sir S. Cotton, employed in the operations against Satuna. Received the thanks of the Major-General Commanding Sind Saugor District for service at Murree.

CAPTAIN E. BRADFORD, P., late 23rd Native Infantry.

Ensign, 11 June 39—Lieut., 16 July 42—Captain, 1 April 54.

SERVICE.—Captain BRADFORD served with the 23rd Native Infantry in the Expedition to Kohat in 1850. Received the thanks of Government. Was present with the 23rd Native Infantry when it mutinied at Mhow on 1st July 1857. Served with the 5th Infantry Hyderabad Contingent and 25th Bombay Native Infantry, part of the Central India Field Force, and present with it in the following actions, *viz.*, at the siege and capture of Rathghur in Bundlecund in January '58; at the siege and capture of Jhansi; at the battle of the Betwa; at the capture of the Mud Fort of Loharree; at the action of Koonch. *Medal and Clasp.* At the operations before, and taking of Calpee. Served with Her Majesty's 79th Highlanders as Interpreter in the following actions in Oude; at the taking of Rampore Russea, 3rd November '58, at the passage of the Gogra before Fyzabad, and subsequent pursuit of the enemy with the Cavalry, and at the affair at Muchlee Gawn.

(72)

MAJOR-GENERAL J. F. BRADFORD, C.B., P., 2nd European Cavalry.

Cornet, 1 Sept. 21—Lieut., 1 May 24—Captain, 27 Apl. 33—Major, 4 Apl. 44—Bt.-Lieut.-Colonel, 19 June 46—Lieut.-Colonel, 20 Oct. 52—Bt.-Colonel, 20 June 54—Major-General, 23 July 58.

SERVICE.—Major-General BRADFORD, C.B., served in Affghanistan, 1842; in the several engagements leading to the re-occupation of Cabul. *Medal.* Present at the battle of Maharajpore, 1843. *Bronze Star.* Battle of Alliwal, 1846. *Medal and Bt.-Lieut.-Colonel.* Army of the Punjab, including the passage of the Chenab, actions of Chillianwallah and Goojerat 1848-49. *Medal, 2 Clasps, and C.B.*

LIEUTENANT H. R. BRADFORD, P., late 36th Native Infantry.

Ensign, 10 Dec. 47—Lieut., 15 Feb. 53.

SERVICE.—Served throughout the Punjab Campaign of 1848-49. Present at the actions of Ramnuggur, Sadoolapore, Chillianwallah, and Goojerat. *Medal and 2 Clasps.* Present with the Regiment at Jullundur on the occasion of the Mutiny of the Native Troops on the 7th June 1857, and accompanied the Column composed of 200 of Her Majesty's 8th Foot and 3 Guns of Major Olpherts' Troops in the subsequent pursuit of the Mutineers towards Umballa, until ordered to return to Jullundur. *Medal.*

ENSIGN G. BRADLEY (unattached.)

Ensign, 20 Sept. 57.

CAPTAIN T. BRADSHAW, 4th Bengal European Cavalry.

Captain, Veteran Establishment, 5 Feb. 1861.

SERVICE.—Captain BRADSHAW served at the Siege and capture of Bhurtpore, under Lord Combermere, 1825-26. *Medal and Clasps.* Served at Jugpore, 1835-36, and through the Shekawatti country, in 1838. Served at Jugpore in 1839 under Brigadier Kennedy. Present at the battles of Meeanee and Hyderabad in Scinde, 1842-43. *Medal and Clasp.* Served in the Sutlej Campaign under Lord Gough, 1845-46. Served during the Mutiny, 1857-58. Present at the siege and capture of Lucknow, under Lord Clyde, March 1858. *Medal and Clasp.*

(73)

ASSISTANT-SURGEON J. BRAKE,† Bengal Medical Establishment.

Asst.-Surgeon, 24 Jan. 55.

SERVICE.—Assistant-Surgeon BRAKE served with 7th Punjab Infantry in charge of Brigadier General Nicholson's Staff and Bourchier's No. 17 Battery on the march to Camp before Delhi, August 1857. Served with 2nd Sikh Cavalry in the Oude Campaign with Brigadier Colin Troup's Columns, at the fight at Biswah, and subsequently in pursuit of Feroze Shah under Captain Campbell and Colonel Brind. Served with General Whitlock's Field Force in Bundlecund from February 1st to April 11th 1859. Had medical charge of Captain Wright's Column. Present at the fight of Tinleepanee, 29th March '59. Served with Brigadier Wheeler's Column in Bundlecund from 13th October '59. In charge of Captain Wright's Column from 15th October to 5th December '59. *Mutiny Medal*. Services mentioned in the Despatch of General Whitlock, published General Order, Commander-in-Chief, No. 790 of '59, and in that of Brigadier Wheeler, not published.

LIEUTENANT A. H. BRAMLEY, P. H., late 44th Native Infantry.

Ensign, 20 Jan. 51—Lieut., 23 Nov. 56.

SERVICE.—Lieutenant BRAMLEY served as Orderly Officer to Brigadier Polwhele, Commanding Agra and Muttra Districts, at the battle against the Neemuch Mutineers, 5th July '57. Also present at the battle of Agra against the Mhow Mutineers, 10th October '57. (*Wounded slightly*). *Medal.*

LIEUTENANT J. B. BRANDER, late 37th Native Infantry.

Ensign, 10 Sept. 56—Lieut., 1 Apl. 58.

SERVICE.—Lieutenant J. B. BRANDER served in the Volunteer Cavalry with Havelock's Force during the Campaign. Present at the battle of Futtehpore, Oung, Pandoo Nuddee, battle and retaking of Cawnpore, Bhittoor, Oonao, Busseerutgunge, Barby-ka-Chowkie. Present at the 2nd recrossing into Oude, at the battle of Munglewar, Alumbaug, and the 1st relief of Lucknow, and subsequent defence of that garrison in the intrenched camp at the Alumbaug, under Sir James Outram. Present at

K

the operations connected with the final storming and capture of Lucknow under His Excellency the Commander-in-Chief. *Medal and two Clasps.*

BREVET-MAJOR M. J. BRANDER, P., late 40th Native Infantry.

Ensign, 10 Dec. 44—Lieut., 18 June 50—Captain, 9 Oct. 57—Bt.-Major, 20 July 58.

SERVICE.—Major BRANDER served with the Burmah Expeditionary Force in 1852-53. Present at the operations in the vicinity and capture of Rangoon, April '52. Accompanied the Martaban Column as Commissariat Officer to the Bengal Troops from Martaban to Tounghoo in January and February '53. Present at two skirmishes with the enemy. *Medal.* Mentioned in the Despatch of Brigadier General S. W. Steel, C.B., Commanding the Martaban Column, and published in General Orders by the Commander-in-Chief, dated March 29th '53. Served as Senior Commissariat Officer and Pay-master to the Goorkha Auxiliary Force, under the Command of Maharajah Jung Bahadoor, from December '57 to June '58. Present at the re-capture of Goruckpore, the storming of the Fort Julalpore in Oude, and the siege and capture of Lucknow in March '58. *Medal and Clasp.* Mentioned in the Despatch of Brigadier General G. H. McGregor, C.B., Military Commissioner, on two occasions, published in General Orders by the Commander-in-Chief, dated 28th January '58 and 2nd April '58. Promoted to *Brevet-Major* for services in the Oude Campaign.

(Received a certificate of high proficiency in Oordoo, 4th July 1849, and also in Hindee, 18th September 1849, from the College of Fort William.)

LIEUTENANT A. M. BRANDRETH, Bengal Engineers.

Lieut., 27 April 58.

LIEUTENANT B. R. BRANFILL, P. H., late 5th Bengal European Cavalry.

Cornet, 14th March 54—Lieut., 5th May 56.

LIEUTENANT C. E. D. BRANSON, General List.

Ensign, 8 Sept. 59—Lieut., 7 July 61.

(75)

BREVET-LIEUTENANT-COLONEL J. BRASYER, C.B., P. H., Unattached List.
Bt.-Major, 19 Jan. 58—Major, 9 Dec. 59—Lieut.-Colonel, 20 Feb. 58.

SERVICE.—Lieutenant-Colonel BRASYER, C.B., served in Affghanistan, with the Force under General Pollock, 1842. Present at the forcing of the Khyber Pass; actions at Mamoo Kheil, Jugdulluck, Tazeen, and Huft Kotul, and assault and capture of Istaliff. *Medal.* Throughout the Campaign on the Sutlej, including the actions of Moodkee, Ferozeshuhur, and Sobraon. *Medal and 2 Clasps, and Ensign's Commission.* Promoted to Captain in consideration of the important services rendered by him at Allahabad in disarming and making prisoners of about a Company of the 6th Regiment Native Infantry, who were on Guard over the Main Gate and State Prisoners in the Fort, on the night of the 6th June 1857, and with but 400 men of his Regiment (Regiment of Ferozepore). Present in conjunction with the few Europeans there— held that Fortress secure until the arrival of more Europeans. In the engagements with the Rebels at Allahabad between the City and Cantonments on the 12th, (*Charger wounded*), Khydgunj 13th, in the Town 16th, and re-occupation of Town and Cantonments 17th June '57, with Major Renaud's moveable Column from 30th June till 12th July, advancing towards Cawnpore, with the Force under General Sir H. Havelock, at the actions of Futtehpore on the 12th, Oung and Pandoo Nuddee 15th, and battle and re-occupation of Cawnpore 16th and 17th July, Bhittoor 18th, actions of Oonao and Busseerutgunge 5th, Boorbeean-ke-Chokee 12th, (*Charger wounded*), and Bhittoor 16th August; *Brevet Major;* landed his Regiment (R. F.) on the Oude side of the River Ganges on the 17th September; two days there, in advance of the Army, to protect the making of a bridge and road for the passage of the Troops; skirmishes of 17th, 18th and 19th; actions of Munglewar 21st, Alumbaug 23rd, and first relief of Lucknow 25th September, (had charger killed at his side, and a horse under him; received five shots, left for dead but recovered). *Medal, Clasps, and C.B.* With the entrenched Camp under General Sir J. Outram at Alumbaug from the 25th November 1857 to the 10th March 1858. Present at the affairs of Gailee, 22nd December 1857, attacks of 12th and 16th January 1858, night attack of 17th February, attack of 18th, affair of 25th, also night attack of the

(76)

25th February 1858; joined the Camp of His Excellency Sir Colin Campbell, Commander-in-Chief, before Lucknow on the 11th; joined the Troops in advance at the Begumkotee on the 12th; operations of the 13th, and on the 14th March under General T. H. Franks; led his Regiment, (R. F.), which on that day stormed and carried the Emam Barra and the Kaissur Bagh, and driving the enemy before it, by turning their own guns on them, established itself in the main square, and planted the British Standard on the top of the principal Palace therein; at the taking of the Iron Bridge, &c., under General Sir J. Outram on the 16th March *(severely wounded,)* and at the subsequent operations about Lucknow. *Medal and Clasp and Lieutenant-Colonel.* With General J. H. Grant's moveable Column at Fyzabad.

ENSIGN J. BRAY (Unattached.)

Ensign, 11 May 58.

ASSISTANT-SURGEON G. BREMNER,† M.D., Bengal Medical Establishment.

Asst.-Surgeon, 10 Feb. 59.

LIEUTENANT J. A. BRERETON, P. H., late 33rd Native Infantry.

Ensign, 12 June 46—Lieut., 30 Dec. 52.

ASSISTANT-SURGEON C. BRETTINGHAM, Bengal Medical Establishment.

Asst.-Surgeon, 4 Aug. 55.

LIEUTENANT C. H. BRIDGES,† late 15th Native Infantry.

Ensign, 4 Feb. 59—Lieut., 15 July 59.

SERVICE.—Lieutenant BRIDGES served at the following operations against the Taipsing Rebels, at the capture of stockades at Wong-ka-Dya 4th April, Chowpoo 17th April, and Nezeean 29th April. At the capture by assault of the walled towns of Kahding 1st May, Chowpoo 12th May, Isoling 20th May, and village of Nawgaw 17th May 1862.

(77)

LIEUTENANT T. W. BRIDGES, Bengal Artillery.
Lieut., 27 Aug. 58.

CAPTAIN D. BRIGGS, P. H., late 17th Native Infantry.
Ensign, 11 June 41—Lieut., 8 Sept. 43—Capt., 27 July 55.

CAPTAIN J. P. BRIGGS, P. H., late 40th Native Infantry.
Ensign, 30 Jan. 42—Lieut., 24 Jan. 45—Captain, 23 Nov. 56.
SERVICE.—Captain BRIGGS served through the Bundlecund Campaign with the 40th Bengal Native Infantry in 1842-43. Served in the 2nd Burmese War, 1852-53. *Medal.* Passed an examination in Burmese.

RIDING-MASTER T. BRIGGS.
Riding-Master, 7 Jan. 59.

LIEUTENANT F. S. S. BRIND, P. H., late 44th Native Infantry.
Ensign, 4 Mar. 57—Lieut., 30 Apl. 58.
SERVICE.—Lieutenant BRIND served with the 66th Goorkha Light Infantry in the defence of the Kumaon Hills and in Rohilcund, 1857-58; in Oude in 1858-59; with Ross' Camel Corps in the operations under Brigadier Wheeler in Bundlecund, September to December '59, and as Adjutant and Quarter-Master of the Left Wing of that Corps, from 13th October to 7th December '59; in the Maroura District, in Command of Detachment of Camel Corps from January '60 to 10th April. Commanded a Column composed of a Troop, 2nd Sikh Cavalry, his own Company, and a Troop Camel Corps and Detachments, Military Police, &c., &c. Was present at the actions of Huldwanee, 1st January 1858, and Chapooraha 10th February 1858, and expedition to Buhairee May 1858. Served with, and in Command of, numerous expeditions in Bundlecund and Saugor Districts against Dowlut Singh and other Rebels, also in Goona District. A captured gun passed over his left foot at Chapoorah, 10th February 1858, injuring it. *Medal.*

(78)

COLONEL J. BRIND, C.B., Bengal Artillery.

2nd Lieut., 3 July 27—Lieut., 15 Oct. 33—Bt.-Captain, 23 July 42—Captain, 3 July 45—Bt.-Major, 20 June 54—Major, 26 June 56—Lieut.-Colonel, 18 Aug. 58—Bt.-Colonel, 26 April 59—Colonel, 18 Feb. 61.

SERVICE.—Colonel BRIND, C.B., commanded the Foot Artillery of the Delhi Field Force from 26th June to end of operations in 1857; commanded the Troops and Light Column in the Mozuffernugger, &c., District for three months, from December '57 to March '58; commanded the 3rd Brigade Horse Artillery and united Artillery Brigade of General Walpole's Field Force during its march from Lucknow to Alligunj, and in the affairs of Rooyea and Allygunj; commanded the Artillery Brigade under Lord Clyde's personal direction through Rohilcund and at the capture of Bareilly; commanded the Artillery Brigade with Brigadier Colin Troup's Column in Oude 1858-59; at the engagements of Modypoor, Russulpoor, Mittowlee, Allygunj, and Biswarrah, also the Light Troops in pursuit; commanded the Light Column in pursuit and defeat of the Rebel Army under Prince Feroze Shah Khan Bahadoor and other Chiefs, taking all their Artillery, ten guns, stores, &c., &c., at Mehuddee; commanded a Cavalry Column in pursuit of Feroze Shah through Oude towards Central India to the point assigned; *made a C.B. for Delhi, and a Brevet-Colonel*, at close of the Campaign. *Medal, with Clasp for Delhi.*

LIEUTENANT W. H. BRIND,† late 2nd European Bengal Fusiliers.

2nd Lieut., 12 Dec. 57—Lieut., 22 Oct. 58.

CAPTAIN E. W. BRISTOW,† Invalid Establishment.

Ensign, 12 Dec. 34—Lieut., 6 July 37—Bt.-Capt., 12 Dec. 49—Captain, 1 Feb. 50—Invalided, 4 Jan. 56.

LIEUTENANT J. S. BRISTOW, Invalid Establishment.

Ensign, 17 Jan. 36—Lieut., 18 Aug. 40—Invalided, 1 Nov. 44.

CAPTAIN J. W. BRISTOW, P., late 19th Native Infantry.

Ensign, 11 Dec. 39—Lieut., 9 Aug. 43—Captain, 26 Apl. 52.

SERVICE.—Captain BRISTOW served on what was technically called "Service in Scinde" from April to November 1842. (Passed in proficiency in Punjabee.)

LIEUTENANT A. W. BRODHURST, late 2nd Bengal European Cavalry.

Cornet, 24 June 57—Lieut., 18 May 58.

SERVICE.—Lieutenant BRODHURST served with the Queen's Bays, in Sir J. Outram's division, at the siege and capture of Lucknow, March 1858, and during the subsequent operations in Oude.

LIEUTENANT H. M. BROMLEY,† late 52nd Native Infantry.

Ensign, 11 June 53—Lieut., 23 Nov. 56.

MAJOR-GENERAL G. BROOKE, C.B., Bengal Artillery.

2nd Lieut., 14 Sept. 08—Lieut., 21 Feb. 10—Captain, 25 Aug. 21—Bt.-Major, 10 Jan. 37—Major, 27 Jan. 37—Lieut.-Colonel, 28 Feb. 42—Colonel, 21 July 51—Major-Genl., 28 Nov. 54.

SERVICE.—Major-General BROOKE, C.B., served in Bundlecund during 1809-10; also throughout the Nepal War under *Sir* D. Ochterlony, 1814-15, including attacks upon Nallaghur, the heights of Ramgurh and Fort Malown; present at the siege of Hattrass, 1817; served throughout the Mahratta Campaign, 1817-18, under Lord Hastings; present at the siege and capture of Bhurtpore, (*blown up,*) 1826. *Medal.* Army of the Sutlej, 1845-46, including the battles of Moodkee, Ferozeshuhur and Sobraon; in the two former of which actions he commanded the whole of the Artillery. (*Medal,* 2 *Clasps, and C.B.*) Army of the Punjab, 1848-49, as a Brigadier Commanding the Horse Artillery. Present at Ramnuggur, also in the actions of Chillianwallah and Goojerat. *Medal and* 2 *Clasps.*

LIEUTENANT-COLONEL J. C. BROOKE, P., late 61st Native Infantry.

Ensign, 12 June 35—Lieut., 3 Oct. 40—Bt.-Captain, 12 June 50—Captain, 15 Nov. 53—Major, 19 Aug. 59—Lieut.-Colonel, 12 June 61.

SERVICE.—Lieutenant-Colonel BROOKE served with the Rajpootana Field Force as Political Officer under Brigadier Parke in pursuit of rebels in Rajpootana from 26th January to 2nd February. Accompanied the Forces as Political Officer under Sir J. Mitchell from 6th to 23rd February 1859. Mentioned in the Right Honorable the Earl Canning's Minute, and received the thanks of Government.

LIEUTENANT W. S. BROOKE, late 2nd Native Infantry.

Ensign, 11 Dec. 58—Lieut., 12 June 59.

BREVET-MAJOR J. H. BROOKS, P. H., late 1st Bengal European Cavalry.

Cornet, 30 Jan. 43—Lieut., 16 Oct. 45—Captain, 20 Feb. 53—Bt.-Major, 20 July 58.

SERVICE.—Major BROOKS served at the battles of Maharajpore, 1843. *Bronze Star.* Alliwal, 1846. *Medal.* And during the Punjab Campaign, including the passage of the Chenab and actions of Chillianwallah and Goojerat, 1848-49. *Medal.* Served with the Sarun Field Force in 1857-58. Present at the battle of Sonepore, 26th December 1857, in Military charge of Gorucknath Regiment of Goorkhas, at the battle of Phoolpore, 20th February 1858. In Military charge of the Ramdul Regiment of Goorkhas, and at the battles of Amorah, 5th March and 17th April 1858. In Military charge of Buruk Regiment of Goorkhas. *Medal and Brevet-Major.*

COLONEL A. BROOME, Bengal Artillery.

2nd Lieut., 13 Dec. 27—Lieut., 9 July 35—Bt.-Captain, 13 Dec. 42—Captain, 3 July 45—Bt.-Major, 20 June 54—Major, 14 Sept. 57—Lieut.-Colonel, 27 Aug. 58—Colonel, 29 Apl. 61.

ENSIGN A. P. BROOME, General List.
Ensign, 28 Aug. 61.

ENSIGN J. H. BROOME, General List.
Ensign, 18 Sept. 60.

ASSISTANT-SURGEON A. R. BROTCHIE, M.B., A.M., Bengal Medical Establishment.
Asst.-Surgeon, 20 Jan. 60.

SURGEON-MAJOR J. P. BROUGHAM,† M.D., Bengal Medical Establishment.
Asst.-Surgeon, 8 March 40—Surgeon, 31 Dec. 53—Surgeon-Major, 8 March 60.

SERVICE.—Surgeon-Major BROUGHAM served in the Goomsur Territory, South-Western Frontier, 1846. Present at the occupation of Sumbulpore, 1848. Present at the battle of Badlee-ka-Serai; siege and capture of Delhi and battle of Narnoul. Served under Sir T. Seaton, K.C.B., in the Doab. Present at the actions of Gungeeree, Puttiallee, and Mynpooree, 1857. Present at the advance on Lucknow by Lord Clyde; affair on crossing the Goomtee; siege and capture of Lucknow, March 1858; Barree, and Nawab Gunge. Present at several engagements with rebels at Durreabad. Mentioned in the Despatch of Sir A. Wilson, K.C.B., also in that of Colonel Gerrard. Mentioned in Orders by Sir T. Seaton in Regimental Orders, July 1856, and October 1858, at Durreabad. *Wounded severely*, 29th October 1858. *Medal and 2 Clasps.*

LIEUTENANT-COLONEL T. BROUGHAM,† Bengal Artillery.
2nd Lieut., 11 Dec. 35—Lieut., 12 Aug. 41—Bt.-Captain, 11 Dec. 50—Captain, 18 March 52—Lieut.-Colonel, 18 Feb. 61.

SERVICE.—Colonel BROUGHAM served in Affghanistan. *Medal.* Present at the battle of Sobraon. *Medal.* And capture of Kangrah, 1846.

L

(82)

LIEUTENANT W. E. D. BROUGHTON,† late 6th Europeans.
Ensign, 13 June 56—Lieut., 26 Sept. 57.
SERVICE.—Served during the Mutiny Campaign. *Medal.*

CAPTAIN C. L. BROWN, P., late 46th Native Infantry.
Ensign, 1 Jan. 44—Lieut., 25 July 49—Bt.-Captain, 1 Jan. 59—Captain, 11 Sept. 59.
SERVICE.—Captain BROWN served with the Force under General Whish throughout the siege and operations in the vicinity of Mooltan, and present at the battle of Goojerat. *Medal and Clasp.*

BREVET-MAJOR E. BROWN, late 1st European Bengal Fusiliers.
2nd Lieut., 29 Dec. 44—Lieut., 10 Feb. 46—Captain, 14 Jan. 56—Bt.-Major, 19 Jan. 58.
SERVICE.—Major BROWN served throughout the Sutlej Campaign; present at the battles of Ferozeshuhur and Sobraon. *Medal and Clasp.* Burmah, 1852-53; present at the re-capture of Pegu, 21st November; relief of its garrison and operations in the vicinity, in December 1852. *Medal.* Present with his Regiment at the battle of Badlee-ka-Serai, 8th June 1857; also with four Companies of his Regiment in an attack made on the Eedgah on the 17th June, under the Command of Colonel Tombs, C.B., Horse Artillery, in which one of the enemy's guns was captured. *Wounded in five places, one dangerously. Medal.*

LIEUTENANT F. D. M. BROWN, V. C., late 1st European Bengal Fusiliers.
2nd Lieut., 8 Dec. 55—Lieut., 7 June 57.
SERVICE.—Lieutenant BROWN, V. C., served with his Regiment (the 1st Bengal Fusiliers) at the battle of Badlee-ka-Serai, 8th June '57. At Nuzzufghur, 25th August '57, with the Force under Brigadier-General Nicholson. Present in all the engagements before the walls of Delhi and at the assault and capture of the city, 14th September '57. Served with his Regiment at Narnoul, 16th November '57, with the Force under Brigadier

Gerrard. Served with his Regiment with the Force under Brigadier Sir T. Seaton, K.C.B., in the actions of Gungeeree, 14th December '57; Puttiallee, 17th December '57; and Mynpooree, 27th December '57. Served with his Regiment with the Force under Command of His Excellency the Commander-in-Chief, at the storm and capture of Lucknow, March '58, and in all the subsequent affairs in which his Regiment was engaged, till it marched into quarters, April '59. *V. C. Medal and 2 Clasps.*

CAPTAIN G. A. BROWN, P., late 21st Native Infantry.

Ensign, 26 Dec. 46—Lieut., 21 April 51—Captain, 25 Aug. 57.

SERVICE.—Captain BROWN served as Adjutant and Interpreter with the 21st (now the 1st) Native Infantry, with the Force under Major-General Sir S. Cotton, K.C.B., in the Hills on the Eusufzaie border, in April and May '58. Present at the destruction of Chinglee and Sattana. Succeeded to the Command of the Regiment on the return of the Force from Chinglee, and commanded it on the attack on Sattana, and during the end of the time the Force was out. Received the best thanks of the Major-General Commanding the Force, in his Despatch of '58.

INSPECTOR-GENERAL OF HOSPITALS, G. G. BROWN, M.D., Bengal Medical Establishment.

Asst.-Surgeon, 20 March 25—Surgeon, 29 Jan. 39—Inspector-General of Hospitals, 26 Aug. 56.

LIEUTENANT G. P. BROWN, Bengal Artillery.

Lieut., 9 Dec. 59.

CAPTAIN G. R. BROWN, P. H., Bengal Artillery.

2nd Lieut., 7 June 44—Lieut., 13 May 46—Captain, 27 April 58.

SERVICE.—Captain BROWN served during the Punjab Campaign, 1848-49. Present at the actions of Sadoolapore, Chillianwallah, and Goojerat. *Medal and 2 Clasps.*

ASSISTANT-SURGEON J. BROWN,† M.D., Bengal Medical Establishment.

Asst.-Surgeon, 24 Jan. 55.

SERVICE.—Assistant-Surgeon BROWN served during the Mutiny, 1857-58. Present at an engagement with the rebels at Allahabad, 16th June '57. Served under Sir H. Havelock. Present at the action at Futtehpore, June '57. Present at the 1st and 2nd advances on Lucknow. Forced entry into Lucknow, 25th September '57, and subsequent defence of the Residency. Served under Sir J. Outram at Alum Bagh. Present at the affair of Ghehilee, attacks of the 12th and 16th January. Night attacks of 17th and 18th February. Affair of 26th February. Present at the capture of Lucknow, including storming of Imambara, capture of Kaiser Bagh, 14th, and taking of the Iron Bridge, 16th March '58. Mentioned in the Despatch of Lieutenant-Colonel Brayser, C.B. Received the thanks of the Governor-General twice, in '56 and in '57. *Medal and 2 Clasps.*

SURGEON J. B. S. BROWN,† Bengal Medical Establishment.

Asst.-Surgeon, 20 Oct. 46—Surgeon, 17 Feb. 60.

SERVICE.—Surgeon BROWN proceeded as a Supernumerary, doing duty with H. M.'s 64th Foot, under General Havelock, on first advance towards Cawnpore from Allahabad, on 7th July '57. Present in nine engagements with the rebels. Nominated to Medical Charge of the Volunteer Cavalry, 10th August '57. *Medal.*

DEPUTY-INSPECTOR-GENERAL OF HOSPITALS, J. C. BROWN,† C.B., Bengal Medical Establishment.

Asst.-Surgeon, 5 July 36—Surgeon, 3 Feb. 50—Deputy-Inspector-General, 1 Dec. 59.

SERVICE.—Deputy-Inspector-General of Hospitals, J. C. BROWN, C.B., served in Affghanistan, from May '40 to the end of '42. *Medal.* With Sir R. Sale's Force, during the defence of Jellallabad. *Medal.* Present at general actions, with Akbar Khan, 7th April and 13th September 1842. Served during the Sutlej Campaign, 1845-46, including the actions of Alliwal and Sobraon. *Medal and Clasp.*

(85)

LIEUTENANT R. BROWN,† late 24th Native Infantry.
Ensign, 12 June 57—Lieut, 18 May 58.

SERVICE.—Lieutenant BROWN served with the 82nd Regiment at the following actions : Kunkur, under Sir T. Seaton, 7th April '58 ; Bunkaguon, 8th October '58 ; capture of Bareilly, by Lord Clyde, 5th May '58; relief of Shahjehanpore, under Sir J. Jones, occupation of Mohumdee, and affair at Shahabad. Served with the 66th Goorkha Light Infantry during the Campaign in Oude, under Brigadier Colin Troup, C.B. Present at the following actions : action at Pusgaon, 19th October '58 ; Russoolpore, 25th October '58 ; and capture of Fort Mittowlee, 8th November '58. *Medal.*

ASSISTANT-SURGEON R. BROWN, Bengal Medical Establishment.
Asst.-Surgeon, 23 July 58.

ASSISTANT-SURGEON T. E. B. BROWN,† M.D., Bengal Medical Establishment.
Asst.-Surgeon, 23 July 58.

2ND CAPTAIN W. BROWN, P. H., Bengal Artillery.
2nd Lieut., 8 June 49—Lieut., 25 July 54—2nd Captain, 27 Aug. 58.

LIEUTENANT W. C. BROWN, Bengal Artillery.
Lieut., 27 Aug. 58.

BREVET-MAJOR W. T. BROWN, C.B., P. H., Bengal Artillery.
2nd Lieut., 12 June 46—Lieut., 3 March 53—2nd Captain, 27 Aug. 58—Bt.-Major, 28 Aug. 58.

SERVICE.—Brevet-Major W. T. BROWN served throughout the Campaign in the Punjab, including the passage of the Chenab. *Medal and Clasp.* Served during the Mutiny Campaign. *Medal, Bt.-Major, and C.B.*

MAJOR C. R. BROWNE, late 60th Bengal Native Infantry.

Ensign, 14 June 27—Lieut., 12 July 33—Bt.-Captain, 14 June 42—Captain, 21 Nov. 45—Bt.-Major, 20 June 54—Major, 17 March 59.

SERVICE.—Major BROWNE served as Political Officer with a Brigade of Madras Troops under Brigadier Watson, in 1842-43. Sent to put down the insurrection in the Saugor and Nerbudda Territories. Served as Deputy Commissioner. Accompanied the Troops under Colonel Ellis, Her Majesty's 24th Regiment, to disarm the 14th Native Infantry at Jhelum. Was present during the fight, and had charger wounded.

LIEUTENANT E. F. BROWNE, P. H., late 15th Native Infantry.

Ensign, 4 Nov. 54—Lieut., 23 Nov. 56.

CAPTAIN H. A. BROWNE, P., 10th Native Infantry.

Ensign, 13 June 52—Lieut., 23 Nov. 56—Captain, 8 July 60.

SERVICE.—Captain BROWNE served with the Army of Burmah in 1852-53-54. Present at skirmishes. Served with the 10th Native Infantry, and as Aide-de-Camp to Major-General Sir J. Cheape, K.C.B. *Medal.* (Has passed an examination in Burmese and received a Certificate in high proficiency in Oordoo.)

ASSISTANT-SURGEON J. BROWNE,† B.A., F.R.C.S.I., Bengal Medical Establishment.

Asst.-Surgeon, 20 Feb. 56.

LIEUTENANT J. BROWNE,† Bengal Engineers.

Lieut., 27 Aug. 58.

SERVICE.—Lieutenant BROWNE served with the Force under Brigadier-General Chamberlain, against the Mahsood Wuzeerees, in 1860, in Command of 2 Companies of Sappers.

LIEUTENANT M. G. BROWNE, Bengal Artillery.

Lieut., 27 Aug. 58.

(87)

BREVET-LIEUTENANT-COLONEL S. J. BROWNE, C. B., V. C., late 46th Native Infantry.

Ensign, 22 Dec. 40—Lieut., 26 Oct. 44—Captain, 10 Feb. 55—Bt.-Major, 20 July 58—Bt.-Lieut.-Colonel, 26 April 59.

SERVICE.—Lieutenant-Colonel BROWNE, V. C., served with the Army of the Punjab, 1848-49. Present at the actions of Ramnuggur, Sadoolapore, Chillianwallah, and Goojerat. *Medal and 2 Clasps.* Served on the Derajat Frontier since '50 (included). Engaged in various minor skirmishes with the Hill Tribes. The Oomerzaie Wuzeeree Expedition, '52. Bozdar Expedition, '57. Narinzee (Eusufzaie), July and August '57. Mentioned in Despatch. At the siege and capture of Lucknow, March '58. Mentioned in Despatch. *Medal and Clasp.* Promoted to *Brevet-Majority* for service at Lucknow. With Sir J. Hope Grant's Column at the action of Koorsee; brought to notice in the Despatch of the Major-General, April '58. Served with Brigadier-General Sir R. Walpole's Column at the actions of Rooyah and Alleegunge. Mentioned in the Despatch of that Officer, May '58. Served with the Army under Lord Clyde, at the capture of Bareilly. Mentioned in Despatch. Commanded a detached Field Force at the action of Mohunpore, near Bareilly, June 1858. Commanded a Field Force of Cavalry and Infantry in the attack and defeat of the enemy at Seupoorah, near Peeleebheet, on 30th August '58, and capture of their guns and camp. *Wounded dangerously in two places. Left arm amputed.* Received the thanks of the Commander-in-Chief, and of Government, October '58. Promoted by Brevet to *Lieutenant-Colonel*. Received the *Military Order of the Bath and the Victoria Cross*.

LIEUTENANT S. J. BROWNE,† late 55th Native Infantry.

Ensign, 20 Jan. 55—Lieut., 23 Nov. 56.

SERVICE.—Lieutenant BROWNE served with the 5th Punjab Infantry during the Oude Campaign, '58, and in the affair of Sitka Ghaut, Nepaul Frontier, 13th February '59. In Command of a Detachment of the

5th Punjab Infantry at Darzee Talas, 12th April '59. *Horse shot under him.* Mentioned in Despatch, 3rd June '59. *Medal.*

CAPTAIN C. H. BROWNLOW, P. H., late 4th Europeans.

Ensign, 20 Dec. 47—Lieut., 10 Sept. 52—Captain, 6 Nov. 59.

SERVICE.—Captain BROWNLOW served during the Punjab Campaign, 1848-49. *Medal.* Present in the operations against the Hussunzaie and Abazaie tribes, and taking of the Black Mountain in Huzara, 1852. *Was shot through the lungs* at the taking of the heights above Shah Moosah Khel, on the Momund Frontier, August 1854. Present at the forcing of the Khanbund Pass, and subsequent operations against the Bozdar tribes, March 1857. Commanded the 8th Punjab Infantry on the expedition beyond the Eusufzaie border, of the Force under Major-General Sir S. Cotton, in April 1858. Served throughout the third China War, including the action of Sinho, taking of the Tonko and Takoo Forts, and subsequent occupation of Pekin. *Medal and Clasps.*

BREVET-MAJOR C. ST. G. BROWNLOW, P. H., late 15th Native Infantry.

Ensign, 26 Sept. 40—Lieut., 28 Sept. 43—Captain, 28 Nov. 54—Bt.-Major, 24 March 58.

SERVICE.—Major BROWNLOW served with the Army of the Punjab in '48. Present at the passage of the Ramnuggur and the actions of Chillianwallah and Goojerat. *Medal and 2 Clasps.* Served as Brigade-Major with the Force under Brigadier McCausland, and mentioned in his Despatch, 9th March '58. *Medal.* Promoted to the rank of *Major* by Brevet, for services in '58.

CAPTAIN F. C. J. BROWNLOW, P. H., late 1st Bengal European Cavalry.

Cornet, 1 Oct. 45—Lieut., 1 Jan. 52—Captain, 23 Nov. 56.

SERVICE.—Captain BROWNLOW served during the Punjab Campaign, 1848-49. Present at the passage of the Chenab, and actions of Chillianwallah and Goojerat. *Medal.*

BREVET-MAJOR H. A. BROWNLOW, Bengal Engineers.

2nd Lieut., 11 Dec. 49—Lieut., 1 Aug. 54—2nd Captain, 27 Aug. 58—Bt.-Major, 28 Aug. 58.

SERVICE.—Major BROWNLOW served as Field Engineer with the Delhi Field Force in '57. *Wounded dangerously* at the storming of Delhi. Mentioned in the Despatch of Lieutenant-Colonel Baird Smith, 9th November '57. Served as Assistant Field Engineer with the Rohilcund Field Force, in '58. Promoted to the rank of *Brevet-Major*. Mentioned *twice* in Lord Canning's Despatch to the Home Government for services at Saharunpore, on the out-break of the Mutiny in '57. *Medal and Clasp.*

CAPTAIN H. R. BROWNLOW, P., Bengal Artillery.

2nd Lieut., 11 June 47—Lieut., 3 March 53—2nd Captain, 27 Aug. 58.

LIEUTENANT A. BRUCE,† late 28th Native Infantry.

Ensign, 20 Oct. 52—Lieut., 23 Nov. 56.

LIEUTENANT A. A. BRUCE, P. H., late 4th Europeans.

Ensign, 15 Aug. 46— Lieut., 15 Nov. 53.

SERVICE.—Lieutenant BRUCE served with his late Regiment (3rd Native Infantry) in the Punjab Campaign, 1848-49, with the Force under Brigadier Wheeler. *Medal.* Served in the expedition under Colonel Mackeson, against the Hussunzaies, in 1852-53.

CAPTAIN A. H. B. BRUCE, P. H., late 43rd Native Infantry.

Ensign, 20 April 46—Lieut., 15 Nov. 53—Captain in Staff Corps, 18 Feb. 61.

ENSIGN A. McC. BRUCE, General List.

Ensign, 4 Nov. 60.

DEPUTY-INSPECTOR-GENERAL OF HOSPITALS, H. A. BRUCE,† M.D., Bengal Medical Establishment.

Asst.-Surgeon, 17 Aug. 30—Surgeon, 5 June 47—Deputy-Inspector-General, 21 May 59.

SERVICE.—Deputy-Inspector-General of Hospitals, H. A. BRUCE, M.D., served against the Coles, 1832-33, in Affghanistan, 1839-40-41. Present at the storm and capture of Ghuznee; crossed the Hindu Koosh with Dennie's Brigade, and was present at the battle of Bameean. Served during the Campaign on the Sutlej, including the actions of Alliwal and Sobraon. *2 Medals and Clasp* for Ghuznee, Alliwal, and Sobraon.

BREVET-LIEUTENANT-COLONEL H. LEG. BRUCE, P. H., Bengal Artillery.

2nd Lieut., 15 Feb. 42—Lieut., 3 July 45—Bt.-Captain, 15 Feb. 57—Captain, 8 June 57—Bt.-Major, 24 March 58—Bt.-Lieut.-Colonel, 26 April 59.

SERVICE.—Brevet-Lieutenant-Colonel H. LEG. BRUCE was present at the battle of Maharajpore. *Bronze Star.* Affair of Budiwal; actions of Alliwal and Sobraon. *Medal and Clasp.* Served with the army of the Punjab, 1848-49, including the actions of Sadoolapore, Chillianwallah, and Goojerat. *Medal and 2 Clasps.* Served during the Mutiny Campaign. *Medal and Brevets of Major and Lieutenant-Colonel.*

LIEUTENANT T. F. BRUCE,† General List.

Ensign, 20 April 59—Lieut., 30 Sept. 60.

ASSISTANT-SURGEON J. L. BRYDEN,† M.D., Bengal Medical Establishment.

Asst.-Surgeon, 4 Aug. 56.

ASSISTANT-SURGEON R. K. BUCKELL,† Bengal Medical Establishment.

Asst.-Surgeon, 20 Nov. 47.

SURGEON H. B. BUCKLE,† Bengal Medical Establishment.

Asst.-Surgeon, 18 March 44—Surgeon, 16 Sept. 57.

SERVICE.—Surgeon BUCKLE served with the 4th Troop, 2nd Brigade Horse Artillery, in the Punjab Campaign, in 1848-49. Present at the passage of the Chenab, and battles of Chillianwallah and Goojerat, and the subsequent pursuit of the Sikh and Affghan Army, and occupation of Peshawur by the Column under General Sir W. Gilbert. *Medal and 2 Clasps.* Served with the 4th Sikh Infantry during the siege, and at the assault of Delhi, 14th September 1857. *Medal and Clasp.* Served with the 4th Sikh Infantry, forming part of the Koorum Field Force, under Brigadier-General Chamberlain, C.B., during the operations against the Cabul Khel Wuzeerees (December and January, 1859-60). Present at the affair at Maidanee. Served with the 4th Sikh Infantry, forming part of the Tâk Field Force under Brigadier-General Chamberlain, C.B., during the operations against the Mahsood Wuzeerees, in April, May, and June '60. Present at the night attack of Palloreew, at the forcing of the Burrharha Pass, and occupation of Ramgoorum and Mukkeew, &c.

LIEUTENANT F. A. BUCKLEY, P. C., late 37th Native Infantry.

Ensign, 17 July 50—Lieut., 22 May 56.

LIEUTENANT JOHN BUCKLEY, V. C., Veteran Establishment.

Lieut., 18 Oct. 58.

SERVICE.—Lieutenant BUCKLEY was present at the mutiny of the Troops on the 11th May 1857, at Delhi. Was one of the nine (and is now the only survivor) of those who defended and blew up the magazine on that occasion. *Was severely wounded in six places.* After the explosion of the magazine, he swam the Jumna with Mrs. Roberts and her son, and saved their lives at the risk of his own. Was present with General Sir A. Wilson's Force at the Hindun; at the battle of the 9th June, and afterwards at the siege of Delhi. *Medal and Clasps. V. C. and Lieutenant on the Veteran Establishment.* Has nearly completed 30 years' active service. "Date of act of bravery, 11th May 1857. For gallant conduct in the defence of the magazine at Delhi, on the 11th May 1857."

(92)

CAPTAIN S. BUDD (Unattached).

Ensign, 11 Apl. 49—Lieut., 14 June 56—Captain, 14 Sept. 57.

SERVICE.—Captain BUDD served against the Coles in 1832. Served in Affghanistan under General Pollock, in 1842. Present at the recapture of Cabul. *Medal.* Served with the Army against Gwalior, 1843. *Bronze Star.* Present at the actions of Buddiwal, Alliwal, and Sobraon. *Medal and Clasp.* Present throughout the Punjab Campaign: *severely wounded* at the battle of Goojerat. *Medal*, and unattached Ensigncy. Served throughout the siege of Delhi *(severely wounded).* *Medal*, and unattached Captaincy. Present at the actions on the Hindun.

LIEUTENANT D. S. BUIST, P. H., late 27th Native Infantry.

Ensign, 20 Dec. 48—Lieut., 23 Nov. 56.

SERVICE.—Lieutenant BUIST served with the Sylhet Light Infantry Battalion, in pursuit of the 34th Mutineers, '57-58. Commanded a Detachment at the action at Binna Caudy (in the Cachar District, 12th January '58). *Medal.* Mentioned in the Despatch of Captain H. B. Stevens, Commanding the Regiment, and was sent with a Detachment to reinforce the station, was attacked by the mutineers and rebel Munnipoorees, which the Detachment repulsed and drove before them. Mentioned by the Officiating Superintendent of Cachar in a Despatch to the Lieutenant-Governor of Bengal, 13th January '58. Received the thanks of Government, 26th January '58. Commanded a Detachment of the Sylhet Light Infantry Battalion employed in the Jynteah Hills, in suppressing the Cossiah insurrection. Skirmishes with the rebels on the 26th and 28th March '60, and capture of the stockaded village of Moong-Gougie. Services brought to the notice of the Lieutenant-Governor of Bengal by Captain Rowlatt, 14th May '60. Received the commendation of the Right Hon'ble Sir Charles Wood, in a Despatch to His Excellency the Governor-General of India, 16th February '61.

LIEUTENANT H. M. BULLER, late 5th Bengal European Cavalry.

Cornet, 4 Jan. 59—Lieut., 3 April 59.

(93)

CAPTAIN A. C. BUNBURY, late 34th Native Infantry.
Ensign, 1 Jan. 44—Lieut., 1 Feb. 50—Bt.-Captain, 1 Jan. 59.

SERVICE.—Captain BUNBURY served during the Sutlej Campaign, 1845-46. Present at the battle of Ferozeshuhur, and at the taking of Kote Kangra. *Medal.*

LIEUTENANT H. F. BUNBURY,† General List.
Ensign, 11 June 59—Lieut., 4 Feb. 61.

BREVET-MAJOR A. BUNNY, P. H., Bengal Artillery.
2nd Lieut., 8 Dec. 43—Lieut., 21 Dec. 45—Captain, 27 April 58—Bt.-Major, 20 July 58.

SERVICE.—Brevet-Major BUNNY served during the Sutlej Campaign. Present at the battle of Sobraon, 1846. *Medal.* At the siege and surrender of Mooltan, including actions, 12th September *(wounded)*, and 7th November 1848; battle of Goojerat, 1849. *Medal and 2 Clasps;* at the siege of Delhi, from battle of Badlee-ka-Serai, 8th June, until assault and capture of the city, 20th September 1857, *(wounded);* present with Greathed's Column at battle of Bolundshuhur, 28th September, and battle of Agra, 10th October; at the relief of Lucknow, from 14th to 22nd November; battle of Cawnpore, 6th December; Futtyghur, 2nd January 1858. Siege of Lucknow under Lord Clyde, March 1858. Served with Walpole's Column at the attack on the Fort of Rooyah, 15th April; Allygunge, 22nd April; Bareilly, 5th May; Mohumdee, 24th May; and Shahabad, 1st June 1858. *Medal and 3 Clasps,* and *Brevet-Majority.*

LIEUTENANT H. M. B. BURLTON, late 5th Europeans.
Ensign, 12 June 55—Lieut., 23 Nov. 56.

SERVICE—Lieutenant BURLTON served with the " 8th King's Own" in various skirmishes, under Brigadier Showers, at Agra, in '58. Served with Meade's Horse at the capture of Gwalior. Commanded the Regiment during the pursuit of the rebels by Sir Robert Napier, and was present at the actions of Joura, Alupore, on the 21st June '58.

Commanded a Detachment of Meade's Horse, attached to Colonel Sandaman's Flying Column, on Field Service, in operations against Tantia Topee, and other rebels, from October '58 to February '59. *Medal.*

LIEUTENANT N. R. BURLTON, P. H., late 40th Native Infantry.

Ensign, 30 Dec. 54—Lieut., 8 June 57.

SERVICE.—Lieutenant BURLTON served with his Regiment during the Sonthal Campaign of '55, under General Lloyd, from July '55 to the close of the Campaign in the beginning of '56. Served with the Sarun Field Force, under Brigadier Rowcroft, in the Sarun and Goruckpore Districts, from October '57 to June '58. Present at the following actions: Sonepore, 25th December '57; capture of Fort of Chandeepore, in Oude, 17th January '58; "Phoolpore," in Oude, 20th February '58; "Amorha," near Fyzabad, on the 5th March '58, and 17th April '58; capture of Fort Nuggur, in the Goruckpore District, on the 29th April '58. Present at the capture of Jugdeespore, in Arrah District, by the Column under Colonel Eyre, in August '57. *Medal.* Mentioned in the Despatches of Colonel Rowcroft, who commanded the Brigade, and Brigadier-General MacGregor, Military Commander with Maharajah Jung Bahadoor's Goorkha Troops. Accompanied the Sarun Field Force as Doing Duty Officer with Maharajah Jung Bahadoor's Troops, and commanded a Detachment from December '57 to June '58, of 50 Sikhs of the Bengal Police Battalion, at that time attached to the Sarun India Force.

LIEUTENANT-COLONEL H. P. BURN, late 4th Europeans.

Ensign, 16 Aug. 24—Lieut., 13 May 25—Captain, 6 July 37—Bt.-Major, 4 Oct. 42—Bt.-Lieut.-Colonel, 20 June 54—Major, 16 Jan. 55—Lieut.-Colonel, 13 March 59—Bt.-Colonel, 1 May 55.

SERVICE.—Lieutenant-Colonel BURN served throughout the Campaign in Affghanistan, 1840-41-42, including the siege of Jellallabad and defeat of Akbar Khan, 7th April 1842. *Medal and Brevet-Major;* also at the re-occupation of Cabul. *Medal.* Served as Deputy-Adjutant-

General with the Force sent across the Jhelum in pursuit of Shere Singh and the Affghans. *Medal.* *(Since retired.)*

CAPTAIN J. BURN, P. H., late 40th Native Infantry.

Ensign, 12 Dec. 45—Lieut., 1 July 51—Captain, 2 Sept. 59.

SERVICE.—Captain BURN served with the 40th Native Infantry throughout the Burmah War of 1852-53, including the storming of the Great Pagoda at Rangoon, on the 14th April 1852, when in Command of the Light Company of his Regiment. *Medal.* Served throughout the Sonthal Campaign of 1855-56. Served as Staff Officer to the Sasseram Field Force, in '58.

BREVET-MAJOR H. K. BURNE, P., late 2nd Native Infantry.

Ensign, 30 Dec. 43—Lieut., 21 Dec. 45—Captain, 6 June 57—Bt.-Major, 4 Nov. 59.

SERVICE.—Brevet-Major BURNE served throughout the Sutlej Campaign, including the actions of Moodkee and Ferozeshuhur. *Medal and Clasp.* Present at the capture of Kote Kangra, and present with the Burmah Force, at the operations in the vicinity of Pegu. *Medal.*

LIEUTENANT J. BURNELL, Veteran Establishment.

Lieut., 3 Jan. 59.

SERVICE.—Lieutenant BURNELL served in the Burmah War, 1825-26 and 1852-54. *Medal.* Present in all the engagements with the Force under General Havelock, from Futtehpore to the taking of Cawnpore, November 1857. *Medal.*

COLONEL F. C. BURNETT, Bengal Artillery.

2nd Lieut., 4 Nov. 27—Lieut., 15 Oct. 34—Bt.-Captain, 4 Nov. 42— Captain, 3 July 45—Bt.-Major, 20 June 54—Major, 27 June 57—Lieut.-Colonel, 27 Aug. 58—Bt.-Colonel, 18 Feb. 61.

SERVICE.—Colonel BURNETT served with Brigadier General Wheeler's Force, during the Punjab Campaign, 1848-49. *Medal.*

COLONEL G. BURNEY, P. C., 10th Native Infantry.

Ensign, 14 Sept. 19—Lieut., 25 May 21—Captain, 11 Nov. 33—Bt.-Major, 23 Dec. 42—Major, 26 Feb. 46—Lieut.-Colonel, 6 Jan. 52—Bt.-Colonel, 28 Nov. 54.

SERVICE.—Colonel BURNEY served in Sylhet, 1824; throughout the operations in Affghanistan, with the Force under General Nott. *Medal and Brevet-Major*, and with the Army of the Sutlej, at Sobraon. *Medal.* Served in Command of the 65th Native Infantry, in China, in 1859-60.

LIEUTENANT-COLONEL F. W. BURROUGHS, late 17th Native Infantry.

Ensign, 8 Jan. 25—Lieut., 19 Oct. 27—Bt.-Captain, 8 Jan. 40—Captain, 1 Oct. 41—Bt.-Major, 11 Nov. 51—Major, 9 Sept. 56—Bt.-Lieut.-Colonel, 4 Feb. 59—Lieut.-Colonel, 27 Dec. 59.

SERVICE.—Colonel BURROUGHS was present at Buddiwal, 1846; served as Aide-de-Camp to General Littler during the Sutlej Campaign, and as Assistant Adjutant-General of Division in the Campaign of the Punjab. Present at Ramnuggur, and with the Force under General Wheeler, at the capture of the heights of Dulla, 1849. *Medal.*

LIEUTENANT R. W. E. BURROWES, General List.

Ensign, 20 Dec. 60—Lieut., 1 Jan. 62.

LIEUTENANT J. P. BURTON,† late 62nd Native Infantry.

Ensign, 11 June 53—Lieut., 23 Nov. 56.

LIEUTENANT-COLONEL R. Y. BUSH, late 13th Native Infantry.

Ensign, 19 May 28—Lieut., 18 Aug. 34—Captain, 1 Feb. 41—Major, 12 Jan. 53—Lieut.-Colonel, 15 July 57.

(97)

LIEUTENANT C. M. BUSHBY,† late 70th Native Infantry.

Ensign, 4 April 54—Lieut., 30 April 58.

SERVICE.—Lieutenant BUSHBY served with the 70th Native Infantry in China, in '58, '59, and till April '60, when the Regiment embarked to return to India.

CAPTAIN G. BUSHBY,† late 4th Bengal European Cavalry.

Cornet, 24 Jan. 46—Lieut., 10 July 52—Captain, 2 Jan. 58.

SERVICE.—Captain BUSHBY served with a Force against the Jhuts, in the Googaira District, in '57. Served under Brigadier Franks in Oude, and present at the siege and capture of Lucknow by Lord Clyde, March '58. *Medal and Clasp.*

CAPTAIN J. T. BUSHBY, late 67th Native Infantry.

Ensign, 10 Aug. 52—Lieut., 17 May 54—Captain, 1 Jan. 62.

SERVICE.—Lieutenant BUSHBY served in Burmah Campaign. *Medal.*

VETERINARY-SURGEON J. G. BUSHMAN.

Veterinary-Surgeon, 7 Jan. 58.

SERVICE.—Veterinary-Surgeon BUSHMAN served with Brigadier Troup's Column, in Oude, '58, '59. *Medal.*

CAPTAIN A. L. BUSK, P. C., late 66th Native Infantry.

Ensign, 12 June 42—Lieut., 9 Dec. 44—Captain, 23 Nov. 56.

SERVICE.—Captain BUSK accompanied the Force under Brigadier Hodgson, against the Sheoranees, on the Dehra Ishmael Khan Frontier, as Assistant Commissioner, in April '53.

LIEUTENANT J. BUTCHART, Bengal Artillery.

Lieut., 10 June 59.

LIEUTENANT-COLONEL J. BUTLER, late 11th Native Infantry.

Ensign, 12 Jan. 21—Lieut., 11 July 23—Captain, 1 Jan. 37—Major, 12 Oct. 45—Lieut.-Colonel, 3 Oct. 51—Bt.-Colonel, 28 Nov. 54.

SERVICE.—Colonel BUTLER served with the late 27th Native Infantry at Chittagong, at the commencement of the first Burmese War, '23, '24. Served under Sir Hugh Wheeler in '48, '49, and commanded the 3rd Native Infantry at the taking of the Fort of " Rungul Munzul" and " Killalwalla," and commanded the Main Column at the taking of the heights of Dulla. *Medal.* (Mentioned in Despatch.) Commanded a Detachment in '49, in disarming the Sikh population in the Baree Doab, in the Punjab. Commanded a Field Force under Colonel Mackeson, in Huzara—the Black Mountain—and against the fanatics of Sattana, on the Indus. Received the thanks of the Governor-General in Council.

SURGEON-MAJOR J. H. BUTLER, P. H., F.R.C.S., Bengal Medical Establishment.

Asst.-Surgeon, 3 Jan. 40—Surgeon, 1 Dec. 53—Surgeon-Major, 13 Jan. 60.

LIEUTENANT T. A. BUTLER, V. C., 1st European Bengal Fusiliers.

2nd Lieut., 9 June 54—Lieut., 23 Nov. 56.

SERVICE.—Lieutenant BUTLER served during the Indian Campaign of '57, '58. Present with his Regiment, from 10th June '57, in all the engagements under the walls of Delhi, including the affair under Brigadier-General Nicholson, on 24th July '57. Present at the storm and capture of Delhi, 14th September '57. Served in the Columns under Brigadier Gerrard and Sir Thomas Seaton, including the actions of Gungeeree, 14th December '57; Puttiallee, 17th December '57; and Mynpooree, 27th December '57, en route to Futtyghur. Present at the storm and capture of Lucknow, under Lord Clyde, and subsequent operations in Oude, under Sir Hope Grant, *wounded slightly.* *Medal and 2 Clasps, and Victoria Cross.* Mentioned in Despatch of Sir J. Outram, 8th March 1858. (Received 1st Class Certificate from Hythe.)

(99)

2ND CAPTAIN F. R. BUTT, P., Bengal Artillery.
2nd Lieut., 11 Dec. 49—Lieut., 2 Oct. 55—2nd Captain, 27 Aug. 58.

SERVICE.—Captain BUTT served under Brigadier General Chamberlain, against the Mahsood Wuzeerees, in May 1860. Received the favorable notice of Government, 24th April 1861.

ASSISTANT-SURGEON W. B. BUTT, Bengal Medical Establishment.
Asst.-Surgeon, 20 March 53.

LIEUTENANT H. R. BUTTANSHAW, P.C.H., late 47th Native Infantry.
Ensign, 24 Dec. 50—Lieut., 27 Oct. 56.

LIEUTENANT T. BUTTANSHAW, P. H., late 20th Native Infantry.
Ensign, 12 Dec. 49— Lieut., 3 Nov. 52.

LIEUTENANT W. H. BUTTANSHAW, late 5th Europeans.
Ensign, 4 Sept. 54—Lieut., 11 June 56.

SERVICE.—Lieutenant BUTTANSHAW served during a portion of the hot season of '57, with a Detachment of the late 5th Regiment employed in protecting the Boossur and Umballa Districts.

LIEUTENANT A. D. BUTTER, late 13th Native Infantry.
Ensign, 12 Dec. 56—Lieut., 27 June 57.

SERVICE.—Lieutenant BUTTER was present at Lahore during the rebellion, at the out-break of the 20th Native Light Infantry. Served during the Oude Campaign, '58, '59, with the Simoor Battalion.

(100)

LIEUTENANT AND BREVET-CAPTAIN C. H. BYERS, P. H., 10th, late 70th Native Infantry.

Ensign, 12 June 42—Lieut., 15 May 50—Bt.-Captain, 12 June 52.

SERVICE.—Captain BYERS served with the Gwalior Army. *Bronze Star*. Served throughout the Punjab Campaign of '48, '49. Present at the affair of Ramnuggur and passage of the Chenab; at the actions of Chillianwallah and Goojerat, and in the subsequent pursuit of the Sikhs and Affghans by the Force under General Gilbert. *Medal and 2 Clasps*. Accompanied the Force from Nepal under His Excellency Maharajah Jung Bahadoor, G.C.B., from 15th December '57 to 2nd May '58, in the capacity of Political Assistant to Brigadier General G. H. Macgregor. Present at the capture and re-occupation of Goruckpore; also at the siege and capture of Lucknow. *Medal and Clasp*.

BREVET-COLONEL B. BYGRAVE, late 31st Native Infantry.

Ensign, 16 Jan. 21—Lieut., 23 July 23—Bt.-Captain, 16 Jan. 36—Captain, 4 May 37—Bt.-Major, 9 Nov. 46—Major, 8 July 48—Lieut.-Colonel, 15 Nov. 53—Bt.-Colonel, 28 Nov. 54.

SERVICE.—Colonel BYGRAVE served on the Sylhet Frontier and in Arracan, during the Burmese War; joined the Army of the Indus as Field Pay Master in November '38, and was employed in Affghanistan until the termination of the Campaign. Present at the storm and capture of Ghuznee. *Medal and 3rd Class Dooranee Order*. Taken prisoner by Mahomed Akbar Khan, during the retreat from Cabul; released, 27th September '42.

ASSISTANT-SURGEON O. BYRNE, Bengal Medical Establishment.

Asst.-Surgeon, 23 July 58.

LIEUTENANT F. M. BIRCH, P. H., late 71st Native Infantry.

Ensign, 4 April 54—Lieut., 31 May 57.

SERVICE.—Lieutenant F. M. BIRCH served during the Indian Mutinies. Present at the disaster at Chinhut, June '57. Mentioned in the

(101)

Despatch of Brigadier Inglis, 25th September '57, as "having cleared a village with a party of skirmishers in a manner to elicit the admiration of the Brigadier-General." Served as A. D. C. to Brigadier Inglis from 2nd July to 25th September '57. Commanded a Detachment of the 71st Native Infantry throughout the whole of the siege, June '57. Engaged in three sorties. Commanded a party of Her Majesty's 84th Foot, 18th August '57, to repulse a grand attack ; and subsequently regained possession of the breach. *Slightly wounded twice. Medal and 2 Clasps.* Favorably mentioned and brought to the notice of the Governor-General and Commander-in-Chief in Despatch of Brigadier Inglis, 25th September '61. Received the thanks of the Governor-General, 8th December '57. Present at the final relief of Lucknow, as A. D. C. to Sir J. Inglis. Received the thanks of the Governor-General, 12th January '58. Present at the advance on the 6th December '57, when the Gwalior Contingent Mutineers were turned out of Cawnpore. Present at the capture of the village of Hurrah, in Oude, March '58.

CAPTAIN W. BRIGGS, P. H., late 71st Native Infantry.

Ensign, 17 Feb. 43—Lieut., 9 July 46—Captain, 31 May 57.

SERVICE.—Captain BRIGGS served with a Force under the Command of Colonel S. Fisher. Present at the attack and defeat of the insurgents under Ram Sing, at Noorpore, in September '48. Served during the Punjab Campaign, '48, '49. *Medal.* Served during the Burmese War, '52. Commanded a Detachment of 250 men in the Aeng Pass. Thanked by Captain Murray and the Officer Commanding in Arracan. *Medal.* Commanded General Reid's Escort of Pathan Cavalry at the battle of Badlee-ka-Serai, 8th June '57. Served throughout the siege and capture of Delhi, '57. *Medal and Clasp.* Served throughout the Rohilcund Campaign, '58, including the battle of Kukuralli, 30th April '58. Present at the battle of Bareilly, under Lord Clyde, 5th and 6th May '58 ; at the attack on the rebels at Shahjehanpore, 18th May '58. Present at the destruction of Mohumdee, 25th May '58. Mentioned in Brigadier Jones' Despatch, 6th May '58. Served in the Oude Campaign, '58, '59. Present at the attack and capture, by storm, of Rampore Kaiseah, 6th November '58. Honorably mentioned in the Brigadier's Despatch, 18th November '58.

Accompanied Colonel Guise into the Terai, in November '59. Thanked in Field Force Orders, 29th December '59.

C

LIEUTENANT W. CABELL, P. H., late 62nd Native Infantry.

Ensign, 26 June 50—Lieut., 29 May 55.

CAPTAIN A. CADELL,† Bengal Engineers.

2nd Lieut., 13 June 45—1st Lieut., 1 Jan. 52—2nd Captain, 27 Aug. 58 —Captain, 18 Feb. 61.

2ND CAPTAIN H. M. CADELL, P. H., Bengal Artillery.

Lieut., 20 Nov. 56—2nd Captain, 21 April 60.

SERVICE.—Captain CADELL served with the Burmah Expedition. Present at the operations in the vicinity and capture of Rangoon, April 1852. *Medal.*

LIEUTENANT R. CADELL, P. H., late 20th Native Infantry.

Ensign, 9 June 49—Lieut., 14 Aug. 53.

LIEUTENANT T. CADELL, P. H., V. C., late 2nd Europeans.

2nd Lieut., 17 April 54—Lieut., 23 Nov. 56.

SERVICE.—Lieutenant CADELL, V. C., served with the 2nd Bengal Fusiliers during the whole of the operations before Delhi. Battle of Badlee-ka-Serai, 8th June 1857. Final assault and capture of the City, 14th September 1857, and subsequent operations with the Moveable Column under Brigadier Showers, C. B., in the District of Delhi. *Medal, Clasp, and Victoria Cross.* Served in the 4th Irregular Cavalry with Brigadier Colin Troup's Column in the Oude

(103)

Campaign of 1858-59. Present at the action at Hindun, under Colonel Brind, in which 13 guns were taken from Ferozeshah. Mentioned in Colonel Brind's Despatch, dated 18th or 19th November '58, and with Colonel Turner's Column, in Bundlecund, in '59. Commanded No. 1 Bundlecund Flying Column, and received the thanks of Government, 29th May 1860.

LIEUTENANT T. CADELL, P. C. H., late 2nd European Bengal Fusiliers.
2nd Lieut., 17 April 54—1st Lieut., 23 Nov. 56.

SERVICE.—Lieutenant CADELL served as Quarter-Master with the 2nd Bengal Fusiliers, during the whole operations before Delhi. Present at the battle of Badlee-ka-Serai, 8th June 1857. Final assault and capture of Delhi, 14th September 1857, and subsequent operations with the Moveable Column under Brigadier Showers, in the District of Delhi.

MAJOR W. M. CAFE, P. H., V. C., late 56th Native Infantry.
Ensign, 11 June 42—Lieut., 12 April 43—Captain, 27 Jan. 49—Major, 29 Aug. 61.

SERVICE.—Major CAFE, V. C., served at the action of Maharajpore. *Bronze Star.* Throughout the Punjab Campaign, including the battles of Sadoolapore, Chillianwallah, and Goojerat, and subsequent pursuit of the Sikhs and Affghans with the Force under General Gilbert. *Medal and 2 Clasps.* Served during the Mutiny Campaign. *Medal and V. C.*

CAPTAIN W. E. CAHILL,† late 40th Native Infantry.
Ensign, 1 Jan. 44—Lieut., 15 Oct. 48—Captain, 8 June 57.

SERVICE.—Captain CAHILL served during the Sonthal Rebellion, '55, under Major General Lloyd. With the Burmah Expedition, '52. Present at the operations in the vicinity and capture of Rangoon, April '52. *Medal.*

(104)

ASSISTANT-SURGEON W. E. CAIRD,† Bengal Medical Establishment.
Asst.-Surgeon, 4 Aug. 57.
SERVICE.—Assistant-Surgeon CAIRD served with Brigadier Barker's Column, in Oude, during cold weather of '58, '59.

LIEUTENANT A. CALLANDER, P., late 58th Native Infantry.
Ensign, 20 Feb. 48—Lieut., 28 Feb. 55.

CAPTAIN J. P. CAMBRIDGE, late 2nd Native Infantry.
Ensign, 12 June 45—Lieut., 22 March 52—Captain, 12 June 61.

ASSISTANT-SURGEON C. CAMERON, Bengal Medical Establishment.
Asst.-Surgeon, 27 July 59.

ASSISTANT-SURGEON J. McL. CAMERON, M.D., Bengal Medical Establishment.
Asst.-Surgeon, 27 July 59.
SERVICE.—Assistant-Surgeon CAMERON served with the 8th and 19th Punjab Infantry throughout the expedition to China, '60.

LIEUTENANT K. W. S. M. CAMERON, Bengal Artillery.
Lieut., 27 July 58.
SERVICE.—Served during the Mutiny Campaign. *Medal.*

CAPTAIN T. M. CAMERON, P. H., late 55th Native Infantry.
Ensign, 15 July 38—Lieut., 3 Oct. 42—Captain, 30 Dec. 47.

(105)

SURGEON A. CAMPBELL, M.D., Bengal Medical Establishment.

Asst.-Surgeon, 8 May 27—Surgeon, 16 Jan. 44—Surgeon-Major, 25 May 61.

SERVICE.—Surgeon CAMPBELL was attacked by 300 Sikimites, and fought for 14 hours in an open stockade, against 800 men, when the enemy had 40 killed and wounded, and his party had 1 killed and 9 wounded, in November '60. Accompanied Colonel Gawler's Force across the Runjeet River, on the 3rd February '61, under fire from the enemy.

ASSISTANT-SURGEON A. D. CAMPBELL,† M.D., Bengal Medical Establishment.

Asst.-Surgeon, 27 Jan. 58.

LIEUTENANT A. E. CAMPBELL,† late 31st Native Infantry.

Ensign, 20 Jan. 51—Lieut., 6 June 57.

SERVICE.—Lieutenant CAMPBELL served during the Sonthal Campaign, '55. With his Regiment during the Mutinies in the Saugor District, '57, '58. *Wounded. Medal.*

CAPTAIN A. H. CAMPBELL, P. H., late 9th Native Infantry.

Ensign, 25 Aug. 41—Lieut., 1 Jan. 45—Captain, 23 Nov. 56.

SERVICE.—Captain CAMPBELL served in the Crimea as Assistant Adjutant-General of Division in the Turkish Contingent, from October '55 till the end of the War. *Obtained 4th Class of the Order of the "Medjidie."* Served as Major of Brigade at Allahabad, and engaged at Munseeta, on the 5th January '58, under Brigadier W. Campbell. Mentioned in Despatch, 22nd January '58. Commanded the 8th Irregular Cavalry during the Campaign in Oude, in '58, '59. Present at capture of town and fort of Sandee, 24th October '58. *Medal.*

LIEUTENANT A. H. F. CAMPBELL, late 4th Europeans.

Ensign, 4th Feb. 58—Lieut.

o

BREVET-COLONEL A. L. CAMPBELL, late 2nd Bengal European Cavalry.

Cornet, 4 July 21—Lieut., 13 May 25—Captain, 12 Jan. 34—Bt.-Major, 19 June 46—Major, 20 Oct. 52—Bt.-Lieut.-Colonel, 20 June 54—Lieut.-Colonel, 17 Sept. 55—Bt.-Colonel, 15 Sept. 57.

SERVICE.—Colonel CAMPBELL served at the action of Maharajpore. *Bronze Star.* Served as Brigade Major to the 2nd Brigade of Cavalry at the battle of Alliwal, and volunteered and served as A. D. C. to Major-General Dick at the battle of Sobraon. *Charger shot under him. Medal, Clasp, and Brevet-Major.* When the 1st Light Cavalry charged into the enemy's entrenched camp, Colonel Campbell cut down a standard bearer, and captured his standard; he also captured a European Sikh Officer of Artillery on the same occasion.

SURGEON A. L. S. CAMPBELL,† Bengal Medical Establishment.

Asst.-Surgeon, 11 July 46—Surgeon, 7 Oct. 59.

SERVICE.—Surgeon CAMPBELL served throughout the first and second siege, and operations before Mooltan, '48, '49. Present at the battle of Goojerat, and at the operations against the Bussey Khel Afreedies, under Lieutenant-Colonel Craigie, March '55. *Medal and 2 Clasps.*

LIEUTENANT C. W. CAMPBELL, late 10th Native Infantry.

Ensign, 20 Dec. 54—Lieut., 30 June 57.

CORNET C. W. CAMPBELL, Cavalry General List.

Cornet, 4 Jan. 61.

SURGEON-MAJOR E. CAMPBELL,† Bengal Medical Establishment.

Asst.-Surgeon, 14 Nov. 39—Surgeon, 15 Nov. 53—Surgeon.-Major, 13 Jan. 60.

SERVICE.—Surgeon-Major CAMPBELL served in the Cabul Insurrection, and present at the storming of Istaliff. *Medal.* Present at the battle of Maharajpore. *Bronze Star.* Served during the Sutlej Campaign, and present at the battles of Moodkee, Ferozeshuhur, Alliwal, and Sobraon. *Medal and 3 Clasps.* Served during the Sonthal Rebellion.

MAJOR-GENERAL G. CAMPBELL, Bengal Artillery.

2nd Lieut., 6 June 23—Lieut., 30 August 26—Bt.-Captain, 6 June 38—Captain, 10 July 40—Bt.-Major, 30 April 44—Major, 21 July 51—Bt.-Lieut.-Colonel, 3 April 46—Lieut.-Colonel, 5 June 56—Bt.-Colonel, 20 June 54—Colonel, 18 Feb. 61—Major-General, 4 July 58.

SERVICE.—Major-General CAMPBELL served in Ava, '24, '25, '26. *Medal.* During the Gwalior Campaign, '45, '46. Present at the battle of Punniar. *Bronze Star, and Brevet Major.* During the Sutlej Campaign, '45, '46. Present at the battles of Ferozeshuhur and Sobraon. *Medal and Clasp, and Brevet-Lieutenant-Colonel.*

LIEUTENANT H. CAMPBELL, P., late 63rd Native Infantry.

Ensign, 11 Dec. 49—Lieut., 12 Feb. 54.

CAPTAIN H. L. CAMPBELL, P. H., late 52nd Native Infantry.

Ensign, 21 April 44—Lieut., 5 Aug. 48—Captain, 13 July 57.

SERVICE.—Captain CAMPBELL served at the first and second siege operations before, and surrender of, Mooltan, including the repulse of the enemy's night attack on the British camp at Mathe Ghôl, 17th August '48. Action of Sooroojkhoond, 7th November '48; attack on the suburbs of Mooltan, 27th December '48, and battle of Goojerat. *Medal and 2 Clasps.*

SURGEON J. CAMPBELL,† M.D., and C.B., Bengal Medical Establishment.

Asst.-Surgeon, 22 Dec. 40—Surgeon, 23 Oct. 54.

SERVICE.—Surgeon CAMPBELL served in Affghanistan in '42, under Sir George Pollock; also in Scinde, '45, '46. *Medal.* Served during the siege of Lucknow. *Medal. Defence Clasp and C.B.*

(108)

LIEUTENANT-COLONEL J. D. CAMPBELL, Bengal Engineers.

2nd Lieut., 11 June 40—Lieut., 1 Feb. 44—Captain, 1 Aug. 54—Bt.-Major, 2 Aug. 54—Lieut.-Colonel, 18 Feb. 61.

SERVICE.—Lieutenant-Colonel CAMPBELL served as Assistant Field Engineer with the Army of Gwalior, '43, '44. Present at the battle of Maharajpore. *Medal.* Served as Assistant Field Engineer on the Scinde Frontier, in '44; with the Army of Pegu, in '52, '53. Present as Senior Engineer at the capture and defence (on two occasions) of Pegu. *Medal.* Served during the Mutiny of '57, in the Agra District, and in Fort of Agra, as Field Engineer.

LIEUTENANT J. E. CAMPBELL, P. H., General List.

Ensign, 10 Dec. 59—Lieut. 1 Oct. 61.

CAPTAIN J. F. CAMPBELL, late 2nd European Bengal Fusiliers.

2nd Lieut., 25 Feb. 43—Lieut., 23 Oct. 45—Captain, 23 Nov. 56.

SERVICE.—Captain CAMPBELL served against the Hill Tribes in Scinde under Sir C. Napier, Punjab Campaign, '48, '49. Present at Ramnuggur, passage of the Chenab, Chillianwallah, Goojerat, and subsequent pursuit under Sir W. Gilbert. *Medal and Clasps.* Served in Burmah, '53. *Medal.* Served throughout the siege and capture of Delhi, '57. *Medal and Clasp.* Mentioned in Despatches of Brigadiers Graves and Longfield.

LIEUTENANT J. G. CAMPBELL,† late 42nd Native Infantry.

Ensign, 20 Aug. 53—Lieut., 9 Nov. 55.

SERVICE.—Lieutenant CAMPBELL served in the Sonthal Campaign in '55, '56. Served in the Saugor District and present at several skirmishes with the rebels in '57, '58, '59. Belonged to the Saugor Garrison under Brigadier Sage. *Medal.*

LIEUTENANT J. H. CAMPBELL, General List.

Ensign, 11 June 59—Lieut., 8 Dec. 60.

(109)

CAPTAIN J. P. W. CAMPBELL, P. H., late 47th Native Infantry.
Ensign, 28 July 42—Lieut., 21 Jan. 46—Captain, 23 Nov. 46.
SERVICE.—Captain CAMPBELL served with the late 47th Native Infantry, with the Army of the Sutlej, in '45, '46. Present at the actions of Moodkee and Ferozeshuhur. *Wounded severely. Medal and Clasp.* Served as Quarter-Master in the expedition under Colonel Mackeson, against the Hussunzaie Tribe, on the Huzara border, in '52, '53. Served as Officiating Staff Officer, Punjab Irregular Force, with the expedition against the Boydar Tribe of Beeloochees, on the Dehra Ghazee Khan border, in '57. Present at the taking of the Khanbund Defile, on the 7th March '57.

LIEUTENANT J. R. CAMPBELL, General List.
Ensign, 8 June 60—Lieut.

CAPTAIN L. G. A. CAMPBELL, P. H., late 53rd Native Infantry.
Ensign, 20 Dec. 46—Lieut., 12 Oct. 51—Captain, 27 June 57.

MAJOR R. CAMPBELL, late 47th Native Infantry.
Ensign, 11 Dec. 37—Lieut., 3 Oct. 40—Captain, 3 Nov. 52.
SERVICE.—Major CAMPBELL served in expeditions in the Naga Hills, in 1845-46-49-50-51, against the Border Tribes, also occasionally on the Bhootan Frontier. Received the thanks of Government for services in the Naga Hills, in 1845-46.

LIEUTENANT R. B. P. P. CAMPBELL, P. H., late 54th Native Infantry.
Ensign, 4 Sept. 55—Lieut., 2 Sept. 57.
SERVICE.—Lieutenant CAMPBELL served in '57 at the capture of Delhi, with the 1st European Bengal Fusiliers, and with the 2nd European Bengal Fusiliers in the subsequent operations in the Meerut, Jhuggur, and Rewarree Districts, with Brigadier Showers' Column. Was attached

to the faithful remnants of the 11th Native Infantry, and engaged in rescuing the Rohilcund refugees. Served in '58 with the 2nd Punjab Cavalry at the seige and capture of Lucknow, with Sir J. H. Grant's Column, at the action of Koorsee; with the Force under Brigadier-General Walpole, at the capture of Rooya and action of Alligunge; with the Army of H. E. the C.-in-C., at the capture of Bareilly, and with a detached Force under Major Browne, at the action of Rohunpore. Served in '59 with the Rohilcund Column against the rebels in the Terai. *Medal and 2 Clasps.* Served in the expedition against the Cabul Khel Wuzeerees, in '59, '60, under Command of Brigadier-General R. Chamberlain.

LIEUTENANT R. D. CAMPBELL, P. H., late 63rd Native Infantry.

Ensign, 15 June 50—Lieut., 19 Jan. 55.

LIEUTENANT W. CAMPBELL, late 71st Native Infantry.

Ensign, 4 March 57—Lieut., 30 April 58.

SERVICE.—Lieutenant CAMPBELL served in the Mutiny, '57. Present at the Mutiny of Lucknow, 30th May, and with the Force that drove the rebels out of the station next day. Served throughout the defence of the Residency of Lucknow, from 30th June to 22nd November '57. Served as a Volunteer with Her Majesty's 78th Highlanders; accompanied the Force under Colonel Napier that went out to the Mootee Munzil, to bring in the sick, wounded, heavy guns, and ammunition left behind by the relieving Force under Sir J. Outram; was sent in to report to Sir J. Outram, at night, that more doolies were required for the sick and wounded. Served at the re-capture of Cawnpore. Lucknow defence. *Medal and Clasp.*

BREVET-COLONEL W. C. CAMPBELL, late 30th Native Infantry.

Ensign, 7 Dec. 24—Lieut., 27 Dec. 25—Captain, 13 Oct. 39—Bt.-Major, 2 Aug. 50—Major, 11 Dec. 51—Bt.-Lieut.-Colonel, 28 Nov. 54—Lieut.-Colonel, 11 May 57—Bt.-Colonel, 28 Nov. 57.

SERVICE.—Brevet-Colonel CAMPBELL served in the Cabul Campaign, '42. Present at the actions at the mouth of the Khyber Pass, January

'42. *Medal.* Served during the Punjab Campaign, '48, '49, as Major of Brigade to the 3rd Infantry Brigade, at the battles of Sadoolapore *(wounded)* and Chillianwallah *(severely wounded)*. *Medal.*

SURGEON H. M. CANNON,† M.B., Bengal Medical Establishment.

Asst.-Surgeon, 1 June 46—Surgeon, 16 Sept. 59.

SERVICE.—Surgeon CANNON was in Medical Charge of the Commander-in-Chief's (Lord Gough's) Head Quarters Staff and Escorts during the whole of the Punjab Campaign of 1848-49. *Medals and 3 Clasps.* "Dr. Henry Cannon was attached to, and in Medical Charge of, the Head Quarters Staff during the Campaign of 1848-49. He maintained that high professional character for which I selected him for the appointment, and obtained the confidence and esteem of all composing my Staff.— (Sd.) GOUGH, *General.*" Received the thanks of the Supreme and Local Governments for services in Rohilcund and North-Western Provinces, during the Mutinies of 1857-58. *Medal.* Was recommended for Brevet rank, but obtaining his full Surgeoncy, he could obtain no Brevet promotion. Repeatedly thanked for good and efficient services, and distinguished on various occasions with parties acting against the mutineers of 1857-58.

LIEUTENANT C. H. CANTOR, late 2nd European Bengal Fusiliers.

2nd Lieut., 13 Dec. 56—1st Lieut., 1 May 58.

SERVICE.—Lieutenant CANTOR served during all the operations before the walls of Delhi, from June to September '57. Was selected as one of the subalterns of the ladder party, on the day of the final assault, 14th September; and served in all the street engagements from that day, till the occupation of the City of Delhi, 20th September '57. Served with the Column under Brigadier Showers, C.B., in the district, during the pursuit of the enemy, till November '57. *Medal and Clasp.*

SURGEON H. CAPE,† Bengal Medical Establishment.

Asst.-Surgeon, 30 Dec. 43—Surgeon, 11 July 57.

SERVICE.—Surgeon CAPE served with the Goorkha Force under Command of Maharajah Jung Bahadoor, and with it was present at the siege and capture of Lucknow. Served with a body of the Oude Military Police, and with it was surrounded and shut up in the Town of Sandula by a large rebel force from Seetapore, under Nurpurt Sing and other leaders. Subsequently took part in the operations of Brigadier Sir G. Barker, with whose Force these Police were incorporated, and was present in two engagements. Services mentioned in the Despatch of Sir G. Barker, 31st December 1858. *Medal and Clasp.*

LIEUTENANT A. W. CAPEL, late 5th Bengal European Cavalry.
Cornet, 8 Sept. 58—Lieut., 5 Feb. 59.

LIEUTENANT F. CARDEN, late 50th Native Infantry.
Ensign, 12 June 58—Lieut., 27 Nov. 59.

DEPUTY-INSPECTOR-GENERAL OF HOSPITALS, G. S. CARDEW,† M.D., Bengal Medical Establishment.
Asst.-Surgeon, 8 Aug. 37—Surgeon, 3 March 51—Surgeon-Major, 13 Jan. 60—Offg. Depy.-Insptr.-Genl., 2 Feb. 61.

SERVICE.—Deputy-Inspector-General of Hospitals G. S. CARDEW served with the 70th Native Infantry throughout the Gwalior Campaign in '43, and was Staff Surgeon to the 3rd Division of the Army. *Bronze Star.* Appointed to the Field Hospital at Gwalior. Temporarily attached to the Delhi Field Force in October '57. Received special thanks through the Adjutant-General of the Army, for services in the Gwalior Field Hospital. *Medal.*

2ND CAPTAIN DE V. F. CAREY,† Bengal Artillery.
2nd Lieut., 8 Dec. 48—Lieut., 10 March 54—2nd Captain, 27 Aug. 58.

LIEUTENANT-COLONEL T. F. CAREY, late 17th Native Infantry.
Ensign, 1 May 43—Lieut., 9 Sept. 49—Captain, 9 Sept. 56—Major, 24 March 58—Lieut.-Colonel, 26 April 59.

SERVICE.—Served during the Mutiny Campaign. *Medal and Clasps, and Brevets of Major and Lieutenant-Colonel.*

(113)

LIEUTENANT S. CARGILL, Bengal Artillery.
Lieut., 27 Aug. 58.

LIEUTENANT-COLONEL H. A. CARLETON, C.B.,† Bengal Artillery.
2nd Lieut., 11 June 30—Lieut., 12 Sept. 39—Bt.-Captain, 11 June 45—Captain, 6 Feb. 48—Bt.-Major, 5 Dec. 55—Major, 18 Aug. 58—Bt.-Lieut.-Colonel, 20 July 58—Lieut.-Colonel, 14 Oct. 58.

SERVICE.—Lieutenant-Colonel CARLETON served under Brigadier-General Sir Colin Campbell, K.C.B., in the operations against the Momunds and Hill Tribes west of Peshawur, in October, November, and December 1851; was present at the siege and capture of Lucknow, in March 1858. *Brevet-Lieutenant-Colonel and C. B.*, also *Medal and Clasp*. Commanded the Artillery in the action at Nawabgunge, in June 1858, under Sir Hope Grant, K.C.B.

MAJOR-GENERAL C. M. CARMICHAEL, C.B., late 5th Bengal European Cavalry.
Cornet, 27 March 06—Lieut., 12 April 10—Bt.-Captain, 27 March 21—Captain, 8 May 21—Major, 30 Dec. 33—Lieut.-Colonel, 1 Nov. 38—Bt.-Colonel, 19 March 49—Colonel, 6 Sept. 51—Major-General, 28 Nov. 54.

SERVICE.—Served at the siege of Kulinger, 1812; Rewah Campaign, 1813; Alwah, 1814; siege and capture of Hatrass, 1816-17; Mahrattah War, 1817-18-19; against Bheels as Major of Brigade to Brigadier J. R. Lumley, in 1823-24; commanded a Light Detachment against Jowra Mairpoor, in 1837; and took Military possession of that country under the orders of Colonel A. Spiers, Political Agent; marched in Command of the 4th Irregular Horse as Volunteer to join the Army of the Indus and Affghanistan; and served the Campaign of 1838-39. Present at the siege and capture of Ghuznee. *C.B. Dooranee Order and Medal.*

LIEUTENANT E. S. R. CARNAC, late 1st Bengal European Cavalry.
Cornet, 4 Jan. 58—Lieut., 18 May 58.

LIEUTENANT D. C. S. L. CARNEGIE,† late 4th Bengal European Cavalry.
Cornet, 20 March 58—Lieut., 21 June 58.

P

CAPTAIN G. F. CARNEGIE, P., late 44th Native Infantry.

Ensign, 11 June 42—Lieut., 9 Jan. 44—Captain, 1 May 55.

SERVICE.—Captain CARNEGIE served with the 3rd Irregular Cavalry throughout the Campaign on the Sutlej, including the battle of Ferozeshah, *Medal;* and subsequent operations against Kôt Kangra with his own Regiment. Served in the Punjab with the 1st Company Pioneers. *Medal.* Passed an examination in Field Engineering; also an examination in the Punjabee language, 10th December 1851.

MAJOR J. W. CARNEGIE, P. C., C.B., late 15th Native Infantry.

Ensign, 23 May 34—Lieut., 1 April 38—Captain, 9 Aug. 48—Bt.-Major, 24 March 48—Major, 30 Sept. 60.

SERVICE.—Major J. W. CARNEGIE, C.B., as Magistrate of Lucknow, by means of his Police, quelled an insurrection in that City on 31st May 1857. Formed one of the original garrison of the Lucknow Residency. Present throughout the whole of the subsequent operations before Lucknow with the Force under Sir J. Outram, G.C.B., and at the siege and capture of Lucknow in March 1858, *where he was twice hit and had a horse shot under him.* Was subsequently employed as Civil Officer with the Kupurthulla Contingent, and was present with it in several actions and skirmishes with the rebels. Afterwards accompanied the Column under the Command of Sir G. Barker, K.C.B. *Brevet Majority, Medal and 2 Clasps.* Permitted to reckon 1 year's extra service for defence of Lucknow Residency. (Since removed from the Army.)

MAJOR-GENERAL A. CARNEGY, C.B., late 15th Native Infantry.

Ensign, 13 Oct. 11—Lieut., 1 Nov. 15—Captain, 25 Jan. 26—Major, 25 Feb. 35—Lieut.-Colonel, 5th Nov. 41—Colonel, 5 Sept. 51—Major-General, 28 Nov. 54.

SERVICE.—Major-General CARNEGY, C.B., served at Kumaoon, 1815; Hattrass, 1817; during the Mahrattah Campaign, 1817-18. Siege and capture of Bhurtpore, 1826. *Medal.* Served during the Sutlej Campaign. *Medal.* During the Punjab Campaign, 1848-49. Commanded the 5th Brigade of the Army at the battle of Goojerat. *Medal and C.B.* *(Since dead.)*

(115)

CAPTAIN W. CARNELL, P.H., late 3rd Europeans.
Ensign, 11 Dec. 46—Lieut., 15 June 49—Captain, 15 Feb. 61.

SERVICE.—Captain CARNELL served throughout the Punjab Campaign, 1848-49. Present at the passage of the Chenab and battle of Goojerat. *Medal and Clasp.* Commanded the Detachment Mhairwarrah Local Battalion, which formed part of the Force under Brigadier General G. St. P. Lawrence, which attacked Awah on the 18th September 1857. *Medal.*

ENSIGN J. G. T. CARRUTHERS, General List.
Ensign, 8 June 60.

SURGEON W. E. CARTE, A.B., Bengal Medical Establishment.
Asst.-Surgeon, 7 Oct. 33—Surgeon, 15 Nov. 42.

LIEUTENANT C. A. E. S. CARTER, late 20th Native Infantry.
Ensign, 11 Dec. 58—Lieut., 30 July 58.

ASSISTANT-SURGEON F. CARTER,† Bengal Medical Establishment.
Asst.-Surgeon, 4 Aug. 55.

SERVICE.—Assistant-Surgeon CARTER served with No. 17 Light Field Battery and Troop, Bengal Horse Artillery; with the Punjab Moveable Column under Brigadier General Nicholson, from its formation on the 18th of May 1857 until the 12th of August 1857. *Medal.*

LIEUTENANT H. CARTER, late 2nd European Bengal Fusiliers.
Ensign, 1 June 59—Lieut., 13 July 60.

MAJOR J. W. CARTER,† late 54th Native Infantry.
Ensign, 24 Feb. 35—Lieut., 3 Oct. 40—Bt.-Captain, 24 Feb. 50—Captain, 15 Nov. 53—Bt.-Major, 20 July 58—Major, 27 May 60.

SERVICE.—Major CARTER served with the 16th Grenadiers throughout the Campaign in Affghanistan, '39, '40, '41, '42, with Sir Robert Sale's (the 1st) Brigade under Lord Keane, at the occupation of Candahar; pursuit at Candahar to Girishk on the Helmund; assault and capture of the fortress of Ghuznee, 23rd July. *Medal.* Defeat of Ghilzie Tribes by Sir James Outram, in Punjab Valley, 22nd September '39. At Candahar, under Sir William Nott, during the Affghan rebellion. Action of Kallu Chuk, 12th January; Kunjee Kuk, Punjwaee, and Tilloo Khan, 7th, 8th, 9th, and 10th, and Baba Wullee (Valley of the Urgundah), 25th March; relief of Kelat-i-Ghilzie, 22nd May; action of Gomaine, 30th August; re-capture of Ghuznee, 5th; action of Benee Budam, 14th; Maidan, 15th; and re-occupation of Cabul, 17th September '42. *Medal.* Affairs with the Rear Guard in the Jugdulluk and Khyber Passes, on the retirement of the Army from Affghanistan, the same year. Served in the 54th Native Infantry during part of the Campaign of the Sutlej, in '46. When in Command of the 5th Infantry Regiment, Gwalior Contingent, in '57, advanced from Augur on 5th June with that Regiment and two 9-pounder guns of Mehidpore Artillery, to the relief of Neemuch during the Mutiny; but the Cavalry of the united Malwah Contingent, which was to have joined the Detachment, having mutinied and murdered all their European Officers and attacked Augur (which was insufficiently protected), he hastened back, and by a forced march of 58 miles in 27 hours, reached and secured that station on the 9th. For this service *received the thanks of the Government of India, and Brevet-Majority.* Appointed District Staff Officer to the Saharunpore and Moozuffernugger Field Force under Colonel Baird Smith, in January '58, and the following April to the Commissariat charge of the Roorkie Field Force, under Brigadier-General Sir John Jones, K.C.B., for service in Rohilcund. Actions of Bagawalla, 17th; Nugeena, 21st; and relief of Moradabad, 25th April; action on the Dojora, 5th; assault and capture of Bareilly, 6th; attack and bombardment of Shajehanpore, defeat of the rebels, and relief of the Garrison, 11th May; action of Bunnai, and pursuit of the rebels to, and destruction of, the Fort of Mohumdee. Repeatedly brought to favorable notice in Sir John Jones' Despatches. *Medal.*

LIEUTENANT T. T. CARTER,† Bengal Engineers.

    Lieut., 27 Aug. 58.

(117)

LIEUTENANT S. CARY, P. H., late 37th Native Infantry.
Ensign, 10 Dec. 54—Lieut., 23 Nov. 56.

SERVICE.—Lieutenant CARY served in the Sonthal Campaign with the Force under Brigadier Bird, from July to December '55; first with Detachment of Calcutta Militia, and subsequently with a Detachment, 39th Native Infantry. Served with the Jounpore Field Force in '58. Present at the actions of Misrutpore, Chanda, Ameerapore, and Sultanpore. Present at the siege and capture of Lucknow, '58. *Medal and Clasp.* Mentioned in the Despatches of Brigadier-General J. H. Franks, C.B., who commanded the Jounpore Field Force, and 4th Division, before Lucknow, 18th February '58, and 14th April '58. Mentioned in the Despatch of His Excellency the Commander-in-Chief, 5th April '58. *(Since dead.)*

LIEUTENANT C. CASE,† late 67th Native Infantry.
Ensign, 14 June 56—Lieut., 27 June 57.

SERVICE.—Lieutenant CASE served during the Mutinies, '57, '58, '59. Present at the action of Shahgunge, near Agra, 5th July '57, under Brigadier Polwhele. Served in the Gwalior District, in '58, under Major McMahon. Served in Bundlecund in '59, under Colonel Lockhart. *Medal.*

LIEUTENANT H. C. CATTLEY, P. H., late 62nd Native Infantry.
Ensign, 20 March 51—Lieut., 23 Nov. 56.

MAJOR G. CAULFIELD,† late 46th Native Infantry.
Ensign, 23 March 35—Lieut., 3 Oct. 40—Bt.-Captain, 23 March 50—Captain, 8 Oct. 50—Major, 1 March 61.

SERVICE.—Major CAULFIELD served with the 2nd Army of the Sutlej, in '48, '49. Present at the actions of Chillianwallah and Goojerat. *Medal and two Clasps.*

LIEUTENANT H. M. CAULFIELD,† late 4th Bengal European Cavalry.
Cornet, 4 Oct. 55—Lieut., 9 Oct. 56.

(118)

MAJOR J. P. CAULFIELD, P. H., late 4th Europeans.

Ensign, 12 Dec. 37—Lieut., 3 Oct. 40—Captain, 3 Oct. 51—Major, 19 Jan. 58.

SERVICE.—Major CAULFIELD served with the Force under Brigadier Sir H. Wheeler, in the Punjab Campaign, '48, '49. *Medal.* Present at the actions of Nudjufghur, 25th August '57, under Brigadier-General Nicholson, and assault of Delhi, 14th September '57. *Wounded slightly. Medal and Clasp.* Present at the action of Narnoul, 14th November '57, in Command of the 1st Bengal Fusiliers as well as the Infantry of the Column, under Colonel Gerrard, and succeeded in action to the Command of the Column, on that Officer's being mortally wounded. Present at the actions of Gungeeree, Puttiallee, and Mynpooree; in Command of the 1st Fusiliers under Brigadier Sir T. Seaton, December '59. *Promoted to rank of Brevet-Major for service in the Campaign.*

LIEUTENANT C. G. CAUTLEY, General List, Cavalry.

Cornet, 4 Sept. 59—Lieut., 4 Sept. 60.

BREVET-COLONEL G. CAUTLEY, late 5th Bengal European Cavalry.

Cornet, 22 Sept. 25—Lieut., 17 May 29—Bt.-Captain, 22 Sept. 40—Captain, 10 July 44—Bt.-Major, 7 June 49—Major, 16 Aug. 59—Bt.-Lieut.-Colonel, 28 Nov. 54—Bt.-Colonel, 28 Nov. 59.

SERVICE.—Brevet-Colonel CAUTLEY served at the battle of Ferozeshuhur. *Medal.* Throughout the Punjab Campaign. Present at the affair of Ramnuggur, and actions of Sadoolapore, Chillianwallah, and Goojerat. *Medal and 2 Clasps.* Received Brevet-Majority for services during the Punjab Campaign.

LIEUTENANT P. L. N. CAVAGNARI, P. H., late 1st European Bengal Fusiliers.

2nd Lieut., 9 April 58—Lieut., 17 March 60.

SERVICE.—Lieutenant CAVAGNARI served with the Corps in Oude, and with a Detachment of his Regiment under Major Wheeler, when 5

(119)

guns were captured from the Nusseerabad Brigade, at Shahdutgunge, 30th October '58. *Medal.*

CAPTAIN G. N. CAVE, P. H., late 21st Native Infantry.

Ensign, 10 Dec. 41—Lieut., 22 March 44—Captain, 27 Feb. 56.

SERVICE.—Captain CAVE commanded a Detachment of the 16th Punjab Infantry with the Column under Command of Major J. L. Vaughan, in the Eusuffzaie country, in July and August '59. Commanded a Wing of the 16th Punjab Infantry in the Column under Colonel Shubrick, in Sohagpore and Rewah, in December '59, and January and February '60.

CAPTAIN G. CAVENAGH,† late 39th Native Infantry.

Ensign, 18 Jan. 45—Lieut., 10 June 49—Bt.-Captain, 18 Jan. 60— Captain, in Staff Corps, 18 Feb. 61.

SERVICE.—Captain CAVENAGH served with Her Majesty's 54th Regiment during the Mutiny in '57, '58, '59. *Medal.* Served with the 16th Native Infantry during the China War, '60. Mentioned in the Despatch of Colonel March, K.L.M., who commanded the British Forces at Shanghai, when attacked by the Rebel Chinese Force in August '60.

COLONEL O. CAVENAGH, P. C., late 32nd Native Infantry.

Ensign, 12 June 37—Lieut., 13 Jan. 42—Captain, 10 Aug. 50—Bt.-Major, 10 Aug. 50—Bt.-Lieut.-Colonel, 28 Nov. 54.—Bt.-Colonel, 28 Nov. 57.

SERVICE.—Colonel CAVENAGH served with the 2nd Irregular Cavalry during the disturbances in Bundlecund, '42. Served with the Army of Gwalior, '43. Present at the action of Maharajpore. *Wounded severely*, left leg being carried away by a round shot, and severe contusions received from his charger being killed and falling over with him. *Bronze Star.* Mentioned in Despatch of Major Oldfield, Commanding 4th Irregular Cavalry. Served with the Army of the Sutlej, '46. Present at the action of Buddiwal, severely wounded in left arm. *Medal.* Promoted to rank of Brevet-Major on obtaining the Regimental rank of Captain, 10th August '50.

ASSISTANT-SURGEON H. CAYLEY,† Bengal Medical Establishment.
Asst.-Surgeon, 29 Jan. 57.

LIEUTENANT A. B. CHALMERS, P. H., General List.
Ensign, 4 March 59—Lieut., 15 June 60.

SURGEON-MAJOR C. B. CHALMERS,† Bengal Medical Establishment.
Asst.-Surgeon, 4 Dec. 40—Surgeon, 28 Sept. 54—Surgeon-Major, 10 Feb. 61.

LIEUTENANT H. B. CHALMERS, P., late 27th Native Infantry.
Ensign, 11 Dec. 47—Lieut., 15 Nov. 53.

SERVICE.—Lieutenant CHALMERS served throughout the Mutiny of '57 '58, at Agra, as Principal Executive Commissariat Officer. Present at the battle fought at Agra, on 5th July '57. *Slightly wounded. Medal.*

LIEUTENANT J. CHALMERS, P. H., A.M., late 39th Native Infantry.
Ensign, 6 Aug. 55—Lieut., 21 April 58.

SERVICE.—Lieutenant CHALMERS, with a body of Pathan Horse, went in pursuit, and was *very severely wounded*, in an engagement with the Mutineers of the 9th Irregular Cavalry, Boota-da-kote, 29th September '57.

LIEUTENANT J. CHALMERS (Unattached).
Lieut., 5 Aug. 59.

LIEUTENANT O. T. CHALMERS,† late 4th Europeans.
Ensign, 10 Dec. 54—Lieut., 19 June 57.

LIEUTENANT R. CHALMERS, P. H., late 45th Native Infantry.
Ensign, 7 Sept. 49—Lieut., 10 Sept. 52.

SERVICE.—Lieutenant CHALMERS served against the rebels as follows: advanced into Major Renaud's Moveable Column towards Cawnpore on

(121)

30th June '57, and carried his Despatch, announcing the massacre of the Cawnpore Garrison, from Sohunda to Allahabad, (40 miles through disturbed country,) joined Havelock's Volunteer Cavalry raised by Major Barrow, and advanced with it to the relief of Cawnpore. Was present at the actions of Futtehpore on the 12th, Aoung and Pandoo Nuddee, 16th; battle and re-occupation of Cawnpore, 16th and 17th; Bithoor, 18th July; at the first crossing into Oude to relief of Lucknow; at actions of Oonao and Busseerutgunge, 1st, 2nd, and 3rd; at the second crossing into Oude to relief of Lucknow. Present at the actions of Munglewar, 21st; Alum Bagh, 23rd; and first relief of Lucknow, 25th September '57, and its subsequent defence for two months, *(twice severely wounded,)* during which time he acted as Field Engineer, and was present as such at the assault and capture of the King's stables and engine house. With the entrenched camp under General Sir J. Outram at Alum Bagh, from 20th November '57 to 12th March '58. Present at Gurtee, and the numerous severe attacks on the Alum Bagh; at the final capture of Lucknow with Colonel Kelly's Moveable Column, in the Azimghur District; from 1st October '58 to 31st January '59 advanced to the Nepal Frontier with it. Present at the action of Ruttunpore with Murray's Jāt Horse, and the numerous minor affairs, terminating in the final destruction and extermination of the rebel army. *Medal and Clasps.*

CAPTAIN S. CHALMERS, P. C., late 53rd Native Infantry.

Ensign, 9 Dec. 52—Lieut., 24 April 55—Captain, 23 Oct. 57.

SERVICE.—Captain CHALMERS served in the Sonthal Insurrection, '55, and as Senior Commissariat Officer in the Jounpore Field Force, under Major-General Franks. Served as Senior Commissariat Officer in charge of the 4th Division of the Army at the capture of Lucknow. *Severely wounded. Medal and Clasp.*

LIEUTENANT W. G. CHALMERS, P. C. H., late 51st Native Infantry.

Ensign, 5 April 54—Lieut., 27 Jan. 57.

SERVICE.—Lieutenant CHALMERS served under General Chamberlain, in the expedition to Upper Meeranzaie and Koorum, against the Hill

Tribes, Zymosht, Wuzeerees, and Torees, in '56. Present at Rawul Pindee in July '57, when the 58th Native Infantry and 2 Companies 14th Native Infantry were disarmed, part of which mutinied. Served with Colonel Davidson's Column in pursuit of the 62nd and 69th Regiments in the Googaira District, September '58. Served in the China Campaign in '60. Present at the landing, 1st August, and occupation of Pehtang, 2nd August; at the affair, 3rd August; battle of Sinho, 12th August; capture of Tonghu, 14th August; Taku Forts, 21st August; action of Chauk Kiawaug, 18th September; action of Tungchow, 21st September; advance on Pekin, 6th October; and final surrender of that city. *Medal and 2 Clasps.*

LIEUTENANT-COLONEL C. T. CHAMBERLAIN, P., late 28th Native Infantry.

Ensign, 12 Dec. 37—Lieut., 26 March 40—Captain, 1st May 52—Major, 2 May 52—Lieut.-Colonel, 30 Dec. 59.

SERVICE.—Lieutenant-Colonel CHAMBERLAIN served with the Army of the Indus, '39, '40, '41, '42. Present at the siege and capture of Ghuznee, '39. *Medal.* In a Cavalry engagement, 27th December '41, *Horse dangerously wounded.* Present at the action of Killu-i-Shah, 12th January '42, and in other actions near Candahar, under Major-General Nott. *Medal.* Served in Scinde, under Sir C. Napier, '43. Served in the Punjab Campaign, '48, '49. Present at the actions of Chillianwallah and Goojerat. *Medal and Clasp.* Wounded in an engagement with Sikh Cavalry, 30th January '49. Received the thanks of the Commander-in-Chief, 30th January '49. Present at the pursuit of the Sikh Army and final surrender at Rawul Pindee, to Sir W. R. Gilbert. Mentioned in the Despatch of Brigadier Hearsey to the Commander-in-Chief, 7th March '49. Promoted to the rank of Brevet-Major for service in the Punjab Campaign. Served at Mooltan during the Mutiny. Disarmed the 62nd and 69th Native Infantry. Engaged against the Googaira rebels. Besieged in the Serai of Cheekawutne for four days. Promoted to the rank of Brevet-Lieutenant-Colonel for services during the Mutiny, '57. Received the thanks of Government, 4th August '59. *Medal.*

(123)

BREVET-COLONEL N. B. CHAMBERLAIN, C.B., P. H., late 16th Native Infantry.

Ensign, 27 Feb. 37—Lieut., 16 July 42—Captain, 1 Nov. 49—Major, 2 Nov. 49—Lieut.-Colonel, 28 Nov. 54—Colonel, 27 Nov. 57.

SERVICE.—Colonel CHAMBERLAIN, C.B., served throughout the Affghan Campaign of '39, '40, '41, '42, during which he was attached to Christie's Corps of Irregular Cavalry. *Wounded on six different occasions. 2 Medals.* Ghuznee, '39; Candahar, Ghuznee, and Cabul, '42. Present with the Governor-General's Body Guard at the battle of Maharajpore. *Bronze Star.* Employed with the Army of the Punjab, at the actions of Chillianwallah and Goojerat. *Medal and Clasp.*

CAPTAIN T. H. CHAMBERLAIN, P. H., late 3rd Europeans.

Ensign, 8 July 42—Lieut., 24 Jan. 45—Captain, 23 Nov. 56.

SERVICE.—Captain CHAMBERLAIN served with the 9th Native Infantry during the Punjab Campaign of '45, '46; and was present with General Wheeler's Force when Phillour surrendered, and which also occupied the Jullunder Doab, immediately after the battle of Sobraon.

LIEUTENANT B. R. CHAMBERS, P. H., late 13th Native Infantry.

Ensign, 20 Dec. 50—Lieut., 10 March 55.

SERVICE.—Lieutenant CHAMBERS served in the Sonthal Campaign with the 13th Native Infantry, in '55, '56. Served throughout the defence of Lucknow as Adjutant, 13th Native Infantry. *Severely wounded,* in receipt of wound pension. *Medal and Clasp, one year's extra service for Lucknow.*

LIEUTENANT C. P. CHAMBERS, late 48th Native Infantry.

Ensign, 14 June 56—Lieut., 30 April 58.

SERVICE.—Lieutenant C. P. CHAMBERS served throughout the Indian Mutiny with the 3rd Europeans. Present at the action near Agra, against the Indore and Mhow Mutineers, on the 16th October '57, also with the Force under Brigadier Sir T. Seaton, at the actions of Gungeeree and Puttiallee, in December '57. Present also with the Mynpooree Moveable Column in the operations at Shereghur Ghaut, in May '58, and with the Agra Column towards Gwalior, in June '58. *Medal.*

MAJOR J. CHAMBERS, P. C., late 21st Native Infantry.

Ensign, 13 Dec. 33—Lieut., 15 March 41—Captain, 27 Aug. 47—Major, 25 Aug. 59.

SERVICE.—Major CHAMBERS was employed in the suppression of the Mutiny as Cantonment Magistrate at Sealkôt in '57. (Received a certificate of high proficiency in the Oordoo Language, and passed examination in Punjabee.)

CAPTAIN R. W. CHAMBERS, P. C., late 11th Native Infantry.

Ensign, 12 June 41—Lieut., 27 March 46—Bt.-Captain, 12 June 56.

SERVICE.—Captain CHAMBERS served during the Sutlej Campaign, '45, '46. *Medal.* Present at the capture of Kôt Kangra, '46.

CAPTAIN R. Y. CHAMBERS, P. H., late 65th Native Infantry.

Ensign, 11 Dec. 46—Lieut., 1 Oct. 55—Captain in Staff Corps, 18 Feb. 61.

SERVICE.—Captain CHAMBERS served in China with the late 65th Bengal Native Infantry, in '58, '59. *Medal.*

LIEUTENANT W. E. CHAMBERS, P. C. H., late 19th Native Infantry.

Ensign, 20 Feb. 57—Lieut., 30 April 58.

LIEUTENANT F. E. A. CHAMIER, P., late 34th Native Infantry.

Ensign, 20 Feb. 50—Lieut., 8 April 57.

SERVICE.—Lieutenant CHAMIER was present as Aide-de-Camp and Interpreter at the actions of Mungalwara and Alum Bagh, and the relief of Lucknow. Mentioned in Divisional Orders, 26th September '59. Mentioned in Sir J. Outram's Despatch, 25th November '57. Received

(125)

thanks of Government, 28th December '57. Present in the same capacity with the 1st Division of the Field on the plains at Alum Bagh, and also in the final capture of Lucknow by Lord Clyde. Mentioned in Despatch of Sir J. Outram. Received thanks of Government. Received thanks of Her Majesty the Queen. *Medal and* 2 *Clasps.*

LIEUTENANT J. U. CHAMPAIN, Bengal Engineers.

Lieut., 13 July 57.

SERVICE.—Lieutenant CHAMPAIN marched with the Bengal Sappers and Miners from Roorkee to Meerut, on the outbreak of the Mutiny in '57. Served with the Force under Brigadier Wilson, and was present at the two actions on the Hindun and Badlee-ka-Serai, and throughout the siege of Delhi. Thanked in Field Force Orders by the General Commanding for constructing a battery in one night, which was afterwards, by the Chief Engineer's orders, called ' Champain's Battery.' *Wounded slightly,* 13th September '57. Commanded the Sappers and Miners on their march from Delhi to Lucknow, including the capture of Futtehpore-Sikree, and minor affairs in the Agra District, under Colonel Cotton. Also at the Alum Bagh under Sir James Outram. Served as Adjutant throughout the siege of Lucknow. Brought to notice of His Excellency the Commander-in-Chief in Brigadier Napier's Despatch, 5th April '58. Served as Executive Engineer under Brigadier Douglas, in the Ghazeepore and Shahabad Districts. Thanked in Captain McMullin's Despatch, 25th August '58. Present at the final capture of Jugdespore, and at various minor affairs in the Oude District, including the pursuit of the rebels to the Kymore Hills. Brought to notice of His Excellency the Commander-in-Chief in Brigadier Douglas' Despatch, 24th December '58. *Medal and* 2 *Clasps.*

LIEUTENANT-COLONEL E. G. J. CHAMPNEYS, late 5th Europeans.

Ensign, 29 March 29—Lieut., 30 May 34—Bt.-Captain, 29 March 44— Captain, 24 Jan. 45—Major, 30 Dec. 52—Lieut.-Colonel, 1 July 57.
(Since retired.)

(126)

ASSISTANT-SURGEON R. C. CHANDRA,† Bengal Medical Establishment.

Asst.-Surgeon, 27 Jan. 58.

SERVICE.—Assistant-Surgeon CHANDRA served during the Mutiny in Medical Charge of the Towana Horse, in the Cawnpore District, during the latter part of '58. Was in Medical Charge of the Regiment when it formed part of the Column under Command of Brigadier the Honorable P. E. Herbert, in pursuit of the Rebel Prince Feroze Shah, and present at the fight on the banks of the Jumna, on the 10th December '58. Held Medical Charge of the expedition under Captain H. Raban, against the Roorkee Hill Tribes, on the South-Eastern Frontier, from 17th December '60 to 6th February '61, and present at the storming of the village of the Roorkee Chief, Rutton Pooeyra, 1st February '61.

LIEUTENANT G. N. CHANNER,† General List.

Ensign, 4 Sept. 59—Lieut., 25 Aug. 61.

LIEUTENANT A. H. CHAPMAN, late 1st Bengal European Cavalry.

Cornet, 20 Sept. 56—Lieut., 9 Jan. 57.

SERVICE.—Lieutenant CHAPMAN served with the Malwah Field Force in '57; at the capture of Dhar and battles at Mundesore, in November '57; and with Her Majesty's 14th Dragoons, with the Central India Field Force, at the capture of Chundehree, action of the Betwa, capture of the Town and Fort of Jhansie, action at Koonch, and capture of Calpee, '58. *Medal and Clasp.*

LIEUTENANT A. R. CHAPMAN, late 1st European Bengal Fusiliers.

Ensign, 4 Jan. 56—Lieut., 24 Sept. 57.

SERVICE.—Lieutenant CHAPMAN served with the Army before Delhi, '57. Present at the action of Badlee-ka-Serai, and skirmishes in the Subzee Mundee, from 9th June to the 13th August '57. Present at the assault and taking of Delhi, 14th August '57. Accompanied the Column under Colonel Gerrard. Present at the battle of Narnoul. Accompanied the Column under Sir T. Seaton. Present at the battle of Gungeerce, Puttiallee, and Mynpooree. Present at the siege and capture of Lucknow, '58. Accompanied the Column under Sir Hope Grant. Present at the affair of Baree, and subsequent operations in Oude. *Medal and 2 Clasps.*

LIEUTENANT E. CHAPMAN,† late 14th Native Infantry.

Ensign, 20 Dec. 50—Lieut., 21 May 57.

LIEUTENANT E. F. CHAPMAN, Bengal Artillery.

Lieut., 27 Aug. 58.

LIEUTENANT H. CHAPMAN, P. H., late 49th Native Infantry.

Ensign, 15 July 56—Lieut., 23 Nov. 56.

SERVICE.—Lieutenant CHAPMAN was present at Meean Meer on the outbreak of the Mutiny, '57. Present at the action of Narnoul, 16th November '57, when serving with 1st Bengal Fusiliers in the Column under Command of Brigadier Gerrard. Present at actions of Gungeeree, 14th; Puttiallee, 17th; and Mynpooree, 27th December '57, with the Column under Brigadier Seaton. Commanded a Detachment of Alexander's Horse in several minor affairs against the rebels in the Etawah District, in '58. Present at the action of Creyah, 16th May '58, *charger twice wounded,* with the Mynpooree Moveable Column. Present at the action of Dewsa, 14th January '59, when Commanding a Detachment of Alexander's Horse. Mentioned in the Despatch of Brigadier Showers, 10th March '59. Served with a second Column under Brigadier Showers, from January to April '59, when in pursuit of the rebels through Rajpootanah and Central India. Served in the Bundlecund Campaign with Brigadier Wheeler's Force, in '59, and with No. 2 Bundlecund Flying Column, in '59, '60, Commanding a Detachment of Alexander's Horse. *Medal.*

LIEUTENANT H. H. CHAPMAN,† late 6th Europeans.

Ensign, 20 Sept. 56—Lieut., 30 April 58.

SERVICE.—Lieutenant CHAPMAN was present at the Mutiny at Benares. *Wounded dangerously. Medal. Wound Pension.*

CAPTAIN H. W. CHAPMAN, P. C. H., late 28th Native Infantry.

Ensign, 20 Dec. 51—Lieut., 20 Dec. 54—Captain, 10 June 57.

SERVICE.—Captain CHAPMAN served in the defence of the Kumaon Hills, against the rebels, '57, '58.

LIEUTENANT J. CHARLES, Bengal Artillery.

Lieut., 27 Aug. 58.

ASSISTANT-SURGEON T. E. CHARLES, M.D.,† Bengal Medical Establishment.

Asst.-Surgeon, 22 Oct. 56.

SERVICE.—Assistant-Surgeon CHARLES served during the Mutiny, '57, '58. In Medical Charge of 400 men of the 1st European Bengal Fusiliers, and 2 Squadrons of Her Majesty's 9th Lancers. Present at the battle of Badlee-ka-Serai, 8th June '57, and throughout the siege of Delhi, till the capture of that City. Served with the Column under Brigadier Gerrard, in the Rewarree District, against the Jeypore and Joudpore rebels. Served under Sir T. Seaton, during his operations in the Doab. Present at the actions of Gungeeree, Puttiallee, and Mynpooree. Served with the Army under Lord Clyde, at Lucknow. Present at the affair on crossing the Goomtee, and with the storming party of the 1st Fusiliers, who took the enemy's first position, at the "Chuckees Kotee," and other points, in their line of defence. Present throughout the siege of Lucknow. *Medal and 2 Clasps.* Served under Sir Hope Grant in Oude. Present during the engagement with the mutineers at Baree, and served other minor operations against the rebels. Mentioned in the Despatch of Major Hume, September '59.

ENSIGN F. W. CHATTERTON, General List.

Ensign, 20 Sept. 59.

LIEUTENANT J. B. CHATTERTON, late 41st Native Infantry.

Ensign, 4 Sept. 56—Lieut., 7 June 57.

(129)

BREVET-LIEUTENANT-COLONEL C. CHEAPE, late 51st Native Infantry.

Ensign, 11 July 23—Lieut., 13 May 25—Bt.-Captain, 11 July 38—Captain, 1 May 43—Bt.-Major, 2 Aug. 50—Major, 27 June 57—Bt.-Lieut.-Colonel, 28 Nov. 54.

SERVICE.—Brevet-Lieutenant-Colonel CHEAPE served at the siege and capture of Mooltan, and action of Goojerat. *Medal and Clasp. (Since retired.)*

LIEUTENANT-GENERAL SIR J. CHEAPE, K.C.B., Bengal Engineers.

2nd Lieut., 3 Nov. 09—Lieut., 29 Dec. 16—Captain, 1 March 21—Bt.-Major, 25 June 30—Lieut.-Colonel, 19 Feb. 44—Bt.-Colonel, 10 June 45—Colonel, 19 Feb. 44—Major-General, 20 June 54—Lieut.-General, 24 May 59.

SERVICE.—Lieutenant-General *Sir* J. CHEAPE, K.C.B., served in the Mahrattah War, '17, '18; Burmese War, '24, '26; was Chief Engineer at Mooltan and Goojerat. *Medal and K.C.B.* Commanded the Force employed in the capture of the Burmese Stockades, 19th March '53. *Medal*, and Honorary Aide-de-Camp to Her Majesty.

SURGEON-MAJOR A. H. CHEEK,† Bengal Medical Establishment.

Asst.-Surgeon, 3 Jan. 40—Surgeon, 1 Dec. 53—Surgeon-Major, 13 Jan. 60.

SERVICE.—Surgeon-Major CHEEK served with the Bundlecund Legion at the siege of Chirgong, and in Bundlecund, '41, '42.

ASSISTANT-SURGEON G. N. CHEEK,† Bengal Medical Establishment.

Asst.-Surgeon, 20 Jan. 55.

SERVICE.—Assistant-Surgeon CHEEK served with Her Majesty's 86th Regiment, C. I. F. F., during the operations before and taking of Calpee and Gwalior. *Medal.*

ASSISTANT-SURGEON G. C. CHESNAYE,† Bengal Medical Establishment.

Asst.-Surgeon, 10 Feb. 1859.

R

(130)

BREVET-MAJOR G. CHESNEY, Bengal Engineers.

2nd Lieut., 8 Dec. 48—Lieut., 1 Aug. 54—2nd Captain, 27 Aug. 58—Bt.-Major, 28 Aug. 58.

SERVICE.—Major CHESNEY served as Brigade Major of Engineers throughout the siege of Delhi. Present at the battle of Badlee-ka-Serai. *Severely wounded* in two places at the assault of Delhi. *Medal and Clasp, and Brevet-Majority.*

LIEUTENANT C. W. R. CHESTER, P., late 19th Native Infantry.

Ensign, 20 Feb. 50—Lieut., 23 Nov. 56.

LIEUTENANT H. D. E. W. CHESTER, P. H., late 36th Native Infantry.

Ensign, 20 Feb. 54—Lieut., 23 Nov. 56.

SERVICE.—Lieutenant CHESTER served in '57, at the siege of Delhi. Present from the 28th June to the final capture, in '58, at the capture of Lucknow, by Lord Clyde; present throughout the siege, including the affair at Moosa Bagh, and with General Sir H. Grant's Column in the vicinity of Lucknow. Present at the affair of Baree, on the 13th April. *Wounded slightly* at Delhi, 14th July '57. *Medal and 2 Clasps.*

ASSISTANT-SURGEON N. CHEVERS, M.D., Bengal Medical Establishment.

Asst.-Surgeon, 1 Aug. 48.

CAPTAIN THE HONORABLE F. A. J. CHICHESTER, P. H., late 5th Bengal European Cavalry.

Cornet, 20 July 49—Lieut., 10 Aug. 50—Captain, 16 Sept. 58.

SERVICE.—Captain CHICHESTER commanded a Wing of the 1st Sikh Irregular Cavalry during the disturbance in the Googaira District. Commanded the 1st Irregular Sikh Cavalry at the final siege and capture of Lucknow, under Lord Clyde, in March '58, and with General Grant's Force in the district. *Medal and Clasp.*

LIEUTENANT H. CHICHESTER, Bengal Artillery.

Lieut., 27 April 58.

(131)

LIEUTENANT A. R. T. CHILTON, Bengal Artillery.
Lieut., 27 Aug. 58.

LIEUTENANT W. C. CHOWNE, P. H., late 12th Native Infantry.
Ensign, 4 Nov. 58—Lieut., 1 March 59.
SERVICE.—Lieutenant CHOWNE served with the 19th Punjab Infantry in the late expedition to China, in '60. *Medal.*

LIEUTENANT A. W. CHRISTIAN, late 22nd Native Infantry.
Ensign, 6 Jan. 59—Lieut., 4 Aug. 59.
SERVICE.—Lieutenant CHRISTIAN accompanied the expedition to China in March '60. Present at the affair of the Chinese rebels against the City of Shanghai, in August '60.

LIEUTENANT H. H. CHRISTIAN,† late 68th Native Infantry.
Ensign, 27 June 49—Lieut., 16 Dec. 54.
SERVICE.—Lieutenant CHRISTIAN served during the War in Burmah, '52, '53. *Medal.*

BREVET-COLONEL J. CHRISTIE, late 1st Bengal European Cavalry.
Cornet, 4 Jan. 23—Lieut., 28 May 24—Bt.-Captain, 4 Jan. 38—Captain, 1 Jan, 46—Major, 3 April 46—Lieut.-Colonel, 7 June 49—Bt.-Colonel, 28 Nov. 54.
SERVICE.—Colonel CHRISTIE served at the siege and capture of Bhurtpore, '26. *Medal.* Commanded the 1st Regiment of Cavalry, Shah Shoojah's Force, during the Campaign in Affghanistan, '39, '40, '42. Present at the storm and capture of Ghuznee, *Medal and 3rd Class Dooranee Order*, and capture of Pushoot. With the Candahar Force under Major-General Nott; engaged in the different operations leading to the re-occupation of Cabul and taking of Istaliff. *Medal.* Battle of Punniar. *Bronze Star.* With the Army of the Sutlej. Present at the actions of Moodkee, Ferozeshuhur, and Sobraon, *Medal, 2 Clasps, and Brevet-Major;* and throughout the Punjab Campaign, including the passage of the Chenab, battles of Chillianwallah and Goojerat, and

subsequent pursuit of the Sikhs and Affghans by the Force under General Gilbert. *Medal and Brevet-Lieutenant-Colonel.*

ASSISTANT-SURGEON A. CHRISTISON,† M.D., Bengal Medical Establishment.

Asst.-Surgeon, 20 Oct. 51.

SERVICE.—Assistant-Surgeon CHRISTISON served with the Field Hospital at the taking of Rangoon, in April '52; and relief of Pegu, in December '52. With the 4th Sikh Local Infantry in the operations after the relief of Pegu. Advance to Prome, and expedition under Sir J. Cheape to Donabew, in '53, till the close of the War. *Medal.* With the Gwalior Cavalry from May 15th to July 2nd '57, against the rebels on the Trunk Road above Agra. At the battle with the Nusseerabad Mutineers at Sussia, near Agra, on the 5th July '57. With Meade's Horse after the taking of Gwalior by Sir H. Rose: in the pursuit and defeat of the enemy by Sir R. Napier. *Medal and Clasp.*

MAJOR L. R. CHRISTOPHER, P., late 71st Native Infantry.

Ensign, 4 Jan. 41—Lieut., 1 Nov. 44—Captain, 28 Dec. 53—Major in the Staff Corps, 18 Feb. 61.

SERVICE.—Major CHRISTOPHER was present at Cawnpore from October '57 to May '58, and during the siege by the rebel forces and Gwalior Contingent, in November and December '57. *Medal.*

ASSISTANT-SURGEON S. C. G. CHUCKERBUTTY,† M.D.,M.R.C.S., Bengal Medical Establishment.

Asst.-Surgeon, 24 Jan. 55.

CAPTAIN C. CLARK, P. H., late 2nd European Bengal Fusiliers.

2nd Lieut., 9 Dec. 44—Lieut., 15 Aug. 47—Bt.-Captain, 9 Dec. 59— Captain, 12 Dec. 59.

SERVICE.—Captain CLARK served throughout the Punjab Campaign of '48, '49. Present at Ramnuggur, passage of the Chenab, battles of Chillianwallah and Goojerat, and subsequent pursuit of the Sikhs and

Affghans by the Force under General Sir W. R. Gilbert. *Medal and 2 Clasps.* Served in Burmah in '53. *Medal and Clasp.* Served in India during the Mutiny, '57. Present with the 88th Connaught Rangers, in the defence of the Town and Cantonments of Cawnpore, under Command of General Windham, *wounded dangerously,* when showing (by order of General Windham) Brigadier Carthew the way into Cantonments, on the 27th November '57. *Medal.*

CAPTAIN E. G. CLARK, P., late 21st Native Infantry.
Ensign, 20 Nov. 47—Lieut., 15 Nov. 58—Captain, 1st Jan. 62.

ASSISTANT-SURGEON H. CLARK,† M.D., Bengal Medical Establishment.
Asst.-Surgeon, 4 Aug. 57.

ASSISTANT-SURGEON S. CLARK,† Bengal Medical Establishment.
Asst.-Surgeon, 24 Nov. 49.

SERVICE.—Assistant-Surgeon CLARK served against the rebels in the Allyghur District during the Mutiny in '57. Was present with the Magistrate and party in a charge against a large body of rebels at Madrack, near Allyghur, on the 30th June '57. *Medal.*

ASSISTANT-SURGEON W. F. CLARK,† Bengal Medical Establishment.
Asst.-Surgeon, 4 June 54.

SERVICE.—Assistant-Surgeon W. F. CLARK served with the 2nd Punjab Infantry at the assault on, and capture of, the Bozdar stronghold, on the Derajat Frontier, in March '57; also during the Campaign in Hindostan in '57, '58. Present at the siege, assault, and capture of Delhi, including the battle of Nudjufghur. Accompanied the Moveable Column under Colonel Greathed after the fall of Delhi. Present at the battles of Boolundshuhur and Agra, the relief of the Lucknow Garrison, the battles of Cawnpore and Khodagunge (near Futtehghur), and the siege and capture of the City of Lucknow, besides many other minor affairs. *Medal and 3 Clasps.*

LIEUTENANT W. W. CLARK,† late 36th Native Infantry.

Ensign, 10 Aug. 48—Lieut., 3 July 56.

SERVICE.—Lieutenant CLARK served during the Mutiny, '57, '58, '59. Present at the Mutiny at Jullunder and at the affairs of Kun-Kul, Hurdwar, Nowrah Ghaut, and Poorawas. *Medal.* Commanded a Field Detachment in Saharunpore and Mozuffurnuggur Districts, from September '57 to April '58. Commanded a Moveable Column in Gwalior District, '59, including affairs of Poorawas. Received the thanks of the Governor-General, 22nd February '60.

CAPTAIN C. D. S. CLARKE, P. H., late 73rd Native Infantry.

Ensign, 2nd Sept. 47—Lieut., 21 May 53—Captain,

SERVICE.—Captain CLARKE served throughout the siege of Lucknow, '57, '58. *Medal and Clasp.*

CAPTAIN C. M. L. CLARKE, P. H., late 37th Native Infantry.

Ensign, 13 Dec. 45—Lieut., 26 April 49—Captain, 13 Dec. 60.

SERVICE.—Captain CLARKE was present during the operations against the Hill Tribes in '55. Served throughout the Indian Mutiny in '57 with No. 21 Field Battery. Was present at the action near Agra against the Neemuch Mutineers, on the 5th July *(horse killed under him)*, also at Etiamadpore, Chelaree, 16th August, Maun Sing's garden, and Mynpooree. *Was wounded in three places* in the action near Allygurh, 24th August. Engaged against the Indore, Delhi, and Mhow Mutineers, under Colonel Greathed, and present at the taking of Futtehpore-Sikree, with the Force of Colonel Cotton. Accompanied the Columns of Colonels Cotton and Riddle. *Medal.* Served throughout the operations in '62, in the Cossyah and Jyntia Hills, as Aide-de-Camp to General St. George Showers.

LIEUTENANT D. R. CLARKE,† late 55th Native Infantry.

Ensign, 11 Dec. 58—Lieut., 23 Aug. 59.

LIEUTENANT H. S. CLARKE, Bengal Artillery.

Lieut., 27 Aug 58.

(135)

COLONEL J. CLARKE, P. C., late 25th Native Infantry.

Ensign, 21 Jan. 28—Lieut., 5 Jan. 37—Bt.-Captain, 21 Jan. 43—Captain, 15 Aug. 44—Bt.-Major, 7 June 49—Major, 27 June 57—Bt.-Lieut.-Colonel, 28 Nov. 54—Bt.-Colonel, 13 April 60—Colonel, 12 Aug. 61.

SERVICE.—Colonel CLARKE served with the 25th Native Infantry in the Jhansie Field Force, in '39, '40; in the Army of the Punjab, '48, '49. Present at the actions of Sadoolapore, Chillianwallah, (where he succeeded to the Command of the Regiment,) and Goojerat. *Medal and 2 Clasps.* Assistant Brigade-Major, 5th Brigade, 3rd Division, 20th February, '49. Mentioned in Despatch of Sir Colin Campbell, 1st March '49. Promoted to the rank of Brevet-Major for service in the Punjab Campaign, '48, '49. Accompanied the Force under Brigadier Seaton, and present at the action of Bunkagaon, 8th October '58. Mentioned in the Brigadier-General's Despatch, 17th November '58. Present as Commissioner in Oude, in the actions of Pusgaon, 19th October '58, and Russoolpore, 25th October '58, under Brigadier C. Troup. *Medal.* *(Since resired.)*

ASSISTANT-SURGEON J. J. CLARKE,† Bengal Medical Establishment.

Asst.-Surgeon, 14 May 53.

SERVICE.—Assistant Surgeon CLARKE joined General Sir H. Havelock's 'Column at Cawnpore on the 6th August '57, after escaping from Banda, through Central India, to Benares. Served under him in Medical Charge of Olphert's Horse Battery of Bengal Artillery, in his operations on both banks of the Ganges, at the action of " Mungawar, " the " Alum Bagh, " and the " penetration to the Lucknow Garrison," on the 25th September '57; under Major-General Sir James Outram, in the defence of Lucknow, until the final relief and evacuation of the Garrison by the General Commanding-in-Chief, in November '57; under General Outram in his various operations during the three months and half he held the Alum Bagh, including surprise at Guilee. And still holding the same Medical Charge, was present at the siege and capture of Lucknow by Lord Clyde, in March '58, under Major-General Sir H. Grant. In Medical Charge of the 1st

(136)

Sikh Irregular Cavalry, in his operations in Oude, from the 10th April to 13th August '58. *Medal and 2 Clasps.*

CAPTAIN M. CLARKE, P. H., late 1st Bengal European Cavalry.

Cornet, 28 July 52—Lieut., 28 Sept. 54—Captain, 10 March 58.

LIEUTENANT W. C. S. CLARKE, P. H., late 3rd Bengal European Cavalry.

Cornet, 24 Nov. 47—Lieut., 30 July 49.

MAJOR J. P. CLARKSON, P. H., late 44th Native Infantry.

Ensign, 10 Dec. 39—Lieut., 6 July 42—Captain, 2 Aug. 51—Major, 1 Jan. 62.

SERVICE.—Major CLARKSON served throughout the Sutlej Campaign, '45, '46. Present at the battle of Ferozeshuhur, *Medal;* and subsequent operations against Kôt Kangra.

CAPTAIN E. B. CLAY, P. H., late 66th Native Infantry.

Ensign, 2 March 45—Lieut., 24 July 50—Bt.-Captain, 2 March 60— Captain, 22 April 60.

SERVICE.—Captain CLAY served against the Hill Tribes under Sir C. Campbell, '51, '52. In the defence of the Kumaon Hills and Rohilcund, against the rebels, in '57, '58, '59. Present at the action of Chapoorah. Served in Brigadier Troup's Column, during the Campaign in Oude, '58, '59. Present at the actions of Pusgaon, 19th October '58; and Russoolpore, 25th October '58; attack and capture of Fort Mittowlee, 8th November '58; and action of Bisenah, 1st December '58. *Medal.* (Passed an examination in Field Engineering.)

LIEUTENANT-COLONEL H. CLAYTON, late 3rd Bengal European Cavalry.

Cornet, 16 Jan. 21—Lieut., 6 March 23—Captain, 18 June 35—Bt.- Major, 30 April 44—Major, 6 Sept. 51—Bt.-Lieut.-Colonel, 20 June 54 —Lieut.-Colonel, 28 Nov. 54—Bt.-Colonel, 18 May 56.

SERVICE.—Colonel CLAYTON was present at the siege and capture of Bhurtpore, '26, *Medal;* also at Maharajpore, '43, as Deputy-Quarter-Master-General of the Cavalry Division. *Bronze Star.*

(137)

SURGEON W. G. W. CLEMENGER,† A.B., M.B., Bengal Medical Establishment.
Asst.-Surgeon, 18 June 46—Surgeon, 16 Sept. 59.

LIEUTENANT M. G. CLERK,† late 4th Europeans.
Ensign, 7 Dec. 55—Lieut., 27 June 57.

SERVICE.—Lieutenant CLERK served with the Army under General Havelock and Major-General Outram, in '57, '58. Present at the actions of Mungulwarrah and Alum Bagh; and at the other actions on the last advance of General Havelock to the relief of Lucknow; remaining in the Alum Bagh with the Force under Colonel Macyntire. Present at the capture of Lucknow, under His Excellency the Commander-in-Chief, '58. *Medal and 2 Clasps.* Mentioned in Despatch of Colonel Eyre, 15th February '58. Served as Assistant Field Engineer in the Alum Bagh, 12th October '58.

LIEUTENANT W. CLIFF, Unattached List.
Ensign, 20 Sept. 57—Lieut., 5 Feb. 61.

SURGEON F. M. CLIFFORD,† Bengal Medical Establishment.
Asst.-Surgeon, 4 April 43—Surgeon, 6 June 57.

SERVICE.—Surgeon CLIFFORD served with the Bundlecund Legion, Cavalry Regiment, throughout the Campaign against the Hill Tribes of Scinde, in '44, '45, under Sir C. Napier; and remained on service on the Scinde Desert Frontier, '45,' 46.

LIEUTENANT R. CLIFFORD, P. H., late 74th Native Infantry.
Ensign, 30 Aug. 53—Lieut., 12 July 56.

SERVICE.—Lieutenant CLIFFORD served in defence of the Kumaon Hills, '57, 58. Rohilcund Campaign, '58, '59. Present at the action of Sisseah Ghaut, 15th January '59. *Medal.* Served with the Column under Brigadier-General Chamberlain, against the Cabul Kehl Wuzzeerees, '59, '60.

s

LIEUTENANT R. C. CLIFFORD, P. H., late 38th Native Infantry.

Ensign, 13 Dec. 56—Lieut., 6 June 57.

SERVICE.—Lieutenant CLIFFORD served with the Left Wing, H. M.'s 54th Regiment, in pursuit of Mutineers of the 34th and 73rd Native Infantry, from Dacca and Chittagong, '57. With the Soraon Field Force, under Lieutenant-Colonel Whistler, from March '58. Served with the 1st Oude Police Cavalry with the Army under Lord Clyde during the winter Campaign in Oude, '58. Present at the first attack on the Fort of Tyroul, in Oude, 21st March '58. *Medal.*

LIEUTENANT R. M. CLIFFORD, late 60th Native Infantry.

Ensign, 25 June 58—Lieut., 22 Oct. 58.

CAPTAIN W. C. CLIFFORD,† late 2nd Bengal European Cavalry.

Cornet, 3 Sept. 44—Lieut., 8 May 49—Captain, 30 April 58.

CAPTAIN P. C. CLIFTON,† late 67th Native Infantry.

Ensign, 18 June 39—Lieut., 3 Nov. 43—Captain, 8 Dec. 53.

LIEUTENANT E. L. CLOGSTOUN, P. H., late 10th Native Infantry.

Ensign, 10 June 48—Lieut., 15 Nov. 53.

CAPTAIN E. CLOSE,† late 32nd Native Infantry.

Ensign, 13 June 37—Lieut., 16 July 42—Bt.-Captain, 13 June 52—Captain 2 April 56.

ENSIGN T. ST. Q. CLUTTERBUCK, General List.

Ensign, 1 Aug. 60.

ASSISTANT-SURGEON J. M. COATES,† M.D., Bengal Medical Establishment.

Asst.-Surgeon, 4 Aug. 1855.

SERVICE.—Assistant-Surgeon COATES served throughout the Mutiny with the 1st Battalion Bengal Military Police, in Patna and Behar, Arrah, Jugdespore, Buxar, Suth, Shahabad, and Rhotas Hills. *Medal.*

(139)

LIEUTENANT W. J. COCHRANE, late 68th Native Infantry.
Ensign, 20 Feb. 58—Lieut., 18 Sept. 60.

LIEUTENANT C. R. COCK, late 20th Native Infantry.
Ensign, 4 Sept. 56—Lieut., 18 Sept. 57.

LIEUTENANT A. COCKBURN,† late 52nd Native Infantry.
Ensign, 20 Jan. 53—Lieut., 27 June 57.

SERVICE.—Lieutenant COCKBURN commanded a Detachment 1st Infantry Nagpore Irregular Force, in the Mundlah District, during the rebellion of '58, '59. Present at the taking of the Town of Ramghur, on 2nd April '58; at the repulse of rebels at the same place, on the 11th April; at the taking of the Fort of Sohagpore in the month of June '58. Present at the capture of the Ranee of Ramghur, in January '59. Was engaged in the pursuit of a party of the Dinapore Mutineers from Sohagpore, and was present at their defeat, 1st February '59, near Shahpoorah. Joined Colonel Shubrick, 3rd Madras European Regiment, with a Detachment 3rd Nagpore Irregular Force, in December '59, when that Officer was engaged in the pursuit of Rummest Singh, and was present at one or two skirmishes in January '60. Received the thanks of Government. *Medal.*

CAPTAIN H. A. COCKBURN, P. H., late 53rd Native Infantry.
Ensign, 13 June 51—Lieut., 7 Feb. 55—Captain, 27 June 57.

SERVICE.—Captain COCKBURN marched from Gwalior on 13th May '57 towards Allyghur, in Command of a Squadron of the 1st Cavalry, Gwalior Contingent, of which Regiment he was Adjutant, and served in the Agra, Hattras, and Allyghur Districts of the Doab, under the orders of the Lieutenant-Governor, North-Western Provinces, until the 2nd July following. On the 22nd May '57, near Hattras, with only about 50 men of the above Regiment, he defeated and dispersed a body of nearly 500 rebels, on which occasion *his charger was slightly wounded.* On the following day he rescued 20 persons, amongst whom were Colonel Cecil, Retired List, Mr. Nichterlein, Indigo Planter, and their families, from the Town of Sasnee. On the 31st May he defeated a body of rebels near Hattras, on which occasion the Official Report from Captain Alexander to the Lieutenant-Governor, North-Western Provinces, stated:— " Lieutenant Cockburn dismounted about 20 men and stormed the village. Every praise is due to Lieutenant Cockburn, a most gallant soldier, who had some very narrow escapes" (his helmet and sword were struck by bullets). " *He killed four men with his own hand.*" On the 5th June he defeated a large body of rebels and saved the Town of Lakhnooa, when his *charger was twice wounded*. On the 5th July '57 he served at the battle of Shahgunge, (Agra,) when he was very *severely wounded by a round shot*, and *his charger was killed under him*. On four occasions he received the thanks of the Government of the North-Western Provinces, and was mentioned in a Despatch of the Lieutenant-Governor, dated 6th June '57. On the 31st May several Officers of the late 9th Native Infantry volunteered to accompany him. Amongst them was Major (now Colonel) Eld, who was very *dangerously wounded*, and had had his horse shot in two or more places. *Medal. Extract of Despatch of the Honorable J. R. Colvin, Lieutenant-Governor, North-Western Provinces, to the Right Honorable the Governor-General, dated Agra, 6th June '57*—" At Hattras there is a party of 120 men of the 1st Regiment, Gwalior Contingent Cavalry, which maintains the communication with Agra, and puts down the open ravages of plunderers in the neighborhood. Some spirited affairs of this kind have been reported; and the Adjutant of the Regiment, Lieutenant H. A. Cockburn, has been marked by his forward activity and courage. Having officiated as Secretary to the Government, North-Western Provinces, during the disturbances, and thus been brought in continual communication with Mr. Colvin, the Lieutenant-Governor, I am aware that that Gentleman entertained a very high opinion of Lieutenant H. A. Cockburn as a dashing, energetic Cavalry Officer. Lieutenant Cockburn was employed from about the middle of May '57 till the 2nd July with his Regiment, the 1st Gwalior Contingent Cavalry, in repressing the bodies of insurgents which appeared at various points in the Agra and Allyghur Districts in the Doab, and engaged them at great odds four or five times, with unvaried success. Mr. Colvin wrote several times to Captain Alexander and Lieutenant Cockburn, but no copies of the letters were kept. These

(141)

letters conveyed the thanks of the Lieutenant-Governor for services rendered against the rebels. Lieutenant Cockburn was so severely wounded by a round-shot on the 5th July that he was a cripple until the end of the year, when he was compelled to visit England."—(Signed) C. B. THORNHILL.

SURGEON R. COCKBURN,† Bengal Medical Establishment.
Asst.-Surgeon, 20 Jan. 47—Surgeon, 25 Sept. 60.

CAPTAIN J. COCKERELL, P. H., late 2nd Bengal European Cavalry.
Cornet, 20 Sept. 48—Lieut., 1 Aug. 49—Captain, 12 Jan. 60.

LIEUTENANT F. CODDINGTON, P. H., Bengal Artillery.
Lieut., 27 April 58.

LIEUTENANT E. G. CODRINGTON, P. H., late 57th Native Infantry.
Ensign, 4 Jan. 56—Lieut., 28 Sept. 57.

SERVICE.—Lieutenant CODRINGTON served in the Campaign of '57,'58. Present with the 1st Sikh Irregular Cavalry during the occupation of the entrenched position of Alum Bagh, in the vicinity of Lucknow, by the Force under Sir James Outram, from the 16th January '58 to the 10th March '58. Present at the following actions: repulse of three separate attacks on 16th January; affair of the 15th February; repulse of night attack on 16th February; ditto of attack on 19th February; ditto ditto on 21st February; affair of the 25th February; repulse of night attack on 25th February; affair of 9th March. Present with the Brigade under Brigadier Campbell, forming part of Lord Clyde's Army, at the siege and capture of Lucknow, in March '58, including the skirmishes on the 19th and 21st March, in the vicinity of the Moosa Bagh. Present with the Moveable Column under Sir H. Grant, during the subsequent operations in Oude, including the actions of Baree, 13th April '58, and Sirsee, 12th May '58. *Medal and Clasp.* Served in the 4th Sikh Infantry with the Koorum Field Force, under Brigadier-General

(142)

Chamberlain, against the Cabul Khel Wuzeerees, in December '59 and January '60, including the affair at Midaneo.

LIEUTENANT K. J. W. COGHILL, P. H., late 2nd European Bengal Fusiliers.

2nd Lieut., 26 Feb. 51—Lieut., 22 Oct. 54.

SERVICE.—Lieutenant COGHILL served with the Army of Delhi, '57. Present at the action of Badlee-ka-Serai on 8th June. Siege of Delhi, from 8th June to 21st September '57. Present at the actions in front of the city, including the 10th, 12th, 19th, 20th, 23rd, 27th, and 30th June, the 8th, 9th, 14th, 18th, and 30th July, 1st, and 2nd August; storming of the city of Delhi, 14th September, and the final struggle on 15th, 16th, 17th, 18th, 19th, and 20th September. Served with Brigadier Showers' Force in the Delhi District, from 1st October to 10th November '57. *Medal and Clasp.*

LIEUTENANT H. COGHLAN, Cavalry General List.

Cornet, 4 June 59—Lieut., 4 June 60.

BREVET-COLONEL J. COKE, C.B., P. C., late 10th Native Infantry.

Ensign, 3 Dec. 27—Lieut., 29 Aug. 35—Bt.-Captain, 3 Dec. 42—Captain, 28 March 48—Bt.-Major, 20 June 54—Major, 18 Nov. 57—Bt.-Lieut.-Colonel, 19 Jan. 58—Bt.-Colonel, 20 July 58.

SERVICE.—Colonel COKE was present at the actions of Chillianwallah *(horse shot under him)* and Goojerat; pursuit of the Sikhs and Affghans under General Gilbert. *Medal and Clasp.* With the Force under Lieutenant-Colonel Bradshaw, in the Eusuffzaie country, in '49, '50; also in the affairs in the Eusuffzaie country and Ranazaie Valley, in '52. Commanded 1st Punjab Infantry at the attack on the Afreedies, in the pass leading to Kohat, under Brigadier Campbell. *Wounded* in a skirmish near the Kohat Pass, November '53. Dersummund, May '55; Summana Mountain, September '55; and Bozdar Hills, March '57. *Wounded.* Commanded Moveable Column at Delhi, from 4th July to 12th August. Was *wounded* at the capture of the guns at Ludlow Castle. Commanded a Brigade in Rohilkund, '58. *Medal and Clasp.*

CORNET J COLLEDGE, Cavalry General List.
  Cornet, 4 Nov. 59.

ASSISTANT-SURGEON J. A. P. COLLES,† M.D., F.R.C S., Bengal Medical Establishment.
  Asst-Surgeon, 27 Jan. 58.
  SERVICE.—Assistant-Surgeon COLLES served with a Detachment under the Command of Captain G. Cleveland, Commanding Moradabad Levy, during the operations in Trans-Gogra, in April and May '59, against Gujada Singh, and other Rebel Chiefs; including an affair in the Durzi-ka-Kua Jungle, near Gonda, on 12th April '59.

LIEUTENANT H. COLLETT, P. H., late 53rd Native Infantry.
  Ensign, 8 June 55—Lieut., 27 June 57.
  SERVICE.—Lieutenant COLLETT served in the expedition against the Eusuffzaies, on the Peshawur Frontier, '58. Present at the affairs of Chingli and Sattana. Served during the Oude Campaign, '58, '59. Present at the storm and capture of the Fort of Rampore Kusseah, 3rd November '58. *Medal.*

LIEUTENANT H. COLLINGWOOD, late 48th Native Infantry.
  Ensign, 26 July 57—Lieut., 18 May 58.
  SERVICE.—Lieutenant H. COLLINGWOOD served in suppressing the Mutiny in '57, '58, with the Jounpore Field Force under Brigadier General Franks, in the actions of Nusrutpore, Chanda, Ummeerpore, and Sultanpore, afterwards with the Main Army under Sir Colin Campbell, at the siege and capture of Lucknow. *Medal and Clasp.*

CAPTAIN C. McF. COLLINS, Invalid Establishment.
  Ensign, 8 Jan. 29—Lieut., 7 Aug. 34—Captain, 7 Nov. 40.

ASSISTANT-SURGEON J. C. COLLINS,† Bengal Medical Establishment.
  Asst.-Surgeon, 22 Dec. 47.

LIEUTENANT F. W. COLLIS, late 30th Native Infantry.
Ensign, 10 Dec. 58—Lieut., 29 March 59.

ASSISTANT-SURGEON J. B. COLLISON,† Bengal Medical Establishment.
Asst.-Surgeon, 24 Jan. 55.

LIEUTENANT J. F. F. COLOGAN,† late 22nd Native Infantry.
Ensign, 20 Sept. 57—Lieut., 15 Aug. 58.

SERVICE.—Lieutenant COLOGAN served with Colonel Maxwell's Column, in the Cawnpore District, '57,'58. Present at the advance on Lucknow, March '58. Served in the Ackbarpore District with Colonel Maxwell's Column, in '58. Present with a Detachment of Her Majesty's 88th sent across the Jumna to join Sir Hugh Rose's Force at the actions before and taking of Calpee, in May '58. Served with the 7th Punjab Infantry as part of Brigadier Berkeley's Saraon Field Force, '58. Present with the above Force at the taking of Forts Dehaigon, Tiroul, and Bhyspore, and left in Command of Detachments of 7th Punjab Infantry, occupying after the capture successively the Forts Dehaigon and Bhyspore. Commanded a Company of the 7th Punjab Infantry sent to skirmish and clear the village of Dehaigon. Served in the Azimpore District with the 7th Punjab Infantry, in '58. Served in Trans-Gogra and Trans-Kaptee with the 7th Punjab Infantry, in '58, '59. *Medal and 2 Clasps.* (Passed examination in Field Engineering.)

LIEUTENANT J. A. S. COLQUHOUN, Bengal Artillery.
Lieut., 10 Dec. 58.

BREVET-CAPTAIN A. COMBE,† late 65th Native Infantry.
Ensign, 13 June 46—Lieut., 24 July 53—Bt.-Captain, 13 June 61.

SERVICE.—Captain COMBE served in China, '58, '59, '60. Was engaged against the Chinese on the 8th January '59, when the Battery and Town of Tshuk Tsing was taken by a combined attack of Gunboats and Land Forces under Major-General Straubenzee.

(145)

CAPTAIN A. K. COMBER, P. H., late 18th Native Infantry.
Ensign, 12 Dec. 45—Lieut., 13 April 52—Captain, 6 June 57.
SERVICE.—Captain COMBER served during the Punjab Campaign, '48, '49. *Medal.* (Passed examination in Bengali.)

CAPTAIN D. COMPTON,† late 2nd Bengal European Cavalry.
Cornet, 26 Aug. 54—Lieut., 13 April 55—Captain, 6 Dec. 57.

CAPTAIN P. J. COMYN, P. H., Invalid Establishment.
Ensign, 9 March 38—Lieut., 26 Aug. 42—Captain, 10 March 49.

ASSISTANT-SURGEON J. H. CONDON,† Bengal Medical Establishment.
Asst.-Surgeon, 10 Feb. 59.

LIEUTENANT A. CONOLLY, Bengal Artillery.
Lieut., 8 June 60.

LIEUTENANT E. R. CONOLLY, P. H., Bengal Artillery.
Lieut., 27 Aug. 58.

LIEUTENANT F. H. CONOLLY,† late 49th Native Infantry.
Ensign, 17 March 55—Lieut., 20 Sept. 56.

LIEUTENANT W. P. CONOLLY, P., late 46th Native Infantry.
Ensign, 11 Aug. 47—Lieut., 1 Nov. 53.
SERVICE.—Lieutenant CONOLLY served in the Punjab Campaign, under Lord Gough, at Chillianwallah and Goojerat. *Medal and 2 Clasps.* On the mutiny of the Joudpore Legion, of which Lieutenant Conolly was Adjutant, he was the only Officer present at Erinpoorah, in Command of two 9-pounder guns, Cavalry and Infantry. He was taken prisoner at the parade ground by the Legion Cavalry, whilst endeavoring to quell the disturbance; was kept six days a prisoner by the mutineers, and several times his life was attempted; he was released on the sixth day by the courage of a few of the mutineers. Served at the taking of

(146)

Roena, a fortified village in Rajpootanah, under Colonel Baines, C.B. Was frequently employed in pursuits after rebels; once in Command of a Squadron of Sikh Horse, with the Political Agent of Marmen, after the Nuggur Parkur Takoor, on the borders of Sindh.

LIEUTENANT C. L. B. CONSTABLE, late 17th Native Infantry.

Ensign, 4 March 56—Lieut., 23 Nov. 56.

SERVICE.—Lieutenant CONSTABLE served throughout the Mutiny, '57, '58. Present at the engagement of Gugha with the Goorkha Force under Major F. Wroughton. Served with the Sarun Field Force under Brigadier Pinkney, in Oude, in '58, '59. *Medal.*

LIEUTENANT F. R. A. B. CONSTABLE,† late 69th Native Infantry.

Ensign, 19 Dec. 57—Lieut., 22 Oct. 58.

ASSISTANT-SURGEON F. G. CONSTANT,† M.D., Bengal Medical Establishment.

Asst.-Surgeon, 10 Feb. 59.

CAPTAIN C. H. COOKES, P. H., Bengal Artillery.

2nd Lieut., 9 Dec. 44—Lieut., 1 Dec. 47—Bt.-Captain, 27 Aug. 58—Captain, 12 March 60.

SERVICE.—Captain COOKES served with the Army of the Punjab, '48, '49, and was present at the actions of Ramnuggur, Sadoolapore, Chillianwallah, and Goojerat. *Medal and 2 Clasps.*

LIEUTENANT J. F. COOKESLEY, Bengal Artillery.

Lieut., 10 June 59.

MAJOR G. R. COOKSON, P. H., late 4th Native Infantry.

Ensign, 1 March 38—Lieut., 2 Jan. 42—Captain, 7 July 46—Major in Staff Corps, 18 Feb. 61.

ASSISTANT-SURGEON H. COOKSON,† Bengal Medical Establishment.

Asst.-Surgeon, 20 Jan. 60.

(147)

CAPTAIN S. B. COOKSON, P. H., late 73rd Native Infantry.

Ensign, 28 Dec. 42—Lieut., 4 April 45—Bt.-Captain, 28 Dec. 57—Captain, 2 June 58.

SERVICE.—Captain COOKSON served with the Army of the Sutlej in '45, '46, and was present at the action of Sobraon. *Medal.* Served in the expedition against the Hussunzaies in '52, under immediate orders of Sir R. Napier. In Command of Rawul Pindee Police Battalion as a Volunteer, with which he accompanied the Force across the Black Mountain. This Force was specially thanked by Government for service done.

BREVET-MAJOR C. COOKWORTHY, P. H., Bengal Artillery.

2nd Lieut., 11 June 42—Lieut., 3 July 45—Bt.-Captain, 11 June 57—Captain, 12 Sept. 57—Bt.-Major, 20 July 58.

SERVICE.—Major COOKWORTHY served at the battle of Sobraon *(Medal);* and throughout the Punjab Campaign, '48, '49, including the actions of Sadoolapore, Chillianwallah, and Goojerat. *Medal and 2 Clasps.*

CAPTAIN J. R. R. COOMBS, P. H., Invalid Pension Establishment.

Ensign, 25 Feb. 43—Lieut., 21 Dec. 45—Captain, 10 Sept. 57.

SERVICE.—Captain COOMBS served during the Sutlej Campaign, '46. Present at the battle of Sobraon. *Medal.*

LIEUTENANT COLONEL C. COOPER, late 23rd Native Infantry.

Ensign, 4 May 24—Lieut., 12 April 26—Bt.-Captain, 4 May 39—Captain, 10 June 40—Bt.-Major, 11 Nov. 51—Major, 8 June 57—Bt.-Lieut.-Colonel, 4 July 58.

SERVICE.—Lieutenant-Colonel COOPER served at the siege of Bhurtpore, '25, '26. *Medal.* Served with the Force against the Afreedies, in the Kohat Pass, February '51.

LIEUTENANT A COPLAND, P. H., 4th Native Infantry.

Ensign, 14 Jan. 54—Lieut., 23 Nov. 56.

SERVICE.—Lieutenant COPLAND served with Colonel Craigie's Force against the Hill Tribes, Peshawur Frontier, March '55.

(148)

LIEUTENANT C. A. COPLAND,† P. H., late 30th Native Infantry.

Ensign, 13 June 57—Lieut., 18 May 58.

SERVICE.—Lieutenant COPLAND served during the Mutiny, '57, '58, '59. Served in Brigadier Rowcroft's Column. Present at the attack of Belwah Fort, in Oude, 2nd March '58; action of Amorah, 5th March; Thelga, 17th April; and actions of Amorah, 25th April and 8th June; action of Hurriah, 18th June; attack and capture of Hurriah; actions of Dumooriergunge, 27th November and 3rd December '58; and Toolsipore, in the Trans-Gogra Campaign. *Medal.* Twice specially mentioned in the Despatches of Brigadier Rowcroft, C.B., 6th March and 19th April '58. (*Since dead.*)

CAPTAIN A. F. CORBETT, P., late 43rd Light Infantry.

Ensign, 13 June 46—Lieut., 14 July 53—Captain, 13 June 61.

(Attained proficiency in Punjabee.)

MAJOR-GENERAL Sir S. CORBETT, K.C.B., late 16th Native Infantry.

Ensign, 7 Sept. 19—Lieut., 9 April 22—Captain, 18 Aug. 25—Bt.-Major, 28 June 38—Major, 19 Sept. 40—Lieut.-Colonel, 26 Dec. 46—Bt.-Colonel, 20 June 54—Colonel, 18 May 56—Major-General, 4 Feb. 59.

SERVICE.—Major-General CORBETT, C.B., served during the Punjab Campaign, '48, '49. Commanded the 25th Native Infantry at the battles of Sadoolapore, Chillianwallah, and Goojerat. *Medal and C. B.* Served the Mutiny Campaign and disarmed the Forces at Lahore, &c. *Medal and K. C. B.*

CAPTAIN T. A. CORBETT, P. H., late 61st Native Infantry.

Ensign, 25 July 42—Lieut., 23 Dec. 45—Bt.-Captain, 25 July 57—Captain, 1 Jan. 62.

SERVICE.—Captain CORBETT served with the Left Wing, 61st Native Infantry, against the insurgents in Bundlecund, in '43, '44. Served throughout the Mutiny in Bengal in '57, in the Punjab, and in the latter part of '58, in Central India. Accompanied the 2nd Brigade Saugor Field Force and various Flying Columns in the capacity of Assistant Commissioner during its operations, Jaloun District, and acted on the Staff of the Brigadier Commanding. *Medal.*

LIEUTENANT E. C. CORBYN, P. H., late 46th Native Infantry.
Ensign, 6 May 57—Lieut., 18 May 58.

SERVICE.—Lieutenant CORBYN was present at Cawnpore in the actions of the 26th, 27th, 28th, and 29th November '57. Served with the Army under Lord Clyde, and was present at the re-occupation of Futtehghur. *Medal.*

ASSISTANT-SURGEON F. CORBYN,† M.D., Bengal Medical Establishment.
Asst.-Surgeon, 20 Sept. 49.

SERVICE.—Assistant Surgeon CORBYN served as Field Assistant-Surgeon at the relief of the Lucknow Garrison, also as Medical Store-keeper to the Army under Lord Clyde. Present at the battle of Cawnpore, at the passage of the Kallah Nuddee, re-occupation of Futtehghur, and siege and capture of Lucknow. *Medal and 2 Clasps.*

ASSISTANT-SURGEON J. C. CORBYN,† M.D., Bengal Medical Establishment.
Asst.-Surgeon, 24 Nov. 51.

SERVICE.—Assistant-Surgeon CORBYN served with the Umritsur Moveable Column. Accompained the Cashmere Force under Colonel R. Lawrence to Delhi, and was present at the siege and capture of that place. *Medal and 2 Clasps.* Served with the Troops at Jhujjur and Rohtuck; had Medical Charge of the 3rd Sikh Cavalry at Lucknow; present at the final capture of that city. The 3rd Sikh Cavalry formed part of the Forces under Sir Edward Lugard, with whom the Regiment was at the relief of Azimghur, and afterwads accompained Brigadier Douglas, in the rapid and celebrated pursuit after the rebel Koer Singh : was present in every action fought by his Regiment. Served with the Azimghur Field Force, from 29th March to 4th June '58, when the rebels were finally expelled the Jugdespore Jungles; also present with the 3rd Sikh Cavalry all through the quelling of the disturbances of the Shahabad and Behar Districts.

LIEUTENANT I. J. CORCORAN, Veteran Establishment.
Lieut., 20 Sept. 58.

2ND CAPTAIN J. E. CORDNER, P. H., Bengal Artillery.

2nd Lieut., 13 Dec. 45—Lieut., 1 Jan. 52—2nd Captain, 27 Aug. 58.

SERVICE.—Captain CORDNER served with Brigadier Chamberlain's Force in the Meeranzaie Valley, in attack on Nussum-ka-Ghurrie, Sunghur, Mela, 2nd September '55. Served with the Koorum Expedition in '56; during the Mutiny in '57; against the rebels of the 55th Native Infantry, 25th May '57; storming of the heights above Sattana, 4th May '58. *Medal.*

MAJOR-GENERAL F. B. CORFIELD, late 5th Bengal European Infantry.

Ensign, 3 April 20—Lieut., 11 July 23—Captain, 22 April 31—Major, 14 March 43—Bt.-Lieut.-Colonel, 7 June 49—Lieut.-Colonel, 3 Dec. 49—Bt.-Colonel, 28 Nov. 54—Colonel, 26 April 59—Major-General,

SERVICE.—Major-General CORFIELD served during the Punjab Campaign, '48, '49. Present at the actions of Chillianwallah and Goojerat. *Medal, 2 Clasps, and Brevet-Lieutenant-Colonel.*

CAPTAIN H. R. CORFIELD,† late 9th Native Infantry.

Ensign, 10 June 43—Lieut., 28 Sept. 45—Captain, 4 April 57.

MAJOR-GENERAL W. R. CORFIELD, late 22nd Native Infantry.

Ensign, 3 Dec. 21—Lieut., 11 Sept. 23—Captain, 30 July 32—Major, 2 Feb. 45—Bt.-Lieut.-Colonel, 7 June 49—Lieut.-Colonel, 31 March 51—Bt.-Colonel, 28 Nov. 54.

SERVICE.—Major-General W. R. CORFIELD was present at the siege and storm of Bhurtpore *(India Medal):* employed in the Cole Country in '36, '37. Served with the Army of the Indus from '38, '39, '40. Present at the storm and capture of Kelat, '39 : battle of Maharajpore. *Bronze Star.* Commanded the 30th Regiment throughout the Punjab Campaign, including the actions of Sadoolapore, Chillianwallah, and Goojerat, and subsequent pursuit of the Sikhs and Affghans to Peshawur, under General Gilbert. *Medal and Brevet-Lieutenant-Colonel.*

CAPTAIN P. G. CORNISH,† Invalid Establishment.

Ensign, 8 Dec. 31—Lieut., 8 Sept. 40—Captain, 8 Dec. 46.

CAPTAIN A. CORY, P. H., late 16th Native Infantry.

Ensign, 3 Oct. 48—Lieut., 13 Dec. 54—Captain, 16 May 61.

SERVICE.—Captain CORY served with the Nepalese Army under H. H. Jung Bahadoor, in '58, also with General Whitlock's Force, in Central India, '58, '59. Present at the capture of Goruckpore, 6th January '58, several minor actions in Oude, January and February '58. Present during several engagements in Central India. Served in the capacity of Staff Officer to a Column under Colonel Primrose, in Bundlecund, October and November '59. *Medal and Clasp.* Mentioned in the Despatches of Brigadier-General Macgregor, 20th July, 25th February, and 30th March '58.

ASSISTANT-SURGEON C. P. COSTELLO,† Bengal Medical Establishment.

Asst.-Surgeon, 10 Feb. 59.

LIEUTENANT-GENERAL W. R. C. COSTLEY, late 9th Native Infantry.

Ensign, 16 Oct. 02—Lieut., 3 June 04—Captain, 9 Dec. 17—Major, 27 Jan. 26—Lieut.-Colonel, 2 Jan. 31—Colonel, 22 Oct. 42—Major General, 20 June 54—Lieut.-General, 2 April 56.

SERVICE.—Lieutenant-General COSTLEY served at Chundrus and at the storming of a fortified village near Allygurh. Present at the battle, siege, and capture of Deig, '04. Engaged in pursuit of Holkar, from Muttra, under Lord Lake; served also during the Nepal War. *Medal.*

LIEUTENANT J. P. COTTAM, Bengal Artillery.

Lieut., 11 Dec. 58.

CAPTAIN C. McC. COTTON, P. H., late 2nd Bengal European Cavalry.

Cornet, 3 March 42—Lieut., 17 Oct. 46—Captain, 16 July 57.

SERVICE.—Captain COTTON served at the battle of Maharajpore. *Bronze Star.*

LIEUTENANT H. COTTON, Bengal Artillery.

Lieut., 27 Aug. 58.

(152)

CAPTAIN W. D. COUCHMAN, P. H., Bengal Artillery.

2nd Lieut., 9 Dec. 44—Lieut., 16 June 48—2nd Captain, 27 Aug. 58—Captain, 6 Feb. 61.

CAPTAIN J. H. COUPER, P. H., late 2nd Native Infantry.

Ensign, 14 Jan. 45—Lieut., 17 Feb. 51—Captain, 16 Feb. 59.

SERVICE.—Captain COUPER served with the expedition under Brigadier Wheeler against Kote Kangra, in '46.

CORNET M. H. COURT,† Cavalry General List.

Cornet, 20 Jan. 60.

CAPTAIN H. R. COURTENAY, P. H., Bengal Artillery.

2nd Lieut., 11 Dec. 41—Lieut., 3 July 45—Captain, 8 June 56.

SERVICE.—Captain COURTENAY served during the Sutlej Campaign, '45, '46. Present at the action of Sobraon. *Medal.* Served during the Punjab Campaign, '48, '49. Present at the actions of Ramnuggur, Chillianwallah, and Goojerat. *Medal and 2 Clasps.*

ASSISTANT-SURGEON S. C. COURTENEY,† M.D., Bengal Medical Establishment.

Asst.-Surgeon, 27 Jan. 58.

LIEUTENANT S. H. COWAN, P. H., Bengal Artillery.

Lieut., 9 Dec. 59.

ASSISTANT-SURGEON A. J. COWIE,† Bengal Medical Establishment.

Asst.-Surgeon, 4 Aug. 54.

LIEUTENANT C. COWIE, P. H., Bengal Artillery.

Lieut., 27 Aug. 58.

ENSIGN T. R. COWIE, General List.

Ensign, 4 July 60.

(153)

LIEUTENANT H. H. P. COWPER, P. H., General List, Cavalry.

Cornet, 4 Sept. 59—Lieut., 4 Sept. 60.

SURGEON C. L. COX,† A.B., F.R.C.S., Bengal Medical Establishment.

Asst.-Surgeon, 27 July 41—Surgeon, 22 Sept. 55.

SERVICE.—Surgeon Cox served throughout the China Expedition with the Army under Lord Gough *(Medal)*; and with the Force under Brigadier-General Wheeler, in the Jullundur Doab, '48, '49. *Medal.*

BREVET-MAJOR C. V. COX,† Bengal Artillery.

2nd Lieut., 11 June 38—Lieut., 14 Aug. 41—Captain, 3 March 53—Bt.-Major, 4 March 53—Bt.-Lieut.-Colonel, 2 June 60—Lieut.-Colonel, 18 Feb. 61.

SERVICE.—Captain (Brevet-Major) Cox was present at the battle of Punniar, '43, *(Bronze Star)*; Moodkee *(slightly wounded)*; Ferozeshuhur and Sobraon, '45, '46. *Medal and 2 Clasps.* Served in the Army of the Punjab, '48, '49, including the passage of the Chenab and actions of Chillianwallah and Goojerat. *Medal, 2 Clasps,* and *Brevet-Major.*

LIEUTENANT E. B. COX,† late 3rd Bengal European Infantry.

Ensign, 11 Dec. 57—Lieut., 15 Feb. 61.

SERVICE.—Lieutenant Cox served during the Mutiny in '58, '59. Present at the action of Dowsa. *Medal.* Accompanied the Force under Brigadier Purnell, in Oude, from the 3rd June till the 16th September '58.

ENSIGN E. R. COX, General List.

Ensign, 4 Sept. 59—Lieut., 24 August 61.

LIEUTENANT F. A. D. COX, 17th Native Infantry.

Ensign, 26 May 57—Lieut., 18 May 58.

SERVICE.—Lieutenant Cox served with Her Majesty's 34th Regiment during the Campaign of '57, '58. Present at the actions of Cawnpore, 27th, 28th, and 29th November '57, under General Windham. The

(154)

capture of the fort at Mean Gunge, Oude, under General Sir H. Grant; the capture of Lucknow. *Medal and Clasps.* The relief of Azimghur, under Sir E. Lugard.

MAJOR-GENERAL H. C. M. COX, late 58th Native Infantry.

Ensign, 24 May 06—Lieut., 13 Aug. 09—Bt.-Captain, 24 May 21—Captain, 1 May 24—Major, 9 Aug. 36—Lieut.-Colonel, 22 Oct. 42—Colonel, 5 June 53—Major.-General, 28 Nov. 54.

SERVICE.—Major-General Cox accompanied the 5th Volunteer Battalion to Java, in '11. Present at the assault and capture of Fort Cornelis, *Medal.* Served at the siege and taking of Hattrass, during the Mahrattah Campaign, '17, and in Oude, '22.

LIEUTENANT J. B. COX, P. H., late 62nd Native Infantry.

Ensign, 11 June 47—Lieut., 28 May 51.

CAPTAIN W. F. COX,† Bengal Artillery,

2nd Lieut., 7 June 44—Lieut., 12 Aug. 46—Captain, 27 April 58.

SERVICE.—Captain Cox was present at the battle of Sobraon, '46 *(Medal)*; Army of the Punjab, '48, '49, including the actions of Chillianwallah and Goojerat. *Medal and 2 Clasps.*

CAPTAIN H. W. H. COXE, P., late 70th Native Infantry.

Ensign, 21 June 41—Lieut., 8 April 50—Bt.-Captain, 21 June 56—Captain, 18 Feb. 61.

SERVICE.—Captain COXE served with the Army of Gwalior, '43. Present (on rear guard) at the battle of Maharajpore. *Bronze Star.* Commanded a Durbar Force, as Assistant Resident, Lahore, for occupation of Pinddadun Khan, after battle of Goojerat, '49. Served as Political Officer at Bunnoo Frontier, '57. Received thanks of Government, 2nd April '51. Accompanied the Expeditionary Force under Brigadier-General Chamberlain, against the Wuzeeree Tribes, '60. Present at the engagements of Palosεen and Bunrah. Received thanks of the Lieutenant-Governor, 9th July '60.

2ND CAPTAIN G. CRACKLOW,† Bengal Artillery.

2nd Lieut., 15 June 57—2nd Captain, 18 Feb. 61.

SERVICE.—Captain CRACKLOW served with the Punjab Column under General Nicholson, at Goordaspore, in the engagement with the Sealkote Mutineers; at the siege and capture of Delhi; with Brigadier Greathead's Column at the battles of Boolundshuhur and Agra, 10th October '57; at the relief of Lucknow, by Sir Colin Campbell; at the defeat and pursuit of the Gwalior rebels, at Cawnpore, 6th December; at the siege and capture of Lucknow, and during the subsequent operations in Oude, during the hot season of '58. *Medal and 3 Clasps.*

LIEUTENANT B. CRACROFT, P. H., late 50th Native Infantry.

Ensign, 15 May 54—Lieut., 21 Feb. 57.

SERVICE.—Lieutenant CRACROFT served throughout the Sonthal Campaign, '55, '56. *(Slightly wounded.)* Served during the Mutiny in Central India, under General Whitlock. Present at the attack and capture of Punwarree Heights, near Kirwee, 29th December '58. Mentioned in the Despatch of General Whitlock, '59. *Medal.*

CAPTAIN J. E. CRACROFT, P., late 69th Native Infantry.

Ensign, 10 July 42—Lieut., 11 Sept. 45—Captain, 10 July 57.

SERVICE.—Captain CRACROFT served during the Sutlej Campaign, '45, 46. Present at the battle of Sobraon *(Medal)*; and with the Force under General Whish, throughout the operations in the vicinity, and siege and surrender of Mooltan and action of Goojerat. *Medal and Clasp.*

SURGEON W. CRADDOCK, M.D., F.R.C.S., P. C. H., Bengal Medical Establishment.

Asst.-Surgeon, 30 Jan. 43—Surgeon, 22 May 57.

SERVICE.—Surgeon CRADDOCK served in China on Field Service as Surgeon of the 70th Bengal Native Infantry, from December '57 to February '58.

(156)

LIEUTENANT F. J. CRAIGIE, P. H., late 21st Native Infantry.

Ensign, 8 Dec. 48—Lieut., 13 April 55.

SERVICE.—Lieutenant CRAIGIE served with the Punjab Irregular Force, in the Koorian Valley, in '56. Present at the taking of Thorewalie. Served with the Bareilly Field Force on the Oude Frontier, in '58, '59. Commanded a party of the 2nd Punjab Cavalry and 24th Punjab Infantry in a successful affair against the rebels at Moreah, on the 29th August; and commanded the Cavalry at the attack on the enemy's position at Seerpoorah, 30th August '58. Present with the Punjab Irregular Force in the affair against the Wuzeeree Hill Tribes, in '60. *Medal.* Received the thanks of Government, 1st October '58.

CAPTAIN H. C. CRAIGIE, P. H., late 1st Bengal European Cavalry.

Cornet, 20 Aug. 48—Lieut., 11 Sept. 51—Captain, 23 Nov. 56.

SERVICE.—Captain CRAIGIE served with the 5th Light Cavalry during the Punjab Campaign, '48, '49. Present at the battle of Goojerat. *Medal.*

CORNET W. B. CRAIGIE,† Cavalry General List.

Cornet, 4 Dec. 59.

2ND CAPTAIN G. A. CRASTER, Bengal Engineers.

2nd Lieut., 11 Dec. 49—Lieut., 1 Aug. 54—2nd Captain, 27 Aug. 58.

SERVICE.—Captain CRASTER served with the expedition to Pegu in '52, '53. Present at the capture of Rangoon and Bassein as Senior Engineer Officer. Mentioned in Major-General Godwin's Despatch, and received the thanks of Government, 21st June '52. *Medal.*

LIEUTENANT W. R. CRASTER, P. H., Bengal Artillery.

Lieut., 27 April 58.

CAPTAIN A. CRAWFORD,† late 9th Regiment.

Ensign, 27 Jan. 44—Lieut., 3 Oct. 48—Bt.-Captain, 27 Jan. 59—Captain, 16 Oct. 61.

SERVICE.—Captain CRAWFORD commanded the Field Detachment, 43rd Native Infantry and 12th Cavalry, at Kishengurh, in the Chutterpore Territory, in Bundlecund.

(157)

LIEUTENANT G. D. CRAWFORD, P. H., late 18th Native Infantry.
Ensign, 14 June 51—Lieut., 1 Jan. 55.

SURGEON J. D. CRAWFORD, A.B., M.B., Bengal Medical Establishment.
Asst.-Surgeon, 11 Aug. 46—Surgeon, 11 Dec. 59.

LIEUTENANT H. C. CREAK, late 4th European Cavalry.
Cornet, 4 March 59—Lieut., 2 Jan. 60.

ASSISTANT-SURGEON A. G. CREWE,† Bengal Medical Establishment.
Asst.-Surgeon, 14 Dec. 53.

LIEUTENANT H. McV. CRICHTON, Bengal Engineers.
Lieut., 27 Aug. 58.

LIEUTENANT A. W. CRIPPS, P., late 26th Native Infantry.
Ensign, 26 Dec. 49—Lieut., 23 Nov. 56.
Has attained proficiency in Punjabee.

CAPTAIN J. M. CRIPPS, P., late 26th Native Infantry.
Ensign, 11 Dec. 39—Lieut., 16 July 42—Capt., 1 Sept. 50.
SERVICE.—Captain CRIPPS served with General Pollock's Army in the advance to Cabul, in '42. Present at the actions of the Khyber Pass, Jugdulluck, Tezeen, and Istaliff, in the Kohistan. *Medal.* Served with the Army of the Sutlej in '45, '46, at the actions of Moodkee, Ferozeshuhur, and Sobraon. *Medal and Clasps.*

CAPTAIN J. CROFTON,† Bengal Engineers.
2nd Lieut., 9 Dec. 44—Lieut., 7 Oct. 51—Captain, 13 Aug. 58.

LIEUTENANT F. W. CROHAN, General List.
Ensign, 31 Jan. 60—Lieut, Jan. 62.

LIEUTENANT P. R. CROLLY,† late 62nd Native Infantry.
Ensign, 9 Dec. 54—Lieut., 1 June 57.

BT.-MAJOR W. A. CROMMELIN, C.B., Bengal Engineers.

2nd Lieut., 10 Dec. 41—Lieut., 5 May 46—2nd Captain, 11 June 54— Captain, 15 April 56—Bt.-Major, 24 March 58.

SERVICE.—Major CROMMELIN, C.B., served in the Sutlej Campaign of '45, '46. *Medal.* Served as Brigade Major of Engineers with the Force under Command of Brigadier Wheeler, in the operations against Fort Kangra and Noorpore, in May '46. Served in the Punjab Campaign. Present at Sadoolapore, Chillianwallah, and Goojerat. Engineer in charge of Pontoon Train with General Gilbert's Force. *Medal and 2 Clasps.* Served as Chief Engineer with Sir H. Havelock's Force on both passages of the Ganges and subsequent actions and defence of Lucknow. *(Wounded.) Medal and Clasp. Brevet-Majority and C. B.*

ASSISTANT-SURGEON P. M. CROSBIE,† A.B., Bengal Medical Establishment.

Asst.-Surgeon, 23 July 58.

SERVICE.—Assistant-Surgeon CROSBIE served in Medical Charge of Detachments of Alexander's Horse and the Agra Police, with Brigadier Showers, C.B., in pursuit of Tantia Topee, in January '59. Was present at the engagement of Dousa, on the 14th January '59. *Medal.*

CAPTAIN R. C. CROSS, late 17th Native Infantry.

Ensign, 18 Jan. 45—Lieut., 15 Nov. 53—Bt.-Captain, 18 Jan. 60— Captain, in Staff Corps, 25 Sept. 61.

SERVICE.—Captain CROSS served in the advance on Cawnpore, July '57 ; with the Army under Sir H. Havelock, K.C.B., and under Sir J. Outram, in '57. Present at the actions of Futtehpore, Aoung, and Pandoo Nuddee : battle and re-occupation of Cawnpore *(horse killed under him by round shot)*, Bithoor, actions of Oonao and Busseerut Gunge, Barby-ky-Chowkee, 2nd action at Bithoor *(horse wounded)*. Protected the building of a bridge of boats and road on the Oude side of the Ganges, 17th September. Present at the skirmishes of 17th, 18th, and 19th September ; action of Mungulwara, Alum Bagh, and relief of Lucknow, 25th September '57 *(slightly wounded)*. Besieged with that garrison for 2 months, and the day before being relieved by Lord Clyde, led 100 men of the Regiment of Ferozepore as part of a storming party to the King's stables and steam engine house. Put up one of the colors of the Regiment of Ferozepore under a heavy fire at one of our outposts to serve as a guide to Lord Clyde's Army, when coming into Lucknow. Served with the entrenched camp under Sir J. Outram, K.C.B., at Alum Bagh, '57, '58. Present at the re-capture of Lucknow by Lord Clyde. Served with a Force under Sir H. Grant at the crossing of the Gogra, at Fyzabad, November '58. Served on the Nepal Frontier, under Brigadier Rowcroft, C.B., in '59. *Medal and 2 Clasps.*

CAPTAIN C. CROSSMAN, Invalid Establishment.

Ensign, 12 June 28—Lieut., 8 Oct. 39—Captain, 12 June 43.

MAJOR F. G. CROSSMAN, P. H., late 45th Native Infantry.

Ensign, 11 Dec. 37—Lieut., 3 Oct. 40—Captain 1 July 50—Bt.-Major, 24 March 58.

SERVICE.—Major CROSSMAN served throughout the Sutlej Campaign, '45, '46. Present at the actions of Moodkee, Ferozeshuhur, Alliwal, and Sobraon. *Medal and 3 Clasps.* Mutiny Campaign. *Medal and Clasps, and Brevet-Major.*

SURGEON-MAJOR A. W. CROZIER,† F.R.C.S., Bengal Medical Establishment.

Asst.-Surgeon, 19 Dec. 39—Surgeon, 1 Dec. 53—Surgeon-Major, 13 Jan. 60.

SERVICE.—Surgeon-Major A. W. CROZIER, F.R.C.S., served with H. M.'s 26th and 55th Regiments in China, in '41, '42, '43. Was at the taking of Amoy, re-capture of Chusan, and occupation of Ningfo. *Medal.* Served in the Gwalior Campaign, and was present at the battle of Punniar, in charge of the 50th Native Infantry. *Bronze Star.* Served in the Sutlej Campaign with 16th Lancers, and was present at the battles of Buddiwal and Alliwal. For his services at the last battle he received the special thanks of Lieutenant-General Sir H. Smith, Commanding. *Medal.* Officiated as Superintending Surgeon in the action on the 5th July '57, near Agra, against the Neemuch and Nusseerabad Mutineers. Had a *horse shot under him*, and was thanked in the Despatch for services performed on the occasion; was in Medical Charge of the 3rd European Regiment in the action of the 10th October, at Agra, against the rebels from Gwalior. Was in Medical Charge of the 3rd in the action with rebels at Oriya. Served the whole of the hot weather Campaign of '58 against the mutineers, in the affairs of Etawah and Mynpooree Districts. Was in charge of the 3rd or Moveable Column under Command of Colonel Riddell, which marched towards Gwalior to cooperate with Central Field Force; thanked by Colonel Riddell in his Despatch for services rendered on the occasion. *Medal.* Twelve times thanked and mentioned for efficient and valuable services.

SURGEON W. CROZIER,† F.U.C., Bengal Medical Establishment.

Asst.-Surgeon, 18 Sept. 42—Surgeon, 10 April 57.

SERVICE.—Surgeon W. CROZIER served during the Sutlej Campaign, '45, '46. Present at the battles of Moodkee and Ferozeshuhur. *Medal and Clasp.*

LIEUTENANT W. G. CUBITT, V.C., P. H., late 13th Native Infantry.

Ensign, 26 July 53—Lieut, 23 Nov. 56.

SERVICE.—Lieutenant CUBITT, V. C., formed one of the Lucknow Garrison (Defence). Served at the action of Chinhut, 30th June '57, and served in the Volunteer Cavalry, and was present during the entire siege of Lucknow. *Medal and Clasp, Victoria Cross, and one year's extra service.*

ASSISTANT-SURGEON P. CULLEN,† Bengal Medical Establishment.

Asst.-Surgeon, 27 July 59.

SERVICE.—Assistant-Surgeon CULLEN served with the 19th Regiment Punjab Infantry throughout the China Expedition of '60. On the 15th May '60 was detached from Kowloon, in Medical Charge of 3 Companies of the 19th Punjab Infantry, and half of the A. Company, 5th Battalion Madras Artillery, to the Island of Chusan.

(161)

2ND CAPTAIN W. B. CUMBERLAND, P. H., Bengal Artillery.

Lieut., 4 July 57—2nd Captain, 18 Sept. 61.

SERVICE.—Captain CUMBERLAND served with the expedition under Brigadier Chamberlain to the Meeranzaie Valley and Upper Koorum, in '56. Also present at the operations in the Bozdar Hills, in '57.

BREVET-COLONEL E. A. CUMBERLEGE, late 40th Native Infantry.

Ensign, 19 Dec. 19—Lieut., 11 July 23—Captain, 29 Nov. 34—Major, 4 April 45—Lieut.-Colonel, 7 April 51—Bt.-Colonel, 28 Nov. 54.

SERVICE.—Colonel CUMBERLEGE served during the Sutlej Campaign, '45, '46. Present at the battle of Sobraon. *Medal.* Served during the Punjab Campaign, '48, '49. *Medal.*

LIEUTENANT H. O. CUMBERLEGE, General List.

Ensign, 15 July 59—Lieut., 18 March 61.

CAPTAIN A. CUMINE, P. H., late 4th Native Infantry.

Ensign, 10 Dec. 44—Lieut., 16 May 48—Captain, 23 Nov. 56.

SERVICE.—Captain CUMINE served under Brigadier Wheeler during the Punjab Campaign, '48, '49. *Medal.* (Passed examination in Field Engineering.)

LIEUTENANT A. J. W. CUMMING, Bengal Engineers.

Lieut., 27 Aug. 58.

LIEUTENANT G. P. CUMMING,† late 4th Bengal Europeans.

Ensign, 12 Dec. 57—Lieut., 6 Nov. 59.

CAPTAIN G. G. CUNLIFFE, P. H., late 41st Native Infantry.

Ensign, 20 March 47—Lieut., 16 July 50—Captain, 26 June 60.

SERVICE.—Captain CUNLIFFE served as a Volunteer in the Nynee Tal Militia, raised for the protection of that place from the 3rd June to 26th December '57, and assisted in that capacity in the surprise and defeat of a body of rebels belonging to Khan Bahadoor Khan, who had occupied

W

Huldwaree on the 17th September '57. Commanded a Detachment of the Kemaon Levy at the action of Churpoorah, 10th February '58. Commanded the Infantry portion of a Field Force under the Command of Captain now Lieutenant-Colonel S. Browne, at the action of Surpoorah, on the 30th August '58, and succeeded to the Command of the Force itself on that Officer being placed *hors de combat* by severe wounds. *(Charger disabled by sword cuts.)* Received the thanks of their Excellencies the Governor-General and Commander-in-Chief for gallant conduct shown on that occasion. *Medal.*

LIEUTENANT-COLONEL A. CUNNINGHAM, Bengal Engineers.

2nd Lieut., 9 June 31—Lieut., 20 May 39—Bt.-Captain, 9 June 46—Captain, 15 Jan. 51—Bt.-Major, 7th June 49—Major, 13 Aug. 58—Lieut.-Colonel, 27 Aug. 58.

SERVICE.—Colonel A. CUNNINGHAM served in the Gwalior Campaign. *Bronze Star.* Punjab Campaign. Present at Chillianwallah and Goojerat. *Medal and 2 Clasps, and Brevet-Major.*

LIEUTENANT A. B. CUNNINGHAM, Bengal Artillery.

Lieut., 11 Dec. 58.

ASSISTANT-SURGEON J. M. CUNNINGHAM,† M.D., Bengal Medical Establishment.

Asst.-Surgeon, 20 Nov. 51.

ASSISTANT-SURGEON R. W. CUNNINGHAM,† M.D., Bengal Medical Establishment.

Asst.-Surgeon, 20 Jan. 60.

CAPTAIN W. R. CUNNINGHAM, P., late 5th Europeans.

Ensign, 31 Jan. 37—Lieut., 12 Nov. 42—Bt.-Captain, 31 Jan. 52—Captain, 15 June 52.

SERVICE.—Captain CUNNINGHAM served with the 6th Native Infantry throughout the Cabul Campaign of '42, under Sir G. Pollock. *Medal.* Present with the same Regiment on the advance on Lahore in '46.

(163)

Served throughout the Punjab Campaign, '48, '49, under Lord Gough, as 2nd in Command, 12th Irregular Cavalry. Present at the affair of Ramnuggur in November '48, and succeeded to the Command of the Corps, on Major Holmes being wounded. Passage of the Chenab and Goojerat, and with Sir Walter Gilbert's Column, in pursuit of the Sikhs and Affghans to Peshawur. *Medal and Clasp.*

CAPTAIN B. CUPPAGE,† late 3rd Bengal European Cavalry.

Cornet, 4 Sept. 53—Lieut., 1 June 55—Captain, 18 Feb. 62.

SERVICE.—Captain CUPPAGE served with the Army before Delhi, from June to September '57. Present at the action of Nudjufghur and all the Cavalry engagements before Delhi. *Wounded severely* at the assault of Delhi, 14th September '57. *Medal and Clasp.* Served as Brigade-Major with the Force under General Johnstone and Lieutenant-Colonel Olpherts, from Umballah to Delhi.

CAPTAIN H. C. CUPPAGE,† late 15th Native Infantry.

Ensign, 23 June 42—Lieut., 5 Oct. 46—Captain, 9 Oct. 58.

SERVICE.—Captain CUPPAGE served throughout the Campaign in the Punjab, including the passage of the Chenab and the actions of Chillianwallah and Goojerat. *Medal and Clasps.* Commanded a detached Squadron of the Jāt Horse when the Corps was employed in guarding the Ghauts of the Ganges against the Rohilcund rebels in the hot weather of '58. Commanded a Squadron, and for some time a Wing of the Regiment attached to Colonel Simpson's Column in the 2nd Oude Campaign, and in the subsequent operations on the Nepal Frontier, under Sir R. Kelly, till the beginning of March '59. *Medal.*

BREVET-LIEUTENANT-COLONEL C. CURETON, P. H., late 38th Native Infantry.

Ensign, 22 Feb. 43—Lieut., 26 Feb. 46—Captain, 25 May 57—Bt.-Major, 20 July 58—Bt.-Lieut.-Colonel, 26 April 59.

SERVICE.—Brevet-Lieutenant-Colonel C. CURETON was present with the Army of the Sutlej in '45, '46. Served as A. D. C. to Brigadier-

(164)

General Cureton, Commanding the Cavalry Division in the Punjab Campaign, and was present at Ramnuggur, passage of the Chenab, and battle of Goojerat; accompanied Sir W. Gilbert's Column in pursuit of the Sikh and Affghan Army in '49; occupation of Peshawur. *Medal and Clasp.* Served against the Sealkôt Mutineers under General Nicholson in '57, and likewise against the Googaira insurgents. Commanded the Mooltanee Regiment of Cavalry throughout the Campaigns in Rohilcund and Oude, '58, '59, including the actions of Bhagwala *(Charger wounded)*; Nagena *(Charger wounded)*; Bareilly, Shahjehanpore, and Bunae, under Brigadier-General J. Jones; Shahabad, under Brigadier Taylor; Búnkagaon, under Sir Thomas Seaton; (in actions under General Jones, Brigadier Taylor, and Sir T. Seaton had also charge of the Intelligence Department,) and Mahadypore, Russoolpore, Fort Mittowlee, and Biswa, under Brigadier C. Troup. *Medal. Has been eleven times mentioned in Despatches, seven times honorably.*

LIEUTENANT A: A. CURRIE, P. H., late 45th Native Infantry.

Ensign, 3 March 49—Lieut., 26 Oct. 50.

LIEUTENANT F. CURRIE, late 1st Bengal European Cavalry.

Cornet, 20 Nov. 58—Lieut., 29 March 59.

ASSISTANT-SURGEON G. V. CURRIE, Bengal Medical Establishment.

Asst.-Surgeon, 14 Jan. 54.

SERVICE.—Assistant-Surgeon CURRIE served with General Sir Sydney Cotton's Field Forces in Eusuffzaie, in '58.

LIEUTENANT H. O. CURRIE,† late 5th Europeans.

Ensign, 4 Feb. 53—Lieut., 6 June 57.

SERVICE.—Present when the 6th Native Infantry mutinied at Allahabad.

ASSISTANT-SURGEON J. A. CURRIE,† M.A., M.D., Bengal Medical Establishment.

Asst.-Surgeon, 4 Dec. 53.

(165)

LIEUTENANT J. R. CURRIE,† late 4th Native Infantry.

Ensign, 26 Jan. 47—Lieut., 15 Sept. 49.

SERVICE.—Lieutenant CURRIE served under Brigadier Wheeler during the Punjab Campaign, '48, '49. *Medal.*

CAPTAIN M. E. CURRIE, P. H., Bengal Artillery.

2nd Lieut., 14 June 45—Lieut., 10 Feb. 49—2nd Captain, 27 Aug. 58—Captain, 23 Aug. 61.

SERVICE.—Captain CURRIE served during the Sutlej Campaign and was present at the battle of Sobraon, '46. *Medal.*

LIEUTENANT E. H. CURTIS.

Cornet, 29 Oct. 59—Lieut., 1 Oct. 61.

CAPTAIN J. C. CURTIS, P. H., late 72nd Bengal Native Infantry.

Ensign, 17 March 41—Lieut., 17 Oct. 43—Captain, 9 Oct. 54.

SERVICE.—Captain CURTIS served with the Army of the Punjab, '48, '49. Present at the siege and surrender of Mooltan, from November '48 to January '49. Present at the surrender of Fort Chuniout, 3rd February '59, and at the battle of Goojerat, 21st February '49. *Medal and Clasps.* Present in Command of 6th Irregular Cavalry at Mooltan, 31st August '58, when the men of the 4th Troop, 3rd Brigade Native Horse Artillery, and of the 62nd and 69th Native Infantry mutinied. Assisted at the extermination of those Regiments between the 31st August and 16th September '58. *Medal.*

ASSISTANT-SURGEON H. C. CUTCLIFFE,† F.R.C.S., Bengal Medical Establishment.

Asst.-Surgeon, 28 May 58.

CAPTAIN G. A. CUYLER, P., late 4th Bengal Europeans.

Ensign, 29 Dec. 44—Lieut., 3 Oct. 51—Bt.-Captain, 29 Dec 59—Captain.

SERVICE.—Captain CUYLER served during the Punjab Campaign, '48, '49, under Brigadier Wheeler, and was present at the assault on the heights of Dullah. *Medal.*

(166)

D

CAPTAIN G. D'AGUILAR, P., late 4th Native Infantry.

Ensign, 22 Dec. 40—Lieut., 24 Jan. 45—Bt.-Captain, 22 Dec. 55—Captain, 1 April 56.

SERVICE.—Captain D'AGUILAR served in the Punjab Campaign, '48, '49. *Medal*. Served in the Kohat Expedition, '51, as Acting Adjutant, 1st Punjab Cavalry. Served with the Huzara Expedition till '52.

ASSISTANT-SURGEON A. M. DALAS,† Bengal Medical Establishment.

Asst.-Surgeon, 20 Feb. 56.

ASSISTANT-SURGEON A. J. DALE,† M.B., Bengal Medical Establishment.

Asst.-Surgeon, 20 Oct. 53.

SERVICE.—Assistant-Surgeon DALE served with the Bengal Fusiliers and 25th Native Infantry immediately after the War in Burmah, in '53. Was present with a Wing of the latter Regiment in quieting the district and capturing dacoits under Moung-ghoung-Ghee, in '54.

LIEUTENANT P. C. DALMAHOY, late 60th Native Infantry.

Ensign, 13 Dec. 56—Lieut., 9 Oct. 57.

SERVICE.—Lieutenant DALMAHOY was present at the siege and capture of Delhi, '57 ; and present at most of the engagements before the walls of that city, previous to its capture. Served with Brigadier Showers' Force in the Delhi District. Present with the Humeerpore Police Battalion in several encounters with the rebels in Bundlecund, in '59, '60 ; and on many occasions during the Campaign commanded an Independent Column of Military Police. Received the thanks of Government for services in Bundlecund and Delhi. *Medal and Clasp*.

MAJOR E. T. DALTON, late 3rd Europeans.

Ensign, 15 June 35—Lieut., 24 Dec. 41—Bt.-Captain, 13 June 50—Captain, 15 Nov. 53.—Major, 18 Feb. 61.

SERVICE.—Major DALTON served in Assam, and was engaged in expeditions against the Frontier Tribes, '39, '40, and '42. Served as Officiating

Political Agent in Upper Assam, in '55. Planned and superintended an expedition which surprised and captured the Mishnee Chief who had murdered the French Missionaries, Messrs. Krick and Bourry, on the Thibetan Frontier. Received the special thanks of the Governor-General. Served in '58, as Commissioner of Chota Nagpore, with the Field Force under Major MacDonell against rebels in Palamow. Received the acknowledgments of Government, 2nd February '58. From May '58 to February '59 was employed against the Singhbhoom insurgents. Received the thanks of Government, 19th July '58, and approval of operations throughout the rains, 14th September '58; and finally the cordial acknowledgments of Government, 28th February '59. Received an intimation of the entire approval of his services from the Secretary of State in a Despatch, 4th November '59, brought to the notice of the Home Government in Despatch of the Governor-General. Received a letter from the Secretary of State, communicating to him the approbation of Her Majesty the Queen for his conduct, as brought to Her Majesty's notice. *Medal.* (Passed examination in Assamese and Bengali.)

ASSISTANT-SURGEON D. B. DALY,† M.D., Bengal Medical Establishment.
Asst.-Surgeon, 4th Aug. 57.

ASSISTANT-SURGEON G. H. DALY,† M.D., Bengal Medical Establishment.
Asst.-Surgeon, 4th Nov. 53.

ASSISTANT-SURGEON W. F. S. B. DALZEL,† M.D., Bengal Medical Establishment.
Asst.-Surgeon, 20 Sept. 52.

SERVICE.—Assistant-Surgeon DALZEL served with the Force under Brigadier Polwhele, in the action at Sussia, near Agra, on the 5th July, and in the action at Agra, against the mutineers, on the 10th October '57, with the first Flying Column from Delhi, commanded by Colonel Greathed. Served with Her Majesty's 9th Lancers, from the 12th October '57 to the 8th February '58, in Medical Charge of the Escort to the Commander-in-Chief, from 1st to 10th November '57. At the

(168)

relief of the Garrison of Lucknow, by the Commander-in-Chief, in November, the relief of Cawnpore in December '57, and subsequent operations against the mutineers with the Brigade, under General Grant, at Serai Ghaut, in December '57. Served at Shumshabad, near Futtehghur, with the Force under the late Brigadier Adrian Hope, in January '58. Served with the 1st Fusiliers, from the 8th February to the 24th March '58. At the siege and capture of Lucknow by the Commander-in-Chief, in March '58. At the capture of Calpee, 23rd May '58. In Medical Charge of the Towana Horse, with the Column commanded by Colonel G. V. Maxwell. In Medical Charge of Meade's Horse, and of the Moveable Column commanded by Major Meade, when Tantia Topee was captured, and brought prisoner into Seaporc, and hanged on the 18th April '59. *Medal and 2 Clasps.*

LIEUTENANT R. C. DANBUZ, Bengal Engineers.

Lieut., 27th Aug. 58.

CAPTAIN C. C. DANDRIDGE, P. H., late 49th Native Infantry.

Ensign, 18 Jan. 45—Lieut., 13 March 48—Captain, 11 Oct. 59.

SERVICE.—Captain DANDRIDGE served with the Army of the Punjab, '48, '49. Present throughout the whole siege operations before Mooltan. Present at the storm and capture of the city of Mooltan. *Medal and Clasp.*

CAPTAIN E. DANDRIDGE, late 73rd Native Infantry.

Ensign, 14 Jan. 46—Lieut., 7 Sept. 52—Captain, 25 Oct. 59.

SERVICE.—Captain DANDRIDGE served with the Army of the Punjab, '48, '49. Served with a Field Detachment under Colonel King, 14th Light Dragoons, in pursuit of the Sikh Jooroo, in June '48. *Medal.* Served with a Field Detachment, engaged in the pursuit and capture of the Rebel Rajah of Toolsipore, in Oude, May '56. Was Staff Officer to Colonel Sherer, at Julpigoree, when the Cavalry mutinied at that station, and during the operations against the Chittagong and Dacca rebels, '57. Thanked by His Excellency the Commander-in-Chief for services during the Mutinies, 25th September '57 and 25th May '58. Commanded a Moveable Column in Bundlecund, and was engaged in repeated expeditions after the rebel leader Dowlut Singh and Burgore Singh, from October '59 to March '60. *Medal.* (Passed in Surveying and Civil Engineering.)

ASSISTANT-SURGEON C. O. DANIELL,† M.D., Bengal Medical Establishment.

Asst.-Surgeon, 27 Jan. 58.

SERVICE.—Assistant-Surgeon DANIELL served in Medical Charge of a Field Battery, Royal Artillery, in the year '55-'56, during the siege and capture of Sebastopol, in the Crimea. *Medal and Clasp, and Turkish Medal.*

ASSISTANT-SURGEON H. R. DANIELL,† Bengal Medical Establishment.

Asst.-Surgeon, 21 Sept. 56.

SERVICE.—Assistant-Surgeon DANIELL served with the Shekawattee Battalion during the latter part of '57, '58, '59, and '60, in the disturbed Districts of Maunbhoom, Singbhoom, and Sumbulpore.

MAJOR J. T. DANIELL, P., 7th (late 47th) Native Infantry.

Ensign, 20 Jan. 29—Lieut., 10 Feb. 35—Bt.-Captain, 20 Jan. 44—Captain, 24 Jan. 45—Bt.-Major, 28 Nov. 54—Major, 1 May 58.

SERVICE.—Major DANIELL served against the Insurgents near Cuttack, '33, and at Punniar, in the Gwalior Campaign. *Bronze Star.*

LIEUTENANT J. W. DANIELL, late 1st European Bengal Fusiliers.

2nd Lieut., 16 June 51—Lieut., 5 Dec. 35.

SERVICE.—Lieutenant DANIELL served in Burmah in '52, '53. Present at the relief of the Garrison of Pegu, 14 December '52. And throughout the operations in the vicinity. Accompanied the Martaban Column under General Steel. *Medal.* Present under Sir Henry Burnard at the battle of Badlee-ka-Serai, on the 8th June '57; in the affair under the walls of Delhi, on the 14th July '57, under Brigadier Chamberlain. *Severely wounded.* Served at the siege and capture of Lucknow in March '58, under Command of Lord Clyde, and in the subsequent operations in Oude, under Sir Hope Grant. *Medal and 2 Clasps.*

(170)

LIEUTENANT L. C. DE L. DANIELL,† late 14th Native Infantry.
Ensign, 6 March 57—Lieut., 18 May 58.

SERVICE.—Lieutenant DANIELL served with Her Majesty's 54th Regiment in the Shahabad and Ghazeepore Districts, also in Oude, '58, '59.

LIEUTENANT M. W. DANIELL, Bengal Artillery.
Lieut., 11 Dec. 58.

CAPTAIN J. J. DANSEY,† late 16th Native Infantry.
Ensign, 10 June 43—Lieut., 10 Oct. 47—Captain, 23 Nov. 56.

SERVICE.—Captain DANSEY served throughout the Sutlej Campaign, '45, '46. Present at the battles of Moodkee, Ferozeshuhur, and Sobraon. *Medal and 2 Clasps.*

ENSIGN F. A. DARLEY, General List.
Ensign, 20 Dec. 59.

CAPTAIN A. DARLING, P., Bengal Artillery.
2nd Lieut., 14 June 45—Lieut., 10 March 49—2nd Captain, 27 Aug. 58.

SERVICE.—Captain DARLING served with the Army of the Punjab, '48, '49, including the actions of Sadoolapore, Chillianwallah, and Goojerat. *Medal and 2 Clasps.*

CAPTAIN T. C. DARNELL, P., late 51st Native Infantry.
Ensign, 11 June 42—Lieut., 7 May 44—Captain, 23 Nov. 56.

SERVICE.—Captain DARNELL served at the action of Punniar. *Bronze Star.* Present at the siege and surrender of Mooltan, and battle of Goojerat. *Wounded. Medal and Clasp.*

CAPTAIN H. Z. DARRAH, P. H., late 41st Native Infantry.
Ensign, 8 June 49—Lieut., 25 May 52—Captain, 13 Feb. 52.

SERVICE.—Captain DARRAH, on the mutiny of the 41st Native Infantry, escaped from Seetapore, 3rd June '57, into Lucknow. Remained on duty at the Muchee Bhawun Fort, and afterwards at the Residency throughout the siege, till the final relief of the Garrison of Lucknow,

November '57. Served as Assistant Baggage-Master in the Field with the 3rd Infantry and Artillery Brigades, till February '58. *Medal and Clasp and* 1 *year's extra service.* (Passsed in Surveying and Civil Engineering.)

LIEUTENANT D. DARROCH,† late 16th Native Infantry.

Ensign, 20 Jan. 59—Lieut., 18 Sept. 60.

COLONEL E. DARVALL, late 3rd Europeans.

Ensign, 1 May 23—Lieut., 6 Jan. 25—Captain, 4 Aug. 36—Bt.-Major, 9 Nov. 46—Major, 11 July 53—Bt.-Lieut.-Colonel, 20 June 54—Lieut.-Colonel, 17 Nov. 57—Bt.-Colonel, 20 June 57.

SERVICE.—Colonel DARVALL served throughout the Burmah War, '24, '26. Present with the Force under Colonel A. Richards during the whole advance from Gwahratta, October '24. Was with the attacking party under Captain Martin, in November '24, marching 18 miles, and carrying the Burmese stockades of Desgaun by night attack. Received the thanks of the Officer Commanding the Detachment. Commanded an outlying picquet during the attack on Colonel Richard's camp, near Rungpore, December '24. Present with the assaulting Column on the Burmese stockades at Rungpore, at the capture of the Fort, pursuit of the Burmese, and liberation of the Assamese captives. *Medal.* Employed as Adjutant to Lord Amherst's Escort to the Upper Provinces, in '26. Present in Oude in '26. At the taking of the Fort in Daoodpore, and the flight of the Killadar Sirteepeehal Sing, in '27. Commanded a Detachment in the Fort of Sertabgur, and held it during the mutiny of the King of Oude's troops, rescuing the Killadar Hajee Imamee, in '27. Commanded 20 miles of the Frontier of Saugor, including the ports of Maltone, Korye, and Kymlassa, during the Bundlecund Insurrection, '48. Served throughout the Indian Mutinies, '57, '58, '59. *Medal.*

LIEUTENANT J. C. C. DAUNT, P. H., V. C., 12th (late 70th) Native Infantry.

Ensign, 20 July 52—Lieut., 20 July 57.

SERVICE.—Lieutenant DAUNT served with the Column commanded by Lieutenant-Colonel Fischer, 27th Madras Native Infantry, during the Mutiny, '57. Served with the Column Commanded by Lieutenant-Colonel English. Her Majesty's 53rd Foot, during '57, '58. Present at the attack and defeat of the Ramghur Light Infantry Battalion, at Chuttra, Chota Nagpore, 2nd October '57. Conduct brought to the especial notice of His Excellency the Commander-in-Chief. Present at the attack and defeat of the 32nd Native Infantry (mutineers) at Nowadah, Behar, 2nd November '57 *(severely and dangerously wounded)*. Conduct brought to the notice of His Excellency the Commander-in-Chief, for submission to Her Majesty, for the decoration of the Victoria Cross. *Medal and V. C.* Served in the capacity of Baggage-Master to the Column under Colonel Fischer. Interpreter to the Column under Colonel English. Commanded 4-gun Bullock Battery on service, G. O. C. C., 12th October '57. Entrusted with the Secret Intelligence Department whilst serving under Colonel English, *vide* letter, dated January '62. Received the thanks of the Government of Bengal, dates of letter about 15th October and 20th November '57. Services in China in '58. Rejoined the 70th Native Infantry at Canton, 1st April '58. Present at the White Cloud Mountain Affair. Present at the repulse of the Chinese at the Landing Pier. Present at the repulse of the Chinese at the Magazine Hill. *Medal.* Dates of acts of bravery, 2nd October and 2nd November '57. Lieutenant Daunt and ———— are recommended for conspicuous gallantry in action on the 2nd October '57, with the mutineers of the Ramghur Battalion, at Chota Behar, in capturing 2 guns, particularly the last, when they rushed at and captured it by pistoling the gunners, who were mowing the Detachment down with grape, one-third of which was *hors de combat* at the time.

LIEUTENANT A. H. DAVIDSON, Bengal Artillery.

Lieut., 15 Feb. 58.

LIEUTENANT-COLONEL C. DAVIDSON, C.B., P., late 51st Native Infantry.

Ensign, 11 May 28—Lieut., 4 Jan. 32—Captain, 8 Sept. 42—Major, 10 May 52—Lieut.-Colonel, 31 May 57.

SERVICE.—Lieutenant-Colonel DAVIDSON served with the Field Force of the Nizam's Contingent, in Command of the 3rd Nizam's Cavalry sent

(173)

to co-operate with the Madras Troops in the capture of Kurnool, under Brigadier Blair. Occupied the fords of the Tomubuddra River, and captured 50 prisoners during the action of Zorapore. Received the Civil Order of the Bath for service in '57. *(Since dead.)*

2ND CAPTAIN E. DAVIDSON, P. H., Bengal Engineers.

2nd Lieut., 11 June 47—Lieut., 1 Aug. 54—2nd Captain, 27 Aug. 58.

LIEUTENANT E. C. DAVIDSON, General List.

Ensign, 10 Dec. 59—Lieut., 1 Jan. 62.

CAPTAIN H. M. DAVIDSON,† late 29th Native Infantry.

Ensign, 21 Aug. 39—Lieut., 22 Dec. 44—Bt.-Captain, 21 Aug. 54—Captain, 23 Nov. 56.

SERVICE.—Captain DAVIDSON served against the rebels North of Jullunder, '48, '49. Present at the storming of the heights of Umb and occupation of the Fort of Oonah. *Medal.* Served under Sir Colin Campbell in Eusuffzaie and Ranezaie, against the Hill Tribes, '52, '53. Present at the defence of Nynee Tal and affair of Huldaonee, 17th September '57.

LIEUTENANT J. P. DAVIDSON,† late 4th Native Infantry.

Ensign, 20 Oct. 51—Lieut., 23 Nov. 56.

SERVICE.—Lieutenant DAVIDSON served in the expedition against the Momund Tribes as Volunteer with 1st Sikh Infantry. Served with the expedition against the Bussee Khel Tribes with 4th Native Infantry, '55. During the Mutiny, '57, '58. Present with 1st Punjab Infantry during the siege, assault, and final capture of Delhi, and battle of Nudjufghur, '57. *Medal and Clasp.* Served with the 1st Punjab Infantry in the re-occupation of the districts of Bijnore and Bareilly and capture of the latter town. Present at the advance on, and re-occupation of, Mohumdee, as Commandant, Shahzada Sooltan Jan's Puttan Ressulla, '58. Served with the first expedition against the Cabul Khel Wuzeerees, '59, '60.

(174)

BREVET-CAPTAIN R. DAVIDSON, P. C., late 64th Native Infantry.
Ensign, 29 Feb. 44—Lieut., 15 Oct. 52—Bt.-Captain, 1st March 59.

LIEUTENANT T. R. DAVIDSON, late 49th Native Infantry.
Ensign, 15 July 56—Lieut., 23 Nov. 56.

SERVICE.—Lieutenant DAVIDSON served as a Volunteer with a Detachment, 1st Punjab Infantry (Rifles), in '57, attached to Brigadier Showers' Column, and was present with them at the taking of the Forts of Rewaree, Tujjur, Kanond, and Bullubghur; and also in two engagements with the Mawottus.

BREVET-COLONEL W. W. DAVIDSON, P. H., late 32nd Native Infantry.
Ensign, 19 July 28—Lieut., 3 April 35—Bt.-Captain, 19 July 43—Major, 1 Jan. 49—Bt.-Major, 16 Jan. 49—Major, 29 Aug. 59—Bt.-Lieut.-Colonel, 28 Nov. 54—Bt.-Colonel, 28 Nov. 57.

SERVICE.—Colonel DAVIDSON served throughout the China Expedition, '42. *Medal.* Served in Command of the 16th Irregular Cavalry, under Brigadier Wheeler, during the Punjab Campaign, '48, '49. Present at the storm and capture of the Fort of Shahpore, and assault of the heights of Noorpoor and Dullah *(severely wounded).* *Medal.* Served with the expedition under Colonel Mackeson, in '52, '53. Commanded the Left Column of attack against the Hussunzaies, on the Black Mountain. Present in the affair with the Momunds near Michnee, '54. On all these occasions Colonel Davidson volunteered his services.

CAPTAIN F. J. DAVIES, P., late 58th Native Infantry.
Ensign, 2nd March 42—Lieut., 4 Feb. 44—Captain, 19 Oct. 53.

SERVICE.—Captain DAVIES served at the battle of Punniar. *Bronze Star.* (Passed examination in Surveying and Civil Engineering.)

CAPTAIN H. N. DAVIES, P. C. H., late 25th Native Infantry.
Ensign, 8 June 44—Lieut., 9 Sept. 53—Captain, 27 June 57.
(Passed examination in Burmese.) Adjutant of the Rangoon Volunteers.

(175)

CAPTAIN J. S. DAVIES, P., late 23rd Native Infantry.
Ensign, 18 Sept. 39—Lieut., 2nd May 43—Bt.-Captain, 18 Sept. 54—Captain, 23 Nov. 56.

LIEUTENANT L. B. J. DAVIES,† late 5th Europeans.
Ensign, 13 Feb. 53—Lieut., 23 Nov. 56.

SERVICE.—Lieutenant DAVIES served with the 3rd European Regiment throughout the Mutiny, '57, '58. Present at the action near Agra, 5th July '57. Against the Neemuch Mutineers at the battle of Agra, 10th October '57; at the affair of Futtehpore-Sikree, 28th October '57. Present with Colonel Cotton's Column towards Muttra and Delhi, in October and November '57. Present in nearly all the minor operations in the Agra District. Present at the re-occupation of Allyghur, August '57. *Medal.*

CAPTAIN S. J. DAVIES, P., late 51st Native Infantry.
Ensign, 27 Sept. 40—Lieut., 12 Nov. 42—Captain, 1 Nov. 53.

SERVICE.—Captain DAVIES served with the Column under Colonel Yates, 51st Native Infantry, in Bundlecund, against the rebels, from November '42 to March '43. Served with the Gwalior Army in '43. Present at the action of Punniar, 29th December '43. *Bronze Star and Clasp.* Employed in outpost duties at Jugraon, Bussean, Moodkee, &c., during the Sutlej Campaign. Proceeded in July '48 with Brigadier Markham's Brigade to Mooltan; was present throughout the siege and surrender of the Fortress, and subsequently at the battle of Goojerat. *Medal and 2 Clasps.* (Passed examination in Civil Engineering.)

LIEUTENANT W. G. DAVIES, P., late 71st Native Infantry.
Ensign, 9 Dec. 48—Lieut., 10 July 52.

LIEUTENANT A. T. DAVIS. General List.
Ensign, 20 Oct. 59—Lieut., 25 Aug. 61.

(176)

LIEUTENANT R. P. DAVIS, late 16th Native Infantry.

Ensign, 22nd Aug. 57—Lieut., 24 July 58.

SERVICE.—Lieutenant DAVIS served with Her Majesty's 6th Regiment with the Jugdespore Field Force, under Brigadier Caulfield.

LIEUTENANT T. A. DAVIS, Bengal Artillery.

Lieut., 27 Aug. 58.

CAPTAIN W. DAVIS, P. H., late 31st Native Infantry.

Ensign, 9 Dec. 42—Lieut., 12 March 46—Captain, 6 June 57.

SERVICE.—Captain DAVIS was present at the battle of Maharajpore. *Bronze Star.* Served with the Army of the Punjab, including the passage of the Chenab. Present in the actions of Sadoolapore, Chillianwallah, and Goojerat, and subsequent pursuit of the Sikhs and Affghans to Peshawur, under General Gilbert. *Medal and Clasp.* Present with the expedition against the Affreedies in the Kohat Pass.

CAPTAIN W. DAVISON, P. H., late 1st Bengal European Fusiliers.

2nd Lieut., 20 April 46—Lieut., 6 July 51—Captain, 10 Oct. 60.

SERVICE.—Captain DAVISON served in Burmah, '52, '53. Present at the relief of the Garrison of Pegu, 14th December '52, and at the operations in the vicinity; accompanied the Martaban Column, and present at the storm and re-capture of Belin, April '53. *Medal.*

LIEUTENANT T DAWES,† late 72nd Native Infantry.

Ensign, 2 Sept. 58—Lieut., 1 March 59.

VETERINARY-SURGEON H. DAWSON, late 4th Bengal European Cavalry.

Veterinary-Surgeon, 9 Aug. 58.

CAPTAIN J. DAWSON, P., late 43rd Native Infantry.

Ensign, 10 Dec. 41—Lieut., 10 March 49—Bt.-Captain, 10 Dec. 56—Captain, 26 April 59.

SERVICE.—Captain DAWSON served with the Force at Gwalior in '43, '44. Present at the battle of Maharajpore. *Bronze Star.* Served during the Sutlej Campaign, '46. Present at the battle of Sobraon. *Medal.* Accompanied General Outram on his advance to Oude; at Dinapore, ordered up in charge of Engineer's stores, arrived too late at Allahabad, sent by Garrison orders to Futtehpore, joined Colonel Powell's party, which surprised and defeated the rebels at the battle of Kudjwa, 1st November '57. *Medal.*

LIEUTENANT T. DAYRELL, P. H., late 58th Native Infantry.

Ensign, 6 Jan. 57—Lieut., 30 April 58.

SERVICE.—Lieutenant DAYRELL served before Delhi in '57. Present at the siege and assault of Delhi from 13th June to November '57. Wounded severely at the assault on Delhi, 14th September '57. *Medal and Clasp.*

HONORARY ASSISTANT-SURGEON J. R. DEANE, Medical Establishment.

Apothecary, 4 Jan. 42—Honorary Asst.-Surgeon, 12 June 60.

SERVICE.—Honorary Assistant-Surgeon DEANE served with the late 2nd Bengal European Fusiliers in Sir C. Napier's Beelooch Campaign, in the year '45. Served with the 3rd Punjab Infantry in the Sheoranee Expedition, in '53. On the Kohut Kothul, in '54. On the Somana Mountain, under Brigadier Chamberlain, in '55; in the Kooren Expedition, in '56. Against the Cabul Khel Wuzeerees, in '59, '60, and in the Muksood Wuzeeree Expedition, in '60. Received thanks of Government, Governor-General's letter, 3rd November '55. Services mentioned in Captain Henderson's Report to Brigadier Chamberlain, on 3rd September '55.

LIEUTENANT H. DeBRETT,† late 57th Native Infantry.

Ensign, 10 Dec. 53—Lieut., 23 Nov. 56.

2ND CAPTAIN F. R. DeBUDE, P. H., Bengal Artillery.

2nd Lieut., 13 June 45—Lieut., 3 Sept. 48—Captain, 27 Aug. 58.

SERVICE.—Captain DeBUDE served in the Punjab Campaign, '48, '49, under Lord Gough. Present at the siege of Mooltan and battle of

Y

Goojerat. *Medal and* 2 *Clasps.* Commanded Artillery Division, Mooltan, from May to September '57. Present at the disarming of the 62nd and 69th Native Infantry, and at the blowing away mutineers. Commanded a Division, Horse Artillery Guns, under Major Chamberlain, against the Insurgent Jāts, from Mooltan to Lahore, '57. Commanded Peshawur Mountain Train Battery against the Cabul Khel Wuzeerees. Present at the affair at Maidanee, '59, '60; and again, from March to June '60, including the action of Burrara, occupation of Kaneegoorum, and retirement in action from Mukeem, when he commanded the Rear Guard.

ASSISTANT-SURGEON F. W. A. DeFABECK,† Bengal Medical Establishment.

Asst.-Surgeon, 23 July 58.

LIEUTENANT C. A. DeKANTZOW, P. H., late 48th Native Infantry.

Ensign, 14 Sept. 53—Lieut., 23 Nov. 56.

SERVICE.—Lieutenant DEKANTZOW was present with the 9th Native Infantry during the operations undertaken against the Hill Tribes in '55. Present at Mynpooree on, during, and subsequent to, the mutiny of the troops at that station, in May '57; receiving Her Majesty the Queen's gracious approbation, and Governor-General's especial thanks, for the services rendered by him at the imminent peril of his life on that occasion. Present with 39 Sowars in action at Bhowgong against the mutineers of the 7th Light Cavalry, 13th, 48th, and 71st Native Infantry (Detachments) from Lucknow, on the 6th June '57, *(wounded on forehead by sabre,)* on which occasion, in hand to hand conflict, he killed the leader of the rebels. Served at Mynpooree in Command of an Irregular Force up to the abandonment of the station, and subsequently as a Volunteer in the action of the 5th July '57, near Agra, *(horse killed under him,)* against the Neemuch Mutineers, Kotah Contingent, 5th July '57. Served as a Volunteer in all the minor operations undertaken against the rebels in the Agra District, up to the 19th August '57, and as Commandant of a Detachment of Agra Militia Cavalry in action near Allyghur, 24th August '57, (mentioned in Despatch,) and subsequent operations of Colonel Montgomerie's Column in that and the Agra District. Present as a Volunteer in the action of the 10th October, at Agra, against the Mhow,

(179)

Indore, and Delhi Mutineers. Served with Sir Hope Grant's Column up to the re-occupation of Mynpooree, and as Commandant of the "Muttra Horse" in Colonel Cotton's Moveable Force during the operations undertaken against the rebels at Futtehpore-Sikree, and elsewhere, in the Muttra District; as also subsequently, under civil power, to February '58, raised the "Futtehghur Organized Police Battalion," and served as Commandant of the same in action at Bungaon, *(1 charger and 1 trooper wounded under him,)* under Sir Thomas Seaton, and elsewhere in the Futtehghur District, (mentioned in Despatch). Present at Shahjehanpore as Commanding the Cavalry at that station, and in action, 3rd May '58, (mentioned in Despatch,) *(charger slightly wounded,)* and the defence of the Jail, and affairs subsequent to the relief of the garrison by Brigadier Jones, including the action of the 15th May *(very dangerously wounded by sabre cuts on face and right arm in hand to hand encounter)*. Present as Commandant of the Rohilcund Auxiliary Levy (raised and organized by him,) in the defence of the Entrenchments and Town of Porvaine, from June to November '58, and in the many and various offensive operations against the enemy at that place; including the attack on the enemy's outpost at Ameenuggur (thanked by the Government of India). Siege of Porvaine (thanked by the Government of India). Served with the Levy on active service against the rebels in the North of the Shahjehanpore District, up to the 28th December '58, and subsequently with the same across the Sarda; move on Pullea and expulsion of the rebels from the Town and Fort of that place, (thanked by the Government of India,) and pursuit of the rebels into the Khyreeghur and Mulwana Districts of Oude. Present as a Volunteer with a Troop of Cavalry and two Companies of the Infantry of the Rohilcund Auxiliary Levy, with Brigadier Dennis' Column, during the pursuit of the rebels in the Khyreeghur jungles and in the two actions fought with the mutineers in January '59 (mentioned in Despatch); served with the Levy in active pursuit of the rebels up to the Nepal Border and subsequent operations undertaken in clearing the district from rebels and marauders, up to the very end of the disturbances (thanked by the Government of India). Has received the gracious approbation of Her Majesty for "excellent service" rendered by him to the State in '57, '58. Been officially and especially reported to the

(180)

Government of India, when leaving Rohilcund, in September '59, for the "valuable services" rendered by the Force under his Command in Rohilcund, and honorably mentioned by the Government of the North-Western Provinces to the Government of India. *Medal.*

LIEUTENANT C. E. DELAFOSSE,† Bengal Artillery.
Lieut., 18 Aug. 58.

BREVET-MAJOR H. G. DELAFOSSE,† late 53rd Native Infantry.
Ensign, 9 Dec. 54—Lieut., 23 Nov. 56—Captain, 11 Sept. 61—Bt.-Major, 12 Sept. 61.

SERVICE.—Major DELAFOSSE served with General Sir Hugh Wheeler's Force in the Garrison of Cawnpore, '57. Present throughout the siege, and was one of the only two survivors of that Garrison. *Honorably mentioned and permitted to reckon one year's additional service for pension. Recommended for Brevet-Majority.* Served as Assistant-Superintendent of Police under General Neil, at Cawnpore, August and September '57. Vacated appointment to join Force under Havelock as Volunteer to Captain W. Olpherts' Battery. Present at second re-crossing into Oude, and the engagements of Mungalwar and Alum Bagh, 25th September; first relief of Lucknow, and subsequent defence of that Garrison. Mentioned in Despatches of Colonel V. Eyre, Commanding Artillery Brigade, General Order. Present in re-taking Cawnpore, December '57. Received thanks of Government. *Medal and Clasp, and Brevet-Major.* Served in the capacity of Orderly Officer with the Force under Colonel Gawler in the Sikhim Campaign, '60, '61. *Brought to the notice of His Excellency the Commander-in-Chief in Despatch of Lieutenant-Colonel Gawler.* (Recommended for V. C. for Mutiny Campaign.)

LIEUTENANT-COLONEL W. H. DELAMAIN, Bengal Artillery.
2nd Lieut., 11 June 30—Lieut., 20 Dec. 39—Bt.-Captain, 11 June 45—Captain, 16 June 48—Bt.-Major, 18 Feb. 56—Lieut.-Colonel, 14 Nov. 58.

CAPTAIN G. DELANE, P. H., late 3rd Bengal European Light Cavalry.

Cornet, 22 Feb. 43—Lieut., 29 Oct. 46—Captain, 24 Dec. 55.

SERVICE.—Captain DELANE served throughout the Punjab Campaign, '48, '49. Present at the passage of the Chenab and battles of Chillianwallah and Goojerat. *Medal.*

2ND CAPTAIN W. DELANE, P. H., Bengal Artillery.

2nd Lieut., 13 Dec. 45—Lieut., 18 March 52—2nd Captain, 27 Aug. 58.

SERVICE.—Captain DELANE served during the Punjab Campaign, '48, '49. Present at the actions of Chillianwallah and Goojerat. *Medal and Clasp.*

LIEUTENANT G. C. DELATOUR, General List.

Ensign, 4 Jan. 60—Lieut., 1 Jan. 62.

LIEUTENANT E. J. DELAUTOUR, Bengal Artillery.

Lieut., 8 June 60.

LIEUTENANT E. W. DELOUSADA, P. H., late 69th Native Infantry.

Ensign, 26 Aug. 58—Lieut., 29 Oct. 60.

ASSISTANT-SURGEON S. DELPRATT,† Bengal Medical Establishment.

Asst.-Surgeon, 6 May 54.

SERVICE.—Assistant-Surgeon DELPRATT served throughout the Sonthal Campaign with the 31st Native Light Infantry and Detachment of 13th, 48th, and 42nd Native Infantry, with the Force under Major-General G. W. A. Lloyd. Present in the action at Chattra against the Ramghur Mutineers, in Medical Charge, Sikh Battalion. *Medal.*

ASSISTANT-SURGEON W. DELPRATT,† Bengal Medical Establishment.

Asst.-Surgeon, 20 Nov. 47.

(Since retired.)

LIEUTENANT R. H. DeMONTMORENCY, P. C. H., late 65th Native Infantry.

Ensign, 4 Jan. 57—Lieut., 30 April 58.

LIEUTENANT T. DENNEHY, P. H., late 2nd Native Infantry.

Ensign, 20th July 51—Lieut., 23 Nov. 56.

SERVICE.—Lieutenant DENNEHY served in the Sonthal Campaign of '55, '56. Commanded a Detachment of 2 Companies of the Regiment in action with the Insurgent Sonthals at Chundkundra and at the foot of the Ural Hills. Received the thanks of the Brigadier Commanding, 15th December '55. Served during the Mutiny of '57, '58. Commanded the Head Quarters Allahabad Military Police Battalion at the action of Manickpore, 30th July; and Gadhamaron, 27th August '58. Received the thanks of the Right Honorable the Governor-General, 24th August and 11th September '58.

2ND CAPTAIN A. D. DENNISS, P. H., Bengal Artillery.

2nd Lieut., 13 Dec. 45—Lieut., 3rd March 53—2nd Captain, 27 Aug. 58.

SERVICE.—Captain DENNISS served in the Punjab Campaign under Brigadier Wheeler, '48, '49. *Medal.*

CAPTAIN E. S. DENNISS, P. H., late 62nd Native Infantry.

Ensign, 2nd April 41—Lieut., 16 July 42—Captain, 1st June 50.

SERVICE.—Captain DENNISS served with the Army of Gwalior, '43, '44. Commanded a Detachment of 100 Sabres 1st Irregular Cavalry and Horse Artillery Guns, and 200 Infantry to the relief of Colonel Crawford Chamberlain, then besieged by the Googaira rebels. Served under Colonel Chamberlain against the Googaira rebels until subdued. Present at the battle of Maharajpore. *Bronze Star.*

(183)

MAJOR G. G. DENNISS, late 1st European Bengal Fusiliers.

2nd Lieut., 8 Feb. 40—Lieut., 1st Nov. 42—Captain, 29 June 49—Major, 14 Sept. 57.

SERVICE.—Major DENNISS served throughout the Sutlej Campaign in '45, '46. Present at the actions of Ferozeshuhur and Sobraon *(severely wounded* in the latter engagement). *Medal and Clasp.* Burmah, '52, '53; present at the re-capture of Pegu, under the Command of General Godwin, 21st November '52, in Command of 9th Company, part of the storming party against the stockade. *Medal.* Present with his Regiment at the battle of Badlee-ka-Serai under the Command of Sir Henry Burnard, on the 8th of June '57, and in the operations against the city of Delhi; succeeded to the Command of the Regiment on Colonel Welchman being *severely wounded*, on the 23rd June '57, in the Subzee Mundee, when he was struck down by a *coup-de-soleil. (Since dead.) Medal and Clasp.*

CAPTAIN E. L. DENNYS, P. H., late 11th Native Infantry.

Ensign, 11 Dec. 38—Lieut., 20 Jan. 41—Captain, 26 July 53.

SERVICE.—Captain DENNYS served with the 11th Native Infantry against the insurgents in Bundlecund, '42. Served throughout the Sutlej Campaign, '45, 46. Present at the action of Ferozeshuhur. *Medal.* Present at the surrender of Kôt Kangra, '46. Present during part of the operations before Delhi, also at the assault and total capture of that City, '57. Accompanied the Column under Brigadier Showers, 27th September, into the district, and returned to Delhi, 1st October. *Medal and Clasp.* (Has passed in Surveying and Civil Engineering.)

MAJOR J. B. DENNYS, P. H., late 38th Native Infantry.

Ensign, 3rd Jan. 40—Lieut., 12 Nov. 42—Captain, 6 Jan. 52.—Major in Staff Corps, 18 Feb. 61.

SERVICE.—Major DENNYS served throughout the Campaign in Affghanistan, under Major General Nott, and present in every action fought under that Officer. From the time of joining his Regiment, held Command of the Light Company in the Field on all occasions. *Medal.* Served during the Sutlej Campaign, '45, '46. In '53, commanded the Kotah Contingent and the Troops ordered from Nusseerabad, to support him in the reduction of the Fort of Kurowlee, in Kurowlee Territory. The Fort was evacuated by the rebels. Received the approbation of the Governor-General on this occasion. Commanded the Kotah Contingent on the outbreak of the Mutinies, and employed some weeks against the rebels in the Agra and Muttra Districts. Served in the Fort at Agra. Present at the attack on the Fort of Abwal, in Rajpootana, under Brigadier General Lawrence, and accompanied Field Forces from Neemuch in civil capacity, in pursuit of Feroze Shah, Tantia Topee, &c.

2ND CAPTAIN G. C. DEPREE, P. H., Bengal Artillery.

2nd Lieut., 14 June 50—Lieut., 9 Dec. 50—2nd Captain, 27 Aug. 58.

ASSISTANT-SURGEON A. C. C. DeRENZY,† B.A., T.C.D., M.R.C.S.

Asst.-Surgeon, 29 July 51.

SERVICE.—Assistant-Surgeon DeRENZY served with the 2nd and 3rd Company of the 5th Battalion Bengal Artillery throughout the War in Burmah, in '52, '53, '54, and was present in the actions at Martaban, Rangoon, and Prome. *Medal and Clasp.* Present when the 15th Native Infantry treacherously fired on their Officers, 28th May 1857. Volunteered to return to Cantonments at Nusseerabad that day in search of Captain Fenwick of the 30th Native Infantry, who was reported missing. Escaped alone afterwards to Beawur. Served throughout the siege of Lucknow in March '58. *Medal and Clasp.* (Passed Examination in Burmese.)

CAPTAIN H. P. DeTEISSIER, P., Bengal Artillery.

2nd Lieut., 11 Dec. 37—Lieut., 17 Aug. 41—Bt.-Captain, 11 Dec. 52 —Captain, 3 March 53.

SERVICE.—Captain DeTEISSIER served in the Campaign on the Sutlej, '45, '46. Present at the battle of Sobraon. *Medal.* Army of the Punjab, '48, '49, including the actions of Chillianwallah and Goojerat. *Medal and 2 Clasps.*

CAPTAIN P. K. H. DEWAAL,† late 34th Native Infantry.

Ensign, 13 June 37—Lieut., 3rd Oct. 40—Captain, 1st Feb. 50.

SERVICE.—Captain DEWAAL served at the taking of Kôt Kangra, '46.

LIEUTENANT J. K. J. DEWAR, Bengal Artillery.

Lieut., 27 Aug. 58.

SURGEON H. DIAPER,† Bengal Medical Establishment.

Asst.-Surgeon, 25 Dec. 40—Surgeon, 1st Feb. 55.

SERVICE.—Surgeon DIAPER detached while doing duty with the 2nd Europeans at Cawnpore on Field Service at Punwaree, in Bundlecund, during the months of August and September '42. Field Surgeon to the Cawnpore Field Force under Major-General Sir J. Outram, G.C.B., from the 2nd September '57, until the final close of the Cawnpore Field Hospital on the 22nd April '59.

LIEUTENANT-GENERAL A. DICK, late 71st Native Infantry.

Ensign, 5 Oct. 04—Lieut., 5 Oct. 04—Captain, 1st Jan. 17—Major, 22 April 26—Lieut.-Colonel, 4 May 31—Colonel, 8 Feb. 43—Major-General, 20 June 54—Lieut.-General, 4 July 56.

SERVICE.—Lieutenant-General DICK served against the Mud Fort of Jurhapoora, and throughout the Campaign under Lord Lake, '05. With the expedition against Java, '11. Present at the storm and capture of Fort Cornelis. *Medal and Clasp.*

LIEUTENANT A. A. DICK, P. H., late 52nd Native Infantry.

Ensign, 20 Dec. 55—Lieut., 13 July 57.

SERVICE.—Lieutenant DICK served with the Kamptee Moveable Column in the Saugor and Nerbudda Territories, from August '57 to February '58. Present at the actions of Kutungee, near Jubbulpore, on 27th September '58; and Moorwarra, on 6th November '58. Mentioned in the Despatch of Major Sullivan, Commanding Detachment, Kamptee Moveable Column, G. G. O., No. 241, of '58. Served with the Saugor Field Division from February '58 to February '59. Present at the action of Banda, on the

19th April '58, and at the capture of Kirwee, in June '58. Also in the action at Sahao, near Jaloun, on 5th September '58. *Wounded severely by sabre cuts* in the latter action. *Medal for Indian Rebellion and Clasp for Central India.* Mentioned in the Despatches of Major Davis, Commanding Cavalry, 2nd Brigade Saugor Field Division, and of Brigadier MacDuff, Commanding 2nd Brigade Saugor Field Division, G. G. O., No. 420, of '58. Brought to the notice of the Commander-in-Chief in the Despatch of Brigadier MacDuff, and in letter No. 330, dated 9th September '58, from Major-General Whitlock, Commanding Saugor Field Division, to the address of Major-General Mansfield, G. G. O., No. 420, of '58. Served in the Districts of Trans-Gogra, Oude, throughout the hot weather Campaign of '59. Present at the actions of Koolee-ka-Bund, near Gonda, on 13th April '59, and capture of the Fort of Bungaon, on the 27th April '59. Mentioned in the Despatches of Captain Jones, Commanding 1st Sikh Irregular Cavalry, and of Lieutenant-Colonel Walker, Commanding Field Detachment, G. G. O., No. 749, of '59. Received the thanks of Government, *vide* G. G. O., No. 749, of '59. Served throughout the China Expedition of '60. Present at the action of Sinho, on 12th August '60. Capture of the Takee Forts, on the 21st August '60. Actions of "Chankia-wan," 18th September; "Palichao," 21st September; and capture and occupation of Pekin, 13th October '60. *Medal for China War and Clasps for "Takee" Forts and "Pekin."* Mentioned in the list of Officers of Her Majesty's Indian Forces recommended to favorable notice by General Sir J. Hope Grant, for their services in China, G. G. O., No. 167, of '61.

MAJOR-GENERAL H. DICK, late 4th Bengal European Infantry.

Ensign, 9 April 08—Lieut., 18 Oct. 12—Bt.-Captain, 9 April 23—Captain, 1st May 24—Bt.-Major, 28 June 38—Major, 13th February 39—Bt.-Lieut.-Colonel, 30 April 44—Lieut.-Colonel, 4 March 45—Bt.-Colonel, 20 June 54—Colonel, 16 Jan. 55—Major-General, 2 April 56.

SERVICE.—Major-General DICK served in Rewah, '13; Mahrattah and Pindaree War, '17, '18, including the reduction of Dhamony, and storm and capture of Ghurrah Mundlah. Commanded the 56th Native Infantry at the battle of Maharajpore. *Bronze Star and Brevet-Lieutenant Colonel.*

(187)

DEPUTY-INSPECTOR-GENERAL OF HOSPITALS W. S. DICKEN, Bengal Medical Establishment.

Asst.-Surgeon, 17 June 29—Surgeon, 6 March 46—Depy.-Insptr.-General, 26 Aug. 58.

SERVICE.—Deputy-Inspector-General of Hospitals W. S. DICKEN served with the Goorkha Army under Maharajah Jung Bahadoor as Senior and Field Surgeon, from December '57 to June '58; was present with it at the re-capture of Goruckpore, and final siege and capture of Lucknow, in March '58. *Medal and Clasp.*

CAPTAIN A. D. DICKENS, P., late 38th Native Infantry.

Ensign, 11 June 42—Lieut., 8 Oct. 43—Captain, 9 May 57—Major, 24 March 58.

SERVICE.—Captain (Brevet-Major) DICKENS served at the siege and capture of Delhi. Accompanied Brigadier Greathed's Moveable Column. Present at the affairs of Boolundshuhur, Allyghur, and defeat of the Gwalior insurgents at Agra. Present at the relief of Lucknow in November '57, and at the defeat of the Gwalior insurgent Force at Cawnpore, by his Excellency the Commander-in-Chief; accompanied the Head Quarter Force to Futtehghur. Present at the engagement of the Kallah Nuddee, and at the final capture and re-occupation of Lucknow in March '58. *Medal, 3 Clasps, and Brevet-Majority.*

CAPTAIN C. H. DICKENS, P., Bengal Artillery.

2nd Lieut., 11 June 38—Lieut., 17 Aug. 41—Captain, 3 March 53.

LIEUTENANT W. L. DICKENS, late 26th Native Infantry.

Ensign, 20 July 57—Lieut., 18 May 58.

COLONEL E. J DICKEY, late 27th Native Infantry.

Ensign, 11 June 23—Lieut., 17 Aug. 24—Captain, 16 June 35—Bt.-Major, 9 Nov. 46—Major, 27 Oct. 48—Lieut.-Colonel, 15 April 54—Bt.-Colonel, 28 Nov. 54—Colonel, 28 Nov. 54.

(188)

BREVET-CAPTAIN F. A. DICKINS, P., 2nd (late 31st) Native Infantry.

Ensign, 12 Dec. 45—Lieut., 21 May 51—Captain, 12 Dec. 60.

SERVICE.—Captain DICKINS served during the Punjab Campaign, '48, '49. Present at the actions of Sadoolapore, Chillianwallah, and Goojerat, and subsequent pursuit of the Sikhs and Affghans to Peshawur. *Medal and 2 Clasps.* Served in an expedition against the Affreedies, under Sir Charles Napier, '48, '49. Volunteered with a Company of his Regiment to scale a hill in the possession of the enemy, who had cut up a Detachment of 40 men, under Ensign Sitwell. Drove off the enemy, and brought down the body of Ensign Sitwell, and the four survivors, for which he was personally thanked by Sir Charles Napier. Served during the Sonthal Campaign, '55. Served during the Mutiny at Saugor, '57. Present at four engagements with rebels at Dumoh, and remained there until September '57. Was detached to take possession of the Fort of Rehli, which had been abandoned by the Police, and was twice attacked by the rebels, and drove them off. Joined the Force of Sir H. Rose at Gurhakotah, and was left in charge of the Fort, with instructions to destroy it, and sell the plunder and stores found in the Fort. Served at Saugor from August '58 to January '59, in hunting down rebels in the Saugor District, while Commanding the Police Battalion. In August '58 co-operated with a Detachment under Captain Finch, in attacking a body of rebels of 1,500 strong, and killed 150 of them. In November '58 co-operated with a Moveable Column under Colonel Reece, and was present with it at the attack on Patrakotah, Luckungur, &c. (Passed examination in Punjabee, Hindee, and Oordoo. Received 1,000 Rupees for proficiency in the Native languages.)

ASSISTANT-SURGEON J. C. DICKINSON,† Bengal Medical Establishment.

Asst.-Surgeon, 29 Jan. 57.

SERVICE.—Assistant-Surgeon DICKINSON served with the Sarun and Goruckpore Field Forces, from 5th November '57 to May '59. Present at the actions of Sonepore, December '57; Phoolpore, in Oude, February '58; Amorah, 5th March '58; at the actions near Thelga, 17th and 25th April '58; at the affair of Debureah, 20th September '58, and at the actions at Dumooriergunge, November and December '58, besides some other minor affairs. *Medal.*

(189)

DEPUTY-INSPECTOR-GENERAL OF HOSPITALS J. B. DICKSON, Bengal Medical Establishment.

Asst.-Surgeon, 26 March 28—Surgeon, 1 Jan. 45—Depty.-Insptr.-General, 26 Aug. 58.

CORNET J. B. B. DICKSON, General List, Cavalry.

Cornet, 20 Jan. 60.

CAPTAIN J. C. DICKSON,† 33rd (late 44th) Native Infantry.

Ensign, 7 April 42—Lieut., 11 May 46—Bt.-Captain, 7 April 57—Captain, 1 July 57.

SERVICE.—Captain DICKSON served in the Sutlej Campaign, '45, '46. Present at the battles of Sobraon and Ferozeshuhur. *Medal and Clasp.* Served as Commandant of all leave men of the Punjab Force in the expedition against Shaik Mohamed Deen, '46. Volunteered and served with the 66th Goorkhas, from 24th July to 8th October '57. Volunteered as Cavalry Trooper from the 66th Goorkhas to Nynee Tal Militia Cavalry. Was present at the action of Hulwanee. Volunteered from Nynee Tal Militia Cavalry to Infantry for the protection of Nynee Tal. Volunteered from Nynee Tal to join his Regiment, and assumed Command of the Force then keeping the Ghauts of Hurdwar, Myapore, and Kunkul. Volunteered his services to Brigadier Jones, Commanding Field Force. Served throughout the Rohilcund Campaign, including the skirmish and capture of Nuggeejabad, Nageersa, re-occupation of Bareilly, Moradabad, relief of Shahjehanpore, skirmish and re-capture of Mohumdee. *Medal.* Served with Brigadier Holdwich's Nepal Frontier Field Force during the whole of the operations on the Nepal Frontier, '58, commanding a Wing of the Mynpooree Levy.

ASSISTANT-SURGEON L. F. DICKSON,† M.D., Bengal Medical Establishment.

Asst.-Surgeon, 4 Aug. 57.

SERVICE.—Assistant-Surgeon DICKSON was present with Shannon's Brigade, under the late Sir W. Peel, at the siege and capture of Lucknow (in Medical Charge of the Field). *Medal and Clasp.* In

(190)

Medical Charge of the 2nd Sikh Police Battalion, whilst engaged in the protection of the Goruckpore Frontier towards Nepal. In Medical Charge of the 20th Punjab Infantry, during several expeditions against flying parties of rebels in the Shahabad District.

2ND CAPTAIN W. DICKSON, P. H., Bengal Artillery.

2nd Lieut., 14 June 45—Lieut., 2 Feb. 51—2nd Captain, 27 Aug. 58.

SERVICE.—Captain DICKSON served during the Punjab Campaign, '48, '49. Present at the battles of Chillianwallah and Goojerat. *Medal and Clasp*.

ASSISTANT-SURGEON T. DILLON,† M.D., Bengal Medical Establishment.

Asst.-Surgeon, 28 June 54.

SERVICE.—Assistant-Surgeon DILLON was in Medical Charge of the Sylhet Light Infantry Battalion and was present in the Field during the first engagement that Regiment had with the mutineers of the 34th Native Infantry at Latoo, in the District of Sylhet. Brought to the notice of the Commander-in-Chief by the Officer Commanding the Head Quarters in the Field, after Major the Hon'ble R. P. Byng was killed in exposing himself under fire to succour wounded men requiring his assistance. *Medal*.

MAJOR H. DINNING,† late 71st Native Infantry.

Ensign, 10 July 39—Lieut., 16 July 42—Captain, 7 Dec. 49—Major, 24 March 58.

SERVICE.—Major DINNING served during the Punjab Campaign, '48, '49. *Medal*. Present at Lucknow on the mutiny of part of the 71st, 30th May '57. Present with the Force which pursued the rebels and drove them from the Cavalry Cantonments and villages near. Present in the Residency during the whole siege of Lucknow. *Medal and Clasp, and one year's extra service.* Mentioned in Brigadier Inglis' Despatch, 26th September '57. Received the thanks of Government, 12th December '57. Promoted to the rank of Brevet-Major. Present at Cawnpore during the operations, from the 30th November to the 6th December '57.

CAPTAIN T. A. DIROM, P. H., Bengal Artillery.
2nd Lieut., 9 June 48—Lieut., 3 March 53—Captain, 27 Aug. 58.

LIEUTENANT A. DIXON,† Bengal Artillery.
Lieut., 27 April 58.

2ND CAPTAIN G. M. DOBBIN, P. H., Bengal Artillery.
1st Lieut., 9 Dec. 50—2nd Captain, 27 Aug. 58.

SERVICE.—Captain DOBBIN served with the Burmese Expedition. Present at the operations in the vicinity and capture of Rangoon, April '52, and attack of the Burmese stockades, 19th March '53. *Medal.*

LIEUTENANT R. A. DOBBIN, late 6th Europeans.
Ensign, 6 July 54—Lieut., 23 Nov. 56.

ENSIGN C. A. DODD, P. H., late 74th Native Infantry.
Ensign, 4 Oct. 57.

SERVICE.—Ensign DODD served during the Mutiny, '57, '58. Present with Her Majesty's 23rd Fusiliers at the action of Kallah Nuddee; siege and capture of Lucknow, and subsequent operations leading to the subjugation of Oude. Joined the Oude Police Force, 1st December '58; served with the 11th Oude Police Infantry during the Trans-Gogra Campaign. *Medal and Clasps.*

LIEUTENANT-COLONEL D. S. DODGSON, P., late 30th Native Infantry.
Ensign, 22 June 38—Lieut., 3 Oct. 40—Captain, 13 Jan. 49—Major, 24 March 58—Lieut.-Colonel, 20 July 58.

SERVICE.—Lieutenant-Colonel DODGSON served throughout the Jaunpore Campaign, '39. In Affghanistan, engaged in the actions of 19th, 23rd, and 24th January '42; at the mouth of the Khyber Pass, forcing of Khyber Pass, 5th April '42; and subsequent operations in Affghanistan. *Medal.* Served throughout the Sutlej Campaign, '46. Present at the battles of Buddiwal and Alliwal. *Medal.* Accompanied General H. Wheeler's Force towards Cashmere, to assist Rajah Goolab Singh, to gain possession of his country from Shaik Emamooddeen. On its return, was appointed

(192)

Staff Officer to that Force, and thanked in Field Force Orders for services performed. Served as Brigade-Major at Benares, 4th June '57, on the mutiny of the Native Brigade. *(Wounded.)* Thanked in Colonel Niel's Despatch, 18th June '57. Served as Assistant Adjutant-General to the Field Forces in Oude, under Command of General Outram. Attached to the Staff of General Havelock, at the battles of Munglewar, 21st; Alum Bagh, 24th; and first relief of Lucknow, 25th September. *(Wounded.)* Received Brevet-Majority, 24th March '58. Served at the defence of the Baillie Guard, final relief of Lucknow, and all operations; recommended for Brevet-Lieutenant-Colonelcy by General Outram, and received that rank, 20th July '58. Served at the repelling of the attack on General Outram's camp, at Alum Bagh, from November '57 to March '58, including capture of enemy's guns and position at Ghylee, and at the capture of Lucknow. *Medal and 2 Clasps.* Thanked by the Governor-General and General Outram, and Colonel Napier, for services during the defence of Lucknow, 22nd and 28th December '57. Thanked by Sir J. Outram for his services at the capture of Lucknow, and his name recorded as deserving of honorable mention, 16th April '58.

CAPTAIN A. S. O. DONALDSON,† late 45th Native Infantry.

Ensign, 24 Jan. 39—Lieut., 21 April 42—Captain, 17 April 51.

SERVICE.—Captain DONALDSON served with the Army of the Sutlej, '45, '46. Present at the action of Moodkee, 18th; Ferozeshuhur, 21st and 22nd December '45. Received the thanks of the Governor-General and the Commander-in-Chief. Present at the battle of Sobraon, 10th February '46; occupation of Lahore, 13th March '46; and formed part of the Garrison till October '46. *Medal and 2 Clasps.* Served under Sir J. Littler with the Force towards Cashmere, December '46. Served in the Punjab Campaign, '48, '49. Commanded Rear Guard of the Army from Barra Muttyan, 19th November '48. Present at the passage of the Chenab, 18th December '48; at the action of Chillianwallah, 13th January '49; and Goojerat, 21st February '49. *Medal and 2 Clasps.* Present with the Regiment during the Mutiny, 13th and 14th May '57, and marched in with the Detachment which laid down its arms. Received the thanks and warm acknowledgments of the Brigadier Commanding.

(193)

CAPTAIN J. DORAN, P. H., late 24th Native Infantry.

Ensign, 11 June 42—Lieut., 20 Sept. 45—Captain, 1st Jan. 55.

SERVICE.—Captain DORAN served with the Army of the Sutlej, '45, '46. Present at the actions of Moodkee and Ferozeshuhur. *Medal and Clasp.* Served in the expedition against the Hussunzaies on the Black Mountain, in Huzara, '52,*'53. Served with Colonel Carmichael's Column in Oude, '58, '59. Served in the expedition to China, '60. *Medal.*

LIEUTENANT R. DOUGAL, late 53rd Native Infantry.

Ensign, 4 Oct. 55—Lieut., 10 Oct. 56.

SERVICE.—Lieutenant DOUGAL served during the Mutiny, '57. In July '57, under Major Allen, proceeded to intercept the Sealkôt Mutineers. Present at the disarming of the cities Poor and Mozuffernuggur, March '58. Served under Brigadier General Jones, at the battles of Bhogowallah, 17th, and Nugeena, 21st April; Bareilly, 5th and 6th May; and Mohurpore, 25th May '58. *Medal.*

LIEUTENANT A. B. DOUGLAS, P. H., late 52nd Native Infantry.

Ensign, 20 April 59—Lieut., 27 May 62.

LIEUTENANT A. L. DOUGLAS, P. H., late 2nd European Bengal Fusiliers.

2nd Lieut., 20 April 55—Lieut., 23 Nov. 56.

COLONEL C. DOUGLAS, late 65th Native Infantry.

Ensign, 16 Aug. 19—Lieut., 29 April 23—Captain, 27 Aug. 28—Bt.-Major, 23 Nov. 41—Major, 10 June 42—Lieut.-Colonel, 27 Oct. 48—Bt.-Colonel, 28 Nov. 54—Colonel, 1 May 58.

LIEUTENANT-COLONEL C. DOUGLAS,† Bengal Artillery.

2nd Lieut., 13 Dec. 33—Lieut., 12 Jan. 41—Bt.-Captain, 13 Dec. 48—Captain, 20 May 51—Bt.-Major, 20 July 58—Lieut.-Colonel, 18 Feb. 61.

SERVICE.—Lieutenant-Colonel DOUGLAS served in Affghanistan in '42. Present at the re-occupation of Cabul. *Medal.* Served with the Central India Field Force under Sir Hugh Rose. *Medal, and Brevet-Major.*

(194)

SURGEON F. DOUGLAS,† M.D., Bengal Medical Establishment.

Asst.-Surgeon, 18 Jan. 45—Surgeon, 16 June 58.

SERVICE.—Surgeon DOUGLAS, M.D., served with the 2nd Brigade Horse Artillery throughout part of the Sutlej Campaign, in '45, '46. Present at the affair of Buddiwal and battles of Alliwal and Sobraon. *Medal and Clasp.* Served as Medical Store-keeper to the Army of the Punjab throughout the Campaign of '48, '49. Present at Ramnuggur and at the battles of Chillianwallah and Goojerat. *Medal and Clasp.* Served as Assistant in the General Field Hospital, during the assault and capture of Lucknow, in March '58. *Medal and Clasp.*

LIEUTENANT H. A. DOUGLAS, Bengal Artillery.

Lieut., 21 Aug. 60.

LIEUTENANT H. McD. DEW. DOUGLAS, late 67th Native Infantry.

Ensign, 29 Aug. 53—Lieut., 23 Nov. 56.

SERVICE.—Lieutenant DOUGLAS served with the Artillery and Agra Infantry Militia. Present at the actions of Sussia, 5th July '59, and Agra, 10th October '59. *Medal.*

CAPTAIN S. DOUGLAS, Unattached List.

Ensign, 10 Feb. 46—Riding-Master, 15 May 46—Baggage-Master, 1 Dec. 48—Lieut., 3 Nov. 51—Riding-Master, 1 March 56—Baggage-Master, 22 May 57—Bt.-Captain, 10 Feb. 61.

SERVICE.—Captain DOUGLAS landed in India on the 16th May '26, and joined the 3rd Troop, 1st Brigade Bengal Horse Artillery. Joined the Army of the Sutlej as Provost Marshal, and was present at the battles of Moodkee, Ferozeshuhur, and Sobraon. Received an Unattached Ensigncy, and a *Medal and 2 Clasps.* Appointed Riding-Master to the 1st Brigade Horse Artillery, 15th May '46. Joined the Army of the Punjab and appointed Baggage-Master. Present at the battles of Ramnuggur, Chillianwallah, and Goojerat. *Medal and 2 Clasps.* Promoted to Lieutenant, Unattached, 3rd November '51. Re-embarked for India from furlough in '55, and received the thanks of the Commander-in-Chief at Bombay, as 2nd in Command of a Detachment of Troops, for the clean and healthy appearance of the men. Rejoined as Riding-Master to the 3rd Brigade. Appointed Baggage-Master to the Delhi Field Force; was at the battle of Badlee-ke-Serai, the siege of Delhi, and afterwards conducted a large convoy of 4,000 country carts, 2,000 camels, and 60 elephants from Allyghur to Cawnpore. With General Sir Hope Grant's Force at the taking of Meeah Gunge. *Medal and Clasp.* Appointed 2nd in Command of the Allahabad Levy for services, and has been recommended for promotion to an Unattached Captaincy.

COLONEL T. M. DOUGLAS, C.B., late 35th Native Infantry.

Ensign, 4 Dec. 06—Lieut., 9 Sept. 08—Captain, 1 May 24—Major, 17 Jan. 29—Lieut.-Colonel, 2 April 34—Bt.-Colonel, 4 Oct. 42—Colonel, 7 Sept. 45—Major-General, 20 June 54—Lieut.-General, 18 March 56.

LIEUTENANT A. DOUIE, Bengal Artillery.

Lieut., 27 April 58.

2ND CAPTAIN W. DOWELL, P. H., Bengal Artillery.

2nd Lieut., 12 June 46—Lieut., 3 March 53—2nd Captain, 27 Aug. 58.

SURGEON-MAJOR E. T. DOWNES, Bengal Medical Establishment.

Asst.-Surgeon, 30 March 26—Surgeon, 1 Jan. 41—Surgeon-Major, 13 Jan. 60.

LIEUTENANT A. E. DOWNING,† late 51st Native Infantry.

Ensign, 4 March 57—Lieut., 30 April 58.

MAJOR-GENERAL D. DOWNING, late 39th Native Infantry.

Ensign, 16 Aug. 19—Lieut., 2 March 22—Captain, 3 July 32—Major, 15 Sept. 39—Lieut.-Colonel, 12 Oct. 45—Bt.-Colonel, 20 June 54—Colonel, 7 May 55—Major-General, 15 Sept. 57.

SERVICE.—Major-General DOWNING served during the Punjab Campaign, under Brigadier Wheeler, '48, '49. *Medal.*

(196)

ENSIGN T. DOYLE (Unattached).
Ensign, 28 Sept. 58.

CAPTAIN C. W. D'OYLY, P. C. H., late 58th Native Infantry.
Ensign, 10 June 42—Lieut., 3 Aug. 44—Captain, 28 Feb. 55.
SERVICE.—Captain D'OYLY served at the battle of Punniar. *Bronze Star.*

LIEUTENANT J. A. DRAKE, late 10th Native Infantry.
Ensign, 26 July 57—Lieut., 18 May 58.

LIEUTENANT-COLONEL J. M. DRAKE, late 46th Native Infantry.
Ensign, 14 Aug. 25—Lieut., 1 April 28—Bt.-Captain, 14 Aug. 40—Captain, 26 Oct. 44—Bt.-Major, 11 Nov. 51—Major, 17 April 56—Lieut.-Colonel, 11 Sept. 59.
SERVICE.—Lieutenant-Colonel DRAKE served during the Punjab Campaign, '48, '49. Present at the affair of Ramnuggur and actions of Sadoolapore, Chillianwallah, and Goojerat. *Medal. (Since dead.)*

ENSIGN T. H. T. DRAKE, General List.
Ensign, 4 Jan. 60.

CAPTAIN H. R. DREW, P. H., late 6th Europeans.
Ensign, 22 Dec. 40—Lieut., 16 Aug. 42—Bt.-Captain, 22 Dec. 55—Captain, 6 May 56.
SERVICE.—Captain DREW served in the late 8th Native Infantry with the Army of the Punjab, '49. Present at first and second sieges of Mooltan, the action at Sooroojkhoond, and battle of Goojerat. *Wounded severely* at Mooltan. *Medal and 2 Clasps.*

COLONEL R. DROUGHT, C.B., P., late 60th Native Infantry.
Ensign, 13 Feb. 24—Lieut., 9 July 25—Captain, 2 Dec. 36—Bt.-Major, 9 Nov. 46—Bt.-Lieut.-Colonel, 20 June 54—Major, 25 Feb. 55—Lieut.-Colonel, 17 March 59—Bt.-Colonel, 29 Aug. 59.
SERVICE.—Colonel DROUGHT served at the siege and capture of Bhurtpore, '25, '26. *Medal.* At the capture of Jhansie, '39, under Brigadier-

General Aubury. Served throughout the Cabul Campaign, '42. Commanded the Advance Guard of Brigadier Wild's Force, in the Khyber Pass, 19th January '42. Commanded his Regiment in the action of the Khyber Pass, and 23rd and 24th January '42; at the forcing of the Khyber Pass, 5th April '42; actions of Gundumuck and Mamoo Khail in the following August, and all the other operations leading to the re-occupation of Cabul, '42, under Major-General Pollock. *Medal*. Commanded the Escort over the Sikh Sirdars and Mooloog, from Lahore to Allahabad, in '49. Served with the 2nd Infantry Brigade as a Field Officer at the siege of Delhi, '57. *Dangerously wounded* near Ludlow Castle, while in Command of the Metcalfe Horse Picquet, 23rd July '57. Mentioned in Brigadier Showers' Despatch. *Medal and C. B.* *(Since retired.)*

LIEUTENANT F. C. W. DRUMMOND,† late 70th Native Infantry.

Ensign, 20 Dec. 57—Lieut., 20 Nov. 58.

SERVICE —Lieutenant DRUMMOND served at the siege and capture of Lucknow with H. M.'s 53rd Foot, under Sir H. Grant, in March '58. *Medal and Clasp*. Present at the affair of Koorsie and the passage of the Goomtee, at Sultanpore, in '58. Served in China with the 70th Native Infantry, '59, '60.

CAPTAIN F. W. DRUMMOND, P. H., late 5th European Cavalry.

Cornet, 2 June 37—Lieut., 8 March 42—Bt.-Captain, 2 June 52—Captain, 1 Nov. 54.

SERVICE.—Captain DRUMMOND served in the Campaign in Bundlecund, in '42. Present at the battles of Punniar, *Bronze Star*, and Ferozeshuhur, *Medal*. Served throughout the Punjab Campaign. Present at the affair of Ramnuggur, and actions of Sadoolapore, Chillianwallah, and Goojerat. *Medal and 2 Clasps*.

MAJOR H. DRUMMOND, Bengal Engineers.

Cornet, 5 May 21—Lieut., 1 May 24—Bt.-Captain, 5 May 36—Captain, 16 Nov. 45—Bt.-Major, 9 Nov. 46—Major, 3 May 56—Bt.-Lieut.-Colonel, 20 June 54—Bt.-Colonel, 30 May 59.

SERVICE.—Major DRUMMOND served during the Sutlej Campaign in '46. *Medal*. Served with Brigadier Wheeler's Column at the capture of

Kôt Kangra, May '46, and present at the advance to Bhimber. Served during the war in Burmah, '52, 53. *Medal.* Served during the Mutiny, '57, '58. Present at the action of Kunkul. Mentioned in the Despatch of Captain H. Boisragon, 26th April '58. Served as Principal Field Engineer with Brigadier-General Jones' Column in Rohilcund. Present at the actions of Anasote, Nujeebabad, Nugeena, Meergunge, Bareilly, Shahjehanpore, Bumee, and Mohumdee. Mentioned in the Despatches of General Jones, 5th May and 3rd June '58. Promoted to Brevet-Majority for service in Rohilcund, '58. Mentioned in the Minute of the Governor-General during the Mutiny, August '59. Received the gracious approbation of Her Majesty the Queen, 11th June '60. *Medal.*

BREVET-COLONEL H. DRUMMOND, late 1st Bengal European Cavalry.

Cornet, 5 May 21—Lieut., 1 May 24—Bt.-Captain, 5 May 36—Captain, 16th Nov. 45—Bt.-Major, 9 Nov. 46—Major, 3 May 56—Bt.-Lieut.-Colonel, 20 June 54—Bt.-Colonel, 20 July 59.

SERVICE.—Colonel DRUMMOND served at the siege and capture of Bhurtpore, '26. *Medal.* Served against the Coles in '32. In Affghanistan, '38, '39. Siege and capture of Ghuznee. *Medal.* Was delivered in December '41 as a hostage to the Nawab Zeman Khan.

MAJOR P. DRUMMOND, P., late 22nd Native Infantry.

Ensign, 13 Jan. 37—Lieut., 1 Nov. 41—Captain, 22 May 49.—Major, 1 Jan. 62.

SERVICE.—Major DRUMMOND served throughout the Punjab Campaign, '48, '49. Present at the action of Sadoolapore. *Medal.* Joined the Column under General Showers, after the fall of Delhi, September '57. Received the thanks of Government, when in Command of a Detachment of the Kemaon Battalion for successful operations against the Insurgent Mawatties, of the Googaira District, in '57, 12th January '58. *Mutiny Medal.*

LIEUTENANT W. L. P. DRUMMOND, P. C. H., late 38th Native Infantry.

Ensign, 9 Dec. 53—Lieut., 9 May 57.

SERVICE.—Lieutenant DRUMMOND served at the siege of Delhi in '57, entering on the 8th June. Present at the action of Badlee-ka-Serai and

(199)

some others; organised and commanded a Regiment of Police Cavalry during the Oude Campaign of '58, in the actions of Sundeela (two days), at Poorwah, Maharajgunge, Simree, Beerah, Doondia Kaira, and a skirmish on the Oude Frontier: four times mentioned in Despatches. *Medal and Clasp for Delhi.* Served in the China Campaign of '60 and '61, with 1st Sikh Cavalry: present at the actions of Singho, Tongko, and at the capture of the Takee Forts; was on the Staff of Sir Robert Napier, also at Chunkia, Whan, and Tungchow. *China Medal and Clasps.*

CAPTAIN C. C. DRURY, P. H., late 34th Native Infantry.

Ensign, 14 April 40—Lieut., 16 July 42—Captain, 14 April 55.

ASSISTANT-SURGEON A. G. DUFF,† M.D., Bengal Medical Establishment.

Asst.-Surgeon, 1 Oct. 56.

SERVICE.—Assistant-Surgeon DUFF served with H. M.'s 60th Rifles and 75th Regiment throughout the Delhi Campaign of '57. Present at the emeute at Meerut, 10th May; with the Force under Brigadier Wilson at both engagements on the Hindun, 30th and 31st May: at the affair of Bhagput, on the Jumna, 20th June, and through the whole of the siege operations against Delhi, from the 20th June to the assault and capture of the city on the 14th September. Joined the Army of occupation at Alum Bagh under General Outram, on the 14th February '58; and was present at the storming and capture of Lucknow under Lord Clyde. *Medal and 2 Clasps.* Present at the operations in Oude under Lord Clyde, which resulted in the evacuation of the Forts of Ameatie and Shunkurpore, and defeat of Banimadho, at Buxar Ghaut, on the 24th November; and at the bombardment and capture of Omriah by Brigadier Evelegh, on the 2nd December; served in Medical Charge of the 3rd Regiment Hodson's Horse, against the rebels on the Nepal Frontier, during April and May '59.

BREVET-CAPTAIN F. DUFFIN, P. H., late 22nd Native Infantry.

Ensign, 29 Dec. 43—Lieut., 3 Aug. 54—Bt.-Captain, 29 Dec. 59.

SERVICE.—Captain DUFFIN served throughout the Campaign on the Sutlej. Present at the action of Moodkee and Ferozeshuhur. *Medal and Clasp.*

MAJOR R. DUFFIN, P. H., late 58th Native Infantry.

Ensign, 11 Dec. 41—Lieut., 3 Feb. 43—Captain, 10 April 49—Major, 8 July 59.

SERVICE.—Major DUFFIN served at the battle of Punniar. *Bronze Star.*

ASSISTANT-SURGEON T. DUKA,† M.D., Bengal Medical Establishment.

Asst.-Surgeon, 4 Jan. 54.

CAPTAIN C. DUMBLETON,† late 4th Bengal European Cavalry.

Cornet, 9 July 40—Lieut., 18 Dec. 45—Bt.-Captain, 9 July 55—Captain, 20 Sept. 55.

SERVICE.—Captain DUMBLETON was present at the battle of Maharajpore. *Bronze Star.*

LIEUTENANT F. W. DUNBAR, P. H., late 37th Native Infantry.

Ensign, 1 Aug. 48—Lieut., 20 May 53.

SERVICE.—Lieutenant DUNBAR served in Burmah under Colonel Cotton, '53, against the Rebel Chief Gounghee. Served throughout the Sonthal Insurrection, '55. Received the thanks of Brigadier Bird for the capture of one of the Chief Rebel Leaders, Ram Manjee. Present at the outbreak at Benares in '57, and in the engagement there with the rebels. Served with the Goorkha Force under Colonel Wroughton in Goruckpore and Azimghur Districts. Served with the Field Force under Colonel Whistler, in '57, against the rebels in the Suraon District, near Allahabad. *Medal.*

DEPUTY-INSPECTOR-GENERAL OF HOSPITALS J. A. DUNBAR,† M.D., Bengal Medical Establishment.

Asst.-Surgeon, 12 Dec. 37—Surgeon, 31 March 51—Surgeon-Major, 13 Jan. 60.

SERVICE.—Deputy-Inspector-General of Hospitals J. A. DUNBAR served with the 43rd Native Infantry with the Army of the Sutlej, in '45, '46. Appointed Staff Surgeon of the 4th, on Sir Robert Dicks' Division. Present at the battle of Sobraon. *Medal.* Appointed to the Medical Charge of Artillery Division at Lahore, in April '46, which formed part of the Army of occupation.

CAPTAIN J. S. DUNBAR, P. C., late 64th Native Infantry.

Ensign, 11 Dec. 41—Lieut., 3 June 48—Bt.-Captain, 11 Dec. 56— Captain, 6 April 60.

ASSISTANT-SURGEON J. DUNCAN,† M.D., Bengal Medical Establishment.

Asst.-Surgeon, 10 Feb. 59.

CAPTAIN C. S. DUNDAS,† Bengal Artillery.

2nd Lieut., 8 July 42—Lieut., 3 July 45—Bt.-Captain, 8 July 57— Captain, 28 Sept. 57.

SERVICE.—Captain DUNDAS was present at the affair of Buddiwal and battle of Alliwal. *Medal.* Served with the Army of the Punjab, '48, '49, and was present at the actions of Ramnuggur, Chillianwallah, *(wounded,)* and Goojerat. *Medal and 2 Clasps.*

CAPTAIN R. B. DUNDAS, P. H., late 38th Native Infantry.

Ensign, 12 Dec. 49—Lieut., 16 Nov. 52—Captain, 23 Oct. 58.

BREVET-COLONEL H. F. DUNSFORD, C.B., P., late 59th Native Infantry.

Ensign, 13 June 35—Lieut., 3 Oct. 38—Captain, 10 June 50—Major, 11 June 50—Lieut.-Colonel, 28 Nov. 54.

SERVICE.—Colonel DUNSFORD, C.B., served as Major of Brigade, 7th Brigade, 3rd Division Army of the Sutlej. Present at the battle of Sobraon. *Medal and Brevet-Major.* Commanded the Troops of the Rajahs of Puttialla and Jheend, during the siege of Delhi. Present at the storm and capture on 14th September '57. *Medal, 2 Clasps, and C. B.* Commanded the Buxar Column of the Shahabad Field Force in October and November '58. Commanded at the attack of Burahpore on the 14th October '58, where the rebels in force were driven out of a strongly entrenched position, and routed with great slaughter. Defeated an attack of the rebels at Sikurreea, on 16th October '58, and in other skirmishes leading to the successful attack on the Town of Jugdespore, on 19th October '58, where he was *very severely wounded.* Served in Assam in '62, during the disturbances there.

LIEUTENANT C. J. DURAND,† late 14th Native Infantry.
Ensign, 4 May 57—Lieut., 18 May 58.

SERVICE.—Lieutenant DURAND served with H. M.'s 42nd Royal Highlanders in the Campaign of '57, '58, against the mutineers, including the actions at Cawnpore, 6th December '57, Seriaghat, Kallah Nuddee, and Shumshabad, siege and capture of Lucknow, attack on the post of Rooya, action at Allyghur, and attack and capture of Bareilly. *Medal and Clasp.*

COLONEL H. M. DURAND, C.B., Bengal Engineers.
2nd Lieut., 12 June 28—Lieut., 20 April 35—Bt.-Captain, 12 June 43—Captain, 30 Nov. 44—Bt.-Major, 7 June 49—Major, 8 June 56—Bt.-Lieut.-Colonel, 28 Nov. 54—Lieut.-Colonel, 13 Aug. 58—Colonel, 20 July 58.

SERVICE.—Colonel DURAND, C.B., headed the explosion party and fired the train at Ghuznee. *Medal.* Present at the battles of Maharajpore. *Bronze Star.* In the actions of Chillianwallah and Goojerat. *Medal and 2 Clasps, and Brevet Major.* As Agent to the Governor-General in Central India in '57, and was present in several affairs, including the siege and capture of Dhar, and actions at Mundroore. *Medal, C.B., and Brevet-Lieutenant-Colonel.*

CAPTAIN H. DURANT, P., late 5th Bengal European Cavalry.
Cornet, 20 Jan. 49—Lieut., 16 April 50—Captain, 17 July 57.

ASSISTANT-SURGEON J. J. DURANT,† Bengal Medical Establishment.
Asst.-Surgeon, 10 Feb. 59.

CAPTAIN H. A. DWYER, P., late 59th Native Infantry.
Ensign, 25 Dec. 40—Lieut., 5 June 45—Bt.-Captain, 25 Dec. 55—Captain, 23 Nov. 56.

SERVICE.—Captain DWYER served with the Army of the Sutlej in '46. Present at the action of Sobraon. *Medal and Clasp.* Served before Delhi in '57. Present at the siege on 14th September '57. *Medal and Clasp.* Served with Brigadier Showers' Column in November '57, and present at the capture of Zuggur. Received the thanks of the Governor-General, 25th May '58, for services in the Gummoo Contingent.

(203)

CAPTAIN J. H. DYAS,† Bengal Engineers.
2nd Lieut., 8 Dec. 43—Lieut., 4 Nov. 47—Captain, 11 Aug. 57.

SERVICE.—Captain DYAS served during the Sutlej Campaign, '45, '46. *Medal.*

LIEUTENANT R. H. DYAS, late 4th Europeans.
Ensign, 4 Sept. 57—Lieut., 3 Nov. 58.

LIEUTENANT F. L. S. DYCE, late 71st Native Infantry.
Ensign, 13 June 57—Lieut., 18 May 58.

LIEUTENANT E. H. DYKE, Bengal Artillery.
Lieut., 27 April 58.

LIEUTENANT G. S. DYSART, P. H., late 23rd Native Infantry.
Ensign, 13 June 52—Lieut., 23 Nov. 56.

SERVICE.—Lieutenant DYSART served with the Malwa Field Force in '57. Present at the actions of Mehidpore, Gorarea, and Mundasore. *Medal and Clasp.* With the Hyderabad Contingent Field Force. Present at the surprise of a body of Rebel Cavalry; also in pursuit of Tantia Topee. Commanded a Detachment in a skirmish with the rebels at Chiculda, November '58. Met with approval of the Governor-General, 21st December '58. Served also in several minor occasions against the Bheels.

E

LIEUTENANT R. H. EADES,† late 42nd Native Infantry.
Ensign, 20 Oct. 58—Lieut., 1 March 59.

2ND CAPTAIN E. L. EARLE, P. H., Bengal Artillery.
Lieut., 14 June 50—2nd Captain, 27 Aug. 58.

ASSISTANT-SURGEON F. J. EARLE,† Bengal Medical Establishment.
Asst.-Surgeon, 20 March 54.

(204)

CAPTAIN J. M. EARLE, P. H., late 24th Native Infantry.

Ensign, 9 Dec. 42—Lieut., 18 Dec. 45—Captain, 23 Nov. 56.

SERVICE.—Captain EARLE served during the Sutlej Campaign, '45, '46. Present at the actions of Moodkee, Ferozeshuhur, Buddiwal, and Alliwal. *Medal and Clasp.*

CAPTAIN W. H. S. EARLE, P. C., late 20th Native Infantry.

Ensign, 17 Feb. 43—Lieut., 31 Dec. 47—Captain, 23 Nov. 56.

SERVICE.—Captain EARLE served in the Punjab Campaign, '48, '49. Present at the actions of Chillianwallah and Goojerat. *Medal and 2 Clasps.* At the fight in the Booree Pass, under Brigadier Boileau, November '53. Operations against the Bussy Khel Afreedies, under Lieutenant-Colonel Craigie, C.B., March '55. Served during the Mutinies, '57, '58, in the Meerut and Boolundshuhur Districts. *Medal.*

SURGEON W. C. B. EATWELL,† M.D., Bengal Medical Establishment.

Asst.-Surgeon, 11 June 41—Surgeon, 1 Aug. 55.

SERVICE.—Surgeon EATWELL served in China from '42 to '45.

ASSISTANT-SURGEON H. A. EBDEN,† M.D., Bengal Medical Establishment.

Asst.-Surgeon, 7 Oct. 47.

SERVICE.—Assistant-Surgeon EBDEN served throughout the Punjab Campaign, '48, '49, as Assistant in the Field Hospital. Present at the actions of Ramnuggur, Chillianwallah, and Goojerat, and accompanied Sir W. Gilbert's Force to Peshawur. *Medal.*

LIEUTENANT A. H. ECKFORD, P., late 69th Native Infantry.

Ensign, 20 Feb. 54—Lieut., 23 Nov. 56.

SERVICE.—Lieutenant ECKFORD was present at the siege and operations before Delhi; was *severely wounded* on the 9th July '57, whilst doing duty with the Sirmoor Battalion, rejoined in August, and was appointed Officiating Adjutant, and continued to act in that capacity till the capture of Delhi; was appointed to act as Deputy Assistant Quarter-Master-

(205)

General to the Meerut Division, and accompanied General Penny's Column into Rohilcund. *Was severely wounded* in action at Kukerowlee on the 30th April '58, *receiving two sabre cuts* in driving back Ghazees from the guns.

LIEUTENANT-GENERAL J. ECKFORD, C.B., late 56th Native Infantry.

Ensign, 1 Jan. 04—Lieut., 17 Sept. 06—Bt.-Captain, 1 Jan. 19—Captain, 20 July 23—Major, 18 July 31—Lieut.-Colonel, 11 March 37—Colonel, 27 Oct. 48—Major-General, 28 Nov. 54—Lieut.-General, 29 April 61.

SERVICE.—Lieutenant-General ECKFORD, C.B., served with Sir Home Popham's expedition. Present at the bombardment of Boulogne and Havre de Grace, and subsequent destruction of the French flotilla (as Midshipman of H. M.'s Frigate *Greyhound*). Present at the capture of Chamur and neighboring parts in Bundlecund, '06 '07 : taking of Java, '11 : battle of Cornelis, and assault of Djokjucurta, '12. *Medal.* Siege and capture of Bhurtpore. *Medal.* Served in Affghanistan with the Force under General Pollock : during the campaign on the Sutlej and in Command of a Brigade with the Army of the Punjab at the passage of the Chenab and action of Sadoolapore. *Medal and C. B.*

LIEUTENANT J. ECKFORD, P. H., Bengal Engineers.

Lieut., 27 April 58.

CAPTAIN J. J. ECKFORD, P. H., late 5th Europeans.

Ensign, 9 June 43—Lieut., 6 April 50—Captain, 29 Jan. 58.

SERVICE.—Captain ECKFORD served with the Army of the Sutlej, '46. In '50, '51, with the 2nd Punjab Infantry on the Kohat and Bunnoo Frontier, against the Hill Wuzeeree Tribes. Present at the siege of of Delhi, '57. Served with the Meerut Volunteers, June '57; against the rebels in the Mynpooree District, May and June '58. Services favorably mentioned by the Governor-General, 7th October '59. *Severely wounded* on 10th May '57, when defending, as Executive Engineer, the Office and Treasury, 6th Division Grand Trunk Road, against an attack made on it by mutinous sepoys and rebels. (Passed examination in Surveying and Civil Engineering.)

ASSISTANT-SURGEON W. EDDOWS, Bengal Medical Establishment.
Asst.-Surgeon, 4 Aug. 56.

MAJOR R. J. EDGELL, P. H., late 53rd Native Infantry.

Ensign, 11 Dec. 40—Lieut., 16 July 42—Captain, 24 April 55—Bt.-Major, 24 March, '58—Major, 2 Oct. 61.

SERVICE.—Major EDGELL served with General Pollock's Force in Affghanistan, in '42. Present at the operations in the Khyber Pass, and at the occupation of Ali Musjid· by the troops under Brigadier Wild. Present at the forcing of the Khyber Pass, and operations in the Mageenah Valley. Present in the Khyber Pass, when the British troops finally left Affghanistan. *Cabul Medal and thanks of Government.* Served with the Army of the Punjab in '48, '49. Occupied with his Regiment the Tête-du-Pont near Ramnuggur, on the Chenab, the day of the battle of Goojerat. *Medal and thanks of Government.* Served throughout the siege of Lucknow, from the 30th June to the 22nd November '57. Present in the action of Chinhut, commanded at the Cawnpore Battery post every third or fourth day throughout the siege, and did duty at "Gubbins's Post" on the intervening days. Present in every attack at these posts. *Medal and Clasp. Brevet-Major. Twice mentioned in General Inglis' Despatch, and received the thanks of Government.*

ENSIGN G. EDMONDS (Unattached List).

Ensign, 5 Oct. 60.

SERVICE.—Ensign EDMONDS served with the Army of the Sutlej, '45. Present at the action of Sobraon. *Medal.* Served in the expedition of the Bhotee Kangra, in May '46, Army of the Punjab, '48. *Medal*, Indian Rebellion, '57. In the Etawah and Jhaloon Districts. Present at the actions of Bijulpore, Silowah, Hurchundpore, Shahpore, Shreghul (*wounded*), Ageetunel, Neemree, Fort Burree, and Bunserai. Mentioned in Despatches, 6th July and 22nd December '58. Thanked by His Excellency the Governor-General, 22nd December '58.

(207)

CAPTAIN F. N. EDMONSTONE, P., late 3rd Bengal European Cavalry.

Cornet, 2 June 37—Lieut., 1 March 43—Captain, 1 Jan. 51—Major, 20 July 58.

LIEUTENANT-COLONEL SIR H. B. EDWARDES, C.B., P. C., late 1st European Bengal Fusiliers.

2nd Lieut., 26 Sept. 40—Lieut., 10 Nov. 43—Captain, 1 March 50— Major, 12 March 50—Lieut.-Colonel, 28 Nov. 54.

SERVICE.—Lieutenant-Colonel EDWARDES, C.B., served as A. D. C. to His Excellency the Commander-in-Chief during the Campaign on the Sutlej, including the actions of Moodkee *(severely wounded)*, and Sobraon. *Medal and Clasp.* Commanded an Irregular Force raised by himself on the Indus, with which, in conjunction with the Troops of the Nawab of Bhawulpore, he twice defeated the Army of Dewan Moolraj, at Kineyree, on the 18th June, and Suddoosam, 1st July '48, taking ten guns. *Medal, C.B., and Local Major.* Served throughout the siege and operations in the vicinity of Mooltan. *Medal and Clasps.*

LIEUTENANT W. F. EDWARDS,† late 45th Native Infantry.

Ensign, 9 Dec. 52—Lieut., 23 Nov. 56.

SERVICE.—Lieutenant EDWARDS served throughout the siege and capture of Delhi, including the action of Moozuffernuggur. Served with Sir J. Douglas' Force in '58, in the Shahabad Campaign, including the action of Berhampore, taking of Jugdespore, and subsequent operations and pursuit of the rebels through the Rotas Hills. *Medal and Clasp.*

LIEUTENANT C. C. EKINS, P. H., late 20th Native Infantry.

Ensign, 20 Dec. 48—Lieut., 1 Jan. 51.

Passed Examination in Field Engineering.

LIEUTENANT-COLONEL L. P. D. ELD, P. C., late 9th Native Infantry.

Ensign, 5 Nov. 25—Lieut., 15 Sept. 33—Bt.-Captain, 5 Nov. 40—Captain, 1 Jan. 45—Bt.-Major, 11 Nov. 51—Major, 4 April 57—Bt.-Lieut.- Colonel, 27 Sept. 59.

(208)

CAPTAIN A. L. ELDERTON, P. C. H., late 2nd European Bengal Fusiliers.

2nd Lieut., 27 Jan. 44—Lieut., 12 July 47—Bt.-Captain, 27 Jan. 59—Captain, 23 Aug. 59.

SERVICE.—Captain ELDERTON served during the Punjab Campaign, including the affair of Ramnuggur, passage of the Chenab, and actions of Chillianwallah and Goojerat. *(Wounded.) Medal and Clasp.* Accompanied the Army under Sir W. R. Gilbert, in pursuit of the Sikhs and Affghans. *Was severely wounded* at the assault of Delhi, and was present during the whole of the siege. Was present with his Regiment during the operations before Delhi, siege and capture of the City, on the 14th September '57. *(Severely wounded.)* (Passed in Surveying, Civil Engineering, and Field Engineering, and obtained a first class certificate in Musketry.)

LIEUTENANT C. P. ELDERTON, Bengal Artillery.

Lieut., 27 Aug. 58.

ENSIGN H. E. ELIOT, General List.

Ensign, 4 Jan. 60.

LIEUTENANT-COLONEL J. ELIOT, P. H., Bengal Artillery.

2nd Lieut., 9 Dec. 36—Lieut., 17 Aug. 41—Bt.-Captain, 9 Dec. 51—Captain, 25 Feb. 53—Lieut.-Colonel, 18 Feb. 61.

CAPTAIN H. E. ELLICE,† late 1st Bengal European Cavalry.

Cornet, 20 Dec. 49—Lieut., 18 Aug. 52—Captain, 1 July 57.

LIEUTENANT E. H. H. ELLIOT, Bengal Artillery.

Lieut., 27 Aug. 58.

BREVET-MAJOR E. K. ELLIOT, P., late 43rd Native Infantry.

Ensign, 7 Feb. 29—Lieut., 2 June 39—Bt.-Captain, 7 Feb. 44—Captain, 21 Jan. 52—Bt.-Major, 28 Nov. 54.

SERVICE.—Brevet-Major ELLIOT served throughout the Affghanistan Campaign, '39, '40, '41, '42, including the operation of the Candahar Force under General Nott. *Medal*.

LIEUTENANT M. ELLIOT, P. H., Bengal Artillery.

1st Lieut., 8 Sept. 57.

CAPTAIN W. R. ELLIOT, P. H., late 6th Europeans.

Ensign, 10 Dec. 39—Lieut., 9 March 42—Captain, 25 Feb. 52.

SERVICE.—Captain ELLIOT served with the Mooltan Field Force and the Army of Punjab, '48, '49. Present at the siege and surrender of Mooltan, and battle of Goojerat. *Medal and 2 Clasps*. In July '57, as Officiating Commissioner of Goojerat, in the Punjab, commanded and led a body of Mounted Police against a party of the mutinous 14th Native Infantry, in the Island of the Jhelum River, and destroyed them. *Medal*.

LIEUTENANT E. D. ELLIOTT, Bengal Artillery.

Lieut., 18 Aug. 58.

ASSISTANT-SURGEON J. ELLIOTT,† M.D., Bengal Medical Establishment.

Asst.-Surgeon, 20 Feb. 54.

BREVET-CAPTAIN A. ELLIS, P., late 31st Native Infantry.

Ensign, 29 Dec. 44—Lieut., 31 March 51—Bt.-Captain, 29 Dec. 59.

SERVICE.—Brevet-Captain ELLIS served throughout the Punjab Campaign. Present at the actions of Sadoolapore, Chillianwallah, Goojerat, and in the pursuit of the Sikhs and Affghans under Sir W. R. Gilbert, in '48, '49. *Medal and Clasp*. Served as Adjutant to the 31st Native Infantry, in the expedition to Kohat, under Sir C. Napier, '50. Served as Interpreter and Quarter-Master in the Mutiny at Saugor, and acted as Adjutant to the 31st Native Infantry and as Superintendent of Saugor Sudder Bazar, in '57, '58. *Medal*.

ENSIGN A. D. ELLIS, P. H., General List.
Ensign, 4 Jan. 60.

CAPTAIN F. J. ELLIS,† late 58th Native Infantry.
Ensign, 10 Dec. 44—Lieut., 22 July 48—Captain, 26 Dec. 58.

ASSISTANT-SURGEON J. ELLIS,† M.B., Bengal Medical Establishment.
Asst.-Surgeon, 10 Feb. 59.

LIEUTENANT N. ELLIS, late 1st European Bengal Fusiliers.
2nd Lieut., 20 Jan. 56—Lieut., 14 Sept. 57.

SERVICE.—Lieutenant ELLIS served during the Mutiny, '57, '58. Present at the action of Badlee-ka-Serai, 8th June '57; in all the engagements before Delhi, and at the storm and capture of that City, 14th September '57. Served in the Columns under Brigadier Gerrard and Sir T. Seaton, K.C.B. Present at the action of Narnoul, 16th November '57; Gungeeree, 14th December 57; Puttiallee, 17th December '59; and Mynpooree, 27th December '57. Served at the siege and capture of Lucknow, March '58, and subsequent operations in Oude, '58, '59. *Wounded* at Delhi and Lucknow. *Medal and 2 Clasps.*

MAJOR R. R. W. ELLIS, P., late 23rd Native Infantry.
Ensign, 5 Nov. 25—Lieut., 17 Dec. 32—Bt.-Captain, 5 Nov. 40—Captain, 10 Feb. 46—Major, 11 Nov. 51.

(Since retired.)

BREVET-CAPTAIN N. W. ELPHINSTONE, P. C., late 4th Native Infantry.
Ensign, 14 June 45—Lieut., 14 Feb. 52—Bt.-Captain, 14 June 60.

SERVICE.—Brevet-Captain ELPHINSTONE served with the Army of the Sutlej, '46. Joined the Head Quarters Camp, and accompanied the Army to Lahore, February '46. Served with the 4th Native Infantry during the Punjab Campaign, under General Wheeler, '48, '49. Present during several skirmishes in the Kangra Hills, January '59. Mentioned in Despatch of Colonel Downing, 19th January '49. *Medal.* Served during the Mutinies of '57 in the Googaira District. Commanded a

(211)

Detachment of Levies and Police in September '57 with which he attacked and destroyed Jamrah, the head quarters of the rebels of Khumul. Commanded a Detachment during the attack of the rebels on the station of Googaira. Accompanied the Forces under Colonel Paton and Colonel Chamberlain, from September '57 to November '57, as Deputy-Commissioner during the Googaira Insurrection. Was present during the attack on Googaira, action near Hurappa, and final attack on Julla. *Medal.* (Received a degree of Honor for attainments in the Persian Language.)

SURGEON H. N. ELTON,† Bengal Medical Establishment.

Asst.-Surgeon, 9 Sept. 43—Surgeon, 27 June 57.

SERVICE.—Surgeon ELTON was appointed to do duty in the Field Hospital, Loodianah, after the battle of Alliwal, in February '46. Appointed to do duty in the Field Hospital, Allahabad, in December '57.

LIEUTENANT J. F. ELTON,† late 37th Native Infantry.

Ensign, 20 Dec. 56—Lieut., 30 April 58.

SERVICE.—Lieutenant J. F. ELTON was present at the outbreak in June '57, at Benares, and present with H. M.'s 10th Foot at the capture of Atrowlea; accompanied Juanpore Field Force and was present at the actions of Chanda, Meereuenpore, Sultanpore, and the assault on the Fort of Dhowar (mentioned in General Frank's Despatches for leading assault) as Orderly Officer to Colonel Longden. Present at the capture of Lucknow, in March '58. *Medal and Clasp.*

LIEUTENANT R. W. ELTON,† late 74th Native Infantry.

Ensign, 8 Dec. 55—Lieut., 11 May 57.

SERVICE.—Lieutenant ELTON was present with his Regiment at the outbreak at Delhi; served in the Meerut Volunteer Horse, and present with it at the defeat of Walledad Khan, at Galowtee, and on several other occasions, when attached to left Wing 1st Belooch Battalion. Was present with the late General Penny's Force at the action of Kurkralee; was with the Commander-in-Chief's Force at the fight before Bareilly, on 5th May '58; and at repulse of rebels by the Commander-in-Chief, on the occasion of their attacking our outposts at Shahjehanpore. In the operations near Mohumdee and relief of Fort Jellallabad. Present with the

Battalion at the taking of Fort Rampore Kussia by Brigadier Wetherell's Force; with Commander-in-Chief's Force at occupation of Forts of Ameytee and Shunkerpore, and at the defeat of Beni Madho at Dundea Keerce; also at the fight at Churda, and taking of Fort Mayeedia. Present at the capture of 14 guns by Brigadier Horsford's Force at Sikha Ghaut, in Nepal. *Medal.*

CAPTAIN W. ELWYN, P. H., late 58th Native Infantry.

Ensign, 23 July 42—Lieut., 24 Jan. 45—Captain, 23 Nov. 56.

SERVICE.—Captain ELWYN served with the Army of Gwalior, '43, '44. Present at the action of Remnai, 29th December '43. *Bronze Star.* Served with the reserve force of the Army of the Punjab, under Sir D. Hill, '49.

ASSISTANT-SURGEON L. EMANUEL, Bengal Medical Establishment.

Asst.-Surgeon, 20 Jan. 60.

CAPTAIN J. EMERSON, P. H., late 26th Native Light Infantry.

Ensign, 24 Sept. 42—Lieut., 10 June 45—Captain, 30 July 57.

SERVICE.—Captain EMERSON served with the Army of the Sutlej, '45, '46. Present at the actions of Moodkee, Ferozeshuhur, Sobraon; and advanced with the Army on Lahore. *Medal and 2 Clasps.*

LIEUTENANT A. ENGLAND, late 44th Native Infantry.

Ensign, 4 Jan. 58—Lieut., 9th Nov. 58.

SERVICE.—Lieutenant ENGLAND served before Lucknow from 20th March to the 20th May '58. Present at the crossing of the Gogra. Served throughout the Trans-Gogra Campaign. *Medal.*

MAJOR W. C. ERSKINE, C.B., late 73rd Native Infantry.

Ensign, 16 April 28—Lieut., 3 Oct. 40—Bt.-Captain, 16 April 43—Captain, 21 Dec. 45—Major, 20 June 54.

SERVICE.—Major ERSKINE served with the Army of the Sutlej, '46. Present at the action of Sobraon. *Medal.* Present at the action of Kuhurrgee, against the mutineers of the late 52nd Native Infantry, 27th September '57. Received the thanks of the Governor-General for conduct during the Mutinies, 7th October '59. As Political Officer accompanied Colonel Miller's Field Force, engaged in operations in these Territories. Mentioned in Colonel Miller's Despatch, 25th June '58. Accompanied the Force under General Whitlock as Political Officer while in the Jubbulpore Division. *Medal.* Received the Order of the Bath, Civil, 9th July '60.

ASSISTANT-SURGEON A. ETESON,† Medical Establishment.

Asst.-Surgeon, 20 May 54.

SERVICE.—Assistant-Surgeon ETESON served with the Artillery at the relief of Arrah and subsequent advance on Jugdespore, August '57, with the Gorucknauth Regiment of Goorkhas in the Sarun Field Force, with the 20th Punjab Infantry, throughout the final operations in Shahabad, October '58. Services mentioned in the Despatch of Major Vincent Eyre, 3rd and 13th August '57; in Brigadier Rowcroft's Despatch, published in General Orders, 5th May '58; in Major Carr's Despatch, 31st December '58; and in Brigadier Douglas' Despatch, dated 31st October '58. *Medal.*

LIEUTENANT H. M. EVANS, late 6th European Bengal Fusiliers.

Ensign, 20 June 58—Lieut., 15 March 59.

LIEUTENANT H. P. EVANS,† late 52nd Native Infantry.

Ensign, 12 June 57—Lieut., 18 May 58.

SERVICE.—Lieutenant EVANS served with H. M.'s 34th Foot in the Mutiny, '57. Present at the defence of Cawnpore, under General Windham, storming of Muongunge, capture of Lucknow, and relief of Azimghur. *Medal and Clasp.* Served with the late 73rd Native Infantry, in the Sikhim Expedition, '60, 61.

CAPTAIN J. M. EVANS, P. C. H., late 6th Europeans.

Ensign, 13 Dec. 45—Lieut., 10 April 52—Captain, 22 Jan. 59.

SERVICE.—Captain EVANS was present as Adjutant with the 7th Native Infantry, when it mutinied, 25th August '57. Served as Staff Officer to the Force under Lieutenant-Colonel O'Brien, at Futtehpore, during the Mutiny, '57. *Medal.*

(214)

LIEUTENANT L. E. EVANS, late 15th Native Infantry.

Ensign, 13 Dec. 56—Lieut., 30 April 58.

SERVICE.—Lieutenant EVANS served throughout the Indian Mutinies of '58 with the 3rd Europeans. Present with the Mynpooree Moveable Column in the operations at Shereghur Ghaut, in May, and with the Agra Column towards Gwalior, in June '58. Served also with the Column under Brigadier Showers, in the action at Dewsa, 14th January '59, against Tantia Topee. *Medal.*

LIEUTENANT T. W. EVANS,† late 47th Native Infantry.

Ensign, 16 Feb. 50—Lieut., 15 Dec. 53.

SERVICE.—Lieutenant EVANS served during the Mutiny, '57, in the Mirzapore District, with the 47th Native Infantry. *Medal.*

CAPTAIN M. F. EVATT, P., late 36th Native Infantry.

Ensign, 25 Feb. 43—Lieut., 30 June 46—Captain, 26 Dec. 56.

SERVICE.—Captain EVATT served in the Sutlej Campaign, '46, with the late 36th Native Infantry.

LIEUTENANT C. H. EWART,† late 25th Native Infantry.

Ensign, 20 Feb. 57—Lieut., 30 April 58.

SERVICE.—Lieutenant EWART served in the Force before Delhi, '57. Was present throughout the whole of the operations before Delhi, including the battle of Badlee-ka-Serai, on the 8th June '57, and the final assault and capture of the City, 14th September '57. *Medal and Clasp.*

ASSISTANT-SURGEON J. EWART,† M.D., Bengal Medical Establishment.

Asst.-Surgeon, 20 Dec. 53.

BREVET-LIEUTENANT-COLONEL R. S. EWART, late 30th Native Infantry.

Ensign, 14 Nov. 26—Lieut., 24 April 32—Bt.-Captain, 14 Nov. 41—Captain, 1 Feb. 44—Bt.-Major, 20 June 54—Major, 9 June 58—Bt.-Lieut.-Colonel, 19 Jan. 58.

SERVICE.—Lieutenant-Colonel EWART served throughout the Cabul Campaign, '42. Present at the actions at the entrance of the Khyber

Pass, on the 19th, 23rd, and 24th January '42, and at the forcing of the Khyber Pass, 5th April '42. *Medal.* Served throughout the Sutlej Campaign, '46. Present at the battle of Alliwal. *Medal.* Served during the Punjab Campaign, '49. Present at the passage of the Chenab, and actions of Chillianwallah and Goojerat, and in the subsequent pursuit of the Sikhs and Affghans. *Medal and 2 Clasps.* Served throughout the operations before Delhi as Assistant Adjutant-General of the Force. Present at the action of Badlee-ka-Serai, 8th June 57, and at the storm and capture of the City. *Medal.* Mentioned in the Despatch of Brigadier-General Sir A. Wilson, Bt., K.C.B., 22nd September '57. Promoted to the rank of Brevet-Lieutenant-Colonel for service before Delhi. *(Since retired.)*

LIEUTENANT G. H. W. EWBANK, Bengal Artillery.

Lieut., 27 Aug. 58.

LIEUTENANT F. V. EYRE, Bengal Artillery.

1st Lieut., 14 Feb. 58.

BREVET-COLONEL V. EYRE, C.B., Bengal Artillery.

2nd Lieut., 12 Dec. 28—Lieut., 28 April 37—Bt.-Captain, 12 Dec. 43— Captain, 19 Sept. 46—Bt.-Major, 20 June 54—Major, 4 July 58—Bt.- Lieut.-Colonel, 11 Dec. 57—Lieut.-Colonel, 27 Aug. 58—Bt.-Colonel, 24 March 58.

SERVICE.—Brevet-Colonel EYRE, C.B., served in Affghanistan, '41, '42. Commanded Horse Artillery in two successful actions under Brigadier Shelton *(severely wounded)*. Taken prisoner on retreat from Cabul. Commanded Field Force for the relief of Arrah, and defeated the rebels under Koer Sing, 2nd and 12th August '57. *Brevet-Colonel and C.B.* Defeated and destroyed a Force of Oude rebels at Koordun Puttee, 11th September. Commanded a heavy gun battery in the actions of Mungulwar, Alum Bagh, and first relief of Lucknow under Major-General Sir H. Havelock. Was Brigadier of Artillery and Cavalry under Sir Jas. Outram, at Lucknow and Alum Bagh, and commanded the Artillery Division at the latter, during the final operations before Lucknow, under His Excellency Sir C. Campbell, G.C.B., March '58. *Medal and 2 Clasps.*

(216)

F

CAPTAIN L. P. FADDY,† late 29th Native Infantry.

Ensign, 1 March 38—Lieut., 5 Sept. 41—Bt.-Captain, 1 March 53—Captain, 3 July 54.

SERVICE.—Captain FADDY served against the rebels north of Jullunder, '48, '49. Present at the storming of the heights of Umballah and occupation of the Fort of Oonah. *Medal. Severely wounded* in an engagement with the rebels under Ram Sing, in the Jullunder Doab.

LIEUTENANT-COLONEL S. B. FADDY, P., late 36th Native Infantry.

Ensign, 24 Feb. 35—Lieut., 1 Feb. 40—Captain, 14 Nov. 46—Major, 31 May 57—Lieut.-Colonel, 9 March 61.

SERVICE.—Lieutenant-Colonel FADDY served in the Sutlej Campaign, '46. *Medal.* Served in the Punjab Campaign, '48, '49. Present at the affair of Ramnuggur, battles of Sadoolapore, Chillianwallah, and Goojerat, and accompanied the pursuing Column to the mouth of the Khyber Pass. *Medal and 2 Clasps.* Mentioned in the Despatches of Major-General Sir J. Thackwell, 18th February '49. Accompanied an Irregular Force for the capture of Sirdars Tall Sing, Murrarceale, and Soorut Sing Meyuteeale. Received the thanks of the Governor-General, 29th October and 8th November '49. Received the approbation of His Excellency the Commander-in-Chief for progress made in constructing accommodation for Troops in the new Cantonments of Umitsur, 30th March '52. Received the acknowledgments of Government for "valuable service rendered to the telegraphic department," 19th January '55.

LIEUTENANT H. C. FAGAN,† late 36th Native Infantry.

Ensign, 20 Dec. 56—Lieut., 5 Sept. 57.

SERVICE.—Lieutenant FAGAN served with the 19th Punjab Infantry with Colonel Carmichael's Brigade in Oude, '58, '59. Served in the late expedition to China, '60. *Medal.*

(217)

CAPTAIN W. T. FAGAN, P. H., late 44th Native Infantry.
Ensign, 28 July 47—Lieut., 9 Feb. 51—Captain, 18 April 58.

SERVICE.—Captain FAGAN served in the Hill Rangers with the Sonthal Field Force, '55, '56. Served in Command of 7th Bengal Police Battalion in the expedition against the Hostile Tribes on the South East Frontier, January and February '61.

LIEUTENANT C. M. S. FAIRBROTHER, late 5th Bengal European Cavalry.
Cornet, 20 Oct. 55—Lieut., 12 Sept. 56.

LIEUTENANT D. W. G. FAIRFIELD, Bengal Artillery.
Lieut., 27 Aug. 58.

LIEUTENANT C. H. FAIRLIE,† late 1st Bengal European Cavalry.
Cornet, 4 Dec. 55—Lieut., 23 Nov. 56.

ASSISTANT-SURGEON J. FAIRWEATHER,† M.D., Bengal Medical Establishment.
Asst.-Surgeon, 4 Aug. 55.

SERVICE.—Assistant-Surgeon J. FAIRWEATHER was present with the 4th Punjab Infantry in the expedition against the Bozdars on the Dehra Ghazee Khan Frontier, in '57. With the same Regiment in an expedition into Eusuffzaie, in July '57, and accompanied it to Delhi. Present at the siege and capture with Brigadier Greathed's Column, at the actions of Boolundshuhur, Allyghur, and Agra, 10th October '57. At Marugunge, under Sir Hope Grant; relief of Lucknow, under Lord Clyde; defeat of Gwalior Troops at Cawnpore, and pursuit and capture of their guns at Seraighat. Passage of Kallah Nuddee, and occupation of Futtehghur; action of Shumshabad under Brigadier Adrian Hope, *(injured by an explosion of the enemy's tumbril,)* and siege and capture of Lucknow. With General Walpole's Force at the attack on the Fort at Rooyah, and engagement of Allygunge. With the Commander-in-Chief's Force at the action of the 5th May '58, and capture of Bareilly. *Medal and 3 Clasps.*

D 1

(218)

CAPTAIN G. FAITHFULL, P. H., late 68th Native Infantry.
Ensign, 12 Dec. 40—Lieut., 3 Dec. 43—Captain, 13 Sept. 53.

SURGEON-MAJOR R. W. FAITHFULL,† Bengal Medical Establishment.
Asst.-Surgeon, 10 Feb. 38—Surgeon, 31 March 51—Surgeon-Major, 13 Jan. 60.
SERVICE.—Surgeon-Major FAITHFULL served in Cabul in '42.

MAJOR R. W. H. FANSHAWE, Invalid Establishment.
Ensign, 12 June 37—Lieut., 3 Oct. 40—Captain, 21 Dec. 45—Major, 5 Feb. 61.
SERVICE.—Major FANSHAWE served in Affghanistan, '39, '40. Present at the storm and capture of Ghuznee. *Medal.* Throughout the Campaign on the Sutlej, including the actions of Ferozepore *(wounded)* and Sobraon. *Medal and Clasp.* In Burmah in '52, '53. Present at the relief of Pegu in December '52; accompanied the Martaban Column to Tonghoo. *Medal.* Received his Majority for his services during the Mutiny.

ASSISTANT-SURGEON T. B. FARNCOMBE,† Bengal Medical Establishment.
Asst.-Surgeon, 20 Feb. 54.
SERVICE.—Assistant-Surgeon FARNCOMBE served in charge of the 31st Native Infantry during the early part of the Sonthal Campaign.

LIEUTENANT J. H. T. FARQUHAR, late 2nd Bengal European Cavalry.
Cornet, 4 Nov. 56—Lieut., 23 Jan. 57.
SERVICE.—Lieutenant FARQUHAR served at the battle of Chinhut, 30th June 57. *(Severely wounded.)* Present throughout the siege of Lucknow, '57. *Medal and Clasp, and 1 year's extra service.*

ASSISTANT-SURGEON T. FARQUHAR,† M.D., Bengal Medical Establishment.
Asst.-Surgeon, 20 Oct. 47.
SERVICE.—Assistant-Surgeon T. FARQUHAR served during the Punjab Campaign, '48, '49.

LIEUTENANT C. E. FARQUHARSON,† late 3rd Bengal European Cavalry.

Cornet, 4 Nov. 56—Lieut., 23 Jan. 57.

SERVICE.—Lieutenant FARQUHARSON served in Oude and in Rohilcund in '58. Present at the battle and capture of Bareilly, May '58. *Medal.*

LIEUTENANT C. J. FARQUHARSON,† late 48th Native Infantry.

Ensign, 4 March 58—Lieut., 29 Oct. 60.

SERVICE.—Lieutenant FARQUHARSON served in the Oude Campaign, '58, '59. *Medal.*

LIEUTENANT F. E. FARQUHARSON, General List, Cavalry.

Cornet, 16 Aug. 59.

MAJOR-GENERAL G. FARQUHARSON, late 46th Native Infantry.

Ensign, 2 Aug. 19—Lieut., 11 June 20—Captain, 20 July 32—Major, 13 March 44—Bt.-Lieut.-Colonel, 7 June 49—Lieut.-Colonel, 21 June 50—Bt.-Colonel, 28 Nov. 54—Colonel, 29 Aug. 59—Major-General, 25 Jan. 61.

SERVICE.—Major-General FARQUHARSON served during the Punjab Campaign, '48, '49. Commanded the 8th Regiment throughout the operations in the vicinity, including the storming of the Dhurmsala, 12th September, and action of Sooroojkhoond, 7th November; siege and surrender of Mooltan, and battle of Goojerat *(dangerously wounded)*. *Medal, Clasp, and Brevet-Lieutenant-Colonel.*

CAPTAIN L. J. FARQUHARSON, P. H., late 3rd Bengal European, Cavalry.

Cornet, 3 Jan. 40—Lieut., 8 May 46—Captain, 21 March 54.

SERVICE.—Captain FARQUHARSON served during the Punjab Campaign, '48, '49. Present at the actions of Chillianwallah and Goojerat. *Medal and 2 Clasps.*

ASSISTANT-SURGEON G. FARRELL,† F.R.C.S., Bengal Medical Establishment.

Asst.-Surgeon, 4 Aug. 56.

SERVICE.—Assistant-Surgeon FARRELL served with the Naval Brigade of H. M.'s S. S. *Shannon*, from August to December '57. Was present at the relief of Lucknow and subsequent actions at Cawnpore, in November in the same year. Served with 2nd Punjab Infantry in the expedition against the Mahsood Wuzeerees, in April and May '60. *Medal and Clasp*.

VETERINARY-SURGEON H. FARRELL, Bengal Veterinary Establishment.

Vety.-Surgeon, 12 April 59.

CAPTAIN O. J. McL. FARRINGTON, P., late 4th Native Infantry.

Ensign, 15 Feb. 40—Lieut., 12 Nov. 42—Captain, 14th Feb. 52.

ASSISTANT-SURGEON J. FAWCUS,† M.D., Bengal Medical Establishment.

Asst.-Surgeon, 10 Feb. 59.

BREVET-SURGEON J. FAYRER, M.D., M.R.C., F.R.C.S.E., P. H., Bengal Medical Establishment.

Asst.-Surgeon, 29 June 50—Bt.-Surgeon, 7 Sept. 58.

SERVICE.—Brevet-Surgeon FAYRER served with the Burmese Field Force during the Burmese War. In Medical Charge of two Companies of H. M.'s 18th Royal Irish Regiment under the Command of Woodright, at the destruction of the stockades on the Rangoon River, previous to the capture of Rangoon, in April '52. Landed at Rangoon in charge of the Field Hospital and continued in that duty throughout the capture of the city stockades, pagoda, and other defences, and also the subsequent operations in the vicinity. Continued to serve in this capacity, and from the 10th December '52 was also officiating as Medical Storekeeper to the Bengal Division of the Army of Burmah, up to August '53, when he was removed to Lucknow. *Medal and Clasp*. Served throughout the siege of Lucknow and the trouble in Oude preceding it. Was a Member of the Council of War assembled by Sir H. Lawrence

(221)

to decide whether to hold or abandon the Residency. Present at Cawnpore when it was relieved by the Commander-in-Chief. Was mentioned in Sir J. Inglis' Despatch of 26th September '57, and received the thanks of Government. Was also included among the Medical Staff mentioned by Sir J. Outram, in his Despatch of 25th November '57. *Medal and Clasp. One year's extra service and Brevet-Surgeon.*

CAPTAIN C. M. N. FELLOWES,† late 3rd Europeans.

Ensign, 12 Jan. 45—Lieut., 15 June 48—Captain, 13 July 58.

SERVICE.—Captain FELLOWES served during the Sutlej Campaign, '45, '46. Present at the action of Sobraon. Served in Bundlecund against the refractory Rajah of Allypora, '51. Served during the Mutiny, '57, '58. Present at the action of 5th July *(wounded)*, Futtehpore, Siekpore, and battle of Agra. Mentioned in the Despatch of Brigadier Polwhele, 5th July '57. *Medal.*

LIEUTENANT H. FELLOWES, P. H., late 31st Native Infantry.

Ensign, 11 Jan. 51—Lieut., 23 Nov. 56.

SERVICE.—Lieutenant FELLOWES served during the Sonthal Campaign, '55, '56. Served during the Mutinies, '57, '58, and '59, in the Saugor and Shahghur Districts. Present in the action of Jahinpore in conjunciton with a part of Sir H. Rose's Force under Brigadier Wheeler, 1st November '58. Present at the capture and re-occupation of Shahghur, 29th March '58. Present at the capture of Town and Fort of Putna, 14th April '58. Thanked in Sir R. Hamilton's Despatch for services in the Field, 17th August '58. *Medal.*

CAPTAIN J FENDALL, P. H., late 17th Native Infantry.

Ensign, 30 Dec. 43—Lieut., 31 Oct. 49—Captain, 23 Nov. 56.

CAPTAIN A. B. FENWICK, P. H., late 5th Europeans.

Ensign, 10 Jan. 37—Lieut., 16 July 42—Bt.-Captain, 10 Jan. 52— Captain, 9 Aug. 54.

SERVICE.—Captain FENWICK served with General Pollock's Force in Affghanistan, in '42. Present in the different engagements leading to the re-occupation of Cabul. *Medal.*

BREVET-MAJOR C. F. FENWICK, late 30th Native Infantry.

Ensign, 21 Jan. 35—Lieut., 13 Oct. 39—Captain, 26 Dec. 46—Bt.-Major, 30 Dec. 59.

SERVICE.—Brevet-Major FENWICK served throughout the Cabul Campaign, '42. Present at the actions on the 19th, 23rd, and 24th January '42, at the mouth of the Khyber Pass. Present at the forcing of the Pass, 5th April. *Medal.* Served throughout the Sutlej Campaign, '46. Present at the action of Alliwal. *Medal.* With the Army of the Punjab, '48, '49. Present at the passage of the Chenab and action of Chillianwallah. *Wounded severely. Medal and Clasp.* Served as Interpreter during the Mutiny, '58, to the 2nd Battalion Rifle Brigade. Present at the capture of Lucknow. *Medal and Clasp.* (*Since retired.*)

LIEUTENANT W. F. FERGUSSON,† late 5th Bengal European Cavalry.

Cornet, 4 Jan. 57—Lieut., 30 April 58.

SERVICE.—Lieutenant FERGUSSON served with the Allahabad Volunteer Cavalry, and was present with General Havelock's Column at all the actions fought by that Force, including the capture of Cawnpore and relief of the Residency. Served with a squadron of the 5th Punjab Irregular Cavalry at the capture of Lucknow, which squadron he commanded at the capture of Bareilly and Shahjehanpore.

LIEUTENANT J. L. FERRIS, late 12th Native Infantry.

Ensign, 4 March 59—Lieut., 2 Feb. 60.

BREVET-CAPTAIN R. J. D. FERRIS, P., late 55th Native Infantry.

Ensign, 10 Dec. 44—Lieut., 30 Dec. 47—Bt.-Captain, 10 Dec. 59.

SERVICE.—Brevet-Captain FERRIS served during the Sutlej Campaign, '45, '46.

MAJOR W. S. FERRIS, P., late 12th Native Infantry.

Ensign, 11 Dec. 37—Lieut., 16 July 42—Captain, 1 Jan. 51—Major, 25 April 58.

SERVICE.—Major FERRIS served throughout the Sutlej Campaign, '45, '46, and was present at the action of Ferozeshuhur. *Medal.* Served also in Burmah in '52, '53. *Medal.* (*Since retired.*)

(223)

LIEUTENANT-GENERAL T. FIDDES, late 42nd Native Infantry.

Ensign, 19 March 05—Lieut., 12 April 05—Captain, 1 Jan. 19—Major, 10 June 26—Lieut.-Colonel, 19 June 31—Colonel, 9 Aug. 43—Major-General, 20 June 54—Lieut.-General, 15 Sept. 56.

SERVICE.—Lieutenant-General FIDDES served at Indore, '05, '06. In Java, '11. *Medal.* Served in Burmah, '24, '25. *Medal.*

VETERINARY-SURGEON J. FIELD, Bengal Veterinary Establishment.

Vety.-Surgeon, 15 July 59.

BREVET-MAJOR H. FINCH, P., late 31st Native Infantry.

Ensign, 19 Aug. 40—Lieut., 24 Jan. 45—Bt.-Captain, 19 Aug. 55—Captain, 28 Nov. 56—Bt.-Major, 20 July 58.

SERVICE.—Brevet-Major FINCH served throughout the Gwalior Campaign. Present at the action of Maharajpore, '43. *Bronze Star.* Served throughout the Punjab Campaign, '48, '49. Present at the passage of the Chenab, actions of Sadoolapore, Chillianwallah, and Goojerat, pursuit of the Sikhs and Affghans to Peshawur, and at the occupation of Attock and Peshawur. *Medal and 2 Clasps.* Present at the forcing of the Kohat Pass, February '50. Present during the Sonthal Campaign, '55, '56, and Commanded 2 Rifle Companies in several skirmishes. Served during the Mutiny, '57, '58. Commanded the station of Dumoh and 500 Native Troops (Cavalry and Infantry) and 2 guns, in July, August, and September '57. Took the Fort of Dumoh, and Rs. 1,30,000, &c., from a mutinous Detachment of the late 42nd Light Infantry; attacked and defeated the rebels at Kounkerea, 19th July '57. Captured the Fort and Town of Hindooreah and 2 guns, 22nd July '57. Defeated the Shahghur Rajah's Force twice when they attacked the station of Dumoh, 28th July and 4th August '57. Present at the fights in Tendee Kera Pass and at Jalimpore, and at the capture and occupation of Shahghur. Commanded a Detachment of half a European Battery, with 400 Infantry and Cavalry, at the fight of Bhopal, on 13th December '57. Commanded a Detachment of Infantry, Cavalry, and 2 guns, and captured the Town and Fort of Putna, 14th April '58. Commanded a Detachment and defeated the rebels who tried to take Fort Gunakota;

taking 70 prisoners and 300 matchlocks, swords, &c., 19th August '58. Captured the Rebel Chief Tulwar Singh and received the Government reward for the same : *wounded* on the 19th July '57. *Medal and Clasps.* Thanked by Major-General Lloyd for services during the Sonthal Campaign, 7th August '55. By the Commissioner of Soorie, for ditto, 11th December '55. Thanked by Brigadier Sage, Commanding Saugor District, for services in the Field, 23rd July '57, and 30th July '57. Thanked by the Right Honorable the Governor-General and His Excellency the Commander-in-Chief for Field Services. Thanked by Brigadier Wheeler, in '58, for Field Services. Thanked by the Lieutenant-Governor of Central Provinces, 12th February '58, for Field Services. Thanked by His Excellency the Commander-in-Chief, 28th May '58, for services at Dumoh. Thanked by the Governor-General, 8th July '58. Thanked by Sir R. Hamilton, 22nd April '58, for Field Services in Despatch of 17 August '58. Thanked by Brigadier Wheeler, 4th September '58, for Field Services. Thanked by Major-General Sir G. C. Whitlock, for Field Services, 28th August '58. Honorably mentioned by Major-General Whitlock, in letter, and thanked by the Governor-General, in General Orders of 9th October '58. Promoted to Brevet-Majority for services during the Mutinies, 20th July '58.

VETERINARY-SURGEON J. FINN, Bengal Veterinary Establishment.

Vety.-Surgeon, 8 Dec. 59.

LIEUTENANT J. FINNIS, late 5th Europeans.

Ensign, 12 Dec. 57—Lieut., 8 Dec. 60.

LIEUTENANT R. F. FIRTH,† late 65th Native Infantry.

Ensign, 17 March 55—Lieut., 14 June 57.

MAJOR G. A. FISHER, late 4th Europeans.

Ensign, 29 Dec. 31—Lieut., 1 Feb. 37—Bt.-Captain, 9 June 46—Captain, 31 Oct. 48—Bt.-Major, 14 Nov. 58—Major, 13 March 59.

(225)

LIEUTENANT G. B. FISHER,† late 32nd Native Infantry.
Ensign, 20 Dec. 56—Lieut., 2 Aug. 57.

LIEUTENANT H. S. V. FISHER, P. H., late 30th Native Infantry.
Ensign, 28 July 50—Lieut., 13 Oct. 55.

LIEUTENANT J. F. L. FISHER, P. H., late 19th Native Infantry.
Ensign, 20 Dec. 48—Lieut., 1 Nov. 50.

LIEUTENANT V. C. FISHER, Bengal Artillery.
Lieut., 11 Dec. 58.

LIEUTENANT W. P. FISHER, P. H., late 4th Europeans.
Ensign, 13 June 51—Lieut., 14 Oct. 55.

SERVICE.—Lieutenant FISHER served at the assault and capture of the Bozdar stronghold, on the Derajat Frontier, in March '57; also during the Mutiny, '57, '58. Present at the siege, assault, and capture of Delhi, including the battle of Nudjufghur. Served under Colonel Greathed after the fall of Delhi. Present at the battles of Boolundshuhur and Agra, relief of Lucknow, battles of Cawnpore and Khodagunge (near Futtehghur), siege and capture of Lucknow, and re-occupation of Bareilly, besides many other minor affairs. *Medal and 3 Clasps.*

LIEUTENANT A. FITZGERALD,† General List.
Ensign, 16 June 59—Lieut., 1 March 61.

BREVET-MAJOR C. M. FITZGERALD, P., late 31st Native Infantry.
Ensign, 20 June 43—Lieut., 17 Aug. 46—Bt.-Captain, 20 June 58—Captain, 14 Aug. 59—Bt.-Major, 15 Aug. 59.

SERVICE.—Major FITZGERALD served as Deputy Assistant Commissary-General in the Burmah War, '52, '53. *Pegu Medal.* Served in the same capacity in Commissariat Charge of the Punjab Moveable Column, June and July '57. Present at the affair of Trimmoo Ghaut, 12th July '57. *(Dangerously wounded.)* Received the commendation of Government for equipping the Column, 18th August '57. Served in Brigadier T. Seaton's Column, from Delhi to Futtehghur, November and December '57. Served with the Army under His Excellency the Commander-in-Chief, at Futtehghur, January '58, as Commissariat Officer. Present at the capture of Lucknow. *Medal and Clasp.* Mentioned in His Excellency the Commander-in-Chief's Despatch, 16th April '58. Received the thanks of Government, 5th April '58. Served as Principal Commissariat Officer with the troops employed in the subjugation of Oude, '58, '59. Present at the engagement with Bein Madhul's force, and the affairs of Bingidia, Majidda, and Raptee. Received the thanks of Lord Clyde, 21st January '59. Promoted to the rank of Brevet-Major for services during the Mutiny, 14th August '59. Joined the Expeditionary Force to China in March '60. Served in the Sikhim Expedition in '60, '61, and honorably mentioned in G. O. G. G., 12th September '61.

ASSISTANT-SURGEON E. A. FITZGERALD,† Bengal Medical Establishment.

Asst.-Surgeon, 27 July 59.

LIEUTENANT E. T. FITZGERALD, P., late 66th Native Infantry.

Ensign, 20 Dec. 55—Lieut., 12 Feb. 58.

SERVICE.—Lieutenant FITZGERALD served in defence of the Kumaon Hills and Rohilcund against the rebels in '57, '58. Present at the action of Chapoorah, 10th February '58.

LIEUTENANT J. FITZGERALD, P. H., late 10th Native Infantry.

Ensign, 16 June 56—Lieut., 30 April 58.

2ND CAPTAIN M. M. FITZGERALD, P. H., Bengal Artillery.

1st Lieut., 9 Dec. 50—2nd Captain, 10 Feb. 60.

SERVICE.—Captain FITZGERALD served with the Force under Brigadier-General Chamberlain in Meranzaie and Koorum, '56, and against the Bozdar Beloochees, in March '57. Present at the siege and capture of Delhi, '57, and accompanied with the Moveable Column under Brigadier Showers. *Medal and Clasp.*

(227)

CAPTAIN W. R. FITZGERALD, P. H., Bengal Artillery.
2nd Lieut., 7 June 44—Lieut., 5 July 46—Captain, 27 April 58.

LIEUTENANT W. H. B. FITZGERALD, late 14th Native Infantry.
Ensign, 15 Aug. 57—Lieut., 22 Aug. 58.

LIEUTENANT A. FITZHUGH, P. H., late 21st Native Infantry.
Ensign, 7 Dec. 55—Lieut., 23 Nov. 56.

2ND CAPTAIN F. FITZROY, Bengal Artillery.
Lieut., 26 July 57—2nd Captain,————.

SURGEON A. FLEMING,† M.D., Bengal Medical Establishment.
Asst.-Surgeon, 29 Sept. 45—Surgeon, 26 April 59.

ASSISTANT-SURGEON J. McN. FLEMING,† M.D., Bengal Medical Establishment.
Asst.-Surgeón, 27 July 59.

LIEUTENANT-COLONEL T. F. FLEMYNG, late 36th Native Infantry.
Ensign, 14 Jan. 24—Lieut., 6 May 25—Bt.-Captain, 14 Jan. 39—Captain, 12 June 41—Bt.-Major, 19 June 46—Bt.-Lieut.-Colonel, 7 June 49—Major, 10 June 52—Lieut.-Colonel, 31st May 57—Bt.-Colonel, 28 May 54.

SERVICE.—Lieutenant-Colonel FLEMYNG served at the siege of Bhurtpore. *Medal.* During the Sutlej Campaign, '45, '46, including the action of Alliwal. *Medal, and Brevet-Majority.* Served during the Punjab Campaign, '48, '49. Present at the passage of the Chenab and actions of Ramnuggur, Sadoolapore, and Chillianwallah. *Medal, Clasp, and Brevet-Colonel.*

LIEUTENANT C. W. FLETCHER, P. H., late 48th Native Infantry.
Ensign, 20 June 50—Lieut., 5 June 53.

SERVICE—Lieutenant FLETCHER served throughout the defence of the residency of Lucknow, from 1st July '57 until its final relief by Lord

Clyde, in November '57; *severely wounded,* shot through left arm. He lost the use of his left hand whilst on duty as Look-out Officer on the top of the Residency, on 18th August '57. *Medal and Clasp, and one year's extra service.*

CORNET H. A. FLETCHER, General List, Cavalry.

Cornet, 4 Sept. 60.

LIEUTENANT R. J. FOLEY,† late 62nd Native Infantry.

Ensign, 26 July 57—Lieut., 18 May 58.

SERVICE.—Lieutenant FOLEY served with the Army under Lord Clyde, '58, '59. Present at the siege and capture of Lucknow, March '58; at the taking of Bareilly and relief of Shahjehanpore. Served in the Oude Campaign, '58, '59. *Medal and Clasp.* Served with the China Expeditionary Force in '60, '61.

MAJOR G. A. St. P. FOOKS, P. H., late 50th Native Infantry.

Ensign, 21 Aug. 40—Lieut., 24 Jan. 45—Bt.-Captain, 21 Aug. 55—Captain, 19 May 58—Major in Staff Corps, 18 Feb. 61.

SERVICE.—Major FOOKS served in the Saugor and Nerbudda Districts, '42, '43. Present at the battle of Punniar, 29th December '43. *Bronze Star.* Served during the Punjab Campaign, '48, '49. *Medal.* Commanded a Detachment of the 37th and 50th Native Infantry during the Sonthal Campaign, '55. Received the thanks of the Brigadier Commanding the Field Force, having been in five skirmishes with the rebels.

CAPTAIN W. K. FOOKS, P. H., Bengal Artillery.

2nd Lieut., 10 Dec. 41—Lieut., 3 July 45—Captain, 30 Oct. 55.

SERVICE.—Captain FOOKS served during the Sutlej Campaign. Present at the battle of Sobraon. *Medal.* Served during the Punjab Campaign, '48, '49. Present at the siege and surrender of Mooltan, battle of Goojerat, and pursuit of the Sikhs and Affghans to Peshawur. *Medal and 2 Clasps.*

LIEUTENANT F. B. FOOTE, late 71st Native Infantry.

Ensign, 11 Dec. 49—Lieut., 1 Sept. 54.

SERVICE.—Lieutenant FOOTE served with the Force under Sir C. Campbell, against the Hill Tribes on the Peshawur Frontier, '51. Served during the Mutinies, '57, '58. Present at the siege and capture of Lucknow, '58. *Medal and Clasp.* Mentioned in the Despatches of Brigadier-General MacGregor, 15th February '58, and 20th March '58. Received the thanks of Government, 19th January '58. Employed in several occasions while in Command of Hoshungabad Military Police Battalion against rebels in the Hoshungabad District, and received thanks of the Lieutenant-Governor, N. W. P., on two occasions.

LIEUTENANT F. M. H. FORBES, P. H., late 39th Native Infantry.

Ensign, 10 Dec. 47—Lieut., 13 Nov. 53.

SERVICE.—Lieutenant FORBES served during the Mutiny of '57, in Eusuffzaie, as Adjutant, 5th Punjab Infantry and Field Staff. Present at the storm and capture of Narinjee, in Eusuffzaie, and other minor affairs which then took place.

BREVET-MAJOR H. FORBES, P. H., late 1st Bengal European Cavalry.

Cornet, 3 Oct. 44—Lieut., 31 March 51—Captain, 25 Oct. 56— Bt-Major, 20 July 58.

SERVICE.—Major FORBES served in the Sutlej Campaign, '46. Present at the actions of Moodkee, *(horse killed under him,)* Ferozeshuhur, and Sobraon. *Medal and 2 Clasps.* Served during the Punjab Campaign, '48, '49. Present at the actions of Chillianwallah and Goojerat. *Medal and Clasp.* Was a Member of the Lucknow Garrison in '57. *Slightly wounded.* Mentioned in the Despatch of Brigadier Inglis, 12th November '57. Present at the battle of Cawnpore, under Lord Clyde. *Slightly wounded.* Served as Brigade Major in the final operations against Lucknow, March '58. Mentioned in the Despatch of Brigadier Campbell, 16th April '58. *Medal and 2 Clasps, and one year's extra service.* Promoted to the rank of Brevet-Major for services at the capture of Lucknow.

(230)

2ND CAPTAIN H. T. FORBES, P. H., Bengal Artillery.

2nd Lieut., 11 Dec. 49—Lieut., 22 Aug. 55—2nd Captain, 27 Aug. 58.

LIEUTENANT L. FORBES, P. H., late 2nd Native Infantry.

Ensign, 20 Sept. 48—Lieut., 17 May 53.

SERVICE.—Lieutenant FORBES served during the Sonthal Campaign, '56. Served during the Mutinies, '57, '58. *Medal*. Commanded the Etawah Yeomanry Levy and Etawah Military Police Battalion at the action of Hurchundpore, the taking of the Fort of Burreh, in the Jumna River, and six other minor affairs. Received thanks of the Government of India, 22nd December '58. Received high commendations of the Governor-General for the operations against Fort Burreh. Recorded for promotion for Brevet-Majority for services during the Mutinies, as soon as he attains the rank of Captain.

LIEUTENANT R. O. H. FORBES, P. H., late 3rd Europeans.

Ensign, 30 Aug. 48—Lieut., 1 Sept. 55.

SERVICE.—Lieutenant FORBES served during the Mutinies, '57, '58. Present at the battle of Agra, 10th October; in the affair of Futtehpore-Sikree, 28th October '57. Also with the Agra Column towards Gwalior, June '58. *Medal*.

CAPTAIN W. FORBES,† late 27th Native Infantry.

Ensign, 25 Jan. 41—Lieut., 16 July 42—Captain, 5 July 49.

SERVICE.—Captain FORBES served during the Sutlej Campaign, '45. Present at the battle of Ferozeshuhur. *Medal*.

LIEUTENANT W. E. FORBES, P. C. H., Bengal Artillery.

Lieut., 10 Dec. 58.

CAPTAIN G. E. FORD,† late 72nd Native Infantry.

Enisgn, 21 Dec. 37—Lieut., 16 July 42—Captain, 17 March 51.

LIEUTENANT H. T. E. FORD, Bengal Artillery.

Lieut., 27 Aug. 58.

(231)

COLONEL J. FORDYCE, Bengal Artillery.

2nd Lieut., 10 May 22—Lieut., 25 March 26—Bt.-Captain, 10 May 37—Captain, 29 April 40—Bt.-Major, 19 June 46—Major, 2 Feb. 51—Bt.-Lieut.-Colonel, 7 June 49—Lieut.-Colonel, 8 June 56—Bt.-Colonel, 28 Nov. 54—Colonel, 18 Feb. 61.

SERVICE.—Colonel FORDYCE served during the Campaign on the Sutlej, '45, '46, including the battles of Ferozeshuhur and Sobraon. *Medal and 1 Clasp.* Served with the Army of the Punjab, '48, '49, including the actions of Chillianwallah and Goojerat. *Medal, 2 Clasps, and Brevet-Lieutenant-Colonel.*

LIEUTENANT W. J. FORLONG,† late 55th Native Infantry.

Ensign, 13 Dec. 56—Lieut., 30 April 58.

SERVICE.—Lieutenant FORLONG served during the Mutiny, '57, '58. Present during the operations against the Gwalior Contingent at Cawnpore, in December '57, and at the siege and capture of Lucknow. *Medal and Clasp.* Served during the Oude Campaign, '58, '59. Present at the engagements of Nawabgunge, occupation of Sultanpore, and other engagements leading to the re-occupation of Oude. Mentioned in the Despatch of Brigadier Horsford, 27th April '59.

COLONEL H. FORSTER, C.B., Retired List.

Cornet, 16—Lieut., 18—Local-Major, 35—Major, 19 June 46—Lieut.-Colonel, 20 June 54—Colonel, 20 June 57.

SERVICE.—Colonel FORSTER served in the Mahrattah and Pindarree Campaigns under Sir D. Ochterlony. Was present when Ameer Khan surrendered, and his Army dispersed, '18. Present with the Force detached under General Sir A. Knox to Sambhur, when Jam Shade Khan surrendered 47 pieces of artillery, and his force was dispersed. Commanded a Squadron and 2 guns to guard the Chumble Ford, near Rampoora Bhanpoora, in '19. Captured some Sirdars from Jawud, attempting to escape; and was detached to the aid of the Political Agent at Rutlam. Surprised and destroyed a body of insurgents near Jhubboa, and recovered much property which they had plundered. Joined the

Troops at Mhow, in '20, under Sir J. Malcolm, and was present at the Settlement of Dhar Provinces. From thence, was employed in suppressing the inroads of the Gonds and Bheels. Received high commendations for the successful results from the General Commanding. Proceeded with 90 Horsemen, in '26,' against Nuthoo, a malcontent in Bhopal District; took his Fort by a *coup-de-main* after a night march of 56 miles, recovered much property, received high commendation from the Commander-in-Chief, and the Political Authorities, and General Stewart, Commanding the Saugor Division : 1,200 head of cattle captured. Was nominated to raise and command the Rungpore Horse during the Burmese War, '26. Served under Major-General Sir J. Arnold at Saugor. Was present at the taking of the Fort at Narhet, and dispersion of the mutineers of Scindiah's troops. On the general reduction of the Army, the Rungpore Cavalry were incorporated in the 6th Irregular Cavalry, and he was employed under Captain Drummond, Assistant Quarter-Master-General. The fortified position in the village of Handsir was attacked; their leader, a Kuzzuk Chief, taken prisoner, several of his followers killed, and the rest dispersed. Received the approbation of the Governor-General in Council, with high commendations from the Chief Political Authorities. The Town and Citadel of Seeker, in June '36, was stormed, and taken with 8 guns, after a sharp action, where many lives were lost on both sides. The Fort of Khialee, in the occupation of noted Kuzzuks, was attacked and taken in '37, the insurgents routed, and the Fort destroyed. In January '38, a Detachment of all arms stormed the Hill Fort of Goodha and took it, the insurgents having refused obedience to the Jeypore Government; also the strong Fort of Dialpoora and Máwá were attacked and taken in Marwar, and the malcontents secured, the Chief brought in prisoner to the Head Quarters at Joonjnoo. Recruited and disciplined a body of 400 sepoys, in '38, for Lieutenant-Colonel McSherry, who was engaged to assist Shah-Soohjah-ool-Moolk during the first Cabul Campaign, and received high commendations for the prompt and efficient aid thus afforded. In '38 proceeded to the strong fortified Town of Tooliasir with a Detachment of all Arms in Beekaneer, to coerce a large body of marauders who had set the Rajah and his Troops at defiance. After a night march of 26 miles through the desert, attacked

(233)

and carried the defences by storm, in which encounter 80 of the marauders were killed, and 120 prisoners taken, with all their plundered property, for which service gratifying public acknowledgments were received, and a presentation of a valuable sword from Maha Rajah Rutten Singh of Beekaneer. In Command of the entire Brigade in '39, and formed a part of the British Division assembled at Joudpore, under Command of Major-General Hampton, to enforce obedience of Rajah Maun Singh to the dictates of the British Government. Proceeded in May '39 with the Brigade to Bugroo, where the refractory Thakoor set the authority of the Political Agent at defiance : this was efficiently performed, and the Thakoor's force dispersed. In '40, the Brigade, joined by a quota of Jeypore Troops placed under his Command, laid siege to the Hill Fort of Kaluk, held by a strong party of insurgents, which after seventeen days' siege surrendered, and the Chief and Garrison taken prisoners. Major Forster was during *the storm severely wounded in three places.* Received the high acknowledgments and approbation of the Governor-, General in Council, and of the Political Authorities present in Camp. In '43, a large assemblage of insurgents took possession of the strong Fort of Khettree and of the Pass of Kotadeh. With the portion of the Brigade left at Joonjnoo, it was determined to attack this formidable position, being joined with a small Force from Jeypore, and Captain (now Major) W. R. forster arriving from his Command at Joudpore, the attack was at once made, the Pass cleared, and after two days' contest the final evacuation of the Fort by the enemy followed, the Forts of Kotepootlee and Khurb also fell, and the insurgents were dispersed. Had the honor to be publicly thanked by the Governor-General in Council, and by the principal Political Authorities in Rajpootanah for these successes. Received high acknowledgments from the Civil Authorities at Hissar, in '44, and the Resident of Delhi, for suppression of dacoities on the British Frontier Districts in that quarter. Received autograph approval of proceedings in Shekawattee from the Governor-General, the Earl of Auckland, with most gratifying expressions of commendation. The entire Brigade joined the British Army in '46, then operating on the Sutlej under General Sir H. Smith. Present at the battle of Alliwal. *Medal. (Horse shot under him.)* The Brigade had the honor to be especially noticed in the Houses of Parliament by His

(234)

Grace the Duke of Wellington, and also Lord Auckland, the late Governor-General of India. The Brigade was subsequently placed under the orders of Brigadier, the late Sir Hugh Wheeler, when his Force crossed the Sutlej for the occupation of Phillour and Jullundur, in the Punjab. Had the honor to receive the congratulations of the Earl of Ellenborough, late Governor-General of India, for the distinguished services of the Shekawattee Brigade, (3rd April '40,) as also high and flattering commendations of Lord Hardinge, who, after personal inspection of the Brigade, offered his public approval on the ground. The Shekawattee Battalion has now the honor to be a numbered Corps of the Line, (13th Regiment,) whose loyalty during the mutinies was severely tested, and found staunch and deserving. During the Mutiny, '57, the Regiment was employed on Field Service, having a Naval Brigade of Europeans, against insurgents in Maunbhoom and Singbhoom Districts; and subsequently in February '58 being appointed Commissioner of Sumbulpore. The following Troops came under his Command, *viz.*, 5th and 40th Madras Native Infantry, the E. Company, 5th Battalion Madras Artillery, a Detachment of the Ramghur Irregular Cavalry and Infantry, besides the Shekawattee Regiment, and six hundred Sebundees under Command of Captain Bird. Colonel Forster has been honored by Her Gracious Majesty with the most Honorable Military Order of the Bath. *India Medal.* *(Since dead.)*

CAPTAIN T. F. FORSTER, P., late 39th Native Infantry.

Ensign, 13 Dec. 45—Lieut., 28 Nov. 49—Captain, 13 Dec. 60.

SERVICE.—Captain FORSTER served as a Volunteer during the Sutlej Campaign, '46. Present at the battle of Alliwal. *Medal.*

MAJOR W. R. FORSTER, (Unattached,) Commandant of the Shekawattee Battalion.

Captain, 29 July 52—Major, 8 Oct. 60.

SERVICE.—Major FORSTER was employed in January '37 with a Detachment of the Shekawattee Brigade, (Cavalry, Infantry, and Guns,) under Major H. Forster, in operations against some insurgents occupying the Village and Fort of Khialee, in Rajpootanah, from whence they were routed, and that stronghold blown up and destroyed. On the 25th January '38, served at the attack and capture by storm of the Hill-Fort of Goodha, in Rajpootanah, occupied by a party of insurgents who refused obedience to the Jeypore Government. In August, September, and October '39, served as 2nd in Command with the Shekawattee Brigade, which Corps formed part of the British Division assembled before Joudpore (in Marwar—Rajpootanah), under Major-General Hampton, to enforce the obedience of Rajah Maun Singh to the dictates of the British Government. In December '40 served with the Shekawattee Brigade, which, in conjunction with a quota of Troops in the service of the Rajah of Jeypore, laid siege to the Hill Fort of Kaluk (in Rajpootanah), held by a strong party of insurgents. Was engaged with the storming party in the assault on the out-works of Kaluk Hill Fort, on the 16th December '40, and served throughout the siege up to the period when the fortress fell. In June '43, proceeded from Joonjnoo, in Shekawattee, to Joudpore, in Command of a Wing of the Shekawattee Brigade (Cavalry and Infantry), and relieved the Joudpore Legion, which, under Captain Winter, marched on to Omercote, to assist General Sir Charles Napier's operations in Scinde. On 6th November '43, served with the Shekawattee Brigade, and was present at the forcing of the Pass of "Kotadeh," and subsequent action of Khettree (in Rajpootanah) with the rebels. In '45, '46, served during the Sutlej Campaign, with the Army under General Sir H. Smith, and on the 28th January '46, commanded the Infantry of the Brigade at the battle of Alliwal. *Medal.* Was present also with the Shekawattee Brigade under Brigadier Sir Hugh Wheeler, when his Force crossed the Sutlej for the occupation of Phillour and Jullundur, in the Punjab, in March and April '47. On the requisition of Colonel J. Sutherland, the Governor-General's Agent in Rajpootanah, for the services of a body of Cavalry, was directed by Major H. Forster, Commanding the Shekawattee Brigade, to proceed in Command of 400 Horse of the Shekawattee Cavalry in pursuit after the noted free-booter Doongur Sing and his band of Kuzzuks, (mounted marauders,)

(236)

who made a sudden and unexpected descent into Agra, attacked the Civil Guard, and after liberating some prisoners from jail, fled into the deserts of Beekaneer, Jessulmere, and Marwar, where, after a long and tedious pursuit, this banditti were broken up and dispersed. During the Mutiny of the Bengal Native Army, and rebellion in India, marched with the Shekawattee Battalion from Midnapore, in December '57, and was present on Field Service with this Corps, and a Naval Brigade of Europeans under Colonel H. Forster, C.B., employed against insurgents in the Maunbhoom and Singbhoom Districts; and subsequently in February '58, proceeded with the Shekawattee Battalion to quell disturbances in the Sumbulpoor District, where the 5th and 40th Madras Native Infantry, the E. Company, 5th Battalion Madras Artillery, and Detachments of the Ramghur Irregular Cavalry and Infantry were also employed. *Medal and Rank of Major.*

CAPTAIN A. G. FORSYTH, P. H., late 3rd Europeans.

Ensign, 7 Feb. 43—Lieut., 29 July 45—Captain, 1 Jan. 57.

SERVICE.—Captain FORSYTH served during the Punjab Campaign, '48, '49. *Medal.* Present at the action of Sadoolapore, '48; the two actions at Agra, '57; and at Dewsa, '58. *Medal.*

PRINCIPAL INSPECTOR-GENERAL G. FORSYTH, Bengal Medical Establishment.

Asst.-Surgeon, 10 Jan. 20—Surgeon, 18 Nov. 30—Principal Insptr-General, 12 Nov. 57.

SERVICE.—Principal Inspector-General FORSYTH served as Senior Surgeon in Shah Soojah's Force in Affghanistan. Present at the capture of Ghuznee, and accompanied the expedition in the Koonar Valley. Present at the capture of the Fort of Pushoot, under Colonel Orchard, and served in the Valley against the Saugoo Khel, under Brigadier Shelton. Served with General Sale's Brigade from the Koord Cabul Pass to Jellallabad, and was present at the affairs of Tazeen, Jugdulluck, and Mamoo Khel; defence of Jellallabad, action of 7th April '42, and re-occupation of Cabul, under General Pollock. *3 Medals and 3rd Class*

Dooranee Order. Several times received the thanks of Government, and of the Governor-General.

LIEUTENANT J. FORSYTH, late 49th Native Infantry.

Ensign, 20 Feb. 57—Lieut., 30 April 58.

SERVICE.—Lieutenant FORSYTH served with a Detachment of the 22nd Punjab Infantry, in Seetapore and Mohumdee Districts, in November and December '58. Served with a Detachment of the 17th Punjab Infantry, in February, March, and April '59, on the Rohilcund Frontier. Served with the 17th Punjab Infantry under Brigadier Wheeler, in '59, and commanded two Companies of the Regiment from the 5th December '59 to 1st April '60.

ENSIGN E. F. FORTESCUE, late 34th Native Infantry.

Ensign, 4 Feb. 58.

CAPTAIN F. R. N. FORTESCUE, P., late 73rd Native Infantry.

Ensign, 20 Sept. 45—Lieut., 7 April 51—Captain, 31 March 60.

SERVICE.—Captain FORTESCUE served during the Punjab Campaign, '48, '49. *Medal.*

LIEUTENANT G. V. FOSBERY,† late 4th Europeans.

Ensign, 20 Jan. 52—Lieut., 1 July 57.

CAPTAIN C. S. FOWLE,† late 22nd Native Infantry.

Ensign, 24 Sept. 42—Lieut., 3 June 45—Bt.-Captain, 24 Sept. 57—Captain, 4 Aug. 59.

SERVICE.—Captain FOWLE served throughout the Punjab Campaign of '48, '49. *Medal.* Present with his Regiment at Fyzabad, at the time it mutinied on the 8th June '57, escaped from that station, and eventually reached Dinapore, after having been twice taken prisoner. On arrival at Dinapore was posted to the 8th Regiment, which mutinied shortly afterwards. Escaped, taking charge of two ladies, from the rebels at Hazareebaugh, in the middle of July '57.

(238)

LIEUTENANT E. S. FOX, P. H., late 72nd Native Infantry.
Ensign, 11 June 53—Lieut., 23 Nov. 56.

LIEUTENANT S. FOX, Veteran Establishment.
Lieut., 31 Aug. 57.

SERVICE.—Lieutenant Fox served with the Joudpore Field Force, '39. With the Bundlecund Field Force, '42, '43. Present at the battle of Maharajpore, '43. *Bronze Star*. With the Army of the Sutlej, '45, '46. Present at the battles of Moodkee, Ferozeshuhur, and Sobraon. *Medal and 2 Clasps*. Served during the Punjab Campaign, '48, '49. Present at the actions of Ramnuggur, Sadoolapore, Chillianwallah, and Goojerat; and accompanied the Field Force under Sir W. Gilbert, on its advance to Peshawur. *Medal and 2 Clasps*.

CAPTAIN A. FRANCIS, P. H., late 68th Native Infantry.
Ensign, 11 June 47—Lieut., 21 Nov. 51—Captain, 15 May 59.

SERVICE.—Captain FRANCIS served in the Burmese War, '52, '53. *Medal*. Served during the Mutiny in Goruckpore and Oude, from January to June '58. Present at the battle of Phoolpore on 20th February '58. Mentioned in Brigadier-General MacGregor's Despatch, 17th March '58; also in Brigadier Rowcroft's Despatch, 20th March '58. Present at the battle of Pandoo Nuddee, 5th March '58. Mentioned in Brigadier-General MacGregor's Despatch, 31st March '58. Also in Captain Plowden's Despatch, Captain Lane's, and in the *Government Gazette*. Present at the siege and capture of Lucknow, March '58. *Medal and Clasp*. Served in the Sarun District under Brigadier Douglas, C.B., '58, '59.

SURGEON C. R. FRANCIS, M.B., P. C. H., Bengal Medical Establishment.
Asst.-Surgeon, 16 Jan. 44—Surgeon, 4 Aug. 57.

(239)

BREVET-MAJOR H. FRANCIS, P. H.,† Bengal Artillery.
2nd Lieut., 8 Jan. 42—Lieut., 3 July 45—Bt.-Captain, 8 Jan. 57—Captain, 1 Feb. 57—Bt.-Major, 26 April 59.
SERVICE.—Major FRANCIS served at the action of Sobraon. *Medal.* Served with the Army of the Punjab. Present at the siege and surrender of Mooltan and battle of Goojerat. *Medal and 2 Clasps.*

LIEUTENANT H. W. FRANKS,† late 20th Native Infantry.
Ensign, 12 June 58—Lieut., 27 Aug. 58.

LIEUTENANT R. R. FRANKS, Bengal Artillery.
1st Lieut., 28 Sept. 57.

LIEUTENANT W. A. FRANKS, late 12th Native Infantry.
Ensign, 4 Oct. 55—Lieut., 19 June 57
SERVICE.—Lieutenant FRANKS served during the Mutiny. *Medal.*

CAPTAIN A. FRASER,† Bengal Engineers.
2nd Lieut., 8 Dec. 43—Lieut., 9 Nov. 48—Captain, 14 Sept. 57.

2ND CAPTAIN A. FRASER,† Bengal Artillery.
2nd Lieut., 12 Dec. 45—Lieut., 1 July 51—2nd Captain, 27 Aug. 58.

LIEUTENANT E. FRASER, Bengal Artillery.
1st Lieut., 27 March 58.

BREVET-CAPTAIN G. L. FRASER, P., late 23rd Native Infantry.
Ensign, 4 July 45—Lieut., 5 June 53—Bt.-Captain, 4 July 60.
SERVICE.—Captain FRASER served in the Sutlej Campaign, '46. In the Punjab Campaign, '49. Present at the action of Goojerat. *Medal and Clasp.* Mentioned in Despatch of Brigadier Markham and General Whish, 1st March '59. Served in the Expedition to Kohat, '50, as Detachment Staff and Special Commissioner with Colonel Maxwell's Moveable Column in the Cawnpore District, from February to June '58.

Present at siege and capture of Calpee. Mentioned in Colonel Maxwell's Despatch, 1st March '59. *Medal and Clasp.*

CAPTAIN G. W. FRASER, P. H., late 27th Native Infantry.

Ensign, 9 June 43—Lieut., 3 Nov. 46—Captain, 23 Sept. 57.

SERVICE.—Captain FRASER served during the Sutlej Campaign, '45, '46. *Medal.*

CAPTAIN J. E. FRASER, P., late 4th Native Infantry.

Ensign, 11 Dec. 40—Lieut., 16 April 44—Captain, 15 Nov. 53.

SERVICE.—Captain FRASER served during the Punjab Campaign, '48, '49. *Medal.* Served during the Mutiny in '57. *Medal.*

LIEUTENANT THE HONORABLE J. H. FRASER,† late 4th Europeans.

Ensign, 20 Feb. 52—Lieut., 23 Nov. 56.

CAPTAIN THE HONORABLE W. M. FRASER, P. H., late 44th Native Infantry.

Ensign, 11 Dec. 49—Lieut., 30 March 53—Captain, 19 June 59.

LIEUTENANT J. F. FREE, Bengal Artillery.

Lieut., 27 Aug. 58.

LIEUTENANT F. P. W. FREEMAN,† late 53rd Native Infantry.

Ensign, 7 Dec. 55—Lieut., 30 April 58.

LIEUTENANT F. P. W. FREEMAN, Bengal Artillery.

Lieut., 8 June 60.

BREVET-MAJOR J. S. FRITH, P. H., Bengal Artillery.

2nd Lieut., 14 June 45—Lieut., 25 March 49—Bt.-Captain, 27 Aug. 58—Bt.-Major, 28 Aug. 58.

SERVICE.—Major FRITH served with Brigadier Wheeler's Force in the Punjab, '48, '49. *Medal.* Served during the Mutiny Campaign. *Medal and Brevet-Majority.*

(241)

ASSISTANT-SURGEON R. FRYER,† Bengal Medical Establishment.
Asst.-Surgeon, 4 Aug. 56.

SERVICE.—Assistant-Surgeon FRYER served with the 64th Foot with Havelock's Force in the advance from Allahabad. Was present at the actions of Futtehpore, Aoung, Pandoo Nuddee, Cawnpore, Oonao, and Busseerutgunge; returned to Cawnpore in charge of sick and wounded on 4th August '57, and was attached to the Field Hospital of that station by the orders of General Neill. Was present during the whole of General Wyndham's engagement with the Gwalior rebels, and at their defeat by Sir Colin Campbell. *Medal.*

2ND CAPTAIN A. R. FULLER, P., Bengal Artillery.
2nd Lieut., 14 Jan. 45—Lieut., 15 Jan. 49—2nd Captain, 27 Aug. 58.

SERVICE.—Captain FULLER served in the action of Shahgunge, near Agra, 5th July '57, under Brigadier Polwhele; at the battle of Agra, 10th October '57, under Colonels Cotton and Greathed. *Medal.*

CAPTAIN W. FULLERTON, P., late 14th Native Infantry.
Ensign, 26 March 39—Lieut., 10 June 42—Captain, 14 Sept. 53.

SERVICE.—Captain FULLERTON served with the Army of Exercise, '43. Present at the action of Maharajpore, 29th December '43. *Bronze Star.* Served during the Sutlej Campaign, '45. Present at the action of Ferozeshuhur on 21st, 22nd, and 23rd December '45. Mentioned in the Despatch of Sir J. Littler, January and February '46. *Medal.*

BREVET-CAPTAIN J. FULTON, P. H., Bengal Artillery.
2nd Lieut., 14 June 45—Lieut., 5 May 49—Bt.-Captain, 27 Aug. 58.

SERVICE.—Captain FULTON served with the expedition to Kôt Kangra, '46, and in the Punjab with the Force under Brigadier Wheeler, '48, '49. *Medal.*

(242)

BREVET-LIEUTENANT-COLONEL FYTCHE, P. H., 12th (late 70th) Native Infantry.

Ensign, 11 Dec. 38—Lieut., 17 Aug. 40—Captain, 1 April 53—Bt.-Major, 9 Dec. 53—Bt.-Lieut.-Colonel, 26 June 60.

SERVICE.—Colonel FYTCHE commanded the Detachment of the Arracan Local Battalion employed against the Walleng Hill Tribes on the Arracan Frontier, in '41, '42, and took the Walleng Hill stockade by storm. Thanked in District Orders, 11th January '42, by Lieutenant-Colonel Pogson, and Service performed brought to the favorable notice of His Excellency the Commander-in-Chief. Served with the Army of the Punjab in '48, '49. Present at the actions of Chillianwallah and Goojerat, *wounded severely*, and in the subsequent pursuit of the Sikhs and Affghans by the Force under General Sir Walter Gilbert. *Medal and 2 Clasps*. Raised and commanded an Irregular Force, with which in conjunction with a party of Seamen and Marines under the Command of Commander Rennie, I. N., he defeated the Burmese Chiefs Ngathein and Moung-tha-bon on the 22nd and 23rd January '53, and the Burmese Governor of the Province of Bassein on the 29th of the same month, capturing nine guns, and upwards of three thousand stand of arms. Received the special thanks and warm approbation of the Governor-General, 19th March '53. Co-operated with the Force under Brigadier-General Sir John Cheape, during the month of March '53, against the Force under Myattoon, in the vicinity of Donabew. *(Wounded.)* Brought to the notice of the Governor-General of India in the Despatch of Brigadier-General Sir John Cheape, and "received the special thanks and full approbation" of the Government of India, 5th May '53. *Pegu Medal and Clasp*, and promoted to the rank of Brevet-Major. Quelled a rebellion of the Burmese in the Bassein District, Pegu, in February '54, with a small Force of Regular Troops, and a Levy of Burmese under his Command, and after three separate engagements, completely routed the insurgents and captured their leaders. Received the special thanks of Government, 18th March '54. Quelled a rebellion of the Karen Tribes in the Bassein District, with the Bassein Police Corps which he commanded, during the months of January and February '57, routing a large body of the

(243)

insurgents under Meng-loung, a pseudo Prince of the Karen Tribe, and taking him prisoner. Received the special thanks of the Governor-General, dated 14th April '57.

G

LIEUTENANT D. GAIR, Bengal Veteran Establishment.

Lieut., 18 May 59.

SERVICE.—Lieutenant GAIR served in the Shekawattee Campaign, '34, '35. With the Army of the Indus, '38, '42. Present at the re-capture of Khelat, of Beloochistan. Capture of Khelai Taz Khan, in '41. *Dangerously wounded* in blowing open the gates. Defence of Khelat-i-Ghilzie, '42. *Medal.* Candahar, Ghuznee, and Cabul. *Medal,* '42. Present at the siege and capture of Delhi in '57. *Medal and Clasp.*

MAJOR-GENERAL W. J. GAIRDNER, C.B., late 63rd Native Infantry.

Ensign, 9 April 08—Lieut., 16 Dec. 14—Bt.-Captain, 9 April 23— Captain, 22 Sept. 24—Major, 16 June 35—Lieut.-Colonel, 12 Jan. 42— Colonel, 10 Sept. 52—Major-General, 28 Nov. 54.

MAJOR J. G. GAITSKEL, late 26th Native Infantry.

Ensign, 4 Aug. 30—Lieut., 1 Jan. 37—Captain, 24 Jan. 45—Bt.-Major, 28 Nov. 54—Major, 27 Aug. 57.

LIEUTENANT-COLONEL F. GAITSKELL, C.B., P., Bengal Artillery.

2nd Lieut., 18 Dec. 23—Lieut., 28 Sept. 27—Bt.-Captain, 18 Dec. 38— Captain, 23 Nov. 41—Bt.-Major, 11 Nov. 51—Major, 17 May 54—Lieut.- Colonel, 14 Sept. 57.

CAPTAIN G. A. GALLOWAY, P. H., late 1st European Bengal Cavalry.

Cornet, 20 Feb. 51—Lieut., 21 Oct. 52—Captain, 10 March 57.

LIEUTENANT C. H. GARBETT, P. H., General List.

Ensign, 27 June 59—Lieut., 23 March 61.

ASSISTANT-SURGEON A. GARDEN,† M.D., Bengal Medical Establishment.

Asst.-Surgeon, 28 March 55.

SERVICE.—Assistant-Surgeon GARDEN served with Goorkha Brigade attached to General Frank's Division. Present at operations against Lucknow, in March '58; also in Medical Charge of the Bengal Yeomanry Cavalry throughout the Mutiny in India, during the years '57, '58, and '59. *Medal and Clasp.*

ASSISTANT-SURGEON A. M. GARDEN,† M.D., Bengal Medical Establishment.

Asst.-Surgeon, 28 March 55.

LIEUTENANT H. C. GARDEN,† late 57th Native Infantry.

Ensign, 26 July 57—Lieut., 18 May 57.

SERVICE.—Lieutenant GARDEN served with the Brigade under General Franks, in Oude. Served with three Companies of the 97th in Bundlecund, under Captain Venables.

BREVET-MAJOR H. R. GARDEN, P., late 2nd Native Infantry.

Ensign, 20 Jan. 45—Lieut., 18 July 49—Captain 25 Dec. 58—Bt.-Major, 26 Dec. 58.

SERVICE.—Major GARDEN served in the Sutlej Campaign. Present with his Regiment in the actions of Moodkee, Ferozeshuhur, and the surrender of Kôt Kangra. *Medal and 2 Clasps.* As Deputy Assistant Quarter-Master-General to the 3rd Infantry Division of the Army of the Punjab. Present at Ramnuggur, Sadoolapore, Chillianwallah, and Goojerat. *Medal and 2 Clasps.* As Assistant Quarter-Master General with Sir C. Napier's Head Quarters at the forcing of the Khyber Pass. As Assistant Quarter-Master-General with the Bengal Division in Burmah, in '52, '53. Present at Prome, capture of Meeaday and Burmese stockade near Donebew, in March '53. *Medal.* As Assistant Quarter-Master-General to General Outram in the advance on Lucknow, in September '57. Actions of Munguwara on the 19th; Alum Bagh, 23rd; entry of Lucknow, 25th September;

(245)

besieged in Lucknow to 18th November. As Assistant Quarter-Master-General to Sir C. Campbell on the withdrawal of Lucknow Garrison, November '57. Relief of Cawnpore and action of the 6th December '57. *Medal, Clasps, and Brevet-Major.*

LIEUTENANT W. A. GARDEN, P. H., late 39th Native Infantry.

Ensign, 11 Dec. 49—Lieut., 4 June 55.

CAPTAIN P. F. GARDINER, P. H., late 29th Native Infantry.

Ensign, 27 Sept. 40—Lieut., 24 Jan. 45—Bt.-Captain, 27 Sept. 55—Captain, 15 June 57.

SERVICE.—Captain GARDINER served against the rebels, north of Jullundur, '48, '49. Present at the storming of the heights of Umb, and occupation of the Fort of Oonah. *Medal.*

LIEUTENANT A. E. GARNAULT, Bengal Artillery.

Lieut., 27 Aug. 58.

LIEUTENANT H. W. GARNAULT, Bengal Engineers.

Lieut., 31 Oct. 58.

SERVICE.—Lieutenant GARNAULT served with the Goorkha Force under Sir Jung Bahadoor, as Assistant Field Engineer, in '58. Present at the taking of the Fort of Berrozepore, Jamattpore, in Oude, 26th February '58. At the action at the Kandoo Nullah, 5th March, and at the siege and capture of Lucknow, March '58. Mentioned in the Despatches of Captain Baring and General MacGregor. Served with the Sarun Field Force under Brigadier Rowcroft, in Goruckpore. Present at the affair of Hurrya, 18th June '58. Mentioned in the Despatch of Colonel Byng. *Medal and Clasp.*

2ND CAPTAIN A. W. GARNETT, Bengal Engineers.

2nd Lieut., 12 June 46—Lieut., 15 Feb. 54—2nd Captain, 27 Aug. 58.

VETERINARY-SURGEON J. W. GARRAD,† Bengal Veterinary Establishment.

Vety.-Surgeon, 14 Feb. 54.

(246)

LIEUTENANT N. D. GARRETT, Bengal Artillery.

Lieut., 27 April 58.

BREVET-COLONEL R. GARRETT, P., late 64th Native Infantry.

Ensign, 24 July 19—Lieut., 29 Aug. 21—Bt.-Captain, 24 July 34—Captain, 1 Dec. 36—Bt.-Major, 9 Nov. 46—Major, 31 July 49—Bt.-Lieut.-Colonel, 20 June 54—Lieut.-Colonel, 28 Nov. 54—Bt.-Colonel, 20 June 57.

SERVICE.—Colonel GARRETT served in Cachar in '24, under Brigadier Innes. Served in '27 against the Bheels, as Detachment Staff to the Force uuder Colonel Burgh.

LIEUTENANT C. J. GARSTIN, P. H., late 29th Native Infantry.

Ensign, 20 Dec. 56—Lieut., 30 April 58.

MAJOR-GENERAL E. GARSTIN, Bengal Engineers.

2nd Lieut., 6 May 15—Lieut., 1 Sept. 18—Captain, 5 July 22—Bt.-Major, 20 April 25—Lieut.-Colonel, 5 Dec. 48—Colonel, 17 March 51—Major-General, 28 Nov. 54.

SERVICE.—Major-General GARSTIN served during the Nepal War, '15, '16; also during the Mahratta War, '17, '18. *Medal.*

LIEUTENANT E. C. GARSTIN,† late 29th Native Infantry.

Ensign, 13 June 56—Lieut., 30 April 58.

SERVICE.—Lieutenant GARSTIN served during the Mutiny, '57, '58. Present at the action of Kudjwah, 1st November '57. Present at the relief of Lucknow by Lord Clyde, and battle of Cawnpore against the Gwalior Contingent. Present at the action of Khodagunge; capture of Lucknow; attack on Fort Rooyah; action of Allygunge; and capture of Bareilly. *Medal and 2 Clasps.* (Passed in Surveying and Civil Engineering.)

MAJOR H. M. GARSTIN, P. H., late 36th Native Infantry.

Ensign, 20 Dec. 42—Lieut., 24 Jan. 45—Captain, 23 Nov. 56—Bt.-Major, 19 Jan. 58.

SERVICE.—Major GARSTIN served during the Sutlej Campaign, '45, '46. Present at the action of Alliwal. *Medal.* Served during the Punjab

(247)

Campaign, '48, '49. Present at the actions of Ramnuggur, Sadoolapore, *(severely wounded,)* Chillianwallah, and Goojerat. *Medal and 2 Clasps.* Specially mentioned by His Excellency the Commander-in-Chief in his Despatch, 5th February '49. Present at the battle of Badlee-ke-Serai, 8th June '57, and served throughout the siege of Delhi as Deputy Assistant Quarter-Master-General attached to Army Head-Quarters. Served in the same capacity at Goorgaon and Rewaree. *Medal and Clasp and Brevet-Major.* Received thanks of Provincial Commander-in-Chief at Delhi, 17th July '57. Favorably mentioned in Despatch of Major-General A. Wilson, 22nd September '57. Received thanks of Governor-General, 5th November '57.

CAPTAIN W. T. GARSTIN, P. H., 12th (late 70th) Native Infantry.

Ensign, 11 Dec. 39—Lieut., 16 July 42—Bt.-Captain, 11 Dec. 54—Captain, 20 July 57.

SERVICE.—Captain GARSTIN served during the Punjab Campaign, '48, '49. Present at the actions of Ramnuggur, Chillianwallah, and Goojerat. *Medal and 2 Clasps.* Served in China, '58, '59, and '60. Present at the action of the White Cloud Mountains in '58. Commanded a Detachment Military Train in the expedition to the Peiho, under Admiral Hope. Present at the attack on the Forts, '59.

LIEUTENANT W. H. GARTON,† late 50th Native Infantry.

Ensign, 14 June 51—Lieut., 23 Nov. 56.

CAPTAIN J. E. GASTRELL, P. C., late 13th Native Infantry.

Ensign, 11 Dec. 35—Lieut., 8 Oct. 39—Captain, 19 March 49.

SERVICE.—Captain GASTRELL served against the Jeypore Insurgents in '38. Served as Detachment Staff and Brigade Quarter-Master in the Bundlecund Campaign, '42, '43. As Sub-Assistant Commissary-General in the Punjab Campaign, '48, '49, and in the subsequent pursuit of the Sikh Army, under Major-General Gilbert. Present at the affair of Ramnuggur, and the battles of Chillianwollah and Goojerat. *Medal and 2 Clasps.* Served in the Sonthal Campaign, '55. Commanded one of the Detached Columns in the final beating up and subjugation of the Tribe.

(248)

LIEUTENANT M. W. GATAKER,† late 2nd Native Infantry.
Ensign, 4th Sept. 58—Lieut., 1 March 59.

MAJOR D. GAUSSEN,† 5th (late 42nd) Native Infantry.
Ensign, 25 May 27—Lieut., 24 July 37—Bt.-Captain, 25 May 42—Captain, 15 Feb. 48—Bt.-Major, 20 June 54—Major, 11 May 60.

SERVICE.—Major GAUSSEN served throughout the Affghan Campaign, '39, '40, '41, and '42; and defence of Khelat-i-Gilzie. *Medal.* Present at the action of Goyne, retaking of Chuznee, and the operations leading to the re-occupation of Cabul, by the Force under General Nott. *Medal.* Present at the battle of Maharajpore. *Bronze Star.* Mentioned in the Despatches of Colonel C. Halkett at the defence of Khelat-i-Ghilzie. Served in the Sonthal Campaign, '55, '56; and in Saugor Garrison and District during the Mutinies. *Medal.* *(Since retired.)*

ASSISTANT-SURGEON C. J. GAYER,† Bengal Medical Establishment.
Asst.-Surgeon, 2 Jan. 56.

SERVICE.—Assistant-Surgeon GAYER served with the advance Force from Allahabad, under Major Renaud, in Medical Charge of the 13th Irregular Cavalry, from 30th June '57 till the 12th July. Served with H. M.'s 84th Regiment, from 13th July till 7th August, in the actions of Futtehpore, Aoung, Pandoo Nuddee, Cawnpore, Oonao, and 1st, 2nd, and 3rd battles at Busseerutgunge. With the battery of Royal Artillery, commanded by Captain Maude, from 8th to 21st August, in the action of Bithoor. Did duty at Cawnpore Field Hospital, from 22nd August to 18th September. Served with H. M.'s 5th Fusiliers, from 19th September to 17th October, in the actions of Muggerawarra, Alum Bagh, and the first relief of Lucknow. Did duty in the Residency with H. M.'s 78th Regiment from 18th October to 27th November. Did duty at Field Hospital from 28th November to 6th December. Present at the defeat of the Gwalior rebels at Cawnpore, 7th December '57. *Medal and Clasp.*

CAPTAIN G. GAYNOR, P. H., late 2nd European Bengal Fusiliers.
2nd Lieut., 29 Jan. 40—Lieut., 12 Nov. 42—Captain, 8 March 49.

(249)

LIEUTENANT F. GELLIE, A. M., P. H., late 9th Native Infantry.

Ensign, 20 Oct. 56—Lieut., 17 Nov. 57.

SERVICE.—Lieutenant GELLIE was present with the late 9th Native Infantry, when that Regiment mutinied at Allyghur on the 20th May '57. Served with the 1st Gwalior Cavalry (Scindia's Contingent), in May and June '57 ; in some minor affairs with rebel villagers, &c., in the Allygurh District. Present when half of this Regiment mutinied at Hattras, on 24th May '57. Served in the Gun Escort in the action near Agra, under Brigadier Polwhele, 5th July '57. Served with the Rifle Company, Agra Militia, in the battle of Agra, under Colonels Cotton and Greathed, and pursuit of the mutineers, 10th October '57. Served with the 3rd Europeans in February '58, against the rebels in the ravines of the Jumna. Served with the "Allygurh Levy" with Colonel Oakes' Column (No. 4), Bundlecund Field Force, under Brigadier F. Wheeler, in October, November, and December '59. *Medal.*

LIEUTENANT A. F. GERARD, late 3rd Europeans.

Ensign, 20 Jan. 58—Lieut., 5 Oct. 60.

SERVICE.—Lieutenant GERARD served during the Mutinies, '57, '58. Present at the relief of Azimghur, under Lord Mark Kerr, on the 6th April '58, and subsequent pursuit of Koer Sing. Present at the action of Amorah, 1st October '58. Present at the attack on Jugdespore, 26th October '58. *Medal.*

BREVET-MAJOR R. C. GERMON, P. H., late 13th Native Infantry.

Ensign, 12 June 39—Lieut., 6 Sept. 42—Bt.-Captain, 12 June 54—Captain, 28 Feb. 55—Bt.-Major, 24 March 58.

SERVICE.—Brevet-Major GERMON served in the Bundlecund Campaign, '42, '43. In the Punjab Campaign, '48, '49. Present at the action of Goojerat. *Medal and Clasp.* Served in the Sonthal Campaign, '55. Action of Chinhut, evacuation of Muchee Bhawun Fort, and defence of Lucknow, '57. Commanded the Judicial Garrison throughout the siege.

(250)

Medal and Clasp Brevet-Major, and one year's extra service. Honorably mentioned in Sir J. Inglis' Despatch, 26th September '57.

CAPTAIN J. S. GIBB, P., Bengal Artillery.

2nd Lieut., 11 June 47—Lieut., 3 March 53—2nd Captain, 27 Aug. 58—Bt.-Major, 28 Aug. 58.

DEPUTY-INSPECTOR-GENERAL OF HOSPITALS, A. GIBBON, Bengal Medical Establishment.

Asst.-Surgeon, 15 June 36—Surgeon, 19 Jan. 50—Surgeon-Major, 13 Jan. 60—Depy-Inspector-General of Hospitals, 18 June 59.

LIEUTENANT W. M. GIBBON, P. H., late 44th Native Infantry.

Ensign, 13 June 51—Lieut., 23 Nov. 56.

CAPTAIN J. J. GIBBS, P. H., late 60th Native Infantry.

Ensign, 24 April 42—Lieut., 21 Sept. 44—Captain, 23 Nov. 56.

SERVICE.—Captain GIBBS served throughout the Sutlej Campaign, in '45, '46. Present at the battle of Sobraon, 10th February '46, and subsequent pursuit of the Sikhs. *Medal.* Served with the 68th Regiment during the War with Burmah, in '52, '53, and '54. *Medal.* Served with Brigadier McCausland's Force in Kumaon and Rohilcund, against the mutineers, in '57, '58. Present in the several engagements of the 14th September, 2nd October '57, and 1st January '58. Present with Brigadier Sir Thomas Seaton's Force in the operations before Shahjehanpore, in September '58. *Medal.* (Has received a certificate of qualification in Civil Engineering.)

CAPTAIN R. D. GIBNEY, P., late 59th Native Infantry.

Ensign, 11 June 42—Lieut., 7 July 45—Bt.-Captain, 11 June 57—Captain, 23 July 57.

CAPTAIN L. W. GIBSON, Invalid Establishment.

Ensign, 13 Feb. 24—Lieut., 22 Sept. 25—Captain, 15 Feb. 36.

ENSIGN P. GIBSON, Unattached List.

Ensign, 11 June 58.

SERVICE.—Ensign P. GIBSON served with the first European Bengal Fusiliers in Burmah, in '52, '53, and '54; accompanied the Martaban Column under the Command of Major-General Sir S. W. Steel, throughout the operations en-route to Shwegyeen. *Medal.* Also present throughout the Indian Mutinies of '57, '58. Present at the action near Agra, against the insurgent Neemuch and Nusseerabad Brigade, 5th July '57, and in the action with the rebels at Oriya; served the whole of the hot weather Campaign of '58, against the mutineers in the affairs of Etawah, Mynpooree, and Shereghur Ghaut; was with the Moveable Column under Command of Colonel Riddel, which marched towards Gwalior to co-operate with the Central India Field Force under His Excellency General Sir Hugh Rose, in June '58. *Medal.*

CAPTAIN E. K. O. GILBERT, P. H., late 27th Native Infantry.

Ensign, 20 Sept. 45—Lieut., 3 Nov. 48—Captain, 4 June 60.

SERVICE.—Captain GILBERT was present with the Force under Brigadier Polwhele, at Agra, on the 5th July '57, against the Neemuch insurgents. (Passed in Surveying and Civil Engineering.)

ENSIGN P. GILL, V.C., Unattached List.

Ensign, 20 Sept. 57.

SERVICE.—Ensign P. GILL, V. C., was present at the battle of Sobraon, 10th Feburary '46; on service to Kôt Kangra, with Brigadier Wheeler's Force, May and June '46. Present at the reduction of the Fort of Rungur Nugul, reduction of the Fort of Kallahwallah, and assault of the Dullah Heights, under Brigadier Wheeler, '48, '49. Present with the Regiment of Khelat-i-Ghilzie, in the operations against the Husseinjai and Akojai Tribes, on the Black Mountain, in December '52. Present on Field Service with the Moradabad Levy, Trans-Gogra, Oudh, from 3rd April '59 until the termination of the Frontier operations. Is in possession of the *Sutlej and Punjab Medals;* also the *Victoria Cross,* for highly distinguished conduct during the Mutiny of the Native Troops at Benares, on the 4th June '57, when he saved the life of Major Barrett,

37th Native Infantry, and the Quarter-Master Serjeant of the 25th Native Infantry, doing duty with the Regiment of Loodianah; also rescued Lieutenant Brown, Pension Pay Master, when surrounded by marauders, who were attempting to plunder the treasure of the office. *Medal.*

CAPTAIN P. H. P. GILL, P. C., 37th Native Infantry.

Ensign, 25 July 42—Lieut., 27 June 46—Captain, 23 Dec. 55.

2ND CAPTAIN A. GILLESPIE, P. H., Bengal Artillery.

2nd Lieut., 10 Dec. 47—Lieut., 3 March 53—2nd Captain, 27 Aug. 58.

LIEUTENANT J. GILLESPIE, P. H., late 61st Native Infantry.

Ensign, 20 Jan. 51—Lieut., 29 Jan. 54.

SERVICE.—Lieutenant GILLESPIE served in the Meounzaie Expedition, under Brigadier-General Chamberlain, in '56. Present at Kohat on the breaking out of the Mutiny in '57, and served throughout the Mutiny on the Frontier. Present at the disarming of the Left Wing, 58th Native Infantry, in June '57. On the Asne Frontier, from May '58 till February '60. From Dehra Ishmael Khan made a forced march to Junk, with a Squadron of 5th Punjab Cavalry, to repulse an attack of the Wuzeerees, and support the outposts, making a distance of 50 miles in one march, and in 12 hours, and bringing the horses up fresh and in good working order. Commanded the Troops at Junk until the expedition of Brigadier-General Chamberlain, assembled there and marched into the Wuzeeree Country. Commanded the Troops in the Goomul Valley in '60, had several slight skirmishes with marauding parties of Wuzeerees, and on several occasions re-took camels and plunder carried away by them. Served on the Bunnoo Frontier as 2nd in Command, 5th Punjab Cavalry.

LIEUTENANT W. A. B. GILLIES, P. H., Bengal Artillery.

Lieut., 27 April 58.

(253)

LIEUTENANT H. GIRARDOT, Bengal Artillery.
1st Lieut., 27 April 58.

CAPTAIN W. B. GIRDLESTONE, P. H., late 67th Native Infantry.
Ensign, 4 Feb. 46—Lieut., 9 July 52—Captain, 28 Nov. 57.
SERVICE.—Captain GIRDLESTONE served in Burmah, in '52, '53, and '54, under General Godwin. Present at the occupation of Rangoon; also at Donabew in the actions of 18th and 19th March '53. *Medal*. In Command of a Detached Company in charge of a fleet of 100 store and ammunition boats on the Irrawaddy, from Donabew to Prome; repulsed a night attack made on his boats at Morrio; struck on the chest and contused by a spent ball. Present and served with the Flying Brigade after the occupation of Lahore, '46. Served throughout the Mutiny of '57. Present in the action near Agra, 5th July; also at the battle of Agra, 10th October '59, and other minor affairs. *Medal*.

SURGEON G. E. GIVINS,† Bengal Medical Establishment.
Asst.-Surgeon, 25 July 46—Surgeon, 7 Oct. 59.
SERVICE.—Surgeon GIVINS served with the 17th Regiment Irregular Cavalry during the Punjab Campaign, in the years '48, '49. Served in the Oude Military Police in Medical Charge of a Regiment of Cavalry and one of Infantry, with the Force under His Excellency Lord Clyde, in '58, '59; also with the Oude Military Police, in the Force under Brigadier Holdich, on the Frontier of Oude, Trans-Raptee, '59, '60. *Medal*.

LIEUTENANT T. B. M. GLASCOCK,† late 50th Native Infantry.
Ensign, 11 Aug. 57—Lieut., 19 May 58.
SERVICE.—Lieutenant GLASCOCK served with H. M.'s 97th Highlanders throughout the siege and capture of Lucknow. Served in the Rohilcund Campaign under General Walpole. Present at the engagements at Rooyah, Allygunge, Bareilly, and taking of Shahjehanpore. Present at the capture of Rampore Kussia, 3rd November '58. Passage of the Gogra, and forcing of the lines of the enemy before Fyzabad, 26th November '58. *Medal*.

(254)

CAPTAIN R. W. GLASSE, P. H., late 14th Native Infantry.

Ensign, 20 May 48—Lieut., 14 Sept. 53—Captain in Staff Corps, 18 Feb. 61.

SERVICE.—Captain GLASSE served during the Mutiny of '57, '58; also served in China with the Loodiana Regiment. *Medal.* Mentioned in Despatch.

CAPTAIN H. L. GLEIG,† late 32nd Native Infantry.

Ensign, 26 Jan. 46—Lieut., 10 Aug. 50—Captain, 29 Aug. 59.

SERVICE.—Captain GLEIG served during the Punjab Campaign, '48, 49. Present at the passage of the Chenab and battle of Chillianwallah. *Medal and Clasp.*

ENSIGN E. H. P. GLOVER, General List.

Ensign, 5 Nov. 60.

SURGEON J. T. GLOVER,† M.D., Bengal Medical Establishment.

Asst.-Surgeon, 14 June 41—Surgeon, 21 April 59.

SERVICE.—Surgeon GLOVER served in the Burmah Campaign in '52, '53. *Medal. (Since invalided.)*

CAPTAIN T. G. GLOVER,† Bengal Engineers.

2nd Lieut., 7 June 44—Lieut., 19 Nov. 49—Captain, 27 April 58.

SERVICE.—Captain GLOVER served during the Punjab Campaign, '48, '49. Present at the siege of Mooltan from September '48 till January '49, including the action at Sooroojkhoond. Present at the battle of Goojerat. *Medal and 2 Clasps.* Mentioned in Despatches by Major-General Whish, '49, by Brigadier Markham, by Sir J. Cheape, and by Colonel Napier, for services at Mooltan. Present at the action of Susseah, near Agra, 5th July '57. *Medal.*

LIEUTENANT J. M. GLUBB, P. H., late 38th Native Infantry.

Ensign, 20 Dec. 54—Lieut., 10 June 57.

SERVICE.—Lieutenant GLUBB was present at Delhi during the out-break in May '57, and escaped to Umballa, proceeded with the Army, in June

'57, to Delhi; also present with Colonel Cotton's Column at the taking of Futtehpore-Sikree, *severely wounded* through both thighs and right heel. *Medal.* (Received 1st class certificate from the School of Musketry at Hythe.)

LIEUTENANT O. M. GLUBB, P., late 37th Native Infantry.

Ensign, 11 Dec. 47—Lieut., 17 March 51.

(Since dead.)

LIEUTENANT F. S. GOAD,† late 69th Native Infantry.

Ensign, 13 June 57—Lieut., 18 May 58.

SERVICE.—Lieutenant GOAD served with H. M.'s 19th Foot in Tirhoot, in '59.

LIEUTENANT G. S. GOAD, P. H., late 49th Native Infantry.

Ensign, 26 July 56—Lieut., 30 April 58.

SERVICE.—Lieutenant GOAD served with the 28th Native Infantry in the Column under Colonel Shubrick, in Rewah and Sohagpore, in '59, '60.

MAJOR-GENERAL C. GODBY, C.B., late 55th Native Infantry.

Ensign, 27 March 06—Lieut., 14 June 09—Bt.-Captain, 27 March 21— Captain, 11 July 23—Major, 14 June 33—Lieut.-Colonel, 1 Feb. 40— Bt.-Colonel, 7 June 49—Colonel, 6 April 50—Major-General, 28 Nov. 54.

SERVICE.—Major-General GODBY, C.B., served during the Nepal War, '15, '16; Cuttack, '17, '18, and '19: siege and capture of Bhurtpore. *(Severely wounded.) India Medal.* Campaign on the Sutlej, including the battle of Alliwal, *Medal and C.B.;* and in Command of a Brigade with the Army of the Punjab, at the action of Chillianwallah. *Medal.* A. D. C. to the Queen.

BREVET-CAPTAIN C. J. GODBY, P. H., late 35th Native Infantry.

Ensign, 20 Feb. 49—Lieut., 15 Nov. 53—Bt.-Captain, 13 June 60.

SERVICE.—Captain GODBY served in the Sutlej Campaign, 45, '46. Present at the action of Alliwal. *Medal.* Subsequent operations in

Jullunder Doab. Served during the Punjab Campaign. Present at the actions of Ramnuggur, Sadoolapore, and Chillianwallah (*wounded dangerously* in a hand-to-hand fight, in defence of the Regimental Colors). *Medal and Clasp.* Wounded by an assassin in December '53, when in charge of Eusuffzaie Frontier. Served with the Guides on the Peshawur Frontier for four years, and thanked by General Cotton for success in clearing the vicinity of Peshawur of Hill robbers.

LIEUTENANT R. F. GODBY, P. H., late 35th Native Infantry.

Ensign, 20 Feb. 49—Lieut., 15 Nov. 53.

SERVICE.—Lieutenant GODBY served in Command of a Wing of the 7th Punjab Infantry with the Punjab Moveable Column under Brigadier-General Nicholson, at Delhi. Served in the Meerut District at Haupper, in July, August, and September '57. Present at the action of Narnoul. Mentioned in Despatches of '58. Present at the actions of Gungairee, Puttiallee, and Mynpooree. Present at the capture of Lucknow, March '58. Served in Oude under Sir H. Grant. Present at the action of Simree. Served under Brigadier Eveligh, on the Lucknow and Cawnpore roads, in '58. Present at the action of Busseerutgunge, in June; commanded the Regiment at the action of Hussengunge, August '58. Mentioned in Despatches of '58. Present at the action of Meagunge, September '58. Served throughout the Oude Campaign, '58, '59, with Brigadier Eveligh's Force. Present in the actions of Simree, Murkutgunge, Daoudeakeeree, and the occupation of Futtehpore. Commanded the Regiment at the action of Pursra. Mentioned in Despatches, '58. Served in the Trans-Gogra Campaign, '59, under Brigadier Horsford. Commanded a Squadron of the Regiment at the action of Burtapore. Mentioned in Despatches, '59. Commanded the 2nd Regiment, Hodson's Horse, on the Nepal Frontier, December '59 and January '60. *Medal and Clasp.* Served in the China Expedition, '60. Present at the actions of Sinho, 12th August; Chunkeiwa and Palichio, 18th and 21st September '60; and occupation of Pekin. During all the China War was 2nd in Command of 1st Sikh Cavalry, and mentioned in Despatches of His Excellency the Commander-in-Chief. *Medal and Clasps.* (*Since dead.*)

VETERINARY-SURGEON S. T. GODDARD, Bengal Veterinary Establishment.
Vety.-Surgeon, 4 Jan. 59.

LIEUTENANT B. J. GOLDIE, Bengal Engineers.
Lieut., 10 Dec. 58.

LIEUTENANT A. GOLDNEY, late 50th Native Infantry.
Ensign, 13 Dec. 56—Lieut., 30 April 58.

SURGEON-MAJOR E. GOODEVE,† M.B., Bengal Medical Establishment.
Asst.-Surgeon, 8 March 41—Surgeon, 17 May 55—Surgeon-Major, 19 July 61.

SERVICE.—Surgeon-Major GOODEVE served during the Sutlej Campaign, '45, '46. *Medal.* During the Punjab Campaign, '48, '49. Present at the actions of Ramnuggur, Chillianwallah, and Goojerat. *Medal and 2 Clasps.*

LIEUTENANT-COLONEL A. G. GOODWYN, P. H., Bengal Engineers.
2nd Lieut., 12 June 37—Lieut., 8 Jan. 41—2nd Captain, 12 June 52—Captain, 1 Aug. 54—Bt.-Major, 2 Aug. 54—Lieut.-Colonel, 18 Feb. 61.

SERVICE.—Colonel GOODWYN served in Affghanistan, '42, *Medal;* in the Sutlej Campaign, *Medal.* Present at Ferozeshuhur and in the Punjab Campaign, Chillianwallah, and Goojerat. *Medal and 2 Clasps.* Served at the second relief of Lucknow under Sir C. Campbell. *Medal and Clasp.*

MAJOR-GENERAL H. GOODWYN, Bengal Engineers.
2nd Lieut., 18 Dec. 23—Lieut., 1 Jan. 26—Bt.-Captain, 18 Dec. 38—Captain, 20 May 39—Bt.-Major, 11 Nov. 46—Lieut.-Colonel, 5 Dec. 48—Bt.-Colonel, 28 Nov. 54—Colonel, 3 Aug. 55—Major-General, 26 June 60.

SERVICE.—Major-General GOODWYN was present at the siege and capture of Bhurtpore, in '25, '26, *India Medal;* and in the late Punjab Campaign. *Medal.*

(258)

LIEUTENANT F. H. GOOLD,† late 47th Native Infantry.

Ensign, 11 Dec. 58—Lieut., 9 Nov. 60.

SERVICE.—Lieutenant GOOLD served against the rebels in Oude, in '59, with H. M.'s 6th Foot. *Medal.*

LIEUTENANT F. I. C. GORDON,† late 5th Europeans.

Ensign, 20 Dec. 51—Lieut., 23 Nov. 56.

(Received a certificate as Instructor of Musketry, from the School of Musketry at Hythe, 15th October '57.)

LIEUTENANT G. G. GORDON,† Bengal Artillery.

1st Lieut., 14 Nov. 57.

CAPTAIN G. H. GORDON,† late 39th Native Infantry.

Ensign, 11 June 42—Lieut., 30 Jan. 46—Bt.-Captain, 11 June 57—Captain, 4 June 59.

SERVICE.—Captain GORDON served at the battle of Punniar. *Bronze Star.*

LIEUTENANT H. T. GORDON,† Bengal Engineers.

Lieut., 13 Aug. 58.

MAJOR J. GORDON, late 5th Europeans.

Ensign, 9 Dec. 36—Lieut., 16 July 42—Captain, 5 May 51—Bt.-Major, 20 July 58—Major, 1 April 59.

SERVICE.—Major GORDON served in the Affghan Campaign under Sir G. Pollock. Served in the Sutlej Campaign, and subsequent occupation of Lahore, in '46, under Sir J. Littler. Served during the Mutinies of '57, '58, including the operations at Allahabad and Cawnpore under Brigadier-General Neill, the relief of Lucknow *(horse shot under him)*, the subsequent defence of Lucknow and occupation of the Alum Bagh, the action of Guhailee, and all attacks that were repulsed during the occupation of the Alum Bagh under Sir J. Outram; and the final capture of Lucknow. *Medal and 2 Clasps.*

LIEUTENANT L. C. GORDON,† Bengal Engineers.
Lieut., 27 Aug. 58.

LIEUTENANT-COLONEL P. GORDON,† late 11th Native Infantry.

Ensign, 26 April 26—Lieut., 7 Aug. 33—Bt.-Captain, 26 April 41—Captain, 20 Nov. 45—Bt.-Major, 3 April 46—Major, 12 Oct. 56—Bt.-Lieut.-Colonel, 20 June 54—Lieut.-Colonel, 13 April 60—Bt.-Colonel, 20 June 57.

SERVICE.—Lieutenant-Colonel GORDON served throughout the Sutlej Campaign, '45, '46. Present at the actions of Moodkee, Ferozeshuhur, and Sobraon. *Medal, 2 Clasps, and Brevet-Major.*

CAPTAIN T. GORDON,† 10th (late 65th) Native Infantry.

Ensign, 24 Jan. 39—Lieut., 1 Feb. 41—Captain, 12 Jan. 53.

SERVICE.—Captain GORDON served in the Azimghur District during the Mutinies of '57. Accompanied his Regiment to China in '60.

CAPTAIN W. GORDON, P. H., late 49th Native Infantry.

Ensign, 11 June 41—Lieut., 14 March 45—Captain, 15 Jan. 53.

SERVICE.—Captain GORDON served throughout the siege of Mooltan, from 1st September '48 to 23rd January '49, as Assistant Field Engineer with Sappers and Miners. Present at the surrender of the Fort Chineole, February '49. Present at the battle of Goojerat, and commanded detached party of 2 Companies Pioneers there. *Medal and 2 Clasps.* (Passed in Surveying and Field Engineering, and received a first class certificate from the School of Musketry at Hythe.)

LIEUTENANT W. GORDON,† late 47th Native Infantry.

Ensign, 12 Dec. 49—Lieut., 11 May 52.

SERVICE.—Lieutenant GORDON served in Burmah against the rebel Mong Gong Gee, '54. During the Mutinies in '57, in charge of the entrenchments at Allahabad and in Command of the outposts of Joussie, Gossegung, and Lohunga. *Medal.* Accompanied the Expeditionary Force to

China. Present with the Army in the march from Taka to Pekin, and present at the operations which led to the capture of that City. *Medal and Clasps.*

CAPTAIN W. R. GORDON, P. H., late 68th Native Infantry.

Ensign, 12 Dec. 45—Lieut., 1 Nov. 49—Captain, 19 Feb. 59.

SERVICE.—Captain GORDON served during the War in Burmah, '52, '53. *Medal.*

LIEUTENANT H. GOSCHEN,† late 3rd Bengal European Infantry.

Ensign, 13 Dec. 56—Lieut., 30 April 58.

SERVICE.—Lieutenant GOSCHEN served throughout the Indian Mutinies. Present in the actions near Agra against the Neemuch Mutineers, 5th July; and the Indore and Mhow rebels, 10th October; also with the Force under Brigadier Sir T. Seaton, at Gungeeree and Puttiallee, in December '57, and with the Agra Column towards Gwalior, in June '58. *Medal.*

MAJOR W. C. GOTT, P. H., late 56th Native Infantry.

Ensign, 2 Feb. 42—Lieut., 11 Dec. 42—Captain, 13 Jan. 49—Major, 27 June 57.

SERVICE.—Major GOTT served with the Army of Gwalior, in '43, '44. Present at the action of Maharajpore. *Bronze Star.* Served with the Army of the Punjab, in '48, '49. Present at the passage of the Chenab, at the actions of Sadoolapore and Chillianwallah. *(Wounded twice.) Medal and Clasp.* Served in the Sonthal Campaign, '55, '56.

BREVET-MAJOR C. J. S. GOUGH, P., V. C., late 5th Bengal European Cavalry.

Cornet, 20 March 48—Lieut., 1 Sept. 49—Captain, 29 June 57—Bt.-Major, 20 July 58.

SERVICE.—Brevet-Major GOUGH served throughout the Punjab Campaign of '48, '49. Present at the actions of Ramnuggur, Sadoolapore,

Chillianwallah, and Goojerat. *Medal and 2 Clasps.* Served at the siege and capture of Delhi, from the 17th July, with the Guide Corps. Commanded the Guide Cavalry in the affairs at Rhotuk, 17th and 18th August, under Major Hodson; engaged in the Cavalry affair in rear of camp, on the 11th September. Served with the Column under Brigadier Showers in the Delhi and Jhujjur Districts. Engaged at the action of Narnoul under Brigadier Gerrard. Served with Hodson's Horse at the actions of Gungeeree, Puttiallee and Mynpooree, under Sir J. Seaton, at the action of Shumshabad, near Futtehghur, *wounded;* under Brigadier A. Hope, served in Command of a Squadron of Hodson's Horse; with the Column under Sir Hope Grant, in Oude, in February '58. Engaged in the action of Meahgunge. Present throughout the siege and capture of Lucknow. *Medal and 2 Clasps, V.C., and Brevet-Majority.*

CAPTAIN and BREVET-MAJOR H. H. GOUGH, P. H., V. C., late 1st Bengal European Cavalry.

Cornet, 4 Sept. 53—Lieut., 9 Aug. 55—Captain, 30 July 62—Bt.-Major, 5 Jan. 61.

SERVICE.—Major H. H. GOUGH served with Hodson's Horse at the siege and assault of Delhi *(wounded);* battles of Boolundshuhur, Allyghur, and Agra; relief of Lucknow; battles of Cawnpore, Serai Ghat, and Khodagunge (near Futtehghur); final capture of Lucknow *(severely wounded and two horses killed under him);* also with the Central India Field Force at the action of Ranode. *Medal and 3 Clasps, and Victoria Cross.*

ASSISTANT-SURGEON G. M. GOVAN, M.D., Bengal Medical Establishment.

Asst.-Surgeon, 20 Dec. 51.

SERVICE.—Assistant-Surgeon GOVAN served throughout the Burmese War, in '52, '53; was present at the capture of the inner stockades and the combined Naval and Military operations, which resulted in the capture of Rangoon. Served with H. M.'s 51st Regiment during '52. Early in '53 proceeded in Medical Charge of Recruits, H. M.'s 18th Royal Irish Regiment, to Prome, and served in the vicinity till the close of the War. *Pegu Medal.* Served in the Delhi District, '59.

(262)

LIEUTENANT B. E. GOWAN, late 15th Native Infantry.
Ensign, 10 June 59—Lieut., 11 Oct 59.

LIEUTENANT-GENERAL G. E. GOWAN, C.B., Bengal Artillery.

1st Lieut., 28 March 06—Captain, 1 Sept. 18—Major, 16 Sept. 29—Lieut.-Colonel, 2 July 35—Colonel, 3 July 45—Major-General, 20 June 54—Lieut.-General, 27 Sept. 59.

SERVICE.—Lieutenant-General GOWAN, C.B., was present at the capture of the Cape of Good Hope, '06. Served in Java, '13, '14, and '15. Present at the siege and bombardment of Hattrass, '17; Pindaree Campaign, under Lord Hastings, '17, '18. Served with Colonel Vanreuen's Detachment at Tonk. Commanded the Artillery with Colonel Ludlow's Field Force, on particular service in Malwa and Meywar, '18, '19, and '20; and under Brigadier Lumley, in operations against the Bheel Tribes, towards the Mhye River, in '24. Commanded the Artillery in the Gwalior Campaign, '43, 44. Present at Maharajpore, *Bronze Star;* also commanded the Artillery in the Campaign of the Sutlej, '45, '46. Present in the affair of Buddiwal and battle of Sobraon. *Medal.* Nominated C.B. in '44, and A.D.C. to the Queen, '46.

CAPTAIN J. Y. GOWAN, P. H., late 18th Native Infantry.
Ensign, 11 June 42—Lieut., 1 Aug. 46—Captain, 6 June 57.

SERVICE.—Captain GOWAN served throughout the Punjab Campaign, '48, 49. *Medal.* Commanded the staunch men of the late 11th Native Infantry, from 8th November '57 to 2nd March '58, in rescuing fugitives from the massacres in Rohilcund. Raised and Commanded an Infantry Levy to apprehend mutineers and rebels, from 19th March to 31st October '58. Accompanied the Force under Major-General Penny, from March to April '58, and that under Colonel R. Jones, from 1st to 10th May '58, as Assistant Commissioner in the operations in the Etah, Mynpooree, Budaon, Furruckabad, and Bareilly Districts. Present at the action of Kakrala, on 30th April, and in the operations before Bareilly, on 5th May '58. In Command of the above-mentioned Levy, occupied the station of Moradabad from 15th May till the arrival of the Force under Brigadier Coke, on 17th June '58. *Medal.*

(263)

CAPTAIN W. M. GOWAN, P. H., Bengal Artillery.

2nd Lieut., 8 Dec. 43—Lieut., 22 Dec. 45—Captain, 27 April 58.

SERVICE.—Captain GOWAN served during the Punjab Campaign, '48, '49. Present at the actions of Chillianwallah and Goojerat. *Medal and* 2 *Clasps.*

CAPTAIN C. H. E. GRÆME, P., late 5th Europeans.

Ensign, 20 Feb. 47—Lieut., 31 March 53—Captain, 17 June 58.

(Passed in Surveying and Civil Engineering, and attained a degree of proficiency in the Punjabee language.)

LIEUTENANT A. W. GRAHAM,† General List.

Ensign, 20 Feb. 59—Lieut., 20 Feb. 60.

LIEUTENANT F. W. GRAHAM, P. H., late 11th Native Infantry.

Ensign, 26 July 47—Lieut., 12 Oct. 56.

SERVICE.—Lieutenant GRAHAM served in Burmah, '52, '53. Present at the operations against Myah Toon, near Donabew, March '53. *Medal.*

CAPTAIN G. A. GRAHAM, P. H., late 28th Native Infantry.

Ensign, 13 Dec. 51—Lieut., 19 Oct. 54—Captain, 10 June 57.

SERVICE.—Captain GRAHAM served during the Bozdar Expedition, in March '57. Present at the forcing of the Khan Bund. Received the thanks of Government, 29th January '58. Present at the attack on Shaick Jana, in Eusuffzaie, under Lieutenant-Colonel Vaughan. Commanded Head Quarters and Detachment of 2nd Punjab Cavalry. Favorably mentioned in Major Vaughan's Despatch, 2nd July '57.

LIEUTENANT G. F. GRAHAM,† late 5th Europeans.

Ensign, 14 Jan. 54—Lieut., 1 Sept. 55.

LIEUTENANT G. F. T. GRAHAM, P. H., late 4th Europeans.

Ensign, 20 Dec. 56—Lieut., 27 Sept. 57.

SERVICE.—Lieutenant GRAHAM served throughout the Mutinies, '57, '58. Present at the affairs in the Etawah District, also with the Column

(264)

under Brigadier Showers, in the action of Dowsa, 14th January '59, against Tantia Topee. Mentioned several times in Despatches.

ASSISTANT-SURGEON H. W. GRAHAM,† Bengal Medical Establishment.

Asst.-Surgeon, 14 Feb. 54.

BREVET-COLONEL J. GRAHAM, late 66th Native Infantry.

Ensign, 20 July 19—Lieut., 1 Dec. 20—Captain, 12 Dec. 33—Bt.-Major, 9 Nov. 46—Major, 4 Jan. 49—Bt.-Lieut.-Colonel, 20 June 54—Lieut.-Colonel, 9 Aug. 54—Bt.-Colonel, 25 Feb. 58.

SERVICE.—Colonel GRAHAM served in Rajpootanah against the rebels, '20, '21. Against the Coles and Chooars, '32, '33.

LIEUTENANT J. GRAHAM, P. C., late 14th Native Infantry.

Ensign, 7 Feb. 49—Lieut., 23 Nov. 56.

SERVICE.—Lieutenant GRAHAM served during the Indian Mutinies of '57, '58. Present at the siege and capture of Lucknow, in March '58; at the affairs of Koorsee, Barnee, and Simree; at the engagement at Newalgunge, in June 58; at the re-occupation of Fyzabad, and at the crossing of the Gogra, November 58. *Medal and Clasp.* Mentioned in Despatch of Major-General Sir H. Grant, 18th July '58. Served as Commissariat Officer in charge of the Force in Command of Major General Outram, on the left bank of the Goomtee, during the siege and capture of Lucknow, March '58; and in the same capacity with Major-General Sir H. Grant, in the Oude Campaign, from April till September '58.

LIEUTENANT J. M. GRAHAM, P. C., late 27th Native Infantry.

Ensign, 11 June 47—Lieut., 18 April 51.

SERVICE.—Lieutenant GRAHAM served throughout the Mutinies in '57, '58, and 59. Commanded the Head Quarters of the Ramghur Irregular Cavalry, and a Company of the 1st Sikh Battalion in an attack on, and defeat of, a body of rebels at Jhurpo, 19th September '57. In the same capacity was besieged for a short time by the rebels in the Palamou District: afterwards held the District for several months with the above

Force and a body of Irregulars, raised for the purpose, against vastly superior numbers. Present in Command of a Detachment with the Force under Major G. G. Macdonell, in the attack on the rebel position at the Palamow Fort, and capture of their guns and camp. Engaged with the rebels at Foungaree Pass, Chemo, Laburmoor, and Paretal. Was with the Force under Colonel Turner in pursuit of the Shahabad rebels, and at the Boogloomara Pass, in the Palamow District. *Medal.* Commanded the 5th Battalion, M. P., in the expedition against the Hill Tribes on the South-East Frontier, in '61. Specially mentioned by the Lieutenant-Governor in his Minute of 30th September '58; also in the Home Despatch of Governor-General, 2nd July '59. Received the "Gracious approbation of Her Majesty" for services in the Mutinies. Services brought to notice of Government by the Lieutenant-Governor of Bengal, 18th March '59. Thanked in various letters and orders, for services performed.

LIEUTENANT O. M. GRAHAM,† late 6th Europeans.

Ensign, 20 Jan. 55—Lieut., 30 July 57.

SERVICE.—Lieutenant GRAHAM served in Commissariat charge of the Force under Colonel Tombs, sent against the Fort of Seonda, Bundlecund. Served at the occupation of the Alum Bagh. With the Force under Lord Clyde at the relief of Lucknow, November '57. Served in the Rohilcund Campaign under Lord Clyde, April and May '58. With Brigadier C. Troup's Column in Oude, from October '58 till March '59. With Brigadier Horsford's Column in Oude, in April and May ,59. On the Nepal Frontier, in November and December '59. Received the thanks of Government. *Medal and Clasp.*

LIEUTENANT R. B. GRAHAM, P. H., late 13th Native Infantry.

Ensign, 14 June 56—Lieut., 30 April 58.

LIEUTENANT S. GRAHAM, Bengal Artillery.

Lieut., 27 April 58.

(266)

CAPTAIN S. F. GRAHAM, P., late 5th Europeans.

Ensign, 4 Aug. 40—Lieut., 1 March 44—Bt.-Captain, 4 Aug. 55—Captain, 23rd Nov. 56.

LIEUTENANT T. C. GRAHAM, late 4th Bengal European Cavalry.

Cornet, 25 Nov. 54—Lieut., 23 Nov. 56.

SURGEON-MAJOR A. GRANT,† Bengal Medical Establishment.

Asst.-Surgeon, 11 Nov. 40—Surgeon, 3 Sept. 54—Surgeon-Major, 11 April 61.

SERVICE.—Surgeon-Major GRANT served throughout the expedition to China, '41, '42, '43, and '44. Present at the capture of Amoy, Chusan, and Chapoo, the storming of Woosung and occupation of Shanghai, and assault and capture of Chian Keang Foos and investment of Nankin. *Medal.* Attached to the Depôt Hospital Army of the Sutlej, '46.

CAPTAIN A. C. GRANT, P. H., late 5th Bengal European Cavalry.

Cornet, 20 Nov. 49—Lieut., 1 Nov. 54—Captain, 16 Aug. 59.

MAJOR-GENERAL C. GRANT, C.B., Bengal Artillery.

2nd Lieut., 22 April 19—Lieut., 2 Aug. 22—Bt.-Captain, 22 April 34—Captain, 17 Jan. 36—Bt.-Major, 30 April 44—Major, 5 July 46—Bt.-Lieut.-Colonel, 19 June 46—Lieut.-Colonel, 5 May 49—Bt.-Colonel, 20 June 54—Major-General, 14 Oct. 58.

SERVICE.—Major-General GRANT served in Bundlecund in '21; also in Oude in '22; and throughout the Ava Campaign, during the years '24, '25, and '26. *Medal.* Present at the capture of Ghuznee, '39. *Medal.* Battle of Maharajpore, '45, *Bronze Star*; Sobraon, '46, *(wounded)*, *Medal and Brevet-Lieutenant-Colonel*; Army of the Punjab, '48, '49, including actions of Ramnuggur, Sadoolapore, Chillianwallah, and Goojerat. *Medal, 2 Clasps, and C.B.*

LIEUTENANT F. H. GRANT, late 3rd Bengal European Cavalry.

Cornet, 20 Oct. 57—Lieut., 18 May 58.

SERVICE.—Served during the Mutiny. *Medal and Clasp.*

(267)

LIEUTENANT F. W. GRANT,† late 22nd Native Infantry.
Ensign, 20 April 57—Lieut., 18 May 58.
SERVICE.—Served during the Mutiny. *Medal and Clasp.*

ASSISTANT-SURGEON G. GRANT,† M.B., Bengal Medical Establishment.
Asst.-Surgeon, 10 Feb. 59.

CAPTAIN H. GRANT, P., late 74th Native Infantry.
Ensign, 24 Aug. 43—Lieut., 16 March 48—Captain, 18 Sept. 57.

SERVICE.—Captain GRANT was present at the breaking out of the Mutiny at Delhi, on the 11th May '57. Served with the 75th Foot at the battle of Badlee-ke-Serai, 8th June '57, and subsequently with the 4th Sikh Infantry and Kumaon Battalion throughout the siege and capture of Delhi. Served with the Kumaon Battalion when forming part of Brigadier Showers' Column at Rewarree, Jhujjur, &c., in October '57; and with the same Corps at Silka Ghaut, in Nepal, and at the affair at Korreealee River, under Brigadier Horsford. *Vide* G. G. O., No. 347 and 823, of '59. *Medal and Clasp.*

CAPTAIN J. A. GRANT, P. H., late 6th Europeans.
Ensign, 26 Jan. 46—Lieut., 22 Oct. 51—Captain, 10 Oct. 59.

SERVICE.—Captain GRANT served during the Punjab Campaign, '48, '49, throughout the operations in the vicinity, including the attack on the Dhurrumsalla, and action of Sooroojkhoond, and siege and surrender of Mooltan, and battle of Goojerat. *Medal and Clasp.*

2ND CAPTAIN J. H. GRANT, P. H., Bengal Artillery.
2nd Lieut., 10 Dec. 47—1st Lieut., 3 March 53—2nd Captain, 27 Aug. 58.

SERVICE.—Captain GRANT served with the Force under Sir C. Campbell, in the Ranzai Valley, May '52. Present at the taking of Pranghur, Nourden, and Sikarkote.

LIEUTENANT J. W. GRANT,† late 42nd Native Infantry.
Ensign, 13 Dec. 56—Lieut., 30 April 58.

ASSISTANT-SURGEON N. J. GRANT,† Bengal Medical Establishment.

Asst.-Surgeon, 18 Dec. 53.

SERVICE.—Assistant-Surgeon GRANT was on continual Field Service on the Peshawur Frontier, in the years '54, '55. Served with the Field Force at annexation of Oude, in '56, and subsequent operations. Sonthal Field Force, in '57. *Wounded dangerously* in action with Rebel Cavalry, June '57. In Medical Charge of Detachment, H. M.'s 37th Regiment, escorting ammunition, '58.

LIEUTENANT-GENERAL SIR P. GRANT, K.C.B., Bengal Infantry.

Ensign, 16 July 20—Lieut., 11 July 23—Captain, 14 May 32—Bt.-Major, 30 April 44—Major, 15 June 45—Bt.-Lieut.-Colonel, 3 April 46—Bt.-Colonel, 2 Aug. 50—Lieut.-Colonel, 29 Aug. 51—Major-General, 28 Nov. 54—Lieut.-General, 25 Jan. 56.

SERVICE.—Lieutenant-General Sir P. GRANT, K.C.B., served at Maharajpore. *Bronze Star and Brevet-Major.* Throughout the Campaign on the Sutlej, including the battles of Moodkee *(twice severely wounded),* and Sobraon, *Medal and Clasp, Brevet-Lieutenant-Colonel, and C.B.:* also with the Army of the Punjab. Present at the passage of the Chenab, actions of Chillianwallah and Goojerat. *Medal and Clasps.*

MAJOR-GENERAL H. M. GRAVES, Infantry.

Ensign, 25 June 22—Lieut., 15 Feb. 24—Captain, 3 May 33—Bt.-Major, 30 April 44—Major, 1 Nov. 49—Bt.-Lieut.-Colonel, 19 June 46—Lieut.-Colonel, 13 Dec. 54—Bt.-Colonel, 20 June 54—Major-General, 27 Aug. 58.

(Since dead.)

LIEUTENANT R. S. GRAVES, P., late 66th Native Infantry.

Ensign, 2 March 49—Lieut., 15 Sept. 54.

SERVICE.—Lieutenant GRAVES served with the 66th Goorkha Regiment on the Peshawur Frontier, against the Hill Tribes, '51, '52. Served with the same Regiment in the defence of the Kumaon Hills and Rohilcund, in '57, '58; with Brigadier Colin Troup's Force, in '59.

(269)

MAJOR-GENERAL J. C. C. GRAY, late 48th Native Infantry.

Ensign, 12 July 14—Lieut., 5 June 16—Captain, 1 Aug. 28—Major, 1 Sept. 41—Lieut.-Colonel, 27 Aug. 47—Bt.-Colonel, 28 Nov. 54—Colonel, 27 June 57—Major-General, 20 July 59.

SERVICE.—Major-General GRAY served during the Nepal War. Present at the siege and capture of Bhurtpore, and at Gureah Kote. *Medal.*

ASSISTANT-SURGEON R. GRAY,† M.B., Bengal Medical Establishment.

Asst.-Surgeon, 27 July 59.

CAPTAIN W. J. GRAY, P. H., Bengal Artillery.

2nd Lieut., 8 Dec. 43—Lieut., 22 Dec. 45—Captain, 27 April 58.

SERVICE.—Captain GRAY served during the Punjab Campaign, '48, '49. Present at the actions of Chillianwallah and Goojerat. *Medal and Clasp.*

CAPTAIN W. GRAYDON, P. H., late 16th Native Infantry.

Ensign, 12 June 39—Lieut., 12 Nov. 42—Bt.-Captain, 12 June 54—Captain, 13 Dec. 54.

SERVICE.—Captain GRAYDON served in the Affghan Campaign of '41, '42. Present at Maharajpore. *(Wounded.)* Served also in the Sutlej Campaign. *2 Medals, 2 Clasps, and Bronze Star.* Candahar, Ghuznee, and Cabul, '42. Maharajpore and Moodkee, Ferozeshuhur and Sobraon.

BREVET-MAJOR W. W. H. GREATHED, C.B., P. H., Bengal Engineers.

2nd Lieut., 9 Dec. 44—Lieut., 14 May 54—2nd Captain, 27 Aug. 58—Bt.-Major, 28 Aug. 58.

SERVICE.—Major GREATHED served at the siege of Mooltan and was present at Goojerat. *Medal and Clasp.* Served throughout the Delhi Campaign, first as Agent to the Lieutenant-Governor, North-Western Provinces, and A. D. C. to the General Commanding, afterwards as Field Engineer. Present at the battles of the Hindun and at Badlee-ka-Serai. *Severely wounded in two places* at the assault of Delhi.

Accompanied Colonel Seaton's Column through the Doab, and present at action of Puttiallee and Futtehghur. Served at the capture of Lucknow. *Medal and* 2 *Clasps, Brevet-Major, and Civil C. B.* Served as A. D. C. to Sir R. Napier at capture of Takoo Fort and advance on Pekin. *Medal and Clasps.*

BREVET-LIEUTENANT-COLONEL G. W. G. GREEN, C.B., P. H., late 2nd European Bengal Fusiliers.

2nd Lieut., 12 June 41—Lieut., 26 Aug. 43—Captain, 24 Nov. 53—Major, 19 Jan. 58—Lieut.-Colonel, 24 March 58.

SERVICE.—Lieutenant-Colonel GREEN served in the expedition under Sir Charles Napier, against the Hill Tribes in Scinde, in '45. During the Punjab Campaign, '48, '49. Present at the battle of Goojerat. *Medal and Clasp.* Served as Brigade-Major to 3rd Infantry Brigade, in the subsequent pursuit of the Sikhs and Affghans to Peshawur, under Sir W. Gilbert. Commanded 2nd Punjab Infantry in the expedition under Brigadier Chamberlain, in the Hungoo Valley, in September '55. Present at the affair with the Rabuck Khel Tribes of Affreedies, 2nd September '55. Commanded 2nd Punjab Infantry under Brigadier Chamberlain, against the Bozdars, on the Derajat Frontier, in March '57. Received the thanks of Government, 29th January '58. Commanded 2nd Punjab Infantry throughout the Mutinies, '57, '58. Present at the siege, assault, and capture of Delhi, including the battle of Nudjufghur, with Colonel Greathed's Column in the actions of Boolundshuhur, Allyghur, and Agra; throughout the final relief of Lucknow by the Army under Lord Clyde, November '57. Present at the operations at Cawnpore, from 30th November to 7th December '57. Battle of Khodagunge, January '58. Throughout the siege and capture of Lucknow, March 58. Campaign in Rohilcund, May '58, and re-capture of Bareilly. *Wounded slightly* at the assault on Delhi, 14th September '57. *C.B. and Medal, and* 3 *Clasps.* Mentioned in Despatch of Brigadier-General Nicholson, 4th December '57. Received the thanks of Government, 10th, 23rd, and 24th December '57, and 5th April '58. Mentioned in Despatch of Brigadier-General Sir H. Grant, 12th April '58. In Despatch of His Excellency the Commander-in-Chief, 8th May '58.

(271)

Promoted to Brevet-Majority for service before Delhi, 19th **January '58.** To the rank of Brevet-Lieutenant-Colonel for services during the relief of Lucknow, 24th March '58. Commanded 2nd Punjab Infantry in the expedition against the Mahsood Wuzeerees, April and May '60. Present at the action with the Wuzeerees at the Burrara Pass, 4th May '60.

LIEUTENANT J. GREEN, Veterinary Establishment.

Lieut., 16 Jan. 54.

ENSIGN R. S. GREEN, General List.

Ensign, 21 August 60.

CAPTAIN T. GREEN,† late 48th Native Infantry.

Ensign, 28 July 39—Lieut., 28 April 41—Captain, 7 Nov. 50.

SERVICE.—Captain GREEN served during the Sutlej Campaign, '45, '46. Present at the actions of Moodkee, Ferozeshuhur, and Alliwal. *Medal and 3 Clasps.* Served during the Mutiny, '57, '58. Present at the battles of Cawnpore and Khodagunge ; and siege and capture of Lucknow, '57. *Medal and Clasps.*

DEPUTY-INSPECTOR-GENERAL OF HOSPITALS W. A. GREEN, Bengal Medical Establishment.

Asst.-Surgeon, 6 June 30—Surgeon, 10 Feb. 47—Surgeon-Major, 30 July 58—Depy.-Inspector-General of Hospitals, 26 Aug. 58.

SERVICE.—Deputy-Inspector-General of Hospitals W. A. GREEN accompanied as Surgeon a party of the Dacca Naval Brigade, on the morning of the 17th November '57, to disarm two Companies of Sepoys (73rd Native Infantry), who offered resistance and fought with the Naval Brigade; was *wounded severely* by a bullet passing through the right thigh. *India Medal.*

CAPTAIN W. C. GREEN,† late 60th Native Infantry.

Ensign, 4 Feb. 41—Lieut., 18 April 43—Bt.-Captain, 4 Feb. 56— Captain, 23 Nov. 56.

SERVICE.—Captain GREEN served throughout the operations in Affghanistan, under General Pollock, '42. *Medal.* Served with the 1st

Bengal Fusiliers at the siege of Delhi, in '57, from 11th June to 24th August. *Medal and Clasp.*

LIEUTENANT H. C. GREENAWAY,† General List.

Ensign, 4 July 59—Lieut., 13 April 61.

BREVET-MAJOR G. G. N. GREENE,† late 70th Native Infantry.

Ensign, 8 Dec. 31—Lieut., 1 July 36—Bt.-Captain, 8 Dec. 46—Captain, 18 March 47—Bt.-Major, 11 Sept. 59.

SERVICE.—Brevet-Major GREENE served with the Army of Gwalior. *Bronze Star.* Present at the passage of the Chenab, affair of Ramnuggur, battles of Chillianwallah and Goojerat; and subsequent pursuit of the Sikhs and Affghans under General Gilbert. *Medal and 2 Clasps. (Since retired.)*

LIEUTENANT J. C. GREENE, Bengal Artillery.

Lieut., 27 Aug. 58.

BREVET-SURGEON H. M. GREENHOW,† F.R.C.S.L., and E., Bengal Medical Establishment.

Asst.-Surgeon, 20 Jan. 54—Bt.-Surgeon, 7 Sept. 58.

SERVICE.—Brevet-Surgeon GREENHOW served with the Oude 12th Irregular Cavalry, throughout the Mutinies in Oude, in '57, '58. Services mentioned, and untiring industry, extreme devotion, and great skill commended, in the Despatch of Brigadier Inglis, Commanding the Lucknow Garrison. *Madal and 2 Clasps, and Brevet-Surgeon.* Received by name the thanks of Government.

LIEUTENANT G. C. GREGORY, P. H., late 58th Native Infantry.

Ensign, 20 Jan. 57—Lieut., 30 April 58.

SERVICE.—Lieutenant GREGORY served throughout the Mutinies, '57, '58; with the Meerut Volunteer Horse in August, September, and October '57; with 1st Belooch Battalion in Brigadier E. R. Wetherall's Force; at the assault and capture of the Fort of Rampore, Kussiah, Oudh; in Lord Clyde's Field Force at the evacuation and occupation of the Forts

Ameitee and Shunkerpore, the action at Buxar, 24th November '58 ; at the taking of the Forts Bujudia and Mejudia, North Oude; and at the action on the banks of the Raptee, 31st December '58. *Medal.*

LIEUTENANT J. GREGORY.
Ensign, 2 July 59—Lieut., 9 April 61.

LIEUTENANT L. J. H. GREY, P. H., late 16th Native Infantry.
Ensign, 13 Dec. 56—Lieut., 15 Sept. 57.

SERVICE.—Lieutenant GREY joined Delhi Force as a Volunteer, 22nd September '57. Present in the actions of Boolundshuhur and Allyghur, and the skirmish of Ackerabad. Detached to reinforce the Garrison of Allyghur, under Lieutenant-Colonel Eld. Served in '57, '58, against the rebels in the Allyghur and Etah Districts. Served in Sir T. Seaton's Column in the Doab Campaign, December '57. Present at the engagements of Gungairee and Puttiallee. Served as a Volunteer with Sir H. Grant's Force in Oude, November and December '58. Present at the attack on Forts Koheia and Kolooee. Present with the Force under Colonel Christie, during his operations (including 2 skirmishes) on the left bank of the Gogra. Served with the expedition under Lieutenant-Colonel Vaughan, to clear the Keronia Sota Pass (skirmish); the final advance to the Nepal Hills, and capture of the enemy's guns at the action of Sitka Ghaut. Served with the Force under Colonel Vaughan on the Nepal Frontier, in '59, including various skirmishes with the rebels in the Nepal Hills. *Medal.*

LIEUTENANT W. M. GRIERSON, P., late 70th Native Infantry.
Ensign, 9 Dec. 48—Lieut., 15 Nov. 53.

LIEUTENANT E. C. GRIFFIN, P. H., Bengal Artillery.
1st Lieut., 8 Jan. 58.

LIEUTENANT R. D. GRIFFIN, P. H., late 64th Native Infantry.
Ensign, 11 Jan. 48—Lieut., 1 Feb. 54.

(274)

CAPTAIN J. C. GRIFFITH, P. H., Bengal Artillery.

2nd Lieut., 9 Dec. 44—Lieut., 31 March 47—Captain, 4 July 58.

SERVICE.—Captain GRIFFITH served during the Sutlej Campaign. Present at the action of Sobraon, *Medal;* and with the expedition to Kôt Kangra.

LIEUTENANT C. J. GRIFFITHS, P. H., late 72nd Native Infantry.

Ensign, 13 June 56—Lieut., 30 April 58.

LIEUTENANT H. GRIMES, General List.

Ensign, 20 July 59—Lieut., 10 May 61.

MAJOR H. S. GRIMES, P., late 46th Native Infantry.

Ensign, 27 June 26—Lieut., 29 Aug. 33—Bt.-Captain, 27 June 41—Captain, 21 April 48—Bt.-Major, 20 June 54—Major, 11 Sept. 59.

CAPTAIN R. G. GRINDALL, P. H., late 6th Europeans.

Ensign, 18 July 40—Lieut., 16 July 42—Bt.-Captain, 18 July 55—Captain, 20 Feb. 56.

SERVICE.—Captain GRINDALL served with the Force under General Whish at the siege and surrender of Mooltan. Present at the battle of Goojerat. *Medal and Clasp.*

BREVET-MAJOR H. R. GRINDLAY, P., late 3rd Bengal European Cavalry.

Cornet, 24 Feb. 37—Lieut., 1 Aug. 42—Bt.-Captain, 24 Feb. 52—Captain, 4 Nov. 52—Bt.-Major, 19 Jan. 58

SERVICE.—Major GRINDLAY served with the Jhansie Field Force under Sir T. Aubury, in '38, '39. Served as Brigade-Major with the Indus Field Force, in '46. During the Punjab Campaign, '48, '49. Present at the actions of Chillianwallah and Goojerat. *Medal and 2 Clasps.* Served as D. A. Q. M. G. with the Punjab Movaeble Column under Brigadier-General Nicholson, in '57. Present at the defeat of the Sealkôt mutineers at Trimmoo Ghaut, 12th

(275)

and 16th July '57. Mentioned in the Despatch of Brigadier Nicholson on that occasion. Present at the siege, assault, and capture of Delhi. Promoted to the rank of Brevet-Major for service in the Field, 19th January '58. *Medal and Clasp.*

CAPTAIN E. A. GRUBB, P., late 24th Native Infantry.

Ensign, 20 Dec. 42—Lieut., 30 Oct. 45—Captain, 9 April 56.

SERVICE.—Captain GRUBB served during the Sutlej Campaign, '45, '46. Present at the battles of Moodkee, Ferozeshuhur *(wounded)*, Buddiwal, and Alliwal. *Medal and 2 Clasps.*

LIEUTENANT G. R. GRYLLS, late 18th Native Infantry.

Ensign, 12 Dec. 57—Lieut., 22 Oct. 58.

SURGEON-MAJOR J. A. GUISE,† Bengal Medical Establishment.

Asst.-Surgeon, 30 May 38—Surgeon, 20 Feb. 52—Surgeon-Major, 13 Jan. 60.

SURGEON-MAJOR R. C. GUISE,† Bengal Medical Establishment.

Asst.-Surgeon, 14 March 37—Surgeon, 11 Feb. 51—Surgeon-Major, 13 Jan. 60.

SERVICE.—Surgeon-Major GUISE served with the 73rd Native Infantry throughout the Sutlej Campaign, and was present at the battles of Moodkee, Ferozeshuhur, and Sobraon. Served with the 73rd Native Infantry during the Punjab Campaign. *2 Medals and 2 Clasps.*

BREVET-MAJOR H. W. GULLIVER,† Bengal Engineers.

2nd Lieut., 12 Dec. 45—Lieut., 15 Feb. 54—2nd Captain, 27 Aug. 58—Bt.-Major, 28 Aug. 58.

SERVICE.—Major GULLIVER served during the Punjab Campaign, '48, '49. Present throughout the operations before, and at the siege of, Lucknow. *Severely wounded* in the trenches, 18th January '49. *Medal and Clasp.* Served with the Delhi Field Force in '57 as Field Engineer; also organised and commanded the 24th Punjab Infantry Pioneers.

Present at the siege of Delhi, from July to September '57. Served in the Agra District in '57, '58. With the Force under Lord Clyde, in January and February '58. Commanded a Detachment of Bengal Sappers and Miners, and the 24th Punjab Infantry, which escorted the Siege Train from Cawnpore to Alum Bagh. Served under Lord Clyde at Lucknow, March '58. Served throughout the siege of Lucknow as Field Engineer and Commandant of the 24th Punjab Infantry Pioneers. *Medal and* 2 *Clasps.* Brought to the notice of the Commander-in-Chief in Colonel Baird Smith's Despatch, 5th November '57. Also in the Despatch of Sir R. Napier, 5th April '58. Promoted to Brevet-Majority, 28th August '58.

CAPTAIN F. J. GULLY, P. H., late 74th Native Infantry.

Ensign, 12 June 46—Lieut., 5 Nov. 51—Captain, 12 June 61.

SERVICE.—Captain GULLY served with the Army of the Punjab at the actions of Sadoolapore, Chillianwallah, and Goojerat, *Medal and Clasp;* also subsequent pursuit of the Sikhs and Affghans to Peshawur, under General Gilbert. *(Wounded at Goojerat.)*

LIEUTENANT W. GULLY, Bengal Artillery.

Lieut., 27 April 58.

LIEUTENANT R. GUNNING, late 14th Native Infantry.

Ensign, 20 Oct. 56—Lieut., 23rd March 58.

LIEUTENANT E. P. GURDON, P., late 33rd Native Infantry.

Ensign, 20 Jan. 52—Lieut., 23 Nov. 56.

SERVICE.—Lieutenant GURDON served at Neemuch during the Mutinies, '57, from August to December. Present at "Nembhaira" with the Neemuch Force under Colonel Jackson; at Jeerun, 23rd October, under Major Simpson. As a Volunteer Gunner with the Garrison of the Fort of Neemuch with the Artillery when the Fort and Station were besieged by the rebels from Mundesore, from 11th to 22nd November, when the rebels raised the siege, owing to the advance on Mundesore, under Brigadier Sir C. Stuart. *Medal.* Mentioned in Despatch of Major Simpson.

(277)

H

ASSISTANT-SURGEON G. B. HADOW,† Bengal Medical Establishment.
Asst.-Surgeon, 20 Jan. 55.
SERVICE.—Served during the defence of Lucknow Residency. *Medal and Clasp, and one year's extra service.*

CAPTAIN A. S. HAIG, P. H., late 55th Native Infantry.
Ensign, 30 Jan. 43—Lieut., 2 May 45—Captain, 14 Sept. 37.
SERVICE.—Captain HAIG served during the Sutlej Campaign, '45, '46. Present at the battle of Sobraon. *Medal.*

ASSISTANT-SURGEON W. J. HAIG,† M.D., Bengal Medical Establishment.
Asst.-Surgeon, 27 Jan. 58.

MAJOR-GENERAL C. HALDANE, late 44th Native Infantry.
Ensign, 6 Feb. 19—Lieut., 26 Aug 26—Bt.-Captain, 6 Feb. 34—Captain, 25 Feb. 35—Major, 19 Dec. 42—Lieut.-Colonel, 9 April 49—Bt.-Colonel, 28 Nov. 54—Colonel, 13 March 59—Major-General, 7 Oct. 60.
SERVICE.—Major-General HALDANE served at the siege and capture of Bhurtpore, '26. *Medal.*

CAPTAIN G. H. HALE, P. H., late 57th Native Infantry.
Ensign, 20 Jan. 51—Lieut., 31 Oct. 53—Captain, 1 Jan. 62.
SERVICE.—Captain HALE served in the Campaign of '57. Present at the Mutiny of the 2nd Oude Irregular Infantry at Secrora. Served with the 12th Irregular Cavalry against the rebels near Benares, on 6th July '57. *(Horse shot.)* Contusion of the chest, action at Azimghur, 19th July; Guggah, near Goruckpore, 13th August. Present, when attacked in camp, with the Goorkha Force under Colonel Wroughton, by Mahomed Hossein. Mentioned in the Despatch of Major G. Boileau, who commanded the 12th Irregular Cavalry on the 6th July '57. Served as British Officer attached to the "Daveedut" Regiment, Goorkha Force, under Colonel Wroughton. *Medal.* Received the thanks of the Brigadier Commanding at Benares, in Brigade Orders of 7th or 8th July '57.

LIEUTENANT-COLONEL J. C. HALKETT, C.B., late 20th Native Infantry.

Ensign, 22 Oct. 22—Lieut., 22 Oct. 24—Captain, 6 Aug. 34—Bt.-Major, 23 Dec. 42—Major, 3 Sept. 49—Bt.-Lieut.-Colonel, 20 June 54—Lieut.-Colonel, 28 Nov. 54—Bt.-Colonel, 15 Sept. 55.

SERVICE.—Lieutenant-Colonel HALKETT served during the Burmese War, '25, '26. Present at the assault and capture of Arracan. *Medal.* Served throughout the Affghanistan Campaign, '39 to '42; including the assault and capture of Ghuznee. *Medal and 3rd class Dooranee Order.* Present at the defence of Khelat-i-Ghilzie. *Medal, C.B., and Brevet-Major.* Present during the operations of the Candahar Force leading to the occupation of Cabul. Present at the battle of Maharajpore. *Bronze Star.*

LIEUTENANT-COLONEL A. HALL, late 3rd Bengal European Cavalry.

Cornet, 9 Feb. 28—Lieut., 1 March 36—Captain, 14 Jan. 42—Major, 14 Nov. 53—Lieut.-Colonel, 5 May 56.

SERVICE.—Lieutenant-Colonel HALL served during the Punjab Campaign, '48, '49. Present at the actions of Ramnuggur, Sadoolapore, Chillianwallah, and Goojerat. *Medal and 2 Clasps.*

BREVET-CAPTAIN C. H. HALL, P. H., late 64th Native Infantry.

Ensign, 29 Dec. 44—Lieut., 15 Nov. 53—Bt.-Captain, 29 Dec. 59.

(Passed Examination in Civil Engineering.)

MAJOR E. HALL, P., late 52nd Native Infantry.

Ensign, 10 Jan. 36—Lieut., 20 Nov. 38—Captain, 5 Aug. 48—Major, 4 Feb. 61.

SERVICE.—Major E. HALL served in the Marwar Field Force against Joopore. Served in the Roy Bareilly District in the first occupation of Oude, in '56. Served in Command of Detachments of 31st Native Light Infantry, 3rd Irregular Cavalry, and Police, against the rebels in the Rehlee Pergunnah of Saugor, from 14th April to 9th May '58. Engaged with the rebels at Rungorea, 20th April '58. Commanded the Allyghur Levy, and No. 4 Column, Bundlecund Field Force, from 7th October to

(279)

7th December '59. Engaged with the mutineers on 8th November '59. Received the thanks of the Governor-General, 9th December '59. Commanded No. 2 Flying Column in Kishenghur District, Bundlecund, from 7th December '59 to 31st March '60, and cleared it of mutineers. These operations were noticed as most satisfactory and highly creditable in a letter from the Government of India, 29th May '60. *Medal.* *(Since retired.)*

MAJOR G. W. M. HALL, P. H., late 26th Native Infantry.

Ensign, 12 June 41—Lieut., 22 Nov. 43—Bt.-Captain, 12 June 56—Captain, 23 Nov. 56—Bt.-Major, 19 Jan. 58.

SERVICE.—Major HALL served in Affghanistan under General Pollock, in '42. Present at the battle of Mamoo Khel, Jugdulluk, Tazeen, storm and capture of Istaliff, and in all the subsequent operations on the return of the Army to India. *Medal.* Served during the Sutlej Campaign, '45, '46. Present at the actions of Moodkee, Ferozeshuhur, Sobraon, and surrender of the Fort of Kôt Kangra. *Medal and 2 Clasps.* Served in Bundlecund, '50, '51. Served under Sir A. Wilson, on the Hindun. Present in the battles of the 30th and 31st May '57. Served with the Delhi Field Force, '57. Present at the assault and capture of Delhi. *(Charger wounded.)* Went towards Agra, escorting heavy guns to Colonel Greathed's Column. Present at the destruction of the Fort of Mynpooree, in '57. Served in Oude, '58, '59, with Brigadier Troup's Column. Served in Bundlecund, under Colonel Turner, in '59. *Medal and Clasp.*

LIEUTENANT-GENERAL H. HALL, C.B., late 21st Native Infantry.

Ensign, 10 Sept. 05—Lieut., 13 March 06—Captain, 5 Oct. 21—Major, 13 Jan. 28—Lieut.-Colonel, 9 Jan. 33—Colonel, 21 Dec. 44—Major-General, 20 June 54—Lieut.-General, 24 Oct. 58.

SERVICE.—Lieutenant-General HALL served at the reduction of the Bundlecund Province, in '06, '07, which included the sieges of Unda, Burgowa, Cheemere, and the surrender of nineteen other forts; as Adjutant of the 4th Light Battalion, at the storming of the fortified hills of Rogoulee, and at the siege of the first class hill fortress of

Adjeeghur, in '09, under Sir G. Martindell; also with the Army under General Sir Gabriel Martindell, which kept Nawab Mheer Khan in check, and prevented his invading our dominions; with a light Force reducing the enterprising Chief, Ghopaul Sing, up the Bundlecund Ghauts, in '10, '11; at the siege of the first class hill fortress of Callenger, in '11, '12, under Sir Gabriel Martindell; also as Deputy Assistant Quarter-Master-General with Sir David Ochterlony's Division of the Grand Army, in the Great Pindarree War of '17, '18, which was carried on by the Marquis of Hastings; subsequently, in the same capacity (Deputy Assistant Quarter-Master-General), till '23 (from '17), on various services, including the reduction of the first class hill fortress of Taraghur, under Sir Alexander Knox; the sieges of Maharajpore and Nussreeda, during the rains of same year, in Rajpootana. The first Campaign of Mhairwarra, in '19; the second in '21, comprising attacks on Jog-Shamghur, fort of Huttoon Burrar, Kôt Kurrana, Ramghur, and Cheetar, which in result finally subdued that destructive race, the Mhairs; in the action of Mongrowl, against the Kotah Rajah, in '21; and the siege of Samba, in '22. During this period, '17 to '23, the various duties of the Guide and Intelligence Department and also general political duties for Sir David Ochterlony were discharged by Lieutenant-General Hall, as well as those of the Quarter-Master-General's Department, and all so satisfactorily, that in '22 the Marquis of Hastings appointed him to the important duties of civilising the turbulent race of Mhairs. And to effect this, he raised a Corps, composed chiefly of that tribe, equal to any of the Line, in discipline; and its fidelity (as well as that of the whole race,) was severely tested during the late out-break of the Bengal Army, on which occasion it aided materially to save the city of Ajmere, its magazine, and all kind of stores, artillery, treasury, and jail, from falling into the hands of the mutineers at Nusseerabad (only 11 miles distant); and also afforded, both at Ajmere and the Head Quarters of the Corps at Beaur, a refuge for the Officers and their families, in short, for all Europeans. The dreadful custom of female infanticide, slavery, sale of women, murder, and universal plunder completely ceased. During his career General Hall received the publicly expressed approbation of the different authorities, from the Governor-General downwards, nearly fifty times.

(281)

MAJOR J. F. D'E. W. HALL, late 22nd Native Infantry.

Ensign, 16 April 36—Lieut., 20 July 39—Captain, 23 April 49—Major, 4 Aug. 59.

(Passed examination in Surveying.)

CAPTAIN J. T. S. HALL,† late 12th Native Infantry.

Ensign, 12 Dec. 40—Lieut., 10 April 43—Captain, 31 Dec. 44.

SERVICE.—Captain HALL served throughout the Sutlej Campaign, and was present at the action of Ferozeshuhur. *Medal.*

LIEUTENANT M. HALL, late 1st European Bengal Fusiliers.

2nd Lieut., 1 March 52—Lieut., 1 Feb. 56.

SERVICE.—Lieutenant HALL served in the Burmese War from 2nd January '53 till its close. *Medal and Clasp.* Present at Allahabad in June, July, and August '57, and joined General Havelock's Force at Cawnpore in September. Appointed Assistant Field Engineer to that Force, and present at the actions of Mungulwar, 21st; Alum Bagh, 23rd; and 1st relief of the Lucknow Garrison, 25th September '57. Present as Assistant Field Engineer, and in charge of the Alum Bagh outpost with the Force under Sir J. Outram, till 9th January '59. Present throughout the Trans-Goomptee operations under Sir J. Outram, and siege and capture of Lucknow, March '58. Also in the subsequent operations in Oude, including the affair at Baree and minor affairs near Durriabad. Mentioned in Despatch of Major Crommelin, and thanked in General Orders. *Medal and 2 Clasps.*

CAPTAIN C. T. HALLETT, P. H., late 72nd Native Infantry.

Ensign, 30 Dec. 43—Lieut., 1 Feb. 48—Captain, 28 Aug. 57.

LIEUTENANT G. T. HALLIDAY,† late 4th Bengal European Cavalry.

Cornet, 20 Nov. 58—Lieut., 29 March 59.

(282)

MAJOR-GENERAL C. HAMILTON, C.B., late 59th Native Infantry.

Ensign, 27 Jan. 18—Lieut., 1 Aug. 18—Captain, 9 Oct. 26—Major, 26 Nov. 36—Lieut.-Colonel, 19 Jan 43—Colonel, 14 July 53—Major-General, 28 Nov. 54.

SERVICE.—Major-General HAMILTON served at the battle of Maharajpore. *Bronze Star and C.B.* Throughout the Sutlej Campaign, '45, '46. Present at the actions of Moodkee and Ferozeshuhur. *Medal and Clasp.* Served with the expedition against Kôt Kangra, '46.

LIEUTENANT-GENERAL C. W. HAMILTON, late 40th Native Infantry.

Ensign, 20 Sept. 1800—Lieut., 20 Sept. 01—Bt.-Captain, 15 June 14—Captain, 16 Dec. 14—Major, 11 July 23—Lieut.-Colonel, 18 May 25—Bt.-Colonel, 18 June 31—Colonel, 6 Aug. 35—Major-General, 23 Nov. 41—Lieut.-General, 11 Nov. 51.

SERVICE.—Lieutenant-General HAMILTON served under Brigadier General Harcourt at the capture of Cuttack and siege of the Forts of Barra Battee and Khoordah. Nepal War, '14, '15. Present at the taking of the Forts of Ramghur, Tarraghur, and Chumbulsoorjghur, and commanded a Column in the attack on the heights of Malown. *Medal.* Pindarree Campaign, '17, '18. Employed at the surrender of the Fort of Tarraghur, and capture of Jumshaid Khan's guns on the Sambhur Lake. Commanded in various engagements with the Insurgent Bheels, '22, '23, and '24.

BREVET-CAPTAIN G. HAMILTON, P. H., late 51st Native Infantry.

Ensign, 9 Dec. 43—Lieut., 1 Oct. 52—Bt.-Captain, 9 Dec. 58.

SERVICE.—Captain HAMILTON served with the Army of the Sutlej, '45, '46, holding the Forts of Dhurmkôt and Jugraon. Served at the occupation of Lahore, '48, '49. Present during the whole of the operations of the first and second sieges and surrender of Mooltan. *Medal and Clasp.* Present at the evacuation of Chineout and battle of Goojerat. *Clasp.*

LIEUTENANT G. F. HAMILTON, Bengal Artillery.

Lieut., 27 April 58.

(283)

LIEUTENANT-COLONEL G. W. HAMILTON, late 17th Native Infantry.

Ensign, 20 June 24—Lieut., 22 Aug. 26—Bt.-Captain, 20 June 39—Captain, 17 March 44—Bt.-Major, 11 Nov. 51—Major, 5 Aug. 54—Lieut.-Colonel, 19 May 58.

SERVICE.—Lieutenant-Colonel HAMILTON served in the Cole Campaign, '32. Present in several actions. Served under Brigadier Paske, in the Chooar Campaign, '32, '33. Present in several actions. Served as Political Officer in charge of Levies in the Campaign on the Nerbudda, '42, '43. Served in same capacity in the Gwalior and Bundlecund Frontier, during the Gwalior Campaign, '43. Received thanks of the Governor-General, 14th February '44. Present at the disarming of the Native Troops at Mooltan, 10th June '57. Accompanied the Googaira Field Force as Commissioner, and was present in action in '57. Served against the Mutineers at Mooltan, in '58. Received the thanks of the Governor-General, 27th September '58. *Medal*. Received intimation of the gracious approbation of Her Majesty for excellent service during '57, '58, on the 11th June '60.

CAPTAIN J. HAMILTON, Veteran Establishment.
Invalided, 18 May 60.

CAPTAIN J. C. HAMILTON,† late 6th Europeans.

Ensign, 12 June 47—Lieut., 25 Feb. 52—Captain, 4 Dec. 59.

SERVICE.—Captain HAMILTON served during the Punjab Campaign, '48, '49. Present at the siege and surrender of Mooltan, 22nd January '48, and at the battle of Goojerat, 21st February '49. *Medal and 2 Clasps*. Present during the Mutiny of the Native Troops at Dinapore, 25th July '57. Volunteered and served in the ranks of H. M.'s 10th Regiment, when the rebels were driven from the station. Commanded No. 6 Company, H. M.'s 10th Regiment, in the Arrah District, including the action at Delawur, and capture of Koer Sing's stronghold at Jugdespore. Served with the Royal Naval Brigade, under Captain Sotheby, R. N., from October '57 to January '58, including the action of Saharunpore, 26th December '57. Served under Sir E. Lugard, in the Arrah District, as

Interpreter and Staff Officer. Served during the Oude Campaign, '58, '59, under Sir R. D. Kelly. Received thanks of Parliament and Government of India and of the Governor-General. 1 *Medal*.

CAPTAIN J. J. HAMILTON, P. H., late 2nd Native Infantry.

Ensign, 9 Aug. 41—Lieut., 4 Oct. 44—Captain, 24 Oct. 54.

SERVICE.—Captain HAMILTON served at the action of Maharajpore, *Bronze Star*; also engaged against a body of insurgents at Gowrie, in the Nizam's Territory, 6th May '49.

BREVET-MAJOR O. HAMILTON, P., late 2nd Bengal European Cavalry.

Cornet, 24 Jan. 39—Lieut., 28 Sept. 41—Captain, 20 Dec. 51—Bt.-Major, 19 Jan. 58.

SERVICE.—Major HAMILTON served under Sir C. Napier against the Hill Tribes in Scinde, in '48; also during the Punjab Campaign, '48, '49. *Medal*.

CAPTAIN T. C. HAMILTON, P. H., late 35th Native Infantry.

Ensign, 13 June 46—Lieut., 17 Nov. 52—Captain, 14 Sept. 59.

2ND CAPTAIN SIR W. HAMILTON, P. H., Bengal Artillery.

2nd Lieut., 8 Dec. 48—Lieut., 3 Sept. 53—2nd Captain, 27 Aug. 58.

CAPTAIN W. C. HAMILTON, late 2nd European Bengal Fusiliers.

2nd Lieut., 5 Jan 45—Lieut., 21 July 48—Captain, 16 Dec. 59.

SERVICE.—Captain HAMILTON served on the Staff of his Regiment throughout the Punjab Campaign, and was present at the actions of Ramnuggur, Chillianwallah, and Goojerat, in which last action his turban was shot through, and his horse killed under him; also with Sir W. R. Gilbert's Force in pursuit of the Affghans to Peshawur. *Medal and 2 Clasps*. Was also present in action against the rebels at Saugor, during the Mutiny, and led the advanced party of a Detachment of the 31st Native Infantry, when attacked by the Patun rebels on the 19th July '57, from whom a gun was taken. *Medal*.

(285)

LIEUTENANT W. R. HAMILTON,† General List.
Ensign, 27 April 59—Lieut., 19 Oct. 60.

LIEUTENANT F. HAMMOND, P. H., late 62nd Native Infantry.
Ensign, 8 Sept. 56—Lieut., 8 Aug. 57.

SERVICE.—Lieutenant HAMMOND was present at the quelling of the disturbances in the Googaira District, in '57. At the outbreak of the 62nd and 69th Native Infantry at Mooltan, in '58.

LIEUTENANT-COLONEL J. H. HAMPTON, late 50th Native Infantry.
Ensign, 11 July 23—Lieut., 18 Nov. 24—Bt.-Captain, 11 July 38—Captain, 7 July 42—Bt.-Major, 11 Nov. 51—Major, 9 Aug. 54—Bt.-Lieut.-Colonel, 22 Aug. 57—Lieut.-Colonel, 19 May 58.

SERVICE.—Lieutenant-Colonel HAMPTON served against the Coles in '33, '34. During the Punjab Campaign, '48, '49. *Medal.* Served during the Sonthal Rebellion, '55, '56. *(Since retired.)*

LIEUTENANT W. HAMPTON, Bengal Invalid Establishment.
Ensign, 21 Aug. 39—Lieut., 12 Jan. 42.

COLONEL W. P. HAMPTON, † 2nd (late 31st) Native Infantry.
Ensign, 3 March 28—Lieut., 8 May 34—Bt.-Captain, 3 March 43—Captain, 24 Jan. 45—Bt.-Major, 20 June 54—Major, 28 Nov. 56—Lieut.-Colonel, 4 June 60.

SERVICE.—Colonel HAMPTON served against the Coles, '36, '37, in Affghanistan and at the capture of Khelat, in '39. Action of Maharajpore. *Bronze Star.* With the Army of the Punjab, '48, '49. Present at the battles of Sadoolapore, Chillianwallah, and Goojerat, and in the subsequent pursuit of the Sikh Army and occupation of Peshawur. *Medal and 2 Clasps.* And with the Force employed against the Affreedies in '50.

LIEUTENANT A. G. HANDCOCK, late 43rd Native Infantry.
Ensign, 11 Dec. 58—Lieut., 20 Aug. 59.

(286)

BREVET-CAPTAIN G. C. HANKIN, P., late 28th Native Infantry.

Ensign, 8 Dec. 43—Lieut., 13 Nov. 45—Bt.-Captain, 8 Dec. 58.
(Passed examination in Punjabee.)

BREVET-CAPTAIN F. H. HANMER,† late 34th Native Infantry.

Ensign, 9 Dec. 44—Lieut., 21 Feb. 52—Bt.-Captain, 9 Dec. 59.

ENSIGN H. B. HANNA, P. H., General List.

Ensign, 4 Jan. 60.

LIEUTENANT-COLONEL S. F. HANNAY, late 44th Native Infantry.

Ensign, 3 April 20—Lieut., 11 July 23—Captain, 1 April 35—Bt.-Major, 9 Nov. 46—Major, 26 July 52—Bt.-Lieut.-Colonel, 20 June 54—Lieut.-Colonel, 8 June 57—Bt.-Colonel, 20 June 57.

(Since dead.)

BREVET-COLONEL J. C. HANNYNGTON, P. C., late 34th Native Infantry.

Ensign, 8 Jan. 25—Lieut., 20 July 25—Bt.-Captain, 8 Jan. 40—Captain, 11 Oct. 43—Major, 6 Oct. 50—Bt.-Lieut.-Colonel, 28 Nov. 54—Lieut.-Colonel, 9 April 56.

SERVICE.—Lieutenant-Colonel HANNYNGTON served against the Coles, '32, '33. *(Since retired.)*

LIEUTENANT A. F. P. HARCOURT, late 30th Native Infantry.

Ensign, 8 June 55—Lieut., 23 Nov. 56.

LIEUTENANT J. E. HARDEN, late 1st European Bengal Fusiliers.

2nd Lieut., 20 Jan. 59.

ENSIGN T. F. HARDY (Unattached).

Ensign, 20 Nov. 58.

SERVICE.—Ensign HARDY served throughout the Burmese War, in '52, '53, with the late 1st European Bengal Fusiliers. Present at the

(287)

relief of the Garrison of Pegu, on the 14th of December '52, and operations in its vicinity; accompanied the Martaban Column under General Steel. *Medal.* Present at the battle of Badlee-ka-Serai, 8th June '57; and in all the subsequent actions under the walls of Delhi. Present at the storm and capture of Delhi, 14th September '57. *(Wounded.) Medal and Clasp.* Served under Command of Brigadier J. G. Gerrard and Sir Thomas Seaton. Present at the actions of Narnoul, 16th November; Gungeeree, 14th; Puttiallee, 17th; and Mynpooree, 27th December '57. Present at the storm and capture of Lucknow, March '58, and all the subsequent operations in Oude under Sir Hope Grant. Ensign's Commission for services during the Mutiny. '57. *Clasp.*

SURGEON-MAJOR E. HARE,† Bengal Medical Establishment.

Asst.-Surgeon, 25 July 39—Surgeon, 25 Aug. 53—Surgeon-Major, 13 Jan. 60.

SERVICE.—Surgeon-Major HARE served at Cabul in '40, at Joolgah and Purwandurra, under General Sale, in the same year. Was in the Garrison of Jellallabad under Sir R. Sale, during the siege. *Medal.* Marched to Cabul under Sir G. Pollock, held charge of the General's Staff. *Medal.* Served in the Burmah Campaign in '52, to '54, in charge of the 1st European Bengal Fusiliers, and re-capture of Pegu. Appointed to the charge of the Burmah Field Hospital. *Medal.* Served as Surgeon of the 2nd Bengal Fusiliers in '57, throughout the siege of Delhi; also at the action of Badlee-ka-Serai, and the final assault and capture of Delhi, 14th September '57. *Medal and Clasp.*

LIEUTENANT THE HON'BLE H. H. HARE, P. H., late 17th Native Infantry.

Ensign, 20 Feb. 57—Lieut., 16 Sept. 57.

SERVICE.—Lieutenant the Hon'ble H. H. HARE served in the Volunteer Cavalry with Major General Sir Henry Havelock's Force during the Campaign in '57, including the actions of Futtehpore, Aong, Pandoo Nuddee, Cawnpore, Oonao, Busseerutgunge, Barby-ka-Chowkie, and Bithoor. Served with the Force under Lord Clyde, at the relief of

Lucknow, in November '57; the defeat of the Gwalior Contingent at Cawnpore, December '57 ; the subsequent Campaign to Futtehghur, and throughout the siege of Lucknow, in March '58. Served in the Military Mounted Police with the Force under Major-General Sir Hope Grant, at the action of Nawabgunge, June '58. *Medal and* 1 *Clasp.*

LIEUTENANT R. T. HARE, P. H., Bengal Artillery.

1st Lieut., 27 April 58.

SERVICE.—Lieutenant HARE served before Delhi, '57. Present at the battle of Badlee-ka-Serai *(slightly wounded)*, and throughout the siege and capture of Delhi. Mentioned in the Despatch of Sir A. Wilson. Present at the affair of Boolundshuhur and action of Agra, with the Force under Lord Clyde ; at the relief of Lucknow, November '57; also at the defeat of the Gwalior Contingent at Cawnpore, 6th December '57. Present at the siege of Calpee. Mentioned in the Despatch of Sir H. Rose, '59. *Medal and* 2 *Clasps.*

SURGEON-MAJOR G. HARPER,† Bengal Medical Establishment.

Asst.-Surgeon, 25 July 39—Surgeon, 25 Aug. 53—Surgeon-Major, 13 Jan. 60.

SERVICE.—Surgeon-Major G. HARPER served with Brigadier Wild's Brigade. Was present at the forcing of the Khyber Pass, and through the subsequent Campaign with Sir George Pollock's Force. *Medal.* Served with the Army throughout the Punjab Campaign. *Medal.*

LIEUTENANT F. D. HARRINGTON, P. H., late 12th Native Infantry.

Ensign, 10 Dec. 54—Lieut., 23 Nov. 56.

SERVICE.—Lieutenant HARRINGTON served throughout the Sonthal Insurrection, '55.

LIEUTENANT H. E. HARRINGTON, P. H., V.C., Bengal Artillery.

1st Lieut., 27 June 57.

SERVICE.—Lieutenant HARRINGTON served during the Mutiny Campaign. *Medal and V.C.* (*Vide* Victoria Cross Roll.) *(Since dead.)*

(289)

MAJOR C. HARRIS, P., late 27th Native Infantry.

Ensign, 9 Feb. 35—Lieut., 8 Oct. 39—Captain, 3 May 47—Major, 4 June 60.

SERVICE.—Major HARRIS served with the Army of the Indus, from October to December '38. Served with Brigadier Shelton's Force in Affghanistan, November '40. Served in a Campaign, in January '41, against the Affghan Tribes of Sungoo Khilloun, in the Valley of Nargeean, near Jellallabad. Served in the Fortress of Ghuznee, June '41. Present in the Fortress at the time it was beseiged by the Affghans, from November '41 to March '42. In February '42 deputed as a hostage with the Affghan Chiefs, for a specific purpose; was a prisoner in the hands of the Affghans, from March till November '42, at Ghuznee, Cabul, and Bamuan. *Medal.* Served with the Army of the Sutlej, '46. In the capacity of Commissariat Officer at the bridge of boats over the Sutlej, employed in forwarding supplies to the Army at Lahore. Served with Brigadier Wheeler's Field Force in Bundlecund, from August to December '59.

LIEUTENANT-GENERAL J. HARRIS, late 4th Europeans.

Ensign, 1 Dec. 03—Lieut., 13 Nov. 04—Captain, 10 June 19— Major, 21 Jan. 29—Lieut.-Colonel, 5 April 34—Colonel, 30 Sept. 45— Major-General, 20 June 54—Lieut.-General, 29 Aug. 59.

CAPTAIN J. C. HARRIS,† Bengal Engineers.

2nd Lieut., 8 Dec. 43—Lieut., 6 Nov. 49—Captain, 27 April 58.

LIEUTENANT J. P. HARRIS, P. H., late 21st Native Infantry.

Ensign, 8 June 54—Lieut., 28 March 56.

LIEUTENANT J. T. HARRIS, P. H., late 2nd European Bengal Fusiliers.

2nd Lieut., 27 June 49—Lieut., 13 Nov. 54.

SERVICE.—Lieutenant HARRIS served with his Regiment during the operations before Delhi. Present at the battle of Badlee-ka-Serai, 8th June '57. *(Wounded through the thigh.) Medal.*

BREVET-COLONEL P. HARRIS, late 1st European Bengal Fusiliers.

Ensign, 18 Feb. 24—Lieut., 13 May 25—Bt.-Captain, 18 Feb. 39—Captain, 8 Oct. 39—Bt.-Major, 30 April 44—Major, 20 July 57—Bt.-Lieut.-Colonel, 20 June 54—Bt.-Colonel, 8 June 56.

SERVICE.—Colonel HARRIS served with the Army of Gwalior, '43, '44. Present at the actions of Maharajpore, *Bronze Star;* and Choundah, 29th December '43. Mentioned in Despatch of Lieutenant-General Sir J. Littler, for "conspicuous gallantry, 30th December '43.

LIEUTENANT P. H. F. HARRIS, P. H., late 70th Native Infantry.

Ensign, 20 Dec. 50—Lieut., 23 Nov. 56.

SERVICE.—Lieutenant HARRIS served with the China Expeditionary Force under General VanStrawbenzee, '58, '59. Present in the White Cloud Expedition against the Branes, June '58.

BREVET-MAJOR W. D. HARRIS, late 2nd European Bengal Fusiliers.

2nd Lieut., 25 Jan. 41—Lieut., 26 Dec. 42—Captain, 1 March 52—Bt.-Major, 19 Jan. 58.

SERVICE.—Major HARRIS served during the Punjab Campaign, '48, '49. Present at the affair of Ramnuggur, passage of the Chenab, and actions of Chillianwallah and Goojerat, and subsequent operations under Major-General Sir H. Gilbert, ending in the final surrender of the Sikh Army, and pursuit of the Affghans under Dost Mahomed through the Valley of Peshawur to the mouth of the Khyber Pass. *Medal and 2 Clasps.* Served as 2nd in Command of the Bengal Fusiliers during the whole of the operations before Delhi, June '57, including the affair of the 12th of August, under Brigadier Showers, at the assault and subsequent capture of Delhi; also with the Moveable Column in October and November, under Brigadier Showers, into the Mharwattie District, in pursuit of the rebels, capturing the Fortress of Jhujjur, and several other fortified places. *Medal and Clasp.* Mentioned in the Despatch of Brigadier Showers to the Commander-in-Chief, 4th December '57. Brevet-Majority for Service before Delhi.

ASSISTANT-SURGEON W. P. HARRIS,† M.D., Bengal Medical Establishment.
Asst.-Surgeon, 23 July 58.

LIEUTENANT A. HARRISON, General List.
Ensign, 20 Feb. 59—Lieut., 20 Feb. 60.

LIEUTENANT C. W. G. HARRISON, Bengal Engineers.
Lieut., 27 Aug. 58.

CAPTAIN E. HARRISON, P. H., Bengal Artillery.
2nd Lieut., 7 June 44—Lieut., 12 Aug. 46—Captain, 27 April 58.

SERVICE.—Captain HARRISON served during the Sutlej Campaign. Present at the battle of Sobraon, '46. *Medal.*

SURGEON J. HARRISON, M.D., P., Bengal Medical Establishment.
Asst.-Surgeon, 5 April 42—Surgeon, 6 Sept. 56.

SERVICE.—Surgeon J. HARRISON served in the Campaign of the Sutlej in '45, '46, and present at the battle of Ferozeshuhur. *Medal.* With the Army of the Punjab, '48, '49, including the actions of Sadoolapore, Chillianwallah, and Goojerat. *Medal and Clasp.*

SURGEON J. B. HARRISON,† M.D., Bengal Medical Establishment.
Asst.-Surgeon, 1 Feb. 43—Surgeon, 31 May 57.

SERVICE.—Surgeon HARRISON served with the 10th Native Infantry in the Army formed by Major-General Sir C. Napier, to co-operate with the Army of the Sutlej. In an affair with the 6th Punjab Cavalry against the Sheoranees, on the Dehra Ishmael Khan Frontier, December '51.

CAPTAIN T. B. HARRISON, P., late 4th Bengal European Cavalry.
Cornet, 20 Dec. 45—Lieut., 9 Oct. 50—Captain, 23 July 58.

(292)

LIEUTENANT T. P. HARRISON, P. H., late 69th Native Infantry.
Ensign, 20 March 50—Lieut., 28 Jan. 56.

LIEUTENANT W. L. S. HARRISON, late 2nd European Bengal Fusiliers.
2nd Lieut., 4 Nov. 57—Lieut., 23 Aug. 59.

ENSIGN W. P. HARRISON, General List.
Ensign, 4 Jan. 61.

BREVET-MAJOR E. HARVEY,† late 4th Bengal European Cavalry.
Cornet, 31 March 30—Lieut., 4 Nov. 54—Bt.-Captain, 31 March 45—Captain, 8 May 49—Bt.-Major, 28 Nov. 54.

2ND CAPTAIN T. N. HARWARD, P. H., Bengal Artillery.
2nd Lieut., 8 Dec. 48—Lieut., 6 March 53—2nd Captain, 27 Aug. 58.

MAJOR C. HASELL, late 48th Native Infantry.
Ensign, 13 Dec. 33—Lieut., 22 June 38—Captain, 24 Jan. 45—Bt.-Major, 28 Nov. 54—Major, 4 Oct. 57.

SERVICE.—Major HASELL commanded the 48th Native Infantry in the Wuzeeree Valley, when six Forts were taken. Commanded the Regiment from Thudgah to Kurnoul, and six times through the Khyber Pass. *(Since dead.)*

MAJOR W. K. HASLEWOOD, Invalid Establishment.
Ensign, 27 June 36—Lieut., 10 Aug. 38—Captain, 1 April 49—Major, 20 Sept. 58.

SERVICE.—Major HASLEWOOD served with the " Army of the Indus" in '38, '39. *Slightly wounded* in the " Bolan Pass." *Dangerously wounded* at the assault and capture of the Fort of Ghuznee, on the 23rd of July '39. Received five sword cuts, one cutting off the head of the right hip joint, and one freely exposing the capsule of the right shoulder joint. Made A. D. C. to the Governor-General, Lord Auckland. *Medal.* Volunteered his services on the breaking out of the Mutiny in '57, and

(293)

at one hour's notice proceeded to Allahabad in Command of a small Detachment of H. M.'s 84th Regiment. Was then placed in Command of two Companies of Invalid Artillery, and was present during General Neill's operations in the vicinity. *Medal*, and made Fort Adjutant, Allahabad. Received the substantive rank of "*Major*."

LIEUTENANT E. G. G. HASTINGS, General List, Cavalry.
Lieut., 26 Aug. 59.

ENSIGN F. E. HASTINGS, General List.
Ensign, 10 Dec. 59.

SURGEON T. HASTINGS, F.R.C.S., Bengal Medical Establishment.
Asst.-Surgeon, 9 Sept. 42—Surgeon, 21 March 57.

BREVET-MAJOR G. C. HATCH, P., late 57th Native Infantry.
Ensign, 12 Dec. 38—Lieut., 11 Nov. 40—Captain, 19 April 51—Bt.-Major, 24 March 58.

ASSISTANT-SURGEON C. HATCHELL,† Bengal Medical Establishment.
Asst.-Surgeon, 23 July 58.

SURGEON C. HATHAWAY,† M.D., Bengal Medical Establishment.
Asst.-Surgeon, 10 Aug. 43—Surgeon, 27 June 57.

CAPTAIN J. G. HATHORN, P. H., Bengal Artillery.
2nd Lieut., 13 June 45—Lieut., 1 Sept. 48—2nd Captain, 27 Aug. 58—Captain, 18 Feb. 61.

MAJOR J. C. HAUGHTON, P.H., late 54th Native Infantry.
Ensign, 15 Feb. 37—Lieut., 16 July 42—Bt.-Captain, 15 Feb. 52—Captain, 15 Nov. 53—Major in Staff Corps, 18 Feb. 61.

SERVICE.—Major HAUGHTON served with the Army of the Indus, '38 to '42. Present in the Bolan Pass, in the vicinity of Khelat-i-Ghilzie, when it was stormed. Was with the Regiment when it resisted successfully a night attack of the defeated troops, Merab Khan. Present in Ghilzie Campaign, '40, and in the action at Abee Tazae, 16th May '40, when the Ghilzies were defeated. Present throughout the siege of Chereekar, and commanded 6th Goorkha Regiment, when it was cut to pieces. *(Badly wounded* and lost right hand.) Present with Army at Cabul during the siege. Left in the hospital in the hands of the enemy, under General Elphinstone's capitulation, and remained in the hands of the enemy till September '42. Served with Broadfoot's Sappers and Miners during the re-occupation of Cabul and march from Affghanistan. Served in seven affairs, where the enemy were defeated, during '46, '47, with the Ramghur Battalion. Has received a pension of £90 for wounds at Chereekar, and in consideration of conduct. (Has received no *Medal* for the Campaign in Affghanistan, and was promised the Brevet of Major, which he subsequently did not obtain.)

LIEUTENANT A. J. D. HAWES, P. H., late 32nd Native Infantry.

Ensign, 6 Jan. 59—Lieut., 9 Nov. 60.

SERVICE.—Lieutenant HAWES served with the Column under Lieutenant-Colonel Gawler, in Sikkim, from the 10th January '61 to the 11th April '61.

LIEUTENANT C. W. HAWES, P. H., late 43rd Native Infantry.

Ensign, 13 Feb. 53—Lieut., 23 Nov. 56.

SERVICE.—Lieutenant HAWES served as Adjutant and Commandant of Cavalry Guides before Delhi, in '57. Commanded the Infantry on several occasions during the siege, assault, and capture of Delhi. Present in every skirmish from the 9th June to 14th September '57. *(Wounded four times.) Medal and Clasp.* Present with Brigadier Showers' Flying Column in the district about Delhi, in '57, after the capture, as Commandant of Guide Cavalry. Served with the Force under Sir S. Cotton in the Sultana Expedition, against the Hill Tribes in Eusuffzaie, in April and May '58, as Commandant of Cavalry and 2nd in Command of Guides.

(295)

CAPTAIN H. J. HAWES, P., late 4th Europeans.
Ensign, 24 Feb. 46—Lieut., 1 Feb. 50—Captain, 27 June 57.

CAPTAIN W. H. HAWES, P., late 63rd Native Infantry.
Ensign, 7 Jan. 46—Lieut., 2 Dec. 49—Captain, 15 Jan. 57.

SERVICE.—Captain HAWES served throughout the Sonthal Campaign in '55. Received the thanks of Government. Served throughout the siege of Lucknow, '57. *Severely wounded* in two places, and received a gratuity of twelve months' pay, 27th July '58. As Acting Interpreter to H. M.'s 53rd Foot, was present at the actions of 6th and 9th December '57, and 2nd January '58. As Brigade-Major and Intelligence Officer to the District Brigade Force, was present at the action of Khankur, 7th April '58. Mentioned in the Despatch of the Brigadier Commanding, 3rd May '58. Accompanied Lord Clyde's Force as 2nd in Command of the Oude Military Police of the Trans-Gogra Division, in '58, and January '59. *Medal and Clasp, and one year's extra service.*

MAJOR-GENERAL R. HAWKES, late 4th Bengal European Cavalry.
Cornet, 29 March 06—Lieut., 9 Nov. 11—Bt.-Captain, 29 March 21—Captain, 13 May 25—Major, 10 Oct. 36—Lieut.-Colonel, 23 Dec. 39—Bt.-Colonel, 28 March 50—Colonel, 4 Feb. 59—Major-General, 28 Nov. 54.

SERVICE.—Major-General HAWKES served during the Mahrattah War, '17, '18. Employed with the dismounted Cavalry at the storm of Choundah, '18. *Medal.*

CAPTAIN J. P. P. T. HAWKEY,† late 74th Native Infantry.
Ensign, 18 July 37—Lieut., 30 April 38—Captain, 1 Dec. 48.

2ND CAPTAIN E. L. HAWKINS, Bengal Artillery.
1st Lieut., 25 June 57—2nd Captain, 18 Feb. 61.

LIEUTENANT F. D. HAWKINS,† late 32nd Native Infantry.
Ensign, 10 Dec. 54—Lieut., 6 June 57.

SERVICE.—Lieutenant HAWKINS served during the Mutinies, '57.

Present at Jullundur. *(Wounded.)* Accompanied Brigadier Johnston's Column of pursuit. Present at Cavalry skirmishes of Molum Brigade and Russoolabad, July '58; at the attack on Fort Borowah, August '58, at Sundala and Jamoo. Mentioned in the Despatch of Sir G. Barker, 13th November '58. Commanded 3rd Oude Police Cavalry at Chilowlee, Subrowlee, and Pooneat, under Colonel Bulwer, also at Maharajgunge and Simree. Mentioned in Despatch of Brigadier Evelegh, 17th December '58. Held the Fort of Toorwah when attacked by " Banee Madhow Sing" with 7,000 men and 3 guns. Received the thanks of the Oude Local Government and of the Governor-General, 20th December '58. Repeatedly brought to the notice of the Oude Local Government by Colonel Bruce and Captain Chamberlain. *Medal.*

LIEUTENANT F. K. HAWKINS, P. H., late 44th Native Infantry.

Ensign, 20 Dec. 54—Lieut., 21 June 57.

SERVICE.—Lieutenant HAWKINS served during the Sonthal Campaign, '55. Present at Benares on the 7th July '57, in the attack on the Dhobys. Served in the Army under General Havelock; commanded a Detachment of the Regiment of Ferozepore, on 19th July '57, at Sydabad, near Allahabad, to protect the Grand Trunk Road. Captured a Mud Fort near the Grand Trunk Road, held by the rebel Joorie Sing, 18th August '57. Served in the defence of Cawnpore, under General Windham, November '57, and subsequent defeat of the Gwalior Contingent, December '57. Served in the Campaign in the Doab, capture of Futtehghur, action of Shumshabad, near Futtehghur, siege and capture of Lucknow, attack on the Fort of Rooya, in Oude, under Brigadier-General Walpole, action of Allygunge, Rohilcund Campaign, and occupation of Bareilly: during a severe engagement in the City of Lucknow succeeded to the temporary Command of the 4th Punjab Rifles, and brought the Regiment out of action. *Medal and Clasp.* Thanked by the Officer Commanding at Allahabad, for taking the Fort held by Joorie Sing, August '57. Mentioned in Despatch of Sir E. Lugard, for the action in Lucknow of 19th March. Served as Interpreter to a Detachment of H. M.'s 37th Foot, from Calcutta to Benares, June '57, and from Allahabad to Cawnpore, October '57. Mentioned in Despatch of Sir E.

Lugard. Served under Colonel Maxwell, in July '58, during the Campaign near Lucknow.

LIEUTENANT H. L. HAWKINS,† late 30th Native Infantry.

Ensign, 11 June 53—Lieut., 8 April 56.

SERVICE.—Lieutenant HAWKINS served at the siege and capture of Kotah, '58. Served in Command of a Detachment of Mayne's Horse, at the action of Seekur, January '59. *Medal and Clasp.*

LIEUTENANT W. L. HAWKINS, † late 30th Native Infantry.

Ensign, 11th June 53—Lieut., 8th April 56.

SERVICE.—Lieutenant HAWKINS served with a Detachment of the late 30th Regiment with the Field Force under Major-General Roberts, at the siege and capture of Kotah, in '58. Served with the Column under Lieutenant-Colonel J. Holmes, in Rajpootanah, in Command of a Detachment of Mayne's Horse, in the action at Sikkim, January '57. *Medal and Clasp.*

MAJOR R. J. HAWTHORNE, late 2nd Bengal European Cavalry.

Cornet, 12 Sept. 28—Lieut., 13 April 37—Bt.-Captain, 12 Sept. 43—Captain, 11 Dec. 48.—Bt.-Major, 20 June 54—Major, 13 April 55.

SERVICE.—Major HAWTHORNE served in Scinde, '45, '46. During the Punjab Campaign, '48, '49. *Medal.*

CORNET E. HAY, Cavalry, General List.

Cornet, 4 Dec. 59.

CAPTAIN G. J. D. HAY, P., late 57th Native Infantry.

Ensign, 20 March 47—Lieut., 4 Nov. 52—Captain, 21 Nov. 58.

SERVICE.—Captain HAY commanded a Squadron, 8th Bengal Cavalry, on 25th May '57, against the mutineers of the 55th Native Infantry, at Hoti Murdoun.

(298)

LIEUTENANT J. HAY, General List.
Ensign, 11 June 59—Lieut., 20 Feb. 61.

ASSISTANT-SURGEON W. H. HAYES, † Bengal Medical Establishment.
Asst.-Surgeon, 4 Aug. 55.

BREVET-CAPTAIN H. HAYLEY, P. H., late 69th Native Infantry.
Ensign, 27 July 44—Lieut., 31 July 49—Bt.-Captain, 27 July 59.
SERVICE.—Captain HAYLEY served during the Punjab Campaign, '48, '49. *Medal.*

LIEUTENANT F. G. HEARN, P. H., General List.
Ensign, 20 May 59—Lieut., 4 Nov. 60.

LIEUTENANT A. HEARSEY, late 5th Bengal European Cavalry.
Cornet, 4 Nov. 58—Lieut., 29 March 59.

LIEUTENANT A. W. HEARSEY,† late 57th Native Infantry.
Ensign, 9 June 55—Lieut., 23 Nov. 56.
SERVICE.—Lieutenant HEARSEY served when the Mutineer Mungal Pandy was seized, and the suppression of the incipient Mutiny at Barrackpore suppressed. Served in General Havelock's Campaign. Present at the actions of Boorbea-ka-Chowkee, Bithoor, skirmish on re-crossing the river at Cawnpore, Mungulwar, Alum Bagh, the affair with the enemy's Cavalry at that place, relief, and subsequent two months' siege of Lucknow. *(Severely wounded.) Medal and Clasps.* Served in the Sumbulpore District with the Skekawattee Battalion, in '58, '59, and '60. Thanked in General Orders, 17th December '57.

LIEUTENANT J. HEARSEY, P. C., late 38th Native Infantry.
Ensign, 8 July 50—Lieut., 1 Jan. 54.

(299)

MAJOR-GENERAL SIR J. B. HEARSEY, K.C.B., late 3rd Bengal European Cavalry.

Cornet, 14 Sept. 08—Lieut., 1 Nov. 09—Captain, 31 Aug. 19—Major, 19 Nov. 35—Lieut.-Colonel, 28 Dec. 38—Bt.-Colonel, 19 March 49—Colonel, 4 Nov. 52—Major-General, 28 Nov. 54.

SERVICE.—Major-General HEARSEY served in Bundlecund, '09, '10. In Rewah, in '12, '13. During the Pindarree Campaign, '17, '18. Present at the battle of Seetabuldee *(dangerously wounded)*; siege and capture of Bhurtpore, '26. *(Wounded.)* *Medal and Clasp.* Commanded one of the Cavalry Divisions during the Punjab Campaign, '48, '49. Present at the battle of Goojerat. *Medal and C.B.*

CAPTAIN A. H. HEATH, P. H., Bengal Artillery.

2nd Lieut., 9 Dec. 44—Lieut., 6 Feb. 48—2nd Captain, 27 Aug. 58—Captain, 12 Nov. 60.

SERVICE.—Captain HEATH served with the Army of the Punjab, '48, '49; including the actions of Sadoolapore, Chillianwallah, and Goojerat. *Medal and 2 Clasps.*

LIEUTENANT M. H. HEATHCOTE, P. H., late 19th Native Infantry.

Ensign, 20 Dec. 54—Lieut., 23 Nov. 56.

CORNET G. H. HEAVISIDE, General List, Cavalry.

Cornet, 20 Oct. 59.

LIEUTENANT W. J. HEAVISIDE, Bengal Engineers.

Lieut., 10 June 59.

CAPTAIN B. HENDERSON, C.B., P., late 48th Native Infantry.

Ensign, 4 Feb. 41—Lieut., 21 April 44—Captain, 5 June 53.

SERVICE.—Captain HENDERSON served throughout the Sutlej Campaign, '45, 46. Present at the actions of Moodkee and Alliwal. *Medal and Clasp.* *(Since dead.)*

SURGEON-MAJOR C. M. HENDERSON,† M.D., Bengal Medical Establishment.

Asst.-Surgeon, 1 Nov. 38—Surgeon, 6 Dec. 52—Surgeon-Major, 13 Jan. 60.

SERVICE.—Surgeon-Major HENDERSON served in Medical Charge of the 68th Native Infantry throughout the Sutlej Campaign, '46. Present at the battle of Sobraon. *Medal.* Served with the 68th Native Infantry during the first occupation of Lahore, in '47. Appointed Medical Storekeeper and Staff Surgeon to Sir J. Littler, in Command of the Lahore Field Force, in '47. Served with the Central India Field Force in '57, '58. Present at the capture of Kôtghur and the affair at Baracha. Held Medical Charge of the Field or General Hospital of the C. I. F. Force at Saugor, from the 9th February to the 7th June '58, when it was broken up. *Medal.*

LIEUTENANT F. HENDERSON, late 16th Native Infantry.

Ensign, 4 April 57—Lieut., 18 May 58.

ASSISTANT-SURGEON G. HENDERSON,† M.D., Bengal Medical Establishment.

Asst.-Surgeon, 27 July 59.

ENSIGN D. C. HENNESSY, General List.

Ensign, 4 July 61.

LIEUTENANT G. R. HENNESSY, P. H., late 34th Native Infantry.

Ensign, 4 Feb. 54—Lieut., 11 Dec. 57.

BREVET-LIEUTENANT-COLONEL J. HENNESSY, late 70th Native Infantry.

Ensign, 3 Feb. 28—Lieut., 10th April 36—Bt.-Captain, 3 Feb. 43—Captain, 24 Jan. 45—Bt.-Major, 20 June 54—Bt.-Lieut.-Colonel, 7 April 60.

SERVICE.—Lieutenant-Colonel HENNESSY served as a Volunteer with H. M.'s 59th Foot, at the siege and capture of Bhurtpore, '25, '26.

(301)

Medal. Served with the Army of Gwalior and present at the battle of Maharajpore. *Bronze Star.*

LIEUTENANT A. B. HEPBURN, late 32nd Native Infantry.

Ensign, 4 Sept. 58—Lieut., 29 Aug. 59.

BREVET-MAJOR C. HERBERT, late 18th Native Infantry.

Ensign, 30 Jan. 41—Lieut., 21 Dec. 45—Captain, 1 Jan. 55—Bt.-Major, 2 Jan. 55.

SERVICE.—Major HERBERT assumed Command of Attock, 1st September '48, and defended it against the rebel force under Sirdar Chuttur Sing, from the 10th November to the 2nd January '49. *Medal,* and Local Major in the Punjab.

LIEUTENANT J. HERSCHEL,† Bengal Engineers.

Lieut., 27 Aug. 58.

MAJOR-GENERAL A. HERVEY, C.B., late 52nd Native Infantry.

Ensign, 27 March 06—Lieut., 2 Jan. 11—Bt.-Captain, 27 March 21— Captain, 1 May 24—Major, 31 Jan. 32—Lieut.-Colonel, 16 March 38— Colonel, 8 March 49—Major-General, 28 Nov. 54.

SERVICE.—Major-General HERVEY, C.B., served during the Nepal Campaign, '14, '15. *Medal.* Jubbulpore, '17; Maharattah Campaign, '17, '18; siege and capture of Mundella, '18; commanded the 1st Infantry Brigade during the siege and operations in the vicinity of Mooltan; commanded the Force at the storming of the Dhurmsalla, on the 12th September '48, the whole of the reserves on the 7th November '48, at the battle of Sooroojkhoond, and the right reserve on the storming and capture of the City of Mooltan; commanded the 1st Infantry Brigade in the action at Goojerat, on the 21st February '49. *Medal, 2 Clasps,* and *C.B.*

(302)

CAPTAIN G. A. F. HERVEY, P. C., Bengal Invalid Establishment.

Ensign, 12 Dec. 34—Lieut., 19 April 39—Captain, 12 Oct. 45.

SERVICE.—Captain HERVEY was employed with the 2nd Volunteer Battalion during the China Expedition, *Medal;* also with the Force under Brigadier Wheeler, in the Punjab, '48, '49.

LIEUTENANT G. L. K. HEWETT, P. H., late 41st Native Infantry.

Ensign, 20 Jan. 57—Lieut., 9 July 57.

SERVICE.—Lieutenant HEWETT served throughout the defence of Lucknow, from June to November '57. *Wounded,* 24th September. Served as Orderly Officer on the Staff of Sir J. Outram, throughout the operations at the Alum Bagh and siege and capture of Lucknow, March '58. *Medal and 2 Clasps, and one year's extra service* for defence of Lucknow.

LIEUTENANT J. N. B. HEWITT, P. H., late 17th Native Infantry.

Ensign, 4 March 54—Lieut., 9 Sept. 56.

SERVICE.—Lieutenant HEWITT served with the 4th Sikh Infantry during the siege of Delhi, '57. Present in all the actions before the walls of Delhi, from 23rd June '57 to 12th September '57. *Medal and Clasp.*

LIEUTENANT-GENERAL W. H. HEWITT, late 27th Native Infantry.

Ensign, 4 Sept. 07—Lieut., 23 Sept. 12—Bt.-Captain, 4 Sept. 22—Captain, 23 May 23—Major, 13 April 30—Lieut.-Colonel, 11 Nov. 35—Bt.-Colonel, 9 Nov. 46—Colonel, 11 March 47—Major-General, 20 June 54—Lieut.-General, 30 Dec. 59.

SERVICE.—Lieutenant-General HEWITT served with the expedition to Java, '11, *Medal;* and during the Burmese War, '24, '25, and '26. *Medal.*

LIEUTENANT R. B. HEWSON, Bengal Artillery.

Lieut., 8 June 60.

LIEUTENANT A. S. HEYLAND, P. H., Bengal Artillery.

Lieut., 27 Aug. 58.

(303)

LIEUTENANT J. M. HEYWOOD, Bengal Engineers.
Lieut., 27 Aug. 58.

LIEUTENANT F. HIBBERT,† late 35th Native Infantry.
Ensign, 12 Dec. 57—Lieut., 12 Nov. 58.

SERVICE.—Lieutenant HIBBERT served during the Mutinies under Lord Clyde, '58, '59. Present at the siege and capture of Lucknow, March '58. Present at the passage of the Gogra, November '58. Served throughout the Trans-Gogra Campaign under Sir H. Grant, '59. *Medal and Clasp.*

2ND CAPTAIN W. HICHENS.† Bengal Engineers.
2nd Lieut., 9 Dec. 50—Lieut., 3 Aug. 55—2nd Captain, 27 Aug. 58.

CAPTAIN R. J. F. HICKEY, P. H., late 1st European Bengal Fusiliers.
2nd Lieut., 13 June 45—Lieut., 17 June 48—Captain, 7 June 57.

SERVICE.—Captain HICKEY served in the Burmese War; present at the storm and re-capture of Pegu, 21st November '52; and relief of the Pegu Garrison, 14th December '52. *Medal.* (Has passed an examination in Surveying.)

VETERINARY-SURGEON T. HICKMAN.†
Vety.-Surgeon, 18 March 54.

CAPTAIN C. F. HICKS,† late 5th Europeans.
Ensign, 25 July 42—Lieut., 6 March 46—Bt.-Captain, 25 July 57—Captain, 29 July 57.

SERVICE.—Captain HICKS served during the Sutlej Campaign. Present with the late 6th Bengal Native Infantry, when it mutinied at Allahabad. Commanded a Detachment of Irregular Cavalry during the operations in the vicinity of Allahabad. Served as a Volunteer in Havelock's Cavalry during the whole of the operations of that Force. *Medal.*

CAPTAIN E. W. HICKS, P., late 67th Native Infantry.

Ensign, 12 June 35—Lieut., 5 Aug. 37—Bt.-Captain, 12 June 50— Captain, 5 Feb. 53.

SERVICE.—Captain E. W. HICKS served during the Burmese War, '52, '53. Present at the capture of Pegu, and at the operations against Mya Thoon, under Major-General Sir J. Cheape, near Donabew. *Medal.* Mentioned in the Despatch of Major Cotton, August '52. Mentioned in the Despatch of Major-General Sir J. Cheape to the Commander-in-Chief, and recommended for Brevet-Majority. Served as Detachment Staff under Major Cotton in the neighborhood of Pounday. Thanked in Detachment Orders.

MAJOR-GENERAL G. HICKS, C.B., late 70th Native Infantry.

Ensign, 1 March 08—Lieut., 14 Sept. 13—Bt.-Captain, 1 March 23— Captain, 9 Nov. 24—Major, 8 Jan. 38—Lieut.-Colonel, 13 March 44— Colonel, 7 May 54—Major-General, 18 Feb. 56.

SERVICE.—Major-General HICKS served in Command of a Brigade throughout the Sutlej Campaign, '45, '46, including the actions of Moodkee, Ferozeshuhur, Buddiwal, and Alliwal. *Medal, 2 Clasps, and C.B.*

COLONEL J. W. HICKS, late 69th Native Infantry.

Ensign, 17 Jan. 24—Lieut., 13 May 25—Captain, 15 Feb. 36—Bt.-Major, 9 Nov. 46—Major, 28 Feb. 50—Bt.-Lieut.-Colonel, 20 June 54—Lieut.-Colonel, 10 Nov. 55—Bt.-Colonel, 15 Feb. 58.

SERVICE.—Colonel HICKS served during the War in Burmah, in '25, '26.

CAPTAIN W. J. HICKS,† late 22nd Native Infantry.

Ensign, 1 Sept. 38—Lieut , 27 June 42—Captain, 29 July 53.

SERVICE.—Captain HICKS served throughout the Punjab Campaign, '48, 49. *Medal.*

BREVET-CAPTAIN E. G. HIGGINS,† late 4th Europeans.

Ensign, 19 March 45—Lieut., 7 Jan. 53—Bt.-Captain, 19 March 60.

SERVICE.—Captain HIGGINS served during the Punjab Campaign, '48, '49. Present at the assault on the Heights of Dullah. *Medal.*

LIEUTENANT C. T. M. HIGGINSON, General List, Cavalry.

Cornet, 16 June 59—Lieut., 16 June 60.

LIEUTENANT H. S. HIGGINSON, Bengal Artillery.

Lieut., 8 June 60.

CAPTAIN C. P. HILDEBRAND, P. H., late 10th Native Infantry.

Ensign, 12 Dec. 49—Lieut., 13 Nov. 55—Captain, 18 Nov. 57.

SERVICE.—Captain HILDEBRAND served in Burmah, '52, '53. *Medal.* (Passed examination in Burmese.)

LIEUTENANT G. E. HILL,† late 32nd Native Infantry.

Ensign, 26 June 47—Lieut., 2 April 56.

SERVICE.—Lieutenant HILL served during the Punjab Campaign, '48, '49. Present with the Force under General Whish at the siege and surrender of Mooltan. *Medal.*

MAJOR G. M. HILL, P., late 17th Native Infantry.

Ensign, 13 June 26—Lieut., 28 Aug. 33—Bt.-Captain, 13 June 41—Captain, 31 Oct. 49—Bt.-Major, 20 June 54—Major, 27 Dec. 59.

BREVET-MAJOR SIR J. HILL, *Bart.*, P. H., late 1st Bengal European Cavalry.

Cornet, 20 Oct. 49—Lieut., 31 Jan. 52—Captain, 1 Jan. 57—Bt.-Major, 20 July 58.

SERVICE.—Major Sir J. HILL served in the defence of the Fort of Neemuch, '57; and subsequently with the Rajpootanah Field Force with the 2nd Bombay Cavalry. Present at the capture of Kotah.

Served as Major of Brigade of the Rajpootanah Field Force at the action of Gwalior, '58, under Sir Hugh Rose. *Medal and Brevet-Majority.*

LIEUTENANT R. B. HILL, P. H., late 60th Native Infantry.

Ensign, 15 Aug. 53—Lieut., 23 Nov. 56.

SERVICE.—Lieutenant HILL served with the Army before Delhi, from June to September '57, as Assistant Field Engineer. Present at the action of the 23rd June, and subsequent engagements before Delhi, also in the trenches of the night attack. *Medal and Clasp.* Served with the Lahore Light Horse with Colonel Smith's Column at Toolseepore, in May '59.

LIEUTENANT R. S. HILL, P. H., late 66th Native Infantry.

Ensign, 4 Aug. 56—Lieut., 12 April 58.

SERVICE.—Lieutenant HILL served in defence of the Kumaon Hills and Rohilcund against the rebels, in '57, '58. Present at Chapoorah, 10th February '58; in Brigadier Troup's Column during the Oude Campaign. Present at the actions of Pusgaon, 19th, and Russoolpore, 25th October '58; attack and capture of Fort Mittowlee, 8th November, and action of Biswah, 1st December '58. *Medal.*

SURGEON J. HILLIARD,† M.D., F.R.C.S.L., Bengal Medical Establishment.

Asst.-Surgeon, 8 Jan. 41—Surgeon, 10 March 55.

SERVICE.—Surgeon HILLIARD served in Bundlecund, in '42. During the Sonthal Insurrection, '56, as Field Surgeon with the Raneegunge Depôt Hospital.

LIEUTENANT G. S. HILLS,† late 38th Native Infantry.

Ensign, 4 Aug. 57—Lieut., 18 May 58.

LIEUTENANT G. S. HILLS,† Bengal Engineers.

Lieut., 27 April 58.

2ND CAPTAIN J. HILLS, P. H., V.C., Bengal Artillery.

1st Lieut., 8 Sept. 57.

SERVICE.—Captain HILLS served during the Mutiny Campaign. *Medal and V.C.* (*Vide* V.C. Roll.)

ASSISTANT-SURGEON A. H. HILSON,† M.D., Bengal Medical Establishment.

Asst.-Surgeon, 29 Jan. 57.

SERVICE.—Assistant-Surgeon HILSON served with "Peel's" Naval Brigade, the Nepalese Troops, and the 18th Punjab Infantry, in the Campaign of '57, '58, and '59. Was present in numerous engagements with the enemy. Services mentioned in the Despatch of Brigadier Rowcroft, 23rd March '58; in the Despatch of Captain Sotheby, Commanding the Naval Brigade, 25th March '58; and in the Despatch of Brigadier Rowcroft, 31st March '58. *Wounded severely* in the face by a musket ball.

CAPTAIN T. W. HILTON,† late 65th Native Infantry.

Ensign, 27 Sept. 41—Lieut., 10 June 45—Bt.-Captain, 27 Sept. 56.

BREVET-CAPTAIN J. HIND,† late 26th Native Infantry.

Ensign, 20 Jan. 45—Lieut., 1 May 49—Bt.-Captain, 20 Jan. 60.

SERVICE.—Captain HIND served throughout the Sutlej Campaign, '45, '46. Present at the actions of Moodkee, Ferozeshuhur, and Sobraon. *Medal and Clasp.*

LIEUTENANT-COLONEL C. T. E. HINDE, late 65th Native Infantry.

Ensign, 3 Jan. 40—Lieut., 16 July 42—Bt.-Captain, 3 Jan. 55—Captain, 23 Nov. 56—Major, 24 Nov. 56—Lieut.-Colonel, 20 July 58.

SERVICE.—Lieutenant-Colonel HINDE served in the Danubian Campaign, '54, with H. H. Omer Pasha. Served as Assistant Adjutant-General at the siege of Silistria, the crossing of the Danube, battle of Guirgeoo, and the occupation of Bucharest. Commanded an Irregular Cavalry Regiment at Ibraila, in '54, to watch the Russians. Served in the Crimean

Campaign until the fall of Sebastopol. In Command of two Regiments of Infantry was present at the siege and the various Cavalry actions before Sepatoria. Served in the Mengrelian Campaign for the relief of Kars. Was present at the battle of Sregur. Served during the Mutinies, '57, '58, and '59. Commanded the combined Forces sent to open the Deccan Road in '57. Took 7 forts and 42 guns. Commanded the central Column of attack on the Punwaree Heights, at the relief of Kirwee, under Major-General Sir G. Whitlock. Commanded one of the Moveable Columns sent to hunt after Desputh and other rebelleaders in Bundlecund. Received the thanks of the Political Authorities, 31st October '58, 21st November '59, and 9th March '60. Mentioned in the Despatch of General Whitlock to the Commander-in-Chief, 27th January '59. Received the thanks of the Governor-General, 1st March '58 and 19th January '59. *Gold Medal* for the Danube. *Medal* for Silistria. English and Turkish *Medal and Clasp* for the Crimea. Mutiny *Medal*. Received the *Order of Medjidee*.

SURGEON-MAJOR H. B. HINTON,† Bengal Medical Establishment.

Asst.-Surgeon, 14 Jan. 39—Surgeon, 31 Dec. 52—Surgeon-Major, 31 Jan. 60.

SERVICE.—Surgeon-Major HINTON served with the Army of Gwalior. Joined the Field Hospital on 31st December '43. Served with the Army of the Sutlej in '46. Present at the actions of Buddiwal, Alliwal, and Sobraon. *Medal and Clasp*. Served in the Depôt Hospital, Ferozepore, during the Punjab Campaign in '48, '49. Served with the 70th Native Infantry during the War in China, in '58, '59, and '60.

BREVET-MAJOR S. J. HIRE, P. H., late 22nd Native Infantry.

Ensign, 12 June 41—Lieut., 22 March 44—Captain, 1 Dec. 55—Bt.-Major, 2 Dec. 55.

SERVICE.—Major HIRE served as A. D. C. on the Staff of His Excellency the Commander-in-Chief, Lord Gough, and was present throughout the Campaign in the Punjab, including the skirmish at Ramnuggur, passage of the Chenab, and battles of Chillianwallah and Goojerat. *Medal and 2 Clasps*. Was mentioned favorably in two Despatches by His

(309)

Excellency the Commander-in-Chief, 5th February '49 and 7th March '49, and his name recorded for a Brevet-Majority on attaining the rank of Captain regimentally. On the conclusion of the Campaign, was appointed Adjutant to the 3rd Irregular Cavalry, and rose successively to the Command of that Regiment.

CAPTAIN C. T. HITCHINS, P. H., late 54th Native Infantry.

Ensign, 7 Jan. 51—Lieut., 31 May 55—Captain, 27 May 60.

(Passed examination in Surveying and Civil Engineering.)

2ND CAPTAIN H. O. HITCHINS, P. H., Bengal Artillery.

1st Lieut., 8 June 57—2nd Captain, 6 Feb. 61.

MAJOR T. F. HOBDAY, P., late 72nd Native Infantry.

Ensign, 17 Dec. 36—Lieut., 3 Oct. 40—Captain, 1 Feb. 48—Major, 28 Aug. 57.

SERVICE —Major HOBDAY served throughout the Campaign on the Sutlej, '45, '46. Present at the actions of Moodkee, Ferozeshuhur, and Sobraon. *Medal and 2 Clasps.* Served throughout the Punjab Campaign, and present at the affair of Ramnuggur. *Medal.*

MAJOR P. R. HOCKIN, P., late 48th Native Infantry.

Ensign, 8 March 41—Lieut., 24 Jan. 45—Bt.-Captain, 8 March 56—Captain, 23 Nov. 56—Major, 8 March 61.

SERVICE.—Major HOCKIN served with the Army of the Sutlej, '46. Present at the actions of Moodkee, Ferozeshuhur, and Alliwal. *Medal and 2 Clasps.* Served during the Punjab Campaign, '49. *Medal.* Served at the siege of Delhi, '57. *Medal and Clasp.* Served in the suppression of the disturbances in the Jhung and Googaira Districts, in September and October '57. Cut up a party of seventeen mutineers of the late 9th Irregular Cavalry.

LIEUTENANT B. P. HODGSON, late 10th Native Infantry.

Ensign, 20 Feb. 58—Lieut., 18 July 60.

CAPTAIN C. J. HODGSON,† Bengal Engineers.
2nd Lieut., 10 June 42—Lieut., 23 May 46—Captain, 17 Aug. 56.

SERVICE.—Captain HODGSON served during the Sutlej Campaign. Present at the action of Sobraon. *Medal.*

LIEUTENANT C. N. HODGSON,† General List.
Ensign, 20 April 59—Lieut., 19 Sept. 60.

BREVET-CAPTAIN H. N. HODGSON, P. H., late 9th Native Infantry.
Ensign, 27 July 44—Lieut., 5 Jan. 50—Bt.-Captain, 27 July 59.

SERVICE.—Captain HODGSON served during the Sutlej Campaign, '46, as Adjutant of the 1st Punjab Infantry. Was with the Regiment in '58, when it formed part of an Expeditionary Force under Brigadier Chamberlain, in the Meranzaie Valley, near Kohat. Present at the affair of Dursune-Mund, 30th April '55.

BREVET-COLONEL J. S. HODGSON, P., late 12th Native Infantry.
Ensign, 3 Feb. 22—Lieut., 1 May 24—Captain, 21 June 34—Bt.-Major, 9 Nov. 46—Major, 28 Aug. 53—Bt.-Lieut.-Colonel, 7 June 49—Lieut.-Colonel, 25 April 58—Bt.-Colonel, 28 Nov. 54.

SERVICE.—Brevet-Colonel HODGSON served in the Campaign of the Sutlej, '45, '46, including the battle of Sobraon. *(Wounded.)* *Medal and Clasp.* Served in the Campaign of the Punjab, '48, '49, and engaged in the various affairs against the insurgents under Ram Sing. *Medal and Brevet-Lieutenant-Colonel.* In '53 commanded a Force employed against the Hill Tribes west of the Derajât.

LIEUTENANT V. J. HODGSON,† late 4th Bengal European Cavalry.
Cornet, 20 Nov. 58—Lieut., 29 March 59.

VETERINARY-SURGEON J. R. HOEY,†
Vety.-Surgeon, 1 April 40.

(311)

LIEUTENANT T. W. HOGG, P. H., late 2nd Bengal European Cavalry.
Cornet, 4 Dec. 57—Lieut., 18 May 58.

LIEUTENANT W. D. HOGG, P., late 41st Native Infantry.
Ensign, 20 Dec. 49—Lieut., 26 March 55.

SERVICE.—Lieutenant HOGG served with the Column under Brigadier Hewitt, from Mooltan, against Ali Morad, Ex-Ameer of Scinde, '52. Served with the Column from Delhi, under Colonel Gerrard, in '57. Present at the action of Narnoul, November '57. Served with the Column under Sir Thomas Seaton, from Delhi to Futtehghur, in December '57 and January '58. Present at the actions of Gungeeree, Puttiallee, and Mynpooree in the former month. Served with the Column under Sir Hope Grant in February '58. Present at the capture of Mecangunge. Served with General Outram's Force in March '58. Present at the siege and capture of Lucknow. *Medal and Clasp.* Served with Sir H. Grant in his expedition against Banee Madho. Present at the affair at Nuggur, in May '58.

LIEUTENANT G. H. W. HOGGAN, P. H., late 4th Native Infantry.
Ensign, 4 April 54—Lieut., 11 Aug. 57.

MAJOR-GENERAL J. HOGGAN, C.B., late 45th Native Infantry.
Ensign, 1 March 08—Lieut., 16 Dec. 14—Bt.-Captain, 1 March 23—Captain, 1 May 24—Major, 8 Oct. 36—Lieut.-Colonel, 22 Dec. 42—Colonel, 14 July 53—Major-General, 28 Nov. 54.

SERVICE.—Major-General HOGGAN, C.B., served at the Nepal War, '15. *Medal.* Suppression of the insurrection at Bareilly, '16; Maharattah Campaign, '17, '18; with the Force under General Pollock in Affghanistan. Present at the forcing of the Khyber Pass, and the operations in the Mazeena Valley. *Medal.* Commanded a Brigade attached to the Army of the Punjab, '58, '59; and engaged at Ramnuggur, Sadoolapore, Chillianwallah, and Goojerat. *Medal and C.B.*

LIEUTENANT J. W. HOGGAN, P., late 45th Native Infantry.

Ensign, 27 June 49—Lieut., 15 May 52.

SERVICE.—Lieutenant HOGGAN served in '57, in Command of a Detachment of the 17th Punjab Infantry, to intercept the Sealkôt mutineers. Present when that Regiment disarmed the "Cities of Poor" and "Mozuffernuggur," March '58. Present at the actions near Bhagonala, 17th, Nugeena, 21st April; and Bareilly, 5th and 6th May '58. Present at the encounter at Mohunpore. *(Severely wounded.)* Thanked by Captain Browne in '58. Formed part of the Saugor Field Brigade under Brigadier Wheeler, '58. *Medal.*

BREVET-COLONEL C. HOGGE, C.B., P. C., Bengal Artillery.

2nd Lieut., 11 Dec. 29—Lieut., 1 Dec. 38—Bt.-Captain, 11 Dec. 44—Captain, 1 Jan. 48—Bt.-Major, 7 June 49—Bt.-Lieut.-Colonel, 28 Nov. 54—Lieut.-Colonel, 27 Sept. 58—Bt.-Colonel, 28 Nov. 57.

SERVICE.—Brevet-Colonel HOGGE, C.B., served with the Army of the Punjab, in '48, '49. Present at the passage of the Chenab and actions of Chillianwallah and Goojerat. *Medal, 2 Clasps, and Brevet-Major.*

LIEUTENANT G. W. HOLDSWORTH, late 3rd Europeans.

Ensign, 13 Dec. 56—Lieut., 30 April 58.

SERVICE.—Lieutenant HOLDSWORTH served throughout the Mutinies of '57, '58, including the action of Sussia, near Agra, 5th July '57, against the Neemuch mutineers. Present at the battle of Agra, 10th October '57; also with Column under Colonel Cotton, at Futtehpore-Sikree, '57. *Medal.*

ENSIGN H. HOLFORD, Unattached List.

Ensign, 20 Sept. 57.

SERVICE.—Ensign HOLFORD served during the Sutlej Campaign, '45, '46. Present at the actions of Ferozeshuhur and Sobraon. *(Wounded severely.) Medal and Clasp.* Served throughout the Burmese War, '52, '53. Present at the re-capture of Pegu, 21st November '52; relief of the Garrison on 14th December '52; and operations in its vicinity.

Accompanied the Martaban Column under General Steel, throughout the operations en route to Tonghoo. *Medal.* Present at the battle of Badlee-ka-Serai, 8th June '57, and all the subsequent operations at the siege of Delhi, including the operations under General Nicholson, at Mozuffurghur, 25th August '57; and assault and capture of Delhi, 14th September '57. Ensign's Commission. *Wounded severely* at the siege of Delhi, '57. Served under Brigadiers Gerrard and Seaton. Present at Narnoul, 16th November '57; Gungeeree, 14th December; Puttiallee, 17th December; and Mynpooree, 27th December '57. Present under Lord Clyde at the storm and capture of Lucknow, March '58; and all the subsequent operations in Oude under Sir H. Grant. *Medal and 2 Clasps.*

CAPTAIN G. HOLLAND, P. H., Bengal Artillery.

2nd Lieut., 11 Dec. 41—Lieut., 3 July 45—Bt.-Captain, 11 Dec. 56— Captain, 10 Feb. 58.

SERVICE.—Captain HOLLAND was present at the battle of Maharajpore, '43. *Medal.* Served during the Sutlej Campaign, '45, '46. Present at the battles of Ferozeshuhur and Sobraon. *Medal and Clasp.* Present with the Expedition to Kangrah, '46; Army of the Punjab, '48, '49, including the actions of Chillianwallah and Goojerat. *Medal and 2 Clasps.*

CAPTAIN T. W. HOLLAND, P. C., late 38th Native Light Infantry.

Ensign, 7 June 44—Lieut., 8 Nov. 49—Captain, 10 June 57.

SERVICE.—Captain HOLLAND served in the Sutlej Campaign, '46. Present at the battle of Sobraon. *Medal.* Served at Meerut during the Mutiny as A. D. C. to Major-General Penny, from July to December '57, the two latter months at Delhi. Accompanied Brigadier Seaton's Column to Futtehghur, as Commissariat Officer, in charge of Head Quarters Camp. Served at the capture of Lucknow as Commissariat Officer of 3rd Infantry Brigade. *Medal and Clasp.* Accompanied the Force under Sir E. Lugard through Oude, to the relief of Azimghur, and in pursuit of Koer Sing to Arrah. Served with the Azimghur Field Force in the operations against Koer Sing's followers in the Jugdespore jungles. Mentioned in the Despatch of Sir E. Lugard, 6th July '58. Served with the Shahabad Field Force, from June '58 to February '59, under Brigadier Douglas, against the rebels in the Jugdespore and Shahabad Districts. Mentioned in the Despatch of Brigadier Douglas, '59.

LIEUTENANT G. H. HOLLEY, late 1st European Bengal Fusiliers.

2nd Lieut., 13 June 58—Lieut., 10 Oct. 60.

SERVICE.—Lieutenant HOLLEY served in Oude, '58, '59. Present with the Column under Major Hume, during which time, on several occasions, was engaged with the rebels and took their guns; served also under Major Wheeler, when 5 guns and camp-stores were captured from the Nusseerabad Brigade, at Shahdutgunge, 30th October '58. *Medal.*

ASSISTANT-SURGEON A. P. HOLMES,† M.D., Bengal Medical Establishment.

Asst.-Surgeon, 27 July 59.

CAPTAIN G. E. HOLMES, P. H., late 72nd Native Infantry.

Ensign, 12 June 40—Lieut., 1 Feb. 43—Captain, 10 May 53.

SERVICE.—Captain HOLMES served during the Punjab Campaign, '48, '49. Present at the 1st and 2nd sieges, and surrender, of Mooltan, and action of Sooroojkhoond; capture of Chineout and battle of Goojerat, 21st February '49. *Medal and Clasp.*

LIEUTENANT W. B. HOLMES,† Bengal Engineers.

Lieut., 27 Aug. 58.

SERVICE.—Lieutenant HOLMES served during the Oude Campaign, '58, '59. *Medal.*

MAJOR C. HOLROYD, P. H., late 36th Native Infantry.

Ensign, 31 Dec. 39—Lieut., 12 Jan. 41—Captain, 1 July 51—Major, 9 March 61.

(Passed examination in Assamese and Bengali.)

(315)

CAPTAIN G. HOLROYD,† late 43rd Native Infantry.

Ensign, 1 March 38—Lieut., 26 Sept. 41—Bt.-Captain, 1 March 53—Captain, 15 Nov. 53.

SERVICE.—Captain HOLROYD served with the Army of the Indus, from December '38 to December '42; Army of Gwalior, '43, '44; Army of the Sutlej, '45, '46. Present at the actions of Candahar, May '42; and the various engagements in its neighborhood: Ghuznee, 8th September '42; Istaliff, *Medal*, 30th September '44; and the whole operations leading to the re-occupation of Cabul, '42, by the Force under Major-General Nott. Present at the battles of Maharajpore and Sobraon. *(Horse shot.)* *Wounded* at Bance Baban, in Affghanistan, 15th September '42. Maharajpore. *Bronze Star and Medal for Sobraon.*

LIEUTENANT W. R. M. HOLROYD, P., late 23rd Native Infantry.

Ensign, 10 Dec. 53—Lieut., 8 June 57.

CAPTAIN E. V. H. HOLT,† late 42nd Native Infantry.

Ensign, 25 July 42—Lieut., 2 March 46—Bt.-Captain, 25 July 57—Captain, 25 Aug. 58.

SERVICE.—Captain HOLT served in the Sutlej Campaign, '45, '46. Present at the actions of Moodkee *(wounded slightly)*, Ferozeshuhur, and Sobraon. *Medal and 2 Clasps.* In the Sonthal Campaign, '55, '56; and in the Saugor District, '57, '58, and '59. Present at two skirmishes with the rebels in '57. *Wounded slightly* at Dumoh, Saugor District, '57. *Medal.* *(Since retired.)*

SURGEON S. A. HOMAN,† Bengal Medical Establishment.

Asst.-Surgeon, 3 March 42—Surgeon, 18 July 56.

SERVICE.—Surgeon HOMAN served with the 2nd Europeans against the Hill Tribes in Scinde, in '45, and during the Punjab Campaign, including the siege and operations in the vicinity of Mooltan and battle of Goojerat, with the 8th Native Infantry. *Medal and 2 Clasps.*

LIEUTENANT F. J. HOME, Bengal Engineers.

Lieut., 27 Aug. 58.

COLONEL R. HOME, late 43rd Native Infantry.

Ensign, 1 Jan. 04—Lieut., 29 Aug. 05—Bt.-Captain, 1 Jan. 19—Captain, 10 Nov. 21—Major, 29 Nov. 34—Lieut.-Colonel, 17 Sept. 41—Colonel, 7 April 51—Major-General, 28 Nov. 54.

(Since dead.)

LIEUTENANT R. HOME,† Bengal Engineers.

Lieut., 14 Sept. 57.

ENSIGN S. B. HOME, General List.

Ensign, 12 Oct. 59.

ENSIGN J. R. McK. HOMFRAY,† General List.

Ensign, 20 Sept. 59.

ASSISTANT-SURGEON D. HOOD,† M.D., Bengal Medical Establishment.

Asst.-Surgeon, 4 Aug. 55.

LIEUTENANT F. H. HOOD, late 30th Native Infantry.

Ensign, 20 Aug. 55—Lieut., 17 Nov. 57.

SERVICE.—Lieutenant F. H. HOOD was present at the mutiny of the 30th Native Infantry at Nusseerabad, 28th May '57. Present at the actions of Ooreyah, and operations at Shereghur Ghaut, May '58. Served with the Agra Moveable Column towards Gwalior, June '58. Commanded the Gwalior Field Force in April, May, and June '60. *Medal.*

BREVET-MAJOR J. HOOD, P. H., late 49th Native Infantry.

Ensign, 29 Jan. 40—Lieut., 5 Nov. 41—Captain, 10 June 50—Bt.-Major, 20 July 58.

SERVICE.—Major HOOD served under General Whish at the siege and capture of Mooltan and action of Sooroojkhoond. *Medal and Clasp.* Present under Brigadier Showers at the capture of Jhujjur Fort. Present at the action of Shumshabad, and siege and capture of Lucknow. *(Dangerously wounded.) Medal and Clasp, and Brevet-Major.*

ASSISTANT-SURGEON J. HOOPER,† Bengal Medical Establishment.
Asst.-Surgeon, 16 Feb. 50.
SERVICE.—Assistant-Surgeon HOOPER served in Medical Charge of the Jheen Rajah's Force during the assault and capture of Delhi, in '57. *Medal and Clasp.*

ASSISTANT-SURGEON W. R. HOOPER,† Bengal Medical Establishment.
Asst.-Surgeon, 10 Feb. 59.

LIEUTENANT J. HOPKINS, Unattached List.
Lieut., 19 Oct. 58.
SERVICE.—Lieutenant HOPKINS served in the actions of Ferozeshuhur and Sobraon, '45, '46. *Medal and Clasp.* Present at the storm and capture of Pegu, 21st November '52. *Medal and Clasp,* and Commission for "Distinguished Conduct." Served also at the relief of the Garrison of Pegu, 14th December '52, and operations in its vicinity.

CAPTAIN H. HOPKINSON, P. H., late 70th Native Infantry.
Ensign, 12 Dec. 37—Lieut., 19 Jan. 40—Bt.-Captain, 12 Dec. 52—Captain, 31 March 53.
SERVICE.—Captain HOPKINSON served as Political Officer against the Hill Tribes of the Kolvelyne, in December '47 and January '48. Present at the surprise of the Akong stockade. Served during the Punjab Campaign, '48, 49. Present at the actions of Chillianwallah and Goojerat, and in pursuit of the Sikh Army and Affghans to Peshawur. *Medal and 2 Clasps.* Present at the capture of Martaban, in April '52. *Medal* for Burmese War, '52. Accompanied General Godwin at the capture of Martaban as Interpreter. Accompanied Major Forster, of the Madras Army, as Principal Assistant Commissioner of Province Amherst. (Passed examination in Burmese.)

ENSIGN W. HOPKINSON, General List.
Ensign, 20 Dec. 59.

LIEUTENANT J. C. HORNE, P., late 6th Europeans.
Ensign, 20 Dec. 48—Lieut., 1 Aug. 53.

(318)

BREVET-MAJOR T. S. HORSBRUGH, P. H., late 32nd Native Infantry.
Ensign, 17 Feb. 29—Lieut., 19 Sept. 36—Bt.-Captain, 17 Feb. 44—Captain, 9 April 49—Bt.-Major, 28 Nov. 54.
(Since retired.)

LIEUTENANT E. C. O'B. HORSFORD,† General List.
Ensign, 11 June 59—Lieut., 26 Jan. 61.

LIEUTENANT E. O'B. HORSFORD,† late 46th Native Infantry.
Ensign, 9 Dec. 48—Lieut., 23 Nov. 56.

LIEUTENANT N. M. T. HORSFORD, P. H., late 27th Native Infantry.
Ensign, 20 Nov. 57—Lieut., 26 May 58.

SERVICE.—Lieutenant HORSFORD served during the Mutinies, '57, '58. Present at the siege and capture of Lucknow, March '58. Served with the Oude Field Force under Major-General Sir H. Grant. Present at the action of Nawabgunge Barabanki, on 13th June '58, and in the subsequent operations leading to the re-occupation of Oude. *Medal and Clasp.*

MAJOR-GENERAL R. HORSFORD, Bengal Artillery.
2nd Lieut., 29 April 19—Lieut., 27 Sept. 23—Bt.-Captain, 29 April 34—Captain, 7 Oct. 36—Bt.-Major, 3 April 46—Major, 31 March 47—Lieut.-Colonel, 21 July 51—Bt.-Colonel, 28 Nov. 54—Colonel, 18 Feb. 61—Major-General, 6 Feb. 06.

SERVICE.—Major-General HORSFORD was present at the siege and capture of Bhurtpore, '25, '26. *Medal.* Sutlej Campaign, '45, '46. Present at the battles of Moodkee, Ferozeshuhur, and Sobraon. *Medal, 2 Clasps, and Brevet-Major.* Army of the Punjab, '48, '49, including actions of Sadoolapore, Chillianwallah, and Goojerat. *Medal, 2 Clasps, and Brevet-Lieutenant-Colonel.*

CAPTAIN W. D. HOSTE, P. H., late 55th Native Infantry.
Ensign, 4 April 43—Lieut., 3 May 45—Captain, 27 Aug. 58.

SERVICE.—Captain HOSTE served in the 1st Sutlej Campaign. In 55 served as Captain of a Division of H. M.'s Land Transport Corps

(319)

in the trenches before Sebastopol. *2 Medals and Clasp.* In '57, as 2nd in Command, 5th Punjab Infantry, he served against the rebels in the Eusuffzaie country, and led the Upper Column of attack against the rebel village of "Ramijee," for which he received the thanks of the Governor-General in Council; also throughout the Oude Campaign of '58, '59, with the Force under Sir Hope Grant. Present at the actions of Barree, Simree, Nawabgunge, and Sultanpore. Also served in the Force under Lord Clyde, and was present in all the minor engagements leading to the re-occupation of Oude, during which time he was attached to the Brigade of Brigadier Horsford, as Assistant Quarter-Master-General. *Three times thanked in General Orders. Medal.*

BREVET-CAPTAIN G. A. F. HOUCHEN, P. H., late 10th Native Infantry

Ensign, 30 Dec. 43—Lieut., 15 Feb. 47—Bt.-Captain, 30 Dec. 58.

SERVICE.—Captain HOUCHEN served with the 55th Native Infantry during the Sutlej Campaign, '45, '46. Present at the battle of Sobraon. *Medal.* (Passed examination in Surveying and Civil Engineering.)

BREVET-COLONEL R. HOUGHTON, late 16th Native Infantry.

Ensign, 21 April 20—Lieut., 11 July 23—Captain, 25 Sept. 34— Bt.-Major, 3 April 46—Major, 1 Oct. 48—Lieut.-Colonel, 5 Dec. 53— Bt.-Colonel, 28 Nov. 54.

SERVICE.—Colonel HOUGHTON served at the siege and capture of Bhurtpore, '26. *Medal.* Throughout the Campaign on the Sutlej; as A. D. C. to Major-General Gilbert at the actions of Moodkee and Ferozeshuhur; as Assistant-Adjutant-General of the 2nd or General Gilbert's Division at Sobraon. *Medal, 2 Clasps, and Brevet-Major.*

GENERAL SIR R. HOUSTOUN, K.C.B., late 4th Bengal European Cavalry.

Cornet, 26 Feb. 96—Lieut., 1 Nov. 98—Captain, 22 Dec. 03—Major, 1 Nov. 09—Lieut.-Colonel, 13 Dec. 18—Colonel, 1 May 24—Major-General, 10 Jan. 37—Lieut.-General, 9 Nov. 46—General, 20 June 54.

SERVICE.—General Sir R. HOUSTOUN served during the Maharattah War. Present at the battles of Delhi and Laswarrie, '03. *Medal.*

(320)

BREVET-MAJOR J. HOVENDEN, Bengal Engineers.

2nd Lieut., 9 Dec. 50—Lieut., 3 Dec. 55—2nd Captain, 27 Aug. 58—Bt.-Major, 28 Aug. 58.

SERVICE.—Major HOVENDEN served at the siege of Delhi. *Severely wounded* at the assault; served also at the capture of Lucknow. Commanded the 24th Punjab Infantry, during the Rohilcund Campaign, under Sir C. Campbell. *Medal, 2 Clasps, and Brevet-Major.*

CAPTAIN E. W. E. HOWARD, P., late 3rd Bengal European Cavalry.

Cornet, 21 May 43—Lieut., 28 Oct. 48—Captain, 5 Dec. 54.

SERVICE.—Captain HOWARD served during the Sutlej Campaign, '45, '46. Present at the battles of Moodkee, Ferozeshuhur, and Sobraon. *Medal and 2 Clasps.* Served throughout the Mutiny, '57, '58. (Passed examination in Punjabee.)

LIEUTENANT G. H. E. HOWARD,† late 24th Native Infantry.

Ensign, 10 Dec. 50—Lieut., 1 Jan. 55.

LIEUTENANT W. HOWEY, late 42nd Native Infantry.

Ensign, 4 Feb. 58—Lieut., 25 Aug. 58.

SERVICE.—Lieutenant HOWEY served during the Mutiny, '58, '59. Present at the capture of the Fort of Tyroul, and throughout the Oude Campaign. *Medal.*

LIEUTENANT R. H. HUDLESTON, P. H., late 69th Native Infantry.

Ensign, 7 Dec. 55—Lieut., 1 June 57.

SERVICE.—Lieutenant HUDLESTON served as Adjutant, 9th Punjab Infantry, in the expedition against Sattana, under General Cotton, in May and June '58.

CAPTAIN H. J. HUGHES, P. H., late 62nd Native Infantry.

Ensign, 11 June 42—Lieut., 17 Dec. 45—Captain, 23 Nov. 56.

2ND CAPTAIN T. E. HUGHES, P. H., Bengal Artillery.

2nd Lieut., 8 June 49—Lieut., 17 May 54—2nd Captain, 27 Aug. 58.

(321)

BREVET-LIEUTENANT-COLONEL W. T. HUGHES, P., late 48th Native Infantry.

Ensign, 28 Dec. 42—Lieut., 19 Feb. 47—Captain, 1 June 57—Bt.-Major, 24 March 58—Bt.-Lieut.-Colonel, 26 April 59.

SERVICE.—Colonel HUGHES served in the Sutlej Campaign, '45, '46. Present at the actions of Moodkee, Ferozeshuhur, and Sobraon. *Medal and 2 Clasps.* Served in the Punjab Campaign, '48, '49. Present at the reduction of the Forts of Rungul-Mungul, Kurrurwallah, and Moraree; and storming of the Dullah Heights. *Medal.* Served on the Peshawur Frontier, under Sir Colin Campbell, '51, '52. Present at the affair on the heights above Michnee. Commanded a Cavalry Picquet, and attacked and routed a large party of Narmad marauders, 3rd January '52. Horse received three sabre wounds. Brought to notice of the Commander-in-Chief in Despatches of Sir Colin Campbell, dated December '51 and 10th January '52. Received the thanks of the Governor-General, 31st December '51, and approbation of the Commander-in-Chief, 15th January '52. Appointed to the Command of 16th Punjab Cavalry, 16th April '52. Served against the Othman Khel Tribes, on the Eusuffzaie Frontier, Peshawur Valley, May and June '52. Present at the affairs at Pranghur and Nardund, and action at Pak-kôt. Received the thanks of the Governor-General and other Commandants. Served on the Trans-Indus Frontier between Kohat and Scinde, from July '52 till May '57. Served throughout the Mutinies, '57, '58. Present at the disarming of the Native Infantry Regiments at Mooltan, June '57. Commanded a Detachment of all Arms at the reduction of the Town of Balleh, Kurnoul District, 14th and 15th July '57. Horse received spear, sword, and bullet wounds. Served against the rebels in the Saharunpore, Mozuffurnuggur, and Meerut Districts, '57, '58; and with Colonel Smyth's Column on the re-occupation of Rohilcund. Promoted to rank of Brevet-Major for Field Services, 17th May '58. Served throughout the Oude Campaign, '58. Mentioned in Brigadier Wetherall's Despatch to the Commander-in-Chief, '58. Served under Sir Hope Grant at the passage of the Gogra and pursuit from Fyzabad, and at Muchlee Gaon. With Brigadier Rowcroft's Column in the Goruckpore District. With the Force under Lord Clyde at Chindah Mujeetra, pursuit from Bankee, and driving of the rebels across the Raptee.

Medal. Promoted to rank of Brevet-Lieutenant-Colonel for Field Services, '59. Served in Trans-Gogra, on the Nepal Frontier, in '59. Present at the taking of the Nana's guns at Silka Ghaut, 9th February '59. Mentioned in Brigadier Horsford's Despatch, '59. Present at the attack on the rebels on the Khoriallee River, 26th April '59. Brought to the notice of the Commander-in-Chief by Brigadier Horsford's Despatch, '59.

VETERINARY-SURGEON H. C. HULSE.

Vety.-Surgeon, 23 Aug. 28.

SERVICE.—Veterinary-Surgeon HULSE served in the Cabul Campaign. *Medal.* With the 10th Light Cavalry in the Gwalior Campaign. Present at the battle of Maharajpore. *Bronze Star.* Present during the Punjab Campaign, '48, '49, at the battles of Chillianwallah and Goojerat. *Medal.* In the Rangoon Campaign and taking of Prome. *Medal.*

BREVET-MAJOR A. HUME, late 1st European Bengal Fusiliers.

2nd Lieut., 22 Dec. 40—Lieut., 22 Nov. 43—Captain, 6 July 51—Bt.-Major, 20 July 58.

SERVICE.—Major HUME served in the Campaign on the Sutlej, including the actions of Ferozeshuhur and Sobraon, '45, '46 : in the latter engagement *twice wounded, once dangerously through the right lung. Medal and Clasp.* Commanded the Regiment in the Trans-Goomtee operations under General Sir J. Outram, and subsequently at the storm and capture of Lucknow, under the personal Command of Lord Clyde. *Medal and Clasp, and Brevet-Major.* Also commanded the Regiment with the Lucknow Field Force under General Sir J. H. Grant.

LIEUTENANT E. T. HUME, Bengal Artillery.

1st Lieut., 27 April 58.

CAPTAIN J. J. HUME, P. H., late 48th Native Infantry.

Ensign, 4 Sept. 43—Lieut., 24 July 47—Captain, 4 Oct. 57.

SERVICE.—Captain HUME was present at the actions of Moodkee, Ferozeshuhur, and Alliwal. *Medal and 2 Clasps.* Present at the action of Huldwanee, in September '57.

(323)

LIEUTENANT W. W. HUME,† late 11th Native Infantry.

Ensign, 5 Aug. 54—Lieut., 1 Feb. 57.

SERVICE.—Lieutenant HUME served at the commencement of the Indian Mutiny with the Meerut Volunteer Cavalry, afterwards as a Volunteer with the Artillery before Delhi, during the siege and capture of that city. *Medal and Clasp.*

LIEUTENANT E. W. HUMPHRY, P. H., Bengal Engineers.

Lieut., 10 May 57.

SERVICE.—Lieutenant HUMPHRY served under Brigadiers Showers, Gerrard, and Seaton, in the Delhi and Allyghur Districts, in '57, as Field Engineer, in Command of a Detachment of Muzbee Sappers. Present at the actions of Narnoul, Gungeeree, Puttiallee, and Mynpooree, and capture of Fort Jhujjur. *Severely wounded* at Narnoul, 16th November '57. Mentioned in the Despatch of Captain Caulfield, '58. Acted as Brigade-Major to the Engineer Brigade, under Sir J. Hope Grant, on the march from Futtehghur to Alum Bagh, February '58. Served as Adjutant of Engineers at the Alum Bagh and capture of Lucknow, February and March '58. Brought to notice of the Commander-in-Chief in the Despatch of Sir R. Napier, 16th March '58. Served with the Force under Brigadier General Walpole, in Oude, and under the Commander-in-Chief, in Rohilcund, in '58; also under Brigadier Troup, in Oude, '58, '59. Present at the attack on Fort Rhuyah, action at Allygunge, capture of Bareilly, '58; capture of Fort Mittowlee, actions of Biswah and Allygunge, '58, '59. Brought to the notice of the Commander-in-Chief in the Despatch of Brigadier Troup, '58. *Medal and Clasp.*

LIEUTENANT J. V. HUNT, P., late 45th Native Infantry.

Ensign, 20 Dec. 50—Lieut., 6 Sept. 56.

SERVICE.—Lieutenant HUNT served with the Force under General Van Cortland, '57, '58. Present at the actions of Odawallah, 17th June '57; Khyrekee, 19th June '57. The action before Hissar, 19th August, and storming and capture of the village of Mungalee, 29th September '57. Commanded the 23rd Punjab Infantry in the action of Narnoul,

16th November '57. Favorably mentioned in the Despatches of General Van Cortland, and received the thanks of Government, 28th August '57 and 16th November '57. Favorably mentioned in the Despatches of Captain Caulfield, regarding the action of Narnoul, 21st December '58. *Medal.*

MAJOR A. HUNTER, P. H., late 25th Native Infantry.

Ensign, 11 June 39—Lieut., 8 Nov. 41—Bt.-Captain, 11 June 54—Captain, 5 March 56—Major, 1 Jan. 62.

2ND CAPTAIN C. HUNTER, P. H., Bengal Artillery.

1st Lieut., 6 July 57—2nd Captain, 29 April 61.

LIEUTENANT C. P. HUNTER, P. H., late 5th Europeans.

Ensign, 20 Jan. 51—Lieut., 18 April 53.

CAPTAIN J. HUNTER, P. H., Bengal Artillery.

2nd Lieut., 14 June 45—Lieut., 21 Feb. 49—2nd Captain, 27 Aug. 58.

SERVICE.—Captain HUNTER served with the Army of the Punjab, '48, '49, including the siege and surrender of Mooltan *(wounded);* battle of Goojerat, and subsequent pursuit of the Sikhs and Affghans. *Medal and 2 Clasps.*

CAPTAIN M. HUNTER, P. H., late 18th Native Infantry.

Ensign, 11 Dec. 45—Lieut., 31 Jan. 53—Captain, 13 Dec. 60.

(Passed examination in Surveying and Civil Engineering.)

LIEUTENANT S. A. HUNTER,† late 34th Native Infantry.

Ensign, 20 Dec. 47—Lieut., 29 June 53.

LIEUTENANT T. A. HUNTER, late 2nd European Bengal Fusiliers.

2nd Lieut., 14 June 56—Lieut., 14 Aug. 57.

SERVICE.—Lieutenant HUNTER served at the siege of Delhi, '57. Present at the action of Badlee-ka-Serai, operations during the siege and

(325)

final assault and capture of the city. Served with the Flying Column under Brigadier Showers, in the Delhi District. Served with the Delhi Field Force in the Bikaneer District, under Major Boyd, '59. Served with the Sikkim Field Force under the Command of Lieutenant-Colonel Gawler, '60, '61. *Medal and Clasp.*

BREVET-MAJOR A. R. E. HUTCHINSON, P. H., late 13th Native Infantry.

Ensign, 30 Jan. 43—Lieut., 22 July 46—Captain, 8 July 57—Bt.-Major, 7 Dec. 58.

SERVICE.—Major HUTCHINSON served in the Punjab Campaign, '48, '49. Present at the battle of Goojerat. *Medal and Clasp.* Served as Assistant Political Officer with the Nerbudda Field Force, in the operations against Dhar, in '57. In Command of 2 Guns, 1 Troop Cavalry, and 2 Companies Infantry, to operate against the rebel Rajah of Amghera. Destroyed the Hill Fort of Lall Ghur, and captured the Rajah. Mentioned in the Minute of the Governor-General during the rebellion. Served as Political Officer, in August '58, with the Force under General Michel, at the action near Rajghur. *Medal.* Mentioned in Despatch, 15th September '58. Received acknowledgment of services from General Michel, 17th September '58. Received thanks of the Governor-General. Served as Political Officer, in December '58, with the Force under Colonel Somerset and Colonel Benson. Mentioned in the Despatch of the latter, 29th December '58. *Brevet-Majority.*

CAPTAIN C. W. HUTCHINSON, P. H., Bengal Engineers.

2nd Lieut., 9 June 43—Lieut., 19 Aug. 47—Captain, 10 March 57.

SERVICE.—Captain HUTCHINSON served with the Army of the Sutlej in '46.

BREVET-MAJOR G. HUTCHINSON, P. H., Bengal Engineers.

2nd Lieut., 7 June 44—Lieut., 15 Jan. 50—Captain, 27 April 58— Bt.-Major, 20 July 58.

SERVICE.—Major HUTCHINSON served throughout the defence of Lucknow, and afterwards as Commanding Engineer with General Outram's

Force at Alum Bagh. Served as Brigade Major of Engineers at the capture of Lucknow. *Medal, 2 Clasps, and Brevet-Major, and one year's extra service.*

LIEUTENANT H. S. HUTCHINSON, Bengal Artillery.

Lieut., 9 Dec. 59.

ASSISTANT-SURGEON J. A. C. HUTCHINSON,† M.D., Bengal Medical Establishment.

Asst.-Surgeon, 20 Nov. 50.

ASSISTANT-SURGEON R. F. HUTCHINSON,† M.D., Bengal Medical Establishment.

Asst.-Surgeon, 3 Dec. 53.

SURGEON-MAJOR T. C. HUTCHINSON,† Bengal Medical Establishment.

Asst.-Surgeon, 16 Oct. 39—Surgeon, 7 Oct. 53—Surgeon-Major, 13 Jan. 60.

SERVICE.—Surgeon-Major T. C. HUTCHINSON was present at the capture of Chusan, '40; and of Amoy, Chinhae, and second capture of Chusan and occupation of Ningfoo, '41, 42. Served throughout the two Campaigns in China, in '40, '41, '42, and '43. *Medal.*

MAJOR-GENERAL E. HUTHWAITE, C.B., Bengal Artillery.

2nd Lieut., 2 Nov. 10—Lieut., 25 Sept. 17—Bt.-Captain, 12 Nov. 25—Captain, 30 Aug. 26—Bt.-Major, 28 June 38—Major, 20 Jan. 42—Lieut.-Colonel, 3 July 45—Colonel, 23 Jan. 54.

SERVICE.—Major-General HUTHWAITE, C.B., served in the Nepal War, in '15, '16; taking of Dwarka and other Forts in Oude, in the hot season of '17; Maharattah War, '17, '18; in Cachar, during the Burmese War, '23, '24; siege and capture of Bhurtpore, '25, '26. *India Medal.* Commanded 3rd Brigade, Horse Artillery, at Ferozeshuhur, *C.B.;* and at Sobraon, '45, '46. *Medal and Clasp.* Brigadier Commanding Foot Artillery with Army of Punjab, '48, '49. Present at the passage of the Chenab and action of Chillianwallah and Goojerat, *Medal and 2 Clasps;* and

(327)

commanded the Artillery with the Force under Sir W. R. Gilbert, in pursuit of the Sikhs across the Jhelum, in '49.

CAPTAIN T. HUTTON, Invalid Establishment.

Ensign, 28 Sept. 25—Lieut., 12 Sept. 27—Captain, 27 Oct. 38.

CAPTAIN G. C. HUXHAM, P. H., late 48th Native Infantry.

Ensign, 13 June 46—Lieut., 29 Sept. 50—Captain, 13 June 61.

SERVICE.—Captain HUXHAM served in the defence of Lucknow, '57. Three times *wounded, once severely*. Received the thanks of Government, 25th March '61 ; of His Excellency the Commander-in-Chief, 30th March '61. *Medal and Clasp, and one year's extra service*.

LIEUTENANT-COLONEL A. HUYSHE, Bengal Artillery.

2nd Lieut., 13 Dec. 27—Lieut., 28 Sept. 35—Bt.-Captain, 13 Dec. 42—Captain, 5 Sept. 45—Bt.-Major, 7 June 49—Major, 25 Sept. 57—Bt.-Lieut.-Colonel, 28 Nov. 54—Lieut.-Colonel, 27 Aug. 58—Bt.-Colonel, 30 Dec. 59.

SERVICE.—Colonel HUYSHE served in the Gwalior Campaign, '43, '44. *Bronze Star*. Army of the Punjab, '48, '49, including the actions of Sadoolapore, Chillianwallah, and Goojerat. *Medal, 2 Clasps, and Brevet-Major*.

LIEUTENANT D. F. HUYSHE, Bengal Artillery.

Lieut., 9 Dec. 59.

MAJOR-GENERAL G. HUYSHE, C.B., late 3rd Europeans.

Ensign, 22 March 20—Lieut., 3 June 22—Captain, 21 Jan. 29—Major, 12 Jan. 37—Bt.-Lieut.-Colonel, 23 Dec. 42—Lieut.-Colonel, 8 Feb. 43—Bt.-Colonel, 14 July 53—Colonel, 15 Nov. 53—Major-General, 28 Nov. 44.

SERVICE.—Major-General HUYSHE, C.B., served in the Burmese Campaign, '25. Commanded the 26th Light Infantry throughout the operations in Affghanistan, under Major-General Sir George Pollock. Present at the forcing of the Khyber Pass, actions at Mamoo Khail *(severely wounded)*, Jugdulluck, and Tazeen, and the capture of Istaliff. *Medal. Brevet-Lieutenant-Colonel and C.B.*

1st CAPTAIN H. HYDE, Bengal Engineers.

2nd Lieut., 7 June 44—Lieut., 26 Feb. 59—Captain, 27 April 58.

SERVICE.—Captain HYDE served at the siege of Mooltan. Present at the battle of Goojerat, '48. *Medal and Clasp.* Served as Field Engineer with General Cotton's Force, in operations against the Hill Tribes of Peshawur, '57.

CAPTAIN E. HYNDMAN, P. H., late 27th Native Infantry.

Ensign, 7 June 44—Lieut., 10 Aug. 47—Captain, 21 Aug. 58.

SERVICE.—Captain HYNDMAN served during the Sutlej Campaign, '45, '46. *Medal.*

I

LIEUTENANT A. T. ILES, late 40th Native Infantry.

Ensign, 12 Dec. 57—Lieut., 2 Sept. 59.

CAPTAIN A. IMPEY,† Bengal Engineers.

2nd Lieut., 11 Dec. 40—Lieut., 5 April 44—Captain, 1 May 55.

SERVICE.—Captain IMPEY served during the Mutiny, '57, '58. Present at the relief of Arrah with Eyre's Column. Served in Oude under Brigadier Berkeley. *Medal.*

LIEUTENANT E. C. IMPEY, P., late 5th Europeans.

Ensign, 10 Dec. 50—Lieut., 15 Nov. 53.

SERVICE.—Lieutenant IMPEY was present at the siege and capture of Kotah by the Field Force under Major-General Roberts, in '58. As Assistant to the Governor-General's Agent in Rajpootanah. Was detached after the siege as Political Officer with Major-General Roberts' Force, on the march from Kotah to Neemuch. *Medal.*

CAPTAIN H. B. IMPEY, P., 12th (late 70th) Native Infantry.

Ensign, 12 Dec. 38—Lieut., 3 Oct. 40—Bt.-Captain, 12 Dec. 53—Captain, 23 Nov. 56.

SERVICE.—Captain IMPEY served with the Army of Gwalior in '43, '44. Present at the battle of Maharajpore. *Bronze Star.* (Received certificates of high proficiency in Hindee and Oordoo.)

ASSISTANT-SURGEON J. INCE,† M.D., Bengal Medical Establishment.

Asst.-Surgeon, 20 Feb. 56.

SERVICE.—Assistant-Surgeon INCE served at the capture of the Fort of Balabete, in the Saugor District, by a Field Force under the Command of Major D. Gaussen, on the 13th June '57. Received the approbation of the Commander-in-Chief. Served at the assault of the Town of Meriowlee, in the Saugor District, by a Field Force under the Command of Lieutenant-Colonel Dalzell, on the 18th September '57. Formed one of the Saugor Garrison relieved by the Central India Field Force, under the Command of Sir Hugh Rose, 3rd February '58.

LIEUTENANT F. H. INGLEFIELD,† late 38th Native Infantry.

Ensign, 20 Feb. 52—Lieut., 23 Nov. 56.

(Qualified to assist in the Instruction of Musketry. Has received a 2nd class certificate from the School at Hythe.)

LIEUTENANT A. D. C. INGLIS, late 18th Native Infantry.

Ensign, 7 Aug. 58—Lieut., 23 Dec. 58.

ENSIGN D. W. INGLIS, General List.

Ensign, 20 Aug. 59.

LIEUTENANT H. INGLIS,† late 41st Native Infantry.

Ensign, 20 Jan. 50—Lieut., 15 April 56.

SERVICE.—Lieutenant INGLIS served at the defence of the Lucknow Residency, from 30th June to 22nd November '57. Served with the

(330)

Baggage Guard at Cawnpore, on 6th December '57, whilst the rebels were being driven out of the City. *Wounded severely* at Lucknow on 18th August '57. *Medal and Clasp, and one year's extra service.*

LIEUTENANT R. H. INGLIS, late 43rd Native Infantry.

Ensign, 28 June 58—Lieut., 22 Oct. 58.

LIEUTENANT J. S. INGRAM, P. H., late 1st European Bengal Fusiliers.

2nd Lieut., 12 Dec. 49—Lieut., 20 March 54.

SERVICE.—Lieutenant INGRAM served in Burmah, '52, '53. Present at the relief of the Garrison, 14th December '52, and operations in the vicinity. Accompanied the Martaban Column under General Steel. *Medal.* (Passed in Surveying.)

CAPTAIN F. C. INNES, P. H., late 60th Native Infantry.

Ensign, 10 Dec. 44—Lieut., 1 March 51—Bt.-Captain, 10 Dec. 59—Captain, 17 Sept. 60.

LIEUTENANT-COLONEL J. C. INNES, P., late 61st Native Infantry.

Ensign, 14 June 28—Lieut., 26 Sept. 33—Bt.-Captain, 14 June 43—Captain, 26 Dec. 44—Bt.-Major, 20 June 54—Major, 3 July 55—Lieut.-Colonel, 15 July 59.

SERVICE.—Lieutenant-Colonel INNES served during the Shekawattee Campaign. Served in the Bundlecund Insurrection.

BREVET-MAJOR J. J. McL. INNES, V.C., Bengal Engineers.

2nd Lieut., 8 Dec. 48—Lieut., 1 Aug. 54—2nd Captain, 27 Aug. 58—Bt.-Major, 28 Aug. 58.

SERVICE.—Major INNES, V.C., served during the whole period of the defence of the Residency of Lucknow. Garrison Engineer of the Mutchi-Bhawun prior to the evacuation. Present at Cawnpore during the action of the 6th December. Served as Field Engineer with Brigadier-General Franks' Column, and present with it at the actions of Nusrutpore, Chanda, Ameerpore, Sultanpore, and Dhowrara. *(Severely wounded.)*

(331)

Present at Lucknow during the siege operations of March '58. *Medal, 2 Clasps, and V.C., and one year's extra service.*

MAJOR-GENERAL P. INNES, late 14th Native Infantry.

Ensign, 16 June 24—Lieut., 28 Aug. 25—Bt.-Captain, 16 Jan. 39—Captain, 12 June 42—Bt.-Major, 30 April 44—Major, 15 April 54—Bt.-Lieut.-Colonel, 3 April 46—Lieut.-Colonel, 4 May 58—Bt.-Colonel, 20 June 54—Major-General, 13 July 58.

MAJOR P. R. INNES, Invalid Establishment.

2nd Lieut., 30 Dec. 43—Lieut., 6 Feb. 46—Captain, 10 May 54—Major, 12 June 60.

SERVICE.—Major INNES served throughout the Sutlej Campaign, '45, '46. Present at the actions of Ferozeshuhur and Sobraon. *(Wounded.) Medal and Clasp.* (Passed in Surveying and Civil Engineering.)

LIEUTENANT W. F. IRELAND, P. H., late 25th Native Infantry.

Ensign, 27 Sept. 52—Lieut., 7 May 54.

SERVICE.—Lieutenant IRELAND commanded the skirmishers of the Loodianah and Ferozepore Regiments of Sikhs, at the attack on Fort Tiroul, in Oude, on the 21st March '58. Commanded the Cavalry of the Centre Column of attack at the storming of the Heights of Punwaree, on the 29th December '58, at which operation all the enemy's guns were taken, and their leaders killed. Commanded a Detachment of Cavalry and Infantry of the Rewah Contingent, attached to the Nowgong Field Force, during the operations on the left bank of the Kaen River, including the actions of Murruree and Saleia, and the pursuit and subsequent dispersion of the enemy on the 23rd March '59. *Medal.*

ASSISTANT-SURGEON W. W. IRELAND,† M.D., Bengal Medical Establishment.

Asst.-Surgeon, 4 Aug. 56.

SERVICE.—Assistant-Surgeon IRELAND served at the siege of Delhi. Present at the battles of Badlee-ka-Serai and Nudjufghur. *(Wounded.) Medal and Clasp.*

(332)

CAPTAIN H. E. IREMONGER, P. H., late 21st Native Infantry.

Ensign, 19 June 42—Lieut., 28 June 44—Captain, 28 Feb. 56.

SERVICE.—Captain IREMONGER served at Murree during the attack on that station in September '57; thanked in Station Orders for his services on the occasion.

CAPTAIN A. IRVINE,† late 24th Native Infantry.

Ensign, 8 June 44—Lieut, 21 Dec. 45—Captain, 31 Jan. 57.

SERVICE.—Captain IRVINE served throughout the Sutlej Campaign. *Medal and Clasps.*

BREVET-CAPTAIN C. IRVINE, P. H., late 51st Native Infantry.

Ensign, 9 Dec. 42—Lieut., 5 Jan. 52—Bt.-Captain, 9 Dec. 57.

SERVICE.—Captain IRVINE served with the Army of Gwalior in '43. Present at the action of Punniar, 29th December '43. *Bronze Star.* Served with the Army of the Sutlej, '46. Present at both sieges of Mooltan, in '48, '49, and at the surrender with Major-General Whish's Column. *Medal.* Served with Colonel Carmichael's Brigade in Oude, '58, '59. Served with the 19th Punjab Infantry in the late expedition to China, '60. *Medal.* (Passed examination in Field Engineering.)

LIEUTENANT J. S. IRVINE, late 2nd Bengal European Cavalry.

Cornet, 20 Dec. 57—Lieut., 18 May 58.

SERVICE.—Lieutenant IRVINE served with the Force under Lord Mark Kerr, in '58. Present at the relief of Azimghur, in April '58, and in the subsequent pursuit on the retreat of the principal portion of Koer Sing's Army. *Medal.*

SURGEON J. IRVING,† M.D., Bengal Medical Establishment.

Asst.-Surgeon, 27 May 47—Surgeon, 9 Nov. 60.

(333)

SURGEON-MAJOR H. IRWIN,† F.R.C.S.T., Bengal Medical Establishment.
Asst.-Surgeon, 13 Jan. 39—Surgeon, 17 Dec. 52—Surgeon-Major, 1 Jan. 60.

SERVICE.—Surgeon-Major IRWIN was attached to Brigadier Wilde's Force, and served under General Pollock during the Affghanistan Campaign, '42. Present at the forcing of the Khyber Pass. *Medal.*

CAPTAIN W. IRWIN,† late 49th Native Infantry.
Ensign, 8 July 42—Lieut., 22 Jan. 47—Captain, 18 May 56.

SERVICE.—Captain IRWIN served at the siege and capture of Mooltan under General Whish, '48. *(Dangerously wounded.) Medal and Clasp.*

CAPTAIN W. B. IRWIN, P. H., late 10th Native Infantry.
Ensign, 12 Dec. 40—Lieut., 24 Jan. 45—Bt.-Captain, 12 Dec. 55—Captain, 18 June 57.

SERVICE.—Captain IRWIN served in Burmah, '52, '53. *Medal.*

ENSIGN E. R. IVES, B.A., General List.
Ensign, 20 Oct. 59.

J

CAPTAIN C. JACKSON,† late 39th Native Infantry.
Ensign, 11 Dec. 38—Lieut., 16 July 42—Captain, 21 Feb. 50.

SERVICE.—Captain JACKSON served at the battle of Punniar. *Bronze Star.*

ASSISTANT-SURGEON C. J. JACKSON,† Bengal Medical Establishment.
Asst.-Surgeon, 4 Aug. 55.

LIEUTENANT C. S. JACKSON, Bengal Artillery.
Lieut., 27 Aug. 58.

ENSIGN E. C. S. JACKSON, General List.
Ensign, 20 Sept. 60.

CAPTAIN E. S. JACKSON, P. H., late 12th Native Infantry.
Ensign, 26 Feb. 51—Lieut., 23 Nov. 56—Captain, 1 Jan. 62.

SERVICE.—Captain Jackson was Adjutant of the 12th Native Infantry when it broke into mutiny at Nowgong, and escaped to Nagode. Engaged in an affair with a party of Bundeelas. Was instrumental in saving the life of Mrs. Kerchoff, wife of Sergeant Kerchoff, whom he rescued from danger by carrying her behind him on horseback.

BREVET-MAJOR G. JACKSON,† late 3rd Bengal European Cavalry.
Cornet, 19 July 28—Lieut., 26 March 38—Bt.-Captain, 19 July 43—Captain, 30 July 49—Bt.-Major, 20 June 54.

SERVICE.—Major JACKSON served in Bundlecund in '42, and in the Punjab with the Force under Brigadier General Sir H. M. Wheeler, in '48, '49. *Medal.* Served under Sir C. Campbell during the operations on the Peshawur Frontier, '51, '52. When in Command of the outpost of "Mutta," repulsed the attack made thereon by the combined Momund Tribes, 8th December '51. *Wounded twice* in an attack on a body of the 26th Light Infantry mutineers, in '57.

LIEUTENANT G. C. JACKSON,† late 2nd Bengal European Cavalry.
Cornet, 20 Oct. 58—Lieut., 5 Feb. 59.

CORNET G. D'A. JACKSON, Cavalry, General List.
Cornet, 20 Nov. 59.

LIEUTENANT H. D. JACKSON, Bengal Artillery.
1st Lieut., 10 July 57.

(335)

ASSISTANT-SURGEON J. R. JACKSON,† M.D., Bengal Medical Establishment.
Asst.-Surgeon, 4 Jan. 55.

SERVICE.—Assistant-Surgeon JACKSON served with the 1st Punjab Infantry in the Meeranzaie Expedition under Brigadier Chamberlain, in '55; in the Koorum Valley Expedition, in '56; in the expedition against the Bozdar Tribe, in March '57. Marched with the Regiment to Delhi, and was at the siege and capture of that city in '57. In the Rohilcund Campaign in '58, with General Jones' Column, including the actions of Bhagawallah, Nageemah, and Meeahwallah, siege and capture of Bareilly, and action of Burnaie, and in the expedition against the Wuzeerees in '59, under Brigadier-General Chamberlain. *Medal and Clasp.*

LIEUTENANT L. D'A. JACKSON,† Bengal Engineers.
Lieut., 27 Aug. 58.

LIEUTENANT W. JACKSON, P. H., late 53rd Native Infantry.
Ensign, 20 Dec. 49—Lieut., 1 Nov. 53.

LIEUTENANT W. V. FITZG. JACOB, P. H., late 6th Europeans.
Ensign, 8 Dec. 55—Lieut., 4 June 57.

ENSIGN F. JADIS, General List.
Ensign, 31 Jan. 60.

MAJOR H. C. JAMES, P. C., late 32nd Native Infantry.
Ensign, 12 June 35—Lieut., 18 July 37—Captain, 16 Aug. 49—Major in Staff Corps, 18 Feb. 61.

SERVICE.—Major JAMES served at Sobraon, '46. *(Wounded.) Medal.* During the Punjab Campaign, '48, '49, present at the actions of Ramnuggur, Sadoolapore, Chillianwallah, and Goojerat. *Medal and 2 Clasps.*

MAJOR H. R. JAMES, C.B., P., late 44th Native Infantry.

Ensign, 21 Aug. 40—Lieut., 1 Aug. 43—Captain, 29 Feb. 52—Major in Staff Corps, 18 Feb. 61.

SERVICE.—Major JAMES, C.B., served with the Force under Major Edwardes. Present at the siege and operations in the vicinity of Mooltan. *Medal.*

LIEUTENANT L. H. S. JAMES, P. H., Bengal Artillery.

Lieut., 11 Dec. 58.

BREVET-MAJOR T. JAMES, P., late 2nd Native Infantry.

Ensign, 10 Dec. 44—Lieut., 8 Dec. 48—Captain, 12 Feb. 58—Bt.-Major, 24 March 58.

SERVICE.—Major JAMES served throughout the Sutlej Campaign, including the actions of Moodkee and Ferozeshuhur, and the expedition against Kôt Kangra. *Medal and Clasp.* Served on the Staff of Sir H. Lawrence, on the night of the 31st May, at Lucknow, when the Native Troops mutinied, and at Chinhut, on the 30th June '57. *(Dangerously wounded.)* Served throughout the siege of Lucknow, and received the special thanks of Government. *Medal and Clasp, Brevet-Majority, and one year's extra service.*

ASSISTANT-SURGEON G. W. JAMESON,† Bengal Medical Establishment.

Asst.-Surgeon, 20 Jan. 60.

BREVET-COLONEL J. W. H. JAMIESON, late 52nd Native Infantry.

Ensign, 16 Jan. 24—Lieut., 13 May 25—Bt.-Captain, 16 Jan. 39—Captain, 4 Sept. 39—Bt.-Major, 7 June 49—Major, 15 Sept. 51—Bt.-Lieut.-Colonel, 28 Nov. 54—Lieut.-Colonel, 10 May 57—Bt.-Colonel, 28 Nov. 57.

SERVICE.—Colonel JAMIESON commanded the Regiment throughout the Campaign of '48, '49. Served at the 1st and 2nd siege operations, and surrender of Mooltan, including the repulse of the enemy's night attack on the British Camp at Mathe Ghol, 17th August '48; action of Sooroojkhoond, 7th November '48; attack on the suburbs of Mooltan, 27th December '48; and battle of Goojerat. *(Wounded.) Medal and Clasp, and Brevet-Major.*

SURGEON-MAJOR W. JAMIESON, Bengal Medical Establishment.

Asst.-Surgeon, 30 Aug. 38—Surgeon, 10 April 52—Surgeon-Major, 13 Jan. 60.

LIEUTENANT H. C. T. JARRETT, P. H., V.C., late 26th Native Infantry.

Ensign, 10 June 54—Lieut., 27 Aug. 57.

SERVICE.—Lieutenant Jarrett served during the Mutinies, '57, '58. *Medal and V.C.* (*See* V.C. Roll.)

LIEUTENANT H. S. JARRETT, P. H., late 3rd Europeans.

Ensign, 13 Dec. 56—Lieut., 11 July 57.

LIEUTENANT W. JEFFREYS, P. H., Bengal Engineers.

Lieut., 1 Oct. 57.

SERVICE.—Lieutenant JEFFREYS served with General Jones' Force in the Rohilcund Campaign. *Medal.*

MAJOR C. V. JENKINS, P. H., late 1st Bengal European Cavalry.

Cornet, 24 Jan. 39—Lieut., 1 Jan. 44—Captain, 31 Jan. 52—Major, 1 July 57.

SERVICE.—Major JENKINS served with the Force in Affghanistan, under General Pollock, '42. *Medal.* Present at the battle of Maharajpore, '43. *Bronze Star.* Alliwal, '46. *Medal.* Served during the Punjab Campaign, '48, '49. *Medal.*

LIEUTENANT C. V. JENKINS, P. H., late 47th Native Infantry.

Ensign, 20 June 48—Lieut., 16 Oct. 51.

(338)

BREVET-COLONEL F. JENKINS, late 61st Native Infantry.

Ensign, 2 Dec. 11—Lieut., 11 May 16—Bt.-Captain, 2 Dec. 26—Captain, 29 April 30—Bt.-Major, 23 Nov. 41—Major, 22 Dec. 45—Lieut.-Colonel, 16 Oct. 51—Bt.-Colonel, 28 Nov. 54.

SERVICE.—Brevet-Colonel JENKINS served during the Nepal War, '14. *Medal.*

LIEUTENANT F. H. JENKINS,† late 57th Native Infantry.

Ensign, 20 Dec. 51—Lieut., 15 Nov. 53.

CAPTAIN H. G. JENKINS,† late 4th Bengal European Cavalry.

Cornet, 26 June 48—Lieut., 27 May 53—Captain, 2 Jan. 60.

SERVICE.—Captain JENKINS served with the Soraon Field Force under Brigadier Rowcroft, '57, '58. Commanded 2nd Squadron European Yeomanry Cavalry. Present at the action of Amorah, *(charger shot under him,)* 5th March '58; at the skirmish near Sibya, 17th April '58; attack on Amorah, 25th April '58; and defeat of the rebels at Fort Nuggur, 29th April '58. *Medal.*

CAPTAIN J. H. JENKINS, P. C., late 44th Native Infantry.

Ensign, 10 Dec. 50—Lieut., 1 May 55—Captain, 1 Jan. 62.

(Received a Degree of Honor for his eminent attainments in the Oordoo language, and a certificate of high proficiency in the Hindee language.)

CAPTAIN R. JENKINS, P. H., late 5th Bengal European Cavalry.

Cornet, 20 Feb. 45—Lieut. 8 May 49—Captain, 22 July 56.

SERVICE.—Captain JENKINS served at the battle of Alliwal. *Medal.* Served during the Punjab Campaign, '48, '49. Present at the affair of Ramnuggur, and actions of Sadoolapore, Chillianwallah *(charger shot)* and Goojerat. *Medal and Clasps.*

LIEUTENANT A. D. JENNINGS,† late 2nd Bengal European Cavalry.

Cornet, 4 July 50—Lieut., 27 Nov. 53.

(339)

LIEUTENANT R. M. JENNINGS, Cavalry, General List.
Cornet, 20 May 59—Lieut., 20 May 60.

CAPTAIN J. JERDAN,† late 43rd Native Infantry.
Ensign, 30 Dec. 43—Lieut., 25 July 50—Bt.-Captain, 30 Dec. 58—Captain, 25 March 60.
SERVICE.—Captain JERDAN served during the Sutlej Campaign, '45, '46. Present at the battle of Sobraon. *Medal.*

CAPTAIN F. V. R. JERVIS, P. H., late 56th Native Infantry.
Ensign, 10 Dec. 42—Lieut., 29 June 45—Captain, 7 Nov. 54.
SERVICE.—Captain JERVIS served during the Gwalior Campaign, '43, '44. Present at the battle of Maharajpore. *Bronze Star.* Served during the Punjab Campaign, '48, '49. Present at the battles of Sadoolapore and Chillianwallah *(severely wounded)*. *Medal and Clasp.* Commanded a Detachment of 3 Companies for nearly two years, during the Sonthal rebellion, '55, '56, and '57, and was several times engaged with the insurgents.

CAPTAIN T. S. JERVIS, Bengal Invalid Establishment.
Ensign, 4 Nov. 27—Lieut., 31 Jan. 35—Captain, 4 Nov. 42.

LIEUTENANT W. S. JERVIS, late 1st European Bengal Fusiliers.
2nd Lieut., 4 Feb. 57—Lieut., 30 April 58.
SERVICE.—Lieutenant JERVIS served in defence of the Town and Cantonments of Cawnpore, under General Windham. Present with his Regiment at the storm and capture of Lucknow, '57, 58. *Medals and Clasp.*

LIEUTENANT C. C. JERVOISE, late 1st Bengal European Cavalry.
Cornet, 4 Nov. 56—Lieut., 23 Jan. 57.

(340)

BREVET-MAJOR A. B. JOHNSON, P. H., late 5th Europeans.

Ensign, 27 July 46—Lieut., 26 Feb. 51—Captain, 5 Oct. 57—Bt.-Major, 20 July 58.

SERVICE.—Major JOHNSON served with the Force under Sir J. Cheape, at the attack on the Burmese stockades, 19th March '53. *Medal.* Mentioned in Despatch. Served during the Mutiny Campaign. *Medal and Brevet-Majority.*

ASSISTANT-SURGEON C. JOHNSON,† Bengal Medical Establishment.

Asst.-Surgeon, 21 June 48.

BREVET-CAPTAIN C. C. JOHNSON, P. H., late 33rd Native Infantry.

Ensign, 7 June 44—Lieut., 4 Jan. 47—Bt.-Captain, 7 June 59.

SERVICE.—Captain JOHNSON served during the Sutlej Campaign, '45, '46. Present at the action of Sobraon. *Medal.* (Passed examination in Field Engineering.)

BREVET-LIEUTENANT-COLONEL E. B. JOHNSON, C.B., P. H., Bengal Artillery.

2nd Lieut., 11 June 42—Lieut., 3 July 45—Bt.-Captain, 10 June 57—Captain, 25 June 57—Bt.-Major, 5 July 57—Bt.-Lieut.-Colonel, 19 Jan. 58.

SERVICE.—Lieutenant-Colonel JOHNSON, C.B., was present at the battles of Ferozeshuhur and Sobraon, '45, '46. *Medal and Clasp.* Served with the Army of the Punjab,' 48, '49, including the actions of Ramnuggur, Chillianwallah, and Goojerat. *Medal and Clasp.* Served during the Mutiny Campaign. *Medal, C. B., and Brevets of Major and Lieutenant-Colonel.*

ASSISTANT-SURGEON J. R. JOHNSON,† Bengal Medical Establishment.

Asst.-Surgeon, 27 July 59.

SERVICE.—Assistant-Surgeon JOHNSON served with the Peshawur Mountain Train and Nos. 2 and 3 Punjab Light Field Batteries, in the Mahsood Wuzeeree Expedition, under Brigadier Chamberlain, during the months of April and May '60; and was present at the attack on the Burmah Heights, 4th May '60.

(341)

VETERINARY-SURGEON W. JOHNSON,† Bengal Veterinary Establishment.
Vety.-Surgeon, 19 June 46.

SERVICE.—Veterinary-Surgeon JOHNSON served during the operations before, and siege and capture of, Mooltan, '48, '49.

MAJOR F. JOHNSTON,† late 62nd Native Infantry.
Ensign, 30 Jan. 41—Lieut., 12 Aug. 41—Captain, 2 Feb. 50—Major, 18 Dec. 57.

LIEUTENANT G. B. JOHNSTON,† late 54th Native Infantry.
Ensign, 12 June 58—Lieut., 21 Dec. 58.

ENSIGN F. E. JOHNSTONE, General List.
Ensign, 4 Aug. 60.

CAPTAIN H. C. JOHNSTONE, P. H., late 5th Europeans.
Ensign, 31 July 40—Lieut., 1 May 46—Captain, 28 Feb. 55.

SERVICE.—Captain JOHNSTONE served in Bundlecund, '42, '43. Commanded the Murree Volunteers in September and October '57, and aided in putting down a rebellion among the surrounding Hill Tribes. *Medal.* Served on the Staff of General Chamberlain as Surveyor with the expedition against the Kabul Khel Wuzeerees, on the North-East Frontier, in December '59 and January '60; also served in the same capacity with the expedition against the Mahsood Wuzeerees, on the North-West Frontier, April and May '60. (Has furnished certificate of qualification as a Surveyor and Civil-Engineer.)

LIEUTENANT J. JOHNSTONE,† late 68th Native Infantry.
Ensign, 20 July 58—Lieut., 19 Feb. 59.

SERVICE.—Lieutenant JOHNSTONE served with the Trans-Gogra Field Force under Brigadier Rowcroft, in '58, '59. *Medal.*

LIEUTENANT J. W. H. JOHNSTONE, P. H., late 18th Native Infantry.
Ensign, 20 Dec. 52—Lieut., 23 Nov. 56.

ENSIGN A. F. JONES, General List.
    Ensign, 20 Nov. 59.

LIEUTENANT G. T. JONES,† late 35th Native Infantry.
    Ensign, 26 Aug. 58—Lieut., 14 Sept. 59.

ASSISTANT-SURGEON H. D. JONES,† Bengal Medical Establishment.
    Asst.-Surgeon, 20 May 54.

LIEUTENANT H. L. JONES, P. H., Bengal Artillery.
    Lieut., 1 Jan. 58.

LIEUTENANT H. T. JONES,† late 31st Native Infantry.
    Ensign, 20 Nov. 57—Lieut., 14 Aug 59.
    SERVICE.—Lieutenant JONES served in Bengal in suppressing the Mutiny in '57, '58, with the Jaunpore Field Force under Brigadier Franks, in the actions of Chanda, Ummeerapore, and Sultanpore; afterwards with the Main Army under Sir Colin Campbell, at the siege and capture of Lucknow. *Medal and Clasp.*

ASSISTANT-SURGEON J. JONES,† M.D., Bengal Medical Establishment.
    Asst.-Surgeon, 20 Feb. 56.

SURGEON-MAJOR J. H. JONES,† Bengal Medical Establishment.
    Asst.-Surgeon, 3 Jan. 40—Surgeon, 1 Dec. 53—Surgeon-Major, 13 Jan. 60.
    SERVICE.—Surgeon-Major JONES served against the Frontier Tribes of Scinde for nearly a year with a Regiment of Irregular Cavalry, raised at Candahar.

BREVET-MAJOR L. B. JONES, P. H., late 56th Native Infantry.
    Ensign, 16 July 42—Lieut., 24 Jan. 45—Captain, 9 March 52—Bt.-Major, 26 April 59.
    SERVICE.—Major JONES served at the action of Maharajpore, *Bronze Star;* and with the Army of the Punjab. Present at the battles of

(343)

Sadoolapore and Chillianwallah, (in which latter engagement he was *twice wounded* and had his *horse killed under him*,) and subsequent pursuit of the Sikhs and Affghans with the force under General Gilbert. *Medal and Clasp.* Served on the Staff of Sir Sydney Cotton, in the expedition against the Hill Tribes of Punjtar and Sittana, April '58. Commanded the first Sikh Irregular Cavalry throughout the operations in Oude, '58, '59, under Lord Clyde. *"Horse killed under him in action at Nurpalgunge Biswarra*, November '58 ; *wounded in action near Gonda*, 13th April '59. Present at the defeat of the rebels at Bungaon, 27th April '59 ; and subsequent operations in Nepal under General Grant. *Medal and Brevet-Majority.*

MAJOR-GENERAL N. JONES, late 49th Native Infantry.

Ensign, 2 Sept. 17—Lieut., 1 Aug. 18—Captain, 21 Sept. 28—Major, 21 July 41—Lieut.-Colonel, 12 Aug. 47—Bt.-Colonel, 28 Nov. 54—Colonel, 31 May 57—Major-General, 30 May 59.

SERVICE.—Major-General JONES served in Burmah, '25, '26.

LIEUTENANT N. J. JONES,† late 15th Native Infantry.

Ensign, 11 Dec. 58—Lieut., 28 May 59.

CAPTAIN W. L. JONES, P. C., late 42nd Native Infantry.

Ensign, 10 June 42—Lieut., 24 Jan. 45—Captain, 23 Nov. 56.

SERVICE.—Captain JONES served throughout the Sutlej Campaign, '45, '46. Present at the battles of Moodkee, Ferozeshuhur, and Sobraon. *Medal and Clasp.*

CAPTAIN C. JORDEN, Bengal Invalid Establishment.

Ensign, 1 July 23—Lieut., 27 May 24—Captain, 16 Dec. 35.

SERVICE.—Captain JORDEN was present at the siege and capture of Bhurtpore, '25, '26. *Medal.*

SURGEON-MAJOR J. JOWETT, Bengal Medical Establishment.

Asst.-Surgeon, 20 Oct. 40—Surgeon, 8 Aug. 54—Surgeon-Major, 21 March 61.

SERVICE.—Surgeon-Major JOWETT served with H. M.'s 49th, 55th, and 18th Regiments throughout the War in China, from '41 to '45. *Medal.* Served with the Army of the Sutlej in the Field Hospital at Ferozepore, in February and March '46.

LIEUTENANT C. N. JUDGE, Bengal Engineers.

Lieut., 27 April 58.

SERVICE.—Lieutenant JUDGE served with Sir H. Havelock in the advance on the Alum Bagh, and at the capture of Lucknow. *Medal and 2 Clasps.*

LIEUTENANT S. A. T. JUDGE, P. H., late 67th Native Infantry.

Ensign, 9 Dec. 52—Lieut., 10 Nov. 55.

SERVICE.—Lieutenant JUDGE served in Burmah. *Medal.*

K.

LIEUTENANT A. E. L. KAYE,† Bengal Artillery.

Lieut., 27 Aug. 58.

BREVET-LIEUTENANT-COLONEL E. KAYE, Bengal Artillery.

2nd Lieut., 12 June 35—Lieut., 1 April 41— Bt.-Captain, 12 June 50— Captain, 1 Jan. 52—Bt.-Major, 2 Jan. 52—Bt.-Lieut.-Colonel, 19 Jan. 58.

SERVICE.—Lieutenant-Colonel KAYE served in Affghanistan in '38, '39, '40. Present at the affair near Fowladee; also in the Campaign on the Sutlej, '45, '46, including the battles of Moodkee, Ferozeshuhur, and Sobraon. *Medal and 2 Clasps.* Served with the Army of the Punjab. Present at the passage of the Chenab, and actions of Chillianwallah and Goojerat; and accompanied the Field Force under Sir W. Gilbert beyond the Jhelum. *Medal, 2 Clasps, and Brevet-Major.*

(345)

SURGEON W. KEATES, P. H., Bengal Medical Establishment.
Asst.-Surgeon, 25 Dec. 40—Surgeon, 27 Dec. 54.

LIEUTENANT F. J. KEEN, P. H., late 35th Native Infantry.
Ensign, 4 Aug. 54—Lieut., 4 June 57.
SERVICE.—Lieutenant KEEN served with the 2nd Punjab Infantry during the Campaign in Hindostan, in '57, '58. Present at the siege, assault, and capture of Delhi. Accompanied the Moveable Column under Colonel Greathed after the fall of Delhi. Present at the battles of Boolundshuhur and Agra, the relief of the Lucknow Garrison, and the battles of Cawnpore and Khodagunge (near Futtehghur); the siege and capture of the city of Lucknow, and the occupation of Bareilly, besides many other minor affairs. *Medal and 2 Clasps.*

BREVET-CAPTAIN J. KEER, P. C., late 60th Native Infantry.
Ensign, 26 July 45—Lieut., 15 Nov. 53—Bt.-Captain, 26 July 60.

LIEUTENANT W. KEILY, Bengal Veteran Establishment.
Lieut., 31 May 52.
SERVICE.—Lieutenant KEILY served at the siege and capture of Bhurtpore, '25, '26. *Medal.* With the Force in Affghanistan, under General Pollock. Present at the forcing of the Khyber Pass, and in all subsequent operations leading to the occupation of Cabul, including those in the Mazeena Valley. *Medal.* Present at the battle of Maharajpore. *Bronze Star.* Served during the Campaign on the Sutlej, including the actions of Ferozeshuhur and Sobraon. *Medal and Clasp.*

LIEUTENANT G. L. KEIR, late 41st Native Infantry.
Ensign, 17 March 55—Lieut., 1 June 57.
SERVICE.—Lieutenant KEIR served throughout the defence of Lucknow, from the 30th June to the 22nd November '57. Present throughout the operations at the Alum Bagh, and capture of Lucknow, March '58. Served during the Oude Campaign, '58, '59. *Medal and 2 Clasps, and one year's extra service.*

Surgeon J. P. KELLY,† Bengal Medical Establishment.

Asst.-Surgeon, 18 June 42—Surgeon, 11 Jan. 57.

Lieutenant H. C. KEMBLE, late 3rd Bengal European Cavalry.

Cornet, 10 June 57—Lieut., 18 May 58.

Service.—Lieutenant Kemble served with the Azimghur Force under Lord Mark Kerr, April '58. Present at the relief of Azimghur. *Medal.*

Major M. F. KEMBLE,† late 41st Native Infantry.

Ensign, 17 Feb. 41—Lieut., 29 Sept. 43—Captain, 16 July 50—Bt.-Major, 24 March 58.

Service.—Major Kemble served throughout the Sutlej Campaign, '45. '46. Present at the battle of Sobraon. *(Wounded.) Medal and Clasp.* Served during the defence of Lucknow, &c. *Medal, Clasp, and Brevet-Major, and one year's extra service. (Since dead.)*

Brevet-Major D. KEMP,† late 5th Europeans.

Ensign, 4 Feb. 46—Lieut., 15 Feb. 51—Captain, 31 Dec. 56—Bt.-Major, 19 Jan. 58.

Service.—Major Kemp served during the Mutiny Campaign. *Medal and Brevet-Major.*

Assistant-Surgeon B. KENDALL,† Bengal Medical Establishment.

Asst.-Surgeon, 4 Aug. 55.

Lieutenant F. H. KENNEDY,† Bengal Invalid Establishment.

Ensign, 12 Jan. 45—Lieut., 21 June 50.

Service.—Lieutenant Kennedy served during the Punjab Campaign, '48, '49. Present at the siege and surrender of Mooltan and battle of Goojerat. *Medal and Clasp.*

BREVET-COLONEL J. D. KENNEDY, P., late 70th Native Infantry.

Ensign, 19 Jan. 28—Lieut., 2 July 33—Captain, 5 July 37—Major, 26 Dec. 46—Lieut.-Colonel, 10 Sept. 52—Bt.-Colonel, 28 Nov. 54.

SERVICE.—Colonel KENNEDY served at the action of Maharajpore. *Bronze Star.* Served during the Sutlej Campaign, '45 '46. *Medal.*

LIEUTENANT J. E. KENNEDY,† late 74th Native Infantry.

Ensign, 12 June 58—Lieut., 23 March 60.

SERVICE.—Lieutenant KENNEDY served with the 1st European Bengal Fusiliers during the Oude Campaign, '58, '59.

LIEUTENANT T. G. KENNEDY, P. H., late 62nd Native Infantry.

Ensign, 24 Dec. 49—Lieut., 3 Oct. 52.

BREVET-MAJOR T. E. KENNION, P., Bengal Artillery.

2nd Lieut., 11 June 42—Lieut., 3 July 45—Bt.-Captain, 11 June 57— Captain, 6 July 57—Bt.-Major, 19 Jan. 58.

SERVICE.—Brevet-Major KENNION was present at the battles of Moodkee, Ferozeshuhur, and Sobraon, '45, '46. *Medal and 2 Clasps.* Served during the Mutiny Campaign. *Medal and Brevet-Major.*

LIEUTENANT W. G. KEPPEL,† late 6th Europeans.

Ensign, 14 March 53—Lieut., 23 Nov. 56.

VETERINARY-SURGEON G. KETTLEWELL.†

Vety.-Surgeon, 5 Dec. 54.

SERVICE.—Veterinary-Surgeon G. KETTLEWELL served with the 1st Troop, 1st Brigade Horse Artillery, throughout the Mutiny, from the outbreak at Jullundur, when the mutineers attacked the guns. Was present at the siege and capture of Delhi, also at the action at Nudjufghur, on the 25th August, under General Nicholson. Served with the Moveable Column under Brigadier Greathed, and was present at the action at Boolundshuhur, 28th September; and at the battle of Agra, on the 10th October; subsequently served with the same Column under Sir Hope Grant; also with the Force under Lord Clyde, at the relief of Lucknow, in November; and at the defeat of the Gwalior Contingent at Cawnpore, in December following; and was present at the siege and capture of Lucknow, in March '58. *Medal and 2 Clasps.* Served with the 1st Sikh Irregular Cavalry during the China Campaign of '60, from the landing of the Force at Kowloon, in April, to the occupation of Pekin; and was present at the action of the 12th August at Singho; on the 18th September at Chun-kia-whee; and on the 21st September near Tungchow. *Medal and Clasps.*

ASSISTANT-SURGEON C. KILKELLY,† A.B., M.B., F.R.C.S., Bengal Medical Establishment.

Asst.-Surgeon, 20 Feb. 56.

ENSIGN T. KINAHAN, Unattached List.

Ensign, 9 Oct. 58.

BREVET-CAPTAIN H. KING, P. H., late 39th Native Infantry.

Ensign, 10 Dec. 42—Lieut., 18 Nov. 46—Bt.-Captain, 10 Dec. 57.

SERVICE.—Brevet-Captain KING served at the battle of Punniar. *Bronze Star.*

ASSISTANT-SURGEON J. B. KING,† M.D., Bengal Medical Establishment.

Asst.-Surgeon, 24 Jan. 55.

BREVET-COLONEL R. R. KINLESIDE, Bengal Artillery.

2nd Lieut., 28 Sept. 27—Lieut., 25 Sept. 34—Bt.-Captain, 28 Sept. 42—Captain, 3 July 45—Bt.-Major, 7 June 49—Major, 25 June 57—Bt.-Lieut.-Colonel, 28 Nov. 54—Lieut.-Colonel, 27 Aug. 58—Bt.-Colonel, 21 Dec. 59.

SERVICE.—Colonel KINLESIDE served with the Army of the Punjab, '48, '49, including the actions of Sadoolapore and Goojerat. *Medal, 2 Clasps, and Brevet-Major.*

SURGEON-MAJOR R. B. KINSEY,† F.R.C.S., Bengal Medical Establishment.

Asst.-Surgeon, 17 Feb. 39—Surgeon, 15 March 53—Surgeon-Major, 13 Jan. 60.

(349)

LIEUTENANT H. J. KINSMAN,† Bengal Artillery.
Lieut., 27 Aug. 58.

LIEUTENANT ST. G. KIRKE, General List.
Ensign, 9 June 60—Lieut., 1 Jan. 62.

LIEUTENANT H. P. KIRKE, P. H., General List.
Ensign, 4 May 60—Lieut., 1 Jan. 62.

SERVICE.—Lieutenant KIRKE was present at Nowgong when the 12th Native Infantry, commanded by Major Kirke, mutinied, and escaped to Nagode. Acted as Interpreter and Quarter-Master as a Volunteer with the Rewah Contingent, in the year '57, '58. Present at the battle of Kirwee and at the storming of the various Forts in that neighborhood. *Medal and commission of Ensign.* Services acknowledged in General Orders.

ASSISTANT-SURGEON W. H. KIRTON,† Bengal Medical Establishment.
Asst.-Surgeon, 4 Aug. 56.

LIEUTENANT C. KITSON, P. H., late 64th Native Infantry.
Ensign, 12 Dec. 57—Lieut., 13 Aug. 58.

SERVICE.—Lieutenant KITSON served with the 53rd Foot at Lord Clyde's capture of Lucknow. *Medal and Clasp.* Served with the Loodiana Regiment in China, in '60.

LIEUTENANT E. KNATCHBULL, late 18th Native Infantry.
Ensign, 1 Sept. 56—Lieut., 12 June 57.

LIEUTENANT-COLONEL R. E. KNATCHBULL, Bengal Artillery.
2nd Lieut., 12 June 28—Lieut., 17 Jan. 36—Bt.-Captain, 12 June 43—Captain, 21 Dec. 45—Bt.-Major, 20 June 54—Major, 28 Sept. 57—Lieut.-Colonel, 27 Aug. 58.

LIEUTENANT F. A. C. KNYVETT, P. H., late 24th Native Infantry.
Ensign, 10 June 54—Lieut., 23 Nov. 56.

(350)

LIEUTENANT-COLONEL W. J. B. KNYVETT, late 30th Native Infantry.

Ensign, 28 March 22—Lieut., 13 May 25—Bt.-Captain, 28 March 37—Captain, 30 March 37—Bt.-Major, 11 Nov. 51—Major, 6 Jan. 52—Bt.-Lieut.-Colonel, 15 Sept. 55—Lieut.-Colonel, 25 May 57.

SERVICE.—Lieutenant-Colonel KNYVETT served during the Bheel Campaign under Colonel Doveton.

L

SURGEON-MAJOR T. S. LACY,† Bengal Medical Establishment.

Asst.-Surgeon, 1 July 40—Surgeon, 27 April 54—Surgeon-Major, 1 July 60.

SERVICE.—Surgeon-Major LACY served with the late 30th Native Infantry throughout the Punjab Campaign, in '48, '49. *Medal and Clasps.*

CAPTAIN F. E. LAING,† late 26th Native Infantry.

Ensign, 10 Dec. 44—Lieut., 18 March 53—Bt.-Captain, 10 Dec. 59—Captain, 27 Dec. 59.

LIEUTENANT SIR A. K. LAKE, Bart.,† late 2nd European Bengal Fusiliers.

2nd Lieut., 20 May 54—Lieut., 23 Nov. 56.

SERVICE.—Lieutenant Sir A. K. LAKE served in all the operations before Delhi: final assault and capture of that city, 14th September '57; and subsequent operations with the Moveable Column under Brigadier Showers, in the Delhi District. *Medal and Clasp.*

LIEUTENANT-COLONEL E. J. LAKE, P. H., Bengal Engineers.

2nd Lieut., 11 June 40—Lieut., 1 Feb. 44—Captain, 21 Aug. 54—Bt.-Major, 22 Aug. 54—Lieut.-Colonel, 18 Feb. 61.

SERVICE.—Lieutenant-Colonel LAKE served with the Army of the Sutlej. Present at the actions of Moodkee *(wounded)* and Alliwal. *Medal and Clasp.* Served During the Campaign in the Punjab. Commanded the Troops of H. H. the Nawab of Bhawulpore throughout the siege and operations in the vicinity of Mooltan. *(Wounded.)* Present at the battle of Goojerat, and subsequent pursuit of the Sikhs and Affghans by the Force under General Gilbert. *Medal, Clasp, and Local Major.*

ASSISTANT-SURGEON M. H. LACKERSTEEN,† M.D., F.R.C.S., Bengal Medical Establishment.

Asst.-Surgeon, 10 Feb. 59.

CAPTAIN C. F. G. LAMB, P., late 62nd Native Infantry.

Ensign, 11 Dec 41—Lieut., 5 July 44—Captain, 11 Feb. 55.

LIEUTENANT G. LAMB,† Bengal Artillery.

Lieut., 27 Aug. 58.

BREVET-CAPTAIN J. LAMB,† late 29th Native Infantry.

Ensign, 3 Feb. 44—Lieut., 1 Oct. 49—Bt.-Captain, 3 Feb. 59.

SERVICE.—Captain LAMB served against the rebels north of Jullundur, '48, '49. Present at the storming of the Heights of Umb, and occupation of the Fort of Oonah. *Medal.*

LIEUTENANT J. LAMB, Bengal Veteran Establishment.

Lieut., 20 Sept. 58.

CAPTAIN T. LAMB, P. H., late 16th Native Infantry.

Ensign, 20 Jan. 47—Lieut., 12 March 52—Captain, 25 Nov. 58.

(Has passed a successful examination in the Vernacular languages of Assam.)

MAJOR W. LAMB, P., late 51st Native Infantry.

Ensign, 4 Feb. 26—Lieut., 25 April 36—Bt.-Captain, 4 Feb. 41—Captain, 1 July 46—Bt.-Major, 20 June 54—Major, 11 Sept. 58—Lieut-Colonel, 27 April 61.

SERVICE.—Major LAMB served at the battle of Maharajpore. *Bronze Star.* Served during the Punjab Campaign, '48, '49. Present at the siege and capture of Mooltan, and battle of Goojerat. *Medal and Clasp.*
(Since retired.)

(352)

LIEUTENANT E. A. C. LAMBERT, P. H., late 1st European Bengal Fusiliers.

2nd Lieut., 12 Dec. 51—Lieut., 14 Aug. 56.

SERVICE.—Lieutenant LAMBERT served in the Burmese War, '52, '53. Present under General Steel, at the operations in the march from Martaban to Tonghoo. *Medal.* Present at the battle of Badlee-ka-Serai, 8th June '57; and at the actions of June 12th, 17th, 19th, 20th, and 23rd *(struck down by sunstroke).* Present at the action of 12th August '57, under Brigadier Showers, at Nudjufghur; 25th August '57, under General Nicholson; and at the assault and capture of Delhi, 14th September '57. Served in Oude, '58, '59, as Sub-Assistant Commissary-General with the Field Force under Colonel Payne, and at Sultanpore, Oude. *Medal and Clasp.*

BREVET-MAJOR F. W. LAMBERT, P. H., late 56th Native Infantry.

Ensign, 9 June 48—Lieut., 1 Oct. 50—Captain, 27 June 57—Bt.-Major, 20 July 58.

SERVICE.—Brevet-Major LAMBERT served with the Force under Major General Gilbert. *Medal.* Served throughout the Burmese Expedition of '52, '53. *Medal.* Served during the Rebellion of '57, '58 : siege of Delhi and Rohilcund. *Medal, Clasp, and Brevet-Major.*

CAPTAIN G. C. LAMBERT, late 1st European Bengal Fusiliers.

2nd Lieut., 20 Feb. 45—Lieut., 11 Feb. 46—Captain, 1 Feb. 56.

SERVICE.—Captain LAMBERT served during the Sutlej Campaign. Present at the battle of Sobraon. *Medal.* Served in the Burmah Campaign, '52, '53. Present at the relief of the Garrison of Pegu, 14th December '52, and the operations in its vicinity. Accompanied the Martaban Column. Present at the storm and re-capture of Belin, in April '53. *Medal.*

LIEUTENANT P. LAMBERT, P. H., Bengal Engineers.

Lieut., 27 Aug. 58.

LIEUTENANT F. LANCE, P. H., late 55th Native Infantry.

Ensign, 13 June 56—Lieut., 14 Sept. 57.

SERVICE.—Lieutenant LANCE served in Rohilcund against the rebels in '58. Present at the defence of the Shahjehanpore Jail, in May '58. Served in the affairs of Mohumudpore, in June '58; and Nooriah, August '58. Present at the action at Sussiah Ghaut, January '59. *(Severely wounded, and horse shot under him.)* Received the thanks of Government, '59. *Medal.*

BREVET-COLONEL J. E. LANDERS, late 9th Native Infantry.

Ensign, 10 Jan. 20—Lieut., 11 July 23—Bt.-Captain, 10 Jan. 35—Captain, 31 March 35—Bt.-Major, 9 Nov. 46—Major, 3 Oct. 48—Lieut.-Colonel, 24 Dec. 53—Bt.-Colonel, 28 Nov. 54.

SERVICE.—Brevet-Colonel LANDERS commanded the Bhopal Contingent in an engagement with a party of insurgents, '46.

LIEUTENANT A. LANDON, General List.

Ensign, 8 June 60—Lieut., 1 Jan. 62.

BREVET-MAJOR C. P. LANE, P., late 3rd Bengal European Cavalry.

Cornet, 20 Jan. 46—Lieut., 8 May 49—Captain, 23 Nov. 56—Bt.-Major, 20 July 58.

SERVICE.—Major LANE served during the Punjab Campaign, '48, '49. Present at the actions of Ramnuggur, Chillianwallah, and Goojerat. *Medal and 2 Clasps.* Served under H. H. Sir Jung Bahadoor, Present at the affair of the Kandooah Nullah, siege and capture of Lucknow, and taking of Fort Jullalpore. *Medal and Clasp.* Brought to the notice of the Governor-General by Brigadier Macgregor, 4th March '58. Promoted to the rank of Brevet-Major for services during the Mutiny.

(354)

MAJOR-GENERAL C. R. W. LANE, C.B., late 5th Europeans.

Ensign, 5 Feb. 07—Lieut., 7 March 13—Bt.-Captain, 5 Feb. 22—Captain, 30 Jan. 24—Major, 30 April 35—Lieut.-Colonel, 26 Dec. 41—Colonel, 25 May 52—Major-General, 28 Nov. 54.

SERVICE.—Major-General LANE, C.B., served at the storming of the Palace of Delhi, '09; throughout the Nepal Campaign, '14, '15; Maharattah War, '17, '18, including the siege and capture of Hattrass, Dhumonee, and Ghurry Mundlah. Siege and capture of Asseergurh, '19; against the Bheels, '23; Burmese War, '25, '26, *Medal;* and with the Force in Affghanistan, under General Nott. Commanded at the defence of Candahar, 10th March '42; and present at the different operations leading to the re-occupation of Cabul by the Candahar Division. *Medal and C.B.*

LIEUTENANT C. S. LANE, P. C., late 56th Native Infantry.

Ensign, 9 Dec. 48—Lieut., 1 Sept. 50.

SERVICE.—Lieutenant LANE served at the siege and capture of Delhi, in September '57, with the Rajah of Jheend's Force, under Colonel Dunsford. *Medal and Clasps.* Served with Columns under General Greathed and Sir H. Grant, including actions of Boolundshuhur, Allyghur, and Agra, in September, October, and November '57. Served as S. A. C. General with the Army under Sir C. Campbell, from 10th November '57 to 15th January '58. Was present at the relief of Lucknow, November '57. *Clasp.*

LIEUTENANT C. T. LANE,† late 16th Native Infantry.

Ensign, 11 Dec. 58—Lieut., 29 March 59.

BREVET-MAJOR H. LANE, P. C., late 5th Bengal European Cavalry.

Cornet, 1 Jan. 44—Lieut., 1 Dec. 48—Captain, 5 May 56—Bt.-Major, 24 March 58.

SERVICE.—Brevet-Major LANE served throughout the Sutlej Campaign, '45, '46. Present at the battles of Moodkee, Ferozeshuhur, Alliwal, and Sobraon. *Medal and* 3 *Clasps.* Served during the Punjab

(355)

Campaign, '48, '49. Present at the affair of Ramnuggur, and actions of Sadoolapore, Chillianwallah, and Goojerat. *Medal and 2 Clasps.* Served during the Mutiny, '57, '58. Present at the relief of the Garrison of Lucknow, by Lord Clyde, in November '57. Served with the Force under Sir J. Outram, at Alum Bagh, 25th November '57, to the 18th March '58. Present at several engagements while in the occupation of that post, on 22nd December '57, 16th January, and 21st and 25th February '58 ; and at the repulse of the enemy's Cavalry, 3,000 strong, which attacked the Camp, 16th March '58. Present during the final storm and capture of Lucknow, March '58. *Medal and 2 Clasps, and Brevet-Major.* Mentioned in Sir James Outram's Despatch, 23rd December '57.

MAJOR-GENERAL J. T. LANE, C.B., Bengal Artillery.

2nd Lieut., 9 June 21—Lieut., 1 May 24—Bt.-Captain, 9 June 36— Captain, 22 Aug. 38—Bt.-Major, 23 Dec. 42—Major, 10 Feb. 49—Bt.- Lieut.-Colonel, 30 April 44—Lieut.-Colonel, 30 Oct. 55—Bt.-Colonel, 20 June 54—Colonel, 18 Feb. 61—Major-General, 8 June 56.

SERVICE.—Major-General LANE, C.B., served with the Force in the Shekawattee Country, '34, '35 ; with the Force before Jhansie and surrender of Fort in '38 ; throughout the Cabul Campaign, '41, '42. Present at the forcing of the Khyber Pass, and other engagements leading to the re-occupation of Cabul. *Medal and Brevet-Major.* Present at the battle of Maharajpore. *Bronze Star and Brevet-Lieutenant-Colonel.* Sutlej Campaign, '45, '46, including the battles of Alliwal and Sobraon. *Medal, Clasp, and C.B.* Army of the Punjab, '48, '49, including actions of Ramnuggur, Chillianwallah, and Goojerat. *Medal and 2 Clasps.*

LIEUTENANT A. M. LANG,† Bengal Engineers.

Lieut., 10 March 57.

SERVICE.—Lieutenant LANG served at the siege of Delhi, '57. Accompanied Colonel Greathed's Column during its march to Lucknow and in various engagements. Present at the relief and final capture of Lucknow, September '57 and March '58, by Lord Clyde ; battle of Cawnpore, and advance on Futtehghur. *Medal and 3 Clasps.*

(356)

LIEUTENANT R. T. M. LANG, General List, Cavalry.
Cornet, 12 Oct. 59—Lieut., 9 Dec. 60

RIDING-MASTER W. LANGDALE.
Riding-Master, 23 Oct. 56.

CAPTAIN E. G. LANGMORE, P., late 27th Native Infantry.
Ensign, 28 July 42—Lieut., 31 Dec. 45—Captain, 23 Nov. 56.
SERVICE.—Captain LANGMORE served during the Sutlej Campaign in '45, '46. Present at the battle of Ferozeshuhur. *Medal.*

BREVET-MAJOR E. H. LANGMORE, P. H., late 71st Native Infantry.
Ensign, 1 March 45—Lieut., 21 Aug. 49—Bt.-Captain, 1 March 60—Bt.-Major, 17 Feb. 61.
SERVICE.—Major LANGMORE served with a Force under Brigadier Wheeler, in the Punjab, in '48, '49. Present at the capture of two Sikh Forts, Ramnuggur and Muraree. *Medal.* Formed one of the Garrison of Lucknow from the 30th of June to the 22nd of November '57. Commanded an important out-post during that period, and was honorably mentioned in Major-General Sir J. Inglis' Despatch, dated 8th December '57, to the Governor-General, and published in General Order No. 1543, dated 8th December '57, from which the following is an extract :—"And Lieutenant Langmore, with the remnant of his Corps (the 71st Native Infantry) held a very exposed position between the Hospital and Water Gate. This gallant and deserving young soldier and his men were entirely without shelter from the weather, both by night and day." Present with the Force under His Excellency the Commander-in-Chief, which drove the Gwalior rebels from Cawnpore in '57. *Medal, Clasp, Brevet-Majority, and one year's extra service.*

LIEUTENANT H. T. LARKINS, General List.
Ensign, 4 Jan. 60—Lieut., 1 Jan. 62.

(357)

BREVET-MAJOR R. LARKINS, P. H., late 49th Native Infantry.

Ensign, 10 Dec. '39—Lieut., 30 Aug. 41—Captain, 13 March 48—Bt.-Major, 20 July 58.

SERVICE.—Major LARKINS served at the siege and capture of Mooltan, '48, '49. *Medal and Clasp.* Served as Captain of Division in H. M.'s Land Transport Corps in the Crimea, up to the fall of Sebastopol. *Medal and Sebastopol Clasps.*

LIEUTENANT L. H. P. DE H. LARPENT,† late 21st Native Infantry.

Ensign, 20 Jan. 51—Lieut., 28 Feb. 56.

SERVICE.—Lieutenant LARPENT commanded a Detachment of his Regiment with the Force under Colonel Vaughan, in the Meranzaie District, in July and August '57. Served as Quarter-Master of his Regiment with the Force under Major-General Cotton, in the Hills in the Eusuffzaie Border, in April and May '58. Present at the destruction of Chinglee Mungul, Thana, and Sultana. Served during the Mutinies of '57, '58.

LIEUTENANT J. H. C. G. LASSALLE, General List.

Ensign, 20 Feb. 60—Lieut., 1 Jan. 62.

LIEUTENANT H. LATHAM, Bengal Artillery.

Lieut., 27 Aug. 58.

COLONEL J. LAUGHTON, Bengal Engineers.

2nd Lieut., 12 June 28—Lieut., 3 Feb. 39—2nd Captain, 12 June 43—Captain, 11 Nov. 46—Bt.-Major, 20 June 54—Major, 10 March 57—Lieut.-Colonel, 27 Aug. 58—Colonel, 18 Feb. 61.

SERVICE.—Colonel LAUGHTON served in Persia, '34, '36. In action with the Russian Troops. Served in Affghanistan, '39. *(Since dead)*

CAPTAIN C. P. St. J. LAW, P. H., late 11th Native Infantry.

Ensign, 10 July 39—Lieut., 16 July 42—Bt.-Captain, 10 July 54—Captain, 12 Oct. 56.

SERVICE.—Captain LAW served throughout the Hill Campaign in Scinde, '44, '45, under Sir C. Napier.

(358)

LIEUTENANT F. A. LAWFORD, P. H., late 50th Native Infantry.

Ensign, 14 June 50—Lieut., 28 Oct. 56.

SERVICE.—Lieutenant LAWFORD served throughout the Oude Campaign with Hodson's Horse.

BREVET-COLONEL G. ST. P. LAWRENCE, C.B., late 2nd Bengal European Cavalry.

Cornet, 5 May 21—Lieut., 1 May 24—Bt.-Captain, 5 May 36—Captain, 5 Jan. 44—Bt.-Major, 9 Nov. 46—Major, 26 Feb. 60—Bt.-Lieut.-Colonel, 7 June 49—Bt.-Colonel, 28 Nov. 54.

SERVICE.—Colonel LAWRENCE served with the Army of the Indus, '39, '40, '41. Present at the capture of Ghuznee. *Medal.* Pursuit of Dost Mahomed Khan, '39, and forcing of the Khoord Cabul Pass by the Force under Sir Robert Sale, October '41. *3rd class Dooranee Order.* Taken prisoner on the 23rd December '41, and released on the 29th of the same month. In retreat from Cabul surrendered as hostage to Akbar Khan, released 21st September '42; fell into the hands of Sirdar Chutter Singh, after the night attack made by the Sikh Army on the Peshawur Agency, October '48. Retreated to Kohat, then made prisoner by Sirdar Sultan Mahomed Khan, liberated 7th March '49, on the submission of the Sirdar to Major-General Gilbert. *Medal and Brevet-Lieutenant-Colonel.*

MAJOR-GENERAL H. LAWRENCE, late 72nd Native Infantry.

Ensign, 30 July 12—Lieut., 16 Dec. 14—Bt.-Captain, 1 Nov. 26—Captain, 19 Jan. 28—Major, 3 Aug. 37—Lieut.-Colonel, 3 Nov. 43—Colonel, 15 April 54—Major-General, 5 Dec. 55.

SERVICE.—Major-General LAWRENCE served on board the *Astell*, East Indiaman, in Command of two guns on her quarter deck, in a severe action fought in the Mosambique Channel on the 3rd July '10, between three Indiamen, and two French Frigates and a Corvette. Served in the operations against and at the attack of the Fortress of Malown, in the Nepal War of '14, '15. Served with the Reserve of the Grand Army during the Maharattah Campaign of '17, '18, and '19; also against the Coles in '35;

and in Command of a Brigade of all arms against the same Tribes, in '36, '37. *Medal.*

ASSISTANT-SURGEON J. J. T. LAWRENCE,† Bengal Medical Establishment.
Asst.-Surgeon, 20 June 54.

BREVET-MAJOR R. C. LAWRENCE, C. B., P. H., late 73rd Native Infantry.
Ensign, 13 June 34—Lieut., 17 Sept. 41—Bt.-Captain, 13 June 49—Captain, 7 April 51—Bt.-Major, 19 Jan. 58.

SERVICE.—Major LAWRENCE served during the Sutlej Campaign, '46. Present at the action of Sobraon. *Medal.* Served as Political Officer in charge of the Cashmere Contingent, under General Wilson, in '57. Present at the assault and capture of Delhi; commanded the 4th Column of assault on Major Reid being wounded. Mentioned in Despatch of General Wilson, to the Commander-in-Chief, 8th October '57. *Medal and Clasp, Brevet-Major, and C.B.*

SURGEON P. G. LAY,† Bengal Medical Establishment.
Asst.-Surgeon, 9 Sept. 42—Surgeon, 13 Feb. 57.

MAJOR F. P. LAYARD, P., late 19th Native Infantry.
Ensign, 11 March 38—Lieut., 16 July 42—Captain, 30 April 51.

SERVICE.—Major LAYARD served as Brigade-Major under Brigadier Wallace, during the War in Scinde, in '42, '43.

LIEUTENANT G. B. LEE, late 6th Europeans.
Ensign, 7 Aug. 58—Lieut., 28 Aug. 60.
(Since dead.)

SURGEON J. LEE,† M.D., Bengal Medical Establishment.
Asst.-Surgeon, 10 Jan. 45—Surgeon, 16 April 58.

BREVET-CAPTAIN E. LEEDS, P. H., late 47th Native Infantry.

Ensign, 7 June 44—Lieut., 22 March 50—Bt.-Captain, 7 June 59.

SERVICE.—Captain LEEDS served with the Army of the Sutlej, '46. Present at the actions of Buddiwal, Alliwal, and Sobraon. *Medal and 2 Clasps.*

ASSISTANT-SURGEON L. H. LEES,† M.D., Bengal Medical Establishment.

Asst.-Surgeon, 27 Jan. 58.

SERVICE.—Assistant-Surgeon LEES served in Medical Charge of the 8th Punjab Infantry throughout the War in China of '60, being present at the action of Sinho, capture of Tonko and Taku Forts, advance on Tientsin and Pekin, and the final surrender and occupation of the latter city. *Medal and 2 Clasps.*

CAPTAIN T. E. B. LEES, P. H., late 43rd Native Infantry.

Ensign, 18 Sept. 40—Lieut., 24 Jan. 45—Bt.-Captain, 18 Sept. 55—Captain, 23 Nov. 56.

SERVICE.—Captain LEES served during the Sutlej Campaign, '45, '46, until the surrender of the Sikhs under the walls of Lahore. Present at the action of Sobraon. *Medal.* Remained on service in the City of Lahore, '46, '47, with the Force left there, to establish the Maharajah Duleep Sing on the throne.

CAPTAIN W. N. LEES, L.L.D., P., late 42nd Native Infantry.

Ensign, 14 June 45—Lieut., 25 July 53—Captain, 11 Sept. 58.

SERVICE.—Captain LEES served during the Sutlej Campaign, '46. Accompanied the Force under Brigadier Wheeler, from Lahore, to coerce the Shaik Imam-ood-deen of Cashmere. (Received certificate of high proficiency in Arabic; a Degree of Honor for eminent attainments in the Persian language; a certificate of high proficiency, and Degree of Honor in Oordoo; and a certificate of high proficiency in Hindee. Received the reward of Rs. 1,000 for proficiency in the Native languages.)

(361)

CAPTAIN A. LeGALLAIS, B.A., P. H., late 46th Native Infantry.
Ensign, 1 Jan. 44—Lieut., 21 April 48—Captain, 14 July 57.

SERVICE.—Captain LeGALLAIS served in the Punjab Campaign, in '48, '49. Present at the affair of Ramnuggur, actions of Sadoolapore, Chillianwallah, and Goojerat. *Medal and 2 Clasps.* Served against the revolted Khurruls and Khateas, in the Googaira District, '57. Commanded a Company of the Goojranwallah Levy attached to Major Chamberlain's Force detached from Mooltan.

BREVET-MAJOR W. B. LEGARD, late 31st Native Infantry.
Ensign, 18 June 28—Lieut., 1 June 34—Bt.-Captain, 18 June 43—Captain, 2 Feb. 45—Bt.-Major, 20 June 54.

SERVICE.—Major LEGARD served with his Regiment in the Saugor District during the Mutiny, '57, '58.

CAPTAIN W. F. LEICESTER, P. H., late 30th Native Infantry.
Ensign, 11 Dec. 47—Lieut., 15 Nov. 53—Captain, 18 Feb. 61.

SERVICE.—Captain LEICESTER served during the Punjab Campaign, '48, '49. Present at the passage of the Chenab and battle of Chillianwallah *(severely wounded)*, '49. (Passed examination in Field Engineering.)

MAJOR R. T. LEIGH, late 6th Europeans.
Ensign, 12 Dec. 40—Lieut., 13 June 44—Captain, 7 May 54—Major in Staff Corps, 18 Feb. 61.

SERVICE.—Major LEIGH served with the Army of the Sutlej, '45, '46. Present at the battle of Ferozeshuhur. *Medal.* Present at several operations against the rebels in Sumbulpore, '57, '58. Favorably noticed by the Lieutenant-Governor of Bengal. (Passed examination in Punjabee.)

LIEUTENANT H. F. LEIGHTON, P. H., late 40th Native Infantry.
Ensign, 11 June 59—Lieut., 18 Feb. 61.

LIEUTENANT F. W. LEMAN, late 4th Europeans.
Ensign, 20th Feb. 58—Lieut., 13 March 59.

x 1

CAPTAIN C. S. LEMARCHAND, P. H., Bengal Artillery.

2nd Lieut., 13 June 45—Lieut., 13 Jan. 49—2nd Captain, 27 Aug. 58—Captain, 18 Feb. 61.

BREVET-COLONEL W. G. LENNOX, late 63rd Native Infantry.

Ensign, 15 Aug. 18—Lieut., 16 Aug. 18—Captain, 23 April. 30—Bt.-Major, 9 Nov. 46—Major, 11 Nov. 47—Lieut.-Colonel, 14th July 53—Bt.-Colonel, 28 Nov. 54.

SERVICE.—Colonel LENNOX served throughout the operations in Affghanistan with the force under General Nott, '39, '40, '41, and '42. *Medal.* At Maharajpore, *Bronze Star*: during the Campaign on the Sutlej, including the battle of Sobraon. *Medal.*

LIEUTENANT J. LEONARD, Bengal Veteran Establishment.

Lieut., 28 April 68.

LIEUTENANT A. Y. LESLIE, General List.

Ensign, 4 March 60—Lieut., 1 Jan. 62.

LIEUTENANT F. M. LESLIE, late 53rd Native Infantry.

Ensign, 20 Dec. 57—Lieut., 2 Feb. 60.

SERVICE.—Lieutenant LESLIE served with the Army under Lord Clyde at Lucknow. Present at the capture of that city. *Medal and Clasp.*

LIEUTENANT F. E. LEWES,† Bengal Artillery.

Lieut., 14 April 58.

SERVICE.—Lieutenant LEWES served during the Mutiny at Peshawur. Present when the 24th, 27th, 51st, and 54th Native Infantry were disarmed. Commanded 2 guns of H. M.'s 87th at Peshawur, at the mutiny of the 51st Native Infantry, and the blowing away of that Regiment. Served with the Peshawur Mountain Train Battery against the Mahsood Wuzeerees, in '60, including the action of Burrara, occupation of Kaneegoorum, retirement in action from Mukeem, on which occasion Lieutenant Lewes was in temporary Command of the battery.

(363)

LIEUTENANT H A. LEWES, P. H., late 20th Native Infantry.

Ensign, 4 Oct. 55—Lieut., 10 May 57.

SERVICE.—Lieutenant LEWES served in the Meerut District with the Force under Brigadier Seaton, from Delhi to Futtehghur, December '57. Served with the Soraon Field Force, July '58. Served under Brigadier Kelly in the Azimghur District and in the Terai. Present under Sir H. Grant, at the attack made on the rebels at Jurwah Pass, Nepal Hills, May '59. Present at the actions of Gungeeree, on 14th; Puttiallee, 17th; and occupation of Mynpooree; 27th December '57. Bungaon, Rohilcund, April '58; Fort Denain and Ferroul, in Oude, July '58. *Wounded severely* by a musket ball at Meerut, on the outbreak of the Mutiny there, 10th May '57. *Medal.*

LIEUTENANT T. H. LEWIN, P. H., late 31st Native Infantry.

Ensign, 12 June 57—Lieut., 18 May 58.

SERVICE.—Lieutenant LEWIN was present at the defence of Cawnpore, under General Windham. Served under General Grant: present at the taking of the fortified Town of Meergunge; present at the siege and capture of Lucknow. *Medal and Clasp.* Took part in the operations against the rebels in Central India, under Brigadier Wheeler. Received the thanks of the Governor-General, 5th August '59.

LIEUTENANT-COLONEL H. LEWIS, P. C., Bengal Artillery.

2nd Lieut., 12 June 37—Lieut., 17 Aug. 41—Bt.-Captain, 12 June 52—Captain, 3 March 53—Lieut.-Colonel, 18 Feb. 61.

ASSISTANT-SURGEON R. LIDDERDALE,† M. D., Bengal Medical Establishment.

Asst.-Surgeon, 27 Jan. 58.

BREVET-MAJOR A. LIGHT, P. H., Bengal Artillery.

2nd Lieut., 11 June 42—Lieut., 3 July 45—2nd Captain, 11 June 57—Captain, 10 July 57—Bt.-Major, 19 Jan. 58.

SERVICE.—Major LIGHT served in the Mutiny Campaign. *Medal and Brevet-Major.*

LIEUTENANT E. LIGHTFOOT, late 59th Native Infantry.

Ensign, 15 July 57—Lieut., 18 May 58.

SERVICE.—Lieutenant LIGHTFOOT served with the Shahabad Field Force in '58. Present at the affairs of Bhurapore, Sikurrea, and capture of Jugdespore. *Medal.* Mentioned in the Despatch of Brigadier Douglas, 18th December '58. Received the concurrence of the Governor-General to the approbation expressed by the Commander-in-Chief, 21st July '59, for the good service rendered by him in reducing mutinous Sepoys into submission.

LIEUTENANT G. A. H. LILLIE, P. H., late 13th Native Infantry.

Ensign, 11 June 47—Lieut., 30 April 51.

2ND CAPTAIN D. LIMOND, Bengal Engineers.

2nd Lieut., 14 June 50—Lieut., 21 Aug. 54—2nd Captain, 27 Aug. 58.

SERVICE.—Captain LIMOND served as Assistant Field Engineer with the Oude Field Force, under Sir H. Havelock, and under Sir J. Outram, in the defence of the Residency of Lucknow. Present at the 2nd crossing of the Ganges; actions of Mungulwar, Alum Bagh, and relief of Lucknow, also at the final storm and capture of that city. Mentioned in the Despatch of the Chief Engineer, Oude Field Force, 25th November '57; in that of General Havelock, 15th November '57; in that of Colonel R. Napier, 5th October '57; in that of Sir J. Outram, 25th November '57. Received the thanks of Government, '57. *Medal and Clasp.*

CAPTAIN J. B. LIND, P., late 24th Native Infantry.

Ensign, 26 May 46—Lieut., 18 Nov. 50—Captain, 26 May 61.

SERVICE.—Captain LIND served in the expedition to Koorum under Brigadier-General Chamberlain. Served during the Mutiny, '57, '58. In Command of *Lind's* Mooltan Horse, was engaged at Jhelum, 7th July '57 (1st charger shot under him, 2nd charger wounded, *slightly contused* on shoulder, and *grazed* on left leg). Served at Delhi with Nicholson's Column. Engaged at Nudjufghur, 25th August '57; and in the night attack of Kisengunge, 14th September '57 (charger wounded

(365)

by a fragment of a shell). Served at Rohtuk, and aided in disarming and quieting the district. Present at the action of Narnoul, 16th November '57 (charger bayonetted under him). With Penny's Column, led the advance in crossing the Ganges. Engaged at Kukraoli, 30th April '58. *(Slightly wounded* in left knee, charger cut down under him.) Present at the action before capture of Bareilly, 5th and 6th May '58. (Struck down by *coup de soleil* on the latter occasion.) Served with the Shahjehanpore Column in Oude, '58, '59. Received the thanks of His Excellency the Governor-General for services at Delhi. *Medal and Clasp.*

GENERAL A. LINDSAY, C.B., Bengal Artillery.

1st Lieut., 14 Aug. 04—Captain, 22 March 13—Major, 12 Aug. 19—Lieut.-Colonel, 1 May 24—Colonel, 2 July 35—Major-General, 28 June 38—Lieut.-General, 11 Nov. 51—General, 11 Sept. 59.

SERVICE.—General LINDSAY, C.B., served with the Subsidiary Force in Gohud and Gwalior under Colonel Bowie, in '05 and '06, and was present at the siege of Gohud, in '06. Was present at the sieges of Kommonah and Gunnowrie, in '07. Served throughout both Campaigns of the Nepal War, with the Dinapore Division of the Army, in '14, '15, and '16, and was *severely wounded* in the attack of the *Fort* and *Stockade* of Hurriarpore, in '16. Served with the Force under Major-General Marshall, in '17, and was present at the siege of Hattrass, and with the left Division of the Grand Army during the Pindarree War, in '17, '18. Was present at the sieges and capture of Dhamoonee and Mundela. Served during the Burmese War with the South-East Division of the Army under Brigadier-General Morrison. Was present at the attack on, and capture of Arracan, in '25. *Medal.*

LIEUTENANT A. LINDSAY, P. H., late 68th Native Infantry.

Ensign, 18 April 57—Lieut., 18 May 58.

SERVICE.—Lieutenant LINDSAY served during the Mutinies, '57, '58. Present at the defence of Cawnpore, and action there on the 6th December '57. At Bhogneepore and Calpee, on 4th February '58. During part of the bombardment of Lucknow, February '58; in the action of

Kukraoli, 29th April '58; capture of Bareilly, 5th and 6th May; action at Shahjehanpore, 18th May; taking of the Fort of Benny, 24th May; and Mohumdee, 25th May '58. *Medal and Clasp.*

LIEUTENANT A. F. LINDSAY, P. H., late 63rd Native Infantry.

Ensign, 6 Jan. 59—Lieut., 19 Aug. 59.

2ND CAPTAIN A. H. LINDSAY, P. H., Bengal Artillery.

2nd Lieut., 11 Dec. 49—Lieut., 12 July 55—2nd Captain, 27 Aug. 58.

SERVICE.—Captain LINDSAY served during the Mutiny in '57, '58. Present at the siege and capture of Delhi, and final storm and capture of Lucknow. *Medal and 2 Clasps.*

LIEUTENANT F. LINDSAY, Bengal Artillery.

Lieut., 11 Dec. 58.

BREVET-CAPTAIN R. C. LINDSAY,† late 24th Native Infantry.

Ensign, 11 Feb. 45—Lieut., 20 May 49—Bt.-Captain, 11 Feb. 60.

LIEUTENANT W. A. LIOT,† Bengal Artillery.

Lieut., 27 Aug. 58.

BREVET-COLONEL J. LIPTRAP, late 45th Native Infantry.

Ensign, 30 Aug. 18—Lieut., 4 Nov. 18—Captain, 19 June 31—Bt.-Major, 9 Nov. 46—Major, 17 Feb. 50—Bt.-Lieut.-Colonel, 20 June 54—Lieut.-Colonel, 7 May 55—Bt.-Colonel, 20 June 57.

SERVICE.—Colonel LIPTRAP served in the Burmese Campaign, '24, '25. Present at the capture of Mahatee and storming of Arracan. *Medal.* Served with the Army of the Indus, '39, '40. Served in the Sutlej Campaign, '45, '46. Present during the occupation of Lahore. Served during the Sonthal Campaign, '55. Received the thanks of Government. Served during the Mutiny, '57. Brought back the men of the 45th Native Infantry, four different times, when they mutinied and marched away with the Colors and Arms. Received thanks in Brigade Orders for daring bravery on the 13th May '57.

(367)

LIEUTENANT-COLONEL J. LIPTROTT, late 14th Native Infantry.

2nd Lieut., 7 Feb. 29—Lieut, 25 Feb. 34—Bt.-Captain, 7 Feb. 44—Captain, 30 April 46—Bt.-Major, 28 Nov. 54—Major, 10 Aug. 56—Lieut.-Colonel, 28 Nov. 59.

SERVICE.—Lieutenant-Colonel LIPTROTT served with the Force under General Pollock, throughout the operations in Affghanistan, '42. *Medal*. Served also during the Campaign on the Sutlej. Present at the battle of Alliwal (horse shot under him). *Medal*.

LIEUTENANT J. T. LISCOMBE,† late 34th Native Infantry.

Ensign, 20 Feb. 51—Lieut., 23 Nov. 56.

MAJOR-GENERAL F. G. LISTER, late 31st Native Infantry.

Ensign, 27 March 06—Lieut., 9 Oct. 08—Bt.-Captain, 27 March 21—Captain, 16 March 24—Bt.-Major, 10 Jan. 37—Major, 4 Sept. 39—Lieut.-Colonel, 30 Sept. 45—Bt.-Colonel, 20 June 54—Colonel, 13 April 55—Major-General, 22 Aug. 57.

LIEUTENANT J. LISTON, late 10th Native Infantry.

Ensign, 7 Dec. 55—Lieut., 17 Oct. 56.

SERVICE.—Lieutenant LISTON served during the operations in Bundlecund, in Command of 5 Companies, late 12th Punjab Infantry, in '59.

LIEUTENANT E. F. LITCHFIELD,† late 42nd Native Infantry.

Ensign, 20 March 55—Lieut., 8 Dec. 56.

LIEUTENANT A. L. C. LITTLEDALE,† late 5th Bengal European Cavalry.

Cornet, 4 Oct. 58—Lieut., 5 Feb. 59.

SURGEON J. H. LITTLER,† M. D., Bengal Medical Establishment.

Asst.-Surgeon, 17 April 42—Surgeon, 28 Sept. 56.

SERVICE.—Surgeon LITTLER served in Medical Charge of the 55th Native Infantry at Hote Murdan, in May '57, when the Force of

Europeans and Sikhs from Peshawur quelled the mutiny of that Regiment. Served in Medical Charge of the Artillery with the Force under Major-General Sir Sydney Cotton, in April and May '58, against some Hill Tribes and fanatics in the Eusuffzaic country.

BREVET-MAJOR B. P. LLOYD, P., late 11th Native Infantry.

Ensign, 3 Jan. 40—Lieut., 24 Jan. 45—Bt.-Captain, 3 Jan. 55—Captain, 23 Nov. 56—Bt.-Major, 24 March 58.

SERVICE.—Major LLOYD served with the Field Force in Bundlecund, in '42, '43 : present at the action of Bhugora, 7th December '42; served through the Gwalior Campaign in '43, '44 ; present at the battle of Maharajpore. *Bronze Star.* Served under Major-General Sir John Grey, at Attaruwallah, 1st January '46 ; and through the remainder of the Sutlej Campaign served in the expedition under Brigadier Wheeler, against Kôt Kangra, in June '46; present at the surrender of that Fortress. Present as Superintendent of Neemuch when the Native Brigade at that station mutinied, 3rd June '57. Regained possession on 6th June with a few Native Horsemen and Police, and succeeded in holding it till reinforced by some Kotah and Boondee Troops, and restored the British authority in the Neemuch District. Present at the action at Jeerum against the rebels, 23rd October '57. Present when the Garrison at Neemuch was besieged by the rebels from the 8th to the 22nd November '57 ; present throughout the siege and conducted the duties of Commandant during that time. Received the thanks of the Commander-in-Chief of the Bombay Army, 19th December '57, and also of Brigadier General Lawrence, 2nd December '57. *Brevet-Majority and Medal.* Mentioned in the Governor-General's Despatch to the Secretary of State, and received a letter, dated the 11th June '60, from the Secretary of State, conveying the gracious approbation of Her Majesty the Queen, of his conduct during the rebellion.

CAPTAIN E. P. LLOYD, P. H., late 24th Native Infantry.

Ensign, 29 Dec. 44—Lieut., 12 Sept. 46—Captain, 1st May 57.

SERVICE.—Captain LLOYD served during the Sutlej Campaign, '46. Present at the actions of Moodkee, Ferozeshuhur, Buddiwal, and

Alliwal, also in the operations against the Forts of Dhurm Kôt and Phillour. *Medal and Clasps.* Served under the late Sir Hugh Wheeler against the insurgents in Cashmere, '47. At the commencement of the outbreak that resulted in the 2nd Sikh Campaign, proceeded with a party of Sikhs from Hooshearpore, and surprised, seized, blew up, and demolished the strong Fort of Choky. Served against the insurgents under Ram Singh, and present at the storming of the enemy's position at Akrot and Aurkabagh. (Passed examination in Assamese and Bengali.)

CAPTAIN G. C. LLOYD,† late 56th Native Infantry.

Ensign, 9 June 49—Lieut., 5 Sept. 53—Captain, 27 June 57.

SERVICE.—Captain LLOYD served in the Sonthal Campaign, '55, '56. Served with the Shahabad Field Force, October and November '58. Present at the attack of Berhampore, 14th October '58. Present at Sikunea, 16th October '58, and other skirmishes leading to the successful attack and taking of Jugdespore. Mentioned in Sir J. Douglas' Despatch.

LIEUTENANT-GENERAL G. W. A. LLOYD, C.B., late 28th Native Infantry.

Ensign, 1 Jan. 04—Lieut., 17 Sept. 06—Bt.-Captain, 1 Jan. 19—Captain, 13 May 25—Major, 3 June 30—Lieut.-Colonel, 7 Jan. 36—Bt.-Colonel, 9 Nov. 46—Colonel, 27 Aug. 47—Major-General, 20 June 54—Lieut.-General, 2 June 60.

SERVICE.—Lieutenant-General LLOYD, C.B., served in China, '08. In Java, '11. *Medal.* During the Pindarree War, '17. *Medal.* Served in China, '41, '42. *Medal and C.B.*

LIEUTENANT J. LOCH, Bengal Artillery.

Lieut., 27 Aug. 58.

ASSISTANT-SURGEON J. H. LOCH,† M.D., Bengal Medical Establishment.

Asst.-Surgeon, 20 Dec. 54.

SERVICE.—Assistant-Surgeon LOCH served with the Oude Field Force from January till June '56, in charge of 4th Company, 1st Battalion

Artillery, &c. Served in Medical Charge of a Detachment of Europeans and Native Troops, in the Serai, against the Dacca mutineers, from December '57 to January '58. Served with H. M.'s 13th Light Infantry, (part of the time in Medical Charge of Head Quarters and Right Wing,) from 30th March '58 to February '59. Was present at the relief of Azimghur and pursuit of Koer Singh. *Medal.*

LIEUTENANT J. L. LOCH,† late 2nd Bengal European Cavalry.

Cornet, 20 Jan. 57—Lieut., 30 April 58.

SERVICE.—Lieutenant LOCH served in the Queen's Bays, in Sir J. Outram's Division, at the siege and capture of Lucknow, March '58, and during the subsequent operations in Oude. *Medal and Clasp.*

LIEUTENANT R. G. LOCH, P. H., late 2nd Bengal European Cavalry.

Cornet, 4 Nov. 58—Lieut., 5 Feb. 59.

LIEUTENANT D. B. LOCKHART,† late 6th Europeans.

Ensign, 10 June 48—Lieut., 21 Aug. 52.

SERVICE.—Lieutenant LOCKHART served in the Sonthal Campaign in July '55. Joined Delhi Field Force in July '57. Present during remainder of the siege. *Severely wounded,* 10th September '57. *Medal and Clasp.*

LIEUTENANT W. S. A. LOCKHART, late 44th Native Infantry.

Ensign, 4 Oct. 58—Lieut., 19 June 59.

SERVICE.—Lieutenant LOCKHART served with Brigadier Eveleigh's Column in Oude, December '58 and January '59.

LIEUTENANT H. B. LOCKWOOD,† late 4th Bengal European Cavalry.

Cornet, 20 Feb. 58—Lieut., 18 May 58.

LIEUTENANT J. C. LOCKWOOD,† late 2nd Bengal European Light Cavalry.

Cornet, 20 Jan. 54—Lieut., 31 Dec. 54.

SERVICE.—Lieutenant LOCKWOOD served as A. D. C. to Major-General Sir S. Cotton, during the Mutiny of '57, with the Force under that Officer which acted during the months of May and June '58, in the Eusuffzaie Valley, against the hostile Chief Mukurul Khan and the Hindoostanee fanatics at Sittana.

CORNET S. D. LOCKWOOD, General List, Cavalry.
Cornet, 4 Nov. 59.

LIEUTENANT C. LODER, Bengal Veteran Establishment.
Lieut., 7 April 56.

ENSIGN G. LOGAN,† late 4th Europeans.
Ensign, 4 Aug. 58.

CAPTAIN C. M. LONGMORE, P. C., late 33rd Native Infantry.
Ensign, 12 Dec. 45—Lieut., 14 March 52—Captain, 12 Dec. 60.

LIEUTENANT A. R. LOUGHNAN, late 13th Native Infantry.
Ensign, 4 Jan. 55—Lieut., 29 May 57.

SERVICE.—Lieutenant LOUGHNAN served throughout the Sonthal Campaign in '55, '56. Present at the engagement at Chinhut, 30th June '57. Commanded an outpost in the defence of Lucknow, '57. *Medal and Clasp, and one year's extra service.* Mentioned in the Despatch of Brigadier Inglis, 9th December '57.

LIEUTENANT W. L. LOUIS,† late 42nd Native Infantry.
Ensign, 8 June 54—Lieut., 23 Nov. 56.

SERVICE.—Lieutenant LOUIS served in the Sonthal Campaign. Served with the Central India Field Force from February to April '58. Served in the Saugor District in '58. Served in the Column under Colonel Primrose and Colonel Ross, and the Field Force in Bundlecund under Brigadier Wheeler, '59.

LIEUTENANT B. LOVEST, Bengal Engineers.
Lieut., 27 Aug. 55.

LIEUTENANT I. LOW, P. H., late 3rd Bengal European Cavalry.
Cornet, 20 Jan. 59—Lieut., 9 Nov. 60.

(372)

LIEUTENANT J. A. LOW, Bengal Artillery.
Lieut., 27 Aug. 58.

LIEUTENANT R. C. LOW, P. H., late 4th Bengal European Cavalry.
Colonel, 26 Aug 54—Lieut., 29 Sept. 58.

SERVICE.—Lieutenant Low served in the Sonthal Campaign, '55. With With the Delhi Field Force in '57. Present at the actions of Badlee-ka-Serai, Nudjufghur, and siege and capture of Delhi. *Medal and Clasp.* Mentioned in the Despatch of Brigadier-General Nicholson, 10th December '57. Mentioned and brought to the notice of the Commander-in-Chief in the Despatch of Major-General Wilson, 9th November '57: received the thanks of Government, '57. Served at the pursuit of the rebels, and taking of Fort Jhujjur, '57. Served at the siege and capture of Lucknow, '58. *Clasp.* As Brigade-Major to the Agra Field Force under Brigadier Showers, in pursuit of rebels in Central India, '59.

ASSISTANT-SURGEON C. LOWDELL,† Bengal Medical Establishment.
Asst.-Surgeon, 20 Oct. 49.

SERVICE.—Assistant-Surgeon LOWDELL served under the Superintending Surgeon at the battle of Agra, 10th October '57. Appointed to Medical Charge of the Bhurtpore Army, 13th May '57. *Medal.*

BREVET-CAPTAIN J. R. A. S. LOWE, P. C., late 56th Native Infantry.
Ensign, 9 Dec. 43—Lieut., 26 July 53—Bt.-Captain, 9 Dec. 58.

(Received certificates of high proficiency in Oordoo and Hindee, and attained the standard of proficiency prescribed by G. G. O., 9th March '52, in the Hindee and Oordoo languages.)

LIEUTENANT N. LOWIS, late 61st Native Infantry.
Ensign, 20 Sept. 57—Lieut., 17 Jan. 59.

SERVICE.—Lieutenant LOWIS served in the Mutinies of '57, '58. Present at the capture of Lucknow, and at various minor engagements in Oude. *Medal and Clasp.*

(373)

LIEUTENANT R. F. LOWIS, Bengal Artillery.
Lieut., 27 Aug. 58.

CAPTAIN W. H. LOWTHER, P. H., late 52nd Native Infantry.
Ensign, 21 Aug. 40—Lieut., 24 Jan. 45—Bt.-Captain, 21 Aug. 55—Captain, 23 Nov. 56.

SERVICE.—Captain LOWTHER served during the Punjab Campaign, '48, '49. Present throughout the 1st and 2nd siege operations before Mooltan, including the action of Sooroojkhoond and battle of Goojerat. *(Wounded.) Medal and 2 Clasps.* Served with the Force employed in the annexation of Oude, '56. Served during the Mutinies, '57, '58. Received a letter of approval from the Lieutenant-Governor of Bengal on the successful capture of the Sarung Rajah, and other conspirators who had tampered with the Troops in Assam. Commanded the first expedition against the Abor Tribes, '58; and served against them again in '59.

LIEUTENANT C. H. LUARD, Bengal Engineers.
Lieut., 27 April 58.

LIEUTENANT F. P. LUARD, P. H., late 1st Bengal European Cavalry.
Cornet, 12 Oct. 52—Lieut., 30 Nov. 53.

SERVICE.—Lieutenant LUARD served during the Mutiny, '57, 58. With the Rajpootana Field Force against the insurgents in Malwa, in '57. Present at the affairs of Minbhera, 19th September; with Volunteer Cavalry, Jeerum, 23rd October, as a Volunteer Gunner. Defence of Neemuch Fort, 8th to 22nd November, as a Volunteer Gunner. Served with the Central India Field Force against the rebels, in '58. Present at the siege and capture of Fort Chundehree, 9th to 17th March; siege and capture of Jhansie, from 20th March to 5th April; actions of Koonch, 7th May; Muttra, 16th May; Gowlowlee, 22nd May; capture of Calpee, 23rd May '58. *Medal and Clasp.* Volunteered and served throughout the War in China, in '60. Present at the actions of Sinho, Chankia-Whan, 18th September; and Tangchow *(wounded)*, 21st September '60.

Medal and 2 Clasps. Mentioned in the Despatches of Captain Simpson for gallant and praiseworthy conduct, 18th February '58; specially by Sir Hugh Rose, for useful service and zeal, 23rd May '58; of Sir Hope Grant, 21st September '60.

MAJOR P. W. LUARD, P. H., late 55th Native Infantry.

Ensign, 13 Dec. 33—Lieut., 1 Dec. 36—Captain, 8 May 45—Bt.-Major, 28 Nov. 54—Major, 27 Aug. 58.

SERVICE.—Major LUARD served with the Army of the Sutlej in '46. Commanded the 17th Punjab Infantry with the Saugor Field Brigade under Brigadier Wheeler, in '59.

CAPTAIN C. P. LUCAS,† late 47th Native Infantry.

Ensign, 10 Dec. 42—Lieut., 19 May 47—Bt.-Captain, 10 Dec. 57—Captain, 1 May 58.

LIEUTENANT G. P. LUCAS, General List.

Ensign, 16 July 60—Lieut., 1 Jan. 62.

BREVET-LIEUTENANT-COLONEL H. B. LUMSDEN, P., C.B., late 59th Native Infantry.

Ensign, 1 March 38—Lieut., 16 July 42—Bt.-Captain, 1 March 53—Captain, 5 Feb. 54—Bt.-Major, 6 Feb. 54—Bt.-Lieut.-Colonel, 15 May 58.

SERVICE.—Lieutenant-Colonel LUMSDEN served in Affghanistan in '42. Present at the forcing of the Khyber Pass, on 5th April '42. Present in the Mazeena and Sungokhale Valleys, under Brigadier Monteith, in May '42. Battle of Tazeen and Huftkotul, forcing of the Jugdulluck Pass, and re-occupation of Cabul, in '42. *Medal.* Present at the battle of Sobraon, 10th February '46. *(Severely wounded.) Medal.* Served with a Sikh Force against fanatics of Koghan and Huzara Tribes in '46. Present at the forcing of Doab Pass, and affair of Balakôt,

November '46. Raised the Corps of Guides, Cavalry and Infantry, 13th December '46. Present at the siege of Mooltan, January '49. Battle of Gojurah, 21st February '49. *Medal and 2 Clasps, and Brevet-Majority.* Commanded the Guides in sixteen hill fights, including the attacks on Bobozie, Pullie, Zormandie, and Shorekhanie, in '49. Lieutenant-Colonel Bradshaw's attacks on Suggow, Pullie, Sherekhanie, Zormandie, and Moora, '50. Sir C. Napier's attack on the Kohat Pass, December '50. Lord Clyde's affairs of Dubb, Nowadkund, Pranghur, and Iskakôt, in May '52. Brigadier Chamberlain's expeditions against the Cabul Khel Mahsood Wuzeerees, in '59, '60. Was in Political Charge of the Eusuffzaies, from December '46 to October '52, including one year's Political Charge of the Peshawur and Kohat Districts. In charge of a Political Mission to Candahar, in '57. *Brevet-Lieutenant-Colonel and C.B. Wounded* by an assassin while in Command of the Guides, 2nd August '60.

CAPTAIN P. S. LUMSDEN, P. H., late 60th Native Infantry.

Ensign, 10 Dec. 47—Lieut., 23 May 54—Captain, 18 Feb. 61.

SERVICE.—Captain LUMSDEN served as D. A. Q. M. G. at the action of Punjpao, 15th April '52; at Nowadund, Pranghur, Iskakôt, and operations in the Ranezee Valley, May '52; at Boree, November '53; at Shah Mooseh Khel, against Momunds (services brought to notice by Colonel Cotton); in Meranzaie Expedition; Cavalry affair at Dursummund, April '55; against the Bussy Khel at Alum, November '55. In Meranzaie and Kooran Expeditions, November '56. (Received special thanks of Local and Supreme Governments.) Served in a special Military Mission to Affghanistan, in '57, '58. (Received the thanks of the Supreme Government.) In July '58 joined Gwalior Force under General Napier. Present at Banode and subsequent pursuit in Central India. *Medal.* (Especially mentioned.) Accompanied the China Expedition, '60. Present at the battle of Sinho, bombardment of Tongchow, assault and capture of Taku Forts, and advance on Pekin. (Especially mentioned and recommended for Brevet-Majority on promotion to Captain.) *Medal and 2 Clasps.*

MAJOR W. LYDIARD,† late 11th Native Infantry.

Ensign, 15 March 26—Lieut., 1 Dec. 36—Bt.-Captain, 15 March 41—Captain, 27 March 46—Bt.-Major, 20 June 54—Major, 13 April 60.

SERVICE.—Major LYDIARD served as Brigade-Major with the Bundlecund Field Force, '42, '43, and the Army of the Sutlej, after the general actions.

ENSIGN M. LYNE (Unattached).

Ensign, 10 June 58.

SERVICE.—Ensign LYNE served under Sir Colin Campbell, in the Peshawur Valley, against the Hill Tribes, in May '52. Served at the siege and assault of Delhi. Present at the battles of Nudjufghur, 25th August '57; Boolundshuhur, 28th September '57; Allyghur, 4th October '57; and Agra, 10th October '57; at the relief of Lucknow, in November '57; Cawnpore, 6th December '57; Serai Ghaut, 9th December '57; Khodagunge, 2nd January '58; and Chota Mhow, 27th January '58. Final capture of Lucknow, March '58. *Medal and 3 Clasps.* Unattached Ensign's Commission.

LIEUTENANT H. H. LYSTER, P. H., V.C., late 72nd Native Infantry.

Ensign, 20 Sept. 48—Lieut., 13 Nov. 54.

SERVICE.—Lieutenant LYSTER served on the Staff of Major-General Hugh Rose, as Interpreter and A.D.C., throughout the whole of the Central India Campaign, from December '57 to July '58, including the following actions and engagements: siege and capture of the Town and Fort of Ruthghur, repulse of the rebels in an attack on the Camp during the siege, action of Baroda *(wounded)* (charger wounded), taking of Baroda, forcing the Pass of Muddinpore, siege and storm of the Town and capture of the Fort of Jhansie, battle of the Betwa, action of Koonch and capture of the Town, (charger wounded in three places), attack on the Camp of the 2nd Brigade at the village of Muttra, attack on the Camp of the 1st Brigade at Goolowlee, taking of the Town and Fort of Calpee, action at and capture of the Morar Cantonments, storming of the Lushker and Fort of Gwalior. *Medal, Clasp, and V.C.*

(377)

M

LIEUTENANT I. F. MacANDREW, P., late 19th Native Infantry.

Ensign, 20 Feb. 46—Lieut., 30 April. 51.

(Passed examination in Surveying and Civil Engineering.)

LIEUTENANT C. E. MACAULAY, P. H., late 51st Native Infantry.

Ensign, 12 Dec. 57—Lieut., 12 March 61.

SERVICE.—Lieutenant MACAULAY served with H. M.'s 5th Fusiliers in the Oude Campaign of '58, '59. Present with that Regiment at the fall of Fort "Amathee," 11th October '58; and at that of Shunkerpore, 15th October '58; and at the battle of "Doondeakhera," on the 24th November '58. Present with that Regiment at the capture of the Fort "Omeriah," 2nd December '58. Served with the 1st Sikh Cavalry through the hot weather Campaign of '59, Trans-Gogra, Oude. *Medal.* Served with the 1st Sikh Cavalry throughout the China Expedition of '60. Present at the action of "Singho, on 12th August '60. Capture of the Taku Forts, on 21st August '60. Actions of "Chankiawun," 18th September; "Palichas," on 21st September; and capture and occupation of Pekin, on 13th October '61. *Wounded severely* at the action of "Singho," on 12th August '60. *Medal for Indian Rebellion, and Medal for China War,* '60. *Clasps for "Taku Forts and Pekin."* Mentioned in list of Officers of H. M.'s Indian Forces recommended to favorable notice by Lieutenant-General Sir Hope Grant for their services in China.

ENSIGN T. G. MACAULAY, P. H., General List.

Ensign, 4 Sept. 59.

BREVET-MAJOR G. S. MACBEAN, P., late 74th Native Infantry.

Ensign, 22 Feb. 43—Lieut., 15 Dec. 47—Captain, 18 June 57—Bt.-Major, 24 March 58.

SERVICE.—Major MACBEAN served in Scinde as only Commissariat Officer, '50. With the Peshawur Force under Colonel Boileau, which attacked and destroyed Boree and other villages. Accompanied the Field Force from Mooltan to coerce Ali Moorad. Served with Major Renaud in June '57; with General Havelock's Force, from July to September '57.

z 1

(378)

In the actions of Futtehpore, Aoung, Pandoo Nuddee, Cawnpore, Oonao, Boorby-ka-Chokee, Busseerutgunge (1st and 2nd), Bithoor, Mungulwarah, Alum Bagh, and the 1st relief of Lucknow, 25th September '57. Received the thanks of Government. Mentioned in Despatches. Present at the final relief of Lucknow. *Medal and 2 Clasps.* As Senior Commissariat Officer in the affairs of Rooya and Allygunge, and of the Army in the Rohilcund Campaign. Present at the re-capture of Bareilly; and received the thanks of the Commander-in-Chief.

ENSIGN G. MacCALL, General List.

Ensign, 7 June 61.

LIEUTENANT D. MACDONALD, P. H., late 25th Native Infantry.

Ensign, 20 Oct. 53—Lieut., 18 Jan. 56.

LIEUTENANT H. MACDONALD,† late 19th Native Infantry.

Ensign, 20 Dec. 49—Lieut., 26 April 52.

SERVICE.—Lieutenant MACDONALD served at the action of Meraigunge and relief of Lucknow, November '57. Served at the relief and battle of Cawnpore, 6th December '57. Pursuit of the Gwalior Contingent to Serai Ghaut. Re-occupation of Bithoor. The actions of Kala Nuddee, Khoodagunge, and entry into Futtehghur; actions of Shumshabad and Mhow; siege and capture of Lucknow, March '58. Served throughout the Oude Campaign, '58. Present at the actions of Rooya and Allygunge. Served throughout the Rohilcund Campaign, '58, including the capture of Bareilly and affair of Shahjehanpore. *Medal and 2 Clasps.*

BREVET-COLONEL J. MACDONALD, late 73rd Native Infantry.

Ensign, 4 April 21—Lieut., 27 Aug. 23—Captain, 26 Sept. 33— Major, 11 April 45—Lieut.-Colonel, 11 April 51—Bt.-Colonel, 28 Nov. 54.

LIEUTENANT J. MACDONALD, P. H., late 18th Native Infantry.

Ensign, 11 Dec. 46—Lieut., 24 May 53.

SERVICE.—Lieutenant MACDONALD served during the Punjab Campaign, '48, '49. *Medal.*

(379)

LIEUTENANT L. MACDONALD,† late 73rd Native Infantry.

Ensign, 8 May 57—Lieut., 18 May 58.

SERVICE.—Lieutenant MACDONALD served with H. M.'s 42nd Royal Highlanders in the Campaign of '57, '58. Present at the actions of Kala Nuddee and Shumshabad. Siege and capture of Lucknow. Attack on the Fort of Rooya, and action of Allygunge. *Medal and Clasp.*

LIEUTENANT W. MACDONALD,† late 25th Native Infantry.

Ensign, 10 Dec. 53—Lieut., 5 March 56.

MAJOR A. A. MACDONELL, P. H., late 40th Native Infantry.

Ensign, 12 Dec. 40—Lieut., 1 Jan. 44—Captain, 19 Nov. 52—Major, 2 Sept. 52.

SERVICE.—Major MACDONELL served during the Sonthal Rebellion, '55, under General Lloyd. (Has passed examination in the Vernacular language of Assam, also passed examination in Bengali.)

LIEUTENANT-COLONEL R. MACDONELL, 4th Bengal European Cavalry.

Cornet, 2 March 26—Lieut., 3 May 29—Bt.-Captain, 2 March 41—Captain, 10 June 42—Major, 27 Nov. 53—Lieut.-Colonel, 23 July 58.

SERVICE.—Lieutenant-Colonel MACDONELL served with the Army in Affghanistan, in '42, under General Pollock. Present at the taking of the Khyber Pass. *Medal.* Served with the Army under Lord Gough in '43. Present at the action of Maharajpore. *Bronze Star.*

CAPTAIN J. MACDOUGALL,† late 19th Native Infantry.

Ensign, 31 July 40—Lieut., 22 Nov. 43—Bt.-Captain, 31 July 55—Captain, 26 Aug. 56.

SERVICE.—Captain MACDOUGALL served under General Franks in '58. Present at the actions of Chanda and Humeerpore, on the 19th, and Sultanpore, 23rd February '58 ; and siege and capture of Lucknow. *Medal and Clasp. Dangerously wounded* by a Sepoy, '41.

(380)

LIEUTENANT W. C. MacDOUGALL, P. H., late 72nd Native Infantry.

Ensign, 20 Feb. 46—Lieut., 17 March 51.

SERVICE.—Lieutenant MacDOUGALL served at the siege and surrender of Mooltan. *(Wounded.)* *Medal.*

LIEUTENANT D. MacFARLAN, P. H., Bengal Artillery.

1st Lieut., 12 Sept. 57.

SERVICE.—Lieutenant MACFARLAN served in the defence of the Lucknow Residency from 30th June '57 to 22nd November '57. *Medal and Clasp, and one year's extra service.* *(Severely wounded.)*

LIEUTENANT C. MacFARLANE, P., late 1st European Bengal Fusiliers.

2nd Lieut., 20 Jan. 51—Lieut., 10 May 54.

SERVICE.—Lieutenant MACFARLANE served during the Burmese War, '52, '53. Present at the capture of Pegu, 21st November '52. *Medal and Clasp.* Served during the Mutinies, 57, '58. Present at the actions of Badlee-ka-Serai, 8th June '57; in many of the affairs before Delhi, from 8th June to 20th September, including the night attack in rear of the Camp, 19th June; Subjee Mundee, 23rd June; Ludlow Castle, 23rd July; and present at the action of Nudjufghur, 25th August. Present at the final assault and capture of Delhi, at the action of Narnoul against the Joudpore Legion and other rebels, and commanded the Regiment after Colonel Gerrard was mortally wounded, and brought it out of action. Present under Sir T. Seaton, in the Doab, at the actions of Gungeeree, Puttiallee, and Mynpooree. Present at the final siege and capture of Lucknow under Lord Clyde, in March '58. *Medal and 2 Clasps.* Present during the Campaign in Oude, and engaged in several minor combats after the capture of the Capital.

LIEUTENANT C. M. MacGREGOR,† late 68th Native Infantry.

Ensign, 20 Oct. 56—Lieut., 17 Nov. 57.

SERVICE.—Lieutenant MACGREGOR served at Delhi in '57. With Sir T. Seaton's Force in the Doab; under Lord Clyde, at the siege of Lucknow; with Sir Hope Grant's Force in Oude; under Brigadiers Horsford and Holdich, on the Nepal Frontier. Present at the actions of Narnoul,

(381)

16th November '57 ; Gungeeree, Puttiallee, Mynpooree, siege and capture of Lucknow, action of Bhumori Ghat *(horse and rider severely wounded)*, 18th September '58. Passage of the Gogra, actions of Muchligaon, Bunkussea, Kumdakôt, Jereva, and Maharajpore *(wounded slightly)*, and Chuppra. *Medal and Clasp.* Mentioned in the Despatch of Major Hume, 14th December '58; in that of Sir R. Napier. Brought to the notice of Government in the Despatch of Sir Hope Grant. Received the thanks of the Governor-General. Served with the Expeditionary Force in China under Sir H. Grant. Present at the action of Singho *(wounded severely* in two places), and capture of Pekin. *Medal and Clasp.* Mentioned in the speech of the Secretary at War, in moving a vote of thanks to the Forces in China.

CAPTAIN E. A. M. MACGREGOR,† late 4th Bengal European Cavalry.

Cornet, 8 June 42—Lieut., 8 May 49—Captain, 23 Nov. 56.

SERVICE.— Captain MACGREGOR served during the Sutlej Campaign in '46. Served with the Sarun Field Force, '57, '58. Present at the actions of 5th March and 27th April, at Amorah.

GENERAL J. A. P. MACGREGOR, late 54th Native Infantry.

Ensign, 4 Feb. 97—Lieut., 30 Oct. 97—Captain, 1 May 05—Major, 12 June 14—Lieut.-Colonel, 1 Aug. 18—Colonel, 1 May 24—Major-General, 10 Jan. 37—Lieut.-General, 9 Nov. 46—General, 20 June 54.

SERVICE.—General MACGREGOR served in Mysore at the siege and capture of Seringapatam, '99: Northern Circars, 1800. *Medal.* Campaign under Lord Lake, Delhi, Deig (two horses shot under him), Kutchowra, Agra, '08, and Bhurtpore, '05. *India Medal.*

LIEUTENANT E. J. MACHELL, Bengal Artillery.

Lieut., 11 Dec. 58.

CAPTAIN L. MACHELL, P. H., Bengal Artillery.

2nd Lieut., 14 June 45—Lieut., 21 Jan. 49—2nd Captain, 27 Aug. 58.

SERVICE.—Captain MACHELL served with the expedition to Kangra in '46, under Brigadier Wheeler; Army of the Punjab, '48, '49, and was present at the battles of Chillianwallah and Goojerat. *Medal and 2 Clasps.*

SURGEON-MAJOR J. MACINTIRE,† Bengal Medical Establishment.

Asst.-Surgeon, 20 July 38—Surgeon, 8 April 52—Surgeon-Major, 13 Jan. 60.

LIEUTENANT D. MACINTYRE, P. H., late 66th Native Infantry.

Ensign, 14 June 50—Lieut., 23 Nov. 56.

SERVICE.—Lieutenant MACINTYRE served against the Hill Tribes on the Peshawur Frontier, under Sir Colin Campbell, in '51, '52. Present in the expeditions under Sir C. Campbell, against the Ranezaie Tribes, Peshawur Frontier, at the destruction of the fortified village of Pranghur, and action at Ishkakôt. Present with the expedition against the Afreedies of the Boree Valley, near Peshawur; accompanied the Koorum Expedition in Affghanistan, in '56. Employed in several occasions in '57, '58, when commanding the extra Goorkha Regiment, in protecting the Hill Passes on the Kalee Kumaon Frontier, from the Rohilcund rebels, and in keeping the district in order.

LIEUTENANT A. K. J. C. MACKENZIE,† late 5th Bengal European Cavalry.

Ensign, 26 Jan. 53—Lieut., 24 Nov. 55.

SERVICE.—Lieutenant MACKENZIE served at the siege and capture of Delhi from the 17th July, with the 1st Punjab Cavalry; engaged in the Cavalry affair in rear of Camp on the 11th of September; served with the Column under Brigadier Greathed; engaged at the actions of Boolundshuhur, Allyghur, Agra, and Kanouje. Present at the relief of Lucknow by Sir Colin Campbell, the skirmishes of Malygunge and Alum Bagh, and the action of Cawnpore. Served with a Column under Sir Hope Grant, in Oude; engaged at Meragunge. Present at the siege and capture of Lucknow, and the affair at Koorsee. Commanded a Squadron, 1st Punjab Cavalry, at the capture of Bareilly, and action of Shahjehanpore. *Medal and Clasp.*

(383)

CAPTAIN A. M. MACKENZIE, P. H., late 56th Native Infantry.
Ensign, 9 Dec. 42—Lieut., 1 Dec. 46—Bt.-Captain, 9 Dec. 57—Captain, 18 Feb. 61.

SERVICE.—Captain MACKENZIE served against the Insurgents in Bundlecund, '43, '44. Commanded the 8th Irregular Cavalry on the mutiny at Bareilly, 31st May '57, on which occasion he tried to induce the Regiment to charge the guns, but failed, owing to the great bulk of the Corps going over to the mutinous Artillery and Infantry at the last moment. He then joined Mr. J. C. Wilson, and in Command of the faithful remnant of the 8th Irregulars, aided him in preserving 48 Christian Refugees, who had been sheltered by friendly Hindoos at Rohilcund. He raised the new 8th Irregular Cavalry (now 6th Bengal Cavalry), and served in Oude throughout the siege and capture of Lucknow. Commanded a portion of his Regiment on the 5th April '58, on which occasion he charged the rebels who had to evacuate the Fort, and after a desperate resistance, cut up the rebel leader, Sultah Sing, and the whole of his Body Guard, upwards of one-fourth of his own men being killed or wounded, including his own charger *wounded*. *Medal and Clasp.*

LIEUTENANT A. R. D. MACKENZIE,† late 1st Bengal European Cavalry.
Cornet, 30 Dec. 54—Lieut., 22 June 56.

SERVICE.—Lieutenant MACKENZIE served during the siege and assault of Delhi, with the Guide Cavalry, and with Brigadier Showers' Column, in the Delhi, Goorgaon, and Jhujjur Districts. With the 1st Sikh Cavalry at the siege and capture of Lucknow. *(Wounded.)* Present at the action of Moosah Bagh, 21st March '58. *Medal and 2 Clasps.*

CAPTAIN F. MACKENZIE, P. H., late 26th Native Infantry.
Ensign, 8 July 40—Lieut., 8 Feb. 43—Bt.-Captain, 8 July 55—Captain, 10 Feb. 56.

SERVICE.—Captain MACKENZIE served throughout the Campaign in Affghanistan with the Army under General Pollock, *Medals*; and also that on the Sutlej, including the actions of Moodkee, Ferozeshuhur, and Sobraon. *(Severely wounded.) Medal and 3 Clasps. (Since retired.)*

LIEUTENANT F. J. N. MACKENZIE, P. H., late 52nd Native Infantry.

Ensign, 17 March 55—Lieut., 27 June 57.

SERVICE.—Lieutenant MACKENZIE served with the Kamptee Moveable Column engaged against the Bhondelas and mutineers of the 52nd Native Infantry, August and September '57.

CAPTAIN H. MACKENZIE, P., late 20th Native Infantry.

Ensign, 20 Feb. 47—Lieut., 20 Sept. 49—Captain, 10 May 57.

SERVICE.—Captain MACKENZIE served during the Punjab Campaign, '48, '49. Present at the actions of Chillianwallah and Goojerat. *Medal and 2 Clasps.* (Passed an examination in Punjabee.)

LIEUTENANT H. L. MACKENZIE,† Bengal Artillery.

Lieut., 10 June 59.

LIEUTENANT H. M. MACKENZIE, Bengal Artillery.

Lieut., 27 Aug. 58.

CAPTAIN J. M. MACKENZIE, P. H., late 58th Native Infantry.

Ensign, 18 Jan. 45—Lieut., 10 Aug. 48—Captain, 8 July 59.

SERVICE.—Captain MACKENZIE served with the Army of Reserve under the late Major-General Sir D. Hill, '48, '49.

LIEUTENANT R. B. MACKENZIE,† late 12th Native Infantry.

Ensign, 4 March 56—Lieut., 10 July 57.

LIEUTENANT C. K. MACKINNON,† late 63rd Native Infantry.

Ensign, 20 July 58—Lieut., 23 Dec. 58.

SERVICE.—Lieutenant MACKINNON served on the Nepal Frontier, in '58, '59.

BREVET-MAJOR W. A. MACKINNON, C.B., P. H., Bengal Artillery.

2nd Lieut., 10 Dec. 41—Lieut., 1 July 45—Captain, 22 Aug. 55—Bt.-Major, 20 July 58.

SERVICE.—Major MACKINNON served during the Sutlej Campaign, '45, '46. Present at the actions of Moodkee, Ferozeshuhur, and Sobraon. *Medal and 2 Clasps.* Served during the Punjab Campaign with Brigadier Wheeler's Force, '48, '49. *Medal.* Served during the Mutiny Campaign. *Medal and Brevet-Major.*

LIEUTENANT-COLONEL R. MACLAGAN, P., Bengal Engineers.

2nd Lieut., 10 Dec. 39—Lieut., 29 Dec. 43—Bt.-Captain, 11 June 54—Captain, 1 Aug. 54—Lieut.-Colonel, 18 Feb. 61.

SERVICE.—Lieutenant-Colonel MACLAGAN served during the Mutiny in the Roorkee and Saharunpore Districts, '57. Services acknowledged by the Government of India, 31st May '59.

LIEUTENANT C. S. MACLEAN, P. H., late 10th Native Infantry.

Ensign, 14 Dec. 53—Lieut., 23 Nov. 56.

SERVICE.—Lieutenant MACLEAN served with the Army before Delhi, '57. Present at the siege and capture of that city. At the actions of Boolundshuhur, Coel, Acrabad, and Agra *(severely wounded).* *Medal and Clasp.* Served in the Chinese Expedition of '60. Present at the actions of Sinho, Chunkee-a-wan, Tung-chow, and the capture of the Taku Forts, and occupation of Pekin. *Medal and 2 Clasps.*

LIEUTENANT J. G. MACLEAN,† General List.

Ensign, 10 Dec. 59—Lieut., 23 Nov. 61.

ASSISTANT-SURGEON L. H. J. MACLEAN,† Bengal Medical Establishment.

Asst.-Surgeon, 14 Jan. 54.

LIEUTENANT J. R. MACLEAY, Bengal Artillery.

Lieut., 27 April 58.

(386)

CAPTAIN H. J. B. MACLEOD,† Bengal Artillery.

2nd Lieut., 11 Dec. 41—Lieut., 3 July 45—Captain, 26 June 56.

SERVICE.—Captain MACLEOD was present at the battles of Ferozeshuhur and Sobraon, '46. *Medal and Clasp.*

LIEUTENANT J. G. MACLEOD,† General List.

Ensign, 9 Dec. 59—Lieut., 28 Sept. 61.

CAPTAIN R. B. MACLEOD, P. H., late 3rd Bengal European Cavalry.

Cornet. 4 Jan. 40—Lieut., 27 Sept. 43—Captain, 6 Sept. 51.

SERVICE.—Captain MACLEOD served with the Army of Gwalior, '43, '44. *Bronze Star.* With the Army of the Sutlej, '45, '46. *Medal and 2 Clasps.* Present at the actions of Maharajpore, Moodkee, Ferozeshuhur, and Sobraon.

CORNET F. W. MACMULLEN, General List, Cavalry.

Cornet, 20 March 60.

BREVET-MAJOR S. F. MACMULLEN,† late 3rd Bengal European Cavalry.

Cornet, 28 March 29—Lieut., 20 Nov. 41—Bt.-Captain, 28 March 44—Captain, 31 Dec. 51—Bt.-Major, 28 Nov. 54.

SERVICE.—Major MACMULLEN served during the Punjab Campaign, '48, '49. Present at the battles of Chillianwallah and Goojerat. *Madal and 2 Clasps.*

LIEUTENANT E. H. MACNAGHTEN,† late 2nd Bengal European Cavalry.

Cornet, 8 Sept. 56—Lieut., 9 Jan 57.

LIEUTENANT F. H. MACNAGHTEN,† late 5th Bengal European Cavalry.

Ensign, 26 Jan 53—Lieut., 24 Nov. 55.

SERVICE.—Lieutenant MACNAGHTEN served in the Towana Horse, in Brigadier Eveleigh's Column, in Oude. Present at the affair of Dhoondia Khairrah.

(387)

CAPTAIN J. D. MACNAGHTEN, P., Bengal Invalid Establishment.
Cornet, 13 June 26—Lieut., 14 Dec. 35—Captain, 13 Jan. 41.

CAPTAIN W. H. MACNAGHTEN,† late 1st Bengal European Cavalry.
Cornet, 20 Sept. 50—Lieut., 20 Oct. 52—Captain, 19 July 57.

LIEUTENANT W. H. MACNAGHTEN, late 5th Bengal European Cavalry.
Cornet, 10 June 58—Lieut., 24 Aug. 58.

ASSISTANT-SURGEON F. N. MACNAMARA,† M. D., Bengal Medical Establishment.
Asst.-Surgeon, 18 June 53.

ASSISTANT-SURGEON N. C. MACNAMARA,† Bengal Medical Establishment.
Asst.-Surgeon, 4 Nov. 54.
SERVICE.—Assistant-Surgeon MACNAMARA served in Medical Charge of the 40th Native Infantry and the European Artillery, as also the Staff of the General Commanding, throughout the Sonthal Rebellion.

LIEUTENANT C. MACPHERSON, Bengal Artillery.
Lieut., 27 Aug. 58.

LIEUTENANT G. E. MACPHERSON, General List.
Ensign, 7 April 60—Lieut., 1 Jan. 62.

SURGEON H. M. MACPHERSON,† Bengal Medical Establishment.
Asst.-Surgeon, 18 Sept. 42—Surgeon, 2 May 57.

SURGEON-MAJOR J. MACPHERSON,† M.D. AND FEL. U.C., Bengal Medical Establishment.
Asst.-Surgeon, 4 Dec. 39—Surgeon, 1 Dec. 53—Surgeon-Major, 13 Jan. 60.
SERVICE.—Surgeon-Major MACPHERSON served in the Depôt Hospital during the Sutlej Campaign, '46.

(388)

LIEUTENANT J. D. MACPHERSON, 10th (late 65th) Native Infantry.

Ensign, 19 Dec. 57—Lieut., 11 Aug. 59.

SERVICE.—Lieutenant MACPHERSON served during the Oude Campaign. Present at the capture of the Fort of Tiroul, 16th July '58.

MAJOR R. D. MACPHERSON, P., late 15th Native Infantry.

Ensign, 12 June 41—Lieut., 24 Jan. 45—Bt.-Captain, 12 June 56—Captain, 23 Nov. 56—Major in Staff Corps, 12 June 61.

SERVICE.—Major MACPHERSON served with the Army in Burmah, '52, '53. Present at the taking of Rangoon, in April '52. *Medal.* Served in the Sonthal Rebellion, '55.

CAPTAIN A. MACQUEEN, P. H., late 42nd Native Infantry.

Ensign, 18 June 39—Lieut., 21 Aug. 43—Bt.-Captain, 18 June 54—Captain, 9 Nov. 55.

SERVICE.—Captain MACQUEEN served throughout the operations of the Candahar Force; at the occupation of Kelat, in '40; Tazee, in '41; at Kimjee Kuk, Punguair, and Tiboo Khan, 7th, 8th, 9th, and 10th March '42. At the action near the Candahar Cantonment, 29th May '42. At Mukoor, on the 27th; Gowaine, on the 28th and 30th August. Re-capture of Ghuznee, 6th September; Bance Badam and Mydon, 14th and 15th September '42. At the occupation of Cabul, 17th September; and Istaliff, 30th September '42. At Tazee, 15th October '42. Present at the battle of Moodkee, 18th December; Ferozeshuhur, 21st and 22nd December '45; Sobraon, 10th February '46. *(Wounded.)* 3 *Medals and* 4 *Clasps.* Present at the defeat of the Gwalior Insurgent Force at Cawnpore, and the engagement at the Kalee Nuddee. Present at the affairs of Baree and Simree, and other engagements in Oude. (Has furnished the certificate of qualification as Assay Master.)

LIEUTENANT A. J. MACQUEEN, late 18th Native Infantry.

Ensign, 13 June 57—Lieut., 18 May 58.

SURGEON-MAJOR A. C. MACRAE,† M.D., Bengal Medical Establishment.
  Asst.-Surgeon, 24 Jan. 39—Surgeon, 16 Jan. 53—Surgeon-Major, 13 Jan. 60.

LIEUTENANT H. MACSWEEN,† Bengal Engineers.
  Lieut., 27 Aug. 58.

LIEUTENANT S. C. MacTIER, P. H., late 24th Native Infantry.
  Ensign, 4 Feb. 59—Lieut., 29 Oct. 60.

SURGEON W. F. MACTIER, M.D., Bengal Medical Establishment.
  Asst.-Surgeon, 3 Dec. 44—Surgeon, 29 March 58.

LIEUTENANT W. D. MACTURK, late 64th Native Infantry.
  Ensign, 26 Aug. 38—Lieut., 24 June 64.

CAPTAIN R. F. MACVITIE, Bengal Invalid Establishment.
  Ensign, 1 May 24—Lieut., 13 May 25—Captain, 26 April 33.

LIEUTENANT T. D. MADDEN,† late 64th Native Infantry.
  Ensign, 13 June 57—Lieut., 18 May 58.
  SERVICE.—Lieutenant MADDEN served during the Mutinies, '57, '58. Present at the actions at Cawnpore, 27th and 28th November '57. Operations on the River Raneegunga, January '58; siege and capture of Lucknow, March '58; actions at Koorsee, 20th March; Banee, 12th April; Nuggur, 12th May; Nawabgunge, 13th June; occupations of Fyzabad, July; and Sultanpore, August '58. Action at Pandoo Nuddee, 26th October; Fort of Ameether; action at Hyderghur, November '58; Churdah, 6th December '58; and action at Sitkaghaut, in Nepal, 9th February '59. Operations on the River Raptee, up to 12th June '59. *(Wounded at Cawnpore.) Medal and Clasp.*

LIEUTENANT T. H. MADDOCK, P. H., late 3rd Europeans.
  Ensign, 28 July 49—Lieut., 15 Nov. 55.
  SERVICE.—Lieutenant MADDOCK served during the Mutinies, '57, '58. Present at the relief of Azimghur, 6th April '58.

LIEUTENANT A. E. MADRAS,† Bengal Veteran Establishment.

Lieut., 12 June 60.

SERVICE.—Lieutenant MADRAS served with the Army of the Indus, '39, '40. Present at the storm and capture of Ghuznee. *Medal.* Served during the Sutlej Campaign, '45, '46. Present at the actions of Ferozeshuhur and Sobraon. *Medal and Clasp.*

LIEUTENANT MAGNIAC, late 1st European Bengal Fusiliers.

2nd Lieut., 20 Feb. 51—Lieut., 17 June 55.

SERVICE.—Lieutenant MAGNIAC served in Burmah, '52, '53. Present at the relief of the Garrison of Pegu, 14th December '52. *Medal.* Served under General Wyndham throughout the attack by the Gwalior rebels on Cawnpore, 26th, 27th, and 28th November '57. Present at the capture of Lucknow, March '58, and subsequent operations in Oude. *Medal and Clasp.*

LIEUTENANT G. E. J. MAIDMAN, P. H., late 24th Native Infantry.

Ensign, 9 June 54—Lieut., 23 Nov. 56.

ASSISTANT-SURGEON A. C. MAINGAY, M.D., Bengal Medical Establishment.

Asst.-Surgeon, 10 Feb. 59.

SERVICE.—Assistant-Surgeon MAINGAY served with the China Expeditionary Force, '60, '61. Present under Brigadier-General Stavely in the operations against the Taiping Tribes, near Shanghai; at the capture of the stockaded village of Chowpoo, 4th April, '62; at the capture of the stockade near Naksiang, 29th April '62; capture, by assault, of the walled town of Khading, 1st May '62; capture, by assault, of the walled town of Sing Poo, 12th May '62; capture of the walled and stockaded village of Nangoo, 17th May '62; capture, by assault, of the walled town of Isuling, 20th May '62, and repulse of an attack made by the rebels on the advance picquets at Mahsiang, 25th May '62.

LIEUTENANT E. P. MAINWARING, General List.

Ensign, 20 Dec. 59—Lieut., 9 Dec. 61.

(391)

BREVET-COLONEL E. R. MAINWARING, late 28th Native Infantry.

Ensign, 9 Jan. 24—Lieut., 13 May 25—Captain, 20 Feb. 38—Bt.-Major, 4 Oct. 42—Major, 13 Dec. 54—Bt.-Lieut.-Colonel, 20 June 54—Lieut.-Colonel, 25 Nov. 58—Bt.-Colonel, 7 May 55.

SERVICE.—Colonel MAINWARING served throughout the whole of the Affghan Campaign in '39, '40, '41, and '42, including the assault and capture of Ghuznee; in the subsequent year was engaged at the night attack at Baboo Kooshgoh and the destruction of Khoodawah; was one of the garrison of Jellallabad, and in the general action and defeat of Akbar Khan, and subsequent operations leading to the re-occupation of Cabul: was attached to the left wing of the Army of Gwalior; and was present on the Staff at the battle of Punniar. Present with the Army on the Sutlej, including the battle of Sobraon; engaged with the Army of the Punjab at the actions of Ramnuggur, Sadoolapore, Chillianwallah, and Goojerat. 5 *Medals*, 2 *Clasps, and a Bronze Star*.

CAPTAIN G. B. MAINWARING, P. H., late 16th Native Infantry.

Ensign, 8 Jan. 42—Lieut., 21 Dec. 45—Captain, 1 Oct. 56.

SERVICE.—Captain MAINWARING served in the Gwalior Campaign, '43: present at the battle of Maharajpore. *Bronze Star*. Served throughout the Sutlej Campaign: present at the battles of Moodkee, Ferozeshuhur, and Sobraon. *Medal and 2 Clasps*.

CAPTAIN R. R. MAINWARING, P. H., late 6th Europeans.

Ensign, 31 Dec. 37—Lieut., 27 Oct. 41—Captain, 10 April 52.

SERVICE.—Captain MAINWARING served with the Army of the Sutlej and was present at Sobraon. Served against the Insurgent Sonthals in '55; and was present during some actions with the rebels during the Indian Mutiny.

BREVET-MAJOR F. C. MAISEY, P. H., late 67th Native Infantry.

Ensign, 9 Dec. 42—Lieut., 8 Sept. 46—Captain, 10 Nov. 55—Bt.-Major, 24 March 58.

SERVICE.—Major MAISEY served throughout the Burmese Campaign, '52, '53. *Medal*. Present as a Volunteer at the attack and capture of Rangoon, 12th, 13th, and 14th April '52. Present at Donabew at the actions on the 2nd, 3rd, and 4th February '53, against the robber Chief Nga Mya Toon. Present as Staff Officer under Sir J. Cheape against the same enemy, from the 6th March '53 to their final defeat and dispersion on the 18th. Present as 2nd in Command with a Detachment of the 67th Native Infantry, and conducted several skirmishes with the enemy under the rebel leaders Gaingee and Gaong Gelay, on the 17th, 18th, and 19th August: personally commanded on the latter date, in the repulse of an attack on the Town at night. *(Wounded.)* Honorably mentioned and thanked for services in February '53, at Donabew, by the Brigadier Commanding at Donabew, by General Godwin, by the Officer Commanding the 67th Native Infantry, and by the Governor-General. Served during the Mutiny of '57 with the Delhi Force. Present at the action of Badlee-ka-Serai, 8th June '57, charger killed while carrying orders to the Troops in attack. Brought to the notice of the Commander-in-Chief in the Despatches of Major-General Sir W. Barnard, 12th June '57; of Major-General Reid, 17th July '57; and of Major-General Sir A. Wilson, 22nd September '57, and received the thanks of the Indian Government. *Medal.*

CAPTAIN G. MAISTER, P. H., Bengal Artillery.

2nd Lieut., 11 June 42—Lieut., 3 July 45—Bt.-Captain, 11 June 57—Captain, 14 Sept. 57.

SERVICE.—Captain MAISTER was present at Maharajpore. *Bronze Star.* Served during the Punjab Campaign. Present at the battles of Chillianwalla and Goojerat, surrender of Sikh Army and occupation of Peshawur. *Medal and 2 Clasps.* Served with the Force under Brigadier Bradshaw in the Eusuffzaie country, in '49, '50. Served under Sir C. Napier at the forcing of the Kohat Pass, '50; affairs against the Momunds and Ootman Khails, in the Eusuffzaie country, in '52; and under Brigadier-General Chamberlain against the Belooch Bozdars, in '57.

LIEUTENANT-COLONEL F. MAITLAND, P., late 5th Europeans.

Ensign, 17 Aug. 26—Lieut., 21 Jan. 38—Bt.-Captain, 17 Aug. 41—Captain, 15 Feb. 51—Bt.-Major, 20 June 54—Major, 31 Dec. 56—Lieut.-Colonel, 18 Nov. 60.

(393)

LIEUTENANT W. G. MAITLAND,† late 39th Native Infantry.
Ensign, 20 Dec. 58—Lieut., 4 June 59.

LIEUTENANT G. E. W. MALET, Bengal Artillery.
Lieut., 11 Dec. 58.

ENSIGN J. H. MALING, General List.
Ensign, 9 June 60—Lieut., 1 Jan. 62.

CAPTAIN G. B. MALLESON, P., late 33rd Native Infantry.
Ensign, 11 June 42—Lieut., 28 Sept. 47—Bt.-Captain, 11 June 57—Captain in Staff Corps, 18 Feb. 61.

LIEUTENANT H. A. MALLOCK, P. H., Bengal Artillery.
Lieut., 25 Sept. 57.

2ND CAPTAIN G. R. MANDERSON, P. H., Bengal Artillery.
1st Lieut., 13 June 51—2nd Captain, 12 March 60.
SERVICE.—Captain MANDERSON served with the Burmah Expedition. Present at the operations in the vicinity and capture of Rangoon, April '52: and with the Force employed under Major Fytche in the Bassein District, in '53. *Medal.*

LIEUTENANT T. C. MANDERSON,† Bengal Engineers.
Lieut., 27 Aug. 58.

SURGEON-MAJOR G. S. MANN, F.R.C.S., Bengal Medical Establishment.
Asst.-Surgeon, 22 Aug. 39—Surgeon, 7 Sept. 53—Surgeon-Major, 13 Jan. 60.
SERVICE.—Surgeon-Major MANN served with the Bengal Volunteer Regiment in China, in the years '40, '41. *Medal.* Served with the 28th Native Infantry at the operations in the Raneezaie Valley, with the Force under Sir Colin Campbell, in '52, and also as Field

B 2

Surgeon to the Eusuffzaie Expedition of '58, under Major-General Sir Sidney Cotton. Services mentioned in the Despatch of Sir Sidney Cotton, in '58.

LIEUTENANT D. G. MANNING,† late 52nd Native Infantry.

Ensign, 12 June 52—Lieut., 23 Nov. 56.

SERVICE.—Lieutenant MANNING served in pursuit of rebels in the Jubbulpore and Seonee Districts, in December '57. Brought to the notice of the Government, 27th February '60.

CAPTAIN H. D. MANNING, P. H., late 19th Native Infantry.

Ensign, 10 June 42—Lieut., 31 Jan. 44—Captain, 23. Nov. 56.

(Has furnished certificates of qualification in Surveying and Civil Engineering.)

LIEUTENANT G. W. MANSON, P. H., late 34th Native Infantry.

Ensign, 11 Dec. 49—Lieut., 5 Aug. 54.

SERVICE.—Lieutenant MANSON served with the Oude Police in '58. Present at the engagement of Selimpore, 24th September '58. Mentioned in the Despatch of Lieutenant Chamberlain, Commanding the Police Force. Joined Colonel Leith Hay's Column in December '58.

MAJOR-GENERAL J. MANSON, late 44th Native Infantry.

Ensign, 1 March 08—Lieut., 16 Dec. 14—Bt.-Captain, 1 March 23—Captain, 13 May 25—Bt.-Major, 28 June 38—Major, 11 July 41—Lieut.-Colonel, 24 April 47—Bt.-Colonel, 28 Nov. 54—Colonel, 29 May 57—Major-General, 15 May 59.

ASSISTANT-SURGEON A. A. MANTELL,† M.D., Bengal Medical Establishment.

Asst.-Surgeon, 24 Jan. 55.

ASSISTANT-SURGEON R. MANTELL,† M.B., Bengal Medical Establishment.

Asst.-Surgeon, 10 Feb. 59.

(395)

LIEUTENANT J. R. MARETT,† late 2nd Native Infantry.
Ensign, 4 Feb. 58—Lieut., 25 Dec. 58.

ENSIGN G. MARLEY, Unattached List.
Ensign, 18 June 61.
SERVICE.—Ensign MARLEY served in the Burmese War in '52, '53. Present at the storm and capture of Pegu, 21st November '52, and at the relief of the Garrison on the 14th December '52 ; and subsequent engagements on the 17th and 18th December '52. *Medal and Clasp.* On the retreat of a party of Europeans defeated at Chinhut, was a Volunteer, and assisted to hold the Iron Bridge, 30th June '57. Served throughout the siege of Lucknow, from June to November '57. Present at the defeat of the Gwalior Contingent, 6th December '57. *Medal and Clasp, and one year's additional service for Lucknow.* Was specially recommended by his Commanding Officer to the Commander-in-Chief for services in the Field, and promoted to the rank of Ensign for the said services. Reported to his Commanding Officer by Lieutenant Sewell for his praiseworthy conduct in assisting to convey Major Bruce *(who was dangerously wounded)* to a place of safety. Reported by Captain Watson to his Commanding Officer for his " excellent conduct and calmness in action as well as for the good example he set to the Guard on the Brigade Mess House, Lucknow Garrison."

CAPTAIN J. MARQUIS, P. H., late 4th Europeans.
Ensign, 17 Feb. 41—Lieut., 5 Feb. 43—Bt.-Captain, 17 Feb. 56—Captain, 23 Nov. 56.
SERVICE.—Captain MARQUIS served in Bundlecund during the Insurrection, '42, '43. Served during the Punjab Campaign, '48, '49. *Medal.* In the expedition against the Hussunzaies, '52, '53. Present at the storm of Delhi, '57. *Medal and Clasp.*

LIEUTENANT E. M. L. MARRIOTT, General List.
Ensign, 9 July 59—Lieut., 29 April 60.

(396)

LIEUTENANT F. H. B. MARSH,† General List.
Ensign, 20 May 59—Lieut., 26 Oct. 60.

LIEUTENANT H. C. MARSH,† late 67th Native Infantry.
Ensign, 20 Feb. 58—Lieut., 22 Oct. 58.

ENSIGN C. H. T. MARSHALL, General List.
Ensign, 12 Oct. 59—Lieut., 28 Aug. 61.

LIEUTENANT C. J. MARSHALL, General List.
Ensign, 9 June 60—Lieut., 1 Jan. 62.

LIEUTENANT H. S. MARSHALL,† General List.
Ensign, 16 June 59—Lieut., 1 March 61.

VETERINARY SURGEON M. J. MARSHALL, Bengal Veterinary Establishment.
Vety.-Surgeon, 22 Dec. 54.

LIEUTENANT R. G. S. MARSHALL, Bengal Artillery.
Lieut., 9 Dec. 59.

CAPTAIN W. B. MARSHALL, P. H., Bengal Artillery.
2nd Lieut., 10 Dec. 41—Lieut., 3 July 45—Captain, 15 Oct. 55.

CAPTAIN W. E. MARSHALL, P. H., T. C., late 48th Native Infantry.
Ensign, 9 Dec. 44—Lieut., 2 July 49—Captain, 21 March 58.
SERVICE.—Captain MARSHALL served during the Sutlej Campaign, '45. '46. Present at the actions of Moodkee, Ferozeshuhur, and Alliwal. *(Slightly wounded.)* *Medal and 2 Clasps.* (Has furnished certificates of qualification in Surveying and Civil Engineering.)

(397)

MAJOR-GENERAL W. H. MARSHALL, late 32nd Native Infantry.

Ensign, 16 Aug. 11—Lieut., 1 Sept. 16—Captain, 10 Oct 25—Major 2 April 34—Lieut.-Colonel, 4 Jan. 41—Colonel, 15 March 51—Major-General, 28 Nov. 54.

SERVICE.—Major-General MARSHALL served at the siege and capture of Bhurtpore, '26. *Medal.*

MAJOR A. P. MARTIN, late 33rd Native Infantry.

Ensign, 19 Nov. 29—Lieut., 14 Nov. 37—Bt.-Captain, 19 Nov. 44—Captain, 11 May 46—Bt.-Major, 28 Nov. 54—Major, 21 July 57.

SERVICE.—Major MARTIN served in the Cole Campaign, '32. Present at the taking of Jhansie, '39. Served at the forcing of the Khyber Pass, '42. Present at the destruction of Forts in the Peshbolack and Shinwaree Valleys and at the affair at Muzeenah. Present in the actions leading to the occupation of Cabul, and return to Peshawur. *Medal.* Served in the Sutlej Campaign, '46. Present at the battle of Sobraon, *Medal.* Served at the taking of Kôt Kangra ; at the siege and fall of Delhi. *Medal and Clasp.* Mentioned in the Despatch of General Grant, 13th January '59.

LIEUTENANT C. MARTIN, P.C., late 1st Bengal European Cavalry.

Cornet, 20 Nov. 51—Lieut., 20 Feb. 53.

SERVICE.—Lieutenant MARTIN served in the Malwa Field Force, in '57. Present at the capture of Dhar, and action of Mundesore, 23rd November 57. *(Wounded severely.) Medal.* Mentioned in the Despatch of Brigadier C. S. Stewart, 29th January '58.

CAPTAIN F. M. MARTIN†, late 52nd Native Infantry.

Ensign, 8 Jan. 42—Lieut., 3 Jan. 46—Bt.-Captain, 8 Jan. 57—Captain 10 May 57.

SERVICE.—Captain MARTIN served at the 1st and 2nd siege operations and surrender of Mooltan, (including the repulse of the enemy's night attack on the British Camp at Mathe Ghol, 17th August '48,) and battle of Goojerat. *Medal and Clasps.*

(398)

CAPTAIN J. P. MARTIN, P., late 4th Europeans.

Ensign, 20 Sept. 49—Lieut., 4 Jan. 56—Captain, 26 Oct. 59.

2ND CAPTAIN J. R. MARTIN, P. H., Bengal Artillery.

2nd Lieut., 8 June 49—Lieut., 31 July 54—2nd Captain, 27 Aug. 58.

SERVICE.—Captain MARTIN served during the Sonthal Campaign,'55.

CAPTAIN E. M. MARTINEAU, P. C., late 10th Native Infantry.

Ensign, 28 Dec. 42—Lieut., 1 Jan. 51—Captain, 11 July 57.

SERVICE.—Captain MARTINEAU served in the Burmese War, '52, '53, and '54. *Medal.* Served with the Delhi Field Force in '57. *Medal.* (Received a first class certificate from the Royal School of Musketry, Hythe.)

CAPTAIN J. MASSON, Bengal Invalid Establishment.

Ensign, 4 Dec. 28—Lieut., 8 July 36—Captain, 4 Dec. 43.

ENSIGN G. MASTERS, Unattached List.

Ensign, 9 Oct. 58.

BREVET-COLONEL R. A. MASTER, C.B., late 2nd Bengal European Cavalry.

Cornet, 12 May 23—Lieut., 13 May 25—Bt.-Captain, 12 May 40—Captain, 10 March 41—Bt.-Major, 7 June 49—Major, 20 Dec. 51—Bt.-Lieut.-Colonel, 28 Nov. 54—Lieut.-Colonel, 13 April 55—Bt.-Colonel, 28 Nov. 57.

SERVICE.—Colonel MASTER, C.B., was present at the siege and capture of Bhurtpore, '25, '26. *Medal.* Commanded the 11th Irregular Cavalry at the battle of Sooroojkhoond, in the vicinity of Mooltan; also during the siege and surrender of that Fortress in '48, '49; and subsequently at the battle of Goojerat, and in the pursuit of the Sikhs and Affghans by the Force under Sir Walter Gilbert. *Medal, 2 Clasps, and Brevet-Major.* Present at the siege and defence of Lucknow, from 30th June to 22nd November '57. *Brevet-Colonel and C.B., and one year's extra service.*

(399)

BREVET-MAJOR J. B. Y. MATHESON, P., late 52nd Native Infantry.

Ensign, 3 Jan. 40—Lieut., 8 April 42—Captain, 24 June 54—Bt.-Major, 20 July 58—Major in Staff Corps, 18 Feb. 61.

SERVICE.—Major MATHESON served with the 11th Irregular Cavalry in the Punjab Campaign: present at the 1st and 2nd siege operations and surrender of Mooltan, including the action of Sooroojkhoond, 7th November '48; battle of Goojerat and subsequent pursuit of Sikhs and Affghans. *Medal and Clasps.* Commanded the 11th Irregular Cavalry in the expedition against the Sonthals, '55, '56. Served throughout the Indian Mutiny in Command of the Benares Horse. Present at the action of Munseytah under Brigadier W. Campbell, Commanding at Allahabad; favorably mentioned in Despatches. Present at the action of Nusrutpore under Brigadier-General Franks, 23rd January '58; mentioned in Despatch. Present at the battle of Sultanpore, commanded the whole of the Cavalry; favorably mentioned in Despatches. Served at the siege and capture of Lucknow. *Medal and Clasps, and Brevet-Majority.* Served in the Shahabad District under Brigadier Douglas, in '58, '59; and subsequently with the Trans-Gogra Brigade under Brigadier Holdich, in the Nepal Frontier, in '59, 60.

LIEUTENANT J. G. S. MATHESON,† late 2nd European Bengal Fusiliers.

2nd Lieut., 20 Dec. 47—Lieut., 12 Nov. 53.

SERVICE.—Lieutenant MATHESON served during the Punjab Campaign, '48, '49. Present at the action of Ramnuggur, passage of the Chenab, battles of Chillianwallah and Goojerat, and subsequent pursuit of the Sikhs and Affghans. *Medal and Clasps.* (*Slightly wounded* at Goojerat.) Served with the Field Force in Tharawaddie, Burmah, '53, '54. (Passed an examination in Burmese.)

ASSISTANT-SURGEON T. MATHEW,† M. B., Bengal Medical Establishment.

Asst.-Surgeon, 4 Aug. 55.

LIEUTENANT C. R. MATHEWS,† late 56th Native Infantry.

Ensign, 20 March 55—Lieut., 30 April 58.

SERVICE.—Lieutenant MATHEWS served in China in '57, and as a portion of the Garrison of Canton, in '58.

SURGEON C. MATHIAS,† Bengal Medical Establishment.

Asst.-Surgeon, 20 Dec. 46—Surgeon, 27 March 60.

SERVICE.—Surgeon MATHIAS served with a Detachment of the Deobee Meenah Corps, at the taking of Kotah, in '58.

LIEUTENANT H. V. MATHIAS, P. H., late 50th Native Infantry.

Ensign, 20 Dec. 49—Lieut., 9 Aug. 54.

SERVICE.—Lieutenant MATHIAS served during the whole of the Sonthal Campaign in '55 '56: was 2nd in Command of the Rewah and Nagode Rajah's Troops, at the opening of the Deccan Road, '57, '58, during which operations the Forts of Kunchunpore Joorah, Myhere City and Fort, Jokye, Kunnwarrah, Bejeeragooghur, and 42 pieces of ordnance were taken. *(Slightly wounded.)* Was 2nd in Command of the Rewah Contingent at the storming of the enemy's position on the Punwarrah Heights, taking all the enemy's guns, killing their leaders, and entirely dispersing their Force. *Medal.* (Has received a first class certificate from the School of Musketry at Umballa.)

COLONEL J. MATHIE, late 2nd European Bengal Fusiliers.

Ensign, 24 Oct. 21—Lieut., 1 Jan. 24—Captain, 8 Sept. 35—Major, 22 Nov. 43—Lieut.-Col., 1st March 50—Bt.-Colonel, 28 Nov. 54—Colonel, 19 Aug. 59.

SERVICE..—Colonel MATHIE served at the siege and capture of Bhurtpore, in '25, '26; commanded one of the Companies of the 1st European Bengal Fusiliers selected to be attached to H. M.'s 59th Regiment of Foot, which led the storming party at the left breach. *Medal.* Was selected by His Excellency the Commander-in-Chief to command the 1st European Bengal Fusiliers with the expedition to Burmah, in '52, '53. *Medal.*

LIEUTENANT-COLONEL H. W. MATTHEWS, late 43rd Native Infantry.

Ensign, 3 March 24—Lieut., 9 Nov. 26—Bt.-Captain, 3 March 39—Captain, 17 Nov. 42—Bt.-Major, 11 Nov. 51—Major, 9 March 55—Bt.-Lieut.-Colonel, 3 Dec. 57—Lieut.-Colonel, 26 April 59.

SERVICE.—Lieutenant-Colonel MATTHEWS served in Affghanistan, '39, '40, '41, '42, and '43, throughout the whole of the operations of the Candahar

Force and the taking of Istaliff *(wounded in the Jugdulluck Pass)*. *Medal.* Present at the battle of Maharajpore. *Bronze Star.* Served during the Campaign on the Sutlej, including the action of Sobraon. *Medal.*

BREVET-MAJOR F. R. MAUNSELL,† Bengal Engineers.

2nd Lieut., 12 June 46—Lieut., 15 Feb. 54—2nd Captain, 27 Aug. 58—Bt.-Major, 28 Aug. 58.

SERVICE.—Major MAUNSELL served during the Mutiny Campaign. *Medal and Brevet-Major.*

CAPTAIN H. D. MAUNSELL,† late 62nd Native Infantry.

Ensign, 11 June 41—Lieut., 22 March 44—Captain, 3 Oct. 52.

BREVET-LIEUTENANT-COLONEL H. H. MAXWELL, P. H., Bengal Artillery.

2nd Lieut., 11 June 42—Lieut., 3 July 45—Bt.-Captain, 10 June 57—Captain, 27 June 57—Bt.-Major, 27 June 57—Bt.-Lieut.-Colonel, 24 March 58.

SERVICE.—Lieutenant-Colonel MAXWELL was present at the battle of Maharajpore, '43. *Bronze Star.* Served as Deputy Assistant Quarter-Master-General of the Artillery with the Army of the Sutlej. Present at the battle of Moodkee, Ferozeshuhur, and Sobraon. *Medal and 2 Clasps.*

LIEUTENANT-COLONEL J. H. MAXWELL, Bengal Engineers.

2nd Lieut., 11 June 40—Lieut., 1 Feb. 43—2nd Captain, 11 June 54—Captain, 1 Aug. 54—Bt.-Major, 2 Aug. 54—Lieut.-Colonel, 18 Feb. 61.

SERVICE.—Lieutenant-Colonel MAXWELL served with the Bundlecund Field Force in '42. Present at the affair with the Insurgents near Jytepore, in December '42. Present and commanded the Sappers and Miners with the Gwalior Field Force under General Grey, at the action of Punniar, on the 29th December '43. Mentioned in the Despatch of the General Commanding, dated 5th January '44. *Bronze Star.* Served in Scinde, in '45, as Field Engineer to the Force in the Hill Campaign under Sir Charles Napier. Brought to the favorable notice of His Excellency. Present at Mooltan throughout the siege operations and surrender in the capacity of Directing Engineer right attack, and afterwards as Brigade-Major of Engineers. Brought to the notice of Government, 23rd January '49. Again in the Despatch of Major R. Napier, late Chief Engineer, Mooltan Field Force, dated 23rd January '49. Also in the Despatch, Major-General Whish, Commanding Mooltan Field Force, 13th February '49. Present at the action of Sooroojkhoond. Favorably mentioned by Colonel Frank, Commanding, dated 8th November '48. Present at the battle of Goojerat in the capacity of Brigade Major of Engineers, and brought to notice by the Chief Engineer of the Army of the Punjab, in his Despatch to the Adjutant-General of the Army, dated Camp Goojerat, 25th February '49, dated 26th February '49. *Medal and 2 Clasps, and Brevet-Majority.*

CAPTAIN P. MAXWELL, P., late 37th Native Infantry.

Ensign, 11 Feb. 45—Lieut., 17 Jan. 49—Captain, 1 April 58.

SERVICE.—Captain MAXWELL served in the Punjab Campaign, '49. *Medal.* Served in the Mutinies, '57, '58. *Medal.* (Passed examination in Punjabee, also passed the Civil Service Examinations, lower and higher standards.)

CAPTAIN R. MAXWELL,† late 45th Native Light Infantry.

Ensign, 12 June 42—Lieut., 28 Aug. 47—Bt.-Captain, 19 June 57—Captain, 1 March 58.

SERVICE.—Captain MAXWELL served with the Turkish Contingent, 55, '56. During the Mutinies, '57, '58. Present at the affair of Munsratta, 5th January '58. *Medal.* Served in China, in '60, '61. Mentioned in the Despatch of Lieutenant-Colonel Marsh, R. M. L. I. Present at Shanghai at the attack of the Chinese Rebel Force, August '60.

SURGEON T. MAXWELL,† M. D., Bengal Medical Establishment.

Asst.-Surgeon, 26 Jan. 46—Surgeon, 5 June 59.

SERVICE.—Surgeon MAXWELL served in Medical Charge of the 46th Native Infantry throughout the Punjab Campaign, '48, '49. Present at the actions of Ramnuggur, Sadoolapore, Chillianwallah, and Goojerat. *Medal and 2 Clasps.* In Medical Charge of the 2nd Punjab Cavalry, in various Field Services, on the Derajat Frontier, from '50 to '57.

(402a)

CAPTAIN H. MAXWELL, P. H., late 1st Bengal Fusiliers.

2nd Lieut., 9 June 48—Lieut., 7 Aug. 42—Captain, 1 Jan. 62—Captaiu in Staff Corps, 18 Feb. 61.

SERVICE.—Captain MAXWELL served in Burmah, '52, '53. Present at the storm and re-capture of Pegu, 21st November '52, *Medal;* also served as Deputy Assistant Quarter-Master-General to the Martaban Column under General Steel, on its advance to Tonghoo. Present as Adjutant of his Regiment in the operations in Trans-Goomtee, under Sir J. Outram, terminating in the final assault and capture of Lucknow under the personal Command of the Right Honorable Lord Clyde, Commander-in-Chief, *Medal and Clasp;* and subsequent operations in Oude, acting as Staff Officer to the Column at Durriabad, accompanying the same into action with the rebels on different occasions, when the rebels were totally defeated and their guns captured. (Has furnished a certificate of qualification in Surveying.)

(403)

Served in '57 against revolted Hill Tribes, in Eusuffzaie. Served in 58 at siege and capture of Lucknow. *Medal and Clasp.* Served in the Campaign in Rohilcund, including the battle of Bareilly, assault of the Fort of Rooya, actions at Allygunge, Mohunpore *(wounded slightly)*, and Philibeet, and on several minor occasions. Services mentioned in the Despatch of the Officer Commanding Force at the action of Philibeet, 27th October '58. *Medal and Clasp.*

LIEUTENANT-COLONEL W. MAXWELL,† Bengal Artillery.

2nd Lieut., 8 Dec. 31—Lieut., 9 June 40—Bt.-Captain, 8 Dec. 46—Captain, 20 June 49—Bt.-Major, 24 March 58—Lieut.-Colonel, 18 Feb. 61.

SERVICE.—Lieutenant-Colonel MAXWELL served with the Army of Reserve, '42, '43; served during the Mutiny, '57, '58 ; commanded the Troops which engaged and defeated, on the 18th September '57, at Huldwanee, the Advance Guard of the Rohilcund Rebel Army. Present at the action of Chumparun, in Rohilcund, 10th February '58. *Medal.* Mentioned in the Despatch of Colonel McCausland, 1st March '58. Promoted to the rank of Brevet-Major, for services during the Mutiny.

LIEUTENANT J. MAY, P. H., late 72nd Native Infantry.

Ensign, 20 Feb. 59—Lieut., 1 Jan. 60.

SERVICE.—Lieutenant MAY served with the Volunteer Cavalry at Lucknow, under the Command of Major Radcliffe, late 7th Bengal Light Cavalry. Served with the Army at Lucknow, '57, '58. Was present at the siege of the Garrison of Lucknow, and served as a Subaltern of Artillery ; and subsequently as Assistant Field Engineer, compiled plans for Colonel Inglis, Commanding the Garrison ; and on the arrival of Sir James Outram, compiled a plan for the final relief of the Garrison by Lord Clyde. Served with the Force at Alum Bagh as Assistant Field Engineer, and compiled a plan for the final capture of Lucknow. Present at the action of Chinhut and various actions at the Alum Bagh *(wounded slightly).* *Medal and 2 Clasps.* Received the thanks of Government in G. G. O., dated 7th December '57. Served as Guide to the Forces under Command of Sir J. Outram ; thanked and honorably mentioned in G. O. G. G., 5th April '58. Accompanied the Forces under Lord Clyde at the final capture of Lucknow.

LIEUTENANT W. MAY, Bengal Veteran Establishment.

Lieut., 3 Feb. 57.

SERVICE.—Lieutenant MAY served at the siege and capture of Hattrass, '16, and during the Pindarree Campaign, '17, '18. During the Burmese War, '25, '26. *Medal.*

LIEUTENANT-COLONEL W. A. J. MAYHEW, late 6th Europeans.

Ensign, 16 Feb. 26—Lieut., 8 Oct. 39—Bt.-Captain, 16 Feb. 41—Captain, 24 Jan. 45—Bt.-Major, 9 Dec. 53—Major, 6 May 56—Lieut.-Colonel, 10 Oct. 59.

SERVICE.—Lieutenant-Colonel MAYHEW served as Assistant Adjutant-General in the Burmah Expedition. Present at the taking of Martaban and operations in the vicinity of, and capture of Rangoon. Served in Pegu, December '52. *Medal and Brevet-Major.* *(Since-retired.)*

2ND CAPTAIN C. W. MAYNARD, P. H., Bengal Artillery.

2nd Lieut., 8 June 49—Lieut., 28 May 55—2nd Captain, 27 Aug. 58.

LIEUTENANT F. N. M. MAYNARD, late 21st Native Infantry.

Ensign, 20 April 57—Lieut., 18 May 58.

SERVICE.—Lieutenant MAYNARD served during the Mutiny, '57, '58. Present at the actions from Cawnpore to Futtehghur and the Ramgunga. Present at the siege and capture of Lucknow, March '58. Present at the taking of Biswar, and other actions under Sir G. Barker, in '58. *Medal and Clasp.*

CAPTAIN C. T. O. MAYNE, P. C. H., late 15th Native Infantry.

Ensign, 22 Aug. 54—Lieut., 23 Aug. 55—Captain, 30 Sept. 60.

(Has passed the higher standard of Civil Examination.)

(405)

CAPTAIN R. G. MAYNE, P. H., late 59th Native Infantry.

Ensign, 10 Aug. 40—Lieut., 4 Jan. 45—Captain, 3 Aug. 55.

SERVICE.—Captain MAYNE served during the Sutlej Campaign, '45, '46. Present at the battle of Sobraon. *Medal.*

CAPTAIN G. McANDREW, P., late 47th Native Infantry.

Ensign, 8 March 41—Lieut., 22 Dec. 45—Bt.-Captain, 8 March 56—Captain, 27 Oct. 56.

SERVICE.—Captain McANDREW served throughout the Sutlej Campaign, '45, '46. Present at the actions of Moodkee, Ferozeshuhur, Buddiwal, Alliwal, and Sobraon. *Medal and 3 Clasps.* Served as Staff Officer with a Detachment of Troops against the Insurgents in the Tharrawadie District of Burmah, in '54. Served during the siege of Delhi, in '57, in Command of Contingent Troops furnished from the Cis-Sutlej States. Served in '57 against the Insurgent Tribes of the Ravie, in the Gogaira District, in Command of a Field Force, consisting of two Horse Artillery Guns, party of Mooltanee Horse, and 400 Military Police. *Medal and 2 Clasps.* Received the thanks of His Excellency the Commander-in-Chief, for services at Delhi, 25th May '57; and of the Governor-General *(twice)* for services in '57, 20th June and 30th November '57.

ENSIGN T. McCARTHY, Unattached List.

Ensign, 23 July 58.

SERVICE.—Ensign McCARTHY served during the siege and capture of Delhi, '57. Present at the actions of Badlee-ka-Serai, 8th June; Nudjufghur, 25th and 26th August '57; and many other minor actions during the siege. Served with the Pursuing Column from Delhi under Colonel Greathed. Present at the actions of Boolundshuhur, 28th September; Allyghur, 6th October; Akrabad, 7th and 8th October; and Agra, 10th October '57. Served with the Force under Lord Clyde throughout the relief of Lucknow, November '57. Battle of Cawnpore, and defeat of the Gwalior Contingent, 5th and 6th December '57. Present at Futtehghur, and throughout the siege; storm and capture of Lucknow, March '58.

Served with General Grant's Column in Oude, '58. Present at the actions of Barree, Nawabgunge, Simree, and Selimpore. Ensign's Commission, Unattached. *Medal and* 3 *Clasps.*

BREVET-COLONEL J. K. McCAUSLAND, C.B., late 29th Native Infantry.

Ensign, 20 Sept. 19—Lieut., 5 Oct. 21—Bt.-Captain, 20 Sept. 34—Captain, 1 July 36—Bt.-Major, 9 Nov. 46—Major, 18 March 47—Bt.-Lieut.-Colonel, 7 June 49—Lieut.-Colonel, 31 March 53—Bt.-Colonel, 28 Nov. 54.

SERVICE.—Brevet-Colonel McCAUSLAND, C.B., served during the Punjab Campaign, '48, '49. Present at the affair of Ramnuggur, passage of the Chenab, and battles of Chillianwallah and Goojerat. *(Severely wounded.) Medal, Clasp, and Brevet-Lieutenant-Colonel.*

LIEUTENANT J. K. McCAUSLAND, late 34th Native Infantry.

Ensign, 11 June 58—Lieut., 22 Oct. 58.

SERVICE.—Lieutenant McCAUSLAND served during the Oude Campaign, '59, under Brigadier Hale. *Medal.*

DEPUTY-INSPECTOR-GENERAL OF HOSPITALS, J. McCLELLAND, Bengal Medical Establishment.

Asst.-Surgeon, 7 April 30—Surgeon, 30 Nov. 46—Inspector-General of Hospitals, 8 Nov. 60.

MAJOR W. McCULLOCH, P., late 13th Native Infantry.

Ensign, 12 Dec. 34—Lieut., 18 Feb. 39—Captain, 30 June 48—Major, 4 Sept. 57.

SERVICE.—Major McCULLOCH served with the Force despatched in '37 from Nusseerabad to reduce the Nagas of Jyepore.

ASSISTANT-SURGEON J. J. McDERMOTT,† M.D., Bengal Medical Establishment.

Asst.-Surgeon, 23 July 58.

SERVICE.—Assistant-Surgeon McDERMOTT served in the Field Hospital, Lucknow, from the middle of October '58 to the 20th November '59.

(407)

Held Medical Charge of the Ameenabad Convalescent Depôt, Lucknow, from the 21st March to the 20th November '59; in addition to duties in the Field Hospital, as mentioned above.

VETERINARY-SURGEON W. McDERMOTT,† Bengal Veterinary Establishment.

Vety.-Surgeon, 11 Feb. 39.

SERVICE.—Veterinary-Surgeon W. McDERMOTT served with Army of the Indus, in '38, '39, and '40, under General Sale, in the Kohistan; of Cabul, Sutlej Campaign, '45, '46; " Ferozeshuhur." *Medal.* Army of the Punjab, " Ramnuggur," " Sadoolapore," " Chillianwallah," " Goojerat," and with the Force in pursuit of Sikhs and Affghans. *Medal and 2 Clasps.*

SURGEON D. McDONALD,† M.D., Bengal Medical Establishment.

Asst.-Surgeon, 20 May 46—Surgeon, 2 Sept. 59.

LIEUTENANT C. McDOUGALL, P. H., late 4th Europeans.

Ensign, 8 June 49—Lieut., 1 June 54.

SERVICE.—Lieutenant McDOUGALL was *severely wounded* in an engagement with the Hill Tribes near Peshawur, in August '54. Served as Interpreter to H. M.'s 79th Highlanders, at the siege and capture of Lucknow, March '58. As Adjutant of Ross's Camel Corps at the taking of Calpee, May '58. *(Severely wounded.) Horse killed* in an engagement with the rebels near Jugdespore, in October '58. *Medal and 2 Clasps.*

LIEUTENANT G. McDOWELL, Bengal Veteran Establishment.

Lieut., 31 July 50.

LIEUTENANT L. McDOWELL, General List.

Ensign, 20 Sept. 60—Lieut., 1 Jan. 62.

LIEUTENANT M. McGRATH, Bengal Veteran Establishment.

Lieut., 3 Jan. 59.

ASSISTANT-SURGEON E..McKELLAR,† Bengal Medical Establishment.
Asst.-Surgeon, 9 July 51.

SERVICE.—Assistant-Surgeon McKELLAR served with H. M.'s 80th Regiment throughout the Burmese War of '52, '53. Present at the capture of Martaban; at the operations before Rangoon on 12th, 13th, and 14th April; in Medical Charge of Major Cotton's Force, at the capture of Prome, in June '52; at the taking of Prome, and the subsequent operations in its vicinity. *Medal.* With the 3rd European Regiment in the actions near Agra, of the 5th July and 10th October '57; and in Medical Charge of Major Montgomerie's Force in the engagement with the rebels near Allyghur, on 24th August; with Colonel Seaton's Column in the actions of Gungeeree and Puttiallee. *Medal.*

CAPTAIN A. McKENZIE, P., late 9th Native Infantry.
Ensign, 12 June 47—Lieut., 24 Dec. 53.—Captain in Staff Corps, 18 Feb. '61.

INSPECTOR-GENERAL OF HOSPITALS, C. McKINNON,† M.D., C.B., Bengal Medical Establishment.

Asst.-Surgeon, 30 March 30—Surgeon, 2 Aug. 46—Inspector-General of Hospitals, 27 Aug. 58.

SERVICE.—Inspector-General of Hospitals, C. McKINNON, M.D., C.B., served in Affghanistan in '39, '40, '41, and '42. Present at the capture of Ghuznee, at the operations in and beyond Bameean in '39, at those on the Kohistan under Sir Robert Sale, '40; at the defence of Kelat-i-Ghilzie, in '41, '42; with the Candahar Division under Sir William Nott, in its advance on Cabul, and present at the action of Gowan and second capture of Ghuznee. Served with the Army of the Punjab in '48, '49, and was present at Ramnuggur and at the battles of Chillianwallah and Goojerat. 4 *Medals.* Ghuznee, Kelat-i-Ghilzie, Candahar, Cabul, and Punjab. *(Since retired.)*

2ND CAPTAIN F. H. McLEOD, P. H., Bengal Artillery.
2nd Lieut., 8 Dec. 48—Lieut., 7 July 53—2nd Captain, 27 Aug. 58.

(409)

CAPTAIN A. L. McMULLIN, P., late 23rd Native Infantry.
Ensign, 17 Feb. 41—Lieut., 24 Jan. 45—Bt.-Captain, 17 Feb. 56—Captain, 12 June 57—Bt.-Captain, 20 July 58.

LIEUTENANT C. N. McMULLIN,† late 73rd Native Infantry.
Ensign, 7 Aug. 48—Lieut., 15 Nov. 53.
(Received a Certificate from the School of Musketry at Hythe. Qualified to assist in the instruction of Musketry.)

CAPTAIN J. R. McMULLIN, P., late 50th Native Infantry.
Ensign, 1 March 38—Lieut., 7 July 42—Bt.-Captain, 1 March 53—Captain, 15 Nov. 53.
SERVICE.—Captain McMULLIN served at the battle of Punniar. *Bronze Star.* Present at the action of Soroojkhoond, siege and capture of Mooltan, and battle of Goojerat. *Medal and 2 Clasps.* (Passed examination in Field Engineering.)

LIEUTENANT E. J. McNAIR, P. H., late 2nd European Bengal Fusiliers.
2nd Lieut., 26 July 56—Lieut., 22 April 58.
SERVICE.—Lieutenant McNAIR served in the Mutiny, '57, '58. Present throughout the siege and capture of Delhi, and at the battle of Badlee-ke-Serai, 8th June '57. *Medal and Clasp.* Served in the Delhi District under Brigadier Showers, and in the Bekaneer District, in '59.

ENSIGN H. A. McNAIR, late 29th Native Infantry.
Ensign, 20 Sept. 58.

LIEUTENANT J. McNAIR,† late 57th Native Infantry.
Ensign, 20 Feb. 58—Lieut., 21 Nov. 58.

LIEUTENANT R. N. McNAIR, General List.
Ensign, 11 June 59—Lieut., 2 Dec. 60.

ENSIGN J. McNALLY, Unattached List.

Ensign, 9 Oct. 58.

SERVICE.—Ensign McNALLY served in the Punjab Campaign, '49. *Medal.* Served before Delhi under General Wilson, at the siege and capture of Delhi, '57; battle of Kurkurowlee, '58; capture of Bareilly, 5th May '58; and action of Mohumdee, May '58. *Medal.*

ENSIGN J. McNAMARA, Unattached List.

Ensign, 9 Oct. 58.

LIEUTENANT C. McNEILE, P. H., late 60th Native Infantry.

Ensign, 11 Dec. 58—Lieut., 1 July 59.

LIEUTENANT J. M. McNEILE, Bengal Engineers.

Lieut., 27 Aug. 58.

CAPTAIN W. McNEILE, P. C., late 5th Europeans.

Ensign, 25 Jan. 41—Lieut, 8 July 48—Bt.-Captain, 25 Jan. 56—Captain, 11 June 56.

(Has received a certificate of high proficiency in Hindee.)

MAJOR McNEILL, P., Bengal Artillery.

2nd Lieut., 11 June 42—Lieut., 3 July 45—Captain, 15 June 57—Bt.-Major, 20 July 58.

SERVICE.—Major McNEILL served in the Gwalior Campaign of '43, '44, and present at the battle of Maharajpore. *Bronze Star.* Served in the Sutlej Campaign of '45, '46, and present at the battles of Ferozeshuhur and Sobraon. *Medal and Clasp.* Served with Brigadier Wheeler's Force, and present at the capitulation of Kôt Kangra, in May '46. Served during the Punjab Campaign of '48, '49, in Command of a Contingent of Native Artillery attached to the Nusseeree Battalion in the Mukwal Dhoon. Served on the Dehra Jât Frontier, '50, '51, and '52, and with the Expeditionary Force against the Scinde Ameer Ali Moorad, in the spring of '52. Served with the Turkish Contingent during the Crimean

(411)

Campaign, '55, '56. On the conclusion of the war was selected by Major-General Michel to conduct a Brigade of Turkish Troops from Kertch to Varna. Received the *4th Class Order of Medjidee* and the *Turkish Crimean Medal*. Served in the Oude Campaign, '57, '58 : present at the several affairs during the advance of the Goorkha Force under Maharajah Jung Bahadoor. Present during the siege and capture of Lucknow, in March '58. Mentioned in Despatches. Received the special thanks of His Excellency the Governor-General in Council. *Medal and Clasp.*

LIEUTENANT A. McNEILL,† Bengal Engineers.

Lieut., 30 Sept. 57.

SERVICE.—Lieutenant MCNEILL was present at the battle of the Hindun and Badlee-ka-Serai, and throughout the siege of Delhi ; served during the subsequent operations in the Doab. *(Wounded at Futtehpore-Sikree.)* Served at the capture of Lucknow and in the Rohilcund Campaign. *Medal and 2 Clasps. (Since resigned.)*

CAPTAIN J. C. McNEILL,† late 12th Native Infantry.

Ensign, 9 Dec. 50—Lieut., 13 Aug. 55—Captain, 31 Aug. 60.

SERVICE.—Captain MCNEILL served during the Mutiny on the staff of Sir E. Lugard as A. D. C. *Medal.*

ENSIGN R. McNIMINEY, Unattached List.

Ensign, 26 Oct. 60.

SERVICE.—Ensign MCNIMINEY was present at the outbreak at Dinapore and at the affair of Jugdespore. *Medal.* Honorably mentioned by His Excellency the Commander-in-Chief for suppressing the mutiny of the 5th Europeans. Promoted for this act of gallantry to an Ensigncy unattached.

BREVET-COLONEL J. D. McPHERSON, P., C.B., late 6th Europeans.

Ensign, 4 Dec. 28—Lieut., 26 Nov. 36—Bt.-Captain, 4 Dec. 43—Captain, 1 Nov. 48—Bt.-Major, 7 June 49—Major, 1 Dec. 55—Bt.-Lieut.-Colonel, 28 Nov. 54—Lieut.-Colonel, 4 Aug. 59—Bt.-Colonel, 5 April 58.

(412)

LIEUTENANT J. R. McPHERSON,† late 3rd Europeans.

Ensign, 22 July 52—Lieut., 23 Nov. 56.

LIEUTENANT J. W. McQUEEN†, late 27th Native Infantry.

Ensign, 4 April 54—Lieut., 4 June 57.

SERVICE.—Lieutenant McQUEEN served during the Mutinies, '57, '58. Present at the siege, assault, and capture of Delhi, in the actions of Boolundshuhur, Allyghur, Acrabad, and Agra. At the engagements of Kanous, Marigunj, and skirmishes near Alum Bagh and Dil-koosha. Present at the relief of Lucknow, March '58, and storming of the Secunderabagh. *(Severely wounded.)* Present at Cawnpore, and with the advance on Futtehghur and Bareilly. Served under Brigadier-General Chamberlain, against the Cabul Khel Wuzeerees, in December '59 and January '60; and against the Mahsood Wuzeerees, in April and May '60. *Medal and 2 Clasps.*

SURGEON-MAJOR D. McRAE,† Bengal Medical Establishment.

Asst.-Surgeon, 24 Jan. 39—Surgeon, 27 Jan. 53—Surgeon-Major, 13 Jan. 60.

2ND CAPTAIN C. J. MEAD, Bengal Artillery.

1st Lieut., 9 Dec. 50—2nd Captain, 27 Aug. 58.

SERVICE.—Captain MEAD served with the Arracan portion of the Burmese Force, in '52. *Medal.*

CAPTAIN J. A. R. MEAD,† Bengal Artillery.

2nd Lieut., 9 Dec. 44—Lieut., 1 Jan. 48—2nd Captain, 27 Aug. 58—Captain, 21 April 60.

MAJOR R. J. MEADE, P. C., late 65th Native Infantry.

Ensign, 1 March 38—Lieut., 17 March 40—Captain, 6 Nov. 48—Major, 20 July 58.

(Passed examination in Surveying and Civil Engineering.)

(413)

BREVET-MAJOR J. G. MEDLEY, P. H., Bengal Engineers.

2nd Lieut., 11 June 47—Lieut., 1 Aug. 54—2nd Captain, 27 Aug. 58—Bt.-Major, 28 Aug. 58.

SERVICE.—Major MEDLEY served at the siege of Delhi (*severely wounded* at the assault), also with Sir T. Seaton's Column at the different actions in which it was engaged. Served at the capture of Lucknow. *(Medal, 2 Clasps, and Brevet-Major.)*

LIEUTENANT J. F. MEIKLEJOHN, Bengal Artillery.

Lieut., 10 Dec. 58.

CAPTAIN H. MELVILL, P. H., late 2nd Bengal European Cavalry.

Cornet, 12 April 49—Lieut., 16 Sept. 50—Captain, 23 March 57.

SERVICE.—Captain MELVILL served in the Kumaon Militia during the year '57. Commanded the Cavalry in an attack made from Nainee Tâl upon a portion of the Rohilcund rebels, on the 18th of September '57. Served with the Oude Police Cavalry from May till September '58; was in Command of a Police Force (Cavalry and Infantry), at Mahon, near Lucknow, when an attack was made on that post by the enemy on the evening of the 7th of August '58. Commanded the Cavalry in an attack made by a Police Force upon the Fort and position of Birwa, 26th August '58.

LIEUTENANT A. B. MELVILLE, P. H., late 67th Native Infantry.

Ensign, 10 Dec. 52—Lieut., 31 Aug. 56.

(Passed examination in Surveying.)

ENSIGN J. S. MELVILLE,† Unattached List.

Ensign, 24 Feb. 58.

LIEUTENANT O. MENZIES, P. H., late 35th Native Infantry.

Ensign, 26 Aug. 54—Lieut., 27 June 57.

SERVICE.—Lieutenant MENZIES served in the Oude Campaign, '58. Present at the storm and capture of the Rampore Kussia Fort, 3rd November '58. Received the thanks of Government, '58.

(414)

LIEUTENANT C. MERCER, General List.
Ensign, 4 March 59—Lieut., 7 April 60.

2ND CAPTAIN C. McW. MERCER, P. H., Bengal Artillery
2nd Lieut., 12 June 46—Lieut., 3 March 53—2nd Captain, 27 Aug. 58.

CAPTAIN T. W. MERCER, P., late 46th Native Infantry.
Ensign, 11 June 42—Lieut., 24 Jan. 45—Bt.-Captain, 11 June 57—Captain, 9 July 57.

SERVICE.—Captain MERCER served during the Punjab Campaign, '48, '49. Present at the actions of Ramnuggur, Sadoolapore, Chillianwallah, and Goojerat. *Medal and 2 Clasps.* (Has passed an examination in Field Engineering, also passed the Civil Service Examinations in the Punjab, lower and higher standards.)

BREVET-CAPTAIN A. MEREWETHER, P. H., late 61st Native Infantry.
Ensign, 16 June 45—Lieut., 18 May 53—Bt.-Captain, 16 June 60.

CAPTAIN T. C. MERRICK, P. H., late 4th Europeans.
Ensign, 10 Dec. 42—Lieut., 1 Jan. 50—Bt.-Captain, 10 Dec. 57—Captain, 1 Feb. 58.

SERVICE.—Captain MERRICK served during the Punjab Campaign, '48, '49, under Brigadier Wheeler, and was present at the assault on the heights of Dullah. *Medal.*

LIEUTENANT H. D. METCALFE,† late 25th Native Infantry.
Ensign, 4 Jan. 54—Lieut., 31 March 56.

SERVICE.—Lieutenant METCALFE served with the Force under Lieutenant-Colonel Cormick, in Oude: present at the affair of Muchleegong, and action of Putreo Nuddee. Served during the China Campaign of '60. Present at the landing at Petang, advance on the Takee Forts, capture of Tankoo, actions of the 18th and 21st September '60, and capture of Pekin. *Medal and 2 Clasps.*

(415)

LIEUTENANT-COLONEL J. METCALFE, C.B., late 4th Europeans.

Ensign, 11 Dec. 35—Lieut., 8 July 39—Captain, 1 Jan. 50—Major, 1 Feb. 58—Lieut.-Colonel, 24 March 58.

CAPTAIN W. METCALFE,† late 35th Native Infantry.

Ensign, 7 Aug. 40—Lieut., 11 March 47—Bt.-Captain, 7 Aug. 55— Captain, 27 June 57.

SERVICE.—Captain METCALFE served in Affghanistan with the Force under General Pollock, on the re-occupation of Cabul, 16th September '42. Present at the actions of the storming of the Khyber Pass, 5th April '42; Jugdulluck Pass, 8th September '42; general action at Tazeen, 13th September '42; and skirmishing at the Khoord Cabul Pass, 14th September '42. *Medal.* Served in the Gwalior Campaign under Lord Gough, '43, '44. Present at the action of Maharajpore, 29th December '43. *Bronze Star.*

LIEUTENANT A. P. MEW,† late 74th Native Infantry.

Ensign, 13 July 53—Lieut., 11 May 57.

CAPTAIN H. MICHELL, Bengal Veteran Establishment.

Captain, 20 Sept. 58.

LIEUTENANT J. W. A. MICHELL, P. H., late 37th Native Infantry.

Ensign, 4 April 58—Lieut., 25 Jan. 61.

LIEUTENANT C. MIDLEMASS, General List.

Ensign, 9 April 59—Lieut., 14 July 60.

LIEUTENANT C. F. MIDDLETON, P. H., late 40th Native Infantry.

Ensign, 12 June 52—Lieut., 17 June 55.

SERVICE.—Lieutenant MIDDLETON served in Burmah in '53. *Medal.* Served throughout the Sonthal Campaign of '55, '56. Served throughout the Mutinies, '57, '58, on the South-Western Frontier, with Detachments of Ramghur Cavalry and Infantry; was also employed in assisting to raise a Corps of Coles and Sonthals, since amalgamated with the 6th Police Battalion.

ENSIGN J. MILERICK, Unattached List.

Ensign, 9 Oct. 58.

SERVICE.—Ensign MILERICK served during the Punjab Campaign, '49. Present at the actions of Chillianwallah and Goojerat. *Medal and 2 Clasps.* Present at the siege and capture of Delhi, '57. Served with the Rohilcund Field Force in '58. Present at the action of Nuggeenah, '58, and at the taking of Bareilly. Present with the Oude Field Force in '58 : present at the action of Russoolpore, 25th October '58 ; at the taking of the Fort of Mittowlee, 8th November '58.

BREVET-MAJOR C. W. MILES, P. H., late 23rd Native Infantry.

Ensign, 4 Sept. 43—Lieut., 8 Aug. 47—Captain, 1 July 57—Bt.-Major, 20 July 58.

SERVICE.—Major MILES served in '57 against the rebels, near Benares *(horse shot)*, and with the Goorkha Force on South-Eastern Frontier of Oude ; also with General Frank's Column in Oude Campaign of '57, '58. Present at the engagements of Nusrutpore, Chanda, Ummeerpore, Sultanpore, final siege and capture of Lucknow, engaged also in protecting Sarun District, '58. *Medal, Clasp, and Brevet-Major.*

LIEUTENANT F. N. MILES, P. H., late 53rd Native Infantry.

Ensign, 11 Dec. 46—Lieut., 28 Oct. 50.

CAPTAIN R. H. MILES, Bengal Invalid Establishment.

Ensign, 5 May 21—Lieut., 11 Sept. 23—Captain, 20 June 33.

CAPTAIN J. C. MILLAR, P. H., late 29th Native Infantry.

Ensign, 29 Dec. 44—Lieut., 10 Nov. 50—Captain, 29 Dec. 59.

SERVICE.—Captain MILLAR served in the Punjab Campaign, '48, '49. Present at the storming of the heights of Umb and the occupation of the Fort of Oonah. *Medal.* Served with the Force under Lord Clyde in

(417)

Eusuffzaie; commanded 2 Companies, 29th Native Infantry, at the affair of Paunch Pass. Present at Jullundur on the 7th June '57, when the 6th Light Cavalry, the 36th and 61st Native Infantry mutinied. *Medal.*

LIEUTENANT J. MILLER,† late 27th Native Infantry.

Ensign, 8 June 55—Lieut., 23 Sept. 57.

LIEUTENANT J. C. MILLER, P. H., late 52nd Native Infantry.

Ensign, 13 June 51—Lieut., 5 Nov. 55.

CAPTAIN A. H. MILLETT, P., late 69th Native Infantry.

Ensign, 11 Dec. 47—Lieut., 17 Nov. 52—Captain in Staff Corps, 18 Feb. 61.

SERVICE.—Captain MILLETT served during the Punjab Campaign, '48, '49. *Medal.*

LIEUTENANT C. G. MILLETT, late 70th Native Infantry.

Ensign, 11 Dec. 58—Lieut., 29 March 59.

SERVICE.—Lieutenant MILLETT served in Oude from December '58 to January '59. Served in China, September '59 to March '60.

CAPTAIN H. L. MILLETT, P. H., late 28th Native Infantry.

Ensign, 20 Jan. 52.—Lieut., 21 July 56—Captain, 27 June 57.

SERVICE.—Captain MILLETT was present at the capture of Bulleh, in the Kurnoul District, 15th July '57; at the disarming of the 62nd and 69th Native Infantry at Mooltan; capture of Thannahbaon, near Mozuffurnuggur; crossing of the Ganges under Brigadier-General Sir J. Jones, advance on Nujeebabad, in Rohilcund; pursuit and dispersion of the rebels at Burrapoora; re-occupation of Bijnore, in Rohilcund, and during the Oude Campaign, '58, '59. Present at the attack and capture of several Forces in Oude; at the pursuit of the rebel army at Rampore Kusseah, under Brigadier Wetherall; crossing of the Gogra; pursuit of the rebels at Fyzabad, and skirmish with the Troops of the Gondah Rajah, at Muchleegaon, under Sir Hope Grant. Present at the capture of Churdah, Nujeedeeah, Bugeedeeah, and Bankee, under Lord

(418)

Clyde, and in an affair with the rebels at Musha, 3rd April '59. *Medal.* Mentioned in the report of Colonel Hughes to the Adjutant General of the Army, 16th July '59. Brought to notice of the Commander-in-Chief by Major R. A. Ramsay, '59. Appointed Detachment Staff Officer to the Moveable Column under Lieutenant-Colonel J. Brind.

LIEUTENANT M. MILLETT,† late 43rd Native Infantry.

Ensign, 4 Sept. 57—Lieut., 18 May 58.

CAPTAIN C. E. MILLS, P., late 28th Native Infantry.

Ensign, 18 Jan. 45—Lieut., 17 April 52—Captain, 31 May 57.

CAPTAIN H. MILLS, P., late 2nd Native Infantry.

Ensign, 20 Oct. 40—Lieut., 16 July 42—Captain, 22 March 52.

SERVICE.—Captain MILLS served with the Bombay Troops at Candahar and with General Nott's Force during the Campaign in Affghanistan, '42. Present in the actions of that Force, from Candahar to Peshawur. *Medal.* Served in the Gwalior Campaign in '43. Present at the action of Maharajpore. *Medal.* Served with the Army of the Sutlej in '45. Present at the actions of Moodkee and Ferozeshuhur. *Medal and Clasp.* Served during the Mutiny. (Has furnished certificate of qualification in Surveying and Civil Engineering.)

LIEUTENANT-COLONEL H. MILNE,† late 21st Native Infantry.

Ensign, 7 March 29—Lieut., 8 Oct. 39—Bt.-Captain, 7 March 44—Captain, 1 May 46—Bt.-Major, 28 Nov. 54—Major, 28 Feb. 56—Lieut.-Colonel, 25 Aug. 59.

SERVICE.—Lieutenant-Colonel MILNE served in Cabul, '38. Present at the assault and capture of Ghuznee, 23rd July '39. *Medal.* Present at the assault and capture of the Fort of Fouladie, near Bamean; at the defeat of the Ameer Dost Mahomed Khan, near Bamean, in October '40; and at Khelat-i-Ghilzie, from August '41 to June '42. Commanded a party when the Affghans assaulted and were repulsed, 21st May '42. Mentioned in Garrison Orders by Major Craigie. *Medal.* Present at

(419)

the action of Ghoain, 30th August; and re-occupation of Ghuznee, 6th September; action of Benee Badam, 16th September; re-occupation of Cabul, in September '42; and in all the subsequent operations consequent on the evacuation of Affghanistan. *Medal.* Served at Chinglai, in the Eusuffzaie Country, in April '58, with Major-General Sir Sydney Cotton. Received the thanks of the Major-General in his Despatch of '58.

LIEUTENANT R. MILNE, late 15th Native Infantry.

Ensign, 12 Dec. 57—Lieut., 18 July 60.

SERVICE.—Lieutenant MILNE served during the Mutinies, '58. Present at the advance on Lucknow, and actions at Chanda, Umeerpore, Sultanpore, and Dowraha, and siege and capture of Lucknow. Present at the relief of Azimghur, and operations in the Jugdespore Jungle.

LIEUTENANT G. MITCHELL, P. H., late 2nd European Bengal Fusiliers.

2nd Lieut., 26 June 56—Lieut., 28 Jan. 58.

SERVICE.—Lieutenant MITCHELL served throughout the siege and capture of Delhi, '57. Present at the battle of Badlee-ka-Serai, 8th June '57, and final assault of Delhi. *Medal and Clasp.*

LIEUTENANT W. C. MITCHELL, P. H., late 4th Native Infantry.

Ensign, 21 Jan. 50—Lieut., 14 Aug. 54.

SERVICE.—Lieutenant MITCHELL served with Brigadier Cotton's Force against the Hill Tribes on the Peshawur Frontier, in August '54. Served during the Mutinies in the Gogaira District, in September, October, and November '57. Commanded the Gogaira Horse and Fort Levies.

BREVET-COLONEL W. ST. L. MITCHELL, late 56th Native Infantry.

Ensign, 5 Feb. 26—Lieut., 6 May 29—Bt.-Captain, 5 Feb. 41—Captain, 5 Nov. 42—Major, 15 June 49—Lieut.-Colonel, 28 Nov. 54.

SERVICE.—Colonel MITCHELL served against the insurgents at Punjabee, in Bundlecund, '42; and throughout the Punjab Campaign, '48, '49.

Present at the passage of the Chenab and battle of Goojerat. *Medal.*
(Since retired.)

LIEUTENANT R. C. W. MITFORD, P. C. H., late 3rd Europeans.
Ensign, 25 July 55—Lieut., 30 April 58.

SERVICE.—Lieutenant MITFORD served with the 3rd Europeans at the outbreak of the Mutiny at Agra, in '57; and was present at the 1st battle of Agra on the 5th July, in which he carried the colors; at the 2nd battle on the 10th October, affair of Futtehpore-Sikree, together with other minor actions in the Agra District. He was appointed to do duty with Hodson's Horse in March '58, and was present with that Corps at the capture of Lucknow by Lord Clyde. *Medal and Clasp.* Commanded a Detachment of Hodson's Horse at Nawabgung, Bara, Bunki, present at the action of Selimpore (charger wounded), and was highly mentioned by the Governor-General in '58, for " gallantry in capturing a party of the rebels in the village of Bibipore, with 20 dismounted Sowars." He then proceeded with 150 Sabres of Hodson's Horse to join Major Bulwer's Force at Jabrowlee, and on the 16th October '58, charged and defeated a large body of Rebel Infantry near that place, receiving a *slight wound.* In the action of Jabrowlee, 23rd October, the Detachment of Hodson's Horse, under his Command, captured 3 of the enemy's guns, and cut up a large number of their Infantry. In this action Lieutenant Mitford was *severely wounded* while assisting an Officer of the Uncovenanted Civil Service, who was attacked by several of the rebels at the same time, and would probably have been cut down, but for timely aid. On partially recovering from the effects of his wound, he joined the 3rd Regiment of Hodson's Horse as Adjutant, and served with them through the Trans-Gogra Campaign of '59, to the final surrender of the rebels in December of that year. Recommended by Lord Clyde for the " Victoria Cross."

CAPTAIN D. MOCATTA, P., late 26th Native Infantry.
Ensign, 9 June 43—Lieut., 21 Dec. 45—Captain, 27 Aug. 57.

CAPTAIN A. K. MOFFAT, P. H., late 58th Native Infantry.

Ensign, 8 Jan. 42—Lieut., 3 March 43—Captain, 16 July 49.

(Passed examination in Surveying and Civil Engineering.)

LIEUTENANT-COLONEL G. MOIR, C.B., P. H., Bengal Artillery.

2nd Lieut., 11 Dec. 38—Lieut., 17 Aug. 41—Captain, 3 March 53— Bt.-Major, 20 July 58—Lieut.-Colonel, 18 Feb. 61.

SERVICE.—Lieutenant-Colonel MOIR, C.B., was present at the battle of Maharajpore, '43. *Bronze Star.* Served throughout the Campaign on the Sutlej, '45, '46, including the battles of Moodkee, Ferozeshuhur, and Sobraon. *Medal and 3 Clasps.* Present at the siege and surrender of Mooltan, '48, '49, and battle of Goojerat. *Medal and 2 Clasps.*

BREVET-LIEUTENANT-COLONEL J. DEW. C. J. MOIR, 28th Native Infantry.

Ensign, 21 June 24—Lieut., 28 Aug. 26—Bt.-Captain, 21 June 39— Captain, 24 Jan. 45—Bt.-Major, 11 Nov. 51—Major, 27 June 57—Bt.- Lieut.-Colonel, 27 Aug. 58.

SERVICE.—Lieutenant-Colonel MOIR served under Sir Colin Campbell against the Hill Tribes in '51, '52. Served during the Sonthal Campaign, '55. *(Since retired.)*

ASSISTANT-SURGEON R. MOIR,† M.D., F.R.C.S., Bengal Medical Establishment.

Asst.-Surgeon, 20 Dec. 53.

ASSISTANT-SURGEON W. MOIR,† A.M., M.B., Bengal Medical Establishment.

Asst.-Surgeon, 20 Jan. 60.

BREVET-CAPTAIN H. C. MOLLER, P., late 11th Native Infantry.

Ensign, 20 Jan. 45—Lieut., 1 Aug. 51—Bt.-Captain, 20 Jan. 60.

SERVICE.—Captain MOLLER served with his Regiment throughout the Sutlej Campaign, '45, '46, under General Lord Gough, *Medal;* was present at the siege of Kôt Kangra under General Wheeler, also at the action of Badlee-ka-Serai, 8th June; affairs of the 12th (horse wounded), 23rd and 30th June; and capture of Delhi. *Medal and Clasp.*

CAPTAIN A. P. S. MONCRIEFF, P. H., late 44th Native Infantry.

Ensign, 22 Feb. 43—Lieut., 10 Jan. 46—Captain, 29 May 47.

SERVICE.—Captain MONCRIEFF served with the Army of the Sutlej, '45, '46, and subsequent operations against Kangra. *Medal.* Served in the Sonthal Insurrection, '55, as Field Engineer. As Field Engineer served during the Mutinies, and received the thanks of Government, 15th October '57. Served against the rebels with the Naval Brigade, '58; as Assistant-Commissioner in charge of Singbhoom, and received the thanks of Government, 25th June '58, 30th June '58, and 19th July '58. *Medal.*

LIEUTENANT C. C. S. MONCRIEFF, P. H., Bengal Engineers.

Lieut., 27 Aug. 58.

SERVICE.—Lieutenant MONCRIEFF served with Brigadier Troup's Column in the Oude Campaign, in '58, '59. Present at the actions of Fort Mittowlee, Biswah, and Mehindee. Mentioned in the Despatch of Colonel Brind, 20th December '58.

CORNET E. A. MONEY, General List, Cavalry.

Cornet, 16 July 60.

LIEUTENANT-COLONEL E. K. MONEY, P., Bengal Artillery.

2nd Lieut., 8 Dec. 31—Lieut., 29 April 40—Bt.-Captain, 8 Dec. 46—Captain, 5 May 49—Bt.-Major, 19 Jan. 58—Lieut.-Colonel, 6 Feb. 61.

SERVICE.—Lieutenant-Colonel MONEY served in Affghanistan in '42; present at the re-occupation of Cabul. *Medal.* Served in Burmah in '52, '53. *Medal.*

LIEUTENANT G. N. MONEY, P. H., late 1st European Bengal Fusiliers.

2nd Lieut., 4 March 53—Lieut., 5 March 56.

SERVICE.—Lieutenant MONEY served in Burmah, '53, '54. Throughout the siege operations before Delhi, including the general actions on

(423)

the 9th, 14th, and 23rd July, 1st and 12th August, and other minor affairs. Present at the storming of the Cashmere Battery Breach on 14th September, and throughout the assault on the city, ending in its capture on 20th September. Served as Staff Officer to Colonel Gerrard's Column in the operations against the Joudpore Legions and other rebels, and at the action of Narnoul (horse killed under him). Mentioned in Despatches. Present at the actions of Gungeeree, Puttiallee, and Mynpooree. Present at Alum Bagh, and throughout the Trans-Goomtee operations in March; at the actions on 1st and 2nd March, assault of the Chukkur Kotee, passage of the Goomtee, and final assault and capture of Lucknow. Present at the affair at Barree; and the subsequent operations in Oude, in '58. *Medal and 2 Clasps.*

LIEUTENANT R. C. MONEY, P. C. H., late 32nd Native Infantry.
Ensign, 20 March 55—Lieut., 12 Feb. 58.

LIEUTENANT R. E. K. MONEY,† late 13th Native Infantry.
Ensign, 9 Oct. 58—Lieut., 21 Dec. 60.

ENSIGN A. MONIES, Unattached List.
Ensign, 30 Dec. 58.

CAPTAIN A. W. MONTAGU, P. H., late 68th Native Infantry.
Ensign, 20 Feb. 48—Lieut., 13 Sept. 53—Captain, 3 Sept. 59.

SERVICE.—Captain MONTAGU served during the Burmese War, '52, '53. *Medal.* Served during the Mutinies, '57, as 2nd in Command of the Regiment of Ferozepore, at Allahabad, in June and July '57. Also with the Trans-Gogra Force on the Nepal Frontier, '58, '59. Present at the action of Toolseepere. *Medal.*

CAPTAIN A. W. J. MONTGOMERIE, P. H., late 2nd Bengal European Cavalry.
Cornet, 4 Oct. 53—Lieut., 12 June 56—Captain, 28 March 60.

SERVICE.—Captain MONTGOMERIE served with the Guide Cavalry at the siege and capture of Delhi, including the battle of Nudjufghur, under

(424)

Brigadier-General Nicholson, and with Brigadier Showers' Column in the Delhi, Goorgaon, and Jhujjur Districts. Served with the 1st Sikh Cavalry with the Force under General Outram, at the Alum Bagh, from the 16th of January to the 2nd March '58, during the siege and capture of Lucknow, from 2nd to 21st March '58, including the action at the Moosa Bagh on the latter date *(slightly wounded)*, and with General Grant's Column in the operations in Oude. Present at the affair of Simree. *Medal and 2 Clasps.*

2ND CAPTAIN T. G. MONTGOMERIE, P. H., Bengal Engineers.

2nd Lieut., 8 June 49—Lieut., 1 Aug. 54—2nd Captain, 27 Aug. 58.

CAPTAIN C. L. MONTGOMERY,† 10th (late 65th) Native Infantry.

Ensign, 12 June 41—Lieut., 24 Jan. 45—Bt.-Captain, 12 June 56—Captain, 15 July 57.

SERVICE.—Captain MONTGOMERY served in the Chota Nagpore District during the Mutinies, '57. With the Sarun Field Force in charge of one of Sir Jung Bahadoor's Brigades, '58. Present at the crossing of the Gogra, and at the battle of Phoolpore.

LIEUTENANT J. MOORE, Bengal Invalid Establishment.

Lieut., 13 Feb. 52.

SERVICE.—Lieutenant MOORE served with the Army of the Indus. Present at the assault and capture of Ghuznee. *Medal.* Served during the Sutlej Campaign, '45, '46. Present at the actions of Ferozeshuhur *(wounded)*, Sobraon *(severely wounded)*, and lost the use of right arm. *Medal, Clasp, and Ensign's Commission.*

LIEUTENANT J. A. H. MOORE, P. H., late 23rd Native Infantry.

Ensign, 11 Dec. 46—Lieut., 10 Oct. 53.

SERVICE.—Lieutenant MOORE served with the Force employed against the Afreedies in the Kohat Pass, February '50. (Has furnished a certificate of qualification in Surveying.)

LIEUTENANT M. J. MOORE, General List, Cavalry.

Cornet, 20 Oct. 59—Lieutenant, 9 April 61.

(425)

BREVET-COLONEL T. MOORE, late 5th Bengal European Cavalry.

Cornet, 11 Dec. 24—Lieut., 13 May 25—Captain, 21 Jan. 39—Bt.-Major, 7 June 49—Major, 1 April 54—Bt.-Lieut.-Col., 28 Nov. 54—Lieut.-Col., 16 Aug. 59—Bt.-Colonel, 27 Sept. 59.

SERVICE.—Colonel MOORE commanded a Detachment of Troops at Punwarri, in Bundlecund, in '42, against a body of insurgents, (*wounded* through the left knee by a matchlock ball). Served during the Punjab Campaign, '48, '49. Present at the affair of Ramnuggur, and actions of Sadoolapore, Chillianwallah, and Goojerat. *Medal and 2 Clasps.* Promoted to Brevet-Majority for services during the Punjab Campaign.

VETERINARY-SURGEON R. MOORHEAD, F.R.C.S., Bengal Veterinary Establishment.

Veterinary-Surgeon, 12 April 58.

ASSISTANT-SURGEON A. MORGAN,† Bengal Medical Establishment.

Asst.-Surgeon, 24 Jan. 55.

SERVICE.—Assistant-Surgeon MORGAN served in Medical Charge of the 50th, 56th, and 40th Native Infantry, and 2nd Irregular Cavalry, during the Sonthal Campaign, in '55, '56. Served in October '57 with a Detachment of H. M.'s 54th Regiment towards Sylhet, until February '58.

BREVET-MAJOR W. D. MORGAN, P. H., late 22nd Native Infantry.

Ensign, 12 Dec. 40—Lieut., 19 Jan. 43—Captain, 15 May 55—Bt.-Major, 20 July 58.

SERVICE.—Major MORGAN served in the Punjab Campaign, '48, '49. Present at the action of Ramnuggur, 22nd November '48. *Medal.* Served at the annexation of Oude, '56. Commanded a Detachment of the 22nd Native Infantry, and captured the city of Fyzabad, 17th February '57. Present at the mutiny of the 22nd Native Infantry, at Fyzabad, on the 8th June '57, and at the mutiny of the Native Troops at Dinapore, 25th July '57. Served as Brigade Major with the Sarun and Goruckpore Field Forces in the Campaigns of '57, '58, '59. Present at the action of Sohunpore, 26th December '57; Phoolpore, 20th February '58; Belwa

Fort, 2nd March; Amorah, 5th March, 17th and 25th April; Doominagunge, on the Raptee, 26th November and 3rd December; battle of Toolseepore and capture of the Fort, 23rd December; and affair on the Nepal Frontier, near Siewa, 29th December '58. *Medal.* Mentioned in the following Despatches: by Brigadier Rowcroft, 28th December '57; by Brigadier-General G. H. Macgregor, 25th February '58; by Brigadier Rowcroft, 22nd February '58, 6th March '58, 19th April '58, 6th and 18th January '59, and 24th January '59. Received the thanks of the Governor-General, 12th January '58. Promoted to the rank of Brevet-Major for services during the Mutinies.

LIEUTENANT M. P. MORIARTY, P. H., late 41st Native Infantry.

Ensign, 13 June 57—Lieut., 18 May 58.

SERVICE.—Lieutenant MORIARTY was present with H. M.'s 34th at the actions at Cawnpore, on the 26th, 27th, and 28th of November '57, under General Windham; likewise at the attack and capture of Fort Meangunge, on the 24th of February, under Sir Hope Grant; also present at several minor engagements, near Bunnee Bridge, in Oude; was also present during the whole of the operations before Lucknow, and at the taking of the city; was present with H. M.'s 93rd Highlanders at the attack on Fort Rooya, and in the action at Allygunge, in Oude, under Major-General Walpole, likewise at the action at, and capture of, Bareilly, in May '58. Was also present with the 66th Goorkha Light Infantry at the actions at Pusgaon, 19th October; Russoolpore, 25th October; and action at Bishwah on the 1st December '58, under Brigadier Troup. *Medal and Clasp.*

ASSISTANT-SURGEON J. C. MORICE,† Bengal Medical Establishment.

Asst.-Surgeon, 8 Oct. 56.

SERVICE.—Assistant-Surgeon MORICE was present with H. M.'s 53rd Foot at the relief of Lucknow, under the Commander-in-Chief, in November '57; also at the actions of Cawnpore and Serai Ghaut, in '57; the Kalee Nuddee and re-occupation of Futtchghur, in '58. Present

(427)

in Medical Charge of a Detachment of the 2nd Punjab Cavalry with Colonel Maxwell's Column, at Akbapore, near Calpee, and with the 5th Punjab Irregulars, at the siege and capture of Lucknow, and at the actions and capture of Bareilly and Shahjehanpore, in May '58; and with the Rohilcund Force at the actions of Russoolpore, and throughout the hot weather of '58 on the Rohilcund Frontier. *Medal and* 2 *Clasps.*

LIEUTENANT J. MORLAND, late 1st European Bengal Fusiliers.

2nd Lieut., 11 Dec. 49—Lieut., 5 March 54.

SERVICE.—Lieutenant MORLAND served in Burmah, in '52, '53. Present at the relief of the Garrison of Pegu, 14th December '52. *Medal and Clasp.* Served throughout the Mutinies, '57, '58. Present at the actions of Futtehpore, Aoung, Pandoo Nuddee, Cawnpore, Oonao, Busseerutgunge, Nawabgunge, Boorbea-ka-Chowky, Bithoor, Mongowa, Alum Bagh, Khodagunge, siege and capture of Lucknow, Koopza, and Allygunge. Served during the Rohilcund Campaign, and subsequent operations in Oude. *Medal and Clasp.* Mentioned in the Despatches of General Havelock, Colonel MacIntire, Lord Clyde, and Major Hume.

BREVET-MAJOR J. MORRIESON, P., late 30th Native Infantry.

Ensign, 5 Feb. 30—Lieut., 2 Dec. 38—Bt.-Captain, 5 Feb. 45—Captain, 19 Jan. 46—Bt.-Major, 28 Nov. 54.

SERVICE.—Major MORRIESON served in the Joudpore Campaign, '39. Served in the 2nd Cabul Campaign, '42. Present at the affairs of the 19th, 23rd, and 24th January '42. Present at the mouth of the Khyber Pass and at the forcing of that Pass under General Pollock. *Medal.* Served in the 1st Punjab Campaign, '46. Present at the battle of Alliwal. *Medal.* Served in the 2nd Punjab Campaign, '48, '49. Present at the passage of the Chenab, and battles of Chillianwallah *(wounded)*, Goojerat, and subsequent pursuit of the Sikhs and Affghans. *Medals and* 2 *Clasps. (Since retired.)*

SURGEON J. S. MORRIESON,† M.D., Bengal Medical Establishment.

Asst.-Surgeon, 27 Jan. 44—Surgeon, 7 Aug. 57.

(428)

LIEUTENANT-COLONEL R. MORRIESON, P., late 52nd Native Infantry.

Ensign, 17 March 27—Lieut., 6 May 29—Bt.-Captain, 17 March 42—Captain, 24 Jan. 45—Bt.-Major, 20 June 54—Major, 10 May 57—Lieut.-Colonel, 4 Feb. 61.

SERVICE.—Lieutenant-Colonel MORRIESON served at the 2nd siege operations of Mooltan, including the attack on the suburbs, 29th December '48, and battle of Goojerat. *Medal and Clasp.*

LIEUTENANT R. MORRIS,† late 1st Bengal European Cavalry.

Cornet, 4 Aug. 57.—Lieut., 18 May 58.

SERVICE.—Lieutenant MORRIS served with H. M.'s 2nd Dragoon Guards during the Lucknow Campaign, '58. Present at the siege and capture of Lucknow, and operations at Koorsee. *Medal and 2 Clasps.*

LIEUTENANT B. W. D. MORTON, P., 30th Native Infantry.

Ensign, 9 June 48—Lieut., 1 Sept. 55.

(Passed an examination in Bengali.)

SURGEON G. E. MORTON, M.D., P. H., Bengal Medical Establishment.

Asst.-Surgeon, 27 Feb. 41—Surgeon, 19 April 55.

SERVICE.—Surgeon MORTON served with the 9th Irregular Cavalry in the 2nd Punjab Campaign of '48, '49. Present at the battle of Chillianwallah and Goojerat. *Medal and Clasps.* Served at the 2nd capture of Lucknow with the Goorkha Force under Maharajah Jung Bahadoor, and present during the other operations of that Force, from the 6th January '58 until their return to Nepal in the following May. *Medal and Clasp.*

LIEUTENANT H. MORTON, P. H., late 5th Europeans.

Ensign, 20 Dec. 55—Lieut., 30 April 58.

SERVICE.—Lieutenant MORTON served in Oude, in May '56. Present in the pursuit and capture of the rebel Rajah of Toolseepore. Served during the Mutiny, '57. Present with a Detachment of the 73rd Native Infantry, near Julpigoree, in an expedition against the two mutinous

(429)

Companies of the same Corps from Dacca, December '57. Served against the rebels in Bundlecund, '59 ; commanded a Detachment of 2 guns of Punjab Artillery, a Squadron of Irregular Cavalry, and 3 Companies Native Infantry for about two months, in frequent expeditions against the rebel leaders Dowlut Singh and Buojore Singh, near the Scinde River. *Medal.*

LIEUTENANT-COLONEL W. E. MORTON, P., Bengal Engineers.

2nd Lieut., 11 June 39—Lieut., 8 Nov. 43—2nd Captain, 11 June 54—Captain, 1 Aug. 54—Lieut.-Colonel, 18 Feb. 61.

SERVICE.—Lieutenant-Colonel MORTON served with the Army of the Punjab in '48, '49: present at the battles of Chillianwallah and Goojerat, and accompanied the pursuing Army to Peshawur. *Medal and Clasp.* Brought to the notice of His Excellency the Commander-in-Chief in the Despatch of Sir W. R. Gilbert, 16th January '49. Mentioned in that of Sir C. Campbell, 23rd February '49, and of Sir W. R. Gilbert, 24th February '49.

CAPTAIN R. S. MOSELEY, P., 10th (late 65th) Native Infantry.

Ensign, 17 Feb. 48—Lieut., 1 April 56—Captain in Staff Corps, 18 Feb. 61.

SERVICE.—Captain MOSELEY served in the expedition to China in '59. Present at an engagement on the 8th January '59, when the battery and village at Shek-tsing was captured by a combined attack of naval and land Forces, under General VanStraubenzee.

LIEUTENANT W. F. MOSLEY,† late 35th Native Infantry.

Ensign, 13 June 57—Lieut., 18 May 58.

SERVICE.—Lieutenant MOSLEY served during the Mutiny, '57, '58. Present at the actions of Amorah, Jugdespore, Doomuriahgunge, and other minor affairs. *Medal.*

ASSISTANT-SURGEON M. W. MOTT,† Bengal Medical Establishment.

Asst.-Surgeon, 20 Dec. 53.

(430)

SURGEON-MAJOR F. J. MOUAT, M.D., F.R.C.S., Bengal Medical Establishment.

Asst.-Surgeon, 3 Jan. 40—Surgeon, 1 Dec. 53—Surgeon-Major, 13 Jan. 60.

MAJOR-GENERAL J. MOULE, late 33rd Native Infantry.

Ensign, Nov. 10—Lieut., 19 Jan. 16—Captain, 29 April 26—Major, 30 June 40—Lieut.-Colonel, 1 April 46—Bt.-Colonel, 20 June 54—Colonel, 9 April 56—Major-General, 27 Jan. 58.

SERVICE.—Major-General MOULE served during the Nepal Campaign, '15, '16. Present at the siege and capture of Bhurtpore, '26. *Medal and Clasp.*

SURGEON J. W. MOUNTJOY,† Bengal Medical Establishment.

Asst.-Surgeon, 20 Oct. 46—Surgeon, 21 Feb. 60.

MAJOR G. G. MOXON, P., late 52nd Native Infantry.

Ensign, 3 Jan. 40—Lieut., 8 April 42—Captain, 24 June 54—Major in Staff Corps, 18 Feb. 61.

SERVICE.—Major MOXON served during the Punjab Campaign, '48, '49. Present throughout the operations before Mooltan, including the 1st and 2nd sieges, and capture of the Town, surrender of the Fortress, repulse of the enemies, and night attack on the Camp at Mutte Tal, 17th August; storming of the Dhurmsala, 12th September; action of Sooroojkhoond, 7th November; attack on the suburbs, 27th December '48; and battle of Goojerat. Brought to the notice of His Excellency the Commander-in-Chief, 13th February '49. *Medal and 2 Clasps.* Served during the Mutinies, '58. Commanded a Detachment of Military Police, and proceeded to the relief of the Deputy Commissioner of Mendlah, who was surrounded by rebels at Shaikpoorah. In December '58 commanded a Force of Irregular Infantry and Cavalry and Military Police, and on the 10th December routed a large body of mutineers and Bondelas under the rebel leader Runmut Singh, killing five of his Sirdars, and capturing the whole of his camp, equipage, and baggage. From December '58 to January '59 was engaged in the pursuit

(431)

of rebels under Himmult Singh, and on three occasions caught up the enemy and defeated them. *Medal.*

LIEUTENANT W. J. W. MUIR,† Bengal Artillery.

Lieut., 11 Dec. 58.

BREVET-COLONEL W. E. MULCASTER, P. H., late 64th Native Infantry.

Ensign, 4 April 37—Lieut., 29 Aug. 40—Captain, 26 Oct. 48—Bt.-Major, 2 Aug. 50—Lieut.-Colonel, 28 Nov. 54—Bt.-Colonel, 28 Nov. 57.

SERVICE.—Colonel MULCASTER served with the Force under General Pollock. Present at the forcing of the Khyber Pass *(severely wounded).* *Medal.* Served during the Campaign on the Sutlej: present at the battles of Moodkee, Ferozeshuhur, and Sobraon, *Medal and 2 Clasps;* and with the Army of the Punjab throughout the siege of Mooltan, including the action of Sooroojkhoond. *Medal and Clasp.*

MAJOR C. F. M. MUNDY,† late 34th Native Infantry.

Ensign, 23 March 35—Lieut., 1 July 40—Captain, 21 Nov. 48.—Major, 18 Feb. 61.

CAPTAIN A. A. MUNRO, P., late 50th Native Infantry.

Ensign, 5 May 46—Lieut., 22 Oct. 49—Captain, 8 March 60.

SERVICE.—Captain MUNRO served during the Punjab Campaign, '48, '49. *Medal.* Served in the Sonthal Rebellion, '55, '56. (Has passed the Civil Service Examinations in the Punjab, lower and higher standards.)

LIEUTENANT C. A. MUNRO, P. H., late 25th Native Infantry.

Ensign, 17 March 55—Lieut., 23 Nov. 56.

SERVICE.—Lieutenant MUNRO served as Interpreter to the Naval Brigade under Captain Peel, in '57. Present at the actions of Kudjwa, near Binkee, 1st November '57; Alum Bagh, during the relief of Lucknow, and at the action of Cawnpore, 6th December '57. *Medal and Clasp.*

LIEUTENANT H. MUNRO, Bengal Artillery.

Lieut., 27 April 58.

(432)

LIEUTENANT J. W. MUNRO, late 38th Native Infantry.

Ensign, 26 Feb. 59—Lieut., 13 July 60.

ENSIGN J. MURPHY, Unattached List.

Ensign, 21 Feb. 60.

LIEUTENANT A. MURRAY,† late 60th Native Infantry.

Ensign, 20 Dec. 56—Lieut., 30 April 58.

SERVICE.—Lieutenant MURRAY served with the Delhi Field Force in '57, under Sir A. Wilson, during the siege and capture of Delhi. Served with Colonel Greathed's Column. Present at the battles of Boolundshuhur, Agra, Allyghur, and Acrabad. Served with Sir Hope Grant's Column on the advance to Oude. Served under Lord Clyde at the final storm and capture of Lucknow, also with Generel Sir J. Outram's Force at Alum Bagh. Present at the affairs at Gaylee, and in the several repulses on the position. Served with the Jhujjur Column under Major Brookes, '58, '59. *Medal and 2 Clasps.*

LIEUTENANT A. H. MURRAY, Bengal Artillery.

Lieut., 27 Aug. 58.

BREVET-CAPTAIN C. MURRAY, P. H., late 70th Native Infantry.

Ensign, 28 Dec. 42—Lieut., 9 Aug. 51—Bt.-Captain, 28 Dec. 57.

SERVICE —Captain MURRAY served with the Army of Gwalior. *Bronze Star.* With the Army of the Punjab, '48, '49 : present at the affair of Ramnuggur, passage of the Chenab, and battles of Chillianwallah and Goojerat *(wounded)*, and in the subsequent pursuit of the Sikhs and Affghans by the Force under General Gilbert. *Medal and Clasp.* Served in the Kohat Expedition under Sir Charles Napier.

2ND CAPTAIN H. MURRAY, Bengal Artillery.

2nd Lieut., 8 June 49—Lieut., 21 May 54—2nd Captain, 27 Aug. 58.

SERVICE.—Captain MURRAY served at the battle of Badlee-ka-Serai, 8th June '57. Present at the siege, storm, and capture of Delhi, and action of Nudjufghur; actions of Boolundshuhur, Agra, Kunoje, relief

(433)

of Lucknow, and actions of Cawnpore, Serai Ghaut, Futtehghur, and Shumshabad. *Medal and 2 Clasps.*

ENSIGN H. MURRAY, Unattached List.

Ensign, 29 Nov. 58.

SERVICE.—Ensign MURRAY served with the Army before Delhi in '57. In Oude in '58. Present at the siege and capture of Lucknow, March '58. In Rohilcund, in April and May '58. And in the North of Oude, '58, '59. Present in the following actions : Badlee-ka-Serai, 8th June '57; Gungeeree, Puttiallee, and Mynpooree, on the 14th, 17th, and 27th December '57; assault and capture of Meangunge (Oude), 24th February '58; actions of Allygunge and Rooya, April '58; battle of Bareilly, 5th May '58; affairs of Pusgaon, Russulpoor, Mittowlee Fort, Mehindee, and Biswah, '58, '59. *Medal and 2 Clasps, and Unattached Ensign's Commission.*

LIEUTENANT H. H. MURRAY,† Bengal Artillery.

Lieut., 27 Aug. 58.

LIEUTENANT H. Y. MURRAY,† late 4th Bengal European Cavalry.

Cornet, 20 June 58—Lieut., 24 Aug. 58.

SERVICE.—Lieutenant MURRAY served in charge of Cavalry Recruits from Raneegunge to Allahabad, in September '58, and proceeded to Cawnpore, and thence to Lucknow.

BREVET-MAJOR J. I. MURRAY, P. H., late 71st Native Infantry.

Ensign, 10 Dec. 42—Lieut., 7 Sept. 45—Captain, 23 Nov. 56.

SERVICE.—Major MURRAY served during the Punjab Campaign, '48, '49. *Medal.* Served as a Trooper at the battle of Shahgunge, 5th July '57. As a Volunteer commanded Rajah Gobind Singh's Jât Horse at the battle of Allyghur, on the 24th August. Mentioned in the Despatches of Major Montgomery and Mr. A. H. Cocks, Special Commissioner, for conspicuous gallantry, &c., and received the public recognition of the Governor-General for eminent service. *(Wounded.) (Charger wounded.)*

(434)

Served as a Volunteer at the battle of Agra, 10th October '57. Employed in November and December in raising the Jât Horse, and in restoring order in the Allyghur and Etah Districts. Commanded at the Cavalry engagements at Kutchla Ghaut, and defeated, with 200 Sabres of Jât Horse, 600 old Irregular Cavalry, and held the Rohilcund rebel army in check till the arrival of General Penny's Force, 11th March '58. Received the thanks of the Governor-General. With the Jât Horse, in April, May, and June, guarded successfully the Ghauts on the Ganges in the Allyghur and Etah Districts, against the Rohilcund rebels. Commanded the Regiment with the Allyghur Column under Brigadier Kelly, throughout the 2nd Oude Campaign, and the operations on the Nepal Frontier. Present at the engagement near Bootwul, 25th March '59. Received the thanks of Government. At the subsequent attack of the rebels in the Hills. Received the thanks of Government, '59. Defeated the Nusseerabad Brigade of rebels at Durriahpore, Goruckpore District. Highly commended and brought to the notice of the Commander-in-Chief by Brigadier Rowcroft, and received the thanks of Government. Commanded a Column in the final operations on the Nepal Frontier, under Brigadier Holdich, in November and December '59. Received the thanks of the Commander-in-Chief, 16th January '60. *Medal*. (Has furnished certificates of qualification in Surveying and Civil Engineering.)

LIEUTENANT P. MURRAY,† Bengal Engineers.

Lieut., 20 Sept. 57.

SERVICE.—Lieutenant MURRAY served as Assistant Field Engineer with the Field Force before Delhi, from 14th August '57 to the capture of the city, 20th September '57. (*Wounded slightly*, 15th September '57.) *Medal and Clasp*. Served as Officiating Major of Brigade, Delhi Engineer Field Force, '57, '58. Present at the actions of Gungeeree, 14th, Puttiallee, 17th, and Mynpooree, 27th December '57, with the Force under Colonel T. Seaton. Served as Assistant Field Engineer with the Army under Lord Clyde, at the capture of Lucknow, March '58. *Clasp*. Served as Assistant Field Engineer with the Force under Brigadier-General Walpole, in Oude and Rohilcund, April '58. Present at the attack on Fort Rooya, 15th April '58; and action at Allygunge,

April '58. Served as Assistant Field Engineer at the defence of the Jail at Shahjehanpore, under Colonel Hall, and present with the Rohilcund Field Force at two actions at Shahjehanpore, under Brigadier-General J. Jones.

2ND CAPTAIN R. MURRAY, P. H., Bengal Artillery.

2nd Lieut., 14 June 45—Lieut., 4 Dec. 42—2nd Captain, 27 Aug. 58.

SERVICE.—Captain MURRAY served during the Punjab Campaign, '48, '49. *Medal.*

VETERINARY-SURGEON R. W. MURRAY, Bengal Veterinary Establishment.

Vety.-Surgeon, 30 May 57.

ENSIGN S. MURRAY, Unattached List.

Ensign, 11 June 58.

HONORARY ASSISTANT-SURGEON T. MURRAY,† M.D., Bengal Medical Establishment.

Apothecary, 13 May 40—Hony. Asst.-Surgeon, 8 June 60.

SERVICE.—Honorary Assistant-Surgeon MURRAY served in the Field Hospital and with H. M.'s 39th in the Gwalior Campaign, '42, '43. *Bronze Star.* Served in Medical Charge of a Detachment of H. M.'s Troops under Command of Captain Swaby, 18th Royal Irish, on board the ship *Buckinghamshire*, when that vessel was totally destroyed by fire at the Sandheads. Served throughout the Mutinies of '57, '58. Formed one of the Volunteer Troop of Cavalry organised at Neemuch for the defence of that station, from July to October '57. Present at the attack on mutineers on the night of the 12th August '57, at Neemuch. Present at the action at Nimbheira, 19th September '57. Present at the action at Jeerun, 23rd October '57. Present in the repulse given to the Mundesore rebels by the Neemuch Troops, on the 8th November '57. Was one of the Neemuch Garrison during the defence of the fortified square against the Mundesore rebels, from 9th to 23rd November '57. Was mentioned in the Despatches of Major Simpson and Major Lloyd. Present in Medical Charge of a Squadron of the 2nd Bombay Light Cavalry, at the siege and capture of Kotah, March '58. *Medal and Clasp.*

LIEUTENANT W. G. MURRAY, P. H., late 68th Native Infantry.
Ensign, 8 June 55—Lieut., 1 May 57.

LIEUTENANT C. K. MYLNE,† late 35th Native Infantry.
Ensign, 10 Dec. 53—Lieut., 23 Nov. 56.

CAPTAIN W. C. R. MYLNE, P. C., late 74th Native Infantry.
Ensign, 20 Feb. 45—Lieut.,*2 Aug. 51—Captain, 22 Aug. 58.

SERVICE.—Captain MYLNE served during the Mutinies, '57, '58, and '59. Present at the action of Pandoo Nuddee, and other affairs previous to the defence of Cawnpore. *(Horse killed under him.)* Mentioned in General Windham's Despatch, 30th November '57. Present at the battle of Cawnpore on the 6th December '57, at Etawah and Mynpooree; and at the operations at Ramgunga, and action of Khankur, 7th April '58. Mentioned in Despatch, 7th April '58. *Medal.*

N

LIEUTENANT C. E. NAIRNE, Bengal Artillery.
Lieut., 27 April 58.

SURGEON-MAJOR J. NAISMITH,† M. D., Bengal Medical Establishment.
Asst.-Surgeon, 12 March 40—Surgeon, 20 Jan. 54—Surgeon-Major, 12 March 60.

SERVICE.—Surgeon-Major NAISMITH served with the Light Brigade of the Army of Reserve which assembled at Ferozepore during the cold season of '42, '43, being there in Medical Charge of the 2nd Light Infantry Battalion.

MAJOR-GENERAL SIR R. NAPIER, K.C.B., Bengal Engineers.
2nd Lieut., 15 Dec. 26—Lieut., 28 Sept. 27—Captain, 25 Jan. 41—Bt.-Major, 3 April 46—Major, 1 Aug. 54—Bt.-Lieut.-Colonel, 7 June 49—Lieut.-Colonel, 15 April 56—Bt.-Colonel, 28 Nov. 54—Colonel, 18 Feb. 61—Major-General, 15 Feb. 61.

SERVICE.—Major-General Sir R. NAPIER was present as Brigade Major in the Sutlej Campaign and actions of '45 '46. *(Severely wounded.)*

Medal and Brevet-Major. Was Acting Chief Engineer during part of the siege of Mooltan *(severely wounded)*; also present at Goojerat. *Medal and Brevet-Lieutenant-Colonel.* Accompanied Sir W. Gilbert's Column in pursuit of the Sikh Army, in '49. Served as Chief of the Staff with General Outram's Force at the 1st relief of Lucknow *(wounded)*, C.B.; as Chief Engineer at the capture of Lucknow. *K.C.B.* Commanded a Brigade at the capture of Gwalior, and in the subsequent pursuit defeated a large force of rebels at Powree, taking 25 guns. Commanded the Gwalior Division, and was present in numerous subsequent affairs in '58. *Medal and Clasp.* Commanded the 2nd Division of the China Expeditionary Force at the capture of the Taku Forts, and advance on Pekin. *Medal and Clasps.* Frequently mentioned in Despatches, &c.

CAPTAIN R. A. NAPPER, P. H., late 55th Native Infantry.

Ensign, 9 Sept. 42—Lieut., 24 Jan. 45—Captain, 23 Nov. 56.

SERVICE.—Captain NAPPER served in Rajpootana, and was present at the attack on the Fort of Beyt, in the Gulf of Cutch, on the 2nd April '58.

LIEUTENANT H. P. P. NASH, P. H., late 25th Native Infantry.

Ensign, 4 March 56—Lieut., 23 Nov. 56.

MAJOR-GENERAL J. NASH, C.B., late 46th Native Infantry.

Ensign, July 13—Lieut., 25 Dec. 17—Captain, 24 Jan. 29—Major, 26 Sept. 41—Bt.-Lieut.-Colonel, 30 April 44—Lieut.-Colonel, 11 Nov. 47—Bt.-Colonel, 20 June 54—Colonel, 15 July 57—Major-General, 9 April 56.

SERVICE.—Major-General NASH, C.B., served throughout the Nepal Campaign, '14, '15: present at the siege and surrender of Malown. *Medal.* Served during the Maharatta War, including the storm and capture of the enemy's guns and camp, 16th December, and city of Nagpore, 24th December '17; siege and surrender of Asseerghur, '19; Lamba, '23; and served throughout the Campaign in Affghanistan, '39, '40, '41, and '42, including the assault and capture of Ghuznee, '39. *Medal.* Commanded the 43rd Light Infantry at the repulse of the enemy at Candahar *(slightly wounded,* 29th May '42), and storm and capture of Istaliff. *Medal*. Commanded the 43rd Native Infantry at the battle of Maharajpore. *Bronze Star and Lieutenant-Colonel*. Campaign on the Sutlej: present at the action of Sobraon. *Medal and C.B.* Commanded the 72nd Native Infantry at the 2nd siege and capture of Mooltan, led the Right Centre Column at the storming of the suburbs of Mooltan. *(Wounded.) Medal.*

CAPTAIN J. D. NASH, Bengal Invalid Establishment.

Lieut., 7 Jan. 25—Captain, 30 May 34.

SERVICE.—Captain NASH served at the siege of Bhurtpore. *Medal.*

MAJOR H. M. NATION,† late 3rd Europeans.

Ensign, 19 Jan. 28—Lieut., 8 Oct. 39—Bt.-Captain, 19 Jan. 43—Captain, 7 June 53—Bt.-Major, 20 June 54—Major, 13 July 58.

(Since retired.)

MAJOR J. L. NATION, P. H., late 57th Native Infantry.

Ensign, 8 March 41—Lieut., 12 Aug. 47—Bt.-Captain, 8 March 56—Captain, 28 Sept. 57.—Major, 8 March 61.

MAJOR A. G. NEDHAM, P., late 74th Native Infantry.

Ensign, 12 June 41—Lieut., 15 March 44—Bt.-Captain, 12 June 56—Captain, 23 Nov. 56—Major in Staff Corps, 12 June 61.

SERVICE.—Major NEDHAM served in Bundlecund in '43. Served throughout the Sonthal Campaign, '55. Received the thanks of Government, December '55. Services at Julpigooree in '57. Brought to the notice of Government by Colonel Sherer, and acknowledged.

CAPTAIN C. NEED, P. H., late 6th Europeans.

Ensign, 14 April 40—Lieut., 16 June 42—Captain, 1 Aug. 53.

SERVICE.—Captain NEED served as Adjutant of the 14th Irregular Cavalry throughout the Punjab Campaign, also when the Regiment surprised the Fort of Govindghur. Commanded a Squadron under Sir J. Lawrence, Bart., at the disarming of the Towns of Sulliana and Kana Kutch, in the Punjab. Served throughout the Rohilcund Campaign, '58,

(439)

as a Volunteer, including the actions of Bagawalla and Nageena (in the latter action charger wounded by sabre cut); relief of Moradabad, action on the Dojura, assault and capture of Bareilly, attack and bombardment of Shahjehanpore, and relief of the Garrison, and the subsequent affairs of the 15th and 18th May, on the latter occasion commanded De-Kantzow's Horse. *Medal.*

MAJOR F. J. NELSON, P. H., 10th (late 65th) Native Infantry.

Ensign, 21 Aug. 40—Lieut., 21 June 43—Bt.-Captain, 21 Aug. 55—Captain, 14 June 57—Major in Staff Corps, 18 Feb. 61.

SERVICE.—Major NELSON served in China with the Force under Major-General Sir C. T. VanStraubenzee, in '58, '59.

LIEUTENANT G. G. NELSON, Bengal Artillery.

Lieut., 27 Aug. 58.

BREVET-CAPTAIN W. NEMBHARD, P., late 55th Native Infantry.

Ensign, 14 June 45—Lieut., 19 Nov. 50—Bt.-Captain, 14 June 60.

SERVICE.—Captain NEMBHARD served in the Sutlej Campaign, '46. In Burmah, in '52, '53. *Medal.* Present during the Mutinies at Dumoh, in July '57, when the Town was attacked by a large force of mutineers and rebels, also on the 5th August, with reinforcements of men and guns, when the enemy a second time attacked the Town and Station of Dumoh. Present at the attack on the Fort of Nursurghur, Dumoh District, on 18th September '57, and on the 27th September, when it was attacked in the Kuttungee Pass, near Jubbulpore, by a body of rebels. *Medal.*

CAPTAIN D. J. F. NEWALL, P. H., Bengal Artillery.

2nd Lieut., 8 June 43—Lieut., 3 Oct. 45—Captain, 27 April 58.

SERVICE.—Captain NEWALL was present at the battle of Sobraon. *Medal.* During the Punjab Campaign, including siege and surrender of Mooltan, '48, '49; and action of Goojerat. *Medal and 2 Clasps.*

LIEUTENANT E. NEWBERY, late 6th Europeans.

Ensign, 11 Dec. 58—Lieut., 29 March 59.

LIEUTENANT F. M. NEWBERY, P. H., General List.

Ensign, 4 March 59—Lieut., 15 July 59.

BREVET-MAJOR G. NEWBOLT, P. C., late 31st Native Infantry.

Ensign, 7 Jan. 29—Lieut., 15 Feb. 36—Bt.-Captain, 7 Jan. 44—Captain, 10 Feb. 47—Bt.-Major, 28 Nov. 54.

SERVICE.—Major NEWBOLT served with the Army of the Indus in Affghanistan, '38, '39, and '40: present at the storm and capture of Ghuznee, *Medal;* during the campaign on the Sutlej and throughout the Punjab Campaign, including the passage of the Chenab, actions of Chillianwallah and Goojerat, and subsequent pursuit of the Sikhs and Affghans to Peshawur under General Gilbert. *Medal.* *(Since retired.)*

BREVET-CAPTAIN L. R. NEWHOUSE,† late 19th Native Infantry.

Ensign, 12 June 40—Lieut., 28 March 50—Bt.-Captain, 12 June 55.

(Since retired.)

LIEUTENANT C. D. G. NEWINGTON, General List.

Ensign, 6 Nov. 60—Lieut., 1 Jan. 62.

CAPTAIN C. D. NEWMARCH,† Bengal Engineers.

2nd Lieut., 9 Dec. 44—Lieut., 28 Feb. 51—Captain, 27 April 58.

SERVICE.—Captain NEWMARCH served during the Burmah Campaign as Assistant Field Engineer, in '53. *Medal and Clasp.*

LIEUTENANT G. NEWMARCH, P. H., Bengal Engineers.

Lieut., 27 June 57.

LIEUTENANT H. F. NEWMARCH, P. H., late 24th Native Infantry.

Ensign, 25 March 50—Lieut., 12 June 54.

LIEUTENANT O. R. NEWMARCH, P., late 44th Native Infantry.

Ensign, 17 March 55—Lieut., 21 July 57.

SERVICE.—Lieutenant NEWMARCH served with the Agra Brigade in '57. Present at the action of the 5th July '51. Served with Brigadier

(441)

Seaton's Column in December '57. Present at the affairs of Gungeeree and Puttiallee. *Medal.*

ASSISTANT-SURGEON I. NEWTON,† Bengal Medical Establishment.
Asst.-Surgeon, 27 July 59.

LIEUTENANT E. G. NEWNHAM,† General List.
Ensign, 4 Aug. 59—Lieut., 5 May 61.

2ND CAPTAIN T. NICHOL, P. H., Bengal Artillery.
2nd Lieut., 8 June 49—Lieut., 20 Feb. 55—2nd Captain, 27 Aug. 58.

ASSISTANT-SURGEON W. NICHOL, M.D., Bengal Medical Establishment.
Asst.-Surgeon, 10 Feb. 59.

LIEUTENANT H. L. NICHOLAS,† Bengal Artillery.
Lieut., 27 Aug. 58.

CAPTAIN R. NICHOLAS,† late 64th Native Infantry.
Ensign, 3 Jan. 40—Lieut., 24 April 42—Bt.-Captain, 3 Jan. 55—Captain, 23 Nov. 56.

SERVICE.—Captain NICHOLAS served on the Peshawur Frontier in '41, '42. Present at the occupation, defence, and subsequent evacuation of the Fort of Ali Mujid in the Khyber Pass, '41. Present at the forcing of the Khyber Pass, and subsequent operations leading to the occupation of Cabul, '42. Served under Sir Charles Napier against the Hill Tribes, '44, '45.

CAPTAIN C. H. NICHOLETTS, P., late 1st Bengal European Cavalry.
Cornet, 19 Feb. 43—Lieut., 23 Oct. 45—Captain, 30 Nov. 53.

SERVICE.—Captain NICHOLETTS served at the battle of Alliwal, '46. *Medal.* With the Rohilcund Field Force as Interpreter to H. M.'s 6th Carabineers, and as Brigade Major to the Field Force at the capture of Bareilly. *Medal.*

(442)

CAPTAIN A. L. NICHOLSON,† late 64th Native Infantry.

Ensign, 12 Oct. 40—Lieut., 11 Dec. 43—Bt.-Captain, 12 Oct. 55—Captain, 18 March 57.

SERVICE.—Captain NICHOLSON served in Affghanistan in '41, '42; as Commissariat Officer to Colonel Turner's Field Force in Shahabad, in '58, '59. Twice mentioned in Colonel Turner's Despatches. Commanded 2 Companies ordered to co-operate with Captain Raban's Force, against the Kokees, in '61.

BREVET-CAPTAIN C. J. NICHOLSON, P., late 54th Native Infantry.

Ensign, 3 Dec. 45—Lieut., 27 July 51—Bt.-Captain, 13 Dec. 60.

SERVICE.—Captain NICHOLSON served during the Punjab Campaign, '48, '49. Present at the actions of Sadoolapore, Chillianwallah, and Goojerat. *Medal and 2 Clasps.*

BREVET-MAJOR H. NICOLL, P., late 50th Native Infantry.

Ensign, 12 Dec. 34—Lieut., 4 Nov. 38—Captain, 22 Oct. 49—Bt.-Major, 19 Jan. 58.

SERVICE.—Major NICOLL served in Bundlecund, '42. In the Gwalior Campaign, '42, '43. Present in the action of Punniar. *Bronze Star.* Served during the Punjab Campaign, '48, '49. *Medal.* Served in the Sonthal Campaign, '55, '56. Served as Brigade Major with the Delhi Field Force, in '57. Present at the action of Badlee-ka-Serai, and at the taking of the heights before Delhi. Mentioned in the Despatch of Brigadier Graves, 8th June '57. Served as Brigade Major throughout the siege of Delhi, and at the assault and final capture of that city. Mentioned in the Despatch of Brigadier Longfield. *Medal and Clasp.* Promoted to the rank of Brevet-Major for services before Delhi.

CAPTAIN J. E. T. NICOLLS, P. II., Bengal Engineers.

2nd Lieut., 10 Dec. 41—Lieut., 11 Nov. 46—Captain, 8 June 56.

SERVICE.—Captain NICOLLS served at the battle of Maharajpore. *Bronze Star.* Served during the Sutlej Campaign, '45, '46. *(Severely wounded.) Medal.*

(443)

CAPTAIN C. W. NIGHTINGALE, P. H., late 18th Native Infantry.

Ensign, 8 June 44—Lieut., 12 Nov. 48—Captain, 6 June 57.

SERVICE.—Captain NIGHTINGALE served during the Punjab Campaign. *Medal.* (Has furnished certificates of qualification in Surveying and Civil Engineering.)

CAPTAIN M. R. NIGHTINGALE, P. H., late 2nd European Bengal Fusiliers.

2nd Lieut., 11 June 42—Lieut., 10 July 44—Captain, 22 Nov. 54.

SERVICE.—Captain NIGHTINGALE served during the Punjab Campaign, '48, '49. Present at the affair of Ramnuggur, passage of the Chenab, and battle of Chillianwallah. *(Very severely wounded.)* *Medal and Clasp.*

LIEUTENANT R. P. NISBET, P. H., General List.

Ensign, 12 Oct. 59—Lieut., 27 July 61.

CAPTAIN J. NISBETT, P. H., late 69th Native Infantry.

Ensign, 12 June 39—Lieut., 3 Oct. 40—Captain, 15 Aug. 50.

SERVICE.—Captain NISBETT served during the Punjab Campaign, '48, '49. Present at the action of Chillianwallah. *(Severely wounded.)* *Medal and Clasp.*

LIEUTENANT C. S. NOBLE, late 72nd Native Infantry.

Ensign, 4 Oct. 58—Lieut., 6 March 59.

LIEUTENANT H. N. NOBLE,† late 44th Native Infantry.

Ensign, 9 Dec. 53—Lieut., 29 May 51.

SERVICE.—Lieutenant NOBLE served with the Agra Force in '57, '58. Present at the action against the rebels on the 5th July '57; at the battle of Agra, 10th October '57. *Medal.* Present at the storming of the large fortified village of Dheepoora; led a small body of Sikhs on the right attack, charged, and took the heights. Present in several other skirmishes.

(444)

ENSIGN G. NOLAN, Unattached List.
Ensign, 14 Sept. 60.

BREVET-CAPTAIN J. T. NORGATE, P. H., late 69th Native Infantry.
Ensign, 30 Dec. 43—Lieut., 29 July 48—Bt.-Captain, 30 Dec. 58.

SERVICE.—Captain NORGATE served with the force under Major Jackson and Lieutenant-Colonel Chamberlain, against the rebels in the Googaira District, October and November '57. Present at the Mutiny at Mooltan, 31st August '58; and sent in pursuit of the mutineers with 50 men of the 11th Punjab Infantry, and 1 Troop, 6th Irregular Cavalry. Came up with the mutineers after a forced march of 57 miles, and destroyed nearly 500 of them. Received the approbation of the Punjab Government, 17th September '58. Received the high approbation of Government, 27th September '58. Received the thanks of the Home Government, 7th April '59. Commanded the 12th Punjab Infantry in the operations against the rebels in Bundlecund, under Brigadier Wheeler, in October, November, and December '59. *Medal.*

LIEUTENANT F. B. NORMAN, P. H., late 14th Native Infantry.
Ensign, 8 Dec. 48—Lieut., 15 April 54.
(Passed examination in Surveying and Civil Engineering.)

LIEUTENANT-COLONEL H. W. NORMAN, C.B., P. H., 2nd (late 31st) Native Infantry.
Ensign, 1 March 44—Lieut., 25 Dec. 47—Captain, 2 Dec. 60—Bt.-Major, 3 Dec. 60—Bt.-Lieut.-Colonel, 4 Dec. 60.

SERVICE.—Lieutenant-Colonel NORMAN, C.B., served as Adjutant to the 31st Native Infantry throughout the Punjab Campaign, including the passage of the Chenab, the action at Sadoolapore, the battles of Chillianwallah and Goojerat, with the subsequent pursuit under Sir W. Gilbert. Present when the Sikh Army laid down its arms and surrendered its cannon at Rawul Pindee, and accompanied the troops that expelled the Affghans from Peshawur. *Medal and 2 Clasps.* Served as Brigade Major to the whole of the troops under the immediate orders of Sir Charles Napier. Engaged against the Affreedies in the Kohat Pass, in February '50. As Major of Brigade or Assistant Adjutant-General present in all the expeditions from Peshawur against the surrounding Hill Tribes, in the years '51, '52, '53, and '54. Served with the 31st Native Infantry, during the Sonthal Insurrection of '55, for more than three months, in Command of a separate Detachment. Served in the field during the Mutiny in '57, '58, and '59; at the battle of Badlee-ka-Serai as Assistant Adjutant-General of the Army, and succeeded to the charge of the Department of the Adjutant-General of the Army in the field, upon Colonel Chester being killed. Served throughout the siege of Delhi, a considerable portion of the time as Acting Adjutant-General. Accompanied the Column that left Delhi after the capture, and was present in the actions of Boolundshuhur, Agra, Maregunge, in Oude, and minor affairs. From the 12th November '57 to the close of the war acted as head of the Department of the Adjutant-General of the Army in the field. Present in this capacity at all the operations attending the final relief of Lucknow *(horse shot)*, from 12th to 25th November; relief of Cawnpore and defeat of the Gwalior Contingent, 28th November to 6th December '57; action at Khodagunge, 2nd January '58, and re-occupation of Futtehghur; siege and capture of Lucknow, 2nd to 21st March; Campaign in Rohilcund, April and May '58 (*wounded* at the action of Bareilly); Campaign in Oude, October '58 to January '59, including actions at Doundia Khera, Burgudia, and Musjidia, and defeat of the Nana's troops on the bank of the Raptee. *Medal and 3 Clasps. Companion of the Bath. Brevets of Major and Lieutenant-Colonel.*

ENSIGN J. NORRIS, Unattached List.

Ensign, 16 Aug. 58.

LIEUTENANT R. NORTON, General List.

Ensign, 21 July 59—Lieut., 13 April 61.

LIEUTENANT C. D. P. NOTT, late 4th Europeans.

Ensign, 27 Sept. 54—Lieut., 10 July 57.

SERVICE.—Lieutenant NOTT served throughout the Oude Campaign, '58, 59. With the Soraon Field Force under Brigadier Pinckney, in '58, and with it on the advance to Pertaubgurh. Present with the Force under His Excellency the Commander-in-Chief in his advance on the Forts of Ahmaetee and Shunkurpore; with Sir Hope Grant's Force at Fyzabad. Present at the passage of the Gogra and subsequent operations against the rebels, Trans-Gogra; with the Force commanded by Brigadier Horsford, Trans-Raptee, in '59; at the action at Jerwah Pass, Nepal Frontier, and subsequent operations in the Terai, up to May '59. Thanked in Despatches. *Medal.*

CAPTAIN R. M. NOTT, P. H., late 64th Native Infantry.

Ensign, 8 March 41—Lieut., 24 Jan. 45—Bt.-Captain, 8 March 56—Captain, 10 July 57.

SERVICE.—Captain NOTT served under General Pollock at the forcing of the Khyber Pass, and subsequent operations in Affghanistan. *Medal.*

LIEUTENANT W. L. NOVERRE, P. H., late 1st European Bengal Fusiliers.

2nd Lieut., 20 Nov. 57—Lieut., 21 Feb. 59.

SERVICE.—Lieutenant NOVERRE served under Brigadier Douglas, in Behar, in '58. *Medal.*

LIEUTENANT R. A. NOWELL, P. H., late 32nd Native Infantry.

Ensign, 20 Jan. 50—Lieut., 23 Nov. 56.

BREVET-LIEUTENANT-COLONEL W. F. NUTHALL, late 18th Native Infantry.

Ensign, 9 Dec. 36—Lieut., 3 Oct. 40—Bt.-Captain, 9 Dec. 51—Captain, 31 Jan. 53—Bt.-Major, 9 Dec. 53—Major, 6 June 57—Bt.-Lieut.-Colonel, 16 June 60.

SERVICE.—Colonel NUTHALL served during the 2nd Burmese War, in '52, and received the thanks of the Commander-in-Chief for his services. During the War, drew together three outposts of the Arracan Battalion in the Aeng Pass, and surprised and captured the Norigan Stockade, at the summit of the Pass. Received the thanks of the Commander-in-Chief, 6th February '53; of the Governor-General, 9th February '53; of the Court of Directors, 9th June '53; and honorably mentioned in the House of Lords. *Brevet-Majority and Medal.* Received the thanks of the

(447)

Governor-General several times for services with the Pegu Light Infantry, '53, '54. (Passed an examination in Burmese.)

CAPTAIN J. M. NUTTALL,† late 5th Europeans.

Ensign, 10 June 42—Lieut., 24 Jan. 45—Captain, 6 June 57.

SERVICE.—Captain NUTTALL served during the Sutlej Campaign. Present at Allahabad when the 6th Native Infantry mutinied, and served in the operations in and about that city during the year '57.

O

CAPTAIN SIR C. W. A. OAKELEY,† *Bart.*,late 5th Bengal European Cavalry.

Cornet, 20 Dec. 48—Lieut., 19 May 50—Captain, 23 June 58.

BREVET-MAJOR E. OAKES,† late 6th Europeans.

Ensign, 2 Feb. 41—Lieut., 13 March 44—Bt.-Captain, 2 Feb. 56—Captain, 23 Nov. 56—Bt.-Major, 24 March 58.

SERVICE.—Major OAKES served during the Punjab Campaign, '48, '49, throughout the operations in the vicinity, including the attack on the Dhurmsala and action of Sooroojkhoond, siege and surrender of Mooltan, and battle of Goojerat. *Medal and Clasp.* Joined Havelock's Force, September '57, and was appointed Assistant Field Engineer, and in that capacity accompanied the Force from Cawnpore in September, for the 1st relief of Lucknow. Entered the Residency on 25th September, accompanied the expedition party at the assault and capture of the King's stables, 16th November. Remained in the Residency during its investiture by the rebel troops, until finally relieved by the Army under Lord Clyde. Was appointed Brigade Major of Engineers to the Force at Alum Bagh, under Sir J. Outram. Was present at the action of " Gailee" and also at the repulses of the numerous attacks, and in the operations ending in the final capture of Lucknow. *Brevet of Major. Medal and 2 Clasps.*

MAJOR G. N. OAKES, P. H., late 46th Native Infantry.

Ensign, 3 Jan. 36—Lieut., 1 July 42—Bt.-Captain, 3 Jan. 51—Captain, 31 Dec. 51.—Major, 18 Feb. 61.

SERVICE.—Major OAKES served during the Punjab Campaign, '48, '49. Present at the actions of Sadoolapore, Chillianwallah, and Goojerat. *Medal and 2 Clasps.*

(448)

CAPTAIN R. E. OAKES, P. H., late 52nd Native Infantry.

Ensign, 11 Dec. 47—Lieut., 1 June 54—Captain, 8 April 62.

SERVICE.—Captain OAKES served at the 2nd siege operations in the vicinity of Mooltan, including the attack on the suburbs, 27th December '48. Served during the Punjab Campaign, '48, '49. Present at the battle of Goojerat. *Medal and Clasp.*

MAJOR W. H. OAKES, P. C., late 45th Native Infantry.

Ensign, 19 June 37—Lieut., 27 Jan. 39—Captain, 2 March 39—Major, 7 Nov. 57.

SERVICE.—Major OAKES served during the Punjab Campaign, '48, '49. Present at the actions of Chillianwallah and Goojerat. *Medal and 2 Clasps.* Served during the Mutiny, '57. *Medal.* *(Since retired.)*

SURGEON R. H. OAKLEY,† Bengal Medical Establishment.

Asst.-Surgeon, 8 Jan. 42—Surgeon, 31 Dec. 55.

SERVICE.—Surgeon OAKLEY served with 69th Native Infantry throughout the war in the Punjab, in '48, 49. Present at the passage of the Chenab, and battles of Chillianwallah and Goojerat. *Medal and Clasp.* Served with 50th and 60th Native Infantry in '55, during the Sonthal Insurrection. Served with 1st Bengal Fusiliers at the siege and capture of Delhi and at the battle of Nudjufghur, in '57. *Medal and Clasp.*

CAPTAIN H. S. OBBARD, P. C.

Ensign, 11 June 42—Lieut., 11 April 45—Bt.-Captain, 11 June 57— Captain, 15 July 59.

SERVICE.—Captain OBBARD served in Bundlecund, '43, '44. During the Punjab Campaign, '49. Present at the mutiny of the Troops at Jullundur, June '57. Accompanied the Pursuing Column when the mutineers had passed Loodianah, and assisted in raising the 21st Punjab Infantry, of which he commanded a Wing, and a Troop of Puthan Cavalry, in the Googaira District, during the rebellion of the Kurals, in October '57. (Passed an examination in Punjabee.)

ASSISTANT-SURGEON D. O'BRIEN,† Bengal Medical Establishment.

Asst.-Surgeon, 20 Jan. 60.

ENSIGN J. O'BRIEN (Unattached).
Ensign, 26 Sept. 57.

LIEUTENANT J. L. G. O'BRIEN, late 44th Native Infantry.
Ensign, 24 June 57—Lieut., 18 May 58.

ASSISTANT-SURGEON PETER O'BRIEN,† F.R.C.S., Bengal Medical Establishment.
Asst.-Surgeon, 20 Nov. 53.

SERVICE.—Assistant-Surgeon O'BRIEN served with the Gwalior Contingent from March '44. In Medical Charge of Field Detachment, engaged in minor affairs in the Narode and Esaughur Districts, in April and May '46, under Captain A. C. Dewar, 1st Cavalry Gwalior Contingent. In the Pahurghur District, in June '49, under Major Parker, 4th Gwalior Contingent, and in the Subulghur District, from March to June '50, under Command of Captain Raikes, 1st Cavalry Gwalior Contingent; joined the Saugor Garrison 14th September '57, engaged with rebels at Tendokhera, 12th January '58. In Medical Charge of Detachment commanded by Captain Sale, 9th Native Infantry. Served with Central India Field Force, commanded by Sir Hugh Rose, from 18th February to 29th May '58, with the 3rd Bombay Europeans. Present at the battle of Muddenpore, the battle of Betwa, the siege, storm, and capture of Jhansie. In Medical Charge of the left Wing at the battle of Koonch, the storm and capture of Loharee, the various actions before Calpee, and the capture of that place. Disabled by sunstroke at Calpee. Thanked in the Despatch of Colonel Gall, H. M.'s 14th Light Dragoons, Commanding at the storm of Loharee. *Medal and Clasp.*

LIEUTENANT W. O'BRIEN,† Bengal Artillery.
Lieut., 27 April 58.

CAPTAIN J. J. O'BRYEN, P. H., late 16th Native Infantry.
Ensign, 22 Nov. 43—Lieut., 2 Nov. 48—Captain, 24 July 58.

SERVICE.—Captain O'BRYEN served throughout the Sutlej Campaign, '45, '46. Present at the actions of Moodkee, Ferozeshuhur, and Sobraon.

(Slightly wounded.) Medal and 2 Clasps. (Has furnished a certificate of qualification in Surveying.)

SURGEON D. J. O'CALLAGHAN,† Bengal Medical Establishment.

Asst.-Surgeon, 8 Jan. 42—Surgeon, 6 Dec. 55.

SERVICE.—Surgeon O'CALLAGHAN served as Assistant-Surgeon in the Royal Navy, '39, '40, and '41, in Europe, West Indies, North and South America, &c. Served with the Army of the Sutlej, '46. Served the Campaign of '57, '58 as Surgeon in Chief Medical Charge of the Foot Artillery of the Army of Delhi; siege, storm, and capture of the city. *Medal and Clasp.* Served in the China Campaign of '60, and expedition to Pekin. *Medal and Clasp.*

ASSISTANT-SURGEON F. ODEVAINE,† Bengal Medical Establishment.

Asst.-Surgeon, 10 Feb. 59.

SERVICE.—Assistant-Surgeon ODEVAINE served with the Turkish Contingent during the Crimean War, from 7th May '55 to 15th June '56. Appointed Assistant-Surgeon to the European General Hospital at Buyukderie (Constantinople), from August '55 to June '56. *Turkish Medal.*

LIEUTENANT C. O'DONEL,† late 48th Native Infantry.

Ensign, 20 Dec. 56—Lieut., 29 June 57.

SERVICE.—Lieutenant O'DONEL served with the Volunteer Cavalry under Colonel Cotton, and was present at the engagement at Sussia, 5th July '57, and retreat into the Fort of Agra. Present at the engagement at Coel, 24th August '57; at the action of Agra, 10th of October, and defeat of the rebels under Tantia Topee. *Medal.* Mentioned in General Orders of the Commander-in-Chief, 25th March '58.

ASSISTANT-SURGEON F. H. O'DONNEL,† M. D., Bengal Medical Establishment.

Asst.-Surgeon, 14 Jan. 54.

SERVICE.—Assistant-Surgeon O'DONNEL served as Field Assistant Surgeon with the Force under Lord Clyde, at the relief of Lucknow, in

November '57; at the battle of Cawnpore, in December '57; at the skirmish at the Kala Nuddee, and re-occupation of Futtehghur, in January '58; at the siege and capture of Lucknow, in February and March '58; with the Lucknow Field Hospital, till 14th March '57. Officiated as Medical Store-keeper to the Oude Field Force, from 1st September '58 to 14th March '59. *Medal and Clasps.*

LIEUTENANT J. W. O'DOWDA, P. H., late 50th Native Infantry.

Ensign, 12 Sept. 54—Lieut., 21 Aug. 57.

SERVICE.—Lieutenant O'DOWDA served during the Sonthal Campaign, '55.

BREVET-CAPTAIN C. S. W. OGILVIE, P., late 5th Europeans.

Ensign, 23 Aug. 45—Lieut., 5 May 51—Bt.-Captain, 23 Aug. 60.

BREVET-CAPTAIN F. D. OGILVIE, P. H., late 46th Native Infantry.

Ensign, 20 April 46—Lieut., 31 Dec. 51—Bt.-Captain, 20 April 61.

SERVICE.—Captain OGILVIE served during the Punjab Campaign, in '48, '49. Present at the affair of Ramnuggur, passage of the Chenab, action of Sadoolapore, Chillianwallah, and Goojerat. *Medal and 2 Clasps.*

BREVET-CAPTAIN J. S. OGILVIE, P. C., late 48th Native Infantry.

Ensign, 13 June 45—Lieut., 29 Sept. 50—Bt.-Captain, 13 June 60—Captain, 25 May 61.

SERVICE.—Captain OGILVIE served as Executive Commissariat Officer during the Sonthal Campaign, '55.

SURGEON H. A. OLDFIELD,† M. D., Bengal Medical Establishment.

Asst.-Surgeon, 25 July 46—Surgeon, 2 Dec. 59.

SERVICE.—Surgeon OLDFIELD served with the 13th Irregular Cavalry during the Punjab Campaign, '48, '49. *Medal.*

LIEUTENANT H. T. OLDFIELD, P. H., late 9th Native Infantry.

Ensign, 11 Dec. 49—Lieut., 7 Sept. 55.

(452)

ASSISTANT-SURGEON C. F. OLDHAM,† Bengal Medical Establishment.
Asst.-Surgeon, 27 July 59.

LIEUTENANT H. G. OLDHAM, late 9th Native Infantry.
Ensign, 4 Feb. 59—Lieut., 14 Dec. 59.
SERVICE.—Lieutenant OLDHAM served with Brigadier Wheeler's Saugor Field Force, in Bundlecund, during '59, '60.

LIEUTENANT H. H. OLDHAM,† late 67th Native Infantry.
Ensign, 4 Nov. 58—Lieut., 11 Sept. 59.
SERVICE.—Lieutenant OLDHAM served with the 8th Punjab Infantry with the China Expeditionary Force in '60. Present at the action of Sinho, capture of Jongkoo, and storm and capture of the North Taku Forts. *Medal and 2 Clasps.*

LIEUTENANT J. S. OLIPHANT,† late 5th Europeans.
Ensign, 4 Jan. 57—Lieut., 30 April 58.

LIEUTENANT T. T. OLIPHANT, late 5th Europeans.
Ensign, 4 April 58—Lieut., 3 Sept. 60.

CAPTAIN W. S. OLIPHANT, P. H., Bengal Engineers.
2nd Lieut., 12 Dec. 45—Lieut., 15 Feb. 54—2nd Captain, 27 Aug. 58—Captain, 18 Feb. 61.
SERVICE.—Captain OLIPHANT served at the siege of Mooltan, and present at the battle of Goojerat, '48. *Medal and Clasp.*

LIEUTENANT-GENERAL T. OLIVER, late 37th Native Infantry.
Ensign, 16 Nov. 03—Lieut., 18 May 05—Captain, 16 Nov. 18—Major, 18 July 27—Lieut.-Colonel, 3 July 32—Colonel, 13 March 44—Major-General, 20 June 54—Lieut.-General, 4 May 58.
SERVICE.—Lieutenant-General OLIVER served during the Nepal War, '15. *Medal.*

(453)

LIEUTENANT A. OLLIVANT, P. H., late 9th Native Infantry.

Ensign, 4 March 57—Lieut., 1 March 58.

SERVICE.—Lieutenant OLLIVANT served during the Indian Mutiny. Served with the Agra Volunteer Horse, in June and July '57, including a skirmish with the rebels at Mudrock. Present at the battle of Shahgunge, near Agra, 5th July, and battle of Agra, October '57. *Medal.*

LIEUTENANT-COLONEL W. OLPHERTS, C.B., P., V.C., Bengal Artillery.

2nd Lieut., 11 June 39—Lieut., 17 Aug. 41—Captain, 3 March 53—Bt.-Major, 19 Jan. 58—Bt.-Lieut.-Colonel, 24 March 58—Lieut.-Colonel, 18 Feb. 61.

SERVICE.—Lieutenant-Colonel W. OLPHERTS, C.B., V.C., was present at the action of Punniar, *Bronze Star;* and served with the Force under Sir Charles Napier against the Hill Tribes in Scinde. Served the Mutiny Campaign. *Medal and Clasps, Brevet of Major and Lieutenant-Colonel, C.B., and V.C.* Mentioned in various Despatches.

LIEUTENANT A. M. OMMANNEY, late 17th Native Infantry.

Ensign, 20 Jan. 59—Lieut., 27 Dec. 59.

SERVICE.—Lieutenant OMMANNEY served under Brigadier Chamberlain against the Mahsood Wuzeerees, in '61.

COLONEL E. L. OMMANNEY, Bengal Engineers.

2nd Lieut., 13 Dec. 27—Lieut., 22 Jan. 34—Bt.-Captain, 13 Dec. 42—Captain, 5 April 44—Bt.-Major, 20 June 54—Major, 15 April 56—Lieut.-Colonel, 1 Oct. 57—Colonel, 18 Feb. 61.

LIEUTENANT E. L. OMMANNEY, P., late 59th Native Infantry.

Ensign, 9 June 55—Lieut., 21 Aug. 57.

SERVICE.—Lieutenant OMMANNEY served with the Army before Delhi in '57. Present at the assault and capture of Delhi, 14th September '57. *Medal and Clasp.*

LIEUTENANT E. P. OMMANNEY, late 49th Native Infantry.
Ensign, 6 June 59—Lieut., 16 April 61.

LIEUTENANT M. W. OMMANNEY,† Bengal Artillery.
Lieut., 27 Aug. 58.

MAJOR A. W. ONSLOW,† late 41st Native Infantry.
Ensign, 13 June 35—Lieut., 28 Feb. 40—Captain, 13 Feb. 50—Major, 24 May 59.

SERVICE.—Major ONSLOW served during the China War, including the capture of Shin Changfoo, and investment of the city of Nankin. *Medal.* Served throughout the Sutlej Campaign, '45, '46. Present at the battle of Sobraon. *(Wounded.) Medal and Clasp. (Since retired.)*

LIEUTENANT W. P. ONSLOW, late 11th Native Infantry.
Ensign, 4 Aug. 58—Lieut., 4 April 60.

LIEUTENANT J. W. ORCHARD,† late 33rd Native Infantry.
Ensign, 20 Dec. 46—Lieut., 1 Oct. 53.

SERVICE.—Lieutenant ORCHARD served throughout the Mutinies, '57, '58. Present at the siege, storm, and capture of Delhi, 14th September '57. Served in the Mewat Country, Jhujjur, and Goorgaon District, '57, '58. Served with the Column under Major Ramsay in the Muttra District, '58. *Medal and Clasp.* Commanded the 6th Punjab Police Battalion and Khoshada Horse, of Dhera Ishmael Khan. Served under Brigadier Chamberlain in the Mahsood Expedition. Present at the forcing of the Berara Pass, March, April, and May '60. Favorably mentioned in the Punjab Report of '60.

LIEUTENANT M. A. D. ORCHARD,† late 3rd Europeans.
Ensign, 21 Jan. 50—Lieut., 17 Dec. 55.

SERVICE.—Lieutenant ORCHARD served during the Mutinies of '57, '58. Present in the actions fought near Agra, on the 5th July '57 and 10th October '57, and other minor operations. *Medal.*

(455)

LIEUTENANT C. E. ORMAN, P. H., late 29th Native Infantry.

Ensign, 11 Jan. 51—Lieut., 14 Jan. 56.

SERVICE.—Lieutenant ORMAN served under Lord Clyde in Eusuffzaie and Ranezaie, and against the Momunds and other Hill Tribes, '51, '52. Served in the defence of the Kumaon Hills. Present at the affair at Huldwanee, against the Rohilcund rebels, 18th September '57.

CAPTAIN A. E. OSBORN, P. H., late 45th Native Infantry.

Ensign, 30 Dec. 43—Lieut., 22 March 49—Captain, 23 Nov. 56.

SERVICE.—Captain OSBORN was present throughout the Punjab Campaign, including the battles of Chillianwallah and Goojerat. *Medal and Clasps.* Served as Orderly Officer to Colonel Gerrard at the action of Narnoul, also present at the minor affairs of Gungeeree, Puttiallee, and Mynpooree. Served with the 1st Bengal Fusiliers at the capture of Lucknow. *Medal and Clasp.*

CAPTAIN D. H. OSBORN, P. H., late 54th Native Infantry.

Ensign, 27 Dec. 45—Lieut., 18 July 48—Captain, 13 May 57.

SERVICE.—Captain OSBORN served with a Column under Sir T. Seaton, at the actions of Gungeeree, Puttiallee, and Mynpooree.

LIEUTENANT H. R. OSBORN, P. H., late 74th Native Infantry.

Ensign, 9 Dec. 50—Lieut , 23 Nov. 56.

SERVICE.—Lieutenant OSBORN served as Brigade Major to the Cavalry portion of the Force employed on the Eusuffzaie Frontier, in April and May '58, under Major-General Cotton, and mentioned in that Officer's Despatch, published in G. O., 17th June '58. (Has passed an examination in Field Engineering.)

LIEUTENANT R. D. OSBORN, P. H., late 26th Native Infantry.

Ensign, 20 Dec. 53—Lieut., 30 July 57.

SERVICE.—Lieutenant OSBORN served during the Mutiny, '57, '58, and '59. Present at the actions of Boolundshuhur and Allyghur, September '57. In Command of a Detachment, 4th Punjab Infantry, at the actions of

Gungeeree and Puttiallee. Present in various operations against the rebels in the Agra District, in '57, '58. Served with Colonel Troup's Column in Oude. Present at the action of Biswah, November and December '58. Served with the Saugor Field Force, from January to May '59. Commanded a Field Detachment in the Ooraie District. Defeated a party of rebels at Tudhoorkee, July '59. Served with the Bundlecund Field Force under Brigadier Wheeler, '59, '60. *Medal.*

LIEUTENANT J. H. W. OSBORNE,† late 44th Native Infantry.

Ensign, 4 July 58—Lieut., 23 Dec. 58.

SERVICE.—Lieutenant OSBORNE served with the 73rd Foot in Brigadier Rowcroft's Column during the Campaign in the Terai, from 4th November '58 to July '59. Present at the attack made by the rebels on the Column under Major Ross, H. M.'s 73rd, and some minor affairs under Majors Ross and Gawler. *Medal.*

SURGEON-MAJOR SIR W. B. O'SHAUGHNESSY, K.T., M.D., F.R.C.S., Bengal Medical Establishment.

Asst.-Surgeon, 8 Aug. 33—Surgeon, 5 Dec. 48—Surgeon-Major, 13 Jan. 60.

(Since retired.)

BREVET-MAJOR R. OUSELEY, P., late 34th Native Infantry.

Ensign, 29 July 39—Lieut., 1 Aug. 41—Captain, 21 Feb. 52—Bt.-Major, 26 April 59.

SERVICE.—Major OUSELEY served during the Campaign in Rohilcund in '58. Present at the actions of Kukraolee, 30th April '58, and Bareilly, 5th May '58. Mentioned in the Despatch of His Excellency the Commander-in-Chief, 8th May '58. Present in Command of 22nd Punjab Infantry, at the relief of Shahjehanpore, 11th May '58. Mentioned in the Despatch of Brigadier Jones. Present at the partial action at Shahjehanpore, 15th May '58, and at the capture of Shahbad, 1st June '58. Mentioned in the Despatch of Lieutenant-Colonel Taylor, and in the Despatch of Brigadier Jones. Received the thanks of the Governor-General. *Medal.* Promoted to the rank of Brevet-Major for service in the Rohilcund Campaign.

(457)

CAPTAIN R. OUSELEY, P. C., late 48th Native Infantry.

Ensign, 11 June 47—Lieut., 1 Oct. 52—Captain, 18 Feb. 61.

SERVICE.—Lieutenant OUSELEY served during the Punjab Campaign, '48, '49. Present at the affair of Ramnuggur, and actions of Sadoolapore, Chillianwallah, and Goojerat. *Medal and 2 Clasps.* Served during the Mutinies, '57, '58. Present at the Mutiny at Lucknow, 30th May '57; at the action of Chinhut, 30th June; at the defence and evacuation of the Muchee Bhawun, 2nd July '57; and throughout the defence of Lucknow. Present during the operations at Cawnpore against the Gwalior Contingent; at the battle of Cawnpore, 6th December '57; at the operations at Tuttya, and west of the Grand Trunk Road; at the occupation of Futtehpore; at the siege and capture of Lucknow, March '58. *Medal and 2 Clasps, and one year's extra service.* Mentioned in the Despatch of Major Apthorp, 20th October '57. Performed the duties of an Artillery Officer, and had charge of 1 eighteen-pounder and 2 nine-pounders at Gubbins' out-post, during the siege of Lucknow, from July to November '57, and commanded the Native Artillery men there posted. Brought to notice of the Commander-in-Chief in the Despatch of Brigadier Inglis, 12th November '57.

LIEUTENANT A. G. OWEN, P. H., late 1st European Bengal Fusiliers.

2nd Lieut., 4 Oct. 55—Lieut., 23 Nov. 56.

SERVICE.—Lieutenant OWEN was present at the battle of Badlee-ka-Serai in all the subsequent engagements under the walls of Delhi, including the affair of Nudjufghur. Present at the storm and capture of Delhi, 14th September '57. *(Dangerously wounded.) Medal and Clasp.*

CAPTAIN A. W. OWEN, P. H., late 11th Native Infantry.

Ensign, 21 Aug. 40—Lieut., 7 April 45—Bt.-Captain, 21 Aug. 55—Captain, 4 April 60.

SERVICE.—Captain OWEN served with the 11th Native Infantry in Bundlecund, against the insurgents, in '42, '43, under Brigadier Young. Present with the Regiment throughout the Sutlej Campaign, in '45, '46. Present at Ferozeshuhur. *Medal.* Present at the capture of Kôt Kangra, in '46. Present with the 11th Regiment on the evening of the 10th May '57.

K 2

(458)

Lieutenant G. A. OWEN, P. H., late 3rd Europeans.
  Ensign, 20 April 58—Lieut., 24 Dec. 60.

Captain S. R. J. OWEN,† A.K.C., late 19th Native Infantry.
  Ensign, 20 June 43—Lieut., 1 March 50—Bt.-Captain, 20 June 58—Captain, 12 Dec. 59.

Lieutenant W. OWEN,† late 61st Native Infantry.
  Ensign, 14 Dec. 53.—Lieut., 23 Nov. 56.

P

Lieutenant C. F. PACKE, P. H., late 4th Native Infantry.
  Ensign, 10 Dec. 47—Lieut., 12 Nov. 50.
  Service.—Lieutenant Packe served with the Force under Brigadier Wheeler, in the Punjab Campaign, '48, '49. *Medal.* Served as a Volunteer with the Army before Delhi, '57. *(Wounded severely.)* (In receipt of a wound pension.) *Medal and Clasp.* (Passed the examination in Field Engineering.)

Lieutenant E. PACKE, late 37th Native Infantry.
  Ensign, 11 Dec. 57—Lieut., 13 Oct. 60.

Lieutenant A. C. PADDAY, Bengal Engineers.
  Lieut., 27 Aug. 58.

Veterinary-Surgeon T. P. PAGE,† Bengal Veteran Establishment.
  Vety.-Surgeon, 21 Nov. 49.

Captain W. H. PAGET, P. H.
  Ensign, 13 June 46—Lieut., 15 Nov. 53—Captain, 8 June 57.
  (Has furnished certificates of qualification in Surveying and Civil Engineering.)

(459)

LIEUTENANT H. A. PAKENHAM,† late 55th Native Infantry.
Ensign, 15 Aug. 57—Lieut., 18 May 58.
SERVICE.—Lieutenant PAKENHAM served with Brigadier Douglas' Force in the Shahabad District, under Colonel Dunsford, '58, '59. Served on the Nepal Frontier in '59, and in China in '60. Present at the actions of Sinho and Chunkia-wan, in China. *Medal and Clasp*.

CAPTAIN C. H. PALLISER, P. H., late 63rd Native Infantry.
Ensign, 11 June 47—Lieut., 15 Nov. 53—Captain, 7 April 60.
SERVICE.—Captain PALLISER served in an expedition against the Shewanee Tribes, on the Dera Jât Frontier, in March '53. Served during the Mutinies, '57, '58. Present at the action of Futtehpore, 12th June '57, and re-occupation of Cawnpore; at the actions of Munglewar, 21st; Alum Bagh, 23rd; and relief of Lucknow, 25th September '57; occupation of Alum Bagh by Sir James Outram; action of Gabelee, 22nd December '57; repulse of rebel attack on the Fort of Jellallabad, 25th February '58; capture of Lucknow, March '58; re-occupation of Fyzabad and Sultanpore, in Oude, by Sir Hope Grant; action of Daoodpore, 22nd October; and repulse and pursuit of the rebels at the Khundoo Nuddee, 26th October '58. *Severely wounded* in the action against the Shewanees, in the Drabund Pass, 14th March '53. (*Wounded* on 2nd July '57 and 25th September '57; *dangerously wounded*, 26th Octobe '58.) *Medal and 2 Clasps*. Mentioned in the Despatch of Sir H. Havelock, 12th July '57. Mentioned in Despatch of Brigadier Horsford, 22nd October '58. (In receipt of a pension of £70 a year for *wound* received at Daoodpore, 26th October '58.)

LIEUTENANT A. P. PALMER, late 5th Europeans.
Ensign, 4 Feb. 57—Lieut., 30 April 58.
SERVICE.—Lieutenant PALMER served throughout the Mutinies, '57, '58, and '59. Present at the action of Nawabgunge, Barabunki, 13th June '58 (*horse killed*); and the minor affairs in the Oude Campaign, till its conclusion on the Nepal Frontier, December '59. *Medal*.

(460)

SURGEON C. PALMER,† M.D., Bengal Medical Establishment.
Asst.-Surgeon, 20 Feb. 46—Surgeon, 26 July 59.

LIEUTENANT C. H. PALMER, late 55th Native Infantry.
Ensign, 12 June 58—Lieut., 27 Aug. 58.

CAPTAIN C. O'B. PALMER, P. H., late 1st European Bengal Fusiliers.
2nd Lieut., 9 June 43—Lieut., 29 Oct. 45—Captain, 20 March 54.

SERVICE.—Captain PALMER served during the Sutlej Campaign, '45, '46. Present at the actions of Ferozeshuhur and Sobraon. *(Slightly wounded.)* *Medal and 2 Clasps.* Served in the Burmah Campaign, '52, '53. Present at the relief of the Garrison of Pegu, 14th December '52, and the operations in its vicinity. Accompanied the Martaban Column under General Steel. *Medal and Clasp.*

BREVET-COLONEL (LIEUTENANT-COLONEL) H. PALMER, P. C., late 48h Native Infantry.
Ensign, 13 Feb. 26—Lieut., 27 June 35—Captain, 16 Oct. 40—Bt.-Major, 3 April 46—Major, 5 June 53—Bt.-Lieut.-Colonel, 20 June 54—Lieut.-Colonel, 4 Oct. 57—Bt.-Colonel, 29 July 57.

SERVICE.—Colonel PALMER was with Brigadier Burgh's Force against the Bheel Tribes, near Mount Aboo, in '27, '28; with the Army of the Indus from '38 to '40, during which was employed:—As Regimental Quarter-Master, 48th Native Infantry; as Brigade Quarter-Master to Brigadier R. Sale's Brigade; as Detachment Staff on different occasions; as Post-Master at Head Quarters for Affghanistan; as Persian Interpreter to Major-General Sir W. Cotton, Commanding in Affghanistan. Present in several affairs with Beloochees and Khyberries. (*Wounded severely* by a matchlock ball through left thigh in a skirmish with Beloochees, at the entrance to the Bolan Pass, on the 20th March '39.) Present at the storming and capture of Ghuznee, 23rd July '39. *Medal for Ghuznee.* Charge of presents from Cabul from His Majesty Shah Shooja-ool-Moolk to the Right Hon'ble the Earl of Auckland, Governor-General of India, and returned to the Provinces in '41. With the Sutlej Army in '45, '46. Commanded the 48th Native Infantry throughout the actions of

(461)

Moodkee, 18th; and Ferozeshuhur, 21st and 22nd December '45. Mentioned in the Reports of Acting Brigadier T. Ryan, Commanding 1st Infantry Brigade, to Major-General Sir H. G. Smith, Commanding the Division. Present in the action of Alliwal, and on the Field was appointed to succeed the Major of Brigade, 1st Brigade, on his retiring severely wounded. *(Wounded slightly.)* Vide Despatch on Alliwal. Mentioned in G. O., 21st February '46. *Promoted to Major by Brevet for service in the Sutlej Campaign. Medal and 2 Clasps.* Served as Brigade Major to the entire Force of all arms, under Brigadier Wheeler, at the reduction of Kôt Kangra, in '46. The Force received the thanks of the Government of India in a letter from the Foreign Department. Served as Brigade Major with the entire Force of Artillery, Cavalry, and Infantry detached from Jullundur under Brigadier Wheeler, to co-operate with one from Lahore, the whole commanded by Sir John Littler, as a demonstration against Cashmere, in '46, '47. Served as Brigade Major to the entire Force of all Arms under General Wheeler, in the Army of the Punjab, in '49. Present at the storming of the Dullah Heights and reduction of three small Forts. The Force received the thanks of the Indian Government in a letter from the Foreign Department. *Medal.* Present in the action of Chinhut on the 30th June '57, in Command of native details from mutinied Regiments. Present in, and commanding the Muchee Bhawun Fort, from the firing of the first rebel shot against it, to the withdrawal of the Garrison during the night of the second day. Organized by written instructions, and commanded at the withdrawal of the Muchee Bhawun Garrison, a service mentioned as follows in Brigadier Inglis' Despatch, dated 26th September '57, omitting to name the Commander:—" The untoward event of the 30th June so far diminished the whole available Force, that we had not a sufficient number of men remaining to occupy both positions. The Brigadier-General, therefore, on the evening of the 1st July, signalled to the Garrison of the Muchee Bhawun to evacuate and blow up that Fortress in the course of the night. The orders were ably carried out, and at 12 P. M. the Force marched into the Residency with their guns and treasure, without the loss of a man; and shortly afterwards the explosion of 240 barrels of gunpowder and 6,000,000 ball cartridges, which were lying in the Magazine, announced to Sir Henry Lawrence and his Officers, who were anxiously waiting

(462)

the report, the complete destruction of that Fort and all that it contained. If it had not been for this wise and strategic measure, no member of the Lucknow Garrison, in all probability, would have survived to tell the tale." Served in the defence of the Lucknow Residency to its relief. *Medal and Clasp.* Commanded a small Detachment of 2 Guns, 80 Cavalry, and 150 Infantry sent from Cawnpore against rebels, in '58. *Extracts from the Report of Acting Brigadier T. Ryan, K.H., of H. M.'s 50th, to Major-General Sir H. G. Smith, K.C.B., Commanding Division, Sutlej Army, 26th December '45* :—" It may not properly be within my province to report upon the battle of Moodkee, on the 18th instant, Brigadier Wheeler having then commanded the Brigade, but I cannot refrain from recording the gallant conduct of the 48th Native Infantry, under Captain Palmer, which kept side by side with H. M.'s 50th throughout the action." And reporting on the action of Ferozeshuhur, 21st and 22nd of December '46—" I must bear testimony to the cool and gallant conduct of Captain Palmer, Commanding the 48th Native Infantry, who led his Regiment into action, more with the precision of a parade than of a battle."*

LIEUTENANT R. H. PALMER, P. H., Bengal Artillery.
Lieut., 27 Aug. 58.

LIEUTENANT W. D. PALMER, late 74th Native Infantry.
Ensign, 14 June 56—Lieut., 18 Sept. 57.

SERVICE.—Lieutenant PALMER served in China in '58, under Major-General Van Straubenzee, at Canton.

ASSISTANT-SURGEON W. J. PALMER,† Bengal Medical Establishment.
Asst.-Surgeon, 7 Sept. 54.

2ND CAPTAIN W. H. PARISH, P. H., Bengal Artillery.
2nd Lieut., 14 June 45—Lieut., 17 April 49—2nd Captain, 27 Aug. 58.

SERVICE.—Captain PARISH served in the Sutlej Campaign, '46, '47; expedition against Kangra, '47; Punjab Campaign, '48, '49. *Medal.*

---

* Colonel Palmer certifies to the strict truth, though not actual position of words, of the above two extracts, the copy given him by Colonel Ryan having been burnt at Lucknow.

(463)

Present at the forcing of the Kohat Pass, November '53. Served throughout the Mutiny, '57, '58.

LIEUTENANT A. W. PARKER, General List.
Ensign, 4 July 59—Lieut., 24 Sept. 59.

LIEUTENANT SIR G. L. M. PARKER,† *Bart.*, late 36th Native Infantry.
Ensign, 13 June 57—Lieut., 18 May 58.

SERVICE.—Lieutenant PARKER served during the Mutinies, '57, '58, and '59. Present at the actions of Pandoo Nuddee, Cawnpore, Boynepore, Rooya, Allygunge, Bareilly, and Pusgaon. *Medal.*

LIEUTENANT N. F. PARKER, General List.
Ensign, 9 April 59—Lieut., 25 July 60.

ASSISTANT-SURGEON R. PARKER,† M.D., Bengal Medical Establishment.
Asst.-Surgeon, 1 Jan. 49.

LIEUTENANT W. J. PARKER, P. H., late 4th Native Infantry.
Ensign, 4 Nov. 58—Lieut., 26 Aug. 60.

LIEUTENANT B. S. B. PARLBY, P. H., late 6th Europeans.
Ensign, 11 Jan. 51—Lieut., 7 May 54.

SERVICE.—Lieutenant PARLBY served in the suppression of the Sonthal Insurrection in '55; with the Force under General Sir John Jones through Rohilcund, in '58. Present at the actions of Bhagoowalla, Nugeena, and Burnaie, on the Oude Frontier. *Medal.*

CAPTAIN B. PARROTT, P. H., late 37th Native Infantry.
Ensign, 19 Aug. 40—Lieut., 16 July 42—Captain, 8 Dec. 50.

SERVICE.—Captain PARROTT served in Affghanistan with the Force under General Pollock. *Medal.*

LIEUTENANT W. PARRY, Bengal Veteran Establishment.
Lieut., 12 July 58.

LIEUTENANT B. J. PARSONS,† late 23rd Native Infantry.
Ensign, 15 May 56—Lieut., 26 April 58.

ASSISTANT-SURGEON F. PARSONS,† Bengal Medical Establishment.
Asst.-Surgeon, 10 Feb. 59.

SERVICE.—Assistant-Surgeon PARSONS served with the Army through the late Campaign in China, '60. Present at the actions of Singho, Chunkia-wan, and Tongchow. *Medal and Clasp.*

✯MAJOR-GENERAL J. PARSONS, C.B., late 50th Native Infantry.
Ensign, 24 May 06—Lieut., 13 Aug. 12—Bt.-Captain, 24 May 21—Major, 22 April 36—Bt-Lieut.-Colonel, 23rd July 39—Lieut.-Colonel, 7 July 42—Bt.-Colonel, 16 July 49—Colonel, 31 March 53—Major-General, 28 Nov. 54.

SERVICE.—Major-General PARSONS, C.B., served at the capture of the Isle of France, '10, '11; Nepal Campaign, '15, '16. *Medal.* Pindarree War, '17, '18; Rajpootanah, '20; with the Army of the Indus, '39. Present at the assault and capture of Ghuznee. *(Wounded.) Medal, Brevet-Lieutenant-Colonel, and 2nd Class Dooranee Order.* Battle of Punniar. *Bronze Star.* Throughout the Campaign on the Sutlej, including the actions of Moodkee, Ferozeshuhur, and Sobraon. *Medal, 2 Clasps, and C.B.*

CAPTAIN J. E. B. PARSONS, P., late 5th Europeans.
Ensign, 20 Dec. 48—Lieut., 15 Nov. 53—Captain, 18 Nov. 60.

CAPTAIN N. J. PARSONS, P. H., late 1st European Bengal Fusiliers.
2nd Lieut., 26 July 45—Lieut., 29 June 49—Captain, 12 March 58.

SERVICE.—Captain PARSONS served with the Army of Burmah, '52, '53. *Medal and Clasp.* Present at the re-capture of Pegu, 21st November '52; at the relief of the Garrison of Pegu, 14th December '52; and throughout the operations in its vicinity accompanied the Martaban Column under General Steel. Present with H. M.'s 64th in defending the Cantonments and Town of Cawnpore, under General Windham, in '57. *Dangerously wounded*, 28th November '57. *Medal.*

LIEUTENANT Q. D. PARSONS, P. H., late 6th Europeans.
Ensign, 20 Jan. 50—Lieut., 20 Feb. 56.

LIEUTENANT J. C. PARTRIDGE, late 1st European Bengal Fusiliers.
2nd Lieut., 20 Sept. 57—Lieut.

SERVICE.—Lieutenant PARTRIDGE served with the Central India Field Force under Sir Hugh Rose, in '57, '58. *Medal and Clasp*. Present with the 2nd Brigade in all the engagements in the Saugor District. Present at the siege and capture of Jhansi; battles of Baitwa and Koonch, actions at, and before Calpee. Present with the 1st Bengal Fusiliers during the operations in Oude. Mentioned in the Despatch of Sir Hugh Rose, '58.

BREVET-SURGEON S. B. PARTRIDGE, F.R.C.S.E., P. C. H., Bengal Medical Establishment.

Asst.-Surgeon, 12 Oct. 52—Bt.-Surgeon, 7 Sept. 58.

SERVICE.—Brevet-Surgeon PARTRIDGE served in the Burmese Campaign of '53. Present with the Force under Sir J. Cheape at Donabew, in March '53. *Medal*. Was a Member of the Lucknow Garrison throughout the defence of the Garrison in '57 subsequent to the relief. Served as Field Assistant-Surgeon with Army Head Quarters. Present at the defeat of the Gwalior rebels at Cawnpore, at the passage of the Kala Nuddee, the re-occupation of Futtehghur, and at the final siege and re-capture of Lucknow. *Medal, 2 Clasps, and 1 year's extra service.* Services mentioned in the Despatch of Brigadier Inglis, Commanding. Received the thanks of the Government of India. Promoted to Brevet-Surgeon for distinguished services at Lucknow.

ASSISTANT-SURGEON C. T. PASKE,† Bengal Medical Establishment.
Asst.-Surgeon, 26 Aug. 52.

SERVICE.—Assistant-Surgeon PASKE served in Burmah with the Field Hospital, '53. *Medal*. Present during the engagement at Azimghur against the Pulwars, July '57. In Medical Charge of the Goorkha Field

Force under Lieutenant-Colonel Wroughton. Present at the actions of Guggah, Koodwah, and Chandah. *Medal.*

LIEUTENANT E. H. PASKE, P., late 53rd Native Infantry.
Ensign, 26 Dec. 46—Lieut., 16 July 49.

CAPTAIN W. PASKE, P. H., late 28th Native Infantry.
Ensign, 11 Feb. 45—Lieut., 1 May 52—Captain, 4 June 57.

SERVICE.—Captain PASKE served during the Punjab Campaign, '48, '49. Present in several expeditions against the Hill Tribes on the Peshawur Frontier, and was present with the Force sent into Eusuffzaie under Lord Clyde. Commanded a Detachment in pursuit of the Jullundur rebels, in '57. Received the special thanks of the Secretary of State for India, of the Governor-General, and of Sir J. Lawrence, for discovering and frustrating a plot formed by the Left Wing, 4th Native Infantry, in '58, to murder their Officers and all the Europeans in the Station.

LIEUTENANT G. J. PASLEY, P. H., late 6th Europeans.
Ensign, 20 Dec. 50—Lieut., 26 April 54.
SERVICE.—Lieutenant PASLEY served in the Sonthal Campaign, '55.

CAPTAIN A. PATERSON, P. H., late 2nd European Bengal Fusiliers.
2nd Lieut., 9 Dec. 43—Lieut., 12 June 47—Captain, 1 May 58.

SERVICE.—Captain PATERSON served during the Punjab Campaign, '48, '49. Present at the affair at Ramnuggur, and actions of Chillianwallah and Goojerat, and subsequent pursuit of the Sikhs and Affghans. *Medal and 2 Clasps.* Served in Burmah in '53, '54. Present at the operations against the rebels in Pegu. *Medal and Clasp.* Served with the Delhi Field Force in the Bikaneer District, under Major Boyd, in '59.

CAPTAIN A. H. PATERSON, P., late 68th Native Infantry.
Ensign, 3 March 42—Lieut., 14 April 44—Captain, 20 April 55.

(467)

SURGEON-MAJOR G. PATON,† A.M., M.D., Bengal Medical Establishment.
Asst.-Surgeon, 24 Jan. 35—Surgeon, 10 Aug. 49—Surgeon-Major, 30 Jan. 60.

SERVICE.—Surgeon-Major PATON served in Scinde and Affghanistan with the Army of the Indus: present at the storm and capture of Ghuznee, *Medal;* at the operations in the Khyber Pass; and was with the Field Hospital in the Campaign of the Sutlej.

COLONEL J. S. PATON, P. H., late 14th Native Infantry.
Ensign, 12 June 37—Lieut., 3 Oct. 40—Captain, 8 Feb. 51—Bt.-Major, 9 Feb. 51—Lieut.-Colonel, 28 Nov. 54—Bt.-Colonel, 28 Nov. 57—Major in Staff Corps, 18 Feb. 61.

SERVICE.—Colonel PATON served with Army of Gwalior in '43. Present and commanded Light Company, 14th Native Infantry, at battle of Maharajpore. *Bronze Star.* Served with Army of Sutlej in '45, '46. Present as Adjutant, 14th Native Infantry, at investment of Ferozepore by Sikh Army, in '45. Present as Adjutant, and also commanded Detachment of 14th Native Infantry at battle of Ferozeshuhur. *Medal.* Mentioned twice in Despatches of this action. Mentioned specially for " gallant behaviour" in the Despatch of Sir W. Gilbert, and Despatch of Sir John Littler. In consequence of the above, at once appointed to the Quarter-Master General's Department and Staff of the 3rd Division, commanded by Sir Robert Dick. Present as D. A. Q. M. G. at battle and storm of the Entrenchments of Sobraon, 10th February '46. *Clasp.* Mentioned in the Despatch of Brigadier Stacy, who succeeded to the Command on Sir Robert Dick being *mortally wounded;* also in that, dated 13th February '46, of the Commander-in-Chief, Lord Gough, and in G. G. O., dated 14th February '46. For Colonel (then Lieutenant) Paton's services in this Campaign, the Court of Directors, in a Public Despatch, recorded their approbation of his conduct, and recommended him to the protection of the Supreme Government in India, as stated in a demi-official communication to the Government of India. Served as Senior Officer, Quarter-Master General's Department, at the reduction of the Hill Fortress of Kôt Kangra, in '46. Mentioned in Despatch of Brigadier Wheeler; also in Field Force Orders, dated

(468)

Kangra, 29th May '46; and acknowledged in letter No. 216, dated 15th June '46, from the Governor-General to the Commander-in-Chief. Served again as Senior Officer, Quarter-Master General's Department, with the Advance Column of the Field Force ordered to Cashmere, in '46. Mentioned in District Orders by Brigadier Wheeler, Commanding the Column; and also in Orders by Sir John Littler. Served as Senior Officer, Quarter-Master General's Department, at the reduction of the Fort of Rungul Mungul, Punjab, '48. Mentioned in the Despatch, dated 15th October '48, of Brigadier Wheeler, Commanding the Force; also in the Orders of the same date. This service acknowledged in a letter from Adjutant-General of the Army, to Officer Commanding Punjab Division. Served in the Punjab Campaign, '48, '49, being attached as D. A. Q. M. G. to the Head Quarters of Lord Gough. Present at the affair of Ramnuggur, on the Chenab, November '48. Appointed *specially* as Senior Departmental Officer to conduct the Column from the Main Army, under Sir Joseph Thackwell, at the passage of the Chenab and battle of Sadoolapore, 1st to 6th December '48. Mentioned twice in the Despatch, dated 6th December '48, of Sir Joseph Thackwell; also acknowledged in that, dated 10th December '48, of the Commander-in-Chief, and in a General Order by the Governor-General. Present with Army Head Quarters at the battle of Chillianwallah. *(Wounded severely.) Medal.* Mentioned in Despatch of His Excellency the Commander-in-Chief, and in G. G. O., dated 27th January '49; also by the Court of Directors, published in G. G. O. Served as D. A. Q. M. G. with the expedition against the Affreedies, and forcing the Kohat Pass, near Peshawur, under Sir Charles Napier. Mentioned in the Despatch, dated 16th February '50, of Sir Colin Campbell. Served with the Force employed to suppress the Googaira Insurrection, Punjab, '57; and commanded the Field Detachment sent from Lahore, which was thrice engaged. Promoted to rank of Major by Brevet for services in the Punjab Campaign. Mentioned twenty-seven times in Despatches and Orders.

CAPTAIN R. M. PATON, P., Bengal Artillery.

2nd Lieut., 10 Dec. 41—Lieut., 20 Feb. 44—Captain, 31 Dec. 54.

SERVICE.—Captain PATON was present in the actions of Moodkee and Ferozeshuhur, '45. *(Wounded.) Medal and Clasp.* Served with the expedition to Kangra, '46, under Brigadier Wheeler; and with Brigadier-General Wheeler's Force, in '48, '49. *Medal.*

LIEUTENANT-COLONEL C. PATTENSON,† late 4th Native Infantry.

Ensign, 4 Dec. 25—Lieut., 8 Oct. 39—Bt.-Captain, 4 Dec. 40—Captain, 22 Aug. 47—Bt.-Major, 11 Nov. 51—Major, 26 April 58—Lieut.-Colonel, 25 Oct. 59.

SERVICE.—Lieutenant-Colonel PATTENSON served during the Punjab Campaign, '48, '49. *Medal.* Commanded 4 Companies, 4th Native Infantry, with a Force under Colonel C. Halket, on the Peshawur Frontier, in '55. (*Wounded severely and dangerously*, 27th March '55.)

LIEUTENANT-GENERAL W. PATTLE, C.B., late 3rd Bengal European Cavalry.

Cornet, 9 Dec. 1800—Lieut., 11 May 05—Captain, 8 June 16—Major, 26 June 26—Lieut.-Colonel, 27 April 33— Bt.-Colonel, 4 July 43—Colonel, 5 Jan. 44—Major-General, 20 June 54—Lieut.-General, 18 July 56.

SERVICE.—Lieutenant-General PATTLE, C.B., served in Oude and Rohilcund, '02; throughout Lord Lake's Campaign, '04, '05. Present at Sarsnee, Bidjyghur, '02; Coel, Allyghur, Delhi, Agra, Laswarrie, Shumlee, and Futtehghur, '03; capture of Deig, '04, *Medal;* assault of Bhurtpore, '05; Campaign in Bundlecund under General Sir Thomas Brown, '10, '11; siege and capture of Kulinger, '12; with the Right Wing of Lord Hastings' Army during the Pindarree War, '17, '18, and '19; and commanded the Cavalry of Sir Charles Napier's Force at the actions of Meeanee and Hydrabad. *Medal, 2 Clasps, C. B., and A. D. C. to the Queen.*

LIEUTENANT J. A. M. PATTON,† late 1st Bengal European Cavalry.
Cornet, 20 April 54—Lieut., 3 May 56.

LIEUTENANT-COLONEL R. PATTON, P., 107th Foot.

Ensign, 3 Jan. 36—Lieut., 3 Oct. 40—Bt.-Captain, 3 Jan. 51—Captain, 15 Nov. 53—Bt.-Major, 28 Nov. 56—Major, 26 April 59—Lieut.-Colonel, 30 July 62.

SERVICE.—Lieutenant-Colonel PATTON served throughout the Indian Mutinies of '57, '58. Present at the action near Agra against the Indore and Mhow mutineers, on 10th October; alsoat Futtehpore-Sikree, with the Column under Colonel H. Cotton, C.B., 28th October '57. *Medal.*

LIEUTENANT-GENERAL M. N. PAUL, late 29th Native Infantry.

Ensign, 23 Nov. 05—Lieut., 23 Feb. 07—Captain, 9 Oct. 18—Major, 11th April 28—Lieut.-Colonel, 15 Sept. 33—Colonel, 2 Feb. 45—Major-General, 20 June 54—Lieut.-General, 17th May 59.

SERVICE.—Lieutenant-General PAUL served at the capture of the Cape of Good Hope, in '05, '06; also at the capture of the Isle of France, in '10, '11. Served during the Goorkha Campaigns of '14, '15, and '16, including the affairs of Jeetghur and Brootwal, in the Maharatta Campaign of '17, '18. Present at the capture of Mundlah. Served with the Volunteer Battalion ordered to Ceylon in '18, '19, and with the 1st Grenadier Battalion at Arracan, in '25, '26. *Medal.*

LIEUTENANT-GENERAL T. H. PAUL, late 20th Native Infantry.

Ensign, 4 Sept. 01—Lieut., 30 Sept. 03—Captain, 16 Dec. 14—Major, 7 Nov. 24—Lieut.-Colonel, 30 July 28—Bt.-Colonel, 22 Jan. 34—Colonel, 9 July 40—Major-General, 23 Nov. 41—Lieut.-General, 11 Nov. 51.

SERVICE.—Lieutenant-General PAUL served at the capture of Java, '10. *(Wounded.) Medal.*

ASSISTANT-SURGEON A. J. PAYNE, M.D., B.A., P. H., Bengal Medical Establishment.

Asst.-Surgeon, 20 Dec. 48.

LIEUTENANT H. P. PEACOCK, P. C. H., late 3rd Bengal European Cavalry.

Cornet, 20th Sept. 56—Lieut., 9 Jan. 57.

BREVET-MAJOR A. PEARSON, P. H., Bengal Artillery.

2nd Lieut., 9 Dec. 42—Lieut., 3 July 45—Bt.-Captain, 9 Dec. 57—Captain, 1 Jan. 58—Bt.-Major, 20 July 58.

SERVICE.—Major PEARSON served throughout the Sutlej Campaign, '45, '46. Was present in the actions of Moodkee, Ferozeshuhur, and

(471)

Sobraon, *Medal and 2 Clasps;* also throughout the Punjab Campaign, '48, '49; and was present in the actions of Ramnuggur, Sadoolapore, Chillianwallah, and Goojerat. *Medal and 2 Clasps.* Was present during the Mutiny of '57, '58, in several affairs in the Muttra and Allyghur Districts; in the actions at Agra, 5th July and 10th October *(wounded);* at the siege of Lucknow and at the capture of the Fort of Birwa, during the operations in Oude, '58, '59. *Medal and Clasp, and Brevet-Majority.*

ASSISTANT-SURGEON F. PEARSON,† Bengal Medical Establishment.

Asst.-Surgeon, 2nd July 48.

LIEUTENANT T. H. PEARSON,† 1st Goorkha Light Infantry.

Ensign, 13 June 57—Lieut., 18 May 58.

SERVICE.—Lieutenant PEARSON served under General Windham at Cawnpore, 27th and 28th November '57. During the attacks made by the rebels on the Fort, November and December '57. Served with H. M.'s 42nd Highlanders under Lord Clyde throughout the operations at, and capture of, Lucknow, March '58. *Medal and Clasp.* Served under Brigadier-General Walpole at the attack on Fort Rooya, April '58; at the action and capture of Bareilly, May '58, under Lord Clyde; also at the defeat of the Gwalior rebels, December '57. Served with the Force under Brigadier Troup, with the 66th Goorkha Light Infantry, against the rebels in Oude, '58, '59. Present at the actions of Pusgaon, 19th October '58; Russoolpore, 25th October '58; attack and capture of Fort Mittowlee, 8th November '58, and action of Biswah, 1st December '58.

LIEUTENANT J. R. PEARSON, P. H., late 27th Native Infantry.

Ensign, 20 Feb. 57—Lieut., 30 April 58.

SERVICE.—Lieutenant PEARSON was present at the mutiny of the late 6th Native Infantry, at Allahabad, in June '57. Served in the operations in re-taking the City and Cantonments of Allahabad from the rebels, with the Force under Sir Henry Havelock. Was present at the actions of Futtehpore, Aong, Pandoo Nuddee, Cawnpore, Oonao, Busseerutgunge

(1st and 2nd), Barby-ka-Chowky, Bithoor, Mungulwar, Alum Bagh, and 1st relief of Lucknow. Served with the Garrison of Lucknow until the final relief of that city. *Medal and Clasp.* Mentioned in Despatch, 30th December '57. Present at the action of Cawnpore, 6th December '57. Served at the re-occupation of Rohilcund, in '58. Served in the Cawnpore District in the pursuit of Ferozeshah, with the Force under Brigadier Herbert, in December '58. Mentioned in Despatch, 24th January '59. Served in the Saugor District in '59, and commanded a Field Detachment, consisting of 1 Squadron of the late 3rd Irregular Cavalry and Detachments of Police Infantry. Received three times the approbration of His Excellency the Governor-General. Received letter from the Secretary of State for India, conveying his approbation for services in the Field. Served as Staff Officer to the Bundlecund Field Force in '59.

2ND CAPTAIN J. R. PEARSON, P. H., Bengal Artillery.

1st Lieut., 27 June 57—2nd Captain, 18 Feb. 61.

SERVICE.—Captain PEARSON served with the Army under Lord Clyde as Deputy Commissary of Ordnance with the Siege Train, proceeded in that capacity from Cawnpore, in April '58, to Rohilcund. Present at the battle of Bareilly, 5th May, affairs of Shahjehanpore, Mohumdee, 24th May, and Shahabad, 1st June '58. *Medal.*

ENSIGN H. J. PEET, General List.

Ensign, 26 June 60.

CAPTAIN F. W. PEILE, Bengal Engineers.

2nd Lieut., 11 Dec. 46—Lieut., 1 Aug. 54—2nd Captain, 27 Aug. 58—Captain, 19 March 62.

CAPTAIN W. B. PEILE,† late 38th Native Infantry.

Ensign, 7 Feb. 49—Lieut., 28 Sept. 51—Captain, 11 March 58.

SERVICE.—Captain PEILE was present at Delhi when the 38th Native Infantry mutined. Served during the Mutiny. *Medal.*

(473)

LIEUTENANT D. S. PEMBERTON, Bengal Artillery.
Lieut., 27 April 58.

MAJOR-GENERAL G. R. PEMBERTON, late 62nd Native Infantry.
Ensign, 24 May 06—Lieut., 22 May 09—Bt.-Captain, 24 May 21—Captain, 1 May 24—Major, 25 June 32—Lieut.-Colonel, 13 Feb. 39—Colonel, 19 March 49—Major-General, 28 Nov. 54.

SERVICE.—Major-General PEMBERTON served with the expedition to Java, '11. Present at the storm and capture of Cornelis. *Medal.*

ASSISTANT-SURGEON G. R. PEMBERTON,† M.D., Bengal Medical Establishment.
Asst.-Surgeon, 20 Jan. 48.

SERVICE.—Assistant-Surgeon PEMBERTON served with the 2nd Fusiliers throughout the Punjab Campaign. Served in the Field Hospital, Army of the Punjab, at Ramnuggur, for a short period. Present at the actions of Chillianwallah and Goojerat, and the pursuit of Affghans and Sikhs to Peshawur. *Medal and 2 Clasps.* Served during the Mutiny of '57, '58, against the Dinapore rebels at Mirzapore.

ASSISTANT-SURGEON J. McL. PEMBERTON,† Bengal Medical Establishment.
Asst.-Surgeon, 9 Dec. 57.

LIEUTENANT R. C. B. PEMBERTON, P. H., Bengal Engineers.
Lieut., 11 Aug. 57.

SERVICE.—Lieutenant PEMBERTON served at the siege of Delhi, '57. *Slightly wounded* at the assault. Present at the capture of Lucknow, in charge of the Engineer Park. *Medal and 2 Clasps.*

LIEUTENANT S. E. PEMBERTON, Bengal Artillery.
Lieut., 9 Dec. 59.

LIEUTENANT G. PENGREE, Bengal Invalid Establishment.
Lieut., 1 Oct. 32—Invalided, 13 Nov. 37.

LIEUTENANT C. R. PENNINGTON, P. H., late 32nd Native Infantry.

Ensign, 4 Oct. 57—Lieut., 18 May 58.

SERVICE.—Lieutenant PENNINGTON served in the Campaign of '57, '58. Present at the siege and capture of Lucknow, March '58. *Medal and Clasp.* Accompanied a Column under Colonel Bulwer into Oude, September '58. Present at the engagements of Jubrowlee and Parna. *(Slightly wounded.)* Brought to the special notice of the Brigadier Commanding. Present at the defeat of Banee Madhoo, on the Ganges, by Lord Clyde, November '58. Served on the Nepal Frontier against the rebels, from June to October '59.

ASSISTANT-SURGEON J. C. PENNY,† M.D., Bengal Medical Establishment.

Asst.-Surgeon, 29 Jan. 57.

SERVICE.—Assistant-Surgeon PENNY served with H. M.'s 23rd Fusiliers throughout the relief of the Garrison of Lucknow, under Sir Colin Campbell, in November '57, and at the defeat of the Gwalior Force at Cawnpore. On duty at the Allahabad Field Hospital, from the 10th December '57 to the 1st January '58. *Medal and Clasp.*

2ND CAPTAIN J. PERCIVALL, P. H., Bengal Artillery.

1st Lieut., 9 Dec. 50—2nd Captain, 19 July 59.

SERVICE.—Captain PERCIVALL served with the Burmese Expedition. Present at the operations in the vicinity and capture of Rangoon, April '52; and attack of the Burmese stockades, 19th March '53. *Medal.*

2ND CAPTAIN ÆNEAS PERKINS, P. H., Bengal Engineers.

2nd Lieut., Dec. 51—Lieut., 17 Aug. 56—2nd Captain, 13 March 61.

SERVICE.—Captain PERKINS served at the battle of Badlee-ka-Serai and siege of Delhi. *(Wounded.)* *Medal and Clasp.*

CAPTAIN E. N. PERKINS, P. H., late 14th Native Infantry.

Ensign, 8 Jan. 42—Lieut., 16 Feb. 46—Bt.-Captain, 8 Jan. 57—Captain, 4 May 58.

SERVICE.—Captain PERKINS served in the Gwalior Campaign, '43, '44. Present at the battle of Maharajpore. Served during the Sutlej Campaign, '45.

(475)

CAPTAIN J. PERKINS, P., late 71st Native Infantry.

Ensign, 16 June 45—Lieut., 7 Dec. 49—Bt.-Captain, 16 June 60—Captain, 18 Feb. 61.

SERVICE.—Captain PERKINS served during the Sutlej Campaign, '46. Present at an attack made on the rebel Ram Singh on the heights of Moorpooria, September '48, *Medal;* as a Volunteer with a Force under Sir C. Napier, that forced the Kohat Pass, February '50. Served with the Force under Lord Clyde against the Mohunnud Tribes. Present at the capture and destruction of Dubb. Received the thanks of Sir C. Campbell, for services at the Fort of Mihinee. Served during the Mutinies, '57; with the Moveable Column under Brigadier-General Nicholson. Present at the action of Timmoor Ghaut. *(Slightly wounded.) (Horse severely wounded.)* Mentioned in General Nicholson's Despatch. *Medal.*

ASSISTANT-SURGEON R. H. PERKINS, Bengal Medical Establishment.

Asst.-Surgeon, 20 April 52.

LIEUTENANT C. W. G. PERREAU, General List.

Ensign, 20 Oct. 59—Lieut., 28 Aug. 61.

LIEUTENANT M. C. PERREAU,† late 47th Native Infantry.

Ensign, 4 Feb. 54—Lieut., 30 April 58.

SERVICE.—Lieutenant PERREAU served with the China Expeditionary Force in '60, '61. Thanked by the Deputy-Commissary-General for services in the Commissariat Department. *Medal.*

ASSISTANT-SURGEON M. J. S. PERREAU,† Bengal Medical Establishment.

Asst.-Surgeon, 27 July 59.

LIEUTENANT W. F. S. PERRY, General List.

Ensign, 22 Nov. 59—Lieut., 19 Sept. 61.

ASSISTANT-SURGEON W. PESKETT,† Bengal Medical Establishment.

Asst.-Surgeon, 26 June 49.

(476)

MAJOR H. L. PESTER, P. H., late 63rd Native Infantry.

Ensign, 8 March 40—Lieut., 24 Jan. 45—Captain, 12 Feb. 54—Major, 1 Jan. 62.

SERVICE.—Captain PESTER served throughout the Sutlej Campaign, '45, '46. Present at the battle of Sobraon. *Medal and Clasp.*

CAPTAIN C. W. PETER, P., late 42nd Native Infantry.

Ensign, 20 Dec. 46—Lieut., 3 Aug. 53—Captain, 11 May 60.

SERVICE.—Captain PETER served during the Sonthal Campaign, '55, '56. In the Saugor District during the Mutiny, in '57, '58, and '59; also as one of the Saugor Garrison. *Medal.*

ASSISTANT-SURGEON F. J. PETTINGAL,† Bengal Medical Establishment.

Asst.-Surgeon, 20 Feb. 56.

SERVICE.—Assistant-Surgeon PETTINGAL served in the Field Hospital Army of the Punjab, throughout the Punjab War, in '48, '49. Proceeded with Detachments of sick and wounded to the Depôt Hospital at Ferozepore, and at the close of the Campaign with sick and wounded Sepoys to Meerut. *Medal and Clasp.*

LIEUTENANT W. PHAIRE, P. C. H., late 54th Native Infantry.

Ensign, 20 Jan. 51—Lieut., 31 Jan. 54.

LIEUTENANT-COLONEL A. P. PHAYRE,† late 4th Europeans.

Ensign, 13 Aug. 28—Lieut., 9 July 38—Bt.-Captain, 13 Aug. 43—Captain, 16 May 49—Bt.-Major, 20 June 54—Major, 10 Jan. 55—Lieut.-Colonel, 22 Jan. 59.

LIEUTENANT A. N. PHILLIPS, P. H., late 19th Native Infantry.

Ensign, 8 Dec. 58—Lieut., 15 Feb. 60.

LIEUTENANT E. A. PHILLIPS.†

Ensign, 8 May 58—Lieut., 24 Aug. 58.

(477)

LIEUTENANT G. F. M. PHILLIPS, P. H., late 30th Native Infantry.
Ensign, 15 July 54—Lieut., 23 Nov. 56.

SERVICE.—Lieutenant PHILLIPS served with the Kotah Contingent in several skirmishes in the Muttra and Allyghur Districts, in '57, and also present when it mutinied. Served with the 3rd Europeans in several skirmishes in '57 with the mutineers. Present at the battle of Sussia, near Agra, 5th July '57. (Horse killed under him.) *Medal.*

CAPTAIN H. PHILLIPS,† late 40th Native Infantry.
Ensign, 7 Jan. 51—Lieut., 6 Aug. 54—Captain, 26 Sept. 61.

SERVICE.—Captain PHILLIPS served in the Burmah War in '52. Present at the operations in the vicinity and capture of Rangoon. *Medal.* Served against the Insurgent Sonthals in '55, under Major-General Lloyd. Served as Staff Officer to a Detachment under the Command of Lieutenant-Colonel Longden. Present at the taking of the Fort of Atrowlia, in Oude, also with the Goorkha Troops under His Highness Maharajah Jung Bahadoor, '57, '58. *Medal.*

MAJOR J. C. PHILLIPS, P., late 3rd Bengal European Infantry.
Ensign, 30 Sept. 30—Lieut., 2 Dec. 36—Bt.-Captain, 30 Sept. 45—Captain, 1 March 51—Bt.-Major, 28 Nov. 56—Lieut.-Colonel in Staff Corps, 18 Feb. 61.

SERVICE.—Major PHILLIPS served throughout the operations in Affghanistan under General Pollock (*wounded* in the Khyber Pass). *Medal.* *(Since retired.)*

BREVET-CAPTAIN W. H. PHILLIPS,† late 59th Native Infantry.
Ensign, 1 Jan. 44—Lieut., 26 Aug. 51—Bt.-Captain, 1 Jan. 59.

SERVICE.—Captain PHILLIPS served during the Sutlej Campaign, '45, '46. Present at the battle of Sobraon. *Medal.* *(Since retired.)*

CAPTAIN H. PHILLPOTTS, P. H., late 15th Native Infantry.
Ensign, 9 June 49—Lieut. 23 July 54—Captain, 16 April 62.
(Passed in Civil Engineering.)

MAJOR J. S. PHILLPOTTS, P. H., late 66th Native Infantry.

Ensign, 15 Feb. 40—Lieut., 25 Nov. 42—Captain, 28 Oct. 50—Major, 1 Jan. 62.

SERVICE.—Major PHILLPOTTS proceeded under Command of Brigadier Chamberlain into Meeranzaie and across the Kurrma River, in '56· Served against the rebels in defence of the Kumaon Hills, in '57, '58. *Medal.*

LIEUTENANT W. PICKARD, late 4th Native Infantry.

Ensign, 20 Feb. 58—Lieut., 22 Oct. 58.

SERVICE.—Lieutenant PICKARD served with the Field Force in Oude, '58.

ASSISTANT-SURGEON J. PICTHALL,† Bengal Medical Establishment.

Asst.-Surgeon, 14 Dec. 53.

SERVICE.—Assistant-Surgeon PICTHALL served with the 2nd Irregular Cavalry, from May to December '56, in the Sonthal District. Served also against the Insurgent Tribes, in '57, in the Googaira District. Received the thanks of the Punjab Government for his valuable services in the management of the Goordaspore Dispensary, concurred in by the Governor-General in letter from Secretary to Government, Foreign Department, dated 13th July '61.

CAPTAIN T. PIERCE, P. C., late 30th Native Infantry.

Ensign, 8 Oct. 44—Lieut., 13 Jan. 49—Bt.-Captain, 8 Oct. 59—Captain, 15 Feb. 61.

SERVICE.—Captain PIERCE served in the Sutlej Campaign, including the action of Alliwal, *Medal;* and with the Army of the Punjab : present at the passage of the Chenab: battles of Chillianwalla *(wounded)*, and Goojerat, and subsequent pursuit of the Sikhs and Affghans with the Force under General Gilbert. *Medal.*

MAJOR H. J. PIERCY, P., late 49th Native Infantry.

Ensign, 13 June 34—Lieut., 17 July 37—Captain, 22 Jan. 47—Major, 11 Oct. 59.

SERVICE.—Major PIERCY served at the siege and capture of Mooltan under General Whish. *Medal and Clasp.*

2ND LIEUTENANT W. H. PIERSON, Bengal Engineers.

2nd Lieut., 10 Dec. 58.

SERVICE.—Lieutenant PIERSON served as Assistant Field Engineer with the Force under Lieutenant-Colonel Gawler, in Sikkim, from January to April '61. Brought to the notice of the Commander-in-Chief in Colonel Gawler's Despatch, 17th May 61. Received the thanks of Government, 14th May '61.

CAPTAIN W. S. PIERSON, P. H., late 54th Native Infantry.

Ensign, 8 June 49—Lieut., 14 Feb. 55—Captain, 6 June 58.

LIEUTENANT C. PIGOU, late 4th Europeans.

Ensign, 13 Dec. 56—Lieut., 20 May 58.

SERVICE.—Lieutenant PIGOU served with the 3rd Europeans through the Indian Mutinies of '57, '58. Present at the actions near Agra against Neemuch mutineers, 5th July, and against Indore and Mhow rebels, 10th October, also with Brigadier Seaton's Column at Gungeeree, 14th December, and Puttiallee, 18th December '57; and with the Agra Column towards Gwalior, in June '58. *Medal.*

LIEUTENANT H. W. PITCHER,† late 13th Native Infantry.

Ensign, 26 July 57—Lieut., 18 May 58.

SERVICE.—Lieutenant PITCHER served during the Mutinies of '58, '59. Present at the affairs of Secundra, 5th January '58; siege and capture of Lucknow, March '58. *Medal and Clasp.* Rooya, 16th April, Allygunge, 21st April, Bareilly, 5th May, operations at Shahjehanpore, May and June '58; storm and capture of the Fort of Rampore Kussia, 3rd November, Passage of the Gogra, 25th November '58; operations on the Nepal Frontier, '59, '60; expedition against the Cabul Khel Wuzeerees, under General Chamberlain, '59, '60; expedition against the Mahmood Wuzeerees April and May '60.

2ND CAPTAIN A. W. PIXLEY, Bengal Artillery.

2nd Lieut., 13 Dec. 45—Lieut., 25 Feb. 53—2nd Captain, 27 Aug. 58.

SERVICE.—Captain PIXLEY served during the Punjab Campaign, '48, '49. Present at the passage of the Chenab. *(Wounded dangerously.)*

(480)

Medal. Mentioned in the Despatch of the Officer who commanded the Division. Served under Lord Clyde in '52, against the Hill Tribes of Peshawur.

ASSISTANT-SURGEON C. PLANK,† Bengal Medical Establishment.

Assistant-Surgeon, 4 Aug. 55.

SERVICE.—Assistant-Surgeon PLANK served in charge of two Companies of H. M.'s 90th Light Infantry with General Outram's Force at the relief of Lucknow, in '57. Proceeded to Cawnpore and was attached to the General Field Hospital on the 10th September '57 to 28th February '58, and was present at the attack of the Gwalior rebels. *Medal and Clasp.*

LIEUTENANT A. L. PLAYFAIR,† late 6th Bengal European Infantry.

Ensign, 5 Aug. 56—Lieut., 7 Nov. 57.

SERVICE.—Lieutenant PLAYFAIR served with the 1st European Bengal Fusiliers at the Alum Bagh, and subsequently in the Trans-Goomtee operations under Major-General Sir James Outram, and was present with that Regiment throughout the storm and capture of Lucknow under Lord Clyde, in March '58. *Medal and Clasp.*

SURGEON G. R. PLAYFAIR,† M. D., Bengal Medical Establishment.

Asst.-Surgeon, 3 Nov. 44—Surgeon, 28 March 58.

SERVICE.—Surgeon PLAYFAIR served with the Troops under Maharajah Jung Bahadoor, from the date they left Goruckpore, 31st January '58, towards Lucknow, until after the capture of that city they returned to Nepal on the 4th June '58, *viâ* Segowlie. *Medal and Clasp.*

LIEUTENANT W. PLAYFAIR, P. H., late 4th Native Infantry.

Ensign, 20 Dec. 49—Lieut., 1 April 56.

SERVICE.—Lieutenant PLAYFAIR served with the 2nd Division Persian Expeditionary Force in '57. Present at the bombardment and capture of Mohumra, 26th March '57. *Medal and Clasp.*

(481)

ASSISTANT-SURGEON W. S. PLAYFAIR, M. D., Bengal Medical Establishment.

Asst.-Surgeon, 4 Aug. 57.

MAJOR A. C. PLOWDEN, P., late 50th Native Infantry.

Ensign, 13 June 37—Lieut., 3 Oct. 40—Bt.-Captain, 13 June 52—Captain, 3 March 53—Bt.-Major, 20 July 58—Major, 18 Feb. 61.

SERVICE.—Major PLOWDEN served against the insurgents in Bundlecund in '42, under General Young, also in the Punjab Campaign. Present at the siege and surrender of the Fortress of Mooltan, repulse of the enemy's night attack on the British Camp under General Whish, at Muttee Thal, and action of Sooroojkhoond, 7th November '48. *Medal and Clasp.* Served with the Goorkha Army under H. H. Maharajah Sir Jung Bahadoor, and held Military Charge of a Division of the Force; engaged and defeated the rebel forces at Peepraitch and Shahgunge, in the Goruckpore District, the enemy at the latter numbering 12,000 strong; at the "Pandoo Nuddee," in Oude, in which action the rebels lost 600 killed; re-capture of Goruckpore and the operations attending the seige and capture of Lucknow, in which his Division took seven guns; succeeded to the charge of the Goorkha Army after the fall of Lucknow, and conducted it through Oude to Segowlie, occupying Fyzabad *en-route*, which was evacuated by the rebels on the approach of the Goorkha Army. *Medal and Clasp.*

BREVET-LIEUTENANT-COLONEL A. W. C. PLOWDEN, P., late 1st Bengal European Cavalry.

Cornet, 19 June 33—Lieut., 23 Dec. 41—Bt.-Captain, 19 June 48—Captain, 21 Oct. 52—Bt.-Major, 22 Oct. 52—Bt.-Lieut.-Colonel, 13 April 60.

SERVICE.—Lieutenant-Colonel PLOWDEN served in Affghanistan, '38, '39; capture of Ghuznee. *Medal.* Sutlej Campaign, '45, 46: present at the affair of Budiwal; actions of Alliwal and Sobraon. *(Horse disabled.) Medal and Clasps.*

LIEUTENANT G. W. C. PLOWDEN, P. H., late 3rd Bengal European Cavalry.

Cornet, 4 April 54—Lieut., 23 Nov. 56.

SERVICE.—Lieutenant PLOWDEN served in the Saharunpore District, in May and June '57. Present at the siege and assault of Delhi, actions of Boolundshuhur, Allyghur, and Agra, and skirmishes at Allahabad and Kanouje. Present at the attack on the Dilkoosha, Secundra Bagh, relief of Lucknow, November '57; battle of Cawnpore, 6th December '57; Serai Ghaut, 8th December '57; Kalee Nuddee, and entrance into Futtehghur. Present at the taking of the Dilkoosha, and siege and capture of Lucknow, March '58. Served in Oude in '58. *Medal and 2 Clasps*. Mentioned in the Despatch of Sir H. Grant, 6th April '58. Has three times brought his Detachment, 5th Punjab Cavalry, out of action, and obtained the Command of it at the taking of Lucknow.

LIEUTENANT H. A. PLOWDEN, P. H., late 51st Native Infantry.

Ensign, 12 Dec. 57—Lieut., 11 Sept. 58.

LIEUTENANT T. J. C. PLOWDEN, General List.

Ensign, 10 Dec. 59—Lieut., 11 Oct. 61.

LIEUTENANT J. F. POGSON, P., Bengal Invalid Establishment.

Lieut., 16 July 42.

SERVICE.—Lieutenant POGSON served at the battle of Moodkee. *(Wounded.) Medal.* (Attained creditable knowledge of Punjabee. Passed examination in Surveying and Civil Engineering.)

CAPTAIN W. Q. POGSON, P., late 43rd Native Infantry.

Ensign, 12 Dec. 38—Lieut., 16 July 42—Bt.-Captain, 12 Dec. 53—Captain, 6 March 54.

SERVICE.—Captain POGSON served in Spain in '37, forming one of the Garrison of San Sebastian. Served in Affghanistan in '40; with the Army of the Sutlej in '46, and with the Army of occupation, Lahore, '46. Served with Brigadier Huish's Column against the insurgents of Cashmere, 4th October '46.

2ND CAPTAIN C. POLLARD, P. H., Bengal Engineers.

2nd Lieut., 12 Dec. 45—1st Lieut., 15 Feb. 54—2nd Captain, 27 Aug. 58·

SERVICE.—Captain POLLARD served during the Punjab Campaign, '48, '49. Present at the siege of Mooltan *(wounded)*, and at the battle of Goojerat. *Medal and Clasp.*

CAPTAIN F. R. POLLOCK, P. H., late 49th Native Infantry.

Ensign, 8 June 44—Lieut., 23 June 47—Captain, 23 Nov. 56.

SERVICE.—Captain POLLOCK served in Political Employ during the siege and capture of Mooltan under Major Edwardes. *Medal and Clasp.*

GENERAL SIR G. POLLOCK, G.C.B., Bengal Artillery.

1st. Lieut., 14 Dec. 03—Captain, 26 March 13—Major, 12 Aug. 19—Lieut.-Colonel, 1 May 24—Colonel, 3 March 35—Major-General, 28 June 38—Lieut.-General, 11 Nov. 51—General, 17 May 59.

SERVICE.—General Sir G. POLLOCK, G.C.B., was present at the following actions: Deig, '04; Bhurtpore, Gwalior, '05; Rewah, '06; Nepal, '15, '16; Burmah, '24, '25, '26. *Medal.* Commanded the Force employed in Affghanistan, '42, for the relief of Jellallabad and re-occupation of Cabul. *Medal and G.C.B.*

CAPTAIN H. T. POLLOCK,† late 35th Native Infantry.

Ensign, 28 Dec. 42—Lieut., 1 April 51—Bt.-Captain, 28 Dec. 57—Captain, 12 Nov. 58.

SERVICE.—Captain POLLOCK served before Delhi, and was engaged in the several actions before that City. *(Severely wounded.) Medal and Clasp.*

MAJOR-GENERAL T. POLWHELE, late 17th Native Infantry.

Ensign, 22 Aug. 15—Lieut., 1 Feb. 18—Captain, 26 July 30—Bt.-Major- 23 Dec. 42—Major, 21 Aug. 43—Bt.-Lieut.-Colonel, 3 April 46—Lieut., Colonel, 17 Jan. 50—Bt.-Colonel, 20 June 54—Colonel, 26 May 59—Major-General, 1 May 58.

SERVICE.—Major-General POLWHELE served in the Nepal Campaign, 16, *Medal;* with the expedition to Ceylon, '18; Burmese War, '24, '25.

Present at the attack and capture of Mahatee and Arracan: throughout the Affghanistan Campaign, in '39, '40, '41, '42; and served as Assistant Adjutant-General throughout the whole of the operations of the Candahar Force under General Nott. *Medal and Brevet-Major.* Commanded the 42nd Regiment during the Sutlej Campaign. Present at the actions of Moodkee, Ferozeshuhur, and Sobraon. *(Wounded) Medal, 2 Clasps, and Brevet-Lieutenant-Colonel.*

CAPTAIN A. POND, P. H., late 3rd Europeans.

Ensign, 11 July 43—Lieut., 26 Dec. 46—Captain, 4 Aug. 57.

SERVICE.—Captain POND served in the Sutlej Campaign, '45, '46. Present at the action of Alliwal, 28th January '46. *Medal.* Detached with 3 Companies, 3rd Europeans, under Captain Patton, for the protection of Berhampore, during the Sonthal Rebellion, '55. Present at the action of Sussia, near Agra, 5th July '57. *(Slightly wounded.)* Present at an engagement with the rebels at the Village of Chawhowlee, surprised, captured, and destroyed the village. In Command of a Wing of the 3rd Europeans under Colonel Hennessy, captured and destroyed a village 30 miles from Agra. Present in action when the Agra Cantonment was attacked by the Gwalior mutineers, 10th October. Present in Command of 4 Companies of Europeans at the taking of Futtehpore-Sikree, 28th October '57. In the same capacity conveyed Commissariat and Ordnance stores to the camp of the Commander-in-Chief at Futtehghur. Served with his Regiment in the Etawah District, restoring order. Commanded 4 Companies of Europeans, which secured the position of Shereghur Ghaut, when 1,500 rebels were driven through the ravines and across the river, and held the Ghaut in action for five or six hours. Mentioned in G. G. O., 9th June '58. With his Regiment at Dholepore, holding the Ghaut until Gwalior fell. *Medal.*

ASSISTANT-SURGEON C. A. POOLE,† Bengal Medical Establishment.

Asst.-Surgeon, 18 March 56.

SERVICE.—Assistant-Surgeon POOLE served with the 1st Regiment Sikh Infantry, throughout the Rohilcund and Oude Campaigns. With the 3rd Regiment Hodson's Horse on the Raptee, in November and December '59.

(485)

Joined the Force, assembling at Roorkee, under Brigadier Jones, in '58. Passed the Ganges and was present at the skirmish on the march to Nujjeerabad, in the action of Wuzeerees and re-occupation of Moradabad. Served in the Budaon District, and was present at the capture of Bareilly. Served in the Phillibeet District at the advance of Colonel Coke on Mohumdee. With a Force under General Jones towards the Ramgunga, joined the Soraon Field Force, and accompanied the Army under Lord Clyde on the advance to Amythee, in November '58. Present at the passage of the Gogra, and at Fyzabad. With a Division under Sir H. Grant was present in the various skirmishes with the rebels in '58, 59; in the action fought at Jerwah by the 1st Sikh Infantry, on 31st March '59. Services mentioned in the Despatch of 1st April '59. *Medal.*

ASSISTANT-SURGEON G. K. POOLE,† Bengal Medical Establishment.

Asst.-Surgeon, 14 March 55.

BREVET-COLONEL D. POTT, 7th (late 47th) Native Infantry.

Ensign, 20 Jan. 29—Lieut., 6 June 33—Captain, 8 Oct. 39—Bt.-Major, 3 April 46—Major, 31 Jan. 54—Bt.-Lieut.-Colonel, 20 June 54—Lieut.-Colonel, 1 May 58—Bt.-Colonel, 22 Aug. 57.

SERVICE.—Colonel POTT served against the insurgents near Cuttack, in '33, with the 47th Native Infantry. Served throughout the Sutlej Campaign, including the actions of Moodkee, Ferozeshuhur, Buddiwal, Alliwal, and Sobraon. Commanded the 47th Native Infantry as a Captain at Moodkee and Ferozeshuhur. *(Horse shot under him at Sobraon.)* *Medal and* 3 *Clasps, and Brevet-Major.* Commanded a Force in the Irrawaddy District, in Pegu, against the rebels in '54. Commanded various parties of troops against the rebels near Mirzapore, during the Mutiny of '57. *Medal.* Commanded the 47th Native Infantry on Foreign Service at Canton, in '58, '59. *Medal.* (Received the special thanks of Lord Canning for services performed during the Mutiny.)

LIEUTENANT-COLONEL S. POTT, Bengal Engineers.

2nd Lieut., 14 Dec. 32—1st Lieut., 31 March 40—Bt.-Captain, 14 Dec. 47—Captain, 15 Feb. 54—Lieut.-Colonel, 24 Aug. 59.

SERVICE.—Lieutenant-Colonel POTT served at the battle of Maharajpore. *Bronze Star.*

(486)

ASSISTANT-SURGEON H. POTTER, M.D., Bengal Medical Establishment.

Asst.-Surgeon, 23 July 58.

SERVICE.—Assistant-Surgeon POTTER served with the 1st Company, 5th Battalion Bengal Artillery, at the capture of Amythee, and the subsequent advance on Shunkerpore, under the Commander-in-Chief, November '58. Served with the Meerut Light Horse, in the pursuit of Ferozeshah and affair with his troops on the banks of the Jumna, under Brigadier the Hon'ble P. Stewart, in December '58. Served with H. M.'s 34th Regiment, part of the Hot Weather Campaign, Trans-Gogra, in '59. *Medal.*

CAPTAIN H. B. A. POULTON, P. H., late 64th Native Infantry.

Ensign, 10 July 42—Lieut., 26 Oct. 48—Bt.-Captain, 10 July 57—Captain, 7 April 61—Captain in Staff Corps, 18 Feb. 61.

SERVICE.—Captain POULTON served against the Hill Tribes in Scinde, under Sir C. Napier, '45.

ASSISTANT-SURGEON F. POWELL,† M. B., Bengal Medical Establishment.

Asst.-Surgeon, 20 Feb. 56.

SERVICE.—Assistant-Surgeon POWELL served in Medical Charge of the 3rd Sikh Infantry, in an expedition under Brigadier-General Chamberlain, against the Bozdars, March and April '57. Also in Medical Charge of that Regiment, in the operations against the rebels, in the Goruckpore District, and on the Nepal Frontier, under Colonel Kelly, in '59. *Medal.*

LIEUTENANT-COLONEL J. POWELL, late 55th Native Infantry.

Ensign, 10 Jan. 24—Lieut., 9 July 25—Captain, 30 Nov. 40—Bt.-Major, 11 Nov. 51—Major, 15 Nov. 52—Lieut.-Colonel, 27 June 57.

LIEUTENANT P. W. POWLETT, P. H., late 58th Native Infantry.

Ensign, 4 Feb. 55—Lieut., 23 Nov. 56.

SERVICE.—Lieutenant POWLETT served during the Mutinies under Lord Clyde, '57, '58. Present at the actions of Allyghur, Agra, Kanouje, and Bunnee Bridge; relief of Lucknow, battle of Cawnpore, action at Kala Nuddee Bridge, and the seige and capture of Lucknow. *(Wounded severely.) Medal and* 2 *Clasps.* Mentioned in the despatch of H. E. the Commander-in-Chief. Merits acknowledged by Government.

MAJOR T. POWNALL, late 39th Native Infantry.

Ensign, 13 June 35—Lieut., 1 July 39—Captain, 10 June 49—Major, 4 June 59.

SERVICE.—Major POWNALL served with the Force sent against the Bheels in '37; with the Force sent against Rajah Maun Singh, of Joudpore, in '39. Served in Bundlecund in '43. Commanded a Detachment of the 39th Native Infantry in the Beeghora Jungles, sent for the protection of wood-cutters. Was attacked and surrounded on all sides on the night of the 10th April '43, and had a volley fired through his tent by a large body of insurgents, who were repulsed before the arrival of some Troops sent to the assistance of Major Pownall. Served with the Brigade under Colonel Yates, in the Gwalior Campaign of '43, under Sir J. Grey, and remained for the protection of the Camp at Punniar. *Bronze Star.* Served during the whole of the Mutiny at Dehra Ismail Khan, '57, 58. *(Since retired.)*

LIEUTENANT-GENERAL R. POWNEY, Bengal Artillery.

1st Lieut., 7 May 05—Captain, 7 Oct. 17—Major, 25 May 26—Lieut.-Colonel, 3 March 35—Colonel, 12 June 44—Major-General, 20 June 54—Lieut.-General, 21 Sept. 59.

LIEUTENANT C. S. PRATT, late 54th Native Infantry.

Ensign, 11 Dec. 58—Lieut., 27 May 60.

LIEUTENANT H. M. PRATT, P. H., late 51st Native Infantry.

Ensign, 4 Nov. 56—Lieut., 30 April 58.

SERVICE.—Lieutenant PRATT was present at the Mutiny of the 51st Native Infantry, in August '57, at Peshawur. Served with the China Expeditionary Force in '60. Present at the actions of Sinho, Tankoo, in reserve at the capture of the Taku Forts, and present at the actions of Chankia-wan and Tungchow, and at the surrender of Pekin. *Medal and 2 Clasps.*

LIEUTENANT C. L. PRENDERGAST, General List.
Ensign, 4 March 60—Lieut., 1 Jan. 62.

CAPTAIN G. A. PRENDERGAST,† late 5th Bengal European Cavalry.
Cornet, 20 March 50—Lieut., 10 Oct. 51—Captain, 30 July 59.

SERVICE.—Captain PRENDERGAST commanded a Squadron of the Mooltanee Regiment of Cavalry detached from Shahjehanpore to the assistance of the Rajah of Powayne, 6th October, and commanded at Powayne during the attack on that place by the rebels under Khan Bahadoor Khan and Ferozeshah, 7th and 8th October '58. Served as Orderly Officer to Brigadier Troup, during the Campaign in Oude, in '58, '59, including the action near Pursgaon, on the 19th, battle of Russoolpore, 25th October, and the attack and capture of Fort Mittowlie, 8th and 9th November '58. *Medal.*

CAPTAIN M. M. PRENDERGAST,† late 4th Bengal European Cavalry.
Cornet, 4 Jan. 54—Lieut., 23 Nov. 56—Captain, 2 July 60.

SERVICE.—Captain PRENDERGAST served against the Tribes in the Googaira District, in '57. Served under Sir J. Outram, at Alum Bagh, March '58; siege and capture of Lucknow; and subsequent operations in Oude, '58. Present at the affair of Bunnee *(slightly wounded)*, 13th April '58. Mentioned in the Despatch of Sir Hope Grant, May '58. Present at the actions of Simree, 13th May '58, and Nawabgunge, 13th June '58. Mentioned in the Despatch of Sir H. Grant, 30th June '58. *Medal and Clasp.*

ASSISTANT-SURGEON C. PRENTIS,† Bengal Medical Establishment.
Asst.-Surgeon, 27 Jan. 58.

SERVICE.—Assistant-Surgeon PRENTIS served with the Field Hospital at Bustee, attached to Brigadier Rowcroft's Force, October '58. Served with the 23rd Native Infantry, when attached to Brigadier Kelly's

(489)

Force, Nepal Frontier. Present at the actions of Ruttenpore, 25th and 28th March '59, and that in the Jarwah Pass, 20th May '59. *Medal.*

CAPTAIN P. PRESANT,† Bengal Artillery.

2nd Lieut., 13 Dec. 45—Lieut., 3 March 53—Captain, 27 Aug. 58.

SERVICE.—Captain PRESANT served during the Punjab Campaign, '48, '49. *Medal.*

CAPTAIN D. K. PRESGRAVE, P. H., late 59th Native Infantry.

Ensign, 29 Dec. 44—Lieut., 10 June 50—Captain, 21 Aug. 57.

SERVICE.—Captain PRESGRAVE served in the Sutlej Campaign, '45, '46. Present at the action of Sobraon, 10th February '46. *Medal.* Mentioned in the Despatch of Lord Gough. Served during the Mutinies, '57, '58. Present at the capture of Delhi, September '57. Accompanied the Moveable Column under Colonel Greathed. Present at the battle of Boolundshuhur and Agra, October '57; advance on Lucknow under Sir H. Grant, including the affairs of Kanouje, Alligunge, and Alum Bagh. Present at the relief of Lucknow under Lord Clyde; and at the defeat of the Gwalior rebels at Cawnpore. *Medal and 2 Clasps.*

CAPTAIN G. PRICE, P. H., late 1st European Bengal Fusiliers.

2nd Lieut., 27 Dec. 45—Lieut., 1 March 50—Captain, 21 Feb. 59.

LIEUTENANT J. C. G. PRICE, Bengal Artillery.

1st Lieut., 14 Sept. 57.

CAPTAIN R. H. PRICE, P. H., late 31st Native Infantry.

Ensign, 1 Sept. 43—Lieut., 10 Feb. 47—Bt.-Captain, 1 Sept. 58—Captain, 4 June 60.

SERVICE.—Captain PRICE served during the Punjab Campaign, '48, '49. Present at the actions of Sadoolapore, Chillianwallah, and Goojerat, and subsequent pursuit of the Sikhs and Affghans; at the disarming of the Sikhs at Rawul Pindee, and occupation of Peshawur. *Medal and 2 Clasps.* Present during the Sonthal Rebellion, '55.

CAPTAIN A. G. PRIESTLEY, P. H., late 41st Native Infantry.

Ensign, 1 May 45—Lieut., 28 Dec. 47—Captain, 1 June 57.

SERVICE.—Captain PRIESTLEY served with the Army of the Sutlej in '46. Present at Benares, in June '57, when the Mutiny broke out. Engaged in several skirmishes. *Medal.* Mentioned in Orders by Brigadier Gordon, 14th June '57. (Has furnished certificates in Surveying and Civil Engineering.)

LIEUTENANT D. PRINGLE, late 58th Native Infantry.

Ensign, 4 Sept. 57—Lieut., 4 Sept. 58.

ASSISTANT-SURGEON R. PRINGLE,† M.D., Bengal Medical Establishment.

Asst.-Surgeon, 4 Oct. 55.

LIEUTENANT A. H. PRINSEP, late 4th Bengal European Cavalry.

Cornet, 20 Oct. 56—Lieut., 23 Jan. 57.

LIEUTENANT C. J. PRINSEP, late 1st Bengal European Cavalry.

Cornet, 6 March 58—Lieut., 21 June 58.

LIEUTENANT F. B. PRINSEP, late 3rd Bengal European Cavalry.

Cornet, 20 April 57—Lieut., 18 May 58.

SERVICE.—Lieutenant PRINSEP served with the Sarun Field Force under Brigadier Rowcroft, '58, '59. Present at the actions of Amorab, Thilga, Doomuriahgunge, Toolseepore, and other minor engagements in Oude, Goruckpore, and on the Nepal Frontier. Mentioned in the Despatch of Captain Sotheby, Naval Brigade, and of Brigadier Rowcroft, 31st March '58. *Medal.*

LIEUTENANT H. A. PRINSEP, P. H., late 3rd Europeans.

Ensign, 20 Dec. 48—Lieut., 21 Feb. 50.

SERVICE.—Lieutenant PRINSEP served during the Mutinies, '57, '58. Present at the battle of Agra, 10th October '57. *Medal.*

(491)

LIEUTENANT-COLONEL C. PRIOR, P. H., late 64th Native Infantry.

Ensign, 13 April 24—Lieut., 13 May 25—Bt.-Captain, 13 April 39—Captain, 17 Jan. 41—Bt.-Major, 11 Nov. 51—Major, 10 July 57—Lieut.-Colonel, 25 April 58.

SERVICE.—Lieutenant-Colonel PRIOR served with Brigadier Wild's Brigade, '41, '42. Present at the relief of the Garrison of Ali Musjid, Khyber Pass; in the several actions from 13th January to 26th January '42. Mentioned in the Despatch of Lieutenant-Colonel Moseley. Present at the storming of the Khyber Pass, 15th April '42, and subsequent operations in Affghanistan, on the advance to Cabul. *Medal.* Served against the Hill Tribes, under Sir Charles Napier, in '45.

BREVET-LIEUTENANT-COLONEL D. M. PROBYN, C.B., V.C., and P.H., late 3rd Bengal European Cavalry.

Cornet, 20 Oct. 49—Lieut., 19 Aug. 53—Captain, 21 Aug. 57—Bt.-Major, 24 March 58—Bt.-Lieut.-Colonel, 15 Feb. 61.

SERVICE.—Lieutenant-Colonel PROBYN served in the Trans-Indus Frontier, from '52 to '57. Present at the operations in the Bozdar Hills, March '57, and other minor affairs. Served throughout the siege of Delhi. Present at the battle of Nudjufghur, 25th August '57, and other minor engagements. Commanded a Detachment, 2nd Punjab Cavalry, at the assault and capture of Delhi, 14th September '57. Mentioned in the Despatch of Brigadier J. H. Grant, November '57. Served with the Flying Column under Colonel Greathed, and in Command of a Detachment, 2nd Punjab Cavalry. Was present at the actions of Boolundshuhur and Malaghur, 28th September, Allyghur, 6th October, Akbarpore, 8th October, and Agra, 10th October '57. Mentioned three times in the Despatches of Colonel Greathed, in '57; by Colonel Cotton, 23rd December '57. Brought to the special notice of the Governor-General, 23rd December '57. Received at the recommendation of Sir Hope Grant the *Victoria Cross*, for gallantry at the battle of Agra, and on other occasions, 22nd February '58. Present at the action of Kanouje, 22nd October '57; at the relief of Lucknow, in November '57. Mentioned twice in Lord Clyde's Despatches, and brought to the notice of the Governor-General, December '57. Received the thanks of the Governor-

(492)

General, 10th December '57. Present at the battle of Cawnpore, 6th December '57; and brought to the notice of the Governor-General in Lord Clyde's Despatch, 24th December '57. Present at the battle of Kala Nuddee, 2nd January '58; and storm and capture of Lucknow, March '58. *Medal and* 3 *Clasps.* Promoted to the rank of Brevet-Major for services in '57, '58. Received the *Order of the Bath,* 3rd August '58. Permitted to retain the Command of the 1st Sikh Irregular Cavalry, as a special reward for his services, while he was on furlough, 18th January '59. Commanded that Regiment throughout the China Expedition of '60. Mentioned in the Despatches of Sir Hope Grant. Recommended by H. R. H. the Duke of Cambridge, that a step of rank might be given him for his services in China, 24th January '61. Brought to the notice of His Excellency the Governor-General, 21st November '60. By Sir Hope Grant promoted to the rank of Brevet-Lieutenant-Colonel, for services in China, '60, '61. *Medal and 2 Clasps.*

LIEUTENANT M. M. PROCTOR, P. H., late 38th Native Infantry.

Ensign, 31 Aug. 52—Lieut., 23 Nov. 56.

SERVICE.—Lieutenant PROCTOR served at the siege and assault of Delhi, in '57. Served with the Kumaon Battalion in the Oude Campaign and on the Nepal Frontier. *Medal and Clasp.*

CAPTAIN J. R. PUGHE, P., late 47th Native Infantry.

Ensign, 3 Jan. 40—Lieut., 20 July 43—Captain, 31 Jan. 54.

SERVICE.—Captain PUGHE served with the Army of the Sutlej in '45, '46. Served in Burmah in 54; in China, '58, '59. Present at the actions of Buddiwal and Atewah. *Medal.* (Received a certificate as Instructor of Musketry from the Royal School of Musketry at Hythe.)

LIEUTENANT A. PULLAN, P. H., late 36th Native Infantry.

Ensign, 14 June 56—Lieut., 26 Dec. 56.

SERVICE.—Lieutenant PULLAN served throughout the siege of Delhi in '57, with the 4th Sikh Infantry. *(Severely wounded.) Medal and Clasp.*

Was present with Colonel Maxwell's Column near Calpee, during March '58, as Adjutant of the 2nd Sikh Police Battalion. Commanded 4 Companies of this Battalion from May to November '58, throughout the Campaign in the Goruckpore Terai, under Brigadier Rowcroft. Mentioned in his Despatches for the defence of Bansee, in September '58. Mentioned three times in Despatches during the Rohilcund Campaign of '48.

CAPTAIN T. PULMAN, Bengal Artillery.

2nd Lieut., 11 June 42—Lieut., 3 July 45—Bt.-Captain, 11 June 57— Captain, 4 July 57.

ASSISTANT-SURGEON J. R. PUREFOY,† M.D., Bengal Medical Establishment.

Asst.-Surgeon, 10 Feb. 59.

Q

VETERINARY-SURGEON J. QUALLETT, Bengal Veterinary Establishment.

Vety.-Surgeon, 21 June 59.

SERVICE.—Veterinary-Surgeon QUALLETT served in the Crimea. Was Superintending Veterinary-Surgeon of the Turkish Contingent Artillery. Subsequently joined the Cavalry under Major-General Shirley, and was ordered to remain on special duty in England after the Contingent was made over to the Sultan.

LIEUTENANT G. QUIN, late 43rd Native Infantry.

Ensign, 11 Dec. 58—Lieut., 26 April 59.

LIEUTENANT T. QUIN, P. H., late 22nd Native Infantry.

Ensign, 20 Feb. 49—Lieut., 17 Oct. 54.

SERVICE.—Lieutenant QUIN served with the Field Force under General N. Chamberlain, in the Meeranzaie Valley, in '55; served with the Field Force under the same Officer in the Meeranzaie and Koorum Valleys, in

'56 ; served with the Force under General Cotton, in Eusuffzaie, in '58. Present at the affair at Sattana. Mentioned in Despatch, G. O. G. G., 3rd June '58.

LIEUTENANT T. J. QUIN,† General List.
Ensign, 4 March 59—Lieut., 11 May 60.

R

MAJOR H. RABAN, P. H., late 36th Native Infantry.
Ensign, 17 Sept. 40—Lieut., 27 Dec. 44—Bt.-Captain, 17 Sept. 55—Captain, 9 Oct. 56—Major in Staff Corps, 18 Feb. 61.

SERVICE.—Major RABAN served during the Sutlej Campaign, '45, '46. Present at the action of Alliwal. *Medal.*

ASSISTANT-SURGEON C. E. RADDOCK,† Bengal Medical Establishment.
Asst.-Surgeon, 29 Jan. 57.

SERVICE.—Assistant-Surgeon RADDOCK served in Medical Charge of Captain Hardy's Battery of Royal Artillery (5th Company, 11th Brigade), at the action of Bunteera, '57, with Sir Hope Grant's Column; and at the relief of the Residency (Lucknow) during the several operations under His Excellency the Commander-in-Chief, '57. In Medical Charge of Captain Middleton's Battery, Royal Artillery, at the battle of Cawnpore, '57 ; with the Commander-in-Chief's Force at Serai Ghaut and Bithoor, with Sir Hope Grant's Column; during the march of the Battery to Jounpore to join General Frank's Column, and at the actions of Chanda and Umrapoora, and the battle of Sultanpore, '58. Marched to Lucknow, and at the siege and capture of Lucknow, '58; with Generals Outram and Lugard's Divisions with the Oude Field Force under Sir Hope Grant, from April to August '58 ; at Baree and the occupation of Fyzabad, at the last-named action in Medical Charge of C. Company, Madras Sappers and Miners. In Medical Charge of the 1st Sikh Cavalry with Brigadier Evelegh's Column, in the Winter Campaign in Oude of '58, '59, including the actions of Meagunge, Poorwa, Morar, Mhow,

(495)

capture of the Fort of Simree Nurpalgunge, Doondea Kheera, capture of the Fort of Oomria; in Medical Charge also of Brigade Staff, in Medical Charge of 4th Irregular Cavalry on service with, in the Summer Campaign in Oude of '59. *Medal and 2 Clasps.*

LIEUTENANT P. B. RAIKES, Bengal Artillery.

Lieut., 21 May 58.

MAJOR R. N. RAIKES, late 67th Native Infantry.

Ensign, 19 Nov. 29—Lieut., 28 June 36—Bt.-Captain, 19 Nov. 44—Captain, 20 Feb. 52—Bt.-Major, 28 Nov. 54—Major, 28 Nov. 57.

SERVICE.—Major RAIKES served in Burmah. *Medal.* Present at the battle of Punniar. *Bronze Star.*

LIEUTENANT-COLONEL G.RAMSAY, P., late 10th Native Infantry.

Ensign, 6 Oct. 30—Lieut., 23 Aug. 34—Captain, 5 May 41—Major, 10 Sept. 52—Lieut.-Colonel, 27 June 57.

MAJOR H. RAMSAY, C. B., P., late 53rd Native Infantry.

Ensign, 14 June 34—Lieut., 8 Jan. 40—Bt.-Captain, 14 June 49—Captain, 15 Dec. 49—Major, 27 June 57.

SERVICE.—Major RAMSAY served during the Punjab Campaign, '48, 49. *Medal.*

LIEUTENANT H. M. RAMSAY, General List.

Ensign, 4 Aug. 60—Lieut., 1 Jan. 62.

LIEUTENANT M. RAMSAY, P. H., late 36th Native Infantry.

Ensign, 20 March 55—Lieut., 31 May 57.

SERVICE.—Lieutenant RAMSAY served during the Mutiny, '57, '58. Present at the mutiny of the Native Troops at Jullundur, and accompanied the Force under Brigadier Johnstone in pursuit. *Medal.*

MAJOR R. A. RAMSAY, P., late 35th Native Infantry.

Ensign, 18 Dec. 36—Lieut., 3 Oct. 40—Bt.-Captain, 18 Dec. 51—Captain, 17 Nov. 52—Bt.-Major, 19 Jan. 58—Major, 14 Sept. 59.

SERVICE.—Major RAMSAY served in the Cabul Campaign, under Lord Keene, '38, '39. Present at the capture of Fort Bakkur, in Scinde, and occupation of Candahar, 13th September '38. Present at the siege, storm, and capture of Ghuznee, 23rd July '39. *Medal.* Present at the occupation of Cabul. Commanded the Kumaon Battalion, during the Mutiny, from May '57 to July '59. Present at the siege, storm, and capture of Delhi, 13th October '57. Mentioned in the Despatch of Brigadier G. Campbell, 9th November '57. Served with Brigadier Showers at the advance on the Goorgaon District, and commanded in the District, from November '57 to October '60. Served in Oude under His Excellency the Commander-in-Chief, December '58. Entered Nepal with Brigadier Horsford's Column, and present at the capture of the rebels' guns at Luddega Ghaut, 9th February '59. Mentioned in the Despatch of Brigadier Horsford, 15th March '59. *Medal and Clasp.*

LIEUTENANT W. E. M. B. RAMSAY, P. H., late 17th Native Infantry.

Ensign, 13 June 56—Lieut., 3 June 57.

COLONEL W. M. RAMSAY, P., late 35th Native Infantry.

Ensign, 21 March 21—Lieut., 21 July 23—Captain, 1 Jan. 36—Major, 5 July 44—Lieut.-Colonel, 28 Sept. 50—Bt.-Colonel, 28 Nov. 54—Colonel, 25 Oct. 59.

SERVICE.—Colonel RAMSAY served in Affghanistan. Present at the taking of Ghuznee. *Medal.* Served in the Burmese War, '24, '25; also at Arracan.

LIEUTENANT H. L. RAMSBOTHAM,† late 47th Native Infantry.

Ensign, 4 Sept. 56—Lieut., 30 April 58.

LIEUTENANT W. L. RANDALL,† late 59th Native Infantry.

Ensign, 15 June 50—Lieut., 5 Feb. 54.

SERVICE.—Lieutenant RANDALL served during the Mutinies, '57, 58. Present at the action of Trimmoo Ghaut, under Brigadier-General

Nicholson, July '57. Present at the assault and capture of Delhi, 14th September '57. Commanded the 1st Punjab Infantry on Lieutenant C. T. Nicholson being wounded, 14th September '57. *Medal and Clasp.* Served with Brigadier Showers' Column in September and October '57; in Command of a Detachment, 1st Punjab Infantry, in the Jhujjur and Rewaree Districts, and with Detached Column under Colonel Scott, against the Mewatees. Commanded the 15th Punjab Infantry in the pursuit of the 62nd and 69th Native Infantry, with the Column under Colonel Davidson, in the Googaira District, September '58. Commanded the 15th Punjab Infantry throughout the China Campaign, '60, and was present at all the engagements, from the landing at Pehtagn, 1st August, to the final surrender of Pekin, 6th October '60. *Medal and Clasp.* Mentioned by Sir Hope Grant, and recommended to the favorable consideration of the Government of India.

LIEUTENANT H. H. RANKIN, General List.

Ensign, 10 Dec. 59—Lieut., 14 Nov. 61.

BREVET-CAPTAIN W. O. RANNIE,† late 32nd Native Infantry.

Ensign, 20 July 45—Lieut., 17 Oct. 55—Bt.-Captain, 20 July 60.

SERVICE.—Captain RANNIE served throughout the Campaign in the Punjab, including the passage of the Chenab and battles of Chillianwallah and Goojerat. *Medal and Clasp.*

CAPTAIN J. F. RAPER,† Bengal Artillery.

2nd Lieut., 9 Dec. 44—Lieut., 7 Jan. 48—2nd Captain, 27 Aug. 58—Captain, 31 May 60.

SERVICE.—Captain RAPER was present at the siege and surrender of Mooltan, '48, '49, and battle of Goojerat. *Medal and 2 Clasps.*

MAJOR T. RATTRAY, P. H., late 64th Native Infantry.

Ensign, 9 Dec. 39—Lieut., 24 June 42—Captain, 1 Feb. 54—Major, 1 April 59.

SERVICE.—Major RATTRAY served in Affghanistan under Sir G. Pollock. *(Severely wounded.) Medal.* Served against the Hill Tribes in Scinde under Sir Charles Napier, '45.

(498)

LIEUTENANT A. J. C. RAWLINS, Bengal Artillery.
Lieut., 9 Dec. 59.

CAPTAIN J. S. RAWLINS, P. H., late 44th Native Infantry.
Ensign, 10 June 43—Lieut., 13 June 49—Captain, 21 July 57.

SERVICE.—Captain RAWLINS served during the Sutlej Campaign, '45, '46: present at the battle of Ferozeshuhur, 20th and 21st December '45, *Medal;* at the passage of the Sutlej, 11th February '46; at the operations before the Fort of Kôt Kangra, March and April '46. Served during the Burmese War, under Major-General Godwin and Sir J. Cheape, in '52, '53. Present at the re-capture of Pegu, 19th December '52, and other operations in its vicinity, from February to March '53. Present at the assault and capture of the enemy's stockade at Donabew, 19th March '52. *(Severely wounded.)* Received the thanks of Major Armstrong for his conduct in the Field at Donabew, 8th April '53. *Medal and Clasp.* Appointed to raise and command a Militia Corps of Europeans and Eurasians at Agra, in June '57. Commanded the Militia when the Station of Agra was attacked by the Neemuch mutineers, 5th July '57. Present at the engagements at Agra, on the 10th October '57, against the Mhow and Indore mutineers. Favorably mentioned in Colonel Cotton's Despatch for his conduct on this occasion, 16th October '57. *Medal.*

LIEUTENANT E. C. B. RAWLINSON, General List, Cavalry.
Cornet, 6 July 59—Lieut., 6 July 60.

LIEUTENANT E. C. RAWSTORNE,† late 9th Native Infantry.
Ensign, 13 June 46—Lieut., 15 Nov. 53.

SURGEON G. H. RAY,† M. D., Bengal Medical Establishment.
Asst.-Surgeon, 3 Jan. 47—Surgeon, 7 Nov. 59.

SERVICE.—Surgeon RAY served with the 2nd European Regiment and was present at Ramnuggur and the passage of the Chenab. Served with the 1st Light Cavalry and was present at the action of Chillianwallah. *Medal and Clasp.* Accompanied a Detachment of sick and wounded to

(499)

Ferozepore, in '49, and rejoined the Army with Hospital Establishments. In Medical Charge of 8th Irregular Cavalry with Field Force under Lieutenant-Colonel Guise, and acted as Post Master to the Force.

CAPTAIN T. RAY, Bengal Veteran Establishment.

Captain, 4 July 60.

SERVICE.—Captain RAY served the Army during Mahratta War, '17, '18, under Lord Hastings. Served in the Burmah War, '24, '25, and '26. *Medal*. Served during the Shekawattee Campaign, '34, under General Stevens. Served in Scinde, '42, '43. Present at the battles of Meanee and Hydrabad, under Sir C. Napier. *Medal*. Served during the Sutlej Campaign, '46. Present at the occupation of Lahore, under Lord Gough. Served during the Mutiny, '57, in the Googaira District, under Colonel Patton. Served in Oude under Brigadier Franks, '58. Present at the siege and capture of Lucknow, in March '58, under Lord Clyde. (Captain Ray has completed upwards of 46 years' service.) *Medal and Clasp*.

LIEUTENANT E. C. W. RAYNSFORD, Bengal Artillery.

1st Lieut., 25 Sept. 57.

CAPTAIN H. E. READ, P. H., late 50th Native Infantry.

Ensign, 10 July 39—Lieut., 14 June 44—Bt.-Captain, 10 July 54—Captain, 23 Nov. 56.

SERVICE.—Captain READ served at the battle of Punniar. *Bronze Star*.

LIEUTENANT B. E. READE, late 67th Native Infantry.

Ensign, 26 July 57—Lieut., 18 May 58.

LIEUTENANT G. E. READE, General List.

Ensign, 15 July 59—Lieut., 5 May 61.

CAPTAIN C. REAY, P., late 32nd Native Infantry.

Ensign, 9 Sept. 42—Lieut., 1 Jan. 49—Bt.-Captain, 9 Sept. 57—Captain, 17 Oct. 57.

LIEUTENANT J. REAY,† late 63rd Native Infantry.

Ensign, 11 Jan. 48—Lieut., 5 Dec. 53.

SERVICE.—Lieutenant REAY served with the Sonthal Field Force, during the Sonthal Rebellion, in '55.

MAJOR G. B. REDDIE, P., late 29th Native Infantry.

Ensign, 15 April 26—Lieut., 24 April 33—Bt.-Captain, 15 April 14—Captain, 6 Dec. 45—Bt.-Major, 20 June 54.—Major, 11 July 61.

SERVICE.—Major REDDIE served with the Army of the Indus, in '38, '39 : present at the capture of Ghuznee. *Medal.* Served during the Punjab Campaign, '48, '49. *Medal.*

ASSISTANT-SURGEON A. K. REED,† Bengal Medical Establishment.

Asst.-Surgeon, 28 Feb. 55.

SERVICE.—Assistant-Surgeon REED served in the Baltic as Assistant-Surgeon of H. M.'s " Conflict," from the 1st April to the 3rd December '54. *Medal.* Served in the Eusuffzaie Country, from the 23rd May to the 5th June '57, in Medical Charge of two Companies of the 87th Fusiliers, against the mutineers of the late 55th Infantry. *Medal.*

LIEUTENANT G. J. REEVES, P. H., late 50th Native Infantry.

Ensign, 8 Dec. 48—Lieut., 3 March 53.

CAPTAIN B. T. REID, P., late 3rd Europeans.

Ensign, 12 June 41—Lieut., 24 Jan. 45—Bt.-Captain, 12 June 56—Captain, 23 Nov. 56.

SERVICE.—Captain REID served during the Punjab Campaign, '48, '49 : present throughout the siege of Mooltan, and as Staff Officer to Colonel Young at the storm of the heights, on 27th and 28th December '48; present at the battle of Goojerat. *Medal and 2 Clasps.* Mentioned in the Despatch of General Whish, 7th March '49. Served as Principal Civil Officer with the Force under Colonel Davidson, in pursuit of the Mooltan mutineers, '58. Received the thanks of Government, 27th

(501)

September '58; also the thanks of the Chief Commissioner, 11th October '58. (Passed an examination in Punjabee.)

COLONEL C. REID, C.B., late 10th Native Infantry.

Ensign, 13 June 35—Lieut., 3 Oct. 40—Bt.-Captain, 13 June 50—Captain, 1 Oct. 52—Major, 2 Oct. 52—Lieut.-Colonel, 19 Jan. 58—Colonel, 26 April 59.

SERVICE.—Colonel REID, C.B., served with the Sirmoor Battalion throughout the Campaign on the Sutlej, including the actions of Alliwal and Sobraon, in which latter engagement he brought the Corps out of action on the death of Captain Fisher. *Medal and Clasp.* Served in Burmah, '52, '53. *Medal.* Served with his Regiment, the Sirmoor Battalion, throughout the siege of Delhi. Commanded the main picquet at Hindoo Rao's house, from the 8th June till the 14th September '57, during which period he sustained and defeated 26 separate attacks upon his position, and one was made on that of the enemy, on the 17th June, when the strong position of Kissengunge was taken, and the enemy's heavy Batteries destroyed. Commanded the 4th Column of attack on the morning of the 14th September '57. *(Severely wounded.)* Brevet-Lieutenant-Colonel and C.B. Served during the Oude Campaign of '58, '59. Colonel and A.D.C. to the Queen. *Medal and Clasp.*

CAPTAIN C. A. REID,† late 20th Native Infantry.

Ensign, 25 Sept. 47—Lieut., 9 March 50—Captain, 6 Feb. 58.

SERVICE.—Captain REID served during the Punjab Campaign, '48, '49. Present at the actions of Chillianwallah and Goojerat. *Medal and Clasp.*

BREVET-COLONEL C. S. REID, Bengal Artillery.

2nd Lieut., 16 Dec. 24—Lieut., 4 April 29—Bt.-Captain, 16 Dec. 39—Captain, 16 Dec. 43—Bt.-Major, 11 Nov. 51—Major, 31 Dec. 54—Bt.-Lieut.-Colonel, 9 Dec. 53—Lieut.-Colonel, 25 Sept. 57—Bt.-Colonel, 28 Nov. 54—Colonel, 18 Feb. 61.

SERVICE.—Colonel REID served with the Burmah Expedition, '52, '53. Present at the taking of Martaban, and at the operations in the vicinity and capture of Rangoon, April '52. Commanded the Artillery with Sir John Cheape's Force, during the operations against the rebel Chief Mya Toon, from the 17th February to 19th March '53. *Severely wounded* at the attack and capture of the stockade near Donabew: right arm amputated. *Medal and Brevet-Lieutenant-Colonel.*

LIEUTENANT-COLNOEL D. REID, Bengal Artillery.

2nd Lieut., 10 Dec. 30—Lieut., 12 Dec. 39—Bt.-Captain, 10 Dec. 45—Captain, 26 Oct. 48—Bt.-Major, 12 Oct. 57—Lieut.-Colonel, 23 Dec. 58.

SERVICE.—Lieutenant-Colonel REID served in Assam in '40, and for nearly 20 years commanded the Local Artillery, and had much to do with jungle fighting, taking of stockades, night attacks, &c. Several times thanked by Government. Served under Colonel Hannay at the taking of Pashee, in the Abor Hills, '59; at the taking of Kenemah, in the Naga Hills, under Major Foquett, '50; and at a severe engagement with the enemy at Kikreewah, also at several attacks on hostile villages.

LIEUTENANT G. D. REID, General List.

Ensign, 20 Jan. 60—Lieut., 1 Jan. 62.

CAPTAIN J. REID, P., late 37th Native Infantry.

Ensign, 24 Sept. 42—Lieut., 30 Dec. 47—Captain, 23 Nov. 56.

SERVICE.—Captain REID served during the Punjab Campaign, '48, '49. *Medal.* Served with the Naval Brigade during the Mutinies, and Sir Jung Bahadoor's Goorkha Force. Present as a Volunteer at the assault and capture of Chandeepore Fort, under Captain Sotheby. Mentioned in Despatch, 25th March '58. Served with the Goorkha Force in Oude, and at the capture of Lucknow. Served with the Force under Sir Hope Grant, from April to October '58. Present at the affairs of Baree and Simree, action at Nawabgunge, occupation of Fyzabad and Sultanpore, and subsequent crossing of the Goomtee. Mentioned by Brigadier Horsford and General Grant in Despatches, 27th May '58, 31st May '58, and 5th October '58. Received Her Majesty's approbation of his services. (Has received a certificate and a Degree of Honor for his high proficiency and eminent attainments in Persian. Has also attained the standard of proficiency in Oordoo and Hindee.)

(503)

ASSISTANT-SURGEON J. REID,† Bengal Medical Establishment.
Asst.-Surgeon, 27 July 59.

LIEUTENANT C. H. REILLY,† Bengal Artillery.
Lieut., 27 Aug. 58.

LIEUTENANT A. G. REMINGTON, late 12th Native Infantry.
Ensign, 13 Feb. 53—Lieut., 23 Nov. 56.

SERVICE.—Lieutenant REMINGTON was present with the Right Wing of the 12th Native Infantry at its mutiny at Nowgong, on the 10th of June '57, and after wandering about for 26 days, during which time the greater part of his party died from exposure and exhaustion, eventually reached Nagode in safety. On the 26th of July accompanied Major Ellis, Political Assistant for Bundlecund, to the Fort of Kulingur, to remonstrate with the Rajah, who had placed his Troops in the Fort in disobedience to the orders of Government. The Rajah proving friendly, the Political Assistant left Lieutenant Remington in charge of the Fort and Rajah's Troops. Continued to hold this position entirely alone for the space of eleven months, when the arrival of General Whitlock's Column at Banda had rendered his presence there no longer necessary. During the above period, the Fort was besieged by the Dinapore mutineers under Koer Sing, on the 11th September, for three days, who ultimately left for Nagode, and inducing the 50th Native Infantry at that station to join them, cut off all communication between the Fort and surrounding country. Was also constantly threatened with the rebel Forces under the Nawab of Banda and Narain Rao of Kirwee, and detected a plot on the part of a portion of the Garrison, to let a party of rebels enter the Fort. Afterwards served in the Police, and effectually disarmed the Banda District.

BREVET-LIEUTENANT-COLONEL F. REMMINGTON,† C.B., Bengal Artillery.
2nd Lieut., 11 Dec. 41—Lieut., 3 July 45—Captain, 18 May 56—Bt.-Major, 19 Jan. 58—Bt.-Lieut.-Colonel, 24 March 58.

SERVICE.—Brevet-Lieutenant-Colonel REMMINGTON served at Maharajpore in '43, *Bronze Star;* during the Sutlej Campaign, '45, '46.

Present at the actions of Ferozeshuhur and Sobraon. *Medal and Clasp.* Served during the Punjab Campaign, '48, '49. *Medal.*

BREVET-MAJOR G. A. RENNY,† V.C., Bengal Artillery.

2nd Lieut., 7 June 44—Lieut., 6 Oct. 46—Captain, 27 April 58—Bt.-Major, 20 July 58.

SERVICE.—Major RENNY served with the Army of the Sutlej. Présent at the battle of Sobraon. *Medal.* Commanded 5th Native Troop, 1st Brigade Horse Artillery, when that Troop fired on the mutinous Cavalry and Infantry at Jullunder, 7th June '57. Served throughout the siege of Delhi, from 23rd June. Commanded No. 4 Siege Battery on the 14th September, heavy Mortar Batteries (manned by the Troop) in the Cashmere Bastion, on the 14th and 15th September, and in the Magazine, from its capture on the 16th, to the capture of the Palace, 20th September '57. *Victoria Cross, Medal and Clasp, and Brevet-Majority.* Commanded the same Troop in Rohilcund, in '58, and in Sir R. Walpole's action at Lisseya, near Philibheet, 15th January '59, when the conduct of the Troop was declared by Lord Clyde to be "beyond all praise."

MAJOR R. RENNY,† late 47th Native Infantry.

Ensign, 31 March 35—Lieut., 15 April 38—Captain, 22 March 50—Major, 1 Jan. 62.

SERVICE.—Major RENNY served with the Army of the Sutlej in '45, '46: present in the actions of Moodkee, Ferozeshuhur, Buddiwal, and Sobraon. *(Twice severely wounded.) Medal and 3 Clasps.* Commanded the 3rd Sikh Infantry in the expedition against the Bozdar Tribes of Beloochees, in March '57, under Brigadier Chamberlain, on the 25th March '59, when the rebels in the Nepal Terai were attacked and defeated by a Force under Sir R. Kelly. Brought to the favorable notice of the Commander-in-Chief, 21st April '59. *Medal.* Commanded the Left Column of attack on the rebel position in the Nepal Hills, 28th March '59, and received the thanks of the Governor-General and the Commander-in-Chief. Commanded a Field Column on the 27th April '59, when he attacked and defeated a large body of rebels in the Gonda District, in Oude, and received the thanks of the

Governor-General and the approval of the Commander-in-Chief, 21st May '59; on the 1st June '59, attacked and defeated a body of rebels on the Nepal Frontier, when his conduct met with the approval of the Governor-General, 1st July '59. Engaged in several minor affairs on the Goruckpore and Oude Frontiers, up to the end of '59, and final dispersion of rebels in the Nepal Frontier. Favorably mentioned in the Despatches of Brigadier Holdich, and received the thanks of the Home Government, from Sir C. Wood, 14th September '60.

LIEUTENANT H. M. REPTON, P. H., late 67th Native Infantry.

Ensign, 9 June 54—Lieut., 30 May 57.

SERVICE.—Lieutenant REPTON served under Colonel Cotton in the Agra and Muttra Districts, '57. Present at the affair at Futtehpore and other minor engagements. Present at the affairs at Jana, Orayiah, and Sheregurh Ghaut. Accompanied the Head Quarters of Alexander's Horse in pursuit of the rebel force under Ferozeshah, in the Futtehghur and Etawah Districts. *Medal.* Served in the Bundlecund Campaign, '59, under Brigadier Wheeler.

BREVET-CAPTAIN W. REVELEY, P. H., 10th (late 65th) Native Infantry.

Ensign, 11 Feb. 45—Lieut., 12 Jan. 53—Bt.-Captain, 11 Feb. 60— Captain in Staff Corps, 18 Feb. 61.

SERVICE.—Captain REVELEY served with the Field Force at Canton, in China, in '58, '59, under Sir C. VanStraubenzee. Present at the capture of Thuk Sen.

ASSISTANT-SURGEON R. RHIND,† Bengal Medical Establishment.

Asst.-Surgeon, 10 Feb. 59.

LIEUTENANT H. C. P. RICE, P. H., late 73rd Native Infantry.

Ensign, 20 Dec. 53—Lieut., 23 Nov. 56.

SERVICE.—Lieutenant RICE accompanied the Sikkim Field Force under Colonel Gawler, from the 1st February '61 to 24th March '61, as Assistant Commissariat Officer in the Sikkim Expedition.

LIEUTENANT-COLONEL J. G. A. RICE,† late 4th Europeans.

Ensign, 5 Feb. 26—Lieut., 9 July 28—Bt.-Captain, 5 Feb. 41—Captain, 6 March 46—Major, 18 April 53—Lieut.-Colonel, 29 July 57.

SERVICE.—Lieutenant-Colonel RICE served during the Affghan Campaign, '42, with the Force under Major-General Pollock. Served during the Sutlej Campaign, '45, '46.

ASSISTANT-SURGEON W. R. RICE,† M. D., Bengal Medical Establishment.

Asst.-Surgeon, 20 Nov. 56.

LIEUTENANT C. RICHARDES, late 63rd Native Infantry.

Ensign, 26th Aug. 51—Lieut., 31 Dec. 55.

SERVICE.—Lieutenant RICHARDES served during the Mutiny, '58. Commanded a Troop of European Cavalry, from Calcutta to Allahabad, in '58. Commanded a Detachment of Ferozepore Sikhs, and Sikh Volunteers, with the Sarun Field Force, under Brigadiers Berkley and Pinkney, in '58. Present at the attack and capture of Fort Dehong; also at the attack on Fort Tiroul, in Oude, 21st March '58. Present at the taking of the Forts of Bycepore and Pertabghur. Commanded in each of these Forts after their capture, and assisted with a Company of Punjab Sappers in destroying the Forts and the surrounding jungle. Received the thanks of the Brigadier on each occasion. *Medal.*

CAPTAIN W. J. S. RICHARDES,† H. M.'s 21st Light Dragoons.

Cornet, 3 May 51—Lieut., 14 Nov. 53—Captain, 9 April 61.

SERVICE.—Captain RICHARDES served with the Force before Delhi, in '57. Present at the siege and capture of Lucknow, March '58. Served with the Rohilcund Field Force. Present at the attack on Fort Rooya, action at Allygunge, and capture of Bareilly, and affairs of Shahjehanpore and Mohumdee. *Medal and Clasp.* Mentioned in the Despatch of General Walpole.

BREVET-MAJOR C. J. RICHARDS, late 25th Native Infantry.

Ensign, 14 June 32—Lieut., 15 May 37—Captain, 12 Feb. 46—Bt.-Major, 1 May 58.

(Since retired.)

(507)

MAJOR S. RICHARDS, P. H., late 55th Native Infantry.

Ensign, 8 March 36—Lieut., 3 Oct. 40—Captain, 15 Feb. 47—Bt.-Major, 13 April 60—Major, 1 Jan. 62.

SERVICE.—Major RICHARDS served during the Sutlej Campaign, '45, '46 : present at the battle of Sobraon. *Medal.*

GENERAL SIR W. RICHARDS, K.C.B., late 26th Native Infantry.

Ensign, 26 Sept. 94—Lieut., 8 Jan. 96—Captain, 21 Sept. 04—Major, 7 Aug. 14—Lieut.-Colonel, 3 Sept. 18—Colonel, 1 May 24—Major-General, 10 Jan. 37—Lieut.-General, 9 Nov. 46—General, 20 June 54.

SERVICE.—General Sir William RICHARDS, K.C.B., was present with the Volunteer Battalion at the siege of Seringapatam, and throughout the operations in Mysore, '99. *Medal.* Served against the Rajah of Palanewur, returned to Bengal, and was employed with his Regiment at the taking of the Fort of Budoon, in April '02; and at Jeitpore, 20th July '04. Served throughout the operations in Bundlecund, in Command of the Native Brigade of Nawab Mahomed Jeewun Khan. In '07 was present at the storming of Kemonah and taking of Gunowur. Served during the Nepal War, '14, '15, and '16. *Medal.* Present at the assault of Kalinger; commanded the Force at Peacock Hill; present at the affair in the Punjore Valley. *Medal.* Marched with the Regiment from Moradabad to Bareilly in 24 hours, and quelled the insurrection there, in '16. In March '21 commanded a Force in the Lurka Cole Country. In '21, till '24, commanded the Fortress of Asseerghur, and the 1st Brigade of General Morison's Force in Arracan, '25. Present throughout the operations in that country. *C.B.*

LIEUTENANT C. L. RICHARDSON, P., late 58th Native Infantry.

Ensign, 10 June 48—Lieut., 7 Dec. 55.

SERVICE.—Lieutenant RICHARDSON served during the Punjab Campaign, '49. *Medal.*

ASSISTANT-SURGEON J. RICHARDSON,† M.B., Bengal Medical Establishment.

Asst.-Surgeon, 27 July 59.

MAJOR J. F. RICHARDSON, C.B., P. H., late 49th Native Infantry.

Ensign, 21 April 41—Lieut., 24 Jan. 45—Captain, 24 Jan. 51—Bt.-Major, 20 July 58—Major, 21 April 61.

SERVICE.—Major RICHARDSON, C.B., served during the Punjab Campaign, '48, '49 : present throughout the siege and capture of Mooltan. *(Wounded dangerously,* 19th September '48, having received 17 *wounds.) Medal and Clasp.* Received a most commendatory letter (autograph) from the Right Honorable Lord Gough. Appointed Adjutant, 10th Irregulur Cavalry, as a reward for these services. Served in Burmah in '54. Raised the Regiment of Bengal Yeomanry Cavalry in '57, and commanded it throughout the Mutinies. Present at the actions of Amorah, 5th March, Thilga, 17th April, Amorah, 25th April and 9th June, Dumooreahgunge, 26th November, Burraree, 28th November; and Toolsipore, 23rd December '58. Brought to the notice of the Commander-in-Chief and the Governor-General in Despatches of Brigadier Rowcroft, 22nd March, 19th April, 30th June, 22nd July, 27th April, 6th August, 17th August, 28th November, and 5th December '58 ; 14th and 24th January '59. Received the thanks of Government, 16th July '59. *Medal and C.B.*

BREVET-MAJOR R. RICHARDSON,† late 1st Bengal European Cavalry.

Cornet, 26 March 39—Lieut., 1 Jan. 46—Bt.-Captain, 26 March 54—Captain, 20 Sept. 54—Bt.-Major, 6 June 56.

SERVICE.—Major RICHARDSON served during the Sutlej Campaign, '45, '46 : present at the actions of Buddiwal, Alliwal, and Sobraon. *Medal and Clasp.*

ENSIGN R. RICHARDSON, Unattached List.

Ensign, 29 Nov. 58.

SERVICE.—Ensign RICHARDSON served in the Campaign against the Hill Tribes in Scinde, under Sir Charles Napier, in '45. Served in the Punjab Campaign, '48, '49: present at the affair at Ramnuggur, passage of the Chenab, battles of Chillianwallah and Goojerat, and subsequent pursuit of the Sikhs and Affghans, under General Gilbert. *Medal and Clasps.* Served during the siege and capture of Delhi, in '57, and with

(509)

Brigadier Showers' Moveable Column in the District. Promoted to Ensign's Commission (Unattached), 29th November '58. *Medal and Clasp.*

LIEUTENANT-COLONEL W. RICHARDSON, P. C., late 73rd Native Infantry.

Ensign, 19 Jan. 28—Lieut., 2 Aug. 39—Captain, 19 Jan. 43—Bt.-Major, 4 April 45—Major, 20 June 54—Lieut.-Colonel, 25 Oct. 59.

SERVICE.—Lieutenant-Colonel RICHARDSON served in the Sutlej Campaign, in '45, '46 : present at the actions of Moodkee, Ferozeshuhur, and Sobraon. *Medal and 2 Clasps.* Favorably mentioned by the Officer Commanding the Regiment in his report of the action of Ferozeshuhur. Served with the Army of the Punjab, '47. *Medal.* Received the thanks of the Government of Bengal for conduct in '57, while he commanded the 2nd Assam Light Infantry.

MAJOR-GENERAL A. F. RICHMOND, C.B., late 24th Native Infantry.

Ensign, 27 Oct. 09—Lieut., 16 Dec. 14—Captain, 1 May 24—Major, 13 May 33—Lieut.-Colonel, 24 Jan. 40—Colonel, 28 March 50—Major-General, 28 Nov. 54.

SERVICE.—Major-General RICHMOND, C.B., was at the siege of Kalinger, in '11 ; in the Nepal War, '14, '15 ; at the assault on Kalunga, at Nalagurh, *wounded,* and Nahun ; at the siege and capture of Bhurtpore, '26. *Medal and Clasp.* Commanded the Regiment in the Affghan Campaign of '42, including the engagement in the Mazeena Valley ; that of Tuzee (where he commanded the Rear Guard), and the advance on Cabul. *Medal and C.B.*

ASSISTANT-SURGEON A. F. RICHMOND,† Bengal Medical Establishment.

Asst.-Surgeon, 23 July 58.

LIEUTENANT G. M. RICHMOND,† late 54th Native Infantry.

Ensign, 12 June 58—Lieut., 22 Oct. 58.

SERVICE.—Lieutenant RICHMOND served with the Expeditionary Force to China, in '60 : present at the action of Sinho, attack and capture of Tonko, and the Taku Forts, and in the subsequent advance on Pekin, and final surrender of that city. *Medal and 2 Clasps.*

(510)

MAJOR E. J. RICKARDS, P. H., late 5th Europeans.

Ensign, 27 March 38—Lieut., 20 Dec. 43—Bt.-Captain, 27 March 53—Captain, 18 April 53—Major, 18 Feb. 61.

SERVICE.—Major RICKARDS served with the 6th Native Infantry in the Cabul Campaign, '42, and with the Army under General Pollock. Served during the Sutlej Campaign, 45, '46.

LIEUTENANT M. P. RICKETTS, P. C., late 4th Europeans.

Ensign, 4 Feb. 55—Lieut., 4 Sept. 57.

SERVICE.—Lieutenant RICKETTS served with the Force under Captain Dunbar, at the relief of the Garrison of Arrah, 29th July '57. Present throughout the siege of Azimghur, March to April '58, and accompanied H. M.'s 37th for the purpose of carrying orders on the occasion of a sortie being made on the Town. Present at one or two skirmishes in the neighborhood, and detained as Station Staff at Azimghur. Served as Staff Officer to the Force under Colonel Milman, on the occasion of a body of rebels being defeated at Atrobea, 21st March '58, and mentioned in the Despatch of Colonel Milman, 25th April '58. *Medal.* (Has passed the higher standard of Civil Examination.)

LIEUTENANT H. V. RIDDELL,† late 2nd European Bengal Fusiliers.

Ensign, 11 Dec. 58—Lieut., 15 May 59.

SERVICE.—Lieutenant RIDDELL served with H. M.'s 19th Foot in the Tirhoot and Chumparun Districts, in '59.

LIEUTENANT R. V. RIDDELL, Bengal Engineers.

2nd Lieut., 10 June 59.

BREVET-COLONEL W. RIDDELL, C.B., late 3rd Europeans.

Ensign, 28 May 23—Lieut., 13 May 25—Captain, 1 Dec. 36—Bt.-Major, 23 Dec. 42—Major, 15 Nov. 49—Bt.-Lieut.-Colonel, 20 June 54—Lieut.-Colonel, 25 Feb. 55—Bt.-Colonel, 5 Dec. 55.

SERVICE.—Colonel RIDDELL served with the 60th Native Infantry at the siege of Bhurtpore, *Medal;* also during the Campaign in Affghanistan,

'42. *Medal and Brevet-Major.* Commanded the 3rd European Regiment during the Mutinies of '57, '58, in the actions near Agra, against the insurgent Neemuch Brigade, 5th July, and against the Indore and Mhow mutineers, 10th October '57. Commanded the Mynpoorie Moveable Column throughout the operations near and at Shereghur Ghaut, 16th May, and the Agra Column towards Dholpore, co-operating with the Central India Field Force under Sir H. Rose, against Gwalior, in June '58. *Medal and C.B. (Since retired.)*

LIEUTENANT C. W. RIGGS,† General List.

Ensign, 20 April 59—Lieut., 31 Aug. 60.

COLONEL H. RIGHY, Bengal Engineers.

2nd Lieut., 12 June 29—Lieut., 20 May 39—Bt.-Captain, 12 June 44—Captain, 1 Dec. 47—Bt.-Major, 28 Nov. 54—Major, 20 Sept. 57—Lieut.-Colonel, 27 Aug. 58—Colonel, 13 March 61.

MAJOR-GENERAL S. D. RILEY, late 47th Native Infantry.

Ensign, 1 Jan. 04—Lieut., 2 July 06—Bt.-Captain, 1 Jan. 19—Captain, 20 Aug. 22—Major, 3 July 32—Lieut.-Colonel, 19 April 39—Colonel, 9 April 49—Major-General, 28 Nov. 54.

SERVICE.—Major-General RILEY served during the Nepal War, '14, '15. *(Wounded.) Medal.* Pindarree Campaign, '17, '18, and at the battle of Maharajpore. *Bronze Star.*

DEPUTY-INSPECTOR-GENERAL OF HOSPITALS, M. McN. RIND, Bengal Medical Establishment.

Asst.-Surgeon, 10 Oct. 29—Surgeon, 6 April 46—Surgeon-Major, 13 Jan. 60.—Deputy-Inspector-General of Hospitals, 25 May 61.

LIEUTENANT M. McN. RIND, late 21st Native Infantry.

Ensign, 6 Jan. 59—Lieut., 25 Aug. 59.

CAPTAIN W. J. RIND, Bengal Invalid Establishment.

Ensign, 27 Jan. 24—Lieut., 14 July 25—Captain, 17 Jan. 39.

(512)

ASSISTANT-SURGEON T. RINGER,† M. D., Bengal Medical Establishment.
Asst.-Surgeon, 17 April 54.

SERVICE.—Assistant-Surgeon T. RINGER served with the Column under Brigadier Franks, in Oude, '58. Present at the siege and capture of Lucknow, by Sir Colin Campbell, in March '58; at the battle and taking of Bareilly, May '58. Served with the Soraon Field Force under Brigadier Berkeley. Present at the capture of the Forts Deghain, Turoul, and Bhyspore, in '58. *Medal and Clasp.*

LIEUTENANT E. P. W. RIPLEY, P. H., late 51st Native Infantry.
Ensign, 20 July 49—Lieut., 18 March 53.

SERVICE.—Lieutenant RIPLEY served throughout the operations in China, in '60, under Sir Hope Grant. *Medal and 2 Clasps.*

LIEUTENANT F. J. RIPLEY, P. H., late 70th Native Infantry.
Ensign, 20 Dec. 51—Lieut., 23 Nov. 56.

LIEUTENANT F. T. RIPLEY,† late 47th Native Infantry.
Ensign, 4 Aug. 57—Lieut., 18 May 58.

MAJOR F. W. RIPLEY, P. H., late 22nd Native Infantry.
Ensign, 12 June 41—Lieut., 24 Jan. 45—Bt.-Captain, 12 June 56—Captain, 23 Nov. 56—Major, 12 June 61.

(Passed an examination in Burmese.)

LIEUTENANT V. RIVAS, Bengal Artillery.
Lieut., 8 June 60.

BREVET-MAJOR C. J. ROBARTS, P. H., late 43rd Native Infantry.
Ensign, 12 June 39—Lieut., 17 Nov. 42—Bt.-Captain, 12 June 54—Captain, 9 March 55—Bt.-Major, 8 March 55.

SERVICE.—Major ROBARTS served in Affghanistan, '40, '41, '42. *Medal.* Served during the Punjab Campaign, '48, '49: present at the siege and surrender of Mooltan, and battle of Goojerat. *Medal.*

(513)

BREVET-COLONEL W. P. ROBBINS, late 15th Native Infantry.

Ensign, 20 June 27—Lieut., 31 May 34—Bt.-Captain, 20 June 42—Captain, 1 Feb. 43—Bt.-Major, 7 June 49—Major, 28 Nov. 54—Bt.-Lieut.-Colonel, 28 Nov. 54—Lieut.-Colonel, 9 Oct. 58—Bt.-Colonel, 28 Nov. 57.

SERVICE.—Colonel ROBBINS served during the Punjab Campaign, '48, '49: present as Orderly Officer to General Gilbert at the battles of Chillianwallah and Goojerat, and as A.D.C. to the General in the pursuit of the Sikhs and Affghans to Peshawur. *Medal and 2 Clasps. (Since dead.)*

MAJOR P. A. ROBERTON,† late 68th Native Infantry.

Ensign, 7 July 38—Lieut., 5 Sept. 42—Captain, 1 Nov. 49—Major, 15 May 59.

SERVICE.—Major ROBERTON served with the Army of the Sutlej in '46: present at the battle of Sobraon. *(Wounded severely.) Medal.* Served during the War in Burmah, '52, '53. *Medal.* Aided in defence of Nynee Tâl, during the Mutiny, '57, '58, and in attacks on the rebels' camp at the Fort of the Kumaon Hills. Present at the re-taking of Bareilly, in May '58. Commanded the 34th Native Infantry in Bundlecund, against the rebels, '59, '60. Favorably mentioned in Colonel Turner's Despatch of a night attack made on the rebels' camp, November '59. *Medal.*

LIEUTENANT-GENERAL A. ROBERTS, C.B., late 1st European Bengal Fusiliers.

Ensign, 18 March 05—Lieut., 19 March 05—Captain, 27 Aug. 22—Major, 24 Sept. 26—Lieut.-Colonel, 28 Sept. 31—Colonel, 10 Nov. 43—Major-General, 20 June 54—Lieut.-General, 13 Oct. 57.

SERVICE.—Lieutenant-General ROBERTS, C.B., served under Lord Lake in the Punjab, in '05, when the Army crossed the Sutlej in pursuit of Holkar and Ameer Khan, in '06. Served in Bundlecund in '07; at the siege of Kemona and Gunowur, in the Doab, under General Dickens; in the Nepal War, '14, '15; at the storm of Kullunga. Commanded the 1st Battery, 13th Native Infantry, in action at Peacock Hill, near the Fort of Jytuk, and was afterwards engaged at Birlake Tebee. *Medal.* Being on Staff employ, joined and marched with his Regiment to Bareilly, where it was sent to quell the insurrection, in April '16. Served in Affghanistan, '38 to '41. Commanded the 4th Brigade of the Army of the Indus. Present at the storm and capture of Ghuznee, succeeding Sir R. Sale in the Command of the Fortress; caused the capture of Hyder Khan, the Governor of the Fortress, and son of Dost Mahomed Khan, for which he received the thanks of the Commander-in-Chief. *Medal and C.B.* Afterwards commanded the Shah's Troops. *2nd Class Dooranee Order.* In '42 commanded the 4th Brigade of the Army of Reserve.

LIEUTENANT A. W. ROBERTS, General List, Cavalry.

Cornet, 20 Feb. 59—Lieut., 12 July 59.

BREVET-MAJOR F. S. ROBERTS, P. H., V.C., Bengal Artillery.

Lieut., 31 May 57—2nd Captain, 12 Nov. 60—Bt.-Major, 13 Nov. 60.

SERVICE.—Major ROBERTS was present at the disarming of the 33rd and 35th Native Infantry, in '57. Served throughout the siege and capture of Delhi *(wounded)*, 14th July; *horse shot*, 14th September '57. *Medal and Clasp.* Mentioned in the Despatch of Sir A. Wilson, 10th December '57. Received the thanks of Government, 4th December '57. Present at the actions, with Colonel Greathed's Column, of Boolundshuhur, *(horse shot)*, Allyghur, Agra, and Kanouje. *(Horse wounded.)* Brought to notice of the Commander-in-Chief in the Despatches of Colonel Greathed, Major Owny, Captain Bourchier, — Thornhill, Esq., and Colonel Cotton, 29th December '57. Received the thanks of Government, 23rd December '57. Present at the relief of Lucknow. *Clasp.* Brought to notice of the Commander-in-Chief by Brigadier-General Grant, 12th December '57. Received the thanks of Government, 10th December '57. Present at the battles of Cawnpore, 6th December, Khodagunge, and occupation of Futtehghur. Brought to notice of the Commander-in-Chief by Brigadier Grant. Mentioned in the Despatch of the Commander-in-Chief, 30th December '57. Received the thanks of Government, 24th December '57. Present at the storm and capture of Meeagunge, action of Koorsee, and capture of Lucknow. *Clasp.* Brought three times to the notice of the Commander-in-Chief by Sir H. Grant, 6th March, and 16th and 28th April '58. Mentioned in the Despatch of the Commander-in-Chief, 16th April '58. Received the thanks of Government, 5th April '58. *Brevet-Majority* for services in '57, '58, and received the *Victoria Cross*, 2nd January '58.

CAPTAIN G. R. ROBERTS, P., late 41st Native Infantry.

Ensign, 7 June 44—Lieut., 1 July 46—Captain, 23 Nov. 56.

SERVICE.—Captain ROBERTS served throughout the Sutlej Campaign, '45, '46. Present at the battle of Sobraon. *Medal and Clasp.*

CAPTAIN H. C. ROBERTS,† late 31st Native Infantry.

Ensign, 11 Dec. 35—Lieut., 3 Oct. 40—Bt.-Captain, 11 Dec. 50—Captain, 27 July 51.

SERVICE.—Captain ROBERTS served in the Cole Country, '36, '37; Affghanistan, '39. Present at the storm and capture of Khelat, and at the battle of Maharajpore. *Bronze Star.* Served during the Mutinies, '57, '58, in the Saugor District.

LIEUTENANT J. ROBERTS,† late 40th Native Infantry.

Ensign, 27 Sept. 52.—Lieut., 23 Nov. 56.

SERVICE.—Lieutenant ROBERTS served during the Sonthal Rebellion, '55, under Major-General Lloyd.

LIEUTENANT W. E. R. ROBERTS,† late 54th Native Infantry.

Ensign, 20 Dec. 50—Lieut., 1 June 56.

SERVICE.—Lieutenant ROBERTS served with the 3rd Europeans in the operations at Shereghur Ghaut, in May '58. Present at the action of Dowsa, 14th January '59, under Brigadier Showers, against Tantia Topee. *Medal.*

ENSIGN D. H. ROBERTSON, General List.

Ensign, 4 Nov. 60.

(516)

CAPTAIN H. L. ROBERTSON, P., 10th (late 65th) Native Infantry.

Ensign, 11 Dec. 38—Lieut., 3 Oct. 40—Captain, 13 Dec. 50.

SERVICE.—Captain ROBERTSON served in Burmah in '55, '56. Commanded the Troops at Azimghur and at the engagements with the rebels, in August '57. *Medal.* Served in China, from April '58 till March '60. *Medal.*

LIEUTENANT R. S. ROBERTSON, P. H., late 6th Europeans.

Ensign, 4 Feb. 54—Lieut., 23 Nov. 56.

SERVICE.—Lieutenant ROBERTSON served with Colonel Eyre's Force in the Shahabad District, in August '57. Present at the capture of Jugdespore and siege and capture of Lucknow. Served with Sir E. Lugard's Force in the Shahabad District, in '58. *Medal and Clasp.*

CAPTAIN A. ROBINSON, P. H., late 19th Native Infantry.

Ensign, 27 Aug. 37—Lieut., 3 Oct. 40—Captain, 31 Dec. 50.

SERVICE.—Captain ROBINSON accompanied expedition against the rebels in the Cossiah and Jyntia Hills, in Command of a Wing, 20 Native Infantry. Present at the capture of the stockade at Ooksae, 11 March '62.

LIEUTENANT C. G. ROBINSON, P. H., Bengal Artillery.

1st Lieut., 5 Oct. 57.

CAPTAIN D. G. ROBINSON, P. H., Bengal Engineers.

2nd Lieut., 9 June 43—Lieut., 16 June 47—Captain, 21 Nov. 56.

SERVICE.—Captain ROBINSON served during the Sutlej Campaign, '45, '46. Present at the battle of Sobraon. *Medal.* Served during the Punjab Campaign, '48, '49. Present at the actions of Chillianwallah and Goojerat. *Medal.*

ASSISTANT-SURGEON H. W. ROBINSON,† B.A., Bengal Medical Establishment.

Asst.-Surgeon, 7 Sept. 54.

CAPTAIN J. I. ROBINSON,† late 5th Bengal European Cavalry.

Cornet, 9 Aug. 49—Lieut., 20 Aug. 51—Captain, 3 April 59.

SERVICE.—Captain ROBINSON served with the 2nd Punjab Irregular Cavalry, at the final siege and capture of Lucknow, by Lord Clyde, in March '58. Present at the affair of Koorsee. Served with the 9th Royal Lancers in the Rohilcund Campaign. Present at the actions of Rooya and Allygunge, capture of Bareilly, and affairs of Shahjehanpore and Mohumdee. *Medal and Clasp.*

LIEUTENANT J. S. ROBINSON,† late 1st Bengal European Cavalry.

Cornet, 4 Jan. 57—Lieut., 27 April 57.

SERVICE.—Lieutenant ROBINSON was taken prisoner the morning after the Mutiny at Meerut, by a party of Goojurs, '57. Present at the Mutiny of Boolundshuhur, May '57. Served as a Private in the Khakee Ressala, Meerut District Volunteers, from the date of raising to 1st September '57, and present in all their actions. Served with the Boolundshuhur Police, on out-post duty, on the banks of the Ganges, in May '58.

LIEUTENANT R. S. ROBINSON, Bengal Artillery.

1st Lieut., 27 April 58.

LIEUTENANT C. S. DEF. ROCHE, late 47th Native Infantry.

Ensign, 11 Dec. 58—Lieut., 20 Aug. 59.

SERVICE.—Lieutenant ROCHE served with H. M.'s 34th from April to May '59, during the latter part of the Oude Campaign.

LIEUTENANT T. F. C. ROCHFORD, late 4th Bengal European Cavalry.

Cornet, 4 April 57—Lieut., 18 May 58.

SERVICE.—Lieutenant ROCHFORD served during the Mutiny, '57, '58. Present at the siege and capture of Lucknow, March '58, under Lord Clyde, also in the operations in Oude under Sir Hope Grant, '58. Present at the actions of Koorsee and Baree, March and April '58. *Medal and Clasp.*

(518)

LIEUTENANT P. RODDY, V.C., Unattached List.

Lieut., 3 Dec. 58.

SERVICE.—Lieutenant RODDY served with General Havelock's 1st advance to Lucknow, and was present at all the different engagements under his Command. Present at the relief and occupation of the Residency of Lucknow, 25th September '57. Present at the defence of Alum Bagh by Sir James Outram. Mentioned in the Despatch of the Major-General, 23rd December '58; also by Major V. Eyre, 8th January '58. Promoted to Ensign's Commission for services in the Field, 24th February '58. Present at the capture of Lucknow by Lord Clyde, March '58. Served during the Oude Campaign, '58. Commanded the Artillery in all the different engagements with the enemy. Promoted to the rank of Lieutenant, and received the decoration of the *V.C.* for services in the Field. Mentioned several times in Despatches. Received the thanks of Government, also of the Oude Local Government, several times, for services. Had his *horse shot* and *wounded slightly* several times. Present on the Oude Frontier at the final capture of the rebels, who found an asylum in the Nepalese Territory, and commanded the Oude Military Police during the moment of their capture. *Medal and 2 Clasps.*

LIEUTENANT B. ROGERS, P. H., late 68th Native Infantry.

Ensign, 8 June 54—Lieut., 23 Nov. 56.

VETERINARY-SURGEON F. ROGERS, Bengal Veterinary Establishment.

Vety.-Surgeon, 6 June 60.

LIEUTENANT R. G. ROGERS, P. H., late 5th Europeans.

Ensign, 9 Dec. 48—Lieut., 28 Aug. 52.

CAPTAIN S. ROGERS,† late 73rd Native Infantry.

Ensign, 19 June 42—Lieut., 24 Jan. 45—Captain, 23 Nov. 56.

SERVICE.—Captain ROGERS served throughout the Sutlej Campaign, '45, '46. Present at the actions of Moodkee, Ferozeshuhur, and Sobraon. *Medal and Clasps.* Served during the Punjab Campaign, '48, '49. *Medal.*

(519)

LIEUTENANT H. A. ROOKE,† late 12th Native Infantry.

Ensign, 20 Feb. 58—Lieut., 4 Aug. 58.

SERVICE.—Lieutenant ROOKE served with H. M.'s 90th Light Infantry during the Mutiny in Oude, in '58, '59; also in the subsequent operations in the Terai, November and December '59. *Medal.*

ENSIGN M. ROSAMOND, V.C., Unattached List.

Ensign, 16 April 58.

SERVICE.—Ensign ROSAMOND entered the Army as a Private Soldier in '41, and was attached to the 2nd Fusiliers. Served the Campaign in Scinde, and against the Hill Tribes in Beloochistan, under Sir Charles Napier. Served in the Punjab Campaign under Lord Gough, and was present at the battles of Ramnuggur, passage of the Chenab, Chillianwallah, and Goojerat. *Medal and 2 Clasps.* Served during the rebellion of '57. *Medal and Victoria Cross.* Received the Cross for meritorious conduct on the 4th June '57, in volunteering and bringing in Captain Brown, Pension Pay-Master, and his wife and infant, and others from a detached bungalow into the Barracks, and for setting fire to the Sepoy lines, with the view of driving out the enemy; also for saving the life of Major Barrett, of the 37th Native Infantry, when a Sepoy was in the act of bayonetting him; also for conveying a message from Major Barrett through a terrific shower of grape, and a cross-fire from the rebels, to the Brigadier. Promoted to an Unattached Ensigncy.

CAPTAIN H. ROSE, P., late 4th Europeans.

Ensign, 11 June 42—Lieut., 1 April 47—Bt.-Captain, 11 June 57—Captain, 15 Nov. 57.

(Has furnished certificates of qualification in Surveying and Civil Engineering.)

SURGEON J. ROSE, Bengal Medical Establishment.

Asst.-Surgeon, 25 May 43—Surgeon, 27 June 57.

LIEUTENANT A. G. ROSS, P. H., late 17th Native Infantry.

Ensign, 4 Nov. 57—Lieut., 12 Dec. 59.

SERVICE.—Lieutenant Ross served with H. M.'s 35th Foot at Arrah, in July '58; with H. M.'s 79th Highlanders in the Oude Campaign,

'58, '59. Present at the capture of the Fort of Rampore Kussia, 3rd November '58. *Medal.*

BREVET-MAJOR A. H. ROSS,† late 42nd Native Infantry.

Ensign, 20 Jan. 30—Lieut., 6 Sept. 39—Bt.-Captain, 20 Jan. 45—Captain, 15 Nov. 53—Bt.-Major, 28 Nov. 54.

SERVICE.—Major Ross served throughout the Campaign in Affghanistan, '39, '40, '41, '42. Engaged in all the operations of the Candahar Force. Commanded the 5th Regiment of Shah Shoojah's Force at the action of Ghirisk, 3rd July '41. *Medal.* Served during the War on the Sutlej, including the battles of Moodkee, Ferozeshuhur, and Sobraon. *Medal and Clasps.* *(Since retired.)*

BREVET-MAJOR C. C. G. ROSS, P. H., late 66th Native Infantry.

Ensign, 4 April 41—Lieut., 16 May 44—Captain, 10 May 52—Bt.-Major, 24 March 58.

SERVICE.—Major Ross served under Lord Clyde against the Peshawur Hill Tribes, in '51, '52. Present at the action of Skakoto, May '52; against the Hill Tribes in '53; in defence of Kumaon, during the Mutiny, under Brigadier M'Causland. Commanded the 66th Goorkha Regiment in the action of Churpoorah. Brought to the notice of the Commander-in-Chief in the Despatch, 12th February '58. Promoted to the rank of Brevet-Major for the above service, 24th March '58. Commanded the 66th Goorkha Regiment during the Campaign of '58, under Brigadier Troup, from 10th November '58 to 17th March '59. *Medal.*

LIEUTENANT D. ROSS, P. H., late 10th Native Infantry.

Ensign, 11 Jan. 51—Lieut., 17 April 55.

SERVICE.—Lieutenant Ross served throughout the Sonthal Rebellion, in '55, '56.

CAPTAIN E. D. R. ROSS, P. H., late 3rd Europeans.

Ensign, 22 Feb. 43—Lieut., 21 Dec. 45—Captain, 21 Jan. 57.

SERVICE.—Captain Ross served with the Army of the Sutlej, in '46. Present at the actions of Moodkee, Ferozeshuhur, and Sobraon. *Medal and 2 Clasps.* Served during the Punjab Campaign, '49. *Medal.* Served with the 3rd Europeans throughout the Indian Mutinies, '57, '58. *Medal.*

(521)

CAPTAIN J. ROSS, P. H., late 71st Native Infantry.

Ensign, 9 March 42—Lieut., 24 Jan. 45—Captain, 30 Dec. 54.

SERVICE.—Captain Ross served with the Force under General Wheeler, in the Sikh Campaign of '48. *Medal.*

SURGEON J. T. C. ROSS,† F.R.C.S., Bengal Medical Establishment.

Asst.-Surgeon, 26 July 45—Surgeon, 24 April 59.

SERVICE.—Surgeon Ross served in Medical Charge of the 71st, 4th Cavalry, and 4th Company, 6th Battalion Artillery, with No. 19 Light Field Battery, in General Wheeler's Brigade, during the Punjab Campaign. Present at the capture of Forts Rungul Nungul and Moraree; went with a guard of 100 men to Kohat to take Medical Charge of 1st Punjab Cavalry, on Field Service there, in February '50. Served under Captain Coke in his expedition to Meeranzaie, on the Cabul Frontier, in the autumn of '51; had additional charge of the 1st Punjab Infantry, during the operations in the Ranezaie Valley, under Sir C. Campbell, in the hot weather of '52. Present at the capture of Pranghur, Skakote, and Erothal. In Medical Charge of 1st Punjab Cavalry, and with general Medical Superintendence of the Brigade under Major Coke, at the affairs of Kohat and Kohtul, in November '53. In Medical Charge of a Battery, Royal Artillery, and 3 Companies, H. M.'s Infantry, at the capture of villages near Allahabad, under Brigadier Campbell, in December '57. Joined the Army under Sir C. Campbell, Commander-in-Chief at Cawnpore. Was present in Medical Charge of the Cavalry on the Field, in the charge which closed the action on the Kala Nuddee, near Futtehghur, in January '58. *Punjab Medal. Mutiny Medal.* Received the thanks of Government.

LIEUTENANT T. G. ROSS,† late 21st Native Infantry.

Ensign, 20 March 50—Lieut., 27 Feb. 56.

2ND CAPTAIN W. A. ROSS, P. H., Bengal Artillery.

2nd Lieut., 14 June 45—Lieut., 23 Sept. 50—2nd Captain, 27 Aug. 58.

SERVICE.—Captain Ross served throughout the Punjab Campaign, including the battles of Chillianwallah and Goojerat. *Medal and 2 Clasps.*

(522)

BREVET-MAJOR O. E. ROTHNEY, P., late 45th Native Infantry.

Ensign, 27 June 41—Lieut., 20 July 43—Captain, 15 May 52—Bt.-Major, 19 Jan. 58—Major, 27 June 61.

SERVICE.—Major ROTHNEY served during the Sutlej Campaign, '45, '46; with Colonel Mackeson's Force against the Hussunzaies, in '52. Commanded the 4th Sikh Infantry in charge of a chain of outposts in Tharrawaddy, in Pegu, in '54, and engaged several times against the rebel leader Goung Gee. Present at Loodianah, 8th June '57, and held the Town and Fort in check, and protected the Cantonment with the main body of the 4th Sikh Infantry; afterwards pursued the mutineers with Major Olphert's Column. Joined the Delhi Field Force, 23rd June '57, and commanded the 4th Sikh Infantry throughout the siege and assault of Delhi, and present in several other engagements in and near Delhi. *Medal and Clasp.* Mentioned in the Despatch of Brigadier W. Jones, 17th September '57. Promoted to the rank of Brevet-Major for service in the siege of Delhi. Commanded the 4th Sikh Infantry, with General Chamberlain's Force, against the Cabul Khel Wuzeerees, in '59, and was present at the affair of Maidanee, 22nd December '59. Commanded the Huzara Goorkha Battalion, with General Chamberlain's Force, against the Mahsood Wuzeerees, in '60. Present at the repulse of the night attack on the camp at Palooseen, 23rd April '60, and at the forcing of the Burrara Pass, 4th May '60. Mentioned in Brigadier Chamberlain's Despatch.

CAPTAIN A. ROTTON, P. H., Bengal Artillery.

2nd Lieut., 14 June 50—Lieut., 28 Oct. 55—2nd Captain, 27 Aug. 58.

ASSISTANT-SURGEON R. ROUSE,† Bengal Medical Establishment.

Asst.-Surgeon, 20 Dec. 54.

CAPTAIN W. S. ROW, P. C., late 33rd Native Infantry.

Ensign, 23 Feb. 42—Lieut., 10 Feb. 46—Captain, 23 Nov. 56.

SERVICE.—Captain Row served during the Sutlej Campaign, '45, '46. Present at the actions of Ferozeshuhur and Sobraon. *Medal and Clasp.*

(523)

COLONEL F. ROWCROFT, C.B., late 62nd Native Infantry.

Ensign, 7 Oct. 19—Lieut., 14 Sept. 21—Captain, 7 Aug. 29—Major, 26 May 43—Lieut.-Colonel, 14 Nov. 49—Bt.-Colonel, 28 Nov. 54—Colonel, 15 May 59.

SERVICE.—Colonel F. ROWCROFT, C.B., commanded the Sarun and Goruckpore Field Force with the Naval Brigade of H. M.'s *Pearl*, in the Goruckpore District, during the Indian War, '57, '58. Served in Command of the Field Force in the successful actions of Shohunpore, 26th December '57; Phoolpore, in Oude, on the Gogra, capturing three guns, 20th February '58; of Amorah, near Fyzabad, capturing eight guns, 5th March '58. Appointed Brigadier from 1st January '58. Commanded in the actions of 17th and 25th April '58, near Amorah; of the 26th November and 3rd December '58, on the Raptee; and present at the battle of Toolseepore, near the Nepal Hills, against Balla Rao and Mahomed Hussun, capturing two guns, 23rd December '58: in the several actions captured sixteen guns. *C. B. and Medal.*

LIEUTENANT F. F. ROWCROFT,† late 2nd Native Infantry.

Ensign, 10 Dec. 53—Lieut., 23 Nov. 56.

CAPTAIN G. C. ROWCROFT, P. H., late 41st Native Infantry.

Ensign, 10 Aug. 49—Lieut., 8 Dec. 52—Captain, 18 Aug. 61.

SERVICE.—Captain ROWCROFT served under Colonel Mackeson against the Hussunzaies, on the Huzara Frontier, in '52. Commanded the Khelat-i-Ghilzie Regiment when employed with the Force under Sir Sydney Cotton, on the Eusuffzaie Frontier, and against the Fanatics of Sittana, in April and May '58. (Passed examination in Field Engineering.)

LIEUTENANT H. C. ROWCROFT,† Bengal Engineers.

Lieut., 10 June 59.

LIEUTENANT H. ROWLAND,† late 63rd Native Infantry.

Ensign, 29 Sept. 57—Lieut., 17 Sept. 58.

(524)

CAPTAIN E. A. ROWLATT, P. H., late 21st Native Infantry.

Ensign, 14 Feb. 39—Lieut., 1 July 41—Captain, 1 Dec. 49.

(Passed an examination in Assamese and Bengali.)

CAPTAIN J. RUGGLES, P. H., late 41st Native Infantry.

Ensign, 13 June 45—Lieut., 28 Sept. 49—Captain, 27 June 57.

SERVICE.—Captain RUGGLES served with the expedition against Kôt Kangra, in '46. Present at the defence of Lucknow, June to November 57. *Medal and Clasp, and one year's extra service.* Joined the China Expedition as a Volunteer, '60, '61. (Has furnished certificates of qualification in Surveying and Civil Engineering.)

LIEUTENANT F. W. RUSSELL, P. H., late 3rd Bengal European Cavalry.

Cornet, 20 Dec. 49—Lieut., 28 Nov. 54.

SERVICE.—Lieutenant RUSSELL served under Colonel Dunsford during the siege and capture of Delhi, 14th September '57. Present at the action of Bun-ke-Jaon under Sir T. Seaton, at the actions of Mahadypore, Russoolpore, the Fort of Mittowlee, Allygunge, and Biswa, under Brigadier Troop, in Oude, '58. *Medal and Clasp.*

LIEUTENANT G. A. RUSSELL, Bengal Artillery.

Lieut., 27 Aug. 58.

LIEUTENANT J. J. RUSSELL, P. H., late 46th Native Infantry.

Ensign, 3 March 50—Lieut., 17 April 56.

SERVICE.—Lieutenant RUSSELL served with "Lind's Mooltanee Horse," in Rohtuck, in '57. Present at the battle of Narnoul, 16th November '57; with Penny's Column at the passage of the Ganges; at the action before and capture of Bareilly, 5th and 6th May '58; advance on Philibheet; actions at Shahjehanpore and Mohumdee, 24th and 25th May '58. Commanded the Regiment (on Lieutenant Lind being sun-stricken) in various dours and skirmishes with the enemy's Sowars in the march from Shahjehanpore to Moradabad, June '58. Served with the Shahjehanpore Column in the North of Oude, in '58, '59. *Medal.*

(525)

2ND CAPTAIN L. RUSSELL, Bengal Engineers.

2nd Lieut., 10 Dec. 47—Lieut., 1 Aug. 54—2nd Captain, 27 Aug. 58.

SERVICE.—Captain RUSSELL served as Brigade-Major of Engineers at the 1st relief of Lucknow, under Sir H. Havelock, and throughout the subsequent defensive operations. *(Wounded.) Medal and Clasp.*

BREVET-CAPTAIN R. W. T. RUSSELL,† late 43rd Native Infantry.

Ensign, 25 June 44—Lieut., 21 Jan. 52—Bt.-Captain, 25 June 59.

SERVICE.—Captain RUSSELL served during the Sutlej Campaign, '45, '46. Present at the action of Sobraon. *Medal. (Since dead.)*

BREVET-MAJOR W. C. RUSSELL, P. C., Bengal Artillery.

2nd Lieut., 11 June 42—Lieut., 3 July 45—2nd Captain, 11 June 57—Captain, 18 Sept. 57—Bt.-Major, 19 Jan. 58.

SERVICE.—Major RUSSELL was present at the battles of Ferozeshuhur and Sobraon, '45, '46. *Medal and Clasp.*

LIEUTENANT T. W. RUTHERFORD, P., late 33rd Native Infantry.

Ensign, 14 June 51—Lieut., 10 April 56.

LIEUTENANT W. E. RUTHERFORD, late 28th Native Infantry.

Ensign, 4 Oct. 58—Lieut., 1 Nov. 59.

MAJOR F. RUTLEDGE, Bengal Invalid Establishment.

Major, 1 Dec. 30.

SERVICE.—Major RUTLEDGE served at the storming of the fortified Hill of Adgurree; also at the siege and capture of the Fort of Adjeghur, in Bundlecund, in '09. Served throughout the Nepal War, and present at the assault of Malown, in '14, '15. Throughout the Mahratta War, including the capture of Nagpore, '16, '17. *Medal and 2 Clasps.*

LIEUTENANT A. N. F. RUXTON, P. H., late 66th Native Infantry.

Ensign, 12 Dec. 49—Lieut., 23 Feb. 56.

SERVICE.—Lieutenant RUXTON served with the Force under Lord Clyde against the Hill Tribes, in '51, '52; and in the Boori Pass, in '53. (Has

(526)

passed an examination in Field Engineering, and furnished the certificate of qualification in Civil Engineering.)

LIEUTENANT H. S. RUXTON, late 56th Native Infantry.

Ensign, 20 July 55—Lieut., 8 Oct. 56.

SERVICE.—Lieutenant RUXTON commanded 2 Companies, 17th Punjab Infantry, in the pursuit and capture of a party of rebels of the late 26th Native Infantry, July '57.

CAPTAIN B. W RYALL, P. H., late 63rd Native Infantry.

Ensign, 14 Jan. 46—Lieut., 6 Nov. 50—Captain, 17 Sept. 58.

SERVICE.—Captain RYALL served throughout the Sonthal Campaign, in '55, '56. Received the thanks of Government for services performed. After escaping from three mutineers, joined the 2nd Hyderabad Cavalry, and with it was present at the forcing of the Khonie Pass, battles of Nigree, Khobrie, and Bandah *(wounded)*, and all subsequent operations, in which the Central India Force, under Major-General Whitlock, was engaged, up to June '58. Commanded the 3rd Sikh Irregular Cavalry during the Shahabad Campaign, from August '58 up to the final capture of Jugdespore, on which occasion was nominated to the Command of all the Southern Detachments of Cavalry, under Brigadier Douglas. Frequently and favorably mentioned in Despatches by Officers Commanding Divisions, Brigades, and Columns. *Medal and Clasp*.

LIEUTENANT E. H. RYAN, P. H., Bengal Artillery.

Lieut., 27 April 58.

MAJOR E. M. RYAN, P. H., late 20th Native Infantry.

Ensign, 12 June 40—Lieut., 7 Aug. 42—Captain, 14 Aug. 53—Major, 18 Feb. 61.

LIEUTENANT T. RYAN, P. H., Bengal Artillery.

1st Lieut., 27 April 58.

LIEUTENANT W. C. B. RYAN, P. H., late 45th Native Infantry.

Ensign, 10 Dec. 50—Lieut., 21 Aug. 54.

(527)

2ND CAPTAIN G. O. RYBOT, P. H., Bengal Artillery.
2nd Lieut., 14 June 45—Lieut., 20 May 51—2nd Captain, 27 Aug. 58.

CAPTAIN S. C. D. RYDER, P., late 14th Native Infantry.
Ensign, 4 Sept. 43—Lieut., 10 Sept. 48—Bt.-Captain, 4 Sept. 58— Captain, 13 April 59.
SERVICE.—Captain RYDER served in the Sutlej Campaign, '45. Present at the battle of Ferozeshuhur, 21st and 22nd December '45. *Medal.* Present at the taking of Mokutsir, January '46. Served in Darjeeling, '49. Commanded an out-post of 2 Companies on the banks of the Runjeet, in Sikkim. Served as Staff Officer to the Troops at Sasseram, under Colonels Corfield and Turner, '58, '59.

MAJOR G. RYLEY,† late 74th Native Infantry.
Ensign, 9 Feb. 36—Lieut., 1 March 38—Captain, 16 March 48—Major, 22 Aug. 58.
(Since retired.)

LIEUTENANT P. C. RYND, P. C. H., late 73rd Native Infantry.
Ensign, 11 June 53—Lieut., 23 Nov. 56.
SERVICE.—Lieutenant RYND was present at the engagement between the Naval Brigade and the mutineers of the late 73rd Native Infantry, at Dacca, on the 22nd November '57.

LIEUTENANT H. E. RYVES, P. H., General List.
Ensign, 11 June 59—Lieut., 22 Nov. 60.

MAJOR W. H. RYVES, P., late 61st Native Infantry.
Ensign, 5 June 29—Lieut., 11 Oct. 38—Bt.-Captain, 28 March 44— Captain, 24 Jan. 45—Bt.-Major, 28 Nov. 54—Major, 15 July 59.
SERVICE.—Major RYVES served with the Force in Shekawattee, '34, '35, Commanding the 3rd Local Horse. Served during the Campaign in Affghanistan, '39, and accompanied Sir J. Outram in pursuit of Ameer Dost

Mahomed Khan to Bamean. Present at the storm and capture of Ghuznee. *Medal.* Commanded the 8th Irregular Cavalry in Bundlecund, '42, '43, with Brigadier Young's Field Force. With Sir S. Cotton's Field Force in Eusuffzaie, in '58.

S

LIEUTENANT E. T. SADLER, P. H., late 19th Native Infantry.

Ensign, 10 Dec. 50—Lieut., 26 Aug. 56.

CAPTAIN F. A. SAGE, P. H., late 11th Native Infantry.

Ensign, 11 June 42—Lieut., 10 Nov. 47—Bt.-Captain, 11 June 57— Captain, 1 Jan. 62.

SERVICE.—Captain SAGE served with the Field Force in Bundlecund, under Brigadier Young, in '43. Served during the Sutlej Campaign, '45, '46. Present at the battle of Ferozeshuhur. *Medal.* Present at the capture of the Fort of Kôt Kangra, in '46. Served in Command of Sappers and Miners, Artillery, Cavalry, and Infantry, in the Saharunpore and Mozuffernuggur Districts, in '57, '58. Crossed the Ganges, on the 24th April '58, and present at the re-occupation of Bijnore.

CAPTAIN S. SAGE,† late 30th Native Infantry.

Ensign, 11 June 42—Lieut., 1 Feb. 44—Captain, 23 Nov. 56.

SERVICE.—Captain SAGE served during the Sutlej Campaign in '46 : present at the action of Alliwal. Mentioned in the Despatch of Brigadier Wilson. *Medal.* Present at the siege and surrender of Kôt Kangra, in '46. Served during the Punjab Campaign, '48, '49. Present at the actions of Ramnuggur, Chillianwallah, and Goojerat, and with the pursuing force to Peshawur. *Medal and 2 Clasps.* Present at the action of Khoda Gunge, under Lord Clyde, January '58. Commanded the 38th Native Infantry throughout the Oude Campaign, '58. Present at the attack and surrender of the Fort of Sandee, October '58. *Medal.*

MAJOR-GENERAL W. SAGE, late 22nd Native Infantry.

Ensign, 24 April 09—Lieut., 16 Dec. 14—Bt.-Captain, 24 April 24—Captain, 13 May 25—Bt.-Major, 28 June 38—Major, 1 Oct. 40—Lieut.-Colonel, 19 Feb. 47—Bt.-Colonel, 28 Nov. 54—Colonel, 18 July 56—Major-General, 13 March 59.

SERVICE.—Major-General SAGE served in Rewah, '12; during the Nepal War, including the capture of Narragurreh, Burruya, and the assault of the heights above Mukwanpore. *Medal.* Served with the Army of the Indus in Affghanistan: present at the storm and capture of Ghuznee. *Medal.*

BREVET-MAJOR R. H. SALE, late 9th Native Infantry.

Ensign, 9 June 31—Lieut., 8 Oct. 39—Bt.-Captain, 9 June 46—Captain, 3 Oct. 48—Bt.-Major, 5 March 59.

SERVICE.—Major SALE served the Mutiny Campaign. *Medal and Brevet-Major. (Since retired.)*

LIEUTENANT C. E. SALKELD, Bengal Artillery.

Lieut., 8 June 60.

LIEUTENANT R. H. SALKELD, P. H., General List.

Ensign, 10 Dec. 59—Lieut., 2 Nov. 61.

CAPTAIN C. S. SALMON,† late 57th Native Infantry.

Ensign, 10 Jan. 34—Lieut., 8 Oct. 39—Captain, 31 Dec. 47.

2ND CAPTAIN T. H. SALT, P. H., Bengal Artillery.

2nd Lieut., 14 June 45—Lieut., 1 Oct. 49—2nd Captain, 27 Aug. 58.

SERVICE.—Captain SALT served with the Army of the Punjab, '48, '49. Present at the actions of Sadoolapore, Chillianwallah, and Goojerat. *Medal and 2 Clasps.*

(530)

MAJOR-GENERAL H. F. SALTER, C.B., late 5th Bengal European Cavalry.

Cornet, 30 April 08—Lieut., 1 Sept. 18—Bt.-Captain, 30 April 23—Captain, 1 May 24—Major, 19 May 38—Bt.-Lieut.-Colonel, 23 July 39—Lieut.-Colonel, 5 Jan. 44—Bt.-Colonel, 16 July 49—Colonel, 27 Sept. 59—Major-General, 28 Nov. 54.

SERVICE.—Major-General SALTER, C.B., served with the Army of the Indus. Present at the assault and capture of Ghuznee, *Medal;* and the operations in the Kohistan. Present at the action of Punniar. *Bronze Star.* Served during the Punjab Campaign, '48, '49, including the siege of Mooltan. *Medal and C.B.*

MAJOR F. O. SALUSBURY, 101st Fusiliers.

2nd Lieut., 9 June 43—Lieut., 9 March 45—Captain, 1 Oct. 53—Bt.-Major, 20 July 58—Major, 30 July 62.

SERVICE.—Major SALUSBURY served with the Army of the Sutlej: present at the battle of Ferozeshuhur, 21st December '45 *(severely wounded),* and 22nd December '45. *Medal.* Served during the Burmese War, '52, '53. Present at the re-capture of Pegu, November '52; and relief of Pegu, December '52; and subsequent operations in the vicinity. *Medal.* Served with the Army under Lord Clyde at the capture of Lucknow *(slightly wounded),* and with the Force under Sir Hope Grant, and with the Force under Brigadier Purnell. *Medal and Clasp, and Brevet-Major.*

CAPTAIN F. SAMLER, Bengal Invalid Establishment.

Ensign, 8 May 27—Lieut., 10 Jan. 33—Captain, 8 May 42.

LIEUTENANT D. T. H. SAMPSON, P. H., late 20th Native Infantry.

Ensign, 20 Aug. 51—Lieut., 18 May 58.

SERVICE.—Lieutenant SAMPSON served with the Force under Major-General Windham, in '57; under Lord Clyde, in '58; under Sir E. Lugard, in April '58; and under Sir R. Kelly, on the Nepal Frontier, in '59. Present at the actions of Cawnpore, 26th, 27th, and 28th November '57; storm and capture of Meeangunge, in Oude,

(531)

February '58; operations before and capture of Lucknow, March '58. Relief of Azimghur, April '58 ; action at Jellalpore, in Oude, October '58 ; action near Botwal (Nepal), 28th March '59. *Medal and Clasp.*

LIEUTENANT A. P. SAMUELLS, General List.

Ensign, 20 Dec. 60—Lieut., 29 March 62.

LIEUTENANT E. W. SAMUELLS,† General List.

Ensign, 9 Dec. 59—Lieut., 26 Sept. 61.

LIEUTENANT W. L. SAMUELLS,† late 11th Native Infantry.

Ensign, 20 Nov. 57—Lieut., 22 Oct. 58.

LIEUTENANT R. G. SANDEMAN, P. C. H., late 14th Native Infantry.

Ensign, 8 Feb. 56—Lieut., 6 Aug. 57.

SERVICE.—Lieuentant SANDEMAN served with Brigadier Showers' Column in the Delhi and Jhujjur Districts; was with the 1st Sikh Cavalry at the siege and capture of Lucknow, also at the affair at Moosa Bagh. *(Wounded.)* Served with the Columns under Sir Hope Grant and Brigadier Evelegh, in Oude, '58, '59. *Medal and Clasp.*

BREVET-COLONEL R. T. SANDEMAN, P., late 33rd Native Infantry

Ensign, 9 Feb. 25—Lieut., 8 April 32—Captain, 12 Feb. 38—Bt.-Major, 3 April 46—Major, 4 Jan. 47—Lieut.-Colonel, 27 Oct. 52—Bt.-Colonel, 28 Nov. 54.

SERVICE.—Colonel SANDEMAN commanded the Regiment throughout the Sutlej Campaign, '45, '46 : present at the battles of Ferozeshuhur and Sobraon. *Medal, Clasp, and Brevet-Major.* *(Since retired.)*

LIEUTENANT-COLONEL A. SANDERS, late 5th Europeans.

Ensign, 11 May 31—Lieut., 12 March 37—Captain, 24 Aug. 43—Major, 29 Feb. 52—Lieut.-Colonel, 29 May 57.

(Since retired.)

(532)

BREVET-MAJOR J. W. SANDERS, P. H., late 41st Native Infantry.

Ensign, 11 June 42—Lieut., 9 Sept. 44—Captain, 26 March 55—Bt.-Major, 24 March 58.

SERVICE.—Major SANDERS Commanded an important outpost, "Sanders' Post," during the entire siege of Lucknow. *Medal and Clasp, Brevet-Major, and one year's extra service.* Mentioned in General Inglis' Despatch, and thanked by the Governor-General in Council.

LIEUTENANT H. B. SANDERSON, P. H., late 22nd Native Infantry.

Ensign, 20 Dec. 56—Lieut., 8 June 57.

MAJOR-GENERAL F. H. SANDYS, late 36th Native Infantry.

Ensign, 11 Feb. 07—Lieut., 22 March 11—Captain, 1 May 24—Bt.-Major, 10 Jan. 37—Major, 1 Oct. 40—Lieut.-Colonel, 30 Jan. 46—Bt.-Colonel, 20 June 54—Colonel, 10 Feb. 56—Major-General, 15 Oct. 57.

SERVICE.—Major-General SANDYS served in the Nepal War of '15, '16; against the insurgents in the Khoordah District, in '17, '18. Served in '24 as Deputy Assistant Quarter-Master-General with the Force under Brigadier Knox; in capture of petty Forts in the Jeypore Territory, '27; Civil and Political Departments, up to '56.

LIEUTENANT T. M. SANDYS, P. H., late 73rd Native Infantry.

Ensign, 9 June 55—Lieut., 30 April 58.

2ND CAPTAIN M. C. SANKEY, P. H., Bengal Artillery.

2nd Lieut., 12 June 46—Lieut., 3 March 53—2nd Captain, 27 Aug. 58.

SERVICE.—Captain SANKEY served with the Army of the Punjab, '48, '49. Present at the siege and surrender of Mooltan. *(Severely wounded.) Medal and 2 Clasps.*

LIEUTENANT R. W. SARTORIUS, late 72nd Native Infantry.

Ensign, 20 Jan. 58—Lieut., 18 May 58.

(533)

SURGEON G. SAUNDERS,† Bengal Medical Establishment.
Asst.-Surgeon, 28 July 42—Surgeon, 20 Jan. 57.

LIEUTENANT G. N. SAUNDERS, P. H., late 24th Native Infantry.
Ensign, 20 Dec. 53—Lieut., 19 Oct. 56.

SERVICE.—Lieutenant SAUNDERS served against the rebels in the Eusuffzaie Country, '57; and led the Left Column of attack against the rebel village of Narinjee, for which he received the thanks of the Governor-General in Council.

LIEUTENANT H. G. SAUNDERS, late 3rd Europeans.
Ensign, 20 Oct. 55—Lieut., 21 Jan. 57.

SERVICE.—Lieutenant SAUNDERS served during the Mutinies, '57, '58. Present at the action of Susseah, near Agra, on the 5th July '57; also at the affair of Shereghur Ghaut, in May '58. Served with the Column towards Gwalior, in June '58. *Medal.*

CAPTAIN J. B. SAUNDERS, P. C., late 4th Bengal European Cavalry.
Cornet, 20 Dec. 49—Lieut., 28 Nov. 54—Captain, 2 Jan. 60.

LIEUTENANT M. S. SAUNDERS, General List, Cavalry.
Cornet, 20 Sept. 59—Lieut., 20 Sept. 60.

LIEUTENANT M. H. SAWARD, Bengal Artillery.
Lieut., 9 Dec. 59.

ASSISTANT-SURGEON M. SCANLAN, Bengal Medical Establishment.
Asst.-Surgeon, 11 Aug. 58.

LIEUTENANT H. SCONCE, P. H., late 74th Native Infantry.
Ensign, 20 Feb. 54—Lieut., 11 May 57.

SERVICE.—Lieutenant SCONCE served with the Army before Delhi, in '57. Present at the siege and capture of that city. *Medal and Clasp.* (Has passed an examination in Assamese and Bengali.)

(534)

LIEUTENANT J. SCONCE, P. H., Bengal Artillery.
1st Lieut., 23 Sept. 57.

CAPTAIN P. G. SCOT, P., late 12th Native Infantry.
Ensign, 10 June 42—Lieut., 1 Sept. 45—Captain, 23 Nov. 56.

SERVICE.—Captain SCOT served with the Army of the Sutlej in '46: present at the action of Ferozeshuhur. *Medal.* Served in the Indian Mutiny Campaign. Was present when the Right Wing of the 12th Native Infantry mutinied at Nowgong. Present at the actions of Mungulwarrah, Alum Bagh, and entry into Lucknow; defence of Lucknow; and in all the attacks on and by the Alum Bagh Force, from November '57 to the 28th February '58. Present at the siege of Lucknow; attack on the rebels at Koorsee and Rooya; and actions of Allygunge and Bareilly. *Medal and 2 Clasps.* Mentioned in General Sir Hope Grant's Despatch.

LIEUTENANT A. SCOTT,† General List.
Ensign, 4 March 60—Lieut., 1 Jan. 62.

SURGEON D. SCOTT,† M.D., Bengal Medical Establishment.
Asst.-Surgeon, 20 Dec. 45—Surgeon, 8 May 59.

SERVICE.—Surgeon SCOTT served throughout the Punjab Campaign, '48, '49, including the skirmish at Ramnuggur, and the actions of Sadoolapore, Chillianwallah, and Goojerat, and subsequent pursuit of the Sikhs and Affghans, *Medal and Clasp;* also with Brigadier Bradshaw's Force in the Eusuffzaie Country, in December '49, and with that under Sir C. Napier, in the Kohat Pass.

LIEUTENANT-GENERAL D. G. SCOTT, late 30th Native Infantry.
Ensign, 10 Sept. 05—Lieut., 19 Dec. 05—Captain, 11 July 23—Major, 7 Dec. 27—Lieut.-Colonel, 29 Oct. 32—Colonel, 7 May 44—Major-General, 20 June 54—Lieut.-General, 23 July 58.

SERVICE.—Lieutenant-General SCOTT served in Bundlecund, '10, '11. Served during the Nepal War, '14, '15. *(Severely wounded.) Medal.*

(535)

CAPTAIN E. H. SCOTT, P. H., late 55th Native Infantry.
Ensign, 2 Sept. 47—Lieut., 10 May 56—Captain, 18 Feb. 61.
SERVICE.—Captain SCOTT served in Command of the Left Wing, 16th Punjab Infantry, with the Bundlecund Field Force, in '59.

LIEUTENANT-COLONEL E. W. S. SCOTT,† Bengal Artillery.
2nd Lieut., 12 Dec. 28—Lieut., 18 Jan. 37—Bt.-Captain, 12 Dec. 43—Captain, 5 July 46—Bt.-Major, 20 June 54—Major, 10 Feb. 58—Bt.-Lieut.-Colonel, 19 Jan. 58—Lieut.-Colonel, 27 Aug. 58.

LIEUTENANT-COLONEL J. C. SCOTT, P., late 20th Native Infantry.
Ensign, 27 June 26—Lieut., 3 Oct. 28—Bt.-Captain, 27 June 41—Captain, 24 Jan. 45—Bt.-Major, 20 June 54—Major, 27 Aug. 58—Lieut.-Colonel, 18 Feb. 61.

LIEUTENANT T. A. SCOTT,† late 28th Native Infantry.
Ensign, 13 June 57—Lieut., 18 May 58.

CAPTAIN T. F. O. SCOTT, P. H., late 41st Native Infantry.
Ensign, 13 Dec. 45—Lieut., 13 Feb. 50—Captain, 24 May 59.
SERVICE.—Captain SCOTT served with the Khelat-i-Ghilzie Regiment in the operations against the Hussunzaies, in the Black Mountains, in '52, '53. (Passed examination in Field Engineering.) *(Since dead.)*

LIEUTENANT T. H. SCOTT, P. H , late 26th Native Infantry.
Ensign, 20 Jan. 56—Lieut., 30 April 58.

ASSISTANT-SURGEON J. B. SCRIVEN,† Bengal Medical Establishment.
Asst.-Surgeon, 11 Jan. 51.
SERVICE.—Assistant-Surgeon SCRIVEN served with the late 1st European Bengal Fusiliers during the Campaign in Burmah, in '52, '53. Accompanied the Martaban Column under General Steel to Tounghoo. *Medal.*

CAPTAIN T. W. SEAGER,† late 27th Native Infantry.

Ensign, 28 July 39—Lieut., 12 Nov. 42—Captain, 18 April 51.

SERVICE.—Captain SEAGER served with the 30th Native Infantry in the Khyber Pass, 19th, 23rd, and 24th January '42, under Brigadier Wild; and on the 5th April '42, under General Pollock, from Peshawur to Jellallabad. *Cabul Medal.* Served during the Sutlej Campaign, '45, '46. *Medal.*

BREVET-COLONEL D. SEATON, late 1st European Bengal Fusiliers.

2nd Lieut., 5 June 29—Lieut., 29 July 36—Captain, 6 Feb. 46—Bt.-Major, 19 June 46—Major, 14 Sept. 56—Bt.-Lieut.-Colonel, 20 June 54—Lieut.-Colonel, 17 March 60—Bt.-Colonel, 15 Oct. 57.

SERVICE.—Colonel SEATON served in the Campaign on the Sutlej, '45, '46. Present at the battles of Ferozeshuhur and Sobraon, in the latter action he commanded the Regiment, and his *horse was shot* under him. *Medal, Clasp, and Brevet-Major.* Served in Burmah in '52, 53. Present at the relief of the garrison of Pegu, 14th December '53; and throughout the operations in the vicinity. Accompanied the Martaban Column under the Command of General Steel. *Medal.*

ASSISTANT-SURGEON E. SELOUS, P. H., Bengal Medical Establishment.

Asst.-Surgeon, 10 Feb. 59.

LIEUTENANT H. W. J. SENIOR, P. H., late 39th Native Infantry.

Ensign, 4 March 59—Lieut., 9 Nov. 60.

ASSISTANT-SURGEON J. A. SEWELL,† M. D., Bengal Medical Establishment.

Asst.-Surgeon, 24 Sept. 56.

SERVICE.—Assistant-Surgeon SEWELL served throughout the Mutinies, '57, '58. Present at the battles of Agra, 5th July, and 10th October '57. In Medical Charge of a Wing, 1st Belooch Battalion, and Lind's Mooltanee Cavalry. Served during the Rohilcund Campaign. Present at the action of Kukrowlee, capture of Bareilly by the Commander-in-

(537)

Chief, affairs of Shahjehanpore, capture of Fort Mohumdee, and relief of Fort Jellallabad. *Medal.*

LIEUTENANT R. M. SEWELL, P. H., late 71st Native Infantry.

Ensign, 20 Dec. 51—Lieut., 23 Nov. 56.

SERVICE.—Lieutenant SEWELL served throughout the Mutiny, '57, '58. Present at the action of Chinhut (*horse shot* under him). Present throughout the siege of Lucknow, from 30th June to 25th November '57. Present at the battle of Cawnpore and defeat of the Gwalior Troops, 6th December '57, under Lord Clyde. Present at the action of Kala Nuddee, and occupation of Futtehghur, January '58. Present throughout the siege and capture of Lucknow, March '58, under Lord Clyde. *Medal and 2 Clasps, and one year's extra service.* Mentioned in the Lucknow Despatches of Brigadier Inglis. Established an Enfield Cartridge manufactory during the siege of Lucknow, and received the special thanks of Sir J. Outram and Sir Henry Havelock. Received the thanks of the Governor-General.

BREVET-COLONEL T. SEWELL, late 25th Native Infantry.

Ensign, 3 Sept. 19—Lieut., 2 Dec. 20—Captain, 7 Dec. 27—Bt.-Major, 23 Nov. 41—Major, 20 Nov. 45—Lieut.-Colonel, 13 Oct. 51—Bt.-Colonel, 28 Nov. 54.

SERVICE.—Colonel SEWELL served at the siege and capture of Bhurtpore. *Medal.* *(Since dead.)*

CORNET G. R. J. SHAKESPEAR, H. M.'s 20th Light Dragoons.

Cornet, 7 Sept. 60.

LIEUTENANT H. A. SHAKESPEAR, late 5th Bengal European Cavalry.

Cornet, 20 Nov. 58—Lieut., 29 March 59.

BREVET-MAJOR H. J. C. SHAKESPEAR, P. H., late 25th Native Infantry.

Ensign, 7 July 34—Lieut., 5 July 37—Captain, 26 Dec. 46—Bt.-Major, 21 Dec. 59.

SERVICE.—Major SHAKESPEAR was present at the siege and capture of the Fort and Town of Baloorgee, in the Deccan, in September '41; and Adjutant of the 2nd Nizam's Cavalry during the operations of the Field Force in that district; commanded the Detachment of 3rd Nizam's Cavalry employed in the Golconda zemindary, February, March, and April '48; commanded the 3rd Nizam's Cavalry and the Detachment that captured the Insurgent Sikhs at Homdah, near Hingolee, January '51; commanded the 5th Nizam's Cavalry and led the 30 dismounted Troopers of that Regiment, who carried by assault the stockaded village of Eshwuntpoora or Devulgaon, near Aurungabad, 22nd September '53, *severely wounded;* commanded the Field Force composed of Nagpore Irregular Troops employed in the Eastern Frontier of the Raepore District and Western Frontier of the Sumbulpore District, in January, February, and March '58; forced the Singora Pass and Niswighat, defended by a body of the Sumbulpore rebels, 19th January '58; commanded the Field Force composed of Nagpore Irregular Troops employed in the Chanda zemindaries, east of the Wynegunga and Prechestur Rivers, May and June '58. *Medal.* *(Since retired.)*

LIEUTENANT-COLONEL J. T. SHAKESPEAR, P. H., late 24th Native Infantry.

Ensign, 8 Feb. 40—Lieut., 13 Aug. 42—Captain, 5 Dec. 49—Major, 1 May 57—Lieut.-Colonel, 26 Jan. 61.

SERVICE.—Lieutenant-Colonel SHAKESPEAR served during the Sutlej Campaign, '45, '46. Present at the battles of Moodkee and Ferozeshuhur. *Medal and Clasp.*

BREVET-COLONEL SIR R. C. SHAKESPEAR, *Kt.*, C.B., Bengal Artillery.

2nd Lieut., 12 June 28—Lieut., 14 May 36—Bt.-Captain, 12 June 43— Captain, 1 May 46—Bt.-Major, 1 Dec. 48—Major, 14 Jan. 58—Bt.- Lieut.-Colonel, 7 June 49—Lieut.-Colonel, 27 Aug. 58—Bt.-Colonel, 28 Nov. 54.

SERVICE.—Colonel Sir R. C. SHAKESPEAR served in Affghanistan, in '39 and '42, *Medal;* Army of the Punjab, '48, '49, including the actions of Chillianwallah and Goojerat *(Wounded.)* *Medal, 2 Clasps, and Brevet-Lieutenant-Colonel.* *(Since dead.)*

(539)

LIEUTENANT C. F. SHARPE, P. C., late 72nd Native Infantry.

Ensign, 20 Dec. 50—Lieut., 23 Nov. 56.

SERVICE.—Lieutenant SHARPE served as Staff Officer with the Moveable Column under Colonel Riddell, in the Etawah District, in '58; and as Staff Officer with the Agra Column towards Gwalior, in '58; and mentioned in Colonel Riddell's Despatch as an efficient Staff Officer. Besieged by the rebels in Sundeela City, Lucknow, 4th and 5th October '58. *Medal.*

CAPTAIN C. SHAW, P. H., late 57th Native Infantry.

Ensign, 11 Jan. 48—Lieut., 11 July 53—Captain, 18 Feb. 61.

CAPTAIN C. R. SHAW, P. H., late 37th Native Infantry.

Ensign, 10 Dec. 47—Lieut., 8 Dec. 50—Captain, 18 Feb. 61.

LIEUTENANT H. A. SHAW, late 3rd Europeans.

Ensign, 12 Dec. 56—Lieut., 11 May 57.

LIEUTENANT-GENERAL S. SHAW, Bengal Artillery.

1st Lieut., 25 Aug. 04—Captain, 6 May 17—Major, 1 May 24—Lieut.-Colonel, 31 May 33—Colonel, 25 March 40—Major-General, 20 June 54—Lieut.-General, 5 March 59.

SERVICE.—Lieutenant-General SHAW served in Java from '13 to '17. Accompanied the expedition to Palambaug, '13; in the expedition to Balli, under General Sir M. Nightingale, in '15.

LIEUTENANT W. D. SHAW,† late 2nd Native Infantry.

Ensign, 4 Sept. 54—Lieut., 3 Sept. 57.

SERVICE.—Lieutenant SHAW served against the Insurgent Sonthals in '55. Served with the Allahabad Military Police as Adjutant at the affairs of Maneekpore, in Oude, and Palput, on the borders of the Rewah Territory.

LIEUTENANT W. F. SHAW,† late 43rd Native Infantry.

Ensign, 12 Dec. 51—Lieut., 23 Nov. 56.

(540)

LIEUTENANT W. B. SHAWE, P. H., late 60th Native Infantry.
Ensign, 8 June 49—Lieut., 15 Jan. 55.

LIEUTENANT W. SHEFFIELD, P. H., Unattached List.
Lieut., 6 Dec. 52.

SERVICE.—Lieutenant SHEFFIELD served with the Army of the Sutlej, '45, '46: present at the actions of Moodkee, Ferozeshuhur *(wounded severely)*, and Sobraon. *Medal and 2 Clasps.* Promoted to Ensign (Unattached) for services during the Sutlej Campaign. Promoted to Lieutenant (Unattached), 6th December '52. *(Since retired.)*

MAJOR-GENERAL SIR J. SHEIL, K.C.B. and K.I.S., late 17th Native Infantry.
Ensign, 4 March 20—Lieut., 11 July 23—Captain, 13 April 30—Major, 17 April 41—Lieut.-Colonel, 11 March 47—Bt.-Colonel, 28 Nov. 54—Colonel, 28 Nov. 56—Major-General, 26 April 59.

SERVICE.—Major-General SHEIL, K.C.B., served at the siege and capture of Bhurtpore. *Medal.*

LIEUTENANT T. M. SHELLEY,† late 11th Native Infantry.
Ensign, 20 Jan. 51—Lieut., 23 Nov. 56.

SERVICE.—Lieutenant SHELLEY was present during the Mutiny at Meerut. Served in the several actions, from 11th August to 29th September, before Delhi, and present at the assault and capture of that city. *(Wounded.) Medal and Clasp.*

MAJOR H. R. SHELTON, P. H., late 38th Native Infantry.
Ensign, 13 Jan. 39—Lieut., 12 Nov. 42—Captain, 28 Sept. 51—Major, 1 Jan. 62.

SERVICE.—Major SHELTON served with the Candahar Force throughout the operations leading to the re-occupation of Cabul. *Medal.*

(541)

LIEUTENANT A. SHEPHERD, late 5th Bengal European Cavalry.
Cornet, 20 Sept. 56—Lieut., 9 Jan. 57.
SERVICE.—Lieutenant SHEPHERD served against the Jhuts, in the Googaira District, during the months of October and November '57. Served with the Column under Brigadier Franks, in Oude, '58. Present at the siege and capture of Lucknow, by Sir Colin Campbell, in March '58; at the battle and taking of Bareilly, in May '58, served with the Soraon Field Force, under Brigadier Berkeley. Present at the capture of Forts Deghain, Turoul, and Bhyspore, '58. *Medal and Clasp.*

CORNET T. SHEPHERD, H. M.'s 20th Light Dragoons.
Cornet, 4 Aug. 60.

ASSISTANT-SURGEON T. W. SHEPPARD,† Bengal Medical Establishment.
Asst.-Surgeon, 10 Feb. 59.

BREVET-COLONEL G. M. SHERER, late 26th Native Infantry.
Ensign, 20 Dec. 21—Lieut., 23 Aug. 24—Captain, 8 July 36—Bt.-Major, 9 Nov. 46—Major, 12 Aug. 47—Lieut.-Colonel, 11 July 53—Bt.-Colonel, 28 Nov. 54.

CAPTAIN J. F. SHERER, P. H., late 49th Native Infantry.
Ensign, 10 Dec. 47—Lieut., 24 Jan. 51—Captain, 18 Feb. 61.
SERVICE.—Captain SHERER served with the Army of Punjab, '48, '49: present throughout the siege operations before Mooltan, including the action of Sooroojkhoond, storm and capture of Mooltan, and surrender of the Fortress. *Medal and Clasp.* Led the Head Quarters of the Sylhet Light Infantry into action, on the 17th December '57, against the mutineers of the 34th Native Infantry, at Latoo, Sylhet District; succeeded to the Command of the Corps on Major Byng being killed at the commencement of the fight, and brought the Corps out of action, after defeating and routing the mutineers. *Medal.*

LIEUTENANT C. SHERIDAN, Bengal Veteran Establishment.
Lieut., 18 Oct. 58.

ASSISTANT-SURGEON T. T. SHERLOCK,† B.A., Bengal Medical Establishment.

Asst.-Surgeon, 4 Aug. 56.

LIEUTENANT J. P. SHERRIFF,† late 35th Native Infantry.

Ensign, 20 Jan. 51—Lieut., 10 July 54.

SERVICE.—Lieutenant SHERRIFF served with the 2nd Punjab Infantry during the Campaign in Hindostan, in '57, '58 : present at the siege, assault, and capture of Delhi, including the battle of Nudjufghur; accompanied the Moveable Column under Colonel Greathed, after the fall of Delhi. Present at the battle of Boolundshuhur, was detached with a portion of the Regiment at Allyghur, and subsequently commanded a mixed Force in the Etawah District, where he had several engagements with the enemy, and on one occasion captured 5 guns, after driving the enemy out of his position. For his conduct on this occasion he received the thanks of the Governor-General. *Medal and Clasps.*

MAJOR J. L. SHERWILL, P., late 39th Native Infantry.

Ensign, 24 Jan. 39—Lieut., 24 Jan. 45—Bt.-Captain, 24 Jan. 54—Captain, 4 June 55—Major, 18 Feb. 61.

SERVICE.—Major SHERWILL served at the battle of Punniar. *Bronze Star.* (Has furnished certificate of qualification in Surveying.)

BREVET-COLONEL M. E. SHERWILL, P. C., late 2nd European Bengal Fusiliers.

2nd Lieut., 7 April 30—Lieut., 3 Oct. 40—Bt.-Captain, 7 April 45—Captain, 12 June 47—Bt.-Major, 7 June 49—Major, 1 May 58—Bt.-Lieut.-Colonel, 28 Nov. 54—Bt.-Colonel, 4 June 60.

SERVICE.—Colonel SHERWILL served throughout the Campaign in the Punjab, '48, '49 : present at the affair of Ramnuggur, passage of the Chenab, battles of Chillianwallah, Goojerat, and subsequent pursuit of the Sikhs and Affghans, and occupation of Peshawur by General Gilbert's Force. *Medal, Clasp, and Brevet-Major. (Since retired.)*

(543)

MAJOR W. S. SHERWILL,† late 66th Native Infantry.

Ensign, 11 June 33—Lieut., 3 Oct. 40—Captain, 22 Feb. 47—Major, 2 April 59.

SERVICE.—Major SHERWILL served as Deputy Assistant Quarter-Master-General to the Field Force under Major-General Lloyd, against the Insurgent Sonthals, in '55. *Since retired.*

SURGEON-MAJOR W. SHILLITO,† F.R.C.S., Bengal Medical Establishment.

Asst.-Surgeon, 7 July 38—Surgeon, 31 March 52—Surgeon-Major, 13 Jan. 60.

ASSISTANT-SURGEON S. M. SHIRCORE,† Bengal Medical Establishment.

Asst.-Surgeon, 2 July 56.

CAPTAIN W. D. A. R. SHORT,† Bengal Engineers.

2nd Lieut., 11 June 41—Lieut., 5 May 44—Captain, 3 Dec. 55—Lieut.-Colonel, 19 Dec. 61.

SERVICE.—Captain SHORT served at the battle of Maharajpore. *Bronze Star.*

LIEUTENANT H. W. SHOUBRIDGE, General List.

Ensign, 21 July 59—Lieut., 16 May 61.

MAJOR C. L. SHOWERS, P., late 14th Native Infantry.

Ensign, 21 Jan. 35—Lieut., 8 Oct. 39—Captain, 27 Oct. 48—Major, 1 Jan. 62.

SERVICE.—Major SHOWERS served during the Punjab Campaign, '48, '49: present at the battle of Goojerat. *Medal.*

BREVET-COLONEL ST. G. D. SHOWERS, C.B., late 2nd European Bengal Fusiliers.

2nd Lieut., 9 Jan. 25—Lieut., 25 June 26—Captain, 22 Feb. 36—Bt.-Major, 9 Nov. 46—Major, 24 April 47—Lieut.-Colonel, 10 May 53—Bt.-Colonel, 28 Nov. 54.

SERVICE.—Colonel St. G. D. SHOWERS, C.B., commanded the 1st Infantry Brigade at the battle of Badlee-ka-Serai, and during the operations before Delhi. *Severely wounded* in two places whilst commanding a Column in a successful attack made on the enemy's position on 12th August '57. Commanded the Moveable Column in the District of Delhi, after the capture of the city. *Medal, Clasp, and C.B.*

LIEUTENANT-GENERAL T. SHUBRICK, late 2nd Bengal European Cavalry.

Cadet 96—Cornet, 22 Sept. 98—Lieut., 29 May 1800—Captain, 18 Aug. 14—Major, 12 Aug. 19—Lieut.-Colonel, 26 June 26—Colonel, 19 April 36—Major-General, 23 Nov. 41—Lieut.-General, 11 Nov. 51.

SERVICE.—Lieutenant-General SHUBRICK served in Oude and Rohilcund, '02; during Lord Lake's Campaigns, '04, '05. Present at the battles of Coel, Allyghur, Delhi, Agra, Laswarrie, Shumlee, and Futtehghur, '03; capture of Deig, '04; Ufzulghur; assault of Bhurtpore, '05; Bundlecund, '10, '11; siege and capture of Kulinger, '13; and Mahratta and Pindarree Wars, '17, '18. *Medal.*

CAPTAIN A. T. SHULDHAM,† late 20th Native Infantry.

Ensign, 25 Feb. 48—Lieut., 25 March 50—Captain, 27 Aug. 58.

SERVICE.—Captain SHULDHAM served during the Punjab Campaign, '48, '49: present at the battle of Goojerat. *Medal.*

BREVET-COLONEL T. H. SHULDHAM, P., late 15th Native Infantry.

Ensign, 6 Oct. 23—Lieut., 16 May 24—Captain, 1 Jan. 37—Major, 30 Sept. 45—Lieut.-Colonel, 15 Sept. 51—Bt.-Colonel, 28 Nov. 54.

SERVICE.—Colonel SHULDHAM served with the expedition to China, '42, '43. *Medal.*

CAPTAIN T. H. SHUM,† late 33rd Native Infantry.

Ensign, 4 April 37—Lieut., 14 July 42—Bt.-Captain, 4 April 52—Captain, 1 Oct. 53.

SERVICE.—Captain SHUM served throughout the Affghan Campaign of '42: present at the forcing of the Khyber Pass, and operations in the Mazeena Valley. *Medal.* Served throughout the Sutlej Campaign, '45,

(545)

'46 : present at the battles of Ferozeshuhur and Sobraon. *Medal and Clasp.* *(Since retired.)*

BREVET-MAJOR D. C. SHUTE, P. H., late 19th Native Infantry.

Ensign, 12 June 37—Lieut., 29 July 40—Captain, 1 Nov. 50—Bt.-Major, 19 Jan. 58.

SERVICE.—Major SHUTE served in Scinde, in '42, '43. Served as Deputy Assistant Quarter-Master General throughout the Sonthal Rebellion of '55, '56. Served in the same capacity with the Annexation Force under Brigadier Wheeler, in '56, '57. Served with the Delhi Field Force under General Barnard throughout the whole operations of storm, siege, and capture; and in the action of Badlee-ka-Serai and Nudjufghur, under Brigadier Nicholson; and with a Column in the District under Brigadier Showers; and for services was thanked in Orders by Government and promoted to Major by Brevet. *Medal and Clasp.*

BREVET-MAJOR T. H. SIBLEY, P. C., late 62nd Native Infantry.

Ensign, 9 Dec. 43—Lieut., 2 Feb. 50—Captain, 18 Dec. 57—Bt.-Major, 19 Jan. 58.

SERVICE.—Major SIBLEY served with the Delhi Field Force in '57 : present at the siege and capture of Delhi, from 23rd June to 21st September '57. Present at the Mutiny at Jullundur. *Medal and Clasp* Mentioned in the Despatch of Sir A. Wilson, 5th November '57. Received the thanks of Government in '57. Promoted to the rank of Brevet-Major for services during the siege of Delhi.

VETERINARY-SURGEON J. SIDDALL,† Bengal Veterinary Establishment.

Vety.-Surgeon, 17 July 44.

SERVICE.—Veterinary-Surgeon SIDDALL served with the 2nd Brigade Horse Artillery during the Punjab Campaign, and was present at the passage of the Chenab and battles of Chillianwallah and Goojerat. *Medal and Clasp.* Served also with the Force commanded by Colonel Eyre, and was present at the actions of Gugiggunge and Behreegunge, on the 2nd August '57; relief of Arrah Garrison, and action at Jugdespore, on 12th August. *Medal.*

(546)

CAPTAIN F. J. SIDEBOTTOM, P. H., late 62nd Native Infantry.
Ensign, 1 Sept. 43—Lieut., 15 May 48—Captain, 1 June 57.
(Since retired.)

ASSISTANT-SURGEON F. SILLIFANT,† Bengal Medical Establishment.
Asst.-Surgeon, 4 Aug. 55.
SERVICE.—Assistant-Surgeon SILLIFANT served during the Mutiny Campaign. *Medal.*

CAPTAIN G. SIM,† Bengal Engineers.
2nd Lieut., 9 June 43—Lieut., 1 Dec. 47—Captain, 27 June 57.
SERVICE.—Captain SIM served during the Sutlej Campaign, '45, '46. Present at the action of Sobraon. *Medal.*

2ND CAPTAIN E. SIMEON, Bengal Artillery.
2nd Lieut., 13 Dec. 45—Lieut., 16 May 52—2nd Captain, 27 Aug. 58.
SERVICE.—Captain SIMEON served during the Punjab Campaign, '48, '49: present at the battles of Ramnuggur, Chillianwallah, and Goojerat, *Medal and 2 Clasps;* and subsequent pursuit to Peshawur of Sikhs and Affghans; with Field Force under Sir C. Campbell, from October to December '51; against Momunds and Hill Tribes west of Peshawur; with Juanpore Field Force under General Franks, at affairs of Chanda, Ameerpore, and Sultanpore, in Oude, in '58. Present at the siege and capture of Lucknow, *Medal and Clasp;* also at Koorsie, under Sir H. Grant, and commanded Bengal Artillery at the affair of Jugdespore, and pursuit of the rebels to Khymore Hills.

CAPTAIN R. G. SIMEON, P., late 4th Bengal European Cavalry.
Cornet, 16 Oct. 39—Lieut., 14 Oct. 44—Captain, 27 Nov. 53.
SERVICE.—Captain SIMEON served throughout the Affghanistan Campaign, under General Pollock, '41, '42. *Medal.* Served in Cabul in '42. Present at the battle of Maharajpore, 29th December '43. *Bronze Star.* *(Wounded slightly.)* Served as Assistant Deputy-Adjutant-General

with Major-General Penny's Column. Present in the Kukralee affair. Mentioned in the Despatch of Colonel R. Jones, '58. Served under Lord Clyde, and present at the capture of Bareilly, May '58. Mentioned in the General Despatches of '58. *Medal.*

CAPTAIN R. S. SIMONDS,† late 4th Europeans.

Ensign, 11 June 47—Lieut., 14 Nov. 49—Captain, 27 June 57.

CAPTAIN A. SIMPSON, A. M., P., Bengal Artillery.

2nd Lieut., 11 June 42—Lieut., 3 July 45—Bt.-Captain, 11 June 57— Captain, 25 Sept. 57.

SURGEON A. SIMPSON,† M.D., Bengal Medical Establishment.

Asst.-Surgeon, 28 Feb. 44—Surgeon, 8 Aug. 57.

SERVICE.—Surgeon SIMPSON joined the Army of the Sutlej, did duty in the Depôt Hospital at Ferozepore from 9th February to 2nd March '46. Served on Field Service with a Detachment of H. M's 35th, in Sarun, from 25th June to 27th October '58, under Brigadier Christie.

ASSISTANT-SURGEON B. SIMPSON, M.D. and A B., P. H., Bengal Medical Establishment.

Asst.-Surgeon, 20 Oct. 53.

COLONEL D. SIMPSON, late 54th Native Infantry.

Ensign, 16 Aug. 19—Lieut., 16 Aug. 22—Captain, 24 April 33—Major, 22 Dec. 44—Lieut.-Colonel, 15 March 51—Bt.-Colonel, 28 Nov. 54— Colonel, 13 April 60.

SERVICE.—Colonel SIMPSON served in Command of a Force against the rebels, in the Hills north of Jullundur, '48, '49. Present at the storming of the heights of Umb, and subsequent occupation of the Fort of Oonah. *Medal.*

LIEUTENANT E. H. C. SIMPSON, P. H., late 39th Native Infantry.

Ensign, 9 Dec. 50—Lieut., 23 Nov. 56.

SERVICE.—Lieutenant SIMPSON served during the Mutiny, '57, '58, with the Force under Sir Henry Havelock, from July to November

'57. Served under Sir James Outram, from November '57 to March '58. Present at the actions of Futtehpore, 12th July '57; Cawnpore, 16th July, Bithoor, August, Mungulwarrah, 21st September, relief of Lucknow, 25th September, and action of Gihlee, 23rd December '57; assault, siege, and final capture of Lucknow by Lord Clyde, March '58. Present at numerous repulses of attacks made by the enemy on the Camp of Sir J. Outram, from December '57 to February '58. *Medal and 2 Clasps.* Mentioned in the Despatch of Sir James Outram, 23rd December '57. In the Despatch of Colonel V. Eyre, 22nd February '58. Received the thanks of His Excellency the Governor-General, 22nd February '58.

MAJOR E. J. SIMPSON, P., late 69th Native Infantry.

Ensign, 24 Jan. 39—Lieut., 24 Aug. 40—Captain, 31 July 49—Major, 8 Dec. 61.

SERVICE.—Major SIMPSON served against the Hill Tribes in Scinde, under Sir C. Napier. Served with the Army of the Punjab, '48, '49: present at the battles of Ramnuggur, Sadoolapore, Chillianwallah, and Goojerat, and pursuit of the Sikhs and Affghans to Peshawur. *Medal and 2 Clasps.* Mentioned in the Despatch of Major-General Thackwell. Present on the Staff of Sir Charles Napier in the expedition against the Affreedies in the Kôhat Pass, in February '50. Present at Meerut during the Mutiny, in '57. *Medal.* Received the thanks of Government, 16th February '58.

LIEUTENANT F. W. SIMPSON,† General List.

Ensign, 2 Aug. 59—Lieut., 28 April 61.

LIEUTENANT G. B. C. SIMPSON, P. H., late 23rd Native Infantry.

Ensign, 9 Dec. 50—Lieut., 1 April 54.

SERVICE.—Lieutenant SIMPSON served with the Malwa Field Force in '57; with the Central India Field Force in '58. Present at the siege of Dhar, Chundehree, and Jhansi, in Bundlecund *(dangerously wounded);* action of Mundesore and battle of Betwa. *Medal and Clasp.* Mentioned in the Despatch of Sir Hugh Rose, 31st May '58.

(549)

LIEUTENANT-COLONEL R. S. SIMPSON, P., late 27th Native Infantry.

Ensign, 1 May 28—Lieut., 7 Feb. 33—Bt.-Captain, 1 May 43—Captain, 24 Jan. 45—Bt.-Major, 20 June 54—Major, 11 Nov. 56—Lieut.-Colonel, 4 June 60.

SERVICE.—Lieutenant-Colonel SIMPSON served with the Army of the Indus in Affghanistan: present at the assault and capture of Ghuznee, *Medal;* with the Army of the Punjab, *Medal;* and with the Burmah Expedition. Present at the capture of Rangoon, April '52. *Medal. (Since retired.)*

LIEUTENANT-COLONEL T. SIMPSON, late 57th Native Infantry.

Ensign, 10 Jan. 28—Lieut., 17 July 32—Bt.-Captain, 10 Jan. 43—Captain, 24 Jan. 45—Bt.-Major, 20 June 54—Bt.-Lieut.-Colonel, 24 March 58.

SERVICE.—Lieutenant-Colonel SIMPSON served against the Coles and Hill Tribes of Kochang Singooree, in '35, '36. Against the Sarka Coles of Singbhoom, in '37. Served in Hazareebaugh and Chota Nagpore, in '57. Present at an engagement with the rebels at Chuttera, on the 3rd October '57, and completely defeated them, capturing their colors, 4 guns, tumbeels, a large amount of Treasure, Military Stores, Ammunition, Arms, Elephants, &c., &c. Mentioned in the report of the Commander-in-Chief, and received the thanks of the Government, 15th October '57. Promoted to the rank of Brevet-Lieutenant-Colonel for services during the Mutinies. *(Since retired.)*

LIEUTENANT-COLONEL E. SISSMORE, P. H., late 69th Native Infantry.

Ensign, 5 Aug. 34—Lieut., 22 April 40—Captain, 29 July 48—Major, 11 July 57—Lieut.-Colonel, 8 Dec. 61.

SERVICE.—Lieutenant-Colonel SISSMORE served during the Punjab Campaign, '48, '49. *Medal. (Since retired.)*

LIEUTENANT F. H. M. SITWELL, P. H., late 31st Native Infantry.

Ensign, 20 Jan. 51—Lieut., 28 Nov. 56.

SERVICE.—Lieutenant SITWELL served in the Sonthal Campaign in Command of a Detachment, 31st Native Infantry, in '55, '56. Served during the Persian Expeditionary Force in '57. *Medal and Clasp.* Served on the personal Staff of Sir J. Outram, from August '57 to

(550)

February '58. Present at the actions of Mungulwarrah and the Alum Bagh, at the relief of Lucknow, September '57. *(Wounded.)* Served during the defence, and was *severely wounded* at the final relief by Lord Clyde. Mentioned in Sir R. Napier's Report, September '57. In Sir J. Outram's Despatch, 25th November '57, and received the thanks of Government. *Medal and Clasp.*

LIEUTENANT H. C. SITWELL, late 5th Bengal European Cavalry.

Cornet, 20 April 57—Lieut., 18 May 58.

SERVICE.—Lieutenant SITWELL was present at the actions fought by General Windham, in defence of Cawnpore, 26th, 27th, and 28th November '57. Was attached to H. M.'s 9th Royal Lancers from 5th December '57 to 15th November '58, and was present during that time at the following actions: defeat of the Gwalior rebels by Lord Clyde, at Cawnpore, Serai Ghaut, Khodagunge, and re-occupation of Futtehghur. Meangunge, Lucknow, siege and capture of Fort of Rooya, Allygunge, Bareilly, Shahjehanpore, Mohumdee. *Medal and Clasp.*

ASSISTANT-SURGEON T. G. SKARDON, Bengal Medical Department.

Asst.-Surgeon, 20 Jan. 60.

CAPTAIN H. SKINNER Unattached List.

Captain, 16 Jan. 52.

(Since retired.)

LIEUTENANT R. M. SKINNER, P. H., late 56th Native Infantry.

Ensign, 7 Dec. 55—Lieut., 15 June 57.

LIEUTENANT G. T. SKIPWITH, Bengal Engineers.

Lieut., 27 Aug. 58.

CAPTAIN J. R. SLADEN, P. H., Bengal Artillery.

2nd Lieut., 11 June 42—Lieut., 3 July 45—Bt.-Captain, 11 June 57—Captain, 25 Sept. 57.

SERVICE.—Captain SLADEN was present at the battle of Maharajpore, '43, *Bronze Star;* Upper Scinde, '45; with the Force under Sir

(551)

C. Napier, against the Belochee Hill Tribes. Served with Major Fordyce's Troop of Horse Artillery at the battle of Goojerat. *Medal and Clasp.* Served with the expedition under Brigadier Chamberlain to the Meeranzaie Valley and Upper Koorum, in '56; also present at the operations in the Bozdar Hills, in '57.

LIEUTENANT J. B. SLATER,† late 22nd Native Infantry.

Ensign, 4 Sept. 58—Lieut., 1 April 59.

SERVICE.—Lieutenant SLATER served with a Detachment of the 1st Battalion H. M.'s 6th Foot in pursuit of mutineers and rebels, in the Azimghur District, in '59.

CAPTAIN M. J. SLATER, P. C., late 5th Europeans.

Ensign, 22 Dec. 40—Lieut., 12 Nov. 42—Captain, 15 Nov. 53.

SERVICE.—Captain SLATER served with General Pollock's Force in Affghanistan, in '42 : present in all the different engagements leading to the re-occupation of Cabul. *Medal.*

SURGEON D. H. SMALL,† Bengal Medical Establishment.

Asst.-Surgeon, 21 Nov. 46—Surgeon, 24 Feb. 60.

CAPTAIN E. SMALLEY, P. H., late 36th Native Infantry.

Ensign, 23 Feb. 43—Lieut., 14 Nov. 46—Captain, 31 May 57.

SERVICE.—Captain SMALLEY served during the Sutlej Campaign, '45, 46: present at the battle of Alliwal. *Medal.* Served during the Punjab Campaign, '48, '49. Present at the actions of Ramnuggur, Sadoolapore, Chillianwallah, and Goojerat. *Medal and 2 Clasps.*

2ND CAPTAIN F. E. SMALPAGE, P. H., Bengal Artillery.

2nd Lieut., 9 June 48—Lieut., 3 March 53—2nd Captain, 27 Aug. 58.

SERVICE.—Captain SMALPAGE served during the Mutiny Campaign. *Medal.*

(552)

BREVET-MAJOR A. S. SMITH, P., late 24th Native Infantry.

Ensign, 3 March 42—Lieut., 1 April 45—Captain, 26 March 54—Bt.-Major, 26 April 59.

SERVICE.—Major SMITH served during the Sutlej Campaign, '45, '46: present in the actions of Moodkee, Ferozeshuhur, Alliwal, and Buddiwal. *Medal and 2 Clasps.* Present at the affair in the Kohat Pass, under Brigadier Coke, in '53. Served with the Sheoranee Expedition, under Brigadier Hodgson; and with the Force under General Chamberlain, in the Meeranzaie Valley, in '55. Commanded the Pathan Ressala of Sooltan Jan, during the Mutiny of '57, '58. Served in the Mozuffernuggur District, previous to, and after the fall of Delhi. Engaged on several occasions. (*Severely wounded* at Thanna Baon, on the 18th September '57.) Served as Orderly Officer to Brigadier Coke with the Roorkee Field Force. Mentioned in Brigadier Coke's Despatch of the action of Nugeena. Joined the Roorkee Field Force with his Ressala, and present at the action of Bareilly, 5th May '58. Served in the Philibheet District under Brigadier Coke. *Medal.* Promoted to the rank of Brevet-Major for services during the Mutiny.

CAPTAIN B. H. SMITH,† late 67th Native Infantry.

Ensign, 20 Aug. 51—Lieut., 8 Dec. 53—Captain, 15 June 60.

SERVICE.—Captain SMITH served with the Force under Major Minchin, and under Sir J. Cheape, at the operations in the vicinity of Donabew. *Medal.*

LIEUTENANT B. N. SMITH, P. H., late 46th Native Infantry.

Ensign, 20 Jan. 49—Lieut., 10 Feb. 55.

CAPTAIN C. F. SMITH, P. H., late 39th Native Infantry.

Ensign, 27 Sept. 40—Lieut., 18 March 45—Bt.-Captain, 27 Sept. 55—Captain, 23 Nov. 56.

SERVICE.—Captain SMITH served at the battle of Punniar. *Bronze Star.*

(553)

SURGEON C. M. SMITH,† Bengal Medical Establishment.

Asst.-Surgeon, 19 March 45—Surgeon, 10 Feb. 59.

SERVICE.—Surgeon SMITH served throughout the first and second siege of Mooltan, '48, '49: present at the action of Sooroojkhoond and the battle of Goojerat. *Medal and 2 Clasps.*

ASSISTANT-SURGEON C. M. SMITH,† M.D., Bengal Medical Establishment.

Asst.-Surgeon, 20 Dec. 54.

ASSISTANT-SURGEON D. B. SMITH,† M. D., Bengal Medical Establishment.

Asst.-Surgeon, 28 Nov. 55.

SERVICE.—Assistant-Surgeon SMITH served with the 1st Brigade Horse Artillery throughout the Campaign of '57, '58. Was present at Meerut on the out-break of the Mutiny, 10th May '57. Present at the two general actions of the Hindun, 30th and 31st May, at Badlee-ka-Serai, taking of the heights at Delhi, 8th June, and at the battle of Nudjufghur, 26th August, throughout the siege and at the storm and capture of Delhi in Medical Charge of Colonel Tomb's Troop of Horse Artillery, at the siege and capture of Lucknow, in March '58; at the affair of Rooya, the engagement of Allygunge, the capture of Bareilly, and the after operations at Mohumdee, Shahabad, Shahjehanpore, &c. Was in Medical Charge of Colonel Smyth's Column at the action of Sussea Ghaut, beyond Philibheet, 15th January '59. *Medal and 2 Clasps.*

LIEUTENANT E. D. SMITH, General List.

Ensign, 20 June 59—Lieut., 9 March 61.

LIEUTENANT-COLONEL E. F. SMITH, late 23rd Native Infantry.

Ensign, 16 Feb. 26—Lieut., 28 July 33—Bt.-Captain, 16 Feb. 41— Captain, 1 April 46—Bt.-Major, 20 June 54—Lieut.-Colonel, 29 April 61.

CAPTAIN F. H. SMITH, P. H., late 34th Native Infantry.

Ensign, 9 April 41—Lieut., 10 Jan. 45—Bt.-Captain, 2 April 56— Captain, 11 Dec. 57.

SERVICE.—Captain SMITH served with the 16th Irregular Cavalry in the Punjab, in '48, '49. *Medal.* Present at the storm and capture of the Fort of Shahpore, assault of the heights of Noorpore, in the engagements of Dunanuggur and heights of Umb, at the storming of the heights of Dullah, with the Force under Colonel Craigie, against the Bussy Khel Affreedies, on the Peshawur Frontier, in '55. Commanded the 2nd Mahratta Horse with the Force under Sir R. Napier, in the defeat and pursuit of the rebels under Ferozeshah, at Ranode, 17th December '58. *Medal.*

LIEUTENANT G. F. SMITH, P. H., late 3rd Bengal European Cavalry.

Cornet, 20 Oct. 55—Lieut., 20 Nov. 56.

LIEUTENANT G. L. SMITH, P. H., late 29th Native Infantry.

Ensign, 5 March 55—Lieut., 23 Nov. 56.

LIEUTENANT H. C. SMITH, P. H., late 9th Native Infantry.

Ensign, 20 Dec. 48—Lieut., 23 Nov. 56.

SERVICE.—Lieutenant SMITH served in the actions against the Hill Tribes on the Peshawur Frontier, in '54, '55. Present at the capture and destruction of the Hill Forts of Dhub and Sardine, in August '54, and the expeditions against the Bussy Khel Affreedies, in December '54 and March '55. Mentioned in the Despatch of Major Eld, in December '54. Served as Interpreter to H. M.'s 19th Foot, with the Force under Brigadier Kelly, on the Nepal Frontier, in '59.

2ND CAPTAIN H. M. SMITH, P. H., Bengal Artillery.

2nd Lieut., 12 Dec. 45—Lieut., 21 July 51—2nd Captain, 27 Aug. 58.

ASSISTANT-SURGEON H. S. SMITH, M.B., Bengal Medical Establishment.

Asst.-Surgeon, 10 Feb. 59.

LIEUTENANT H. U. SMITH, P. H., late 46th Native Infantry.

Ensign, 4 Oct. 57—Lieut., 11 Sept. 59.

SERVICE.—Lieutenant SMITH served in the Oude Campaign in '57: present at the taking of Futtehghur, under Brigadier Walpole, and at the siege and capture of Lucknow, under Lord Clyde. Served in the Trans-Gogra Campaign, '58, 59, under Lieut.-Colonel Pratt. *Medal and Clasp*.

CAPTAIN J. SMITH, P. H., late 51st Native Infantry.

Ensign, 29 July 41—Lieut., 1 May 43—Captain, 13 May 55.

SERVICE.—Captain SMITH served during the Campaign in Bundlecund, in '42, '43. Served in Gwalior, in '43, '44. Present at the battle of Punniar, 29th December '43. *Bronze Star*. Served during the Sutlej Campaign, in '46; during the Punjab Campaign, '48, '49. Present throughout the siege operations before Mooltan, until its fall, including the attack on the enemy's position, 12th September '48; action of Sooroojkhoond, 7th November '48; the assault of the Suburbs, on the 27th December; at the battle of Goojerat, 21st February '49. *Medal and 2 Clasps*. Commanded Detachments of Bengal Military Police, in the Sumbulpore District, against rebels, in February '61.

LIEUTENANT J. SMITH, V.C., Bengal Veteran Establishment.

Lieut., 1 Jan. 60.

SERVICE.—Lieutenant SMITH served in the Campaign in Affghanistan: present at the affair at Ali Musjid, and retreat through the Khyber Pass with Brigadier Wild's Force; storming of the Khyber Pass, Mammoo Khel, Jugdulluck, Mazeena Valley, Tazeen Valley, Huft Kotul, with General Pollock's Force. *Cabul Medal*. Punjab Campaign, siege of Mooltan, and battle of Goojerat. *Medal and 2 Clasps*. Capture of Delhi and blowing in the Cashmere gate. *Medal, Clasp, and Victoria Cross, and the thanks of the Governor-General*. Present with Brigadier Barker's Force, in Oude. *(Vide V. C. Roll.)*

LIEUTENANT J. B. SMITH, P., late 5th Europeans.

Ensign, 26 June 56—Lieut., 30 April 58.

CAPTAIN J. W. SMITH, P. H., late 22nd Native Infantry.

Ensign, 11 Dec. 40—Lieut., 16 July 42—Captain, 15 Sept. 55.

SERVICE.—Captain SMITH served with the Army of the Punjab, '48, '49. Present at the action of Sadoolapore. *Medal*. Served at Ramnuggur, holding the Bridge Heads.

(556)

LIEUTENANT L. SMITH,† late 36th Native Infantry.

Ensign, 13 Dec. 56—Lieut., 12 June 57.

SERVICE.—Lieutenant SMITH served as a Volunteer with H. M.'s 8th Foot, in repulsing the rebels from the guns at Jullundur, 7th June '57. Served with the Kumaon Battalion in Oude, '58; and under Brigadier Horsford, in the Nepal Frontier, '59. Present in a skirmish, 9th February '59, and at the action of Sikta Ghaut, 15th March '59. *Medal.*

LIEUTENANT M. C. SMITH, 101st Regiment of Foot (Royal Bengal Fusiliers.)

Ensign, 11 June 58—Lieut., 22 Oct. 58.

LIEUTENANT M. G. SMITH, P. H., late 59th Native Infantry.

Ensign, 10 April 51—Lieut., 5 April 55.

CAPTAIN O. L. SMITH, P. H., late 48th Native Infantry.

Ensign, 12 June 47—Lieut., 7 Nov. 50—Captain, 18 Feb. 61.

LIEUTENANT R. SMITH,† late 59th Native Infantry.

Ensign, 26 Aug. 52—Lieut., 23 Nov. 56.

SERVICE.—Lieutenant SMITH served with the Delhi Field Force in '57. Served with the Mounted Police Force at Delhi, in '57, '58. Present at the occupation of Jhujjur.

MAJOR R. A. SMITH,† late 19th Native Infantry.

Ensign, 11 June 36—Lieut., 18 June 37—Captain, 28 March 50—Major, 12 Dec. 59.

BREVET-COLONEL R. B. SMITH, C.B., Bengal Engineers.

2nd Lieut., 9 Dec. 36—Lieut., 28 Aug. 44—2nd Captain, 9 Dec. 51—Captain, 15 Feb. 54—Bt.-Major, 16 Feb. 54—Bt.-Lieut.-Colonel, 19 Jan. 58—Bt.-Colonel, 26 April 59.

SERVICE.—Colonel SMITH, C.B., served during the Sutlej Campaign, '45, '46: present at the action of Sobraon. *Medal.* Served during the

(557)

Punjab Campaign, '48, '49: present at the battles of Sadoolapore, Chillianwallah, and Goojerat. *Medal and 2 Clasps.* Served the Mutiny Campaign. *Medal and Clasp and C.B., and Brevets of Colonel and Lieutenant-Colonel. (Since dead.)*

LIEUTENANT R. W. SMITH, Bengal Artillery.

Lieut., 9 Dec. 59.

SURGEON T. SMITH,† M.D., Bengal Invalid Establishment.

Asst.-Surgeon, 16 March 48—Surgeon, 15 March 53.

2ND CAPTAIN T. P. SMITH, P. H., Bengal Artillery.

2nd Lieut., 11 Dec. 49—Lieut., 15 Oct. 55—2nd Captain, 27 Aug. 58.

CAPTAIN W. SMITH, late 28th Native Infantry.

Ensign, 12 June 46—Lieut., 10 April 49—Captain in Staff Corps, 18 Feb. 61.

SERVICE.—Captain SMITH served with the 58th Native Infantry in the Reserve Force under Major-General Hill, of the Army of Punjab of '48, '49. Served in Military Charge of two Regiments of Goorkhas (Nepalese Troops), throughout the Campaign against the mutineers of '57, '58. Was present at the actions fought by the Goorkha Troops, and with them accompanied Brigadier-General Franks' Column, 4th Division of the Army, throughout Oude. Was present at the attack on Chandah and affair of Umeerapoor, on the 19th February '58; and battle of Sultanpore, on the 24th of the same month, at which action he acted on the Personal Staff of General Franks, as his Orderly Officer and extra A.D.C. Received the General's thanks on the Field for services rendered on that day. Was also mentioned in his Despatch, and afterwards the same approbation of his services was expressed by General Franks, Commanding 4th Division of the Army, *vide* his letter to Colonel Birch. Was present throughout the siege and capture of Lucknow; holding Military charge of two Regiments of Goorkhas during the whole of that time; and was, for services at the attack on the Begum Kotee at Lucknow, mentioned in the Despatch of General Lugard amongst the Roll of Officers who were deemed deserving of Honorable mention. Received the thanks of Government. Received the thanks of the Commander-in-Chief. His conduct having been brought to the favorable notice of the Commander-in-Chief by the above letter, he received the thanks of the Court of Directors. The above thanks were given to him for his conduct at the outbreak in India, in June '57. *Medal and Clasp.*

ASSISTANT-SURGEON W. C. SMITH,† M. D., Bengal Medical Establishment.

Asst.-Surgeon, 29 Jan. 57.

SERVICE.—Assistant-Surgeon SMITH served against the mutineers in the Sonthal and Behar Districts; served with Colonel Cotton's Force in putting down the rebels in Fulamow, and in the relief of Lieutenant Graham and party of Sikhs shut up in a native Fort in that District. Served with the Rohilcund Force in June '58, till August '59.

LIEUTENANT W. G. SMITH, P. H., General List.

Ensign, 11 Aug. 59—Lieut., 6 May 61.

CAPTAIN W. H. SMITH, P. H., late 56th Native Infantry.

Ensign, 20 Dec. 45—Lieut., 12 May 49—Captain, 20 Dec. 60.

SERVICE.—Captain SMITH served throughout the Punjab Campaign, '48, '49: present at the passage of the Chenab and battles of Chillianwallah and Goojerat. *Medal.*

LIEUTENANT H. SMITHETT, Bengal Artillery.

Lieut., 21 April 58.

SERVICE.—Lieutenant H. SMITHETT served in the Campaign of '57, '58: was present with the Force under Sir Henry Havelock in its *first* advance to Lucknow, in Command of three guns of Captain W. Olphert's Light Field Battery, and present at the actions of Busseerutgunge, on 5th and 12th August. Served with Sir James Outram's Division in the advance to Lucknow. Present at passage of the Ganges, on 19th September; Mungulwarrah, 21st September; Alum Bagh, 23rd, and 1st relief of Lucknow, 25th September. Was besieged in the Garrison of

(559)

Lucknow from 26th September till 17th November '57, during which time *was wounded, first in October, by a shower of grape shot in seven places, and again, on 17th November, severely in the head by a musket ball.* During the siege, commanded late 2nd Company, 3rd Battalion Bengal Artillery, with No. 12 Light Field Battery attached. Was present with Sir James Outram's Division at the Alum Bagh, during December '57, and January and February '58, and in all the assaults and engagements there, including the action at Guilee, on 22nd December, where he commanded four Horse Field Guns. Present at the final siege and capture of Lucknow, under Lord Clyde, in March and April '58. *Medal and 2 Clasps.* (Several times mentioned in Despatches.)

CAPTAIN J. B. SMYLY, P., late 29th Native Infantry.

Ensign, 14 June 45—Lieut., 15 March 51—Bt.-Captain, 14 June 60— Captain, 18 Feb. 61.

SERVICE.—Captain SMYLY served during the Punjab Campaign, north of Jullundur, '48, '49, including the storming of the heights of Moorpore, and capture of the Forts of Shahpore and Oonah. *Medal.* (Attained the standard of proficiency in Punjabee.)

CAPTAIN E. SMYTH, P., late 13th Native Infantry.

Ensign, 10 July 42—Lieut., 15 July 45—Bt.-Captain, 10 July 57— Captain, 18 June 57.

SERVICE.—Captain SMYTH served throughout the Punjab Campaign, '48, '49 : present at the passage of the Chenab and battle of Goojerat. *Medal and Clasp.*

BREVET-COLONEL G. M. C. SMYTH, late 5th Bengal European Cavalry.

Cornet, 14 Aug. 20—Lieut., 3 Oct. 21—Captain, 24 July 28—Bt.-Major, 23 Nov. 41—Bt.-Lieut.-Colonel, 11 Nov. 51—Major, 21 Oct. 52—Lieut.-Colonel, 3 May 56—Bt.-Colonel, 28 Nov. 54.

SERVICE.—Colonel SMYTH was present at the siege and capture of Bhurtpore, '26. *Medal.* Served during the Affghanistan Campaign, '38, '39 : present at the capture of Ghuznee. *Medal.* Served during the Sutlej Campaign, '45, '46: present at the actions of Buddiwal, Alliwal, and Sobraon. *Medal and Clasp.*

LIEUTENANT-COLONEL J. H. SMYTH, C.B., Bengal Artillery.

2nd Lieut., 9 June 31—Lieut., 11 April 40—Bt.-Captain, 9 June 46—Captain, 5 May 49—Bt.-Major, 19 Jan. 58—Bt.-Lieut.-Colonel, 24 March 58—Lieut.-Colonel, 12 March 60.

SERVICE.—Lieutenant-Colonel SMYTH served at the action of Punniar. *Bronze Star.*

LIEUTENANT R. G. SMYTH, Bengal Engineers.

Lieut., 15 Aug. 58.

MAJOR N. R. SNEYD, P. H., late 57th Native Infantry.

Ensign, 11 Jan. 39—Lieut., 7 Jan. 41—Captain, 11 July 53—Major, 18 Feb. 61.

SERVICE.—Major SNEYD served with the Army of Gwalior in '43: present at the battle of Maharajpore. *Bronze Star.* Mentioned in the Despatch of His Excellency Sir Hugh Gough, 4th January '44.

BREVET-MAJOR T. R. SNOW, P., late 4th Bengal European Cavalry.

Cornet, 18 June 39—Lieut., 28 Oct. 42—Bt.-Captain, 18 June 54—Captain, 13 Jan. 55—Bt.-Major, 19 Jan. 58.

SERVICE.—Major SNOW served with the Army in Scinde, '43, '44. Present at the actions of Meenee and Hyderabad. (*Horse shot* under him.) *Medal.* Served against the Tribes in the Googaira District, under Sir J. Lawrence, in '57. (*Wounded*, 30th September '57, and *horse wounded* by a sabre cut; *wounded severely*, 16th October '57.) *Medal.* Promoted to the rank of Brevet-Major for services in '57.

LIEUTENANT W. SNOW,† late 63rd Native Infantry.

Ensign, 20 Jan. 56—Lieut., 30 April 58.

SERVICE.—Lieutenant SNOW served during the Mutinies in the

(561)

Goruckpore and Ghazeepore Districts, in '58, '59. *Medal.* Served against the Cabul Khel Wuzeerees in '59, under Brigadier-General Chamberlain.

CAPTAIN B. SOADY, P. H., late 24th Native Infantry.

Ensign, 1 April 44—Lieut., 6 Oct. 50—Bt.-Captain, 1 April 59—Captain, 1 Jan. 62.

CAPTAIN M. R. SOMERVILLE,† late 61st Native Infantry.

Ensign, 12 June 41—Lieut., 25 Jan. 43—Captain, 3 July 55.

SERVICE.—Captain SOMERVILLE served with the 61st Native Infantry in Bundlecund, in '42, '43. Served in the Campaign on the Oude Frontier, in '58, '59. *Medal.* *(Since dead.)*

LIEUTENANT H. SPALDING, late 2nd European Bengal Fusiliers.

2nd Lieut., 20 Feb. 58—Lieut., 9 Oct. 59.

SERVICE.—Lieutenant SPALDING served against the rebels in Oude, in '58. Present at the passage of the Goomtee and occupation of Sultanpore. *Medal.*

CAPTAIN J. G. SPARKE, P. H., late 21st Native Infantry.

Ensign, 17 Feb. 43—Lieut., 24 Jan. 45—Bt.-Captain, 17 Feb. 58—Captain, 7 Sept. 58.

CAPTAIN J. H. SPEKE, P. H., late 46th Native Infantry.

Ensign, 8 June 44—Lieut., 8 Oct. 50—Bt.-Captain, 8 June 59—Captain, 1 March 61.

SERVICE.—Captain SPEKE was engaged by Government in an expedition to explore Eastern Africa, in '54, '55; was taken prisoner there, *and received* 11 *spear wounds.* Served with the Turkish Contingent in '55, '56. (Has passed an examination in the Turkish language.)

MAJOR J. K. SPENCE, late 20th Native Infantry.

Ensign, 21 May 26—Lieut., 6 Aug. 34—Bt.-Captain, 21 May 41—Captain, 3 Sept. 49—Bt.-Major, 20 June 54—Major, 18 Feb. 61.

SERVICE.—Major SPENCE served in Affghanistan, '39, '40. *Medal.*

CAPTAIN T. SPENCER, Bengal Veteran Establishment.

Captain, 1 Nov. 56.

SERVICE.—Captain SPENCER served at the siege and capture of Hattrass, '17. Throughout the Pindarree Campaign under Lord Hastings, '17, '18; with the expedition to China under Sir Hugh Gough, '42, '43. *Medal.* Throughout the siege and capture of Mooltan, under General Whish, and battle of Goojerat, '48, '49. *Medal and Clasp.* Was present at Mooltan during the Mutiny, '57, '58. *(Since retired.)*

LIEUTENANT F. VAN H. SPERLING, late 5th Europeans.

Ensign, 15 May 56—Lieut., 5 Oct. 57.

CAPTAIN E. J. SPILSBURY, P. H., late 67th Native Infantry.

Ensign, 16 Jan. 44—Lieut., 28 Feb. 50—Captain, 23 Nov. 56.

SERVICE.—Captain SPILSBURY served in Burmah, '52, '53. *Medal.* (Has passed an examination in Burmese.)

BREVET-COLONEL A. C. SPOTTISWOODE, late 37th Native Infantry.

Ensign, 25 Feb. 24—Lieut., 13 May 25—Captain, 14 Nov. 33—Bt.-Major, 9 Nov. 46—Major, 17 March 51—Bt.-Lieut.-Colonel, 20 June 54—Lieut.-Colonel, 22 May 56—Bt.-Colonel, 23 July 58.

SERVICE.—Colonel SPOTTISWOODE served at the siege and capture of Bhurtpore. *Medal.* Served during the Affghanistan Campaign, '38, '39. *(Since retired.)*

LIEUTENANT R. C. D'E. SPOTTISWOODE, late 3rd Bengal European Cavalry.

Cornet, 20 March 58—Lieut., 21 June 58.

LIEUTENANT F. P. SPRAGGE, Bengal Engineers.

Lieut., 10 June 59.

CAPTAIN C. H. D. SPREAD, Bengal Invalid Establishment.

Ensign, 1 July 36—Lieut., 7 Feb. 38—Captain, 6 June 45.

ASSISTANT-SURGEON H. W. SPRY,† Bengal Medical Establishment.
Asst.-Surgeon, 4 Oct. 53.

SURGEON J. SQUIRE,† Bengal Medical Establishment.
Asst.-Surgeon, 30 April 45—Surgeon, 1 April 59.

LIEUTENANT B. T. STAFFORD, P. H., late 18th Native Infantry.
Ensign, 9 Dec. 48—Lieut., 12 Aug. 53.

SERVICE.—Lieutenant STAFFORD served during the China Expedition, in '62. *Medal.* Present in the following operations against the Taipsing rebels: capture of stockades at Wong-ka-Dya, 4th April; of the stockaded village of Chowpoo, 17th April; and stockades near Nezeean, 29th April; present at the capture, by assault, of the walled towns of Kahoing, 1st May; Chingpoo, 12th May; Munchiao, 17th May; Isoling, 20th May; and repulse of superior force of rebels at Nezeean, 25th May '62.

BREVET-MAJOR J. F. STAFFORD, P. H., late 4th Native Infantry.
Ensign, 12 Jan. 45—Lieut., 1 July 48—Captain, 11 Aug. 57—Bt.-Major, 26 April 59.

SERVICE.—Major STAFFORD served during the Punjab Campaign, '48, '49, *Medal;* with the Force under Brigadier Chamberlain in the Meeranzaie Valley. Present at the action of Darsummund, May '55. Served during the Mutiny, '57, '58, '59. Present at the actions of Gungeeree, Puttiallee, and Mynpooree, December '57; Bungaon (Rohilcund), in April '58; with Brigadier Kelly's Force in Nepal, and present at Ruttunpore, 25th March '59; and commanded the Right Column of attack at the affair on the 28th March '59. *Medal.* Present with the Force under Sir Hope Grant at the action in the Juowah Pass, 20th May '59. Mentioned in the Despatches of Brigadier Kelly, both in '59, and also in the Despatch of Sir Hope Grant, in '59. Favorably recommended to the notice of the Governor-General by Lord Clyde, '59. Received the thanks of Government in '59. Promoted to the rank of Brevet-Major for services in the Oude Campaign of '58.

(564)

BREVET-MAJOR W. J. F. STAFFORD, P., late 36th Native Infantry.

Ensign, 9 Sept. 40—Lieut., 25 July 44—Captain, 15 Feb. 53—Major, 19 Jan. 58.

SERVICE.—Major STAFFORD served during the Mutiny, '57, '58. Present at the siege and capture of Delhi, commanded the 1st European Bengal Fusiliers on the day of assault, 14th September '57, until the final evacuation of the city by the rebels on the 20th September '57. (*Wounded in two places*, 14th September '57.) *Medal and Clasp*. Served as Brigade Major with the Hurreeanah Field Force, under General Van Cortland. Present under Brigadier Showers, at the surrender of Jhujjur, in October '57. Commanded a Detachment of Hurreeanah Field Force at the action of Narnoul, 16th November '57. Mentioned in the Despatch of Captain Caulfield, 16th January '58. Received the thanks of Sir John Lawrence for conduct at Narnoul, 1st December '57. Commanded the 22nd Punjab Infantry at the action of Kukrowlee, under General Penny, and at the taking of Bareilly, under Lord Clyde. Mentioned in the Despatch of Lord Clyde, 8th May '58. Promoted to the rank of Brevet-Major for services at Delhi, in '57. Served during the expedition in China, in '60, '61, in Command of the 22nd Punjab Infantry. *Medal*. Present at the following operations against the Taipsing rebels: capture of stockades at Wong-ka-Dya, 4th April '62; of the stockaded village of Chowpoo, 17th April, and of the stockades near Nezeean, 29th April, at the capture, by assault, of the walled towns of Kahoing, 1st May, Chingpoo, 12th May, Munchiao, 17th May, Isoling, 20th May, and repulse of an immensely superior Force of rebels at Nezeean, 25th May '62. Present at the relief of Kahoing, 26th May '62. Commanded Detachments, 31st Punjab Native Infantry and 22nd Punjab Native Infantry, sent to co-operate with the Naval Force under Sir Hope Grant, for the relief (effected) of Chingpoo, 10th June '62.

MAJOR F. G. STAINFORTH, P. C., late 61st Native Infantry.

Ensign, 4 Aug. 41—Lieut., 26 Dec. 44—Captain, 29 Dec. 55—Major in Staff Corps, 4 Aug. 61.

(565)

LIEUTENANT G. B. STAINFORTH, P., late 61st Native Infantry.

Ensign, 20 Jan. 53—Lieut., 3 July 55.

SERVICE.—Lieutenant STAINFORTH served during the siege and capture of Delhi, in '57. *Medal and Clasp.* Served against the Cabul Khel Wuzeerees, in '59; against the Mahsood Wuzeerees in '60, and was present at the night attack on the British Camp at Poluseen, and the forcing of the Burrara Pass.

LIEUTENANT R. STAINFORTH, P. H., late 56th Native Infantry.

Ensign, 20 June 57—Lieut., 18 May 58.

SERVICE.—Lieutenant STAINFORTH served during the Mutiny, '57, '58. Present at the actions of Akberpore, taking of Lucknow by Lord Clyde, in March '85; Nawabgunge, Barabunki, under Sir Hope Grant. Present with the Rifles on the banks of Ramgunga; fight at Kawab Pass, under Brigadier Horsford. *Medal and Clasp.* Mentioned in the Despatch of Brigadier Horsford, March '59.

CAPTAIN S. STALLARD, P. H., Bengal Artillery.

2nd Lieut., 11 Dec. 41—Lieut., 3 July 45—Bt.-Captain, 17 Nov. 56.

BREVET-LIEUTENANT-COLONEL H. J. STANNUS, P. H., late 5th Bengal European Cavalry.

Cornet, 31 Dec. 40—Lieut., 12 Nov. 42—Captain, 16 April 50—Bt.-Major, 17 April 50—Major, 7 April 60—Bt.-Lieut.-Colonel, 28 Nov. 54.

SERVICE.—Colonel STANNUS served in the Campaign of '42, in Affghanistan, at the forcing of the Khyber Pass, and the battle of Mamoo Khail. *Medal.* Commanded a Detachment of the Regiment on escort with His Excellency the Commander-in-Chief, at the battle of Maharajpore. *Bronze Star.* Throughout the Campaign on the Sutlej. Present at the actions of Moodkee, Ferozeshuhur, Alliwal, and Sobraon. *Medal and 3 Clasps.* Served with the Army of the Punjab, at the action of Ramnuggur, and commanded the 3rd Troop of the Regiment on escort with he Commander-in-Chief, at the battles of Chillianwallah and Goojerat. *(Severely wounded.) Medal.*

CAPTAIN D. STANSBURY,† late 60th Native Infantry.

Ensign, 12 Dec. 34—Lieut., 13 March 37—Bt.-Captain, 12 Dec. 49—Captain, 15 Nov. 59.

SERVICE.—Captain STANSBURY served throughout the operations in Affghanistan, with the Force under General Pollock. *Medal.* *(Since retired.)*

LIEUTENANT H. H. STANSFELD,† late 6th Europeans.

Ensign, 13 Dec. 56—Lieut., 11 Oct. 57.

2ND CAPTAIN F. S. STANTON, Bengal Engineers.

2nd Lieut., 9 Dec. 50—Lieut., 1 May 55—2nd Captain, 27 Aug. 58.

CAPTAIN T. STAPLES, P. H., late 58th Native Infantry.

Ensign, 27 Jan. 44—Lieut., 10 Nov. 47—Captain, 4 Sept. 58.

(Has passed an Examination in Field Engineering.)

LIEUTENANT R. T. P. STAPLETON,† late 1st Bengal European Cavalry.

Cornet, 20 Nov. 52—Lieut., 17 Sept. 55.

SERVICE.—Lieutenant STAPLETON served in defence of the Fort of Neemuch, '57 (horse shot under him); accompanied the Rajpootanah Field Force, and was present at the capture of Kotah and action of Gwalior, '58, under Sir Hugh Rose. *Medal.*

LIEUTENANT E. H. STEEL, Bengal Artillery.

Lieut., 8 June 60.

BREVET-MAJOR J. A. STEEL, P. H., late 17th Native Infantry.

Ensign, 11 June 42—Lieut., 24 Jan. 45—Captain, 15 Jan. 56—Bt.-Major, 20 July 58.

SERVICE.— Major STEEL served the Mutiny Campaign. *Medal and Brevet-Major.*

LIEUTENANT J. N. STEEL, General List.

Ensign, 20 Jan. 60—Lieut., 1 Jan. 62.

(567)

LIEUTENANT J. P. STEEL, Bengal Engineers.

Lieut., 27 Aug. 58.

CAPTAIN W. F. STEPHENS, P. H., late 5th Bengal European Cavalry.

Ensign, 1 Jan. 44—Lieut., 4 June 48—Captain, 31 Dec. 54.

SERVICE.—Captain STEPHENS commanded a Detachment of the Regiment on escort duty with the Commander-in-Chief at Moodkee. *Medal.*

CAPTAIN F. J. STEPHENSON, P. C., late 3rd Europeans.

Ensign, 10 Dec. 44—Lieut., 19 Aug. 54—Bt.-Captain, 10 Dec. 59—Captain, 1 Jan. 62.

SERVICE.—Captain STEPHENSON served during the Mutiny in '57. Present at the action of Susseah, near Agra, 5th July '57; and at the action in the Fort of Agra, 10th October '57. *Medal.*

LIEUTENANT G. B. STEVENS, late 38th Native Infantry.

Ensign, 11 Dec. 58—Lieut., 29 March 59.

MAJOR H. B. STEVENS, P. H., late 41st Native Infantry.

Ensign, 11 June 41—Lieut., 21 June 44—Captain, 25 May 52—Bt.- Major, 26 April 59—Major, 11 July 61.

SERVICE.—Major STEVENS served during the Sutlej Campaign, '45, '46: present at the battles of Ferozeshuhur and Sobraon. *Medal and Clasp.* Commanded the Sylhet Light Infantry Battalion, and engaged with the mutineers, in '57, of the 34th Native Infantry, and succeeded in destroying the entire body, for which he received the thanks of Government, 26th January and 3rd February '58; also the great satisfaction of His Excellency Lord Clyde, 27th February '58. Promoted to the rank of Brevet-Major, 26th April '59. *Medal.*

MAJOR J. STEVENS, Bengal Invalid Establishment.

Ensign, 20 May 19—Lieut., 28 June 21—Captain, 18 July 31.

SERVICE.—Major STEVENS served at the siege of Bhurtpore. *Medal.* Served also with the Force under Major-General Sir G. Pollock, during the Affghan Campaign, '42.

(568)

ENSIGN T. P. STEVENS, Unattached List.

Ensign, 8 Jan. 59.

SERVICE.—Ensign STEVENS served during the Sutlej Campaign, '45, '46: present at the battles of Moodkee, Ferozeshuhur, and Sobraon. *Medal and 2 Clasps.* Served during the Punjab Campaign, '48, '49. Present at the action of Deenanuggur, and reduction of the Fort of Oonah, December '48. Served with Colonel Butler's Force on the Jullunder Doab, in January '49. *Medal.* Served against the Hill Tribes, Peshawur Frontier, in '50, '51. Present at the action, near Subkundur, in April '51, and several skirmishes in the Hills. Served throughout the siege and capture of Delhi, from 1st August '57, and several times engaged in the suburbs during the siege. Served in the Agra District in '57. Present at Futtehghur, 7th January '58, at Alum Bagh, 7th February '58. Present at the actions near the Fort of Jellallabad, 21st and 25th February '58. Present at the siege and capture of Lucknow, March '58. Present at the actions of Rugun, 15th April, Allygunge, 18th April, and battle and capture of Bareilly, 5th and 7th May '58. *Medal and 2 Clasps.* Received the Commission of Ensign (Unattached) for several acts of bravery, during the Campaign, 8th January '59.

LIEUTENANT E. STEVENSON, P. H., late 3rd Europeans.

Ensign, 20 Feb. 51—Lieut., 23 Nov. 56.

SERVICE.—Lieutenant STEVENSON served with the Force under Brigadier Showers. Present at the action of Dowsa, 14th January '59, against Tantia Topee. *(Not in the service.)*

LIEUTENANT J. STEVENSON, P. H., late 33rd Native Infantry.

Ensign, 18 June 53—Lieut., 23 Nov. 56.

SERVICE.—Lieutenant STEVENSON served during the Mutiny, '57, '58. Present at the capture of Delhi, '57; at the actions of Boolundshuhur, 28th September, Malaghur, 6th October, and Agra, 10th October '57. Present at the action of Bantarah, 9th November, Alum Bagh, 14th November, at the occupation of the Martiniere, action at Secunderabagh, and occupation of the Barracks, 17th and 18th November '57. Present

(569)

at the relief of Lucknow, November '57; at the battle of Cawnpore; action of Kala Nuddee; re-occupation of Futtehghur. Re-entered Oude with Lord Clyde's Force, 9th February '58. *Severely wounded* by explosion of powder whilst engaged in blowing up a Magazine in Fort Futtehpore, Chowdrassee. Present during the storm and capture of Lucknow under Lord Clyde, March '58. Present at Fort Rooya, 15th April; at the action near Allygunge, 22nd April; at the action of Bareilly, 5th May; and at Seerpoorah, 30th August '58. (*Severely wounded* on the head by a tulwar cut.) *Medal and Clasps.*

CAPTAIN R. C. STEVENSON, P. H., late 3rd Europeans.

Ensign, 8 March 38—Lieut., 12 Nov. 42—Bt.-Captain, 8 March 53—Captain, 21 Sept. 54.

SERVICE—Captain STEVENSON served with the Column under Brigadier Showers: present at the action at Dowsa, on the 14th January '59, against a body of rebels headed by Tantia Topee. *(Since retired.)*

LIEUTENANT A. STEWART, P., late 16th Native Infantry.

Ensign, 4 Feb. 55—Lieut., 1 Oct. 56.

LIEUTENANT A. McL. STEWART, P. H., late 64th Native Infantry.

Ensign, 20 June 52—Lieut., 18 March 57.

SERVICE.—Lieutenant STEWART served during the Mutiny, '57. Proceeded to Fort Mackerson with 20 Jeezailchees to hold 'the keep,' during the disarming of 2 Companies, 24th Native Infantry, in August '57. Served with the Delhi Field Force in September '57. Present at the taking of Jhujjur. Served under Lord Clyde in '58. Present at the actions of Shumshabad and Mhow, near Futtehghur, 27th January '58. Present at the siege and capture of Lucknow, March '58. *Severely wounded*, 10th March '58. *Medal and Clasp.* Present at the attack on Rooya, 5th April '58, under General Walpole, in Rohilcund. Mentioned in the Despatch of Captain W. M. Cafe. Present at the action at Allygunge, Rohilcund, 18th April '58, and taking of Shahjehanpore. Present at the siege and capture of Bareilly, 5th to 7th May '58.

ASSISTANT-SURGEON C. STEWART,† M. A., Bengal Medical Establishment.

Asst.-Surgeon, 26 Feb. 51.

SERVICE.—Assistant-Surgeon STEWART served with the 1st European Bengal Fusiliers at the relief of Pegu and the subsequent operations in the Field under General Godwin; was attached to the advanced Guard of General Steel's Column from Martaban to Shwegyeen. *Medal.* Served in Medical Charge of Major Gottreux's Force at the assault and re-capture of Beeling, and of Major Selon's Detachment in the expedition to Womgyee. Served under Major Nuthall in the operations against the rebel Chief Goungyee.

CAPTAIN C. T. STEWART,† Bengal Engineers.

2nd Lieut., 12 June 46—Lieut., 15 Feb. 54—2nd Captain, 27 Aug. 58—Captain, 14 Dec. 61.

SERVICE.—Captain STEWART served at the capture of Lucknow, '58, in charge of the Telegraph Department. *Medal, Clasp, and Brevet-Major.*

LIEUTENANT D. J. STEWART, P. H., General List.

Ensign, 20 Sept. 59—Lieut., 23 July 61.

BREVET-LIEUTENANT-COLONEL D. M. STEWART, P., late 9th Native Infantry.

Ensign, 12 Oct. 40—Lieut., 3 Jan. 44—Captain, 1 June 54—Bt.-Major, 19 Jan. 58—Bt.-Lieut.-Colonel, 20 July 58.

SERVICE.—Colonel STEWART served against the Hill Tribes on the Peshawur Frontier, in '54, '55. Mentioned in Sir Sydney Cotton's Despatch. Commanded the Volunteers serving in the Allyghur District, in May and June '57. All communication with the Upper Provinces having been cut off, volunteered to carry Despatches from the Government, North-West Provinces, to the Officer Commanding the Troops at Delhi. On arriving in Camp in June 57, was appointed Deputy Assistant Adjutant-General of the Field Force, and served in that capacity throughout the siege. Received the thanks of the Provincial Commander-in-Chief.

(571)

Mentioned in General Wilson's Despatches. Promoted to Brevet-Major for services at Delhi. *Medal and Clasp.* Served at the siege and capture of Lucknow as Assistant Adjutant-General of the Army, and was promoted to Brevet-Lieutenant-Colonel for services on that occasion. *Clasp for Lucknow.* Served throughout the operations in Rohilcund, in '58, as Assistant Adjutant-General of the Army. Mentioned in the Commander-in-Chief's Despatches.

LIEUTENANT G. STEWART, P. H., late 17th Native Infantry.

Ensign, 20 Sept. 56—Lieut., 1 Sept. 57.

ASSISTANT-SURGEON G. L. STEWART, M.D., P. H., Bengal Medical Establishment.

Asst.-Surgeon, 4 Aug. 55.

SERVICE.—Assistant-Surgeon STEWART served before Delhi, and throughout the siege, assault, and capture of the city, '57, '58. *Medal and Clasps.* Served with the expedition in the Eusuffzaie Country, under Sir S. Cotton, in '58.

ASSISTANT-SURGEON H. STEWART,† Bengal Medical Establishment.

Asst.-Surgeon, 22 July 47.

SERVICE.—Assistant-Surgeon STEWART served at the siege of Mooltan, '48, '49. *Medal and Clasp.* Served in Medical Charge of the Reserve Foot Artillery at the siege of Delhi, '57. *Medal and Clasp.*

2ND CAPTAIN J. STEWART, P. H., Bengal Artillery.

1st Lieut., 8 June 57—2nd Captain, 18 Feb. 61.

LIEUTENANT J. C. STEWART,† late 6th Europeans.

Ensign, 4 Sept. 57—Lieut., 17 June 58.

SERVICE.—Lieutenant STEWART served during the Mutiny, in '57, '58: present at the capture of Meangunge; served during the siege and capture of Lucknow. *Medal and Clasp.* Present at the affairs of Barree and Nuggur, under Sir J. Hope Grant.

(572)

ASSISTANT-SURGEON J. F. STEWART,† M. D.
 Asst.-Surgeon, 20 Feb. 56.

LIEUTENANT J. M. STEWART,† late 35th Native Infantry.
 Ensign, 20 Oct. 58—Lieut., 14 Dec. 60.

CAPTAIN R. STEWART, P. H., late 22nd Native Infantry.
 Ensign, 12 June 46—Lieut., 11 Nov. 53—Captain, 18 Feb. 61.

SERVICE.—Captain STEWART served throughout the Punjab Campaign, '48, '49. *Medal.* Commanded a Force of a Detachment, Sylhet Light Infantry, and Roorkee Levy, in pursuit of the Munniporee Princes; engaged with, and defeated them at Bishenpore, in Munnipore, 24th November '52. Served in Cachar against the mutineers of the 34th Native Infantry, in '57, '58. Received the repeated notice of the Government of Bengal, and the commendation of the Governor-General. Mentioned with distinction in the Governor-General's Minute during the Mutiny. Received Her Majesty's approval of his conduct during the Mutinies.

CAPTAIN W. F. STEWART, P. H., late 45th Native Infantry.
 Ensign, 8 Dec. 48—Lieut., 28 July 50—Captain, 16 March 58.

LIEUTENANT W. J. STEWART, P. H., Bengal Artillery.
 Lieut., 27 April 58.

SERVICE.—Lieutenant STEWART served under Sir James Outram before Lucknow, in '58. Served in the Alum Bagh till the final capture of Lucknow. *Medal and Clasp.*

CAPTAIN E. ST. GEORGE, P. C., late 1st European Bengal Fusiliers.
 2nd Lieut., 14 June 45—Lieut., 14 May 46—Captain, 23 Nov. 56.

SERVICE.—Captain ST. GEORGE served with the Army of the Sutlej in '45, '46 : present at the actions of Moodkee, Ferozeshuhur, and Sobraon. *Medal and 2 Clasps.* Served during the Burmese War, in '52, '53. *Medal and Clasp.* Served at the storm and capture of Lucknow, under

Lord Clyde, in March '58. (*Dangerously wounded*, 9th March '58.) *Medal and Clasp*. (Has received certificates of high proficiency in Oordoo and Hindee, and has also a Degree of Honor for his eminent attainments in Oordoo.)

LIEUTENANT SIR R. DEL. ST. GEORGE, *Bart.*, Bengal Artillery.

Lieut., 27 April 58.

SERVICE.—Lieutenant ST. GEORGE was present at the actions on the Hindun, 30th and 31st May '57; at the siege of Delhi, in '57; in charge of two 6-pounder guns in the Saharunpore District, '57, '58 ; commanded the Artillery at the affair near Hurdwar, 10th of January '58 ; served in the Trans-Gogra District, '58, '59, and on the several affairs near Gondah. *Medal and Clasp*.

BREVET-MAJOR T. G. ST. GEORGE,† late 17th Native Infantry.

Ensign, 22 May 30—Lieut., 1 Nov. 38—Bt.-Captain, 22 May 45—Captain, 18 March 53—Bt.-Major, 28 Nov. 54.

LIEUTENANT M. K. ST. JOHN,† late 49th Native Infantry.

Ensign, 1 March 52—Lieut., 18 May 56.

SERVICE.—Lieutenant ST. JOHN served during the Mutiny Campaign with Alexander's Horse. *Medal*. Served in the China Campaign with the 1st Sikh Irregular Cavalry, and was present in the actions of Sinho, Tongchow, and occupation of Pekin. *Medal and 2 Clasps*.

LIEUTENANT O. B. C. ST. JOHN, Bengal Engineers.

Lieut., 27 Aug. 58.

LIEUTENANT-COLONEL G. W. STOKES, late 59th Native Infantry.

Ensign, 4 Feb. 26—Lieut., 2 July 28—Bt.-Captain, 4 Feb. 41—Captain, 15 June 45—Bt.-Major, 20 June 54—Major, 21 Aug. 57—Lieut.-Colonel, 21 Feb. 61.

SERVICE.—Lieutenant-Colonel STOKES served with the Army of the Sutlej in '45, '46. Commanded the 59th Native Infantry from February

'46 till the Army broke up. Served with the Jullundur Force under Brigadier Wheeler, in '46, and commanded the 59th Native Infantry from October to December '46. Commanded the Pathan Cavalry during the Mutinies, from August '57 to February '59. Commanded an attack on the mutineers at the village of Moradungger, between Meerut and Delhi, on the 18th September '57, on which occasion the rebels were driven out, and the road opened between the two Stations. Guarded the whole length of the Ganges River, in the Boolundshuhur District, up to the 9th July '58. Present at the action of Gungeeree, 14th December '57. Served under Lord Clyde, in Oude, in '58. *Medal.* *(Since retired.)*

CAPTAIN E. G. STONE, P. H., late 40th Native Infantry.

Ensign, 20 Jan. 50—Lieut., 2 Jan. 53—Captain, 26 Aug. 60.

SERVICE.—Captain STONE served during the Sonthal Rebellion in '55, under Major-General Lloyd. Served with the Burmah Expedition in '52. Present at the operations in the vicinity, and capture of Rangoon, in April '52. *Medal.*

LIEUTENANT P. STORY,† late 66th Native Infantry.

Ensign, 11 Dec. 57—Lieut., 8 Nov. 58.

SERVICE.—Lieutenant STORY served under Brigadier C. Troup, during the Oude Campaign, '58, 59. Present at the action of Pusgaon, 19th October '58; Russoolpore, 25th October, attack and capture of Fort Mittowlee, 8th November, and action of Biswah, 1st December '58. *Medal.*

MAJOR-GENERAL P. F. STORY, C.B., late 3rd Bengal European Cavalry.

Cornet, 20 Oct. 25—Lieut., 10 July 26—Captain, 28 Oct. 32—Major, 28 Oct. 42—Bt.-Lieut.-Colonel, 4 July 43—Lieut.-Colonel, 2 Oct. 51—Bt.-Colonel, 1 Feb. 54—Major-General, 13 April 55.

SERVICE.—Major-General STORY served throughout the Scinde Campaign, in '43 : present at the battles of Meeance and Hyderabad. *Medal, C.B., and Brevet-Lieutenant-Colonel.*

(575)

LIEUTENANT J. STOTESBURY, Bengal Veteran Establishment.
Lieut., 14 Sept. 57.

SERVICE.—Lieutenant STOTESBURY served at the siege and capture of Delhi, in '57. *Medal and Clasp.*

BREVET-CAPTAIN R. STOTHERT, P. H., late 4th Native Infantry.
Ensign, 18 Jan. 45—Lieut., 20 Oct. 48—Bt.-Captain, 18 Jan. 60.

SERVICE.—Captain STOTHERT served with the Force under Brigadier Wheeler, during the Punjab Campaign, '48, '49. *Medal.*

CAPTAIN H. STRACHEY,† late 66th Native Infantry.
Ensign, 12 June 35—Lieut., 7 Nov. 40—Captain, 19 July 48.

LIEUTENANT-COLONEL R. STRACHEY, Bengal Engineers.
2nd Lieut., 10 June 36—Lieut., 24 Feb. 41—Bt.-Captain, 10 June 51— Captain, 15 Feb. 54—Bt.-Major, 16 Feb. 54—Lieut.-Colonel, 2 July 60.

LIEUTENANT G. STRAHAN,† Bengal Engineers.
Lieut., 10 Dec. 58.

MAJOR G. STRANGWAYS, P. H., late 71st Native Infantry.
Ensign, 16 June 38—Lieut., 3 Oct. 40—Captain, 21 Aug. 49—Major, 16 Feb. 61.

SERVICE.—Major STRANGWAYS served with the 71st Native Infantry at the defeat and dispersion of a body of dacoits who entered the Shahehanpore District, in May and June '41. Commanded the 71st Native Infantry and re-captured the Bareilly Jail from the prisoners, who had risen and overpowered the Guard, in July '42. Received the thanks of Major-General Waters. Served during the Punjab Campaign, '48, '49. Led the advance party of a Detachment, 71st Native Infantry, at the attack and defeat of the rebels under Ram Sing, who occupied the heights in front of Noorpoor, in September '48. Received the thanks of Lieutenant-Colonel Fisher. Present at the capture of the Fort of Rungul Nuggur, in November '48. Served also in pursuit of bodies of insurgents, in '48, '49. *Medal.* Commanded the 71st Native Infantry on the night of the Mutiny at Lucknow, 31st May '57. Commanded the faithful detachment of that corps throughout the entire defence of Lucknow, from 31st June to November '57. (*Wounded* on the 4th July '57.) *Medal and Clasp and one year's service.* Received the thanks of Government. Present with the Army under Lord Clyde at the battle of Cawnpore, in December '57.

ENSIGN A. STRATTON, Unattached List.

Ensign, 9 Oct. 58.

LIEUTENANT H. P. STREATFIELD,† General List.

Ensign, 4 Nov. 59—Lieut., 10 Sept. 61.

LIEUTENANT D. M. STRONG,† General List.

Ensign, 10 Dec. 59.

ENSIGN C. STROUD, Unattached List.

Ensign, 20 Sept. 57.

SERVICE.—Ensign STROUD served during the Gwalior Campaign: present at the action of Punniar, 29th December '43. *Bronze Star.* Served during the Sutlej Campaign in '45, '46. Present at the actions of Ferozeshuhur and Sobraon. *Medal and Clasp.* Served during the Punjab Campaign, '48, '49. Present in the actions of Chillianwallah and Goojerat, and pursuit of the Sikhs and Affghans to Peshawur. *Medal and 2 Clasps.* Served during the siege and capture of Delhi, '57. Received Ensign's commission for distinguished service.

CAPTAIN N. M. STROVER, P. H., Bengal Invalid Establishment.

Ensign, 27 Feb. 41—Lieut., 19 Nov. 42—Captain, 17 Dec. 55.

SERVICE.—Captain STROVER served with the late 25th Native Infantry throughout the Punjab Campaign of '48, '49, including the passage of the Chenab and battles of Sadoolapoor, Chillianwallah, and Goojerat. *Medal and 2 Clasps.* Served with the late 3rd Europeans during

(577)

the rebellion of '57. Present at the action, near Agra, against the Neemuch mutineers 5th July '57; also commanded the Detachment of the 3rd Europeans in the engagement at Maun Singh's Garden, near Allyghur, 24th August '57. Mentioned in Despatch. *Medal.*

CAPTAIN C. B. STUART,† late 4th Europeans.

Ensign, 11 Dec. 38—Lieut., 18 April 41—Captain, 7 Jan. 53.

SERVICE.—Captain STUART served during the Punjab Campaign, '48, '49, with the Force under Brigadier Wheeler. *Medal.* (Has furnished certificates of qualification in Surveying and Civil Engineering.)

LIEUTENANT H. B. STUART, late 18th Native Infantry.

Ensign, 20 Jan. 54—Lieut., 23 Nov. 56.

ENSIGN W. T. STUART,† Unattached List.

Ensign, 9 Oct. 60.

SERVICE.—Ensign STUART served during the Mutiny, '57, '58. Present at the action on the Hindun, 30th and 31st May '57, under Sir A. Wilson. Present at the action of Badlee-ka-Serai, and storming of the heights before Delhi, 8th June '57. Present throughout the siege, storm, and capture of Delhi, to 20th September '57. Served with the Force under Colonel Cotton, at Futtehpore-Sikree, 28th October '57. Served in the Agra, Muttra, and Allyghur Districts in '57. Served in Rohilcund and Oude with the Force under Brigadier Colin Troup. Present at the action and capture of Fort Mittowlee, 8th November '58, Allygunge, 17th November, and Biswah, 1st December '58. *Medal and Clasp.* Promoted to the rank of Ensign Unattached, 9th October '60.

LIEUTENANT F. A. STUBBS,† Bengal Artillery.

Lieut., 11 Dec. 58.

2ND CAPTAIN F. W. STUBBS, P. H., Bengal Artillery.

2nd Lieut., 11 June 47—Lieut., 3 March 53—2nd Captain, 27 Aug. 58.

SERVICE.—Captain STUBBS commanded a heavy Battery with the Column under Sir J. Jones, in Rohilcund, in '58. Present in the actions of Nugeenah, Meergunge, capture of Bareilly (mentioned in Despatches), relief of Shahjehanpore, and affairs at the same place (mentioned in Despatches), Shahabad (mentioned in Despatches), and Mohumdee; with Brigadier Colin Troup's Column in Oude, in '58, '59. Present at the actions of Pusgaon (mentioned in Despatches), Russoolpore (mentioned), capture of Mittowlee (mentioned), and Biswah. *Medal.*

CAPTAIN W. H. STUBBS, P., late 33rd Native Infantry.

Ensign, 11 June 42—Lieut., 7 Sept. 46—Bt.-Captain, 11 June 57—Captain, 21 July 57.

SERVICE.—Captain STUBBS served during the Sutlej Campaign, '45, '46. Present at the battles of Ferozeshuhur and Sobraon. *Medal and Clasp.*

LIEUTENANT H. W. STUDDY, P. H., late 32nd Native Infantry.

Ensign, 12 Oct. 54—Lieut., 11 May 57.

LIEUTENANT T. J. C. A. STUDDY, P. H., Bengal Artillery.

Lieut., 27 Aug. 58.

ASSISTANT-SURGEON G. S. SUTHERLAND,† M.D., Bengal Medical Establishment.

Asst.-Surgeon, 4 Aug. 57.

SERVICE.—Assistant-Surgeon SUTHERLAND served with the Field Hospital of the Army in Oude at the capture of Lucknow, and in charge of the 1st Troop, 1st Brigade Horse Artillery, during subsequent operations in Oude, in '38, '39, with Moveable Columns under Sir Hope Grant and Brigadier Evelegh. *Medal and Clasp for Lucknow.*

SURGEON-MAJOR J. SUTHERLAND,† M.D., Bengal Medical Establishment.

Asst.-Surgeon, 4 Sept. 41—Surgeon, 16 April 55—Surgeon-Major, 14 July 61.

SERVICE.—Surgeon-Major SUTHERLAND was attached to the European Hospitals at Ferozepore after the battle of Sobraon, till the Army of the Sutlej was broken up.

ASSISTANT-SURGEON P. W. SUTHERLAND,† Bengal Medical Establishment.

Asst.-Surgeon, 6 May 54.

SERVICE.—Assistant-Surgeon SUTHERLAND served at Peshawur with the Peshawur Light Horse, during the Mutiny of '57, and as a Volunteer at Murree against the Hill Tribes in the same year. *Medal.* Served with Murray's Jât Horse in '59 and '60, on the Nepal Frontier.

LIEUTENANT S. S. SUTHERLAND, P.H., late 42nd Native Infantry.

Ensign, 13 June 56—Lieut., 14 Sept. 57.

SERVICE.—Lieutenant SUTHERLAND served during the Mutiny, '57. Present at the two actions at Dumoh, in July '57. Commanded a Squadron, 3rd Irregular Cavalry, at the affair of Ballakote, 1st September '57. Present at the attack on Murriowlee, 18th September '57. Commanded the storming party at the assault and capture of Bhapail, 14th December '57. Brought to the prominent notice of the Brigadier Commanding Saugor Division for gallant behaviour in leading the storming party at Bhapail, by Captain Finch, 17th December '57. *Medal.*

BREVET-COLONEL W. SWATMAN, P., late 2nd European Bengal Fusiliers.

Ensign, 24 Oct. 27—Lieut., 24 Aug. 33—Captain, 17 March 40—Major, 11 March 47—Lieut.-Colonel, 12 Jan. 53—Bt.-Colonel, 28 Nov. 54.

(Since dead.)

BREVET-CAPTAIN J. D. SWAYNE, P. H., late 11th Native Infantry.

Ensign, 12 Dec. 45—Lieut., 13 Oct. 51—Captain, 18 Feb. 61.

LIEUTENANT J. R. G. SWEENY, late 2nd Bengal European Cavalry.

Cornet, 4 April 58—Lieut., 21 June 58.

MAJOR E. SWETENHAM, Bengal Invalid Establishment.

2nd Lieut., 1 Sept. 18—Lieut., 18 May 21—Captain, 28 Sept. 27—Major, 20 May 39.

SERVICE.—Major SWETENHAM served at the siege and capture of Bhurtpore. *Medal.*

(580)

LIEUTENANT E. SWETENHAM, P. H., late 45th Native Infantry.

Ensign, 13 Dec. 56—Lieut., 7 Nov. 57.

SERVICE.—Lieutenant SWETENHAM served with the Huzara Field Force in '58. In the expedition against the Hill Tribes in Eusuffzaie. Present at the action on the heights above Sattana. (Has furnished the certificate of qualification in Surveying and Civil Engineering.)

CAPTAIN G. SWINEY, P. H., late 6th Europeans.

Ensign, 30 Jan. 42—Lieut., 5 Dec. 45—Captain, 9 Jan. 55.

SERVICE.—Captain SWINEY served during the Sutlej Campaign, '45, '46. During the Sonthal Rebellion, '55, '56. During the Mutiny, in '57, '58, '59. Present at the mutiny of the 7th Native Infantry at Dinapore, 25th July '57. Served with the Force under Lord M. Kerr. Present at the relief of Azimghur, in the engagement with the rebels under Koer Sing, 6th April '58, and other skirmishes. Employed as Commissariat Officer with the Azimghur Garrison, until its relief by Sir E. Lugard, April '58. *Medal.* Served with the Force under Brigadier McDuff, and present at the action of Suhao, in Bundlecund, 4th September '58. Engaged with a body of rebels at Burrah, in the Jaloun District, 12th November '58. Received the thanks of the Deputy Commissioner. Commanded the Jaloun Military Police in an engagement with the mutineers at Rohain, 14th May '59. Received the thanks of the Lieutenant-Governor, North-Western Provinces, 1st June '59. Employed in various occasions with the rebels, from July '58 to March '60.

LIEUTENANT G. C. SWINEY, late 5th Bengal European Cavalry.

Cornet, 20 Oct. 57—Lieut., 18 May 58.

LIEUTENANT-COLONEL F. W. SWINHOE, P., Bengal Artillery.

2nd Lieut., 11 June 40—Lieut., 13 Jan. 42—Captain, 1 July 53—Lieut.-Colonel, 18 Feb. 61.

SERVICE.—Lieutenant-Colonel SWINHOE served in Scinde in '45, in the Campaign against the Belochee Hill Tribes. Present at the siege and surrender of Mooltan and battle of Goojerat, '48, '49. *Medal and 2 Clasps.*

CAPTAIN H. SWINHOE,† late 30th Native Infantry.

Ensign, 4 Aug. 42—Lieut., 24 Jan. 45—Captain, 11 May 57.

SERVICE.—Captain SWINHOE served during the Sutlej Campaign, '45, '46, including the action of Alliwal. *Medal.* During the Punjab Campaign, '48, '49. Present at the passage of the Chenab, battles of Chillianwallah (*severely wounded*) and Goojerat, and pursuit of the Sikhs and Affghans under General Gilbert. *Medal.*

LIEUTENANT-GENERAL S. SWINHOE, late 73rd Native Infantry.

Ensign, 18 March 05—Lieut., 27 March 05—Captain, 1 Jan. 18—Major, 14 June 25—Lieut.-Colonel, 9 May 30—Colonel, 23 June 42—Major-General, 20 June 54—Lieut.-General, 15 Sept. 55.

LIEUTENANT G. SWINLEY, Bengal Artillery.

Lieut., 6 Nov. 60.

COLONEL G. H. SWINLEY, Bengal Artillery.

2nd Lieut., 6 June 23—Lieut., 28 Sept. 27—Bt.-Captain, 6 June 38—Captain, 10 July 40—Bt.-Major, 30 April 44—Major, 21 July 51—Bt.-Lieut.-Colonel, 3 April 46—Lieut.-Colonel, 26 June 56—Bt.-Colonel, 20 June 54—Major-General, 4 July 58.

SERVICE.—Major-General SWINLEY served with the Force in Cachar, in '24, '25, under Major-General Shuldham. Present at the battles of Moodkee, Ferozeshuhur, and Sobraon, '45, '46. Commanded a Troop of Horse Artillery in these actions. *Medal,* 2 *Clasps, and Brevet-Major.* Present with Brigadier-General Wheeler's Force in the Punjab, '48, '49. *Medal.*

CORNET S. A. SWINLEY, General List, Cavalry.

Cornet, 20 April 61.

LIEUTENANT A. SWINTON, Bengal Artillery.

Lieut., 27 April 58.

LIEUTENANT A. SWINTON, Bengal Artillery.

Lieut., 9 Dec. 59.

(582)

LIEUTENANT G. SWINTON,† Bengal Engineers.

Lieut., 27 April 58.

ASSISTANT-SURGEON B. W. SWITZER,† M.D., Bengal Medical Establishment.

Asst.-Surgeon, 27 Jan. 58.

CAPTAIN J. SYKES, P., late 66th Native Infantry.

Ensign, 14 June 45—Lieut., 13 Aug. 50—Bt.-Captain, 14 June 60—Captain, 18 Feb. 61.

SERVICE.—Captain SYKES served with the Army of the Sutlej, during the advance on Lahore. Served on the Bunnoo and Kohat Frontier, from May '51 to February '56. Accompanied the Force under Brigadier General Nicholson, in December '53, on the Omerzaie Wuzeerees, Bunnoo Frontier, and attacked and surprised them at night. Served in an Expedition in the Hungoo Valley, in '55, under Brigadier Chamberlain. Commanded the Left Wing, 2nd Punjab Infantry, forming a portion of Brigadier Coke's Column of attack on the border of the Affreedies, in their fastnesses, and secured the heights. Engaged in several minor affairs, in Command of out-posts against the marauding parties from the hills, and in repulsing attacks on villages.

LIEUTENANT J. M. SYM,† late 58th Native Infantry.

Ensign, 11 Dec. 58—Lieut., 15 July 59.

2ND CAPTAIN P. M. SYME, P. H., Bengal Artillery.

2nd Lieut., 14 June 45—Lieut., 21 June 50—2nd Captain, 27 Aug. 58.

LIEUTENANT H. C. A. SZEZEPANSKI, P. H., late 40th Native Infantry.

Ensign, 13 June 57—Lieut., 18 May 58.

SERVICE.—Lieutenant SZEZEPANSKI served during the Mutinies, '57, '58. Present at the actions at Cawnpore, 25th, 26th, and 27th November '57; and present at the subsequent operations. Present at the action of Kala Nuddee, under Lord Clyde, and served in pursuit of the rebels in Bundlecund. *Medal.*

T

LIEUTENANT J. S. TAIT, P. H., General List.

Ensign, 20 June 59—Lieut., 18 March 61.

SERVICE.—Lieutenant TAIT served in defence of the Arrah House, in July and August '57; as Volunteer with the Field Force under Colonel V. Eyre, in the operations against Koer Sing, at Jugdespore, August '57. Served under Sir James Outram, at the relief of Lucknow, as Assistant Field Engineer. Present at the actions of Mungulwarrah and Alum Bagh in Oude. Served with the Oude Field Force under Sir J. Outram, at Alum Bagh, '57, '58. Served as Assistant Field Engineer with the Force under Lord Clyde, at the final assault and capture of Lucknow, March '58. *Medal and 2 Clasps.*

MAJOR H. C. TALBOT, Bengal Invalid Establishment.

Ensign, 17 Jan. 24—Lieut., 13 May 25—Captain, 11 Oct. 38—Major, 11 April 51.

ASSISTANT-SURGEON E. O. TANDY,† Bengal Medical Department.

Asst.-Surgeon, 10 Feb. 59.

ASSISTANT-SURGEON E. TAYLER,† Bengal Medical Establishment.

Asst.-Surgeon, 1 Aug. 53.

ASSISTANT-SURGEON A. TAYLOR,† Bengal Medical Establishment.

Asst.-Surgeon, 4 Aug. 55.

CAPTAIN A. TAYLOR,† late 25th Native Infantry.

Ensign, 11 June 47—Lieut., 15 Nov. 53—Captain, 17 Oct. 57.

SERVICE.—Captain TAYLOR served during the Punjab Campaign, '48, '49. Present in the actions of Ramnuggur, Sadoolapore, Chillianwallah, and Goojerat. *Medal and Clasps.*

LIEUTENANT A. F. TAYLOR, General List.

Ensign, 12 Nov. 59—Lieut., 11 Sept. 61.

LIEUTENANT A. H. TAYLOR, late 3rd Bengal European Cavalry.
Cornet, 4 Nov. 58—Lieut., 5 Feb. 59.

LIEUTENANT C. C. TAYLOR, P. H., late 56th Native Infantry.
Ensign, 20 Dec. 50—Lieut., 25 Feb. 55.

SERVICE.—Lieutenant TAYLOR was Adjutant of the Regiment of Ferozepore and was present under Colonel Brasyer, on the night of the 6th June '57, in the Fort at Allahabad, when a Company of the mutinous Sepoys of the 6th Native Infantry were disarmed and made prisoners by the Sikhs. Present also at the engagements with the rebels between the city and the Cantonments of Allahabad, on the 12th, at Kidgunj on the 13 June '57 *(Severely wounded.) Medal.*

LIEUTENANT C. S. S. TAYLOR, P. H., Bengal Artillery.
1st Lieut., 29 Oct. 58.

CAPTAIN F. S. TAYLOR, Bengal Engineers.
2nd Lieut., 11 June 47—Lieut., 1 Aug. 54—2nd Captain, 27 Aug. 58.

LIEUTENANT G. C. B. TAYLOR,† late 1st Bengal European Cavalry.
Cornet, 20 Jan. 58—Lieut., 18 May 57.

CAPTAIN H. A. TAYLOR, P. H., late 74th Native Infantry.
Ensign, 3 Feb. 44—Lieut., 1 Dec. 48—Captain, 6 Oct. 57.

BREVET-COLONEL J. L. TAYLOR, late 32nd Native Infantry.
Ensign, 23 Jan. 25—Lieut., 26 Dec. 26—Captain, 12 Jan. 37—Bt.-Major, 3 April 46—Major, 18 June 50—Bt.-Lieut.-Colonel, 20 June 54—Lieut.-Colonel, 10 Feb. 56—Bt.-Colonel, 14 March 57.

SERVICE.—Colonel TAYLOR served with the Army in '25, '26. *Medal.* Served in Cabul under General Pollock, in '42. *Medal.* Served as Brigade Major during the Sutlej Campaign, in '45, '46. Present at the battles of Moodkee, Ferozeshuhur, and Sobraon. *Medal and 2 Clasps.*

(585)

LIEUTENANT J. W. TAYLOR, P. H., Bengal Artillery.

Lieut., 10 Dec. 58.

LIEUTENANT L. W. TAYLOR, Bengal Artillery.

Lieut., 27 Aug. 58.

LIEUTENANT M. G. TAYLOR, late 14th Native Infantry.

Ensign, 26 May 58—Lieut., 13 April 59.

LIEUTENANT P. T. H. TAYLOR, Bengal Artillery.

Lieut., 27 Aug. 58.

BREVET-LIEUTENANT-COLONEL R. G. TAYLOR, P., late 2nd Bengal European Cavalry.

Cornet, 26 Feb. 40—Lieut., 5 Jan. 44—Captain, 15 Dec. 51—Bt.-Major, 16 Dec. 51—Bt.-Lieut.-Colonel, 21 Dec. 59—Major, 18 Feb. 61.

SERVICE.—Lieutenant-Colonel TAYLOR served with the Army of Gwalior, in '45 : present at the action of Punniar. *Bronze Star.* Served during the Sutlej Campaign, '45, '46. Present at the action of Moodkee. *(Severely wounded.) Medal.* Served in the Punjab Campaign, '48, '49. Present at Bunnoo, and also before Mooltan. *Medal and Clasp.* Received the thanks of Government. Promoted to Brevet-Major on becoming a Captain for services in the Punjab Campaign. Present at the disarming of the 4th Native Infantry, in '57, at the Fort of Kangra. Served in the expedition against the Mahsood Wuzeerees, in '60.

CAPTAIN T. TAYLOR, P. H., late 14th Native Infantry.

Ensign, 6 March 46—Lieut., 5 March 50—Captain, 18 Feb. 61.

SERVICE.—Captain TAYLOR served as Volunteer in H. M.'s 24th against the mutineers of the 14th Native Infantry, at Jhelum, 7th July '57.

MAJOR-GENERAL T. M. TAYLOR, late 1st European Light Cavalry.

Cornet, 27 March 09—Lieut., 1 Sept. 18—Bt.-Captain, 16 Sept. 23— Captain, 13 May 25—Major, 1 March 36—Lieut.-Colonel, 5 Aug. 39— Bt.-Colonel, 14 Nov. 49—Colonel, 22 Aug. 55—Major-General, 28 Nov. 54.

SERVICE.—Major-General TAYLOR served with the expedition employed in the capture of Java, and in the Pindaree Campaign, '16, '17, and '18.

(586)

LIEUTENANT T. R. TAYLOR, General List.
Ensign, 9 Dec. 59—Lieut., 26 Sept. 61.

LIEUTENANT A. B. TEMPLE, P. H., late 49th Native Infantry.
Ensign, 26 Dec. 49—Lieut., 18 July 55.

SERVICE.—Lieutenant TEMPLE served with the Army of Delhi, and under Brigadier Showers, in the Goorgaon and Jhujjur Districts, in '57, and with the Army of Oude under Lord Clyde, in '58, '59. Present at the siege, storm, and capture of Delhi, and brought out of action a Detachment of the Kumaon Battalion the day of the final assault. Present at the action of Sussia Ghaut, 9th February '59, when Brigadier Horsford's Column captured all the guns remaining in the hands of the rebels. (*Wounded slightly* at Delhi, 6th August '57, when commanding one of the Right Picquets.) *Medal and Clasp.* Served as Staff Officer with the Column under Major Ramsay, on the Delhi and Muttra Road, in August '58.

LIEUTENANT E. TEMPLE,† late 25th Native Infantry.
Ensign, 15 May 56—Lieut., 17 Dec. 56.

CAPTAIN H. J. TEMPLER,† late 5th Europeans.
Ensign, 10 July 43—Lieut., 17 Nov. 50—Bt.-Captain, 10 July 58—Captain, 1 April 59.

SERVICE.—Captain TEMPLER served with the Army of the Sutlej, '46. Present at the actions of Cawnpore, 5th and 6th December '57; operations on the Goomtee, 6th, 7th, and 9th March '58; siege of Lucknow, 10th to 16th March '58; Koorsie, 23rd March '58; Calpee, 22nd and 23rd May '58. *Medal and 2 Clasps.* Ranode, 17th December '58; Nainwas, 5th April '59. Mentioned in the Despatch of Brigadier-General Sir R. Napier, 14th February '59.

CAPTAIN J. F. TEMPLER,† late 3rd Europeans.
Ensign, 13 Dec. 45—Lieut., 9 Dec. 54—Captain, 13 Dec. 60.

SERVICE.—Captain TEMPLER served with the Force employed against the Affreedies in the Kohat Pass, in February '50. *(Since retired.)*

(587)

BREVET-MAJOR J. F. TENNANT, P. H., Bengal Engineers.

2nd Lieut., 11 June 47—Lieut., 1 Aug. 54—2nd Captain, 27 Aug. 58—Bt.-Major, 28 Aug. 58.

SERVICE.—Major TENNANT was present at the siege of Delhi as Field Engineer, from the 20th August '57. Mentioned in the Despatch of Colonel Baird Smith. Served under Sir J. Outram at Alum Bagh, and present at two attacks on the Jellallabad Fort. Present at the storm and capture of Lucknow, March '58; and served with Sir J. Outram's Force on the left of the Goomtee. Mentioned in Sir James Outram's Despatch. *Medal and 2 Clasps.*

MAJOR A. H. TERNAN, P., late 4th Europeans.

Ensign, 24 Jan. 39—Lieut., 19 April 42—Captain, 20 Sept. 53—Major, 18 Feb. 61.

SERVICE.—Major TERNAN served in Bundlecund, '42, '43, and engaged several times with the rebels; during the Sutlej Campaign, '46. Present as a Volunteer at the action of Alliwal, and other minor affairs before Loodianah. *Medal.* Mentioned in the Despatch of Brigadier Godby. Served during the Punjab Campaign, '49. *Medal.* Mentioned in Despatch. Served as Deputy-Commissioner under Captain Woolley, in numerous expeditions against the rebels in the Nursingpore, Saugor, and Jubbulpore Districts, in '57, '58. Mentioned in the Despatch of Captain Woolley, 28th December '57. Commanded a party of the 3rd Irregular Cavalry at the attack and complete defeat of the Saugor rebel, Gungun Singh, of Deeolee, 23rd November '57. *(Horse killed under him.)* Received the thanks of the Lieutenant-Governor of the Central Provinces, 4th January '58, and of the Commissioner of Jubbulpore, on the capture of another Rebel Chief, 16th December '57. Served with the Central India Field Force under Sir Hugh Rose, as Deputy Commissioner of Jaloun. *Medal and Clasp.* Present at the forcing of the Wuddunpoor Pass, 3rd March; at the action of Betwah, 1st April; siege and capture of Jhansie, 3rd April; action of Koonch, 7th May; at the different affairs at Gololi, 20th, 21st, and 22nd May; and taking of Calpee, 23rd May '58. Mentioned in the Despatch of Sir Hugh Rose, 22nd June '58. Served under Brigadier MacDuff, and present at the various attacks on the rebels of the Jaloun District, '58, '59, as Deputy-Commissioner. Present at the action of Sahao as A. D. C. to the Brigadier. Mentioned in his Despatch, 5th September '58, and in that of Major-General Whitlock, 9th September '58. Mentioned in the Minute of His Excellency the Governor-General, 2nd July '59. Services brought to the notice of Her Majesty the Queen, 11th June '61.

CAPTAIN C. S. J. TERROT, P., late 29th Native Infantry.

Ensign, 11 Dec. 37—Lieut., 3 Oct. 40—Bt.-Captain, 11 Dec. 52—Captain, 27 Aug. 53.

SERVICE.—Captain TERROT was present at the attack on Ram Sing's positions on the heights of Noorpoor, 19th September '48. In the attack on the Huldwanee, near Nynee Tal, September '57. Campaign in Rohilcund, '58, including the actions of Buggawal, Nugeena, relief of Moradabad, actions on the Dojura, assault and capture of Bareilly, attack and relief of Shahjehanpore, capture of the Fort of Bunni, pursuit of the enemy to the banks of the Goomtee, destruction of the Fort of Mohumdee, and destruction of Shahabad, action of Bunkagaon, Oude Campaign, including the actions of Russoolpore and Pusgaon, and capture of Fort Mittowlee. *Medal.*

LIEUTENANT E. T. THACKERAY,† V. C., Bengal Engineers.

Lieut., 27 April 58.

SERVICE.—Lieutenant THACKERAY served during the Mutiny, '58, 59. Present at the battles of the Hindun, Badlee-ka-Serai, siege of Delhi, and subsequent operations in the Doab. Present at the capture of Lucknow, and through the Rohilcund Campaign. Served also during the Oude Campaign of '58, '59. *Medal and 2 Clasps, and V. C.*

LIEUTENANT A. S. THAIN, P. H., late 13th Native Infantry.

Ensign, 20 Feb. 54—Lieut., 23 Nov. 56.

SERVICE.—Lieutenant THAIN served during the Sonthal Campaign, '55, '56. Present at the Mutiny of his Regiment at Lucknow, 30th

May '57, and subsequent dispersion of the mutineers. Present at the action of Chinhut, 30th June '57. Served in the defence of Lucknow, from June to November '57. Commanding Innes' outpost during several months of the siege. *Medal and Clasp, and one year's service.* Mentioned in the Despatch of Sir J. Inglis, 26th September '57. Present with the Army under Lord Clyde in operations in the vicinity of Lucknow, subsequent to the relief of the Garrison. Present at the defeat, by Lord Clyde, on the 10th December '57, of the Gwalior Contingent at Cawnpore. Carried Despatches from the Governor-General to Sir James Outram, at Lucknow, in March '58. Present during part of the operations, resulting in the final capture of Lucknow. *Clasp.* Engaged in December '58, as Commandant of the Cavalry, portion of the Cawnpore Military Police, under Brigadier Herbert, in pursuit of Ferozeshah, through the Cawnpore and Etawah Districts. Commanded the District Police Battalion, in '59, '60, in the pacification of the Chundehree District, in Bundlecund.

LIEUTENANT G. G. THAIN, late 2nd Native Infantry.

Ensign, 25 July 57—Lieut., 18 May 58.

LIEUTENANT W. T. A. THAIN, General List.

Ensign, 10 Dec. 59—Lieut., 13 Oct. 61.

MAJOR R. THATCHER, late 9th Native Infantry.

Ensign, 1 April 29—Lieut., 31 March 35—Bt.-Captain, 1 April 44— Captain, 24 Jan. 45—Major, 28 Nov. 54.

CAPTAIN F. G. THELLUSSON,† late 29th Native Infantry.

Ensign, 21 April 41—Lieut., 29 March 46—Bt.-Captain, 12 June 56— Captain, 11 July 61.

CAPTAIN J. P. A. THEOBALD,† late 3rd Bengal European Cavalry.

Cornet, 27 Dec. 45—Lieut., 12 April 49—Captain, 20 Nov. 56.

SERVICE.—Captain THEOBALD served during the Punjab Campaign, '48, '49. *Medal.*

ASSISTANT-SURGEON H. THOM,† M.D., Bengal Medical Establishment.

Asst.-Surgeon, 4 Aug. 55.

SERVICE.—Assistant-Surgeon THOM served with the 1st Sikh Infantry, in the expedition against the Bozdars, under General Chamberlain, '57. Served during '58 with the 5th Punjab Infantry, under Sir Hope Grant, throughout the Campaign in Oude, and in Byswarrah and Trans-Gogra, under the Commander-in-Chief, November '58. Served in Medical Charge of this Regiment, until the termination of operations on the Nepal Frontier, December '59. Present at Baree, April '58; Simree, May '58; Nawabgunge, June '58; Sultanpore, August '58; and Sitka Ghaut, February '59. *Medal.*

LIEUTENANT A. B. E. THOMAS, P. H., late 4th Europeans.

Ensign, 4 Feb. 55—Lieut., 20 March 57.

LIEUTENANT C. W. THOMAS,† late 3rd Bengal Cavalry.

Cornet, 20 Oct. 56—Lieut., 9 Jan. 57.

SERVICE.—Lieutenant THOMAS served with the Rohilcund Field Force in '58. Present at the actions of Bugawallah, Nugeena, relief of Moradabad, skirmish on the Dogura, assault and capture of Bareilly, and action at Shahjehanpore, 18th May '58. *Medal.*

CAPTAIN E. THOMAS, P., late 3rd Europeans.

Ensign, 12 June 39—Lieut., 6 March 41—Bt.-Captain, 12 June 54—Captain, 15 Oct. 54.

SERVICE.—Captain THOMAS served with the Army of Reserve, in '42; with the Army of Gwalior, with the 70th Native Infantry. Present at Maharajpore, *Bronze Star.* With the Army of the Punjab, '48, '49. Present at the actions of Ramnuggur, passage of the Chenab, Chillianwallah, and Goojerat, and pursuit of the Sikhs and Affghans to Peshawur. *Medal and 2 Clasps.* Served under General Wyndham at Cawnpore. Present at the attack by the Gwalior Troops, and final defeat of the Force under Lord Clyde, 2nd and 6th December '57. *(Since retired.)*

(591)

LIEUTENANT F. H. THOMAS, P. H., General List.
Ensign, 4 Jan. 60—Lieut., 1 Jan. 62.

MAJOR J. N. THOMAS,† late 39th Native Infantry.
Ensign, 9 Feb. 36—Lieut., 25 July 39—Captain, 1 Nov. 49—Major, 1 Jan. 62.
SERVICE.—Major THOMAS served against the Bheels in '37. Present at the action of Punniar. *Bronze Star.*

LIEUTENANT R. M. B. THOMAS, P. H., late 46th Native Infantry.
Ensign, 6 Jan. 59—Lieut., 9 Nov. 60.

LIEUTENANT C. S. THOMASON, Bengal Engineers.
Lieut., 6 June 57.
SERVICE.—Lieutenant THOMASON served throughout the siege of Delhi, and was present at the battle of Badlee-ka-Serai. *Medal and Clasp.*

LIEUTENANT C. H. THOMPSON, Bengal Artillery.
Lieut., 9 Dec. 59.

CAPTAIN E. THOMPSON, P. H., late 4th Europeans.
Ensign, 24 Sept. 42—Lieut., 14 July 48—Captain, 23 Nov. 56.

CAPTAIN E. THOMPSON, P., late 67th Native Infantry.
Ensign, 12 Dec. 49—Lieut., 21 March 53—Captain, 11 Sept. 59.
SERVICE.—Captain THOMPSON was present at the operation in the vicinity of Donabew, under Sir J. Cheape. *Medal.* Present at the capture of Pegu, in June '52.

CAPTAIN F. J. THOMPSON, P. H., Bengal Invalid Establishment.
Ensign, 6 Feb. 36—Lieut., 16 July 49—Captain, 21 July 48.
SERVICE.—Captain THOMPSON served against the Hill Tribes in Scinde, under Sir C. Napier. Served during the Punjab Campaign, '48, '49:

Present at the passage of the Chenab, battles of Chillianwallah and Goojerat, and subsequent pursuit of the Sikhs and Affghans under General Gilbert. *Medal and Clasp.*

CAPTAIN G. H. THOMPSON, P., late 6th Europeans.

Ensign, 8 Dec. 43—Lieut., 6 Nov. 48—Captain, 10 Jan. 55.

SERVICE.—Captain THOMPSON was present with the late 7th Native Infantry, when it escorted the siege train from Delhi to the Sutlej, in '45, '46. Joined the Army of the Sutlej at Lahore, in March '46, and formed one of the Lahore Garrison in '47, '48. Accompanied the Force under Major Fisher as a Volunteer, in September '48, against the rebels under Ram Singh, in the Noorpoor Hills, Kangra District. Present with his Regiment at Jullundur, in '48, '49, when it held that station during the 2nd Punjab War.

LIEUTENANT J. THOMPSON,† late 58th Native Infantry.

Ensign, 2 March 49—Lieut., 23 Nov. 56.

LIEUTENANT P. THOMPSON, P. H., Bengal Artillery.

Lieut., 17 Nov. 57.

BREVET-MAJOR R. L. THOMPSON, P. H., late 10th Native Infantry.

Ensign, 18 Sept. 40—Lieut., 16 July 42—Bt.-Captain, 18 Sept. 55—Captain, 18 June 57—Bt.-Major, 20 July 58.

SERVICE.—Major THOMPSON served in Burmah, in '52, '53. *Medal.* Served in Bengal with Havelock's Columns from its first taking the field in '57; including the actions of Futtehpore, Aoung, Pandoo Nuddee, Cawnpore, Oonao, Busseerutgunge (1st and 2nd), Barbya-ka-Chowkee, Bhitoor, and the several actions leading to and ending in the relief of the Residency of Lucknow and subsequent defence. Served with Outram's Force at Alum Bagh, including an attack on the enemy's outpost at Gahilee *(horse shot under him)*, and present in the operations ending in the final capture of Lucknow. *Medal and Clasp.*

LIEUTENANT A. H. THOMSON, P. H., late 3rd Europeans.

Ensign, 10 Dec. 54—Lieut., 1 Jan. 57.

SERVICE.—Lieutenant THOMSON served throughout the Indian Mutinies: present at the battle of Agra, 10th October '57; the operations at Shereghur Ghaut, in May '58; and with the Column towards Gwalior, in June '58. *Medal.*

2ND CAPTAIN D. THOMSON, P. H., Bengal Artillery.

2nd Lieut., 12 June 46—Lieut., 3 March 53—2nd Captain, 27 Aug. 58.

SERVICE.—Captain THOMSON served during the Punjab Campaign under Sir H. Wheeler, '48, '49. *Medal.* Served throughout the operations before Delhi, and present at the final capture of that city. *Medal and Clasp.*

BREVET-CAPTAIN F. R. THOMSON,† late 29th Native Infantry.

Ensign, 11 June 42—Lieut., 7 April 46—Bt.-Captain, 11 June 57.

SERVICE.—Captain THOMSON served against the rebels North of Jullundur, '48, '49. Present at the storming of the heights of Umb, and occupation of the Fort of Oonah. *Medal.*

LIEUTENANT G. C. THOMSON, P. H., late 51st Native Infantry.

Ensign, 9 July 51—Lieut., 7 Sept. 54.

SERVICE.—Lieutenant THOMSON served with the Army before Delhi in '57, from the 31st July to the final assault and capture of the city. Commanded a Detachment of Kumaon Battalion in the action of Ludlow Castle, under the walls of Delhi, 12th August '57, when four guns were captured from the rebels. Mentioned in the Despatch of Brigadier Showers, 12th August '57. Served under Lord Clyde at Futtehghur, in Command of a Squadron of the 17th Irregular Cavalry. Served with several different Columns in the Jumna Doab. Present at Cawnpore, under Sir J. Inglis, during the operations, leading to the final capture of Lucknow. Present throughout the Rohilcund Campaign, including the capture of Bareilly, 5th May '58, and several other engagements. Mentioned in the Despatch of Lord Clyde, 8th May '58. *Medal and Clasp.*

LIEUTENANT G. W. THOMSON,† Bengal Artillery.

Lieut., 27 Aug. 58.

LIEUTENANT-GENERAL H. THOMSON, late 1st Bengal European Cavalry.

Cornet, 31 Aug. 99—Lieut., 22 Dec. 03—Captain, 15 April 16—Major, 27 Oct. 18—Lieut.-Colonel, 29 April 25—Cornet, 1 Dec. 29—Major-General, 28 June 38—Lieut.-General, 11 Nov. 51.

SERVICE.—Lieutenant-General THOMSON served during the Campaign under Lord Lake: present at the battles of Laswarrie, in '30, and Ufzulghur; also at the assault and capture of Bhurtpore, '05. *Medal.*

LIEUTENANT J. THOMSON, P. H., late 34th Native Infantry.

Ensign, 12 Dec. 51—Lieut., 23 Nov. 56.

CAPTAIN J. E. THOMSON, P., late 62nd Native Infantry.

Ensign, 19 June 42—Lieut., 24 Jan. 45—Captain, 9 April 56.

BREVET-MAJOR M. THOMSON, P. H., late 53rd Native Infantry.

Ensign, 20 Dec. 53—Lieut., 4 June 55—Captain, 17 May 58—Major, 1 Feb. 60.

SERVICE.—Major THOMSON served throughout the Mutiny of '57, '58: in the trenches at Cawnpore during the massacre—one of the only two survivors of Cawnpore Garrison. *(Wounded five times and had one horse shot under him.)* Medal, Brevet-Majority, *one year's extra service*, and recommended for *the Victoria Cross.**

SURGEON-MAJOR T. THOMSON,† M.D., Bengal Medical Establishment.

Asst.-Surgeon, 21 Dec. 39—Surgeon, 1 Dec. 53—Surgeon-Major, 13 Jan. 60.

SERVICE.—Surgeon-Major THOMSON served with the 27th Native Infantry at Ghuznee, where he was made prisoner. Served during the Sutlej Campaign, '45, '46; also during the Punjab Campaign, '48, '49.

---

* Major Thomson published the account of his wonderful escape from the treachery of the Nana Sahib.

DEPUTY-INSPECTOR-GENERAL OF HOSPITALS, W. THOMSON, Bengal Medical Establishment.

Asst.-Surgeon, 9 May 24—Surgeon, 2 April 38—Deputy-Inspector-General of Hospitals, 21 March 56.

BREVET-MAJOR W. A. A. THOMSON, P. H., late 4th Bengal European Cavalry.

Cornet, 21 May 41—Lieut., 24 March 43—Bt.-Captain, 21 May 56—Captain, 12 July 56—Bt.-Major, 13 July 56.

SERVICE.—Major THOMSON served throughout the Scinde Campaign in '43, on the Staff of Sir Charles Napier, as A.D.C.: present at the battles of Meeanee and Hyderabad. *Medal.*

BREVET-COLONEL W. B. THOMSON, C.B., P., late 57th Native Infantry.

Ensign, 30 June 26—Lieut., 8 April 28—Captain, 3 Aug. 57—Bt.-Major, 3 April 46—Major, 21 Sept. 54—Bt.-Lieut.-Colonel, 20 June 54—Lieut.-Colonel, 13 July 58—Bt.-Colonel, 29 May 57.

SERVICE.—Colonel THOMSON served during the Sutlej Campaign, '45, 46: present at the battle of Ferozeshuhur. *Medal and Brevet-Majority.* Served throughout the Mutiny, '57, '58. Present at the siege and capture of Delhi, 14th September '57. *Medal and Clasp and C.B.* *(Since retired.)*

CAPTAIN W. B. THOMSON, P. H., late 13th Native Infantry.

Ensign, 8 June 49—Lieut., 28 Feb. 55—Captain, 8 June 61.

ASSISTANT-SURGEON W. J. THOMSON,† Bengal Medical Establishment.

Asst.-Surgeon, 10 Feb. 59.

ASSISTANT-SURGEON J. H. THORNTON,† M.P., B.A.

Asst.-Surgeon, 9 Jan. 56.

SERVICE.—Assistant-Surgeon THORNTON served with a Detachment of H. M.'s 5th Fusiliers, at the relief of Arrah (2nd August), and at the capture of Jugdespore, 11th August '57. Was present with a Force under the Command of Brigadier Wilson, at the action of Soorajpore, 18th October; proceeded with Major Barnston's Force to Alum Bagh, and served with the Garrison of that post from 25th October to 27th November '57; was then attached to H. M.'s 90th Light Infantry, and was present with that Regiment at several engagements with the enemy near Alum Bagh, and at the assault and capture of Lucknow, in March '58. Served with the 1st European Bengal Fusiliers at various operations against the enemy in the vicinity of Durriabad. *Medal and Clasps.*

CAPTAIN C. G. THORP, P. H., late 69th Native Infantry.

Ensign, 12 June 46—Lieut., 17 July 54—Captain, 12 June 61.

SERVICE.—Captain THORP served during the Punjab Campaign, '48, '49. *Medal.*

SURGEON E. C. THORP,† M.D., Bengal Medical Establishment.

Asst.-Surgeon, 20 Jan. 47—Surgeon, 16 July 60.

SERVICE.—Surgeon THORP served throughout the Punjab Campaign: present at both sieges of Mooltan; night attack on the British Camp of Muttee Thâl, 17th August '48; action of Sooroojkhoond, 7th November, and attack on the Suburbs of Mooltan, 27th December '48; and joined the Army under Lord Gough at Goojerat. *Medal and 2 Clasps.* Served under Captain Raban against the Kookie Hill Tribes, '60, '61.

MAJOR R. THORPE, Bengal Invalid Establishment.

Lieut., 21 Oct. 18—Captain, 23 May 28—Major, 23 Nov. 41.

SURGEON E. B. THRING,† Bengal Medical Department.

Asst.-Surgeon, 24 April 41—Surgeon, 6 July 55.

SERVICE.—Surgeon THRING served with the 1st Native Infantry throughout the Mutinies in the Saugor District, in the year '57, '58.

SURGEON R. S. O. THRING,† M.D., Bengal Medical Establishment.

Asst.-Surgeon, 20 April 45—Surgeon, 11 March 59.

SERVICE.—Surgeon THRING served with H. M.'s 62nd Foot at the battle of Ferozeshuhur, on 21st and 22nd December '45. *Medal.* Served

(597)

with the Field Hospital during the siege of Mooltan, and during the remainder of the Punjab Campaign, including the battle of Goojerat, and pursuit of the Sikh Army to Peshawur, with the 11th Irregular Cavalry. *Medal and 2 Clasps.*

LIEUTENANT-COLONEL H. E. L. THUILLIER, Bengal Artillery.

2nd Lieut., 14 Dec. 32—Lieut., 1 Sept. 40—Bt.-Captain, 14 Dec. 47—Captain, 2 Feb. 51—Lieut.-Colonel, 18 Feb. 61.

LIEUTENANT H. R. THUILLIER, P. H., Bengal Engineers.

Lieut., 27 Aug. 58.

MAJOR F. A. V. THURBURN, P. H., late 4th Native Infantry.

Ensign, 11 Dec. 41—Lieut., 24 Jan. 45—Captain, 23 Nov. 56—Major, 11 Dec. 61.

SERVICE.—Major THURBURN served with the Army of Gwalior, '43 : present at the action of Maharajpore. *Bronze Star.* Served with the Army of the Sutlej, '45, '46: present at the defence of Ferozepore and the action of Ferozeshuhur. *Medal.* Served against the Rohillas of the Bhopal State, in Central India, in October '46. Present at the action of Kalia Kheree, 6th October '46 ; commanded there the Infantry and 2 nine-pounders of the Bhopal Contingent. Received for this service the thanks of Lord Hardinge, who was pleased to order that Captain Thurburn's name, with those of others engaged, should be placed in honorable record in the Adjutant-General's Office. Served in the Turkish Contingent Cavalry from 20th March to 9th August '55. Served during the suppression of the Indian Rebellion of '57, '58. Accompanied the Force under Brigadier Campbell in the attack on the rebels near Papamow (Allahabad), on the 6th January '58. Brought to the notice of His Excellency the Commander-in-Chief, in his Despatch, as having rendered assistance to the Royal Artillery during the action. *Medal.* Accompanied the Force under General Walpole, from 9th April '58 to May '58, in the capacity of Civil Officer, in the expedition from Lucknow into Rohilcund. Present in the attack on the Fort of Rooheea, 15th April '58, and the affair of Allygunge, 22nd April '58. Brought to the notice of H. M.'s Government in the Supplementary Civil Service Minute of the

Governor-General of India, dated 30th December '59. Received the approbation of Her Majesty for services at Lucknow and with Major-General Walpole's Column, conveyed in the letter of the Secretary of State for India to his address, dated the 11th June '60.

MAJOR J. TICKELL, P., late 73rd Native Infantry.

Ensign, 9 Sept. 40—Lieut., 13 Jan. 43—Captain, 19 July 53—Major, 18 Feb. 61.

SERVICE.—Major TICKELL served during the Sutlej Campaign, '45, '46 : present at the actions of Moodkee, Ferozeshuhur *(horse shot under him)*, and Sobraon. *Medal and 2 Clasps.* Received the thanks of the Officer Commanding the 73rd Native Infantry. Served during the Punjab Campaign, '47, '48. *Medal.* Served during the Mutiny at Julpigoree, in '57. Aided in preserving the 73rd Native Infantry and the peace of the district, and in suppressing several attempts at Mutiny at Julpigoree. In December '57 commanded a Detachment of 73rd Native Infantry and 11th Irregular Cavalry set out to attack the Dacca mutineers. In this expedition the Squadron of Irregular Cavalry mutinied in Camp, and in attempting to desert and join the Dacca mutineers, were engaged, defeated, and being captured, several were hung. Received the thanks of the Officer Commanding at Julpigoree for this service. *Medal.* Brought to the notice of the Commander-in-Chief, 15th September '57, and received the acknowledgment of His Excellency's approval of his conduct, 25th September '57, where it is added, " Captain Tickell is already known to Sir C. Campbell as a meritorious Officer." Good services also acknowledged by Government and promised to be brought to the notice of the Crown. (Has furnished a certificate of qualification in Surveying and Civil Engineering.)

BREVET-MAJOR S. R. TICKELL, P. C., late 31st Native Infantry.

Ensign, 12 June 29—Lieut., 4 Aug. 36—Bt.-Captain, 12 June 44— Captain, 25 Dec. 47—Bt.-Major, 28 Nov. 54—Major, 18 Feb. 61.

SERVICE.—Major TICKELL served with the Force against the Coles and Choohars, in '33, '34, '35, and '36. Served with the Ramghur Field

Force against the Coles, in '37. Received the approbation of Government for suppressing the above Insurrection.

2ND CAPTAIN E. TIERNEY, P. H., Bengal Artillery.

2nd Lieut., 11 Dec. 49—Lieut., 24 June 55—2nd Captain, 27 Aug. 58.

LIEUTENANT J. A. TILLIARD, Bengal Artillery

Lieut., 27 Aug. 58.

CAPTAIN H. V. TIMBRELL, Bengal Artillery.

2nd Lieut., 7 June 44—Lieut., 29 Dec. 46—Captain, 21 May 58.

SERVICE.—Captain TIMBRELL served during the Sutlej Campaign, '45, '46: present at the battles of Ferozeshuhur and Sobraon. *Medal and Clasp.*

LIEUTENANT-COLONEL G. TIMINS, late 34th Native Infantry.

Ensign, 25 Jan. 25—Lieut., 7 April 28—Bt.-Captain, 25 Jan. 40—Captain, 10 Jan. 45—Bt.-Major, 11 Nov. 51—Major, 19 May 58—Lieut.-Colonel, 5 March 59.

SERVICE.—Lieutenant-Colonel TIMINS served during the Cole Campaign, '32, '33.

LIEUTENANT-GENERAL S. H. TOD, late 60th Native Infantry.

Ensign, 14 Sept. 99—Lieut., 28 Oct. 99—Captain, 26 Feb. 13—Major, 11 July 23—Lieut.-Colonel, 12 Jan. 25—Bt.-Colonel, 1 Dec. 29—Colonel, 5 April 34—Major-General, 28 June 38—Lieut.-General, 11 Nov. 51.

SERVICE.—Lieutenant-General TOD served at the siege and capture of Bhurtpore. *Medal.*

LIEUTENANT F. F. J. TOKE,† late 63rd Native Infantry.

Ensign, 22 Jan. 57—Lieut., 30 April 58.

LIEUTENANT A. C. TOKER, P. H., General List.

Ensign, 4 May 60—Lieut., 1 Jan. 62.

(600)

MAJOR F. C. TOMBS, P. C., late 18th Native Infantry.

Ensign, 24 Feb. 37—Lieut., 12 April 41—Bt.-Captain, 24 Feb. 52—Captain, 24 May 53—Major, 10 June 61.

SERVICE.—Major TOMBS served during the Punjab Campaign, '48, '49: present at the siege and surrender of Mooltan and battle of Goojerat. *Medal and Clasp.*

BREVET-COLONEL H. TOMBS, C.B., V.C., P. H., Bengal Artillery.

2nd Lieut., 11 June 41—Lieut., 15 Jan. 44—Captain, 25 July 54—Bt.-Major, 1 Aug. 54—Bt.-Lieut.-Colonel, 19 Jan. 58—Bt.-Colonel, 20 July 58.

SERVICE.—Colonel TOMBS, C.B. and V.C., was present at the battle of Punniar, *Bronze Star;* at the actions of Moodkee and Ferozeshuhur, affair of Buddiwal, and battle of Alliwal, as A.D.C. to Sir Harry Smith. *Medal and 2 Clasps.* Army of the Punjab, '45, '46, as Deputy Assistant Quarter-Master-General of the Artillery, including the actions of Ramnuggur, passage of the Chenab, Chillianwallah, and Goojerat. *Medal and 2 Clasps.* Served during the Mutiny at the siege and capture of Delhi, &c., &c. *Medal and Clasp, V.C., and Brevets of Lieutenant-Colonel and Colonel.* Brigadier Wilson thus alludes to the acts for which Colonel Tombs received the *Victoria Cross.* " Yesterday, the 9th instant (July '57), Second Lieutenant J. Hills was on picquet duty with two guns at the mound to the right of the Camp. About 11 o'clock A. M., there was a rumour that the enemy's Cavalry were coming down on this post. Lieutenant Hills proceeded to take up the position assigned to him in case of alarm; but before he reached the spot, he saw the enemy close upon his guns before they had time to form up. To enable him to do this, Lieutenant Hills boldly charged single-handed the head of the enemy's Column, cut down the first man, struck the second, and was then ridden down, horse and all. On getting up and searching for his sword, three more men came at him (two mounted); the first man he wounded with his pistol; he caught the lance of the second in his left hand, and wounded him with his sword; the first man then came on again and was cut down; the third man (on foot) then came up and wrenched the sword from the hand of Lieutenant Hills (who fell in the struggle), and the enemy was about to cut him down, when Major Tombs (who had gone up to visit his two guns) saw what was going on, rushed in, and shot the man and saved Lieutenant Hills. By this time the enemy's Cavalry had passed by, and Major Tombs and Lieutenant Hills went to look after the wounded men, when Lieutenant Hills observed one of the enemy passing with his (Lieutenant Hills') pistol. They walked towards him, the man flourishing his sword and dancing about. He first cut at Lieutenant Hills, who parried the blow, and he then turned on Major Tombs, who received the blow in the same manner. The second attack on Lieutenant Hills was (I regret to say) more successful, as he was cut down with a bad sword cut on the head, and would have been, no doubt, killed, had not Major Tombs rushed in and put his sword through the man. I feel convinced that such gallant conduct on the part of these two Officers has only to be brought properly forward to meet with an appropriate reward. Major Tombs was saved from a severe sword cut on the head by the wadded head dress he wore." Mentioned in General Reed's Despatch, 14th July '57, for being conspicuous for distinguished gallantry. Frequently mentioned in Despatches.

ASSISTANT-SURGEON A. P. TOMKYNS,† Bengal Medical Establishment.

Asst.-Surgeon, 20 Sept. 54.

MAJOR-GENERAL G. TOMKYNS, late 19th Native Infantry.

Ensign, 28 Feb. 07—Lieut., 5 Jan. 11—Bt.-Captain, 28 Feb. 22—Captain, 1 May 24—Major, 5 March 35—Lieut.-Colonel, 23 Nov. 41—Colonel, 16 Oct. 51—Major-General, 28 Nov. 54.

SERVICE.—Major-General TOMKYNS served during the Mahratta War, in '17, '18.

CAPTAIN A. D. TOOGOOD,† late 2nd European Bengal Fusiliers.

2nd Lieut., 12 Jan. 45—Lieut., 21 Feb. 49—Bt.-Captain, 12 Jan. 60—Captain, 11 May 60.

SERVICE.—Captain TOOGOOD served during the Punjab Campaign, '48, '49: present at the affair of Ramnuggur, passage of the Chenab, battles of Chillianwallah and Goojerat *(wounded)*, and subsequent pursuit of the

Sikhs and Affghans by the Force under General Gilbert. *Medal and Clasp.* Served with the Turkish Contingent in the Crimea, during the occupation of Kertch by that Force.

LIEUTENANT H. L. A. TOTTENHAM,† late 67th Native Infantry.

Ensign, 20 Dec. 53—Lieut., 23 Nov. 56.

SERVICE.—Lieutenant TOTTENHAM served during the Mutiny, '57, '58. Present at the action of Shahgunge, near Agra, 5th July '57 *(slightly wounded)*, as a Mounted Escort to the guns, under Colonel Cotton, and as a Volunteer at Agra, on the 10th October '57. Served with the Kumaon Battalion against the rebels in Nepal, under Brigadier Horsford, '58, '59. *Medal.*

ASSISTANT-SURGEON S. C. TOWNSEND,† Bengal Medical Establishment.

Asst.-Surgeon, 1 June 52.

SERVICE.—Assistant-Surgeon TOWNSEND served with the Field Hospital and with the 18th Royal Irish during the Burmese War, from October '52 to August '53. *Medal.*

CAPTAIN R. M. J. TOZER, late 45th Native Infantry.

Ensign, 28 Dec. 42—Lieut., 8 May 47—Captain, 21 Aug. 54.

SERVICE.—Captain TOZER served throughout the Sutlej Campaign, '45, '46. Present at the battles of Moodkee, Ferozeshuhur, and Sobraon. *Medal and Clasp.* Served during the Punjab Campaign, '48, '49. Present at the actions of Chillianwallah and Goojerat. *Medal.*

2ND CAPTAIN G. B. TRAILL, P. H., Bengal Artillery.

1st Lieut., 27 July 57—2nd Captain, 1 Oct. 61.

COLONEL J. TRAVERS, C.B. and V.C., P. H., late 2nd Grenadiers.

Ensign, 11 June 38—Lieut., 7 June 41—Captain, 7 Jan. 46—Bt.-Major, 8 Jan. 46—Major, 16 Feb. 59—Bt.-Lieut.-Colonel, 20 June 54—Bt.-Colonel, 6 Dec. 56—Lieut.-Colonel, 1 Jan. 62.

SERVICE.—Colonel TRAVERS served throughout the Campaign in Affghanistan, '40, '41, and '42. Served in Bhopal State, '46. Served in Seronge and adjoining States, '56. Served in the Mutinies in '57. Present in the actions of Lundi Khanah, Khamind. Mentioned in the Despatch, and name brought to the special notice of Government of India by Major General Sir W. Nott. Present during the five days' operations in March '42. Mentioned in General Nott's Despatch. Baba Wullee *(wounded)*. Mentioned in Despatch, 27th March. Two Cavalry actions, 28th August. Goirie, 31st August. The re-capture of Ghuznee. Benee Badaum, 14th September. Mydaum, 15th September; also in many attacks upon the Rear Guard and Forage Parties of General Nott's Army; also Sobraon. Commanded the Nusseeree Goorkha Battalion in the action, and mentioned in the Despatch: at Kullea Karee, and commanded the Cavalry, and mentioned in the Despatch. Commanded at Indore, 1st July. Brought to the special notice of the Government of India. *Sabre wound* at Baba Wullee. 3 *Medals for Candahar, Ghuznee, Cabul, Sobraon, and for India*, '57, *Victoria Cross and C.B-ship*. Mentioned in the Despatch of Major Griffin, who commanded the Field Force in the action of Khamind, 17th August '41. Publicly thanked upon parade, in front of the line, by Major-General Sir W. Nott, for his services on this occasion, and his conduct brought by him to the special notice of the Government of India. Served as a Volunteer with Skinner's Horse, and received on the Field, in February '42, the acknowledgments of Major-General Sir W. Nott, for the attack made by him, with a few horsemen, upon a superior body of the enemy. For the above service the Major-General attached him to the 1st or Skinner's Irregular Cavalry, with which Corps he served until the termination of the war. Mentioned in the Despatch of Brigadier Wymer, Commanding Brigade in action at Baba Wullee, 27th March '42. Mentioned in the Despatch of Lord Gough, also in the Despatch of General Sir Harry Smith, Commanding a Division of the Army in the battle of Sobraon, 10th February '46. Mentioned in the Despatch of Major Sanders, Commanding Bhopal Contingent, in action at Kullea Karee, 10th October '46; and received the "best thanks" of the Governor-General for his services on this occasion. Received the acknowledgments of the Agent, Governor-General, Central India, for services in the Field, in '56. Received the acknowledgments of the Governor-General "for the manner he conducted the operations against the rebel Sunkur Sing," in '56, and "which were crowned with success." Brought to the special notice of Government by Colonel Durand, in his Despatch. Promoted to the rank of Major by Brevet for services in the Campaign of Affghanistan. *Brevets of Colonel and Lieutenant-Colonel for the Mutiny Campaign.*

LIEUTENANT V. W. TREGEAR, P. H., General List.

Ensign, 11 June 59—Lieut., 16 Feb. 61.

LIEUTENANT F. TRENCH, P. H., late 2nd Bengal European Cavalry.

Cornet, 20 Jan. 57—Lieut., 30 April 58.

SERVICE.—Lieutenant TRENCH was present at the siege and capture of Delhi. Served with Hudson's Horse with Brigadier Showers' Column in the Delhi, Goorgaon, and Jhujjur Districts; with Brigadier Sir T. Seaton's Column in the Doab, including the engagements of Gungeeree, Puttiallee, and Mynpooree; also at the siege and capture of Lucknow, March '58. *Medal and Clasp.*

MAJOR H. LEP. TRENCH, P. H., late 35th Native Infantry.

Ensign, 17 Sept. 40—Lieut., 13 Jan. 42—Bt.-Captain, 17 Sept. 55—Captain, 23 Nov. 56—Major, 19 Jan. 58.

SERVICE.—Major TRENCH served with the Force under General Pollock: present at the forcing of the Khyber Pass, and in the different engagements leading to the re-occupation of Cabul, *Medal;* and also throughout the Hindustan Campaign of '57, '58, including the battle of Nudjufghur *(horse killed under him),* the several engagements under the walls, and final assault of Delhi, as Orderly Officer to Brigadier-General Nicholson. Immediately on the fall of Delhi, accompanied the Force under General Showers as Brigade-Major throughout the operations in the Goorgaon District. Served as Brigade-Major with the Column under Sir T. Seaton. Present at the actions of Gungeeree, Puttiallee, and Mynpooree. *Medal and 2 Clasps.*

(605)

SURGEON J. N. TRESIDDER,† Bengal Medical Establishment.
Asst.-Surgeon, 1 March 45—Surgeon, 30 Oct. 58.

SERVICE.—Surgeon TRESIDDER served with the Army of the Sutlej, '45, '46, as Field Assistant Surgeon. Served with the Army of the Punjab, '48, '49, as Field Assistant Surgeon. Served during part of the Mutiny as Senior Assistant Surgeon with H. M.'s 42nd Royal Highlanders, '57, '58. *2 Medals and 2 Clasps.*

LIEUTENANT J. F. TREVANION, 1st Native Infantry.
Ensign, 29 Sept. 57—Lieut., 7 Sept. 58.

SERVICE.—Lieutenant TREVANION served during the Mutinies in '58, with the Azimghur Field Force, under Brigadier-General Sir E. Lugard. Served in the operations in the Jugdespore jungles. *Medal.*

LIEUTENANT J. TREVENEN, P. H., late 24th Native Infantry.
Ensign, 14 June 50—Lieut., 29 Aug. 54.

LIEUTENANT E. A. TREVOR, Bengal Engineers.
Lieut., 27 Aug. 58.

LIEUTENANT S. T. TREVOR, Bengal Engineers.
Lieut., 6 June 57.

2ND CAPTAIN W. S. TREVOR, Bengal Engineers.
2nd Lieut., 11 Dec. 49—Lieut., 1 Aug. 54—2nd Captain, 27 Aug. 58.

SERVICE.—Captain TREVOR served with the Army of Ava, in '52, '53, as Assistant Field Engineer. Present at the operations preceding the capture of Rangoon, April '52; attack on the Burmese intrenchments under Sir J. Cheape, March '53; and several skirmishes with the enemy; *severely wounded* at the escalade and capture of the white house stockade, on the 12th April '52; *slightly wounded* at the assault and capture of entrenched position, on 19th March '53. *Medal.* Mentioned in the Despatch of General Godwin, and brought to the notice of the

Governor-General, 1st May '52. Mentioned in the Despatch of Sir J. Cheape, 25th April '53. Received the thanks of Government, 1st May '53. Served with the Darjeeling Field Force under Captain Curzon, at Julpigoree; and present at an engagement with the Mutineers of the 75th Native Infantry, from Dacca, on the 12th December '57, at Cherabunder. *Medal.*

MAJOR W. M. TRITTON, Bengal Invalid Establishment.

Ensign, 4 July 21—Lieut., 1 Nov. 23—Captain, 30 Jan. 30—Major, 22 Nov. 43.

MAJOR R. N. TRONSON, P. H., late 2nd European Bengal Fusiliers.

2nd Lieut., 24 July 39—Lieut., 15 Aug. 42—Captain, 30 July 48—Major, 18 Feb. 61.

SERVICE.—Major TRONSON served with the Army of Reserve in '42; with Lord Gough's Army during the Punjab Campaign, '48, '49. Present in the affair of Ramnuggur, passage of the Chenab, and battles of Chillianwallah, and Goojerat. *Medal and* 2 *Clasps.* Engaged in the disarming of the Troops at Mooltan, 10th June '57. Commanded a Detachment of Irregular Troops and Horse and Foot Police during the rebellion of the Nomad Tribes, on the Sutlej, in '57. Repulsed with slaughter a night attack of 2,000 men, and destroyed several of the enemy's villages and strongholds. Marched 55 miles, the greater portion through water, in twenty consecutive hours, with an active enemy on the flank, to the rescue of the city of Pāk Puttun. The rapidity with which this movement was performed ensured in the opinion of the Local Authorities its success, and was the means of preventing the disaffected in Bhauwulpore and Sirsa from joining the Googaira insurgents, and of saving the many rich towns and villages on the Sutlej, and of stopping the progress of rebellion along its banks. *Medal.* Served against the mutineers at Mooltan, in August and September '58.

LIEUTENANT J. M. TROTTER, General List.

Ensign, 19 Dec. 60—Lieut., 1 Jan. 62.

(607)

CAPTAIN L. J. TROTTER, late 2nd European Bengal Fusiliers.

2nd Lieut., 20 Feb. 47—Lieut., 20 Aug. 52—Captain, 1 Jan. 62.

SERVICE.—Captain TROTTER served during the Punjab Campaign, '48, '49. Present at the affair of Ramnuggur, passage of the Chenab, battles of Chillianwallah and Goojerat; and subsequent pursuit of the Sikhs and Affghans, with the Force under General Gilbert. *Medal and Clasp.*

CAPTAIN R. A. TROTTER,† late 43rd Native Infantry.

Ensign, 10 March 34—Lieut., 10 Oct. 39—Bt.-Captain, 10 March 49—Captain, 14 July 53.

SERVICE.—Captain TROTTER served throughout the Affghan Campaign, '39, '40, '41, and '42, *Medal*, including the re-occupation of Khelat: defence of Khelat-i-Ghilzie, *Medal;* and taking of Istaliff. Present at the battle of Maharajpore. *Bronze Star. (Since retired.)*

BREVET-COLONEL C. TROUP, late 68th Native Infantry.

Ensign, 16 July 20—Lieut., 11 July 23—Bt.-Captain, 16 July 35—Captain, 8 Oct. 39—Bt.-Major, 19 June 46—Major, 24 July 47—Lieut.-Colonel, 5 June 53—Bt.-Colonel, 28 Nov. 54.

SERVICE.—Colonel TROUP served against the Bheels in '27: throughout the operations in Affghanistan, '39,' 40, '41, and '42 : present at the storm and capture of Ghuznee. *Medal.* Taken prisoner during the retreat from Cabul, January '42. Commanded the 48th Regiment at the battle of Alliwal. *Medal and Brevet-Major.*

COLONEL H. TROUP, late 6th Europeans.

Ensign, 16 July 20—Lieut., 11 July 23—Captain, 27 June 30—Major 16 May 44—Lieut.-Colonel, 13 Aug. 50—Bt.-Colonel, 28 Nov. 54—Colonel, 11 Sept. 59.

SERVICE.—Colonel TROUP served against the Hill Tribes under Sir Colin Campbell, in '51, '52,

(608)

LIEUTENANT-COLONEL R. TROUP,† late 63rd Native Infantry.

Ensign, 24 Oct. 27—Lieut., 5 April 34—Bt.-Captain, 24 Oct. 42—Captain, 1 Oct. 48—Bt.-Major, 20 June 54—Major, 31 Dec. 55—Lieut.-Colonel, 19 Aug. 59.

SERVICE.—Lieutenant-Colonel TROUP served during the Sutlej Campaign, in '46 : present at the battle of Sobraon. *Medal and 2 Clasps.*

LIEUTENANT W. B. TROUP, Bengal Artillery.

Lieut., 27 Aug. 58.

MAJOR C. P. TROWER, P. H., late 23rd Native Infantry.

Ensign, 12 June 37—Lieut., 3 Oct. 40—Bt.-Captain, 12 June 52—Captain, 15 Nov. 53—Major, 18 Feb. 61.

SERVICE.—Major TROWER served with the expedition against the Affreedies, in the Kohat Pass, under Sir C. Napier, in February '50. Served under Colonel Hungerford in Command of the Garrison at Mhow, in July '57, when he walled Magarnee, as that station was held by a very small Force, until relieved by Brigadier Stuart, Bombay Army. Favorably mentioned by Colonel Hungerford in his report of the doings at the said Garrison, July '57.

GENERAL J. TRUSCOTT, late 74th Native Infantry.

Ensign, 13 Oct. 99—Lieut., 28 Oct. 99—Captain, 4 March 12—Major, 6 Nov. 18—Lieut.-Colonel, 1 March 24—Colonel, 4 March 30—Major-General, 2 June 38—Lieut.-General, 11 Nov 51—General, 27 Jan. 58.

SERVICE.—General TRUSCOTT served at the battle of Delhi. *Medal.*

BREVET-COLONEL A. TUCKER, C.B., late 4th Bengal European Cavalry.

Cornet, 4 Feb. 27—Lieut., 9 Jan. 29—Captain, 23 Dec. 39—Bt.-Major, 4 July 43—Major, 28 Nov. 54—Bt.-Lieut.-Colonel, 20 June 54—Bt.-Colonel, 2 April 56—Lieut.-Colonel, 1 Jan. 62.

(609)

LIEUTENANT H. ST. G. TUCKER,† late 29th Native Infantry.
Ensign, 4 Feb. 55—Lieut., 23 Nov. 56.

SERVICE.—Lieutenant TUCKER served at Nainee Tal, in '57. Served with the 19th Punjab Infantry in the expedition to China, in '60. *Medal.*

SURGEON ST. G. W. TUCKER,† M.D., Bengal Medical Establishment.
Asst.-Surgeon, 14 March 45—Surgeon, 22 Dec. 58.

LIEUTENANT W. F. TUCKER, General List.
Ensign, 20 Dec. 59—Lieut., 1 Jan. 62.

CAPTAIN W. R. TUCKER, P. H., Bengal Engineers.
1st Lieut., 13 June 51—2nd Captain, 31 Aug. 59.

LIEUTENANT A. TULLOCH, P. H., late 20th Native Infantry.
Ensign, 20 Jan. 53—Lieut., 10 May 57.

SERVICE.—Lieutenant TULLOCH served with the Simoor Rifle Regiment before Delhi, '57; *wounded slightly,* 17th June '57, at Hindoo Rao's house, by the bursting of a shell; *severely wounded,* 14th July '57. *Medal and Clasp.* Served with the China Expeditionary Force, '60, '61. *Medal.* (Passed an examination in Punjabee.)

CAPTAIN E. TULLOCH, P. H., late 69th Native Infantry.
Ensign, 10 Dec. 39—Lieut., 2 Feb. 42—Captain, 17 Nov. 52.

SERVICE.—Captain TULLOCH served during the Punjab Campaign, '48, '49. Present at the passage of the Chenab, and the battles of Chillianwallah and Goojerat. *Medal and 2 Clasps.*

LIEUTENANT-GENERAL J. TULLOCH, C.B., late 51st Native Infantry.
Ensign, 23 Nov. 05—Lieut., 2 Feb. 07—Captain, 11 July 21—Major, 24 Jan. 29—Lieut.-Colonel, 30 April 34—Colonel, 23 Oct. 45—Major-General, 20 June 54—Lieut.-General, 11 Sept. 59.

SERVICE.—Lieutenant-General TULLOCH, C.B., served at the Cape of Good Hope, '06; at Bhowaree, in '09; Bundlecund, in '10; and Java, in

'11 *Medal and Clasp;* during the Mahratta War, in '16, '17, including the battle of Nagpore, and subsequent storm of that city. *Medal.* Served in Arracan in '25 ; with the Force under General Pollock in Affghanistan, in '42. Present at the forcing of the Khyber Pass, and the different engagements leading to the re-occupation of Cabul, and assault and capture of Istaliff. *Medal and C.B.*

MAJOR J. S. D. TULLOCH, P., late 17th Native Infantry.

Ensign, 14 Jan. 32—Lieut., 9 July 40—Bt.-Captain, 14 Jan. 47—Captain, 15 Nov. 53—Major, 18 Feb. 61.

(Passed an examination in Punjabee.)

CAPTAIN J. S. TULLOH, P. H., Bengal Artillery.

2nd Lieut., 8 Dec. 43—Lieut., 23 Jan. 46—Captain, 27 April 58.

SERVICE.—Captain TULLOH served during the Sutlej Campaign, '45, '46. Present at the actions of Ferozeshuhur, Buddiwal, and Alliwal. *Medal and Clasp.* Served with the expedition to Kangra, '46, under Brigadier Wheeler, as A. D. C., during the Punjab Campaign, '48, '49. Present at the actions of Ramnuggur, Chillianwallah, and Goojerat. *Medal and 2 Clasps.*

CAPTAIN R. H. TULLOH, P. H., late 16th Native Infantry.

Ensign, 9 June 48—Lieut., 1 Feb. 54—Captain, 11 Feb. 60.

CAPTAIN R. H. D. TULLOH, P., late 39th Native Infantry.

Ensign, 9 Feb. 36—Lieut., 25 July 39—Captain, 1 Nov. 49.

SERVICE.—Captain TULLOH served at the battle of Punniar. *Bronze Star.*

CAPTAIN T. TULLOH,† late 33rd Native Infantry.

Ensign, 4 April 37—Lieut., 3 Oct. 40—Bt.-Captain, 4 April 52—Captain, 30 Dec. 52.

SERVICE.—Captain TULLOH served throughout the Affghan Campaign of '42 : present with the Regiment in every engagement. *Medal.* Served

(611)

during the Sutlej Campaign of '45, '46, including the battles of Ferozeshuhur *(horse short under him)*, and Sobraon *(wounded)*. *Medal and Clasp.*

VETERINARY-SURGEON A. TURNBULL,† Bengal Veterinary Establishment.

Vety.-Surgeon, 13 March 47.

SERVICE.—Veterinary-Surgeon A. TURNBULL served with the Army of the Punjab, at Ramnuggur, Sadoolapore, Chillianwallah, and Goojerat. *Medal and Clasp.* Was present at the relief of Lucknow with the Military Train; occupation of Alum Bagh under Sir J. Outram; siege and capture of Lucknow; relief of Azimghur and pursuit of Koer Singh under Sir E. Lugard, and subsequent operations in the Jugdespore jungles.

LIEUTENANT-COLONEL A. D. TURNBULL, P. H., Bengal Engineers.

2nd Lieut., 12 June 37—Lieut., 22 Oct. 41—Bt.-Captain, 12 June 52—Captain, 1 Aug. 54—Lieut.-Colonel, 18 Feb. 61.

SERVICE.—Lieutenant-Colonel TURNBULL served during the Sutlej Campaign, '46. Placed in charge of the bridge of boats on that river. *Medal.* Received the thanks of the Commander-in-Chief. Served with Colonel Maxwell's Brigade at Calpee, in the construction of Batteries at Calpee, and firing the Mortar Batteries at Delouli during the advance on Calpee. Brought to the notice of Sir Hugh Rose in Despatch, 18th May '58, and mentioned by Sir Hugh Rose, in the Calpee Despatches for " high services," 22nd June '58. Served with the Central India Force as Assistant Quarter-Master-General, and present at the capture of Gwalior under Sir Hugh Rose. Served as Chief Engineer under Sir R. Napier, at the capture of Fort Powri, and mentioned in his Despatch. *Medal and Clasp.*

SURGEON F. TURNBULL,† M. D., Bengal Medical Establishment.

Asst.-Surgeon, 11 Feb. 45—Surgeon, 30 Sept. 58.

SERVICE.—Surgeon TURNBULL served with the Army of the Sutlej in the Field Hospital at Ferozepore, from January to March '46. Served with the Sappers and Miners during the 1st and 2nd siege, and surrender of Mooltan, from July '48 to January '49, and with the Army of the

Punjab at the battle of Goojerat. *Medal and 2 Clasps.* Proceeded with the Sappers and Miners from Roorkee to Meerut, and was present in the Camp on the 17th May '57, when a portion of the Corps mutinied and shot the Commanding Officer, Captain E. Fraser. Served in Medical Charge of a combined Force of Artillery, Cavalry, and Infantry against the insurgents in the Meerut District, in September '57; and with the Sappers in the Agra District, against the insurgents, in November and December '57. Joined Sir James Outram's Force at Alum Bagh, with the Engineer Brigade, in the beginning of February '58, and served at the subsequent siege of Lucknow, in March; afterwards marched with Brigadier Walpole's Column from Lucknow, on 5th April, through Oude to Bareilly. Present at the attack on 15th April, and at the battle and re-capture of Bareilly, on the 6th May '58. Served with Sappers and Miners under Brigadier C. Troup's Column, from November '58 to February '59, in the various operations against the rebels in the Seetapore and Mohumdee Districts, including the capture of Fort Mittowloo. *Medal and Clasp.*

MAJOR M. J. TURNBULL, P., late 2nd Bengal European Cavalry.

Cornet, 28 June 36—Lieut., 10 March 41—Captain, 10 Aug. 50—Major, 18 Feb. 61.

SERVICE.—Major TURNBULL served in Scinde, '45, '46. Served during the Punjab Campaign under General Wheeler, '48, '49. *Medal.*

MAJOR A. TURNER,† late 4th Europeans.

Ensign, 13 June 34—Lieut., 28 June 37—Bt.-Captain, 13 June 49—Captain, 14 Nov. 49—Major, 18 Feb. 61.

SERVICE.—Major TURNER served during the Punjab Campaign, '48, '49. *Medal.*

COLONEL F. TURNER, C.B., Bengal Artillery.

2nd Lieut., 11 June 30—Lieut., 11 March 39—Bt.-Captain, 11 June 45—Captain, 7 Jan. 48—Bt.-Major, 22 Aug. 55—Bt.-Lieut.-Colonel, 19 Jan. 58—Lieut.-Colonel, 11 Oct. 58—Colonel, 24 March 58.

SERVICE.—Colonel TURNER, C.B., served in Affghanistan in '38, '39, '40, '41, and '42, and was present in the several engagements during that period, including Candahar, Ghuznee, and Cabul. *Medal.*

LIEUTENANT F. R. TURNER, P. H., late 33rd Native Infantry.

Ensign, 17 March 55—Lieut., 1 July 57.

SERVICE.—Lieutenant TURNER served with the Nusseeree Battalion in the Jumna Doab, in '57. Present at the action of Thannah Bhowun in Command of 1,000 Horse and Foot Levies of Police. Marched from Agra to Jhansie, detached in October '58 with 175 men, to hold the line of the Dhassam, between Gooserai and Toree Futtehpore, during the pursuit of Tantia Topee. Commanded Detachments of Police in several minor engagements with the enemy in the above and in the Chundehree Districts.

LIEUTENANT J. P. TURTON, P. H., late 26th Native Infantry.

Ensign, 9 Dec. 48—Lieut., 10 Feb. 56.

ASSISTANT-SURGEON J. E. TUSON,† Bengal Medical Establishment.

Asst.-Surgeon, 17 June 53.

LIEUTENANT F. TWEDDELL,† General List.

Ensign, 27 Aug. 59—Lieut., 16 May 61.

SURGEON-MAJOR H. M. TWEDDELL, Bengal Medical Establishment.

Asst.-Surgeon, 3 June 25—Surgeon, 16 April 39—Surgeon-Major, 13 Jan. 60.

SERVICE.—Surgeon-Major TWEDDELL served with the Saugor and Nerbudda Field Force, in '42, '43. Served during the Gwalior Campaign, *Bronze Star;* also during the Sutlej Campaign. *Medal.*

CAPTAIN W. H. TWEEDALE, Bengal Invalid Establishment.

Cornet, 5 Feb. 26—Lieut., 5 Oct. 36—Captain, 5 Feb. 41.

LIEUTENANT W. TWEEDIE, late 4th Europeans.

Ensign, 20 Jan. 57—Lieut., 30 April 58.

SERVICE.—Lieutenant TWEEDIE served during the Mutiny, '57, '58, and '59. Present at the engagement which attended the disarming of the Native

Troops at Benares, 4th June '57. *(Dangerously wounded.)* Volunteered for active service, and joined Havelock's Column at Hauppur. Present at the action of Bithoor, and all the actions, ending in the relief and defence of Lucknow. Served with General Outram's Division at Alum Bagh, including the repulse of the enemy's numerous attacks. Present with the 78th Highlanders throughout the operations resulting in the final storm and capture of Lucknow, also with Lord Clyde's Army, in its advance through Rohilcund, and storming and capture of Bareilly. *Medal and 2 Clasps*. Served with the Field Force under General Beatson, in the operations against, and pursuit of, Tantia Topee, in the Mhow and Nerbudda Districts, in '59.

MAJOR-GENERAL G. TWEMLOW, Bengal Artillery.

2nd Lieut., 6 Aug. 12—Lieut., 1 Aug. 18—Bt.-Captain, 6 Aug. 27—Captain, 16 Sept. 29—Major, 15 Jan. 44—Lieut.-Colonel, 1 July 47—Colonel 6 March 54—Major-General, 17 May 59.

SERVICE.—Major-General TWEMLOW served with the Army of Observation, on the Nepal Frontier, '13, '14; Nepal Campaign, '15, '16, *Medal;* Pindarree and Mahratta Campaign; sieges of Chandah and Asseerghur, '17, '18; from '21 to '23 served in the Nizam's Army, and on three several occasions received the high approbation of the Governor-General in Council, *viz.*, for the capture of the Forts of Jamood, Baroda, and Byrooghur, and an autograph letter of thanks from the Governor-General.

LIEUTENANT A. W. TWYFORD, late 3rd Bengal European Cavalry.

Cornet, 20 Dec. 57—Lieut., 18 May 58.

SERVICE.—Lieutenant TWYFORD served during the Mutiny, '58. Served with the Force under Sir Hope Grant at Lucknow, April '58. *Medal.*

CAPTAIN E. J. L. TWYNAM, P. H., late 25th Native Infantry.

Ensign, 21 Aug. 51—Lieut., 2 May 54—Captain, 4 Nov. 60.

(Has furnished certificates of qualification in Surveying and Civil Engineering.)

MAJOR H. D. TWYSDEN,† late 33rd Native Infantry.

Ensign, 9 Sept. 40—Lieut., 29 Jan. 46—Captain, 3 Oct. 53—Major, 1 Jan. 62.

SERVICE.—Major TWYSDEN served throughout the Affghan Campaign of '42 : present at the forcing of the Khyber Pass and operations in the Mazeena Valley; also at the engagements in the advance on Cabul. *Medal.* Served throughout the Sutlej Campaign, '45, '46, including the battles of Ferozeshuhur and Sobraon. *Medal and Clasp.*

LIEUTENANT J. H. TYLER, P. H., late 20th Native Infantry.

Ensign, 20 Dec. 49—Lieut., 23 Nov. 56.

CAPTAIN W. G. B. TYLER, P. H., late 42nd Native Infantry.

Ensign, 20 Jan. 48—Lieut., 15 Nov. 53—Captain, 18 Feb. 61.

LIEUTENANT H. TYNDALL, P. H., late 61st Native Infantry.

Ensign, 20 Aug. 52—Lieut., 12 April 54.

SERVICE.—Lieutenant TYNDALL was present at the Mutiny of the 61st Native Infantry, 7th June '57. Served with General Johnson's Column of pursuit. Served in the expedition against the rebels near Googaira and Mooltan, '57, '58. *Medal.* Served in the expedition against the Mahsood Wuzeerees, in April and May '60. Present at the action at the Burrara Pass, 4th May '60.

MAJOR E. TYRWHITT, P. H., late 51st Native Infantry.

Ensign, 10 July 42—Lieut., 1 July 46—Bt.-Captain, 10 July 57—Captain, 11 Sept. 58—Major, 10 July 62.

SERVICE.—Major TYRWHITT served with the Army of Gwalior in '43 : present at the battle of Punniar. *Bronze Star.* Present at the siege of Mooltan, '48, '49. *Medal and Clasp.* (*Severely wounded*, December '48.) Present at the battle of Sooroojkhoond *(wounded)*, November '48. Received the thanks of Government for the capture of a rebel in the Huzara Hills, in '53, when in Command of 2 Companies, Khelat-i-Ghilzie Regiment. Received the thanks of Government for services against the Bussy Khel Tribes, while Commanding the Frontier Fort Mackeson, in '55.

SURGEON H. W. TYTLER,† Bengal Medical Establishment.

Asst.-Surgeon, 23 Feb. 42—Surgeon, 14 July 56.

CAPTAIN J. A. TYTLER, V.C., P. H., late 66th Native Infantry.

Ensign, 10 Dec. 44—Lieut., 19 July 48—Captain, 2 April 59.

SERVICE.—Captain TYTLER served with the Force under Sir Colin Campbell against the Hill Tribes, in '51, '52; and in the Boori Pass, '53; in defence of the Kumaon Hills and Rohilcund against the rebels, in '57, '58. Present at action of Chapoorah. *(Severely wounded.)* *Victoria Cross.* Served in the Campaign in Oude under Brigadier Troup, '58, '59. Present at the actions of Pusgaon, 19th October '58; Russoolpore, 25th October '58; attack and capture of Fort Mittowlee, 8th November '58, and present at the action of Biswah, 1st December '58. *Medal.*

BREVET-COLONEL J. M. B. F. TYTLER, C.B., late 37th Native Infantry.

Ensign, 17 Feb. 41—Lieut., 12 Nov. 42—Captain, 17 March 51—Bt.-Major, 18 March 51—Bt.-Colonel, 28 Nov. 54.

SERVICE.—Colonel TYTLER served under Sir G. Pollock at the relief of the Jellallabad Garrison, '42. *(Severely wounded at the Khyber Pass.)* Served during the Sutlej Campaign, '45, '46. Present at the actions of Moodkee and Ferozeshuhur. *Medal and 3 Clasps.* Served during the Punjab Campaign, '48, '49. Present at the actions of Chillianwallah and Goojerat. *Medal and 2 Clasps.* Served under Sir H. Havelock, in '57. Present at the actions of Futtehpore, Aoung, Pandoo Nuddee, Cawnpore, Oonao, Busseerutgunge, Boorby-ka-Chowkee, Bithoor, Mungulwarra, Alum Bagh, and relief of Lucknow. *(Dangerously wounded.)* *Medal and Clasp.* Received *C. B.-ship and Brevet-Colonelcy* for distinguished service in the Field, '58.

MAJOR R. C. TYTLER, P., late 38th Native Infantry.

Ensign, 16 Feb. 35—Lieut., 25 Sept. 37—Captain, 26 Feb. 46—Major, 16 May 58.

SERVICE.—Major TYTLER served during the whole of the operations in Scinde and Affghanistan, '39, '40, '41 and '42. Present in all the engagements leading to the re-occupation of Cabul, by the Force under General Nott. *Medal.* Served at Maharajpore, '43. *Bronze Star.* Served in charge of the Commissariat Depôt at Busseean and Wudnee during the first Punjab Campaign.

LIEUTENANT R. F. C. A. TYTLER,† General List.

Ensign, 2 Oct. 60—Lieut., 1 Jan. 62

U

LIEUTENANT G. C. UDNY,† late 5th Europeans.

Ensign, 14 June 56—Lieut., 27 June 57.

MAJOR R. UNWIN, P., late 16th Native Infantry.

Ensign, 9 Sept. 40—Lieut., 29 Dec. 43—Captain, 11 June 55—Major, 18 Feb. 61.

SERVICE.—Major UNWIN served with Major-General Nott's Force from Candahar to Cabul, '42: present at the taking of Ghuznee, *Medal;* at the battle of Maharajpore, 29th December '43. *Bronze Star.* Served throughout the Sutlej Campaign : present at the battles of Moodkee, Ferozeshuhur, and Sobraon, '45. *Medal and 2 Clasps.* Served during the Punjab Campaign, '48, '49. *Medal.* Present at the capture of Lucknow, March '58; action at Allygunge, and capture of Bareilly, May '58. *Medal and Clasp.*

LIEUTENANT W. H. UNWIN, P. H., late 56th Native Infantry.

Ensign, 20 Dec. 57—Lieut., 18 May 58.

LIEUTENANT J. UPPERTON, P., late 46th Native Infantry.

Ensign, 10 June 54—Lieut., 9 July 57.

LIEUTENANT H. B. URMSTON, P., late 62nd Native Infantry.

Ensign, 20 July 47—Lieut., 15 Aug. 51—Captain, 18 Feb. 61.

SERVICE.—Lieutenant URMSTON served in the expedition against the Hussunzaies, in Huzara, under Colonel Mackeson, in '52, '53:

present as Assistant Commissioner with the Force under Sir Sydney Cotton, in the attack on Shah Mooseh Khel, near Mitchoree, Peshawur Frontier, September '54. (Passed the Punjab Civil Examination, lower and higher standards, also the Colloquial Examination in Pushtoo.)

LIEUTENANT B. C. URQUHART, P. H., late 29th Native Infantry.

Ensign, 11 Dec. 49—Lieut., 26 Aug. 55.

CAPTAIN F. D. URQUHART, P. H., Bengal Artillery.

2nd Lieut., 13 June 45—Lieut., 19 July 48—2nd Captain, 27 Aug. 58—Captain, 18 Feb. 61.

LIEUTENANT I. M. URQUHART, late 18th Native Infantry.

Ensign, 4 Feb. 59—Lieut., 18 Sept. 60.

V

LIEUTENANT A. VALLINGS, late 41st Native Infantry.

Ensign, 20 Sept. 58—Lieut., 24 May 59.

SERVICE.—Lieutenant VALLINGS served with H. M.'s 6th Foot in the Sikkim Expedition, '61.

CAPTAIN B. G. VANDER-GUCHT, P. H., late 2nd Native Infantry.

Ensign, 20 Sept. 45—Lieut., 1 Dec. 51—Captain, 8 Feb. 62.

SERVICE.—Lieutenant VANDER-GUCHT served with the expedition under Brigadier Wheeler, Kôt Kangra, in '46.

LIEUTENANT T. E. VANDER-GUCHT, P. H., late 5th Bengal European Infantry.

Ensign, 20 Dec. 50—Lieut., 9 Aug. 54.

SERVICE.—Lieutenant VANDER-GUCHT served with the Force under Sir Sydney Cotton, in the Eusuffzaie Country, April and May '58. Present at the attack on the heights above Sattana, 4th May '58. *(Severely and dangerously wounded.)*

(619)

CAPTAIN A. D. VANRENEN, P. H., late 71st Native Infantry.

Ensign, 7 July 49—Lieut., 28 Dec. 53—Captain, 7 July 61.

LIEUTENANT-COLONEL D. C. VANRENEN, P. H., Bengal Artillery.

2nd Lieut., 10 Dec. 39—Lieut., 13 Jan. 42—Captain, 28 April 53—Lieut.-Colonel, 18 Feb. 61.

CAPTAIN J. A. VANRENEN, P. C., late 54th Native Infantry.

Ensign, 10 Dec. 47—Lieut., 29 Aug. 54—Captain, 15 June 57.

SERVICE.—Captain VANRENEN served at the defence of the Residency of Lucknow, from June to November '57. Present at the defeat of the rebels at Cawnpore, 5th and 6th December '57. *Wounded* in Lucknow, 17th August '57. *Medal and Clasp.* Allowed to count *one year's extra service* for defence of Lucknow Residency.

BREVET-LIEUTENANT-COLONEL J. L. VAUGHAN, P. C., late 21st Native Infantry.

Ensign, 12 Oct. 40—Lieut., 16 July 42—Captain, 30 June 50—Bt.-Major, 6 June 56—Bt.-Lieut.-Colonel, 26 April 59.

SERVICE.—Lieutenant-Colonel VAUGHAN served as A. D. C. to Sir John Littler at the battle of Maharajpore. *Bronze Star.* Served with the Anglo-Turkish Contingent in the Crimea, from October '55 to the end of the War, as Assistant Deputy Quarter-Master-General. *Brevet-Major and 4th Class of the Medjidie.* Commanded a Field Force in Eusuffzaie, '57; and was twice thanked by Government, particularly for the attacks on the fortified village of Nerinjee, 21st July and 3rd August. Commanded the 5th Punjab Infantry in all the operations in Oude, subsequent to the capture of Lucknow, '58; and mentioned in the Despatches for the affairs of Baree and Simree, battle of Nawabgunge, passage of the Goomtee at Sultanpore, &c., &c. *Brevet-Lieutenant-Colonel.* Commanded a Column of Troops on the Raptee, '59, and repeatedly defeated bodies of the rebels, particularly on the 14th and 18th June. Commanded the whole of the Troops on the Upper Raptee in the operations which led to the final surrender of the rebels, December '59. *Medal.* (Passed the College Examination as Interpreter.)

ASSISTANT-SURGEON T. S. VEALE,† Bengal Medical Establishment.

Asst.-Surgeon, 27 Jan. 58.

LIEUTENANT E. VENOUR, late 40th Native Infantry.

Ensign, 4 March 57—Lieut., 9 Oct. 57.

SERVICE.—Lieutenant VENOUR served as a Volunteer with H. M.'s 10th Foot against the Dinapore mutineers at Arrah. *(Severely wounded.)* Received wound compensation. *Medal.*

ASSISTANT-SURGEON A. M. VERCHERE,† B.A., Bengal Medical Establishment.

Asst.-Surgeon, 23 July 58.

SERVICE—Assistant-Surgeon VERCHERE served with H. M.'s 1st Bengal European Fusiliers during the Winter Campaign in Oude, '58, '59. Served with 1st Punjab Infantry throughout the Expedition against the Mahsood Wuzeerees, in April and May '60, under Brigadier-General Chamberlain, Commanding Punjab Irregular Force.

MAJOR G. VERNER, late 9th Native Infantry.

Ensign, 24 July 30—Lieut., 20 April 35—Captain, 4 March 48—Bt.-Major, 18 May 56—Major, 1 Jan. 62.

BREVET-MAJOR J. E. VERNER, late 60th Native Infantry.

Ensign, 12 Sept. 28—Lieut., 7 Jan. 36—Bt.-Captain, 12 Sept. 43—Captain, 10 Aug. 49—Bt.-Major, 20 June 54.

SERVICE.—Major VERNER served throughout the operations in Affghanistan, with the Force under General Pollock. *Medal.* Commanded the Cavalry Bundlecund Legion against the insurgents in Bundlecund and at the taking of Chirgong, in '41. Commanded the same Regiment against the Hill Tribes in Scinde, under Sir Charles Napier, in '44, '45.

LIEUTENANT-COLONEL H. VETCH, late 54th Native Infantry.

Ensign, 15 June 23—Lieut., 13 May 25—Bt.-Captain, 15 June 38—Captain, 13 June 42—Bt.-Major, 11 Nov. 51—Major, 29 Aug. 54—Bt.-Lieut.-Colonel, 29 May 59—Lieut.-Colonel, 6 June 58.

SERVICE.—Lieutenant-Colonel VETCH served in Burmah, '25, '26, *Medal;* against the Cossyahs, in '29, '30. Captured a standard in the attack on the Dewangiri Rajah, at Soobung Kottah, in '36.

LIEUTENANT E. D. H. VIBART, P. H., late 54th Native Infantry.

Ensign, 4 Sept. 54—Lieut., 26 Nov. 56.

SERVICE.—Lieutenant VIBART served with the 1st European Bengal Fusiliers at the siege of Delhi, including the battle of Nudjufghur, 25th August '57; and storm and capture of Delhi. Present at the action of Narnoul, 16th November '57; and subsequently accompanied the Column under Sir Thomas Seaton, to Futtehghur. Present at the affairs of Gungeeree, Puttiallee, and Mynpooree. Served with the 2nd Punjab Infantry at the siege and capture of Lucknow. Served with several Moveable Columns under Sir Hope Grant and General Walpole. Present at the capture of Bareilly, 5th May '58. *Medal and 2 Clasps.*

CAPTAIN M. J. VIBART,† Bengal Invalid Establishment.

2nd Lieut., 11 June 40—Lieut., 20 Jan. 42—Captain, 7 July 53.

CAPTAIN G. F. F. VINCENT, P., late 30th Native Infantry.

Ensign, 21 June 43—Lieut., 1 Oct. 46—Captain, 9 June 58.

SERVICE.—Captain VINCENT served during the Sutlej Campaign, '45, '46; and in two expeditions against the Angamee Naga Tribes, in the Hills of Assam, in '49, '50. Present at the action of Alliwal, and at the taking of Fort Konomah, in the Naga Hills, 10th December 50. *Medal.* Mentioned in the Despatch of Major Foquett, November '60. Commanded a Detachment, 1st Assam Infantry Battalion, against a refractory Hill Tribe in North Assam. Received the thanks of the Government of India, 10th May '47; of the Government of Bengal, 17th January '51; of the Government of India, 12th February '51; of the Government of Bengal,

25th January '53. Served as Political Officer in an expedition to the Angamee Naga Hills, Assam, in '49; also in March '50. Volunteered and remained in the Naga Hills till November '50, in Command of 80 Sepoys, and held Civil, Military, and Political control over 100,000 men. (Passed examinations in Assamese and Bengali.)

LIEUTENANT E. A. VINE,† General List.

Ensign, 20 Oct. 59—Lieut., 29 Aug. 61.

LIEUTENANT A. VIVIAN, P. H., late 20th Native Infantry.

Ensign, 9 Dec. 54—Lieut., 31 Jan. 57.

SERVICE.—Lieutenant VIVIAN commanded a Ressala of Pathan Horse during the Mutiny, in '57, '58, and '59. Assisted in the suppression of the rebellion of the Jât Tribes of the Ravee, in the Googaira District, in '57. Served with Brigadier Franks' Column in the advance on Lucknow, in February '58. Present at the capture of the Fort of Dhowrara, 4th March '58. Served during the operations before, and capture of, Lucknow, under Lord Clyde, in March '58. *Medal and Clasp*. Stationed at Oonao, on the Lucknow and Cawnpore Road, from April to November '58, assisting in keeping the road clear from the rebels, during which time had frequent skirmishes with the enemy. Served with Colonel Kelly's Column in the operations on the Nepal Frontier, in '59. Present at the attack on the rebels' position in the Hills near Booswul, on the 28th March. Mentioned in Colonel Kelly's Despatch, 30th March '59. Served with the 3rd Punjab Cavalry in the expedition under Brigadier-General Chamberlain, against the Mahsood Wuzeerees, in April '60.

ASSISTANT-SURGEON E. J. VIVIAN,† Bengal Medical Establishment.

Asst.-Surgeon, 20 Nov. 50.

SERVICE.—Assistant-Surgeon VIVIAN served with the 1st Troop and 3rd Battalion Bengal Horse Artillery, in the action with the Jhelum mutineers, on the 7th July '57.

BREVET-CAPTAIN BARON F. VON ANDLAU, P. H., 28th Native Infantry.

Ensign, 13 Dec. 45—Lieut., 18 June 60—Captain, 13 Dec. 60.

SERVICE.—Captain VON ANDLAU was present at the siege, storm, and capture of Delhi, from August to October '57. Served with Brigadier Showers' Column for the subjugation of the Goorgaon and Jhujjur Districts, in 57. Served under His Excellency the Commander-in-Chief, in '58, '59, in Oude. Served in Nepal with Brigadier Horsford's Column, and present at the capture of the rebel guns at Suddeya Ghaut, 9th February '59. *Medal and Clasp.* *(Since dead.)*

CAPTAIN BARON F. A. VON MEYERN, P. H., late 53rd Native Infantry.

Ensign, 8 June 40—Lieut., 17 June 42—Captain, 15 Nov. 52.

SERVICE.—Captain VON MEYERN served with Brigadier Wild's Brigade, and was *severely wounded* in the Khyber Pass. *Medal.* Present at the battle of Punniar. *Bronze Star.* *(Since retired.)*

LIEUTENANT-COLONEL F. E. VOYLE, P., late 39th Native Infantry.

Ensign, 9 June 31—Lieut., 17 Oct. 38—Captain, 18 Nov. 46—Major, 4 June 55—Lieut.-Colonel, 4 June 59.

SERVICE,—Lieutenant-Colonel VOYLE served with the Force under Colonel Shardon against the Bheels, in '37. Served with the Army of Reserve at Ferozepore, in '42, and in 57 against the Googaira rebels, and was present at the three night attacks on the Detachment under Captain Tronson, which ended in their defeat, and the relief of the Town of Pāk Puttun. *Medal.* Mentioned in the Punjab Military Report. Served as Interpreter and Quarter-Master of the 39th Native Infantry, in '37 and '42.

LIEUTENANT-COLONEL G. E. VOYLE, P. H., Bengal Artillery.

2nd Lieut., 11 Dec. 40—Lieut., 24 Aug. 42—Captain, 15 Sept. 53—Lieut.-Colonel, 18 Feb. 61.

SERVICE.—Lieutenant-Colonel VOYLE served in the Sutlej Campaign, '45, '46, including the affair of Buddiwal and battles of Alliwal and

Sobraon. *Medal and Clasp.* Served with the expedition to Burmah. Present at the taking of Martaban, and operations in the vicinity and capture of Rangoon, April '52. *Medal.*

LIEUTENANT B. G. VYVYAN, General List.

Ensign, 8th June 60—Lieut., 1 Jan. 62.

LIEUTENANT R. O. VYVYAN, General List.

Ensign, 4 Feb. 60—Lieut., 1 Jan. 62.

W

LIEUTENANT E. G. WACE, P. H., late 33rd Native Infantry.

Ensign, 1 July 57—Lieut., 18 May 58.

SERVICE.—Lieutenant WACE served with the Force under Major-General Windham, at Cawnpore, November and December '58; also under Brigadier Maxwell, in front of Calpee, February and March '58. Present at the actions on the 25th, 26th, 27th, and 29th November, against the Gwalior Contingent, and throughout the defence of Cawnpore, in '57. Present at the taking of Fort Rooya and action of Allygunge, April '58. Served with the Army under Lord Clyde, in the advance on Bareilly, 5th and 6th May '58. Served with the Oude Field Force under Brigadier Troup, '58, '59. Present at the actions of Pusgaon, Russoolpore, and capture of Fort Mittowlee, 8th November '58. *Medal and Clasp.*

MAJOR G. M. WADDILOVE, P. H., late 24th Native Infantry.

Ensign, 17 Feb. 41—Lieut., 11 Oct. 43—Captain, 6 Oct. 50—Major, 26 Jan. 61.

SERVICE.—Major WADDILOVE served throughout the Sutlej Campaign, '45, '46. Present at the actions of Moodkee, Ferozeshuhur, Buddiwal, and Alliwal. *Medal and Clasp. (Since retired.)*

CAPTAIN H. F. WADDINGTON, P., late 52nd Native Infantry.

Ensign, 8 Dec. 43—Lieut., 15 July 48—Captain, 27 June 57.

SERVICE.—Captain WADDINGTON served during the 1st siege operations before Mooltan, including the repulse on the enemy's night attack on the British Camp at Muttee Thâl, 17th August '48. *Medal and Clasp.*

ASSISTANT-SURGEON A. R. WAGHORN,† Bengal Medical Establishment.

Asst.-Surgeon, 22 June 54.

SERVICE.—Assistant-Surgeon WAGHORN served with the Light Battery, and subsequently with heavy guns at the siege of Delhi, in '57. Served with the 23rd Punjab Infantry, &c., with the Columns under Majors Redmond and Brooks, in February, March, and April '59. *Medal and Clasp.*

LIEUTENANT A. J. WAKE, Bengal Artillery.

1st Lieut., 10 Feb. 58.

LIEUTENANT E. B. WAKE, late 3rd Bengal European Cavalry.

Cornet, 20 Oct. 53—Lieut., 26 April 56.

LIEUTENANT E. Y. WALCOTT, P., late 57th Native Infantry.

Ensign, 20 June 52—Lieut., 16 March 56.

LIEUTENANT A. WALKER, P. H., Bengal Artillery.

1st Lieut., 27 April 58.

BREVET-MAJOR E. W. E. WALKER, P. H., Bengal Artillery.

2nd Lieut., 9 Dec. 44—Lieut., 1 July 47—Captain, 18 Aug. 58—Bt.-Major, 28 Aug. 58.

SERVICE.—Major WALKER served with the expedition to Kôt Kangra, '46, and throughout the Campaign in the Punjab, including the actions of Sadoolapore, Chillianwallah, and Goojerat. *Medal and 2 Clasps.*

MAJOR J. L. WALKER, P. H., late 71st Native Infantry.

Ensign, 13 June 34—Lieut., 22 March 39—Captain, 1 May 47—Major, 31 May 57—Lieut.-Colonel, 16 Feb. 61.

(626)

SURGEON J. P. WALKER, M.D., P. H., Bengal Medical Establishment.
Asst.-Surgeon, 5 April 45—Surgeon, 24 Feb. 59.

SERVICE.—Surgeon WALKER served during the Punjab Campaign, '48, '49. *Medal.*

LIEUTENANT R. J. WALKER, P. H., late 61st Native Infantry.
Ensign, 11 June 53—Lieut., 29 Dec. 55.

LIEUTENANT T. N. WALKER, late 2nd European Bengal Fusiliers.
Ensign, 14 March 54—Lieut., 23 Nov. 56.

SERVICE.—Lieutenant WALKER served with the 2nd Bengal Fusiliers during all the siege operations before Delhi, *wounded* on the 18th July; at the final assault and capture of the city, 14th September '57. *(Wounded.)* Served in the subsequent operations with the Moveable Column under Brigadier Showers, in the District of Delhi; also with the 17th Punjab Infantry, in the Campaign in Rohilcund, under Brigadier Jones, in '58, including the actions of Bagawalla, Nugeena, and relief of Moradabad. *Medal and Clasp.* (Received a first class certificate from the School of Musketry at Hythe.)

ASSISTANT-SURGEON W. WALKER,† M.A., M.D., Bengal Medical Establishment.
Asst.-Surgeon, 4 Aug. 55.

SERVICE—Assistant-Surgeon WALKER served with the 2nd Company, 5th Battalion Artillery, and No. 21 Light Field Battery, during the year '57.

CAPTAIN R. H. WALL, P. H., late 16th Native Infantry.
Ensign, 11 Dec. 49—Lieut., 9 Sept. 55—Captain, 19 May 62.

LIEUTENANT A. J. WALLACE,† late 33rd Native Infantry.
Ensign, 4 Jan. 58—Lieut., 8 Jan. 61.

1st LIEUTENANT N. H. WALLACE,† 101st Foot.

2nd Lieut., 9 Dec. 54—Lieut., 23 Nov. 56.

SERVICE.—Lieutenant WALLACE was present with the 1st Fusiliers at the battle of Badlee-ka-Serai, 8th June '57; in all the subsequent operations under the walls of Delhi, including the affair in the rear of Camp, 19th of June '57; and under General Nicholson, at Nudjufghur, on he 24th of July '57. Present at the storm and capture of Delhi, 14th September '57. Served in the Columns under the Command of Brigadiers Gerrard and Sir Thomas Seaton. Present at the actions of Narnoul, 16th November '57; Gungeeree, 14th December '57; Puttiallee, 17th December '57; and Mynpooree, 27th December '57. En route to Futtehghur: present with Lord Clyde's Army at the siege and capture of Lucknow, in March '58, and subsequent operations in Oude under Sir Hope Grant. *Medal and 2 Clasps.*

MAJOR W. F. N. WALLACE, P. H., late 74th Native Infantry.

Ensign, 11 Dec. 37—Lieut., 16 July 42—Captain, 1 Feb. 49—Major, 1 Jan. 62.

SERVICE.—Major WALLACE served with Major-General Hampton's Force against the Fortress of Joudpore, '39. Commanded a Detachment, 2nd Sikh Infantry, at the storm and capture of the rebel leader Ram Singh's position on the heights of Noorpore, '48; affair of Deenanuggur, and hill insurrection of Tera Soojenpore, and occupation of that Fort. Present at the Mutiny at Delhi, 11th May '57. Commanded the Main Guard on the attack by the 3rd Cavalry and Meerut mutineers at the Cashmere Gate. *Medal.*

CAPTAIN W. R. WALLACE, † late 51st Native Infantry.

Ensign, 27 Sept. 40—Lieut., 12 Nov. 42—Captain, 1 Nov. 53.

SERVICE.—Captain WALLACE served at the action of Punniar. *Bronze Star.* Served during the Punjab Campaign, '48, '49: present at the siege and surrender of Mooltan, and battle of Goojerat. *Medal and Clasp.*

(628)

LIEUTENANT H. E. WALLER,† late 40th Native Infantry.

Ensign, 10 Aug. 52—Lieut., 23 Nov. 56.

SERVICE.—Lieutenant WALLER served during the Sonthal Rebellion in '55, under General Lloyd.

LIEUTENANT J. E. WALLER, General List.

Ensign, 4 July 59—Lieut., 28 April 61.

ASSISTANT-SURGEON N. D. S. WALLICH,† Bengal Medical Establishment.

Asst.-Surgeon, 20 Dec. 48.

SERVICE.—Assistant-Surgeon WALLICH served with the Scinde Camel Corps in the operation against Sheoranees, under Brigadier Hodgson, in April '53. Served with the 4th Punjab Cavalry in the expedition into the Meeranzaie Valley, under Brigadier Chamberlain, in the spring and autumn of '55. Served with the 1st Punjab Cavalry in the attack on the Raubeah Khel Oonuckzaies. Served with the 4th Punjab Cavalry in the expedition into the Koorum Valley, under Brigadier Chamberlain, in the end of '56.

LIEUTENANT-GENERAL C. A. G. WALLINGTON, late 18th Native Infantry.

Ensign, 13 Feb. 04—Lieut., 3 June 04—Captain, 1 Oct. 15—Major, 14 Dec. 26—Lieut.-Colonel, 4 April 32—Colonel, 20 Dec. 43—Major-General, 20 June 54—Lieut.-General, 4 March 58.

SERVICE.—Lieutenant-General WALLINGTON served at the siege and capture of Bhurtpore. *Medal.*

ASSISTANT-SURGEON E. WALLIS, Bengal Medical Establishment.

Asst.-Surgeon, 27 July 59.

(629)

BREVET-LIEUTENANT-COLONEL C. G. WALSH, P. C., late 14th Native Infantry.

Es ign, 25 December 27—Lieut., 8 Oct. 39—Bt.-Captain, 25 Dec. 42—Captain, 10 Sept. 48—Bt.-Major, 20 June 54—Major, 13 April 59—Bt.-Lieut.-Colonel, 20 July 58.

SERVICE.—Lieutenant-Colonel WALSH served during the Sutlej Campaign, '45, '46: present at the battle of Ferozeshuhur. *Medal.* Served in China in 1860, in Command of the Loodiana Regiment. *Medal.*

LIEUTENANT C. J. WALTER, General List.

Ensign, 2 Oct. 60—Lieut., 1 Jan. 62.

LIEUTENANT C. K. M. WALTER, P. H., late 73rd Native Infantry.

Ensign, 20 March 52—Lieut., 26 Feb. 56.

SURGEON J. K. WALTER,† Bengal Medical Establishment.

Asst.-Surgeon, 20 Feb. 46—Surgeon, 26 July 59.

SERVICE.—Surgeon WALTER served as a Surgeon during three years of the Carlist War in Spain: present at the destruction of the fortifications on the heights of Ayete, for the relief of San Sebastian; also at the capture of Venta, taking of Hernani, battle of Andoin, and storm and capture of Srun. (Received a *Medal and Riband* from the Spanish Government.)

LIEUTENANT J. S. WALTERS, late 28th Native Infantry.

Ensign, 9 Dec. 53—Lieut., 14 Sept. 56.

SERVICE.—Lieutenant WALTERS served with the 1st European Bengal Fusiliers at the battle of Badlee-ka-Serai, 8th June '57; also in some of the subsequent engagements under the walls of Delhi. *Medal.*

LIEUTENANT-COLONEL R. WARBURTON, P., Bengal Artillery.

2nd Lieut., 9 June 31—Lieut., 18 March 40—Bt.-Captain, 9 June 46—Captain, 21 Feb. 49—Bt.-Major, 13 March 59—Lieut.-Colonel, 5 Jan. 60.

SERVICE.—Lieutenant-Colonel WARBURTON served in Affghanistan in '39, '40, '41, and '42: present at the assault and capture of Ghuznee. *Medal.*

(630)

Delivered over in December '41 as a hostage to Nawab Mahomed Zuman Khan, by whom he was transferred, in July '42, into the charge of Mahomed Akbar. With the Army of Gwalior at the battle of Maharajpore. *Bronze Star.*

LIEUTENANT D. WARD, P. H., Bengal Engineers.

Lieut., 12 Oct. 57.

SERVICE.—Lieutenant WARD served as Assistant Field Engineer in '57, '58, and '59, with the following Forces:—With the Force under Sir A Wilson on the Hindun, Badlee-ka-Serai, and throughout the siege of Delhi. Mentioned as attached to Reserve at the assault of the City, in the Chief Engineer's Despatch. Served with Colonels Riddell and Cotton's Columns in the Agra District, and at the taking of Futtehpore-Sikree; with Sir J. Outram's Force at Alum Bagh, and at the siege and capture of Lucknow; with Sir R. Walpole's Force at Rooya, Allygunge, and Bareilly; with Lord Clyde's Force at Pertabghur and Amoatie; with Sir H. Grant's Force at the passage of the Gogra, at Fyzabad; with Colonel Rowcroft's Force in the Goruckpore District, and at Toolseepore. *Medal and 2 Clasps.*

CAPTAIN E. WARD, † late 22nd Native Infantry.

Ensign, 20 Feb. 54—Lieut., 10 Aug. 56—Captain, 30 July 60.

LIEUTENANT E. B. WARD, P. H., late 48th Native Infantry.

Ensign, 14 June 56—Lieut., 12 June 57.

LIEUTENANT F. W. WARD, Bengal Artillery.

Lieut., 27 Aug. 58.

CAPTAIN G. WARD, P. H., late 5th Bengal European Light Cavalry.

Cornet, 1 Dec. 43—Lieut., 17 Feb. 49—Captain, 12 Sept. 56.

SERVICE.—Captain WARD served throughout the Sutlej Campaign, '45, '46: present at the battle of Ferozeshuhur. *Medal and Clasp.* Served throughout the Punjab Campaign, '48, '49: present at the affair of Ramnuggur, and actions of Sadoolapore, Chillianwallah, and Goojerat. *Medal and 2 Clasps.* Served at the siege and capture of Delhi, '57; with Hodson's

(631)

Horse at the affairs of Kurkowda, 15th, and Rhotuck, 17th and 18th August '57; and led the Regiment into action the day of the assault, September '57. *Medal and Clasp.*

LIEUTENANT H. C. E. WARD, P. H., late 5th Europeans.

Ensign, 20 April 55—Lieut., 28 Nov. 56.

SERVICE.—Lieutenant WARD served as a Volunteer at the latter part of the siege, and at the assault of Delhi, 14th September '57. Served with the Guides in Brigadier Showers' expedition in the Delhi District; and was present with a Detachment of Guides at the battle of Narnoul, 16th November '57. Served with the Guides in General Cotton's expedition on the Eusuffzaie Frontier, and also in General Chamberlain's expedition against the Cabul Khel Wuzeerees. Mentioned in the Despatch of Major Brind, 1st October '57, and in that of Captain Caulfield, 24th November '57. *Medal and Clasp.*

LIEUTENANT P. WARD, P. H., late 25th Native Infantry.

Ensign, 5 Feb. 54—Lieut., 16 June 56.

LIEUTENANT R. H. WARD,† General List.

Ensign, 20 Feb. 60—Lieut., 1 Jan. 62.

BREVET-CAPTAIN W. J. WARD, P., late 51st Native Infantry.

Ensign, 25 July 42—Lieut., 2 Aug. 50—Bt.-Captain, 25 July 57.

SERVICE.—Captain WARD served at the battle of Punniar. *(Twice wounded slightly.) Bronze Star.* Served during the Punjab Campaign, 48, '49: present at the siege and surrender of Mooltan, and battle of Goojerat. *Medal and Clasp.*

BREVET-MAJOR C. WARDE, P., late 68th Native Infantry.

Ensign, 10 June 43—Lieut., 14 Aug. 46—Captain, 8 June 57—Bt.-Major, 26 April 59.

SERVICE.—Major WARDE served during the Burmese War, in '52, '53. Served during the Sutlej Campaign, '45, '46: present at the battle of Sobraon. *Medal.*

LIEUTENANT C. A. M. WARDE, Bengal Artillery.
Lieut., 27 Aug. 58.

LIEUTENANT S. G. WARDE,† late 11th Native Infantry.
Ensign, 12 June 53—Lieut., 23 Nov. 56.

SURGEON C. F. WARNEFORD,† M. D., Bengal Medical Establishment.
Asst.-Surgeon, 30 Dec. 43—Surgeon, 11 July 57.

SERVICE.—Surgeon WARNEFORD served with the Depôt Hospital during the Sutlej Campaign, '45, '46. Served throughout the Punjab Campaign, '48, '49: present at the affair of Ramnuggur and battle of Goojerat. *Medal and Clasp.*

BREVET-MAJOR A. C. WARNER, P. H., 20th Hussars.
Cornet, 4 Oct. 53—Lieut., 28 Aug. 54—Captain, 1 Oct. 57—Bt.-Major, 19 Nov. 59.

SERVICE.—Major WARNER formed one of the Garrison of Lucknow from the 30th of June till the 22nd November '57. Was brought to the favorable notice of the Governor-General in Council in the Despatch of Sir J. Inglis, dated 25th September '57; and thanked by the Governor-General in Council in General Order No. 1543, dated 8th December '57. Was present with the Force under His Excellency the Commander-in-Chief which drove the Gwalior rebels from Cawnpore, at the action of Khodagunge, and re-occupation of Futtehghur. Served as Aide-de-Camp to Brigadier-General Walpole, during the siege and capture of Lucknow, in March '58, and at the action and re-occupation of Bareilly, in May '58. Mentioned in Despatches on both occasions. *Medal and 2 Clasps, Brevet-Majority, and one year's extra service.*

MAJOR E. C. WARNER,† 20th Hussars.
Cornet, 25 Jan. 41—Lieut., 3 June 44—Captain, 2 May 54—Major, 30 July 62.

SERVICE.—Major WARNER served at the action of Punniar, *Bronze Star;* with the Army of the Punjab. Present throughout the operations in the vicinity and siege and surrender of Mooltan. *Medal.*

(633)

1st LIEUTENANT W. H. WARNER,† late 1st European Bengal Fusiliers
2nd Lieut., 13 Dec. 56—Lieut., 12 March 58.

SERVICE.—Lieutenant WARNER was present with his Regiment at the battle of Badlee-ka-Serai, under the Command of Sir Henry Barnard, in all the subsequent operations under the walls of Delhi, including the affair under General Nicholson at Nudjufghur, 24th July '57, up to the assault and capture of that city on the 14th of September '57. Served with his Regiment in the Columns under the Command of Brigadiers Gerrard and Seaton. Present at the action of Narnoul, 16th November '57; Gungeeree, 14th December '57; Puttiallee, 17th December '57; and Mynpooree, 27th December '57. Present with the Army under Lord Clyde at the storm and capture of Lucknow, in March '58, and all the subsequent operations in Oude under Sir Hope Grant. *Medal and 2 Clasps.* Served with a Detachment of the 1st European Bengal Fusiliers under Major Wheeler, when they captured 5 guns from theNusseerabad Brigade, at Shahdutgunge, on the 30th October '58.

BREVET-MAJOR W. E. WARRAND, P. H., Bengal Engineers.

2nd Lieut., 8 June 49—Lieut., 1 Aug. 54—2nd Captain, 27 Aug. 58.— Bt.-Major, 28 Aug. 58.

SERVICE.—Major WARRAND served at the siege of Delhi. *(Severely wounded, arm amputated.) Medal, Clasp, Brevet-Major, and Wound Pension.*

MAJOR-GENERAL G. WARREN, late 1st European Bengal Fusiliers.

Ensign, 6 Oct. 18—Lieut., 30 Jan. 20—Captain, 13 April 30—Major, 25 Feb. 37—Bt.-Lieut.-Colonel, 23 July 39—Lieut.-Colonel, 6 Aug. 43— Bt.-Colonel, 16 July 49—Colonel, 5 Dec. 53—Major-General, 28 Nov. 54.

SERVICE.—Major-General WARREN served at the siege of Bhurtpore in '26. Commanded one of the Companies selected for the escalade at the Jungeena Gate. *(Severely wounded.) Medal.* Served with the Army of the Indus in Affghanistan, in '39. Present at the assault and capture of Ghuznee, *again severely wounded. Medal, 3rd Class Dooranee Order,* and *Brevet-Lieutenant-Colonel.* Commanded the Bengal Brigade in the Expeditionary Force to Burmah under Major-General Godwin: present at the operations in the vicinity of Rangoon, in April '52. *Medal.*

(634)

LIEUTENANT H. DEG. WARTER, Bengal Artillery.
1st Lieut., 27 April 58.

LIEUTENANT A. WATERFIELD, late 4th Bengal European Cavalry.
Cornet, 4 Oct. 57—Lieut., 18 May 58.

LIEUTENANT H. A. W. WATERFIELD, P. H., late 27th Native Infantry.
Ensign, 10 May 48—Lieut., 28 Sept. 54.

LIEUTENANT H. G. WATERFIELD,† late 34th Native Infantry.
Ensign, 4 Aug. 57—Lieut., 19 May 58.

SERVICE.—Lieutenant WATERFIELD served with H. M.'s 82nd in the N. W. Provinces, in suppressing the Mutiny, in '57, '58, including the operations at and defence of Cawnpore under General Windham ; the defeat of the rebels on the 6th December '57, under Lord Clyde. Was present at the action of Kalee Nuddee, also that of Khankur, under Sir T. Seaton, 7th April '58. Was engaged at the defence of the Jail at Shahjehanpore, under Colonel Hale, and operations subsequent to the relief under Sir J. Jones. Capture of the Forts of Buneral, Mahowdie, and Shahabad. Present at the action of Bun-ka-gaon under Sir T. Seaton. Served also with the 66th Goorkha Light Infantry in the Oude Campaign of '58, '59. Present at the action of Pusgaon, 19th October ; battle of Russoolpore, 25th October ; attack and capture of the Fort of Mittowlee, 8th November ; and action of Biswah, 1st December '58. *Medal and Clasp.*

LIEUTENANT W. G. WATERFIELD, P., late 23rd Native Infantry.
Ensign, 3 Oct. 52—Lieut., 23 Nov. 56.

SERVICE.—Lieutenant WATERFIELD served at Meerut at the outbreak of the Mutiny in '57. Present at the actions on the Hindun River, 31st May and 1st June '57. Mentioned in the Despatches. Present at the battle of Badlee-ka-Serai, and throughout the siege of Delhi. *Medal and Clasp.* Served as Political Officer to the Force that marched from Delhi to Jeypore, under Major Redmond, in pursuit of Tantia Topee and other rebels.

LIEUTENANT J. WATERHOUSE, Bengal Artillery.
Lieut., 10 June 59.

CAPTAIN T. P. WATERMAN, P., late 13th Native Infantry.
Ensign, 11 June 38—Lieut., 16 July 42—Bt.-Captain, 11 July 53—Captain, 28 Nov. 54.
SERVICE.—Captain WATERMAN served during the Punjab Campaign, '48, '49: present at the passage of the Chenab and battle of Goojerat. *Medal and Clasp.*

LIEUTENANT-GENERAL E. F. WATERS, C.B., late 68th Native Infantry.
Ensign, 1 Nov. 1800—Lieut., 1 July 03—Captain, 1 Sept. 15—Major, 11 July 23—Lieut.-Colonel, 13 May 25—Bt.-Colonel, 18 June 31—Colonel, 16 Nov. 35—Major-General, 23 Nov. 41—Lieut.-General, 11 Nov. 51.
SERVICE.—Lieutenant-General WATERS, C.B., served at the assault and capture of Allyghur, battle of Delhi, and throughout the Campaign under Lord Lake, '03, '04, and '05; Nepal War, '15; Assam, '24. *Medal and Clasp.*

ASSISTANT-SURGEON J. WATKINS,† Bengal Medical Establishment.
Asst.-Surgeon, 11 Aug. 50.

LIEUTENANT-COLONEL E. D. WATSON, P., late 44th Native Infantry.
Ensign, 7 March 37—Lieut., 26 June 40—Captain, 13 June 49—Major, 21 July 57—Lieut.-Colonel, 1 Jan. 62.

ASSISTANT-SURGEON G. A. WATSON,† Bengal Medical Establishment.
Asst.-Surgeon, 4 Aug. 55.
SERVICE.—Assistant-Surgeon WATSON served with the 2nd Company, 6th Battalion Artillery, during the Mutiny of the Native Troops at Mhow, in July '57; and the subsequent occupation of the Fort of Mhow. Served at the siege of Dhao, the actions before Goorarea and Mundesore, and the Campaign in Central India, from October to December '57. *Medal.*

(636)

BREVET-MAJOR G. E. WATSON,† Bengal Engineers.

2nd Lieut., 11 Dec. 46—Lieut., 1 Aug. 54—2nd Captain, 27 Aug. 58—Bt.-Major, 28 Aug. 58.

SERVICE.—Major WATSON served with Sir H. Havelock's Force during the first advance on Lucknow, and as Brigade-Major of Engineers at the relief of Lucknow, under Sir C. Campbell, and subsequent operations. Present at the capture of Lucknow. *Medal, 2 Clasps, and Brevet-Major.*

CAPTAIN J. E. WATSON, P. H., Bengal Artillery.

2nd Lieut., 8 Dec. 43—Lieut., 19 Dec. 45—Captain, 27 April 58.

SERVICE.—Captain WATSON served with the Army of the Punjab, '48, '49, including the actions of Sadoolapore *(wounded)*, Chillianwallah, and Goojerat. *Medal and 2 Clasps.*

CAPTAIN J. T. WATSON, P. H., late 12th Native Infantry.

Ensign, 20 Dec. 46—Lieut., 3 Sept. 53—Captain, 6 Aug. 58.

SERVICE.—Captain WATSON was with the 7th Oude Infantry during the Mutiny at Lucknow. Served during the entire defence of the Residency, and was present during the operations against the Gwalior rebels in Cawnpore, December '57. *Medal and Clasp, and one year's extra service.* Accompanied the Mooltan Special Field Force under Brigadier Hewitt, to Subzul Kôt, in Scinde, in '52, to coerce Meer Ali Moorad.

CAPTAIN T. WATSON,† 4th (late 33rd) Native Infantry.

Ensign, 12 Dec. 35—Lieut., 24 Jan. 40—Bt.-Captain, 12 Dec. 50—Captain, 14 March 52.

SERVICE.—Captain WATSON served at the taking of Jhansie in '38. Served in Cabul under Sir G. Pollock, in '42 : present at the forcing of the Khyber Pass, and relief of Jellallabad, to the re-taking of Cabul, *Medal,* including the affairs of Dacca, Mugeena Valley, Jugdulluck, Tazeen, and Huft Kootul. Present at the annexation of Oude, at the capture of the Toolsepore Rajah, after a forced march of 50 miles. Served under Sir E. Lugard in '58, against the mutineers at Jugdespore. *Medal.* Received the thanks of the Adjutant-General of the Army, for the capture of the Toolsepore Rajah. *(Since retired.)*

LIEUTENANT T. J. WATSON, P. H., late 46th Native Infantry.

Ensign, 20 Feb. 51—Lieut., 23 Nov. 56.

SERVICE.—Lieutenant WATSON served between Delhi and Futteghur, and present at all the engagements that took place with Brigadier Seaton's Column. Present at the siege of Lucknow, and one or two engagements with the Oude Field Force, under Sir Hope Grant. Commanded a Squadron, Hodson's Horse, and present at one engagement. Was honorably mentioned in the Despatches. *Medal and Clasp.*

ASSISTANT-SURGEON W. WATSON, M. B., Bengal Medical Establishment.

Asst.-Surgeon, 1 Aug. 54.

SERVICE.—Assistant-Surgeon WATSON was present at Sussia Ghaut, near Agra, on the 5th July '57; with Brigadier Showers' Column in the Goorgaon District, 1st to 9th November '57. *Wounded slightly* on the head at Sussia, on 5th July '57.

CAPTAIN W. C. WATSON, P. H., 7th (late 47th) Native Infantry.

Ensign, 24 Feb. 39—Lieut., 15 Jan. 42—Captain, 15 Dec. 53.

SERVICE.—Captain WATSON served with the 47th Native Infantry on special service in Arrakan, in '42. Served with the Sutlej Campaign of '46, and proceeded to Lahore in charge of 750 men for the Army of the Sutlej, and received one year's batta. Served in Burmah from '54 to '57. Served in China, and present at minor engagements around Canton, in '58, '59.

LIEUTENANT J. L. WATTS,† Bengal Engineers.

Lieut., 27 June 57.

SERVICE.—Lieutenant WATTS was present at Allyghur at the Mutiny of the 9th Native Infantry, on the 20th May '57. Present at the Mutiny of 2 Squadrons, 1st Gwalior Cavalry, at Hattrass. Retired to Agra, 17th June '57. Present at the actions at Agra on the 5th July and 10th

October; also out in the District with Major Montgomery's Force. Served with General Penny's Column. Present at the action of Kukrowlie, and served with the Commander-in-Chief's Column. Present at the re-occupation of Bareilly. *Medal.*

LIEUTENANT R. A. WAUCHOPE, late 57th Native Infantry.

Ensign, 4 Oct. 55—Lieut., 17 Feb. 58.

SERVICE.—Lieutenant WAUCHOPE served with the 4th Sikh Infantry during the siege of Delhi. Was present at the storming of the Water Bastion, with the 2nd Column, on the 14th September '57; at the subsequent and last fighting, and at the taking of the Burn Bastion on the evening of the 19th. *Medal and Clasp.* Served with the Force under Colonel Gawler against the Hill Tribes in Sikkim, in '60, '61.

LIEUTENANT-COLONEL A. S. WAUGH, Bengal Engineers.

2nd Lieut., 13 Dec. 27—Lieut., 13 Dec. 27—Bt.-Captain, 13 Dec. 42—Captain, 19 Feb. 44—Bt.-Major, 10 June 54—Major, 3 Aug. 55—Lieut.-Colonel, 20 Sept. 57.

LIEUTENANT L. WAVELL, P. H., late 45th Native Infantry.

Ensign, 14 June 56—Lieut., 25 Aug. 57.

SERVICE.—Lieutenant WAVELL served at the taking of the stockade of Wong-Ka-dya, 3rd* April; of Chapoo, 17th April; capture of the Towns of Nah-Ding, 1st May; Tsing Poo, 12th May; Nanjim, 17th May; and Cho-King, 20th May '62.

LIEUTENANT G. A. WAY, P. H., late 58th Native Infantry.

Ensign, 5 March 55—Lieut., 14 March 58.

SURGEON-MAJOR A. WEBB, M. D., Bengal Medical Establishment.

Asst.-Surgeon, 20 March 35—Surgeon, 10 Oct. 49—Surgeon-Major, 13 Jan. 60.

(639)

SURGEON C. K. WEBB,† Bengal Medical Establishment.
Asst.-Surgeon, 1 July 46—Surgeon, 25 Sept. 59.

SERVICE.—Surgeon WEBB served with the 2nd Punjab Infantry through the Rohilcund Campaign to the capture of Bareilly, '58; and with the 4th Punjab Infantry in the expedition under General Chamberlain, against the Mahsood Wuzeerees, in April and May '60. *Medal.*

LIEUTENANT E. J. WEBBER,† General List.
Ensign, 10 Dec. 59—Lieut., 2 Oct. 61.

LIEUTENANT A. G. WEBSTER, late 1st Bengal European Cavalry.
Cornet, 20 Dec. 56—Lieut., 10 March 57.

LIEUTENANT H. B. WEBSTER, late 4th Bengal European Cavalry.
Cornet, 4 Dec. 57—Lieut., 18 May 58.

LIEUTENANT H. W. WEBSTER, late 45th Native Infantry.
Ensign, 26 July 57—Lieut., 18 May 58.

CAPTAIN R. F. WEBSTER,† late 3rd Europeans.
Ensign, 30 Dec. 43—Lieut., 15 March 48—Captain, 15 May 58.

CAPTAIN T. E. WEBSTER,† late 63rd Native Infantry.
Ensign, 11 June 47—Lieut., 21 Sept. 51—Captain, 19 Aug. 59.

CAPTAIN J. WEDDERBURN,† late 69th Native Infantry.
Ensign, 12 Dec. 40—Lieut., 12 Sept. 44—Captain, 28 Nov. 54.

SERVICE.—Captain WEDDERBURN was engaged at the battles of Chillianwallah and Goojerat, *Medal and 2 Clasps;* also in Scinde, in the Campaign against the Hill Tribes, under Sir Charles Napier, in '45.

LIEUTENANT A. J. T. WELCHMAN, P. H., General List.
Ensign, 20 Dec. 59—Lieut., 1 Jan. 62.

BREVET-COLONEL J. WELCHMAN, C.B., late 1st European Bengal Fusiliers.

Ensign, 1 June 21—Lieut., 11 July 23—Captain, 5 March 36—Bt.-Major' 9 Nov. 46—Major, 28 March 48—Lieut.-Colonel, 14 July 53—Bt.-Colonel, 28 Nov. 54.

SERVICE.—Colonel WELCHMAN, C.B., served in Burmah in '52, '53: present at the relief of the garrison of Pegu, 14th December '52, and operations in its vicinity. Accompanied the Martaban Column, under the Command of Major-General Godwin, to Thong-Gheen and Tonghoo. *Medal.* Commanded the Regiment in the action fought at Badlee-ka-Serai, on the 8th June '57; and on the 23rd June in the Subzee Mundel. *(Severely wounded.) Medal.*

CAPTAIN G. WELD, P. H., late 14th Native Infantry.

Ensign, 27 Aug. 44—Lieut., 27 Oct. 48—Bt.-Captain, 27 Aug. 59— Captain, 18 Feb. 61.

SERVICE.—Captain WELD served during the Sutlej Campaign, '45, '46: present at the battle of Ferozeshuhur. *(Severely wounded.) Medal.*

LIEUTENANT E. WELLS, General List, Cavalry.

Cornet, 21 July 59—Lieut., 21 July 60.

CAPTAIN L. F. WELLS,† late 2nd Bengal European Cavalry.

Cornet, 20 Oct. 55—Lieut., 23 Nov. 56—Captain, 31 March 60.

SERVICE.—Captain WELLS served under Brigadier-Generals Chamberlain and Nicholson in the Punjab Moveable Column: present at the action of Nimmoo Ghaut, marched with General Nicholson to Delhi, and served at its siege and capture. Served under Brigadier Showers in the Delhi, Goorgaon, and Jhujjur Districts; also with Brigadier Seaton's Column in the Doab. Present at the actions of Gungeeree and Puttiallee. *Medal and Clasp.*

2ND CAPTAIN D. J. WELSH, P. H., Bengal Artillery.

1st Lieut., 30 May 57—2nd Captain, 28 July 60.

(641)

CAPTAIN H. M. WEMYSS, P. H., late 1st European Bengal Fusiliers.

2nd Lieut., 9 Dec. 48—Lieut., 18 April 53—Captain, 18 Feb. 61.

SERVICE.—Lieutenant WEMYSS was present with his Regiment at the battle of Badlee-ka-Serai, 8th June '57 ; and in some of the subsequent operations before Delhi. Present at the siege and capture of that city, 14th September '57. *(Slightly wounded.) Medal.*

BREVET-COLONEL W. B. WEMYSS, late 1st Bengal European Cavalry.

Cornet, 22 May 26—Lieut., 3 Dec. 28—Captain, 10 Oct. 36—Bt.-Major, 9 Nov. 46—Major, 2 Oct. 51—Bt.-Lieut.-Colonel, 20 June 54—Lieut.-Colonel, 28 Nov. 54—Bt.-Colonel, 20 July 59.

SERVICE.—Colonel WEMYSS served throughout the Campaign in Scinde, in '43 : present at the battles of Meeanee and Hyderabad. *Medal.*

ASSISTANT-SURGEON R. WESTCOTT,† Bengal Medical Establishment.

Asst.-Surgeon, 4 Aug. 56.

SERVICE.—Assistant-Surgeon WESTCOTT served with the Bhopal Contingent in the suppression of the Mutiny, from May to July '57; in Medical Charge of 22nd Punjab Infantry throughout the Campaign in Rohilcund, and was present at the action of Kukralah, capture of Bareilly, relief of Shahjehanpore, and subsequent affairs on the 15th and 18th May, and the capture of Shahabad, and remained on active Field Service in Rohilcund, until February '59. *Medal.* Served with the Field Force under Command of Colonel Turner, during the operations against the rebels in Bundlecund, '59.

CAPTAIN G. R. WESTMACOTT, P. H., late 23rd Native Infantry.

Ensign, 20 Jan. 50—Lieut., 15 Nov. 53—Captain, 20 Jan. 62.

LIEUTENANT I. P. WESTMORLAND, Bengal Engineers.

Lieut., 27 Aug. 58.

BREVET-MAJOR C. S. WESTON, P. H., late 36th Native Infantry.

Ensign, 4 Jan. 40—Lieut., 9 Dec. 42—Captain, 10 July 52—Bt.-Major, 20 July 58.

SERVICE.—Major WESTON served during the Sutlej Campaign: present at Alliwal, *Medal*, and during the Punjab Campaign: present at Ramnuggur, Sadoolapore, and Chillianwallah. *(Wounded.) Medal and Clasp.* Served also with the Nepal Force in '58. *(Severely wounded.) Medal and Brevet-Major. (Since retired.)*

BREVET-MAJOR G. R. WESTON, P. H., 10th (late 65th) Native Infantry.

Ensign, 10 Dec. 39—Lieut., 21 Feb. 42—Bt.-Captain, 10 Dec. 54—Captain, 1 Oct. 55—Bt.-Major, 24 March 59.

SERVICE.—Major WESTON was in Political Charge and vested with special powers at the capture of the Durriabad Forts. *Brevet Major, Medal, and 2 Clasps.* Oude, in March and April '50. Formed one of the old Garrison Lucknow Residency, from 30th June to 22nd November '57. *One year's extra service.* Present throughout the whole of the subsequent operations before Lucknow with the Force under Sir J. Outram, and at the siege and capture of Lucknow, in March '58. *(Since retired.)*

SURGEON-MAJOR T. A. WETHERED, M.D., Bengal Medical Establishment.

Asst.-Surgeon, 27 May 38—Surgeon, 11 Jan. 52—Surgeon-Major, 13 Jan. 60.

SERVICE.—Surgeon-Major WETHERED served during the Sutlej Campaign of '45, '46, in charge of the European Depôt Hospital at Ferozepore. Served during the Sikh Campaign of '48, '49, in Medical Charge of 58th Native Infantry, which formed part of Sir Dudley Hill's Reserve Force. Served as Principal Medical Officer with the Force under Command of Sir Hope Grant, when it crossed the Gogra, on 25th November '58, till it was broken up. Served with the Force under Brigadier Holditch, at the foot of the Nepal Hills, '58, '59, and '60. Present in the actions of Muchligaon and Bunkussia, Trans-Gogra, Oude. *Mutiny Medal. (Since retired.)*

(643)

BREVET-COLONEL A. WHEATLEY, late 4th Bengal European Cavalry.

Cornet, 9 Jan. 24—Lieut., 13 May 25—Captain, 3 Dec. 38—Bt.-Major, 7 June 49—Major, 16 April 50—Lieut.-Colonel, 14 Nov. 53—Bt.-Colonel, 28 Nov. 54.

SERVICE.—Colonel WHEATLEY was present at the battle of Punniàr. *Bronze Star.* Commanded the Regiment with the Army of the Punjab, during the latter part of the action at Ramnuggur *(slightly wounded)*, and at the battles of Sadoolapoore, Chillianwallah, and Goojerat. *Medal and Brevet-Major.*

LIEUTENANT F. WHEELER, P., late 39th Native Infantry.

Ensign, 9 June 54—Lieut., 15 June 57.

CAPTAIN G. WHEELER, P. H., late 29th Native Infantry.

Ensign, 11 Dec. 47—Lieut., 3 July 54—Captain, 18 Feb. 61.

LIEUTENANT H. I. WHEELER, late 38th Native Infantry.

Ensign, 6 March 57—Lieut., 18 May 58.

(Has received a 2nd class certificate from the School of Musketry, Hythe.)

LIEUTENANT P. WHEELER, P. H., late 15th Native Infantry.

Ensign, 4 July 55—Lieut., 6 June 57.

LIEUTENANT R. WHEELER, P. H., late 61st Native Infantry.

Ensign, 8 Dec. 55—Lieut., 30 April 58.

BREVET-COLONEL F. WHELER, C.B., P., late 1st Bengal European Cavalry.

Cornet, 18 Aug. 19—Lieut., 30 June 21—Captain, 7 July 33—Bt.-Major, 9 Nov. 46—Major, 15 Dec. 51—Bt.-Lieut.-Colonel, 7 June 49—Lieut.-Colonel, 28 Nov. 54—Bt.-Colonel, 28 Nov. 54.

SERVICE.—Colonel WHELER served in Bundlecund, '21, '22. In

Affghanistan, '39, '40 : present at the assault and capture of Ghuznee, *Medal;* and pursuit of Dost Mahomed Khan. *3rd Class Dooranee Order.* Present at the siege and capture of Mooltan, and battle of Soorooj-khoond, in the Punjab Campaign, '48, '49. *Medal and Brevet-Lieutenant-Colonel.* Favorably mentioned in Brigadier Markham's and General Whish's Despatches. Commanded Saugor District, '58, '59; three times in action at Zalimpore, Dowlutpore, and Goonapoora, against the rebels. Commanded 7 Columns of Troops in Bundlecund, '59, against the rebels. Thanked by Lord Clyde in General Orders. *Medal and Clasp, and C.B.-ship.*

BREVET-MAJOR T. WHELER, P. H., late 1st European Bengal Fusiliers.

2nd Lieut., 10 Dec. 44—Lieut., 4 March 46—Captain, 5 March 56—Bt.-Major, 26 April 59.

SERVICE.—Major WHELER served during the Campaign on the Sutlej : present at the actions of Buddiwal, Alliwal, and Sobraon, *Medal and Clasp;* with the Burmah Field Force: present at the re-capture and relief of Pegu, in November and December '52; and served with the Martaban Column under General Steel, *Medal ;* with Lord Clyde's Army at the capture of Lucknow, in March '58 ; and commanded the Force that defeated the Nusseerabad Brigade at Sahadutgunge, on the 30th October '58. *Medal and Clasp.*

BREVET-COLONEL G. P. WHISH, P. C., late 60th Native Infantry.

Ensign, 19 Nov. 29—Lieut., 1 Dec. 36—Bt.-Captain, 19 Nov. 44—Captain, 15 Nov. 49—Bt.-Major, 7 June 49—Major, 1 Jan. 62—Major in Staff Corps, 18 Feb. 61—Bt.-Lieut.-Colonel, 28 Nov. 54—Bt.-Colonel, 2 June 60.

SERVICE.—Colonel WHISH served in the Campaign in Affghanistan with the Force under General Pollock, *Medal;* as Assistant Adjutant-General to the Mooltan Field Force, and to the 1st Infantry Division, Army of the Punjab ; and was present at the action of Goojerat. *Medal,*

Clasp, and Brevet-Major. (Received a certificate of high proficiency in Oordoo.)

LIEUTENANT H. E. WHISH, P., T.C., late 26th Native Infantry.

Ensign, 9 June 49—Lieut., 23 Nov. 56—Captain, 9 June 61.

SERVICE.—Captain WHISH served as a Volunteer at the siege of Mooltan. *Medal and Clasp.* (Has furnished certificates of qualification in Surveying and Civil Engineering.)

CAPTAIN M. B. WHISH, P. H., late 29th Native Infantry.

Ensign, 13 June 37—Lieut., 14 Feb. 40—Captain, 15 March 51.

SURGEON A. WHITE,† M.D., Bengal Medical Establishment.

Asst.-Surgeon, 30 Jan. 41—Surgeon, 10 April 55.

SERVICE.—Surgeon WHITE served with the 3rd Light Dragoons throughout the Campaign in Affghanistan with the Force under General Pollock. Present at the forcing of the Khyber Pass, and subsequent operations in Affghanistan, *Medal ;* in Medical Charge of the 63rd Native Infantry. Served during the Sutlej Campaign, '45, '46 : present at the battle of Sobraon. *Medal and Clasp.* Served on the Burmese Frontier during the 2nd Burmese War, '52, '53. *Medal and Clasp.* Served in Oude, in Medical Charge of the 19th Punjab Infantry, during the Mutiny of '57, '58. *Medal and Clasp.*

SURGEON J. WHITE,† M.D., Bengal Medical Establishment.

Asst.-Surgeon, 9 March 47—Surgeon, 26 Sept. 60.

SERVICE.—Surgeon WHITE served during the Punjab Campaign, '48, '49 : present at the battles of Chillianwallah and Goojerat. *Medal and 2 Clasps,* and with the Force under Sir W. Gilbert, in pursuit of the Sikhs and Affghans. Served in the Eusuffzaie Country under Brigadier Bradshaw, December '49. Present at Nourhuve when the 55th Native Infantry mutinied, 21st May '57. Served in the Peshawur Division during the Mutiny, '57, '58.

ASSISTANT-SURGEON J. B. WHITE,† Bengal Medical Establishment.

Asst.-Surgeon, 23 July 58.

SERVICE.—Assistant-Surgeon WHITE served in Medical Charge of the Abor Expeditionary Force, in February and March '59. Services mentioned in Despatches of Lieutenant-Colonel Hannay.

ASSISTANT-SURGEON J. H. WHITE,† Bengal Medical Establishment.

Asst.-Surgeon, 29 Jan. 57.

SERVICE.—Assistant-Surgeon WHITE served with the 12th (late 70th) Native Infantry, during the China Campaign, from 21st December '57 to 12th November '58. Served in Medical Charge of 5th Troop, 1st Brigade Horse Artillery, and Field Force under Command of Lieutenant-Colonel Smyth, Horse Artillery, in the Rohilcund District, from 11th February '59 till the breaking up of the Column in April.

CAPTAIN J. S. D. WHITE, P. H., late 40th Native Infantry.

Ensign, 11 June 41—Lieut., 12 Sept. 44—Captain, 6 Aug. 54.

SERVICE.—Captain WHITE served in Burmah in '52 : present at the operations in the vicinity and capture of Rangoon, in April '52. *Medal.* Served in the Bundlecund Campaign of '42, '43. *(Since dead.)*

CAPTAIN M. J. WHITE, P. H., late 26th Native Infantry.

Ensign, 10 Dec. 44—Lieut., 7 June 47—Bt.-Captain, 10 Dec. 59—Captain, 25 July 60.

SERVICE.—Captain WHITE served throughout the Sutlej Campaign, '45, '46 : present at the actions of Moodkee, Ferozeshuhur, and Sobraon. *Medal and Clasp.* (Has attained a degree of proficiency in Punjabee.)

CAPTAIN S. D. WHITE, P. C., late 3rd Europeans.

Ensign, 10 Dec. 44—Lieut., 15 Nov. 53—Bt.-Captain, 10 Dec. 59.

SERVICE.—Captain WHITE served during the Sutlej Campaign, '45, '46 : present at the battle of Sobraon. *Medal and Clasp.* Served throughout the Mutinies, '57, '58. Present at the actions near Agra, 5th July, and near Allyghur, 24th August '57; operations near Shereghur Ghaut, 16th May, and with the Agra Column near Gwalior, June '58. Present with the Column under Brigadier Showers, in the action at Dowsa, January '59, against Tantia Topee. *Medal.* (Received a certificate of high proficiency in Hindee, and has attained the standard of proficiency in Oordoo and Hindee.)

ASSISTANT-SURGEON W. WHITE,† F.R.C.S., Bengal Medical Establishment.

Asst.-Surgeon, 4 July 48.

SERVICE.—Assistant-Surgeon WHITE served with the Army of the Punjab: present at the battle of Goojerat, *Medal;* also served with the expedition to Burmah. Present at the operations in the vicinity and capture of Rangoon, April '52. *Medal.*

LIEUTENANT A. WHITING,† late 59th Native Infantry.

Ensign, 26 Aug. 52—Lieut., 23 Nov. 56.

BREVET-CAPTAIN R. C. WHITING,† late 70th Native Infantry.

Ensign, 8 June 44—Lieut., 31 March 53—Bt.-Captain, 8 June 59.

SERVICE.—Captain WHITING served with the Army of the Punjab at the battles of Chillianwallah and Goojerat. *(Severely wounded.) Medal and Clasp.*

SURGEON-MAJOR R. WHITTALL,† Bengal Medical Establishment.

Asst.-Surgeon, 25 Dec. 40—Surgeon, 31 Dec. 54—Surgeon-Major, 14 June 61.

SERVICE.—Surgeon-Major WHITTALL served with the 26th Native Infantry throughout the Campaign in Affghanistan, under General Pollock, in '42: present at the forcing of the Khyber Pass, at the battles of Mammoo Khel, Jugdulluck, and Tazeen. Served with Sir J. McCaskill's Division in Kohistan, and was present at the capture of Istaliff. *Medal.* Served during the Sutlej Campaign, '45, '46: present at the battle of Sobraon. *Medal.*

(648)

LIEUTENANT J. E. WHITTING, late 68th Native Infantry.

Ensign, 4 Sept. 57—Lieut., 5 Oct. 58.

LIEUTENANT F. E. WIGGENS, General List.

Ensign, 10 Dec. 59—Lieut., 8 Dec. 61.

CAPTAIN E. R. WIGGINS,† late 35th Native Infantry.

Ensign, 8 March 41—Lieut., 24 Jan. 45—Bt.-Captain, 8 March 56—Captain, 4 June 57.

SERVICE.—Captain WIGGINS accompanied the Force under General Pollock. Present at the forcing of the Khyber Pass, and in the different engagements leading to the re-occupation of Cabul. *Medal.* *(Since retired.)*

CAPTAIN F. C. WIGGINS,† late 70th Native Infantry.

Ensign, 8 March 41—Lieut., 18 March 47—Bt.-Captain, 8 March 56—Captain, 11 Jan. 59.

SERVICE.—Captain WIGGINS served with the Army of the Punjab at the battles of Chillianwallah and Goojerat: present at the action of Ramnuggur and passage of the Chenab, and in the subsequent pursuit of the Sikhs and Affghans by the Force under General Gilbert. *Medal and Clasp.* *(Since retired.)*

LIEUTENANT E. R. C. WILCOX, P. H., late 4th Europeans.

Ensign, 13 June 52—Lieut., 18 July 56.

CAPTAIN E. J. WILD, P. H., late 40th Native Infantry.

Ensign, 13 June 46—Lieut., 26 July 52—Captain, 29 Jan. 60.

SERVICE.—Captain WILD served with the Burmah Expedition of '52. Present at the operations in the vicinity and capture of Rangoon, in April '52. *Medal.*

LIEUTENANT-COLONEL D. WILKIE, P., late 4th Native Infantry.

Ensign, 28 Sept. 25—Lieut., 22 Aug. 27—Bt.-Captain, 28 Sept. 40—Captain, 31 March 45—Bt.-Major, 11 Nov. 51—Major, 15 Nov. 53—Lieut.-Colonel, 26 April 51.

(649)

DEPUTY-INSPECTOR-GENERAL OF HOSPITALS, J. WILKIE, M. D., Bengal Medical Establishment.

Asst.-Surgeon, 26 Feb. 33—Surgeon, 17 April 48—Deputy-Inspector-General of Hospitals, 3 Sept. 58.

LIEUTENANT W. H. WILKINS, P. H., Bengal Artillery.

Lieut., 27 Aug. 58.

LIEUTENANT A. R. WILKINSON, General List.

Ensign, 4 Jan. 60—Lieut., 1 Jan. 62.

MAJOR-GENERAL C. D. WILKINSON, C. B., late 6th Europeans.

Ensign, 16 Aug. 11—Lieut., 1 March 16—Captain, 14 June 25—Major, 26 June 33—Lieut.-Colonel, 26 March 40—Colonel, 28 Sept. 50—Major-General, 28 Nov. 54.

SERVICE.—Major-General WILKINSON served during the Sutlej Campaign, '45, '46. Commanded a Brigade at the action of Sobraon. *Medal* and *C.B.*

MAJOR O. WILKINSON, P. H., late 4th Bengal European Cavalry.

Cornet, 27 Jan. 44—Lieut., 12 Aug. 48—Captain, 30 April 58—Bt.-Major, 20 July 58.

SERVICE.—Major WILKINSON served as a Volunteer in the Jullundur Doab, '48, '49 : present at the reduction of Fort Rungul Nungul. Present as a Volunteer with the Army of Punjab: present at Ramnuggur. (*Slightly contused* on the side from a bullet.) *Medal.* As a Volunteer under Sir S. Cotton, against the Momund Tribes, in '54. Served during the Mutiny of '57, '58, and '59; as Sub-Assistant Commissary-General with Brigadier Campbell's advance on Lucknow ; under Sir H. Grant, in Oude, '58. Present at the storm and capture of Meeangunge. (Received a blow on the head from a musket.) Served throughout the final siege and capture of Lucknow, including the repulse of the enemy's attack on Alum Bagh, defeat of a body of Fanatics near Moosah Bagh, and other minor Cavalry skirmishes. Served under Sir E. Lugard. Present at the affair of Tigree, 2 guns captured, capture of Jugdespore, Jhitoorah, Metahi, 2 guns captured, and other skirmishes. Served as Deputy Assistant Quarter-Master-General to the Shahabad Field Force, under Brigadier Douglas. Present throughout the Campaigns in Jugdespore, Khymore Hills, Palamow, Behar, including night surprise of the enemy's Camp at Tulya-Duhar, and affairs at Karee Sath, and Mujowleea. Major Wilkinson was seven times mentioned in Despatches during the Mutiny: by Sir H. Grant, Brigadier Campbell, Sir E. Lugard (twice), Brigadier Douglas (twice), and by Colonel Haggart. Received *Brevet-Major* for services during the Mutiny. *Medal and Clasp.*

LIEUTENANT A. WILLES, late 2nd European Bengal Fusiliers.

2nd Lieut., 9 Dec. 50—Lieut., 22 Nov. 54.

SERVICE.—Lieutenant WILLES was present with his Regiment during the whole of the operations before Delhi, including battle of Badlee-ka-Serai, 8th June '57, final storming and capture of the city on 14th September '57. Served in the Moveable Column under Brigadier Showers, in the District of Delhi. *Medal and Clasp.*

CAPTAIN J. I. WILLES, P., late 69th Native Infantry.

Ensign, 22 Feb. 43—Lieut., 29 May 48—Captain, 11 July 57.

SERVICE.—Captain WILLES served during the Punjab Campaign, '48, '49. *Medal.* Served against the Hill Tribes in Scinde, under Sir Charles Napier, in '45.

VETERINARY-SURGEON A. C. WILLIAMS,† Bengal Veterinary Establishment.

Vety.-Surgeon, 5 Oct. 43.

SERVICE.—Veterinary-Surgeon WILLIAMS served with the Azimghur Field Force under Sir E. Lugard, in '58.

LIEUTENANT B. WILLIAMS,† late 51st Native Infantry.

Ensign, 27 Sept. 54—Lieut., 19 May 57.

(651)

2ND CAPTAIN E. C. S. WILLIAMS, P. H., Bengal Engineers.

2nd Lieut., 9 June 48—Lieut., 1 Aug. 54—2nd Captain, 27 Aug. 58.

SERVICE.—Captain WILLIAMS served with the Burmah Expedition in '52. Present at the operations in the vicinity and capture of Rangoon, in April '52. *(Slightly wounded.) Medal.*

LIEUTENANT F. H. WILLIAMS,† General List.

Ensign, 4 Jan. 60—Lieut., 1 Jan. 62.

BREVET-CAPTAIN G. A. WILLIAMS, P. H., late 26th Native Infantry.

Ensign, 23 Aug. 45—Lieut., 1 April 50—Bt.-Captain, 23 Aug. 60.

SERVICE.—Captain WILLIAMS served with the 4th Sikh Infantry in Burmah, '52, '53, and '54: present with the expedition to the Tonghoo Pass, in the Arracan Mountains, that escorted the elephants that arrived from Bengal to Prome, in February '53—*for this service received one month's batta.* Served with the expedition into the Podonymew District, in February '53; and at the subsequent pursuit and destruction of the King of Ava's Troops under Moung Shoey Moung. Commanded the first Detachment of British Troops that ever crossed the Frontier between Prome and Tonghoo, in January '54. Served with the expedition under Colonel Poole, Madras Army, on the Tonghoo Frontier, in February '54, and on the return of the Detachment back to Prome across the Frontier. Commanded at the storming of the entrenched Village of Yeh. Served in the disturbed Tharrawaddy District, nine months in Command of the advanced out-post of Tapoon. *Medal, Clasp, and six months' batta.* Commanded three Companies of the 4th Sikh Infantry at the engagement in June '57, on the banks of the Sutlej, near Loodiana, with the Jullundur mutineers. *(Dangerously wounded.)* Received thanks of His Excellency the Governor-General in Council. *Medal.*

MAJOR G. W. WILLIAMS, C.B., P., late 29th Native Infantry.

Ensign, 15 May 26—Lieut., 21 Aug. 32—Bt.-Captain, 15 May 41—Captain, 24 Jan. 45—Bt.-Major, 20 June 54—Major, 15 June 57.

ASSISTANT-SURGEON H. F. WILLIAMS,† M.D., Bengal Medical Establishment.

Asst.-Surgeon, 20 Nov. 50.

CAPTAIN H. P. WILLIAMS, P., late 72nd Native Infantry.

Ensign, 18 Jan. 45—Lieut., 20 Feb. 51—Bt.-Captain, 18 Jan. 60—Captain, 21 Oct. 60.

SERVICE.—Captain WILLIAMS served during the Punjab Campaign, '48, '49: present at the siege and surrender of Mooltan, and battle of Goojerat. *Medal and Clasp.*

LIEUTENANT H. W. WILLIAMS, late 64th Native Infantry.

Ensign, 20 Feb. 59—Lieut., 13 July 60.

SURGEON J. WILLIAMS,† F.R.C.S., Bengal Medical Establishment.

Asst.-Surgeon, 19 June 47—Surgeon, 11 Feb. 61.

SERVICE.—Surgeon WILLIAMS served with the 7th Irregular Cavalry throughout the 1st and 2nd sieges of Mooltan, in '48, '49. *Medal and Clasp.* Served also under Sir Colin Campbell against the Hill Tribes in the neighborhood of Peshawur.

LIEUTENANT L. H. WILLIAMS,† late 5th Europeans.

Ensign, 10 Dec. 50—Lieut., 10 April 53.

CAPTAIN J. WILLIAMSON, P. H., late 49th Native Infantry.

Ensign, 20 Jan. 45—Lieut., 13 April 48—Bt.-Captain, 20 Jan. 60—Captain, 18 Feb. 61.

SERVICE.—Captain WILLIAMSON served as Major of Brigade with the Field Force employed in the Meeranzaie Valley, in '55, under Brigadier Chamberlain. Present with the Troops engaged at Dursummund with the Hill Tribes.

LIEUTENANT H. G. WILLIS, Bengal Artillery.

Lieut., 11 Dec. 58.

(653)

LIEUTENANT E. H. WILLOCK, General List, Cavalry.
Cornet, 4 Dec. 59—Lieut., 1 Jan. 62.

LIEUTENANT G. W. WILLOCK, General List, Cavalry.
Cornet, 20 Oct. 59—Lieut., 21 Feb. 61.

ENSIGN W. WILLOCKS, Unattached List.
Ensign, 30 Dec. 58.

CAPTAIN J. E. L. WILLOWS, P. H., late 10th Native Infantry.
Ensign, 23 June 42—Lieut., 29 March 50—Bt.-Captain, 23 June 57—Captain, 11 July 57.
SERVICE.—Captain WILLOWS served in Burmah, '52, '53. *Medal.*

LIEUTENANT R. E. WILMOT, General List.
Ensign, 4 March 60—Lieut., 1 Jan. 62.

MAJOR-GENERAL SIR A. WILSON, *Bt.*, K.C.B., Bengal Artillery.
2nd Lieut., 10 April 19—Lieut., 7 July 20—Bt.-Captain, 10 April 34—Captain, 13 Oct. 34—Lieut.-Colonel, 3 July 45—Bt.-Colonel, 28 Nov. 54—Colonel, 14 Oct. 58—Major-General, 14 Sept. 57.
SERVICE.—Major-General Sir A. WILSON, *Bt.*, K.C.B., was present at the siege and capture of Bhurtpore, in '26, *Medal;* and commanded the Artillery with Brigadier Wheeler's Force in the Jullundur Doab, '48, '49. *Medal.* Served during the Mutiny Campaign. *Medal, Clasps, and K.C.B.*

DEPUTY-INSPECTOR-GENERAL OF HOSPITALS, A. WILSON, Bengal Medical Establishment.
Asst.-Surgeon, 10 March 27—Surgeon, 25 Sept. 43—Deputy-Inspector-General of Hospitals, 30 July 58.

ASSISTANT-SURGEON C. C. W. WILSON,† Bengal Medical Establishment.
Asst.-Surgeon, 26 Aug. 54.

LIEUTENANT F. A. WILSON, Bengal Artillery.
Lieut., 8 June 60.

MAJOR H. M. WILSON, P., late 6th Europeans.

Ensign, 6 July 39—Lieut., 23 Feb. 42—Captain, 22 Oct. 51—Bt.-Major, 24 March 58—Major, 18 Feb. 61.

SERVICE.—Major WILSON served during the Punjab Campaign, '48, '49: present throughout both sieges of Mooltan, including the storming of the Dhurmsalla, action near Sooroojkhoond, and battle of Goojerat. *Medal and 2 Clasps.* Present at the Mutiny of the Native Troops at Jullundur, 7th June '57. Served with the Delhi Field Force during the siege, and present at the storm and capture of Delhi, 22nd September '57. Present at the action of Boolundshuhur, 20th September; Allyghur, 3rd October; battle of Agra, 10th October '57. Served under Lord Clyde at the taking of Dilkoosha and La Martiniere, storming of the Sekunder Bagh, and relief of the Lucknow Garrison, 22nd November '57. Present at the battle of Cawnpore, 6th December '57. *Medal and 2 Clasps.* Promoted to the rank of Brevet-Major for services during the Mutiny. Mentioned in the Despatches of Sir A. Wilson, '57; Lord Clyde, '57 (twice); Lieutenant-Colonel Greathed, '58; and Lieutenant-Colonel Cotton, '57. Received the thanks of Government four times, '57.

ASSISTANT-SURGEON J. WILSON,† Bengal Medical Establishment.

Asst.-Surgeon, 7 May 56.

SERVICE.—Assistant-Surgeon WILSON served with the 4th Sikh Cavalry in Brigadier Showers' Column in pursuit of Tantia Topee and Ferozeshah. Marched from Delhi, 14th January '59, and returned 18th May.

CAPTAIN J. E. D. WILSON,† late 42nd Native Infantry.

Ensign, 20 Jan. 53—Lieut., 7 May 55—Captain, 1 Jan. 62.

MAJOR T. F. WILSON, C.B., P. H., late 13th Native Infantry.

Ensign, 24 April 38—Lieut., 1 July 42—Captain, 15 June 49—Major, 18 Feb. 61.

SERVICE.—Major WILSON commanded a Detached Company of his Regiment (the late 13th Native Infantry) at the capture of the Fort of

"Chirgong," April '41 : the Company had five men *wounded* on the occasion. Mentioned in the Despatches. Commanded a Company of his Regiment at the action of "Punwarree," in Bundlecund, in June '42, when two Companies of the late 13th Native Infantry and a Squadron of the late 8th Light Cavalry defeated upwards of 3,000 Bundeelahs; more than 80 of the enemy, together with their leader, were left dead on the Field, and the two Companies had 20 men killed and wounded. Served throughout the Punjab Campaign of '48, '49 : passage of the Chenab and battle of Goojerat. *Medal and Clasp.* Appointed Deputy Assistant Adjutant-General to the late Sir Henry Lawrence, 21st May '57. Served in the action in the old Cantonments of Lucknow, on the night of the 30th and morning of the 31st May '57, and at the battle of Chinhut, 3rd June '59, with Sir H. Lawrence, when he was mortally hit, and was himself *slightly wounded* by a piece of the same shell. Served as Deputy Assistant Adjutant-General to the old Lucknow Garrison, throughout the entire siege, from the 30th June to 22nd November '57. Prominently mentioned in the Despatches, and thanked in the *Government Gazette*, 8th December '57, " For courage, activity, and sound judgment in a very high degree." Service again acknowledged in *Government Gazette*, 11th January '58. *Medal, Clasp, C.B., and Brevet-Major, and one year's extra service.* Deputy Assistant Adjutant-General to General Windham, at the Bombardment of Cawnpore, December '57 ; at the affairs on the Jumna with Brigadier Herbert's Detachment, December '58. Mentioned in Despatches.

CAPTAIN T. H. WILSON,† late 57th Native Infantry.

Ensign, 27 June 41—Lieut., 31 Dec. 47—Bt.-Captain, 27 June 56— Captain, 17 Nov. 57.

SURGEON-MAJOR T. W. WILSON,† M.D., Bengal Medical Establishment.

Asst.-Surgeon, 14 March 37—Surgeon, 22 Dec. 50—Surgeon-Major, 13 Jan. 60.

BREVET-MAJOR W. WILSON, Bengal Artillery.

2nd Lieut., 10 Dec. 47—Lieut., 3 March 53—2nd Captain, 27 Aug. 58— Bt.-Major, 28 Aug. 58.

(656)

LIEUTENANT E. B. WIMBERLEY, B.A., P. H., late 3rd Europeans.

Ensign, 20 Oct. 55—Lieut., 4 Aug. 57.

SERVICE.—Lieutenant WIMBERLEY served throughout the Mutinies: present at the actions near Agra, against the Neemuch Mutineers, 5th July, and against the Indore and Mhow Insurgents, 10th October; in the engagement at Maun Sing's Garden, near Allyghur, 24th August; the affair at Futtehpore-Sikree, with the Force under Colonel Cotton, 28th October '57. *(Slightly wounded.)* Present also with the Mynpooree Moveable Column in the operation at Shereghur Ghaut (Acting Adjutant), in May, and with the Agra Column towards Gwalior, in June '58. *Medal.*

LIEUTENANT R. J. WIMBERLEY, P. H., General List.

Ensign, 20 Sept. 59—Lieut., 7 July 61.

CAPTAIN W. WINSON, P. H., late 45th Native Infantry.

Ensign, 3 March 50—Lieut., 10 June 53—Captain, 3 March 62.

LIEUTENANT-COLONEL A. WINTLE, P. H., Bengal Artillery.

2nd Lieut., 11 June 41—Lieut., 6 June 43—Captain, 10 March 54—Lieut.-Colonel, 29 April 61.

SERVICE.—Lieutenant-Colonel WINTLE was present at the battle of Maharajpore, '43, *Bronze Star;* and served during the Sutlej Campaign, including the action of Sobraon. *Medal.*

LIEUTENANT A. T .WINTLE, Bengal Artillery.

Lieut., 8 June 60.

BREVET-COLONEL E. WINTLE, late 24th Native Infantry.

Ensign, 20 Sept. 19—Lieut., 25 April 22—Bt.-Captain, 20 Sept. 34—Captain, 5 Feb. 35—Major, 9 July 46—Lieut.-Colonel, 10 July 52—Bt.-Colonel, 28 Nov. 54.

SERVICE.—Colonel WINTLE served with the Force under Brigadier Wheeler during the Punjab Campaign, '48, '49. *Medal. (Since retired.)*

(657)

CAPTAIN E. H. C. WINTLE, P. H., late 61st Native Infantry.

Ensign, 8 Jan. 42—Lieut., 24 Jan. 45—Captain, 23 Nov. 56.

LIEUTENANT H. R. WINTLE, late 28th Native Infantry.

Ensign, 20 Feb. 57—Lieut., 30 April 58.

SERVICE.—Lieutenant WINTLE served during the Mutiny. *Medal.*

LIEUTENANT D. W. WISE, P. H., late 3rd Bengal European Cavalry.

Cornet, 14 April 49—Lieut., 1 Jan. 51.

ASSISTANT-SURGEON J. F. N. WISE,† M. D., Bengal Medical Establishment.

Asst.-Surgeon, 16 July 56.

ASSISTANT-SURGEON J. C. WISHAW,† Bengal Medical Establishment.

Asst.-Surgeon, 23 July 58.

LIEUTENANT-COLONEL W. K. WOOLLEN,† late 19th Native Infantry.

Ensign, 4 Jan. 34—Lieut., 22 Sept. 36—Captain, 24 Jan. 45—Bt.-Major, 28 Nov. 54—Major, 26 Aug. 56—Lieut.-Colonel, 12 Dec. 59.

(Since retired.)

CAPTAIN A. O. WOOD,† late 14th Native Infantry.

Ensign, 14 April 40—Lieut., 1 March 44—Captain, 15 April 54.

SERVICE.—Captain WOOD served during the Gwalior Campaign, '43, '44: present at the battle of Maharajpore. *Bronze Star.* Served during the Sutlej Campaign, '45, '46: present at the defence of Ferozepore and battle of Ferozeshuhur. *Medal. Severely wounded* through the leg by a grape shot at Jhelum, 8th July '57. Was Orderly Officer to Colonel Gerrard under a heavy fire of musketry for twelve consecutive hours.

CAPTAIN J. C. WOOD, P., late 30th Native Infantry.

Ensign, 12 Dec. 45—Lieut., 11 Dec. 51—Captain, 12 Dec. 60.

SERVICE.—Captain WOOD served during the Punjab Campaign, '48, '49: present at the passage of the Chenab and battle of Chillianwallah *(Very severely wounded.) Medal.*

(658)

LIEUTENANT E. H. WOODCOCK, P. H., late 55th Native Infantry.

Ensign, 1 March 47—Lieut., 14 Nov. 54.

SERVICE.—Lieutenant WOODCOCK served with the 1st European Bengal Fusiliers during the latter part of the siege, and at the capture of Delhi. *(Severely wounded.) Medal and Clasp.*

LIEUTENANT H. F. WOODCOCK,† General List.

Ensign, 27 March 60—Lieut., 1 Jan. 62.

LIEUTENANT H. T. WOODCOCK, P. H., General List.

Ensign, 20 Aug. 59—Lieut., 16 May 61.

CAPTAIN S. C. WOODCOCK, P. H., Bengal Artillery.

2nd Lieut., 10 Dec. 41—Lieut., 1 March 44—Captain, 20 Feb. 55.

SERVICE —Captain WOODCOCK was present at the battle of Sobraon, '46. *Medal.*

LIEUTENANT F. H. WOODGATE,† late 11th Native Infantry.

Ensign, 20 Feb. 57—Lieut., 30 April 58.

SERVICE.—Lieutenant WOODGATE served with the Volunteer Cavalry and was present with General Havelock's Force in the advance from Allahabad, in the actions of Futtehpore, Aoung, Pandoo Nuddee, and Cawnpore. Present at Oonao, Busseerutgunge, 29th July '57, and Busseerutgunge, 5th August '59; Barby-ka-Chowkee, Bithoor, Mungulwarra, and Alum Bagh, first assault and relief of Lucknow. Served as Assistant Field Engineer during the remainder of the defence of Lucknow. Present with the Army of occupation under Major-General Sir James Outram, and at the final assault and capture of Lucknow. Commanded the Cavalry of the Kupoorthulla Contingent in all the actions in which that Force was engaged, including the storm and capture of Gohunia, and several minor affairs. Received the thanks of the Right Hon'ble the Governor-General of India in his Order, dated 15th of April '59. *Medal and 2 Clasps.*

(659)

LIEUTENANT H. WOODHOUSE,† P. H., late 30th Native Infantry.
Ensign, 11 Dec. 58—Lieut., 1 Feb. 61.

LIEUTENANT C. L. WOODRUFFE, late 68th Native Infantry.
Ensign, 28 June 58—Lieut., 22 Oct. 58.

VETERINARY-SURGEON J. S. WOODS,† Bengal Veterinary Establishment.
Vety.-Surgeon, 31 May 50.

SURGEON W. WOLLEY, Bengal Invalid Establishment.
Asst.-Surgeon, 24 Aug. 11—Surgeon, 1 June 13.

MAJOR-GENERAL H. L. WORRALL, late 4th Bengal European Cavalry.
Cornet, 16 Aug. 19—Lieut., 22 May 22—Captain, 26 June 26—Major, 12 Jan. 34—Lieut.-Colonel, 12 Nov. 38—Bt.-Colonel, 19 March 49—Colonel, 21 Oct. 52—Major-General, 28 Nov. 54.

LIEUTENANT H. R. B. WORSLEY,† late 47th Native Infantry.
Ensign, 13 June 52—Lieut., 23 Nov. 56.

LIEUTENANT J. H. WORSLEY, late 71st Native Infantry.
Ensign, 19 July 54—Lieut., 31 May 57.

SERVICE.—Lieutenant WORSLEY served throughout the defence of Lucknow, from the 30th of June till the 22nd of November '57; was mentioned in the Despatches of Major-General Sir J. Inglis, and thanked by the Governor-General, 8th December '57. Present with the Force under His Excellency the Commander-in-Chief which drove the Gwalior rebels from Cawnpore, at the actions of Khodagunge and re-occupation of Futtehghur. Was present during the siege and capture of Lucknow in March '58, and at the affairs of Baree and Nuggur, under Sir J. Hope Grant. Commanded a Regiment of Sikh Military Police at the relief of Sandeelah and in the action of Jhummoo, under Brigadier Barker, Royal Artillery. Mentioned in Despatches. Also in the Baiswarrah (Oude), under Brigadier Evelegh, at the action of Poorwah, capture of Simree, the affairs of Beerah and Dhoondeah Khera, and the capture of Doomrah and Trans-Gogra, until end of Oude Campaign. *Medal and 2 Clasps, and one year's extra service.*

LIEUTENANT R. WORSLEY, P. H., late 15th Native Infantry.

Ensign, 12 June 58—Lieut., 30 Oct. 58.

CAPTAIN J. Y. WORTHINGTON, P. H., Bengal Artillery.

2nd Lieut., 11 Dec. 46—Lieut., 3 March 53—2nd Captain, 27 Aug. 58.

SERVICE.—Captain WORTHINGTON was present at the siege and surrender of Mooltan, '48, '49, and action of Goojerat. *Medal.*

ASSISTANT-SURGEON D. WRIGHT,† M.D., A.M., Bengal Medical Establishment.

Asst.-Surgeon, 28 May 58.

CAPTAIN J. A. WRIGHT, P. H., late 28th Native Infantry.

Ensign, 12 June 40—Lieut., 24 Jan. 45—Bt.-Captain, 12 June 55—Captain, 30 April 58.

SERVICE.—Captain WRIGHT served during the Punjab Campaign, '48, '49: present at the affair of Ramnuggur, passage of the Chenab, and battles of Chillianwallah and Goojerat, and subsequent pursuit of the Sikhs and Affghans, by the Force under General Gilbert. *Medal and Clasp.*

MAJOR T. WRIGHT, P., T. C., late 46th Native Infantry.

Ensign, 8 Jan. 42—Lieut., 15 Dec. 44—Captain, 17 April 56—Major in Staff Corps, 8 Jan. 62.

SERVICE.—Major WRIGHT served during the Punjab Campaign, '48, '49: present at the actions of Ramnuggur, Sadoolapore, Chillianwallah, and Goojerat. *Medal and 2 Clasps.* (Passed examination in Surveying.)

ASSISTANT-SURGEON T. P. WRIGHT, Bengal Medical Establishment.

Asst.-Surgeon, 20 Feb. 56.

SERVICE.—Assistant-Surgeon WRIGHT served with the 1st Division of the Goorkha Force, from the Nepal Frontier, through Chumparun, to

Goruckpore, Jounpore, Azimghur, and the South-East Frontier of Oude, from June '57 to March '58, including the affair of Guggah, 13th December '57; the action of Mondree, 20th September '57; capture of Fort Atrowlea, October '57, and its re-capture, November '57. Acting Civil Surgeon of Azimghur, from March to May '58, and was in the retrenchment during the whole period of its investment by *the* rebel Kooer Singh, till relieved by General Lugard, 26th March to 15th April '58. Mentioned in Despatches of General Sir J. H. Franks, and received thanks of Government. *Medal.*

LIEUTENANT-COLONEL F. T. WROUGHTON, C.B., P. H., late 6th Europeans.

Ensign, 18 Feb. 38—Lieut., 3 Oct. 40—Captain, 2 June 47—Bt.-Major, 20 July 58—Major, 10 Oct. 59—Lieut.-Colonel, 1 Jan. 62.

SERVICE.—Lieutenant-Colonel WROUGHTON, C.B., served in the Punjab Campaign, '49 : present throughout the operations in the vicinity, including the attack on the Dhurmsalla, *wounded*, and siege and surrender of Mooltan and battle of Goojerat. *Medal and Clasp.* Served during the Mutinies, '57, '58. Had Military Charge and Command of Colonel Pulwan Sing's Division of Nepalese Troops; with these Troops he kept clear, for four months, the Frontier Districts of Azimghur and Jounpore. Commanded in the affairs of Bughah, 18th August '57, at the attack on the intrenched dwelling of Rajah Idanut Jehan (a noted rebel in the Jounpore District), leading to his capture and execution, after a prolonged bombardment of his house. Present at the affair of Khoodwah on the 19th October '57, which ended in the signal defeat of the enemy, and capture of their camp. Received the thanks of the Lieutenant-Governor, Central Provinces. Commanded at the severe action of Chanda (1st), when 1,000 Goorkhas attacked and beat off 5,000 Oude Troops, capturing their artillery, ammunition, and camp. Received the thanks of the Lieutenant-Governor, Central Provinces. Received the special thanks of the Governor-General in Council in December '57, for services performed whilst in Military Charge of the Nepalese Troops. Marched through Oude with Brigadier-General Franks' Column. Was present at the attack on Chanda (2nd), and affair of Umeerapore, on the 19th

February '58, and battle of Sultanpore, on the 24th of the same month. Was present throughout the siege and capture of Lucknow. Promoted to Major by Brevet. *Medal and Clasps, and C.B.*

CAPTAIN H. R. WROUGHTON, P. C., late 40th Native Infantry.

Ensign, 20 Jan. 45—Lieut., 21 Feb. 51—Captain, 15 Oct. 57.

SERVICE.—Captain WROUGHTON served with the Burmah Expedition: present at the operations in the vicinity and capture of Rangoon, April '52. *Medal.* Served against the Insurgent Sonthals in '55, under Major-General Lloyd. Accompanied the Column under General Franks, as Commissariat Officer. Present at the actions of Chanda, Hameerpoor, Sultanpoor, and siege and capture of Lucknow, '58. *Medal and Clasp.* Served as Commissariat Officer with General Sir H. Grant's Column, Trans-Raptee, in '58, '59.

MAJOR R. C. WROUGHTON, P., late 12th Native Infantry.

Ensign, 13 Jan. 39—Lieut., 24 Aug. 42—Captain, 28 Aug. 53—Major, 1 Jan. 62.

SERVICE.—Major WROUGHTON served throughout the Sutlej Campaign, and was present at the action of Ferozeshuhur. *Medal. (Charger killed under him.)* Served also in Burmah as Sub-Assistant Commissary-General in, '52, '53. *Medal* for Pegu. Served in a Civil capacity with General Wheeler's Force on its march to Cashmere, in '46.

LIEUTENANT W. WROUGHTON, late 54th Native Infantry.

Ensign, 4 Sept. 52—Lieut., 23 Nov. 56.

SERVICE.—Lieutenant WROUGHTON served at Delhi in September '57. Joined the Kumaon Battalion and served with Showers' Column at Jhujjur, Kanoud, and in the Goorgaon District. Commanded Mullick Futteh Shere Khan's Tewanee Horse in the assault and capture of Goosarah and Roopraka. Served in several skirmishes in the Goorgaon District. Served with Ramsay's Column of Observation at Muttra, and Redman's Column in the Ulwar District. *Medal.*

(663)

CAPTAIN W. WYLD, P., late 3rd Bengal European Cavalry.

Cornet, 9 Feb. 36—Lieut., 24 Oct. 39—Captain, 1 Aug. 49.

SERVICE.—Captain WYLD served at the battle of Maharajpore, 29th December '43. *Bronze Star.* Served during the Sutlej Campaign: present at the battles of Moodkee, Ferozeshuhur, and Sobraon. *Horse killed under him. Medal and 2 Clasps.* Mentioned in General White's Despatches. Commanded a Squadron in the Jugadharee and Saharunpore Districts, May to July '57, and was frequently engaged with the Goojurs.

ASSISTANT-SURGEON J. D. WYLIE,† M.D., Bengal Medical Establishment.

Asst.-Surgeon, 4 April 55.

LIEUTENANT G. B. WYMER, Bengal Artillery.

Lieut., 10 June 59.

LIEUTENANT-GENERAL SIR G. P. WYMER, K.C.B., late 38th Native Infantry.

Ensign, 15 Aug. 04—Lieut., 21 Sept. 04—Captain, 1 Aug. 18—Major, 11 July 28—Lieut.-Colonel, 26 Sept. 33—Bt.-Colonel, 23 Dec. 42—Colonel, 10 June 45—Major-General, 20 June 54—Lieut.-General, 8 June 56.

SERVICE.—Lieutenant-General Sir G. P. WYMER, K.C.B., served during the Nepal War, '14, '15. *Medal.* Served in Affghanistan in '39, '40, '41, and '42: present throughout the operations of the Candahar Force under General Nott. *Medal, C.B., and A. D. C. to the Queen.*

CAPTAIN H. P. W. WYNCH, P. H., late 59th Native Infantry.

Ensign, 28 July 49—Lieut., 10 Nov. 51—Captain, 28 July 61.

LIEUTENANT P. H. M. WYNTER, P. H., late 32nd Native Infantry.

Ensign, 4 May 57—Lieut., 18 May 58.

(664)

Y

LIEUTENANT P. S. YORKE,† late 12th Native Infantry.

Ensign, 9 June 55—Lieut., 6 June 57.

SERVICE.—Lieutenant YORKE joined the 2nd Bengal Fusiliers and served with them at Delhi in all actions from the 23rd June to 15th August '57. Joined 2nd Sikh Cavalry in January '58, and served with it in the Delhi District, in Major Ramsay's Column, in May, June, and July '58. *Medal and Clasp.* (Received a 1st class certificate from the Umballah School of Musketry, '57.)

ASSISTANT-SURGEON A. YOUNG,† Bengal Medical Establishment.

Asst.-Surgeon, 20 Oct. 53.

LIEUTENANT-COLONEL C. B. YOUNG, Bengal Engineers.

2nd Lieut., 11 Dec. 35—Lieut., 25 Jan. 41—Bt.-Captain, 11 Dec. 50—Captain, 15 Feb. 54—Lieut.-Colonel, 2 Jan. 60.

SERVICE.— Lieutenant-Colonel YOUNG, C. B., was present at Maharajpore, *Bronze Star;* and served in the Punjab Campaign: present at Chillianwallah and Goojerat. *Medal.* Served in Burmah, '52, '53 : capture of Prome. *Medal.*

CAPTAIN C. M. YOUNG, P., Bengal Artillery.

2nd Lieut., 9 Dec. 42—Lieut., 3 July 45—2nd Captain, 9 Dec. 57—Captain, 14 Jan. 58.

ASSISTANT-SURGEON D. YOUNG,† M. D., Bengal Medical Establishment.

Asst.-Surgeon, 20 March 50.

LIEUTENANT-GENERAL F. YOUNG, late 66th Native Infantry.

Ensign, 19 July 02—Lieut., 18 March 05—Captain, 8 Jan. 16—Major, 21 Jan. 26—Lieut.-Colonel, 1 Nov. 30—Colonel, 3 Oct. 42—Major-General, 20 June 54—Lieut.-General, 18 Feb. 56.

SERVICE.—Lieutenant-General YOUNG served with the Bengal Volunteers at the taking of Balasore, and operations on the Coast, '03, '04 ; with the Army under Lord Lake, in '05. Present at the assault of

Bhurtpore, Nepal War, '14, '15, and '16, including the actions of Nalapanee, Nahun, and Jeetuk. Served in Rajpootanah, in '17, '18. *Medal.* Commanded a Detachment employed in the capture of the Ghurrah of Kooryah, in '24.

LIEUTENANT G. YOUNG, P. H., late 66th Native Infantry.

Ensign, 20 Aug. 58—Lieut., 22 April 60.

LIEUTENANT G. G. YOUNG, P. H., late 16th Native Infantry.

Ensign, 13 June 56—Lieut., 23 Nov. 56.

CAPTAIN H. E. YOUNG,† late 64th Native Infantry.

Ensign, 19 March 39—Lieut., 17 Jan. 41—Captain, 15 Nov. 53.

SERVICE.—Captain YOUNG served throughout the Campaign in Affghanistan, under Sir G. Pollock. Present at the forcing of the Khyber Pass, 5th April '42. *Medal.* Honorably mentioned in Detachment Orders when Commanding the Rear Guard, in the retreat from the Fort Ally Musjid, in the Khyber Pass, Cabul, 24th January '42. In April '42 took a Despatch of great importance from Brigadier Wild, to Major-General Sir J. McCaskill, running the gauntlet through the enemy, from the top of Lundekhanna Pass, in the Khyber, to the foot of it; out of the five sepoys who accompanied him, only two survived, the other three were shot dead. He was thanked by Brigadier Wild, and Sir J. McCaskill, in person. During the retreat from the Fort of Ally Musjid, in the Khyber Pass, Cabul, 24th January '48, Captain Young went back under a very severe fire from the Fort, which the enemy entered the moment it was evacuated by the English Force, and saved the life of Ensign R. M. Nott, now Captain, in the 64th Native Infantry, who was lying in a deserted doolee, prostrate from sickness; also rallied a party of one Havildar and some 20 Sepoys, which he headed, and who were the means of saving the lives of one Native Officer and several Sepoys. The above was done in the face of a victorious and barbarous enemy.

LIEUTENANT H. G. YOUNG, Bengal Artillery.

Lieut., 27 Aug. 58.

(666)

LIEUTENANT H. L. YOUNG,† General List.
Ensign, 4 March 60—Lieut., 1 Jan. 62.

LIEUTENANT H. R. YOUNG, P. H., late 31st Native Infantry.
Ensign, 20 Jan. 59—Lieut., 4 June 60.

LIEUTENANT-COLONEL J. YOUNG, P. H., Bengal Artillery.
2nd Lieut., 11 June 39—Lieut., 17 Aug. 41—Captain, 3 March 53—Bt.-Major, 19 Jan. 58—Lieut.-Colonel, 18 Feb. 61.

SERVICE.—Lieutenant-Colonel YOUNG served throughout the siege of Delhi, '57, including the action of Badlee-ka-Serai. *Wounded slightly* before Delhi. *Medal and Clasp.* Mentioned in the Despatch of Sir A. Wilson, 5th November '57. Promoted to the rank of Brevet-Major for services before Delhi, 5th March '58.

LIEUTENANT J. M. YOUNG, Bengal Artillery.
Lieut., 27 Aug. 58.

CAPTAIN J. N. YOUNG, P., late 3rd Europeans.
Ensign, 21 Aug. 40—Lieut., 16 July 42—Bt.-Captain, 21 Aug. 55—Captain, 9 Dec. 54.

SERVICE.—Captain YOUNG served with the 53rd Native Infantry at the forcing of the Khyber Pass by the Troops under General Pollock, and the march on Jellallabad, and with the 35th Light Infantry, at the forcing of the Jugdulluck Pass, the action in the Tazeen Valley, the defeat of Mahomed Akbar Khan, on the Huft-Kohtul, and the occupation of Cabul, '42. *Medal.*

BREVET-LIEUTENANT-COLONEL K. YOUNG, C.B., P. C., late 50th Native Infantry.
Ensign, 16 Jan. 24—Lieut., 13 May 25—Bt.-Captain, 16 Jan. 39—Captain, 14 June 44—Bt.-Major, 11 Nov. 51—Major, 19 May 58—Bt.-Lieut.-Colonel, 12 Oct. 57.

SERVICE.—Lieutenant-Colonel YOUNG served in the operations in Bundlecund, Saugor, and Nerbudda Territories, in '42, '43. Served with the Delhi Field Force, from May to September '57, as Judge Advocate-General of the Army. Present at the actions of Badlee-ka-Serai, 8th June '57, and at the assault and operations before Delhi, and capture of that city, on the 14th September '57. Served as Judge Advocate-General with the Army of Lucknow, from February to April '58. *Medal and 2 Clasps.* Mentioned in the following Despatches of Major-General Sir H. Barnard, 8th June '57; of that of Major-General J. Reed, 14th July '57 and 17th July '57; of Major-General Sir A. Wilson, 22nd September '57; of His Excellency the Commander-in-Chief, 22nd March '58. Received the thanks of Government, 5th November '57, 4th December '57, and 5th April '58. Received the Order of Campanion of the Bath, 18th June '58. *(Since dead.)*

CAPTAIN R. YOUNG, P. H., Bengal Engineers.

2nd Lieut., 7 June 44—Lieut., 16 June 50—Captain, 27 April 58.

SERVICE.—Captain YOUNG served during the Sutlej Campaign. Present at the siege of Kôt Kangra, in April '46. Served throughout the siege of Mooltan, and was noticed by General Whish in his Order, 23rd January '49. *Medal.* Commanded 2,000 Irregulars and reduced the Fort of Hurrund, in the Lower Derajat, and disarmed the disaffected Futleypultun, for which he received the warm approbation of the Governor-General.

LIEUTENANT W. S. YOUNG,† 8th (late 59th) Native Infantry.

Ensign, 13 June 51—Lieut., 3 Aug. 55.

LIEUTENANT G. D. A. YOUNGHUSBAND,† late 66th Native Infantry.

Ensign, 12 Dec. 56—Lieut., 3 April 58.

SERVICE.—Lieutenant YOUNGHUSBAND served in the defence of the Kumaon Hills against the rebels in '57, '58. Present at Chapoorah, 10th February; with Brigadier Troop's Column during the Oude Campaign; present at the actions of Pusgaon, 19th, and Russulpore, 25th October; attack and capture of Fort Mittowlee, 8th November; and action of Bisawah, 1st December '58. *Medal.*

LIEUTENANT-COLONEL H. YULE, P., Bengal Engineers.

2nd Lieut., 11 Dec. 38—Lieut., 1 Jan. 42—2nd Captain, 11 Dec. 53—Captain, 1 Aug. 54—Lieut.-Colonel, 18 Feb. 61.

SERVICE.—Lieutenant-Colonel YULE served in the Sutlej Campaign, *Medal;* and in the Punjab Campaign, at the action of Chillianwallah. *Medal.* *(Since retired.)*

DATES

ON WHICH THE
VARIOUS REGIMENTS
OF THE
LATE BENGAL ARMY
WERE RAISED.

1st	Lt. Cavalry,	7th Dec.	1787	6th	Lt. Cavalry,	29th May	1800
2nd	,,	22nd Jan.	1842	7th	,,	5th Apl.	1805
3rd	,,	3rd Oct.	1796	8th	,,	5th Apl.	1805
4th	,,	20th Feb.	1797	9th	,,	13th May	1825
5th	,,	29th May	1800	10th	,,	13th May	1825

1st Fusiliers raised,		1754	3rd	Europeans,	15th Nov. 1853
,, so designated, 11th April	1848	4th	,,	3rd Sept. 1858
2nd ditto raised,		1839	5th	,,	3rd Sept. 1858
,, so designated, 18th Jan.	1850	6th	,,	3rd Sept. 1858

1st	Regt.	Native Infantry,	1775	19th	Regt.	Native Infantry,		1776
2nd	,,	,, ,,	1762	20th	,,	,,	,,	1776
3rd	,,	,, ,,	1763	21st	,,	,,	,,	1776
4th	,,	,, ,,	1763	22nd	,,	,,	,,	1778
5th	,,	,, ,,	1758	23rd	,,	,,	,,	1778
6th	,,	,, ,,	1763	24th	,,	,,	,,	1779
7th	,,	,, ,,	1763	25th	,,	,,	,,	1795
8th	,,	,, ,,	1763	26th	,,	,,	,,	1797
9th	,,	,, ,,	1761	27th	,,	,,	,,	1797
10th	,,	,, ,,	1763	28th	,,	,,	,,	1797
11th	,,	,, ,,	1763	29th	,,	,,	,,	1797
12th	,,	,, ,,	1763	30th	,,	,,	,,	1798
13th	,,	,, ,,	1764	31st	,,	,,	,,	1798
14th	,,	,, ,,	1764	32nd	,,	,,	,,	1798
15th	,,	,, ,,	1764	33rd	,,	,,	,,	1798
16th	,,	,, ,,	1765	34th	,,	,,	,,	1846
17th	,,	,, ,,	1765	35th	,,	,,	,,	1798
18th	,,	,, ,,	1765	36th	,,	,,	,,	1800

37th Regt. Native Infantry,				1800	56th Regt. Native Infantry,			1815
38th	,,	,,	,,	1800	57th	,,	,,	,,	1815
39th	,,	,,	,,	1800	58th	,,	,,	,,	1815
40th	,,	,,	,,	1802	59th	,,	,,	,,	1815
41st	,,	,,	,,	1803	60th	,,	,,	,,	1815
42nd	,,	,,	,,	1803	61st	,,	,,	,,	1823
43rd	,,	,,	,,	1803	62nd	,,	,,	,,	1823
44th	,,	,,	,,	1803	63rd	,,	,,	,,	1828
45th	,,	,,	,,	1803	64th	,,	,,	,,	1823
46th	,,	,,	,,	1803	65th	,,	,,	,,	1823
47th	,,	,,	,,	1824	66th	,,	,,	27th Feb, 1850
48th	,,	,,	,,	1804	67th	,,	,,	,,	1823
49th	,,	,,	,,	1804	68th	,,	,,	,,	1823
50th	,,	,,	,,	1804	69th	,,	,,	,,	1825
51st	,,	,,	,,	1804	70th	,,	,,	,,	1825
52nd	,,	,,	,,	1840	71st	,,	,,	,,	1325
53rd	,,	,,	,,	1804	72nd	,,	,,	,,	1825
54th	,,	,,	,,	1804	73rd	,,	,,	,,	1825
55th	,,	,,	,,	1815	74th	,,	,,	,,	1825

THE
ARMY ON THE BENGAL ESTABLISHMENT,
EXCLUSIVE OF
REGIMENTS OF EUROPEANS
OF
HER MAJESTY'S ARMY.

NATIVE INFANTRY REGIMENTS.

21st Regiment Native Infantry has become 1st Regiment Native Infantry.

31st	,,	,,	,,	2nd*	,,	,,
32nd	,,	,,	,,	3rd	,,	,,
33rd	,,	,,	,,	4th	,,	,,
42nd	,,	,,	,,	5th*	,,	,,
43rd	,,	,,	,,	6th*	,,	,,
47th	,,	,,	,,	7th	,,	,,
59th	,,	,,	,,	8th	,,	,,
63rd	,,	,,	,,	9th	,,	,,
65th	,,	,,	,,	10th	,,	,,
70th	,,	,,	,,	11th	,,	,,
Kelat-i-Ghilzie Regiment			,,	12th (The Kelat-i-Ghilzie) Regt. N. I.		
Shekhawattee Battalion			,,	13th (The Shekhawattee)		,,
Regiment of Ferozepore			,,	14th (The Ferozepore)		,,
,, ,, Loodianah			,,	15th (The Loodianah)		,,
,, ,, Lucknow			,,	16th (The Lucknow)		,,
Loyal Poorbeah Regiment			,,	17th (The Loyal Poorbeah)		,,
Alipore Regiment			,,	18th (The Alipore) Regt. N. I.		,,
7th Punjab Infantry			,,	19th (Punjab) Regt. N. I.		
8th	,,		,,	20th	,,	,,
9th	,,		,,	21st	,,	,,
11th	,,		,,	22nd	,,	,,
15th	,,		,,	23rd	,,	,,(Pioneers.)
16th	,,		,,	24th	,,	,,
17th	,,		,,	25th	,,	,,
18th	,,		,,	26th	,,	,,
19th	,,		,,	27th	,,	,,
20th	,,		,,	28th	,,	,,
21st	,,		,,	29th	,,	,,

* These Corps still retain the honorary designation of "Light Infantry," *vide* paragraph 12 of G. G. O. No. 400 of 1861.

NATIVE INFANTRY REGIMENTS.—(*Continued.*)

22nd Punjab Infantry	has become	30th (Punjab) Regt. N. I.
23rd ,,	,,	31st ,, ,,
24th ,,	,,	32nd ,, ,, (Pioneers.)
Allahabad Levy	,,	33rd (The Allahabad) Regt. N. I.
Futtehghur ,,	,,	34th (The Futtehghur) ,,
Mynpoorie ,,	,,	35th (The Mynpoorie) ,,
Bareilly ,,	,,	36th (The Bareilly) ,,
Meerut ,,	,,	37th (The Meerut) ,,
Agra ,,	,,	38th (The Agra) ,,
Allygurh ,,	,,	39th (The Allygurh) ,,
Shahjehanpore Levy	,,	40th (The Shahjehanpore) ,,
1st Gwalior Infantry	,,	41st (The Gwalior) ,,
1st Assam Light Infantry Battalion	,,	42nd (Assam) Light Infantry.
2nd ,, ,, ,,	,,	43rd (Assam) ,,
Sylhet ,, ,, ,,	,,	44th (Sylhet) ,,

GOORKHA REGIMENTS.

66th or Goorkha Regiment	... 1st Goorkha Regiment.*
Sirmoor Rifle Regiment	... 2nd Goorkha (The Sirmoor Rifle) Regiment.
Kemaoon Battalion	... 3rd Goorkha (The Kemaoon) Regiment.
Extra Goorkha Regiment	... 4th Goorkha Regiment.
25th Punjab Infantry (or Hazara Goorkha) Battalion	... 5th Goorkha Regiment. [Attached to P. I. F.]

EUROPEAN CAVALRY.

19th Hussars.	21st Hussars.
20th ,,	

EUROPEAN INFANTRY.

101st Royal Fusiliers.	107th Regiment of Foot.
104th Regiment of Foot.	

NATIVE CAVALRY.

1st Bengal Cavalry, now 1st Irr. Cavalry.			6th Bengal Cavalry, now 8th Irr. Cavalry.			
2nd	,,	2nd ,,	7th	,,	17th	,,
3rd	,,	4th ,,	8th	,,	18th	,,
4th	,,	6th ,, —	9th	,,	1st Hodson's Horse.	
5th	,,	7th ,,	10th	,,	2nd	,,

Vide G. G. O. No. 400 of 3rd May, and No. 990 of 29th October 1861.
* This Corps still retains the honorary designation of "Light Infantry," *vide* paragraph 12 of G. G. O. No. 400 of 1861.

NATIVE CAVALRY.—(Continued.)

11th Bengal Cavalry, now 1st Seikh Cavalry.
12th   „   2nd   „
13th   „   4th   „
14th   „   Murray's Jat Horse.
15th   „   Cureton's Mooltanee Cavy.
16th Bengal Cavalry, now Rohilcund Horse.
17th   „   Robart's Horse.
18th   „   2nd Mahratta Horse.
19th   „   Fane's Horse.

ROYAL BENGAL ARTILLERY.
2ND ROYAL HORSE BRIGADE.*

1st Troop 1st Brigade Bengal Artillery will become   A Battery.
2nd   „   „   B   „
3rd   „   „   C   „

4th Troop 1st Brigade Bengal Artillery will become D Battery.
5th   „   „   E   „
1st Troop 3rd Brigade   F   „
2nd   „   „   G   „

5TH ROYAL HORSE BRIGADE.

1st Troop 2nd Brigade Bengal Horse Artillery will become   A Battery.
2nd   „   „   B   „
3rd   „   „   C   „

4th Troop 2nd Brigade Bengal Horse Artillery will become   D Battery.
3rd Troop 3rd Brigade   E   „
4th   „   „   F   „

16TH BRIGADE ROYAL ARTILLERY.

1st Co. 1st Battalion will become No. 1 Battery.
2nd   „   „   2   „
3rd   „   „   3   „

4th Co. 1st Battalion will become No. 4 Battery.
1st Co. 6th   „   „   5   „

19TH BRIGADE ROYAL ARTILLERY.

1st Co. 2nd Battalion No. 1 Battery.
2nd   „   „   2   „
3rd   „   „   3   „

4th Co. 2nd Battalion No. 4 Battery.
2nd Co. 6th Brigade   „   5   „

22ND BRIGADE ROYAL ARTILLERY.

1st Co. 3rd Battalion No. 1 Battery.
2nd   „   „   2   „
3rd   „   „   3   „

4th Co. 3rd Battalion No. 4 Battery.
3rd Co. 6th Battalion   „   5   „

24TH BRIGADE ROYAL ARTILLERY.

1st Co. 4th Battalion No. 1 Battery.
2nd   „   „   2   „
3rd   „   „   3   „

4th Co. 4th Battalion No. 4 Battery.
4th Co. 6th Battalion   „   5   „

25TH BRIGADE ROYAL ARTILLERY.

1st Co. 5th Battalion No. 1 Battery.
2nd   „   „   2   „

3rd Co. 5th Battalion No. 3 Battery.
4th   „   „   4   „

BENGAL ENGINEERS.

---

* Vide G. G. O., No. 494 and 924, of 1861.

HONORARY DISTINCTIONS

Have been granted to the undermentioned Regiments, in commemoration of their Services, in the following Campaigns, Battles, Actions, &c.

ARTILLERY REGIMENT—*Ubique.*

Plassey, battle of ...... 23rd June 1857.
G. G. O., 23rd Feb. 1829. { 1st European Bengal Fusiliers. 1st Native Infantry.

Buxar, battle of ...... 23rd Oct. 1764.
G. G. O., 23rd Feb. 1829. { 1st European Bn. Fus. 2nd N. Infantry (Grs.) 3rd ditto. 5th ditto. 8th ditto. 9th ditto. 10th ditto.

Korah, battle of ...... 10th June 1776.
G. G. O., 23rd Feb. 1829. { 1st Native Infantry. 10th ditto... 2 Honorary colors.

Guzerat, campaign in, from 1778 to 1784 inclusive.
G. G. O., 23rd Feb. 1829. { 1st European Bn. Fus. 2nd N. Infantry (Grs.) 3rd ditto. 5th ditto. 7th ditto. 11th ditto. 13th ditto.

Carnatic, campaign in the, from 1781 to 1784 inclusive.
G. G. O., 23rd Feb. 1829. { 4th Native Infantry. 5th ditto. 12th ditto. 22nd ditto.

Mysore, campaign in the, from 1790 to 1793 inclusive.
G. G. O., 23rd Feb. 1829. { 4th Native Infantry. 6th ditto. 13th ditto. 16th ditto (Grs.)

Seringapatam, assault and capture of, 4th May 1799.
G. G. O., 23rd Feb. 1829. { 14th Native Infantry. 16th ditto (Grs.) 36th ditto. 37th ditto. 38th ditto (L. I.) 39th ditto.

Allyghur, action near, and assault and capture of, 29th Aug. and 4th Sept. 1803.
G. G. O., 23rd Feb. 1829. { 7th N. I. 23rd ditto. 35th do. (L. I.) } { Honorary colors, and extra Jemadars.

Delhi, battle of......... 11th Sept. 1803.
G. G. O., 23rd Feb. 1829. { 2d Lt. Cavy.† 3rd ditto.† 1st N. I. 5th ditto. 22nd ditto. 23rd ditto. 28th ditto. } Honorary standards, colors, and extra Jemadars.

G. O. C. C., 15th Aug. 1839. } 29th Native Infantry.

G. G. O., 23rd Feb. & 25th Apl. 1829. { 30th ditto. 31st ditto. 35th do. (L. I.) } { Honorary colors, and extra Jemadars.

Laswarrie, battle of.... 1st Nov. 1803.
G. G. O., 23rd Feb. 1829. { 1st Light Cavalry. 2nd ditto.† 3rd ditto. 4th ditto (Lancers). 6th ditto.

---

† *Vide* G. G. O. No. 553 of 24th October 1851.

Laswarrie, battle of ......1st Nov. 1803.
G. G. O., 23rd Feb. 1829.
- 1st Native Infantry.
- 12th ditto.
- 21st ditto.
- 24th ditto.
- 30th ditto.
- 31st ditto.
- 33rd ditto.

Deig, battle of ...... 13th Nov. 1804.
G. G. O., 23rd Feb. 1829.
- 2nd Light Cavalry.
- 3rd ditto. †
- 1st Eur. B. Fusiliers.
- 5th Native Infantry.
- 7th ditto.
- 9th ditto.
- 30th ditto.
- 31st ditto.
- 44th ditto.

Java, campaign in, Aug. and Sept. 1811.
G. G. O., 23rd Feb. 1829.
- Gov. Genl.'s Body Guard.
- 25th Native Infantry.
- 40th ditto.

Seetabuldie, Cavalry charge .... 27th November 1817.
- 6th Light Cavalry.

Bhurtpore, assault and capture of, 18th January 1826.
G. G. O., 30th May 1826.
- 3rd Light Cavalry.
- 4th ditto (Lancers).
- 6th ditto.
- 8th ditto.
- 9th ditto.
- 10th ditto.
- 1st European Bn. Fus.
- 6th Native Infantry.
- 11th ditto.
- 15th ditto.
- 18th ditto.
- 21st ditto.
- 23rd ditto.
- 31st ditto.
- 32nd ditto.
- 33rd ditto.
- 35th ditto (L. I.)
- 36th ditto.
- 37th ditto.
- 41st ditto.
- 58th ditto.
- 60th ditto.
- 63rd ditto.
- 1st Irregular Cavalry.

Arracan, campaign in, from 1824 to 1826 inclusive.
G. G. O., 22nd April 1826.
- 26th N. Infantry (L. I.)
- 40th ditto.
- 42nd ditto (L. I.)
- 49th ditto.
- 62nd ditto.
- 2nd Irregular Cavalry.

Assam, campaign in, from 1824 to 1826 inclusive.
G. G. O., 22nd April 1826.
- 46th Native Infantry.
- 57th ditto.

Ava, campaign in, from 1824 to 1826 inclusive.
G. G. O., 22nd April 1826.
- Governor Genl.'s Body Guard.
- 40th Native Infantry.

Affghanistan, campaign in, 1838-39.
G. O. G., 19th Nov. 1839.
- 2nd Light Cavalry.†
- 3rd ditto.†
- 1st European Bn. Fus.
- 16th N. Infantry (Grs.)
- 31st ditto.
- 35th ditto (L. I.)
- 37th ditto.
- 42nd ditto } (L. I.)
- 43rd ditto }
- 48th ditto.
- 4th Irregular Cavalry.

Ghuznee, assault and capture of, 23rd July 1839.
G. O. G. G., 19th Nov. 1839.
- 2nd Light Cavalry.†
- 3rd ditto.†
- 1st European Bn. Fus.
- 16th N. Infantry (Grs.)
- 35th ditto (L. I.)
- 48th ditto.
- 4th Irregular Cavalry.

Kelat, assault and capture of, 13th November 1839.
G. O. G. G., 15th Feb. 1840.
- 31st Native Infantry.

Kelat-i-Ghilzie, defence of.........1842.
G. O. G. G., 4th Oct. 1842.
- Kelat-i-Ghilzie Regt.

---

† *Vide* G. G. O. No. 553 of 24th October 1851.

Candahar, actions, &c., in the vicinity of, 1842.

G. O. G. G., 4th Oct. and 13th Dec. 1842,
- 2nd N. Infy. ⎫
- 16th ditto ⎬ (Grs.)
- 38th ditto ⎫
- 42nd ditto ⎬ (L. I.)
- 43rd ditto ⎭
- Kelat-i-Ghilzie Regt.
- 1st Irregular Cavalry.

Ghuznee, re-capture of, 6th Sept. 1842.

G. O. G. G., 4th October 1842.
- 2nd N. Infy. ⎫
- 16th ditto ⎬ (Grs.)
- 38th ditto ⎫
- 42nd ditto ⎬ (L. I.)
- 43rd ditto ⎭
- Kelat-i-Ghilzie Regt.

Cabul, capture of......17th Sept. 1842.

G. O. G. G., 4th Oct. & 8th Nov. 1842.
- 1st Light Cavalry.
- 5th ditto.
- 10th ditto.
- 2nd N. Infantry (Grs.)
- 6th ditto
- 16th ditto (Grs.)
- 26th ditto (L. I.)
- 30th ditto.
- 33rd ditto.
- 35th ditto
- 38th ditto ⎬ (L. I.)
- 42nd ditto
- 43rd ditto
- 53rd ditto.
- 60th ditto.
- 64th ditto.
- Kelat-i-Ghilzie Regt.
- 3rd Irregular Cavalry.

Jellalabad, defence and battle of, 27th April 1842.

G. O. G. G., 30th April 1842.
- 5th Light Cavalry.
- 35th N. Infantry (L. I.)

Meeanee, battle of...... 17th Feb. 1843.

G. O. G. G., 5th Mar. & 11th April 1843.
- 9th Light Cavalry.

Hyderabad, battle of...24th Mar. 1843.

G. O. G. G., 11th April 1843.
- 9th Light Cavalry.

Maharajpore, battle of, 29th Dec. 1843.

G. O. G. G., 4th Jan. 1844.
- Govr. Genl.'s Body Guard.
- 1st Light Cavalry.
- 4th ditto (Lancers).
- 5th ditto ⎫ Detach-
- 8th ditto ⎬ ments.
- 10th ditto.
- 2nd N. Infantry (Grs.)
- 14th ditto.
- 16th ditto (Grs.)
- 31st ditto.
- 39th ditto (6th Co.)
- 43rd ditto (L. I.)
- 56th ditto.
- Kelat-i-Ghilzie Regt. (flank Companies.)
- 4th Irregular Cavalry.

Punniar, battle of...... 29th Dec. 1843.

G. O. G. G., 4th Jan. 1844.
- 2nd Lt. Cavy. (2 Squad.)
- 5th ditto (2 Squad.)
- 8th ditto.
- 39th Native Infantry.
- 50th ditto.
- 51st ditto.
- 58th ditto.
- 8th Irregular Cavalry.

Moodkee, battle of...... 18th Dec. 1845.

G. O. G. G., 12th Aug. 1846.
- Govr. Genl.'s Body Guard.
- 4th Lt. Cavy (Lancers).
- 5th ditto.
- 2nd N. Infantry ⎫
- 16th ditto ⎬ (Grs.)
- 24th ditto.
- 26th Light Infantry.
- 42nd ditto
- 45th Native Infantry.
- 47th ditto.
- 48th ditto.
- 73rd ditto.
- 4th Irr. Cavy. ⎫
- 8th ditto ⎬ Detachts.
- 9th ditto.

Ferozeshuhur, battle of, 21st and 22nd December 1845.

G. O. G. G., 12th Aug. 1846.
- Govr. Genl.'s Body Guard.
- 4th Lt. Cavy. (Lancers.)
- 5th ditto.
- 8th ditto.

Ferozeshuhur, battle of, 21st and 22nd December 1845.

G. O. G. G., 12th Aug. 1846.
- 1st European Bn. Fus.
- 2nd N. Infantry (Grs.)
- 12th ditto.
- 14th ditto.
- 16th ditto (Grs.)
- 24th ditto.
- 26th ditto (L. I.)
- 33rd ditto.
- 42nd ditto (L. I.)
- 44th ditto.
- 45th ditto.
- 47th ditto.
- 48th ditto.
- 54th ditto.
- 73rd ditto.
- 3rd Irregular Cavalry.
- 4th ditto ⎫
- 8th ditto ⎬ Detachments.
- 9th ditto ⎭

Aliwal, battle of......28th Jan. 1846.

G. O. G. G., 12th Aug. 1846.
- Govr. Genl.'s Body Guard.
- 1st Light Cavalry.
- 3rd ditto.
- 5th ditto.
- 24th Native Infantry.
- 30th ditto.
- 36th ditto.
- 47th ditto.
- 48th ditto.
- 66th or Goorkha Regt.
- 4th Irregular Cavalry.
- Nusseree Battalion.
- Sirmoor Battalion.
- Shekhawattee Brigade (now Battalion.)

Sobraon, battle of......10th Feb. 1846.

G. O. G. G., 12th Aug. 1846.
- Govr.-Genl.'s Body Guard.
- 3rd Light Cavalry.
- 4th ditto (Lancers).
- 5th ditto.
- 1st European Bn. Fus.
- Det. 1st Co. 7th N. Infy.
- 16th N. Infantry (Grs.)
- 26th ditto (L. I.
- 33rd ditto.
- 41st ditto.
- 42nd ditto ⎱ (L. I.)
- 43rd ditto ⎰
- 47th ditto.
- 59th ditto.
- 63rd ditto.

Sobraon, battle of......10th Feb. 1846.

G. O. G. G., 12th Aug. 1846.
- 66th or Goorkha Regt.
- 68th Native Infantry.
- The Head-quarters and Rt. Wing, 2nd Irr. Cav.
- 8th Irregular Cavalry.
- 9th ditto.
- Nusseree Battalion.
- Sirmoor Battalion.

Punjab, campaign in......1848 & 1849.

G. G. O., 7th Oct. 1853.
- 1st Light Cavalry.
- 5th ditto.
- 6th ditto.
- 7th ditto.
- 8th ditto.
- 11th ditto (now 2nd.)
- 2nd European Ben. Fus.
- 1st Native Infantry.
- 3rd ditto.
- 4th ditto.
- 8th ditto.
- 13th ditto.
- 15th ditto.
- 18th ditto.
- 20th ditto.
- 22nd ditto.
- 25th ditto.
- 29th ditto.
- 30th ditto.
- 31st ditto.
- 36th ditto.
- 37th ditto.
- 45th ditto.
- 46th ditto.
- 49th ditto.
- 50th ditto.
- 51st ditto.
- 52nd ditto.
- 53rd ditto.
- 56th ditto.
- 69th ditto.
- 70th ditto.
- 71st ditto.
- 72nd ditto.
- 73rd ditto.
- 2nd Irregular Cavalry.
- 3rd ditto.
- 7th ditto.
- 9th ditto.
- 11th ditto.
- 12th ditto.
- 13th ditto.
- 14th ditto.

Punjab, campaign in......1848 & 1849.

G. G. O.,
7th Oct.
1853.
- 15th Irregular Cavalry.
- 16th ditto (the Head Qrs. and Detachments.)
- 17th ditto (Left Wing).
- 1st Sikh Local Infy.
- 2nd ditto.
- Corps of Guides (Det.)

Mooltan, siege of....22nd Jan. 1849.

G. G. O.,
7th Oct.
1853.
- 11th (now 2nd) Lt. Cavy.
- 8th Native Infantry.
- 49th ditto.
- 51st ditto.
- 52nd ditto.
- 72nd ditto.
- 7th Irregular Cavalry.
- 11th ditto.
- 14th ditto } (Det.)
- Corps of Guides

Chillianwalla, battle of....13th Jan· 1849.

G. G. O.,
7th Oct.
1853.
- 1st Light Cavalry.
- 5th ditto.
- 6th ditto.
- 8th ditto.
- 2nd European Ben. Fus.
- 15th Native Infantry.
- 20th ditto.
- 25th ditto.
- 30th ditto.
- 31st ditto.
- 36th ditto.
- 45th ditto.
- 46th ditto.
- 56th ditto.
- 69th ditto.
- 70th ditto.
- 3rd Irregular Cavalry.
- 9th ditto.

Guzerat, battle of....21st Feb. 1849.

G. G. O.,
7th Oct.
1853.
- 1st Light Cavalry.
- 5th ditto.
- 6th ditto.
- 8th ditto.
- 2nd European Ben. Fus.
- 8th Native Infantry.
- 13th ditto.
- 15th ditto.
- 20th ditto.
- 25th ditto.
- 30th ditto.
- 31st ditto.
- 36th ditto.
- 45th ditto.
- 46th ditto.
- 51st ditto.
- 52nd ditto.
- 56th ditto.
- 69th ditto.
- 70th ditto.
- 72nd ditto.
- 3rd Irregular Cavalry.
- 9th ditto.
- 11th ditto.
- 12th ditto
- 13th ditto.
- 14th ditto (Detachment.)
- Corps of Guides (Det.)

Pegu, campaign in.

G. O. P. C.,
18th May
1855.
- 1st European Ben. Fus.
- 2nd ditto. Head Qrs. and 4 Comps.
- 10th Native Infantry.
- 40th ditto.
- 67th ditto.
- 68th ditto.
- 4th Sikh Local Infy.
- Arracan Local Battalion.
- Ramgurh Irregular Cavy.

N. B.—Original dates of raising the several Corps were published in G. O. G. G., 20th May 1824—Revised ditto first inserted in the "Adjutant General's Quarterly Army List" for October 1844.

MUTINY.*
1857.

HORSE ARTILLERY.

The SPHINX, *with the words* "EGYPT," "AVA," *and* "BHURTPORE."

1st brigade, head quarters, "Bhurtpore." "Moodkee." "Ferozeshuhur." "Subraon." "Punjab." "Chillianwalla." "Guzerat."
1st troop, "Egypt." "Deig." "Ava." "Moodkee." "Ferozeshuhur." "Alliwal."
2nd troop, "Bhurtpore." "Moodkee." "Ferozeshuhur." "Subraon." "Punjab."
3rd troop, "Cabul, 1842." "Moodkee." "Ferozeshuhur." "Subraon." "Punjab."
2nd brigade, head quarters, "Bhurtpore." "Alliwal." "Subraon." "Punjab." "Chillianwalla." "Guzerat."
1st troop, "Bhurtpore." "Alliwal." "Subraon." "Punjab." "Chillianwalla." "Guzerat."
2nd troop, "Bhurtpore." "Ava." "Ghuznee." "Affghanistan." "Maharajpore." "Subraon." "Punjab." "Chillianwalla." "Guzerat."
3rd troop, "Bhurtpore." "Cabul, 1842." "Maharajpore." "Alliwal." "Subraon." "Punjab." "Chillianwalla." Guzerat."
3rd brigade, head quarters, "Bhurtpore." "Ferozeshuhur." "Subraon." "Punjab." "Chillianwalla." "Guzerat."
1st troop, "Bhurtpore." "Punniar." "Moodkee." "Ferozeshuhur." "Subraon." "Punjab." "Chillianwalla." "Guzerat."
2nd troop, "Bhurtpore." "Maharajpore." 2 guns, G. G. Escort. "Moodkee." 2 guns G. G. Escort. "Ferozeshuhur." "Alliwal." "Subraon." "Punjab." "Chillianwalla." "Guzerat."
3rd troop, "Punniar." "Ferozeshuhur." "Subraon." "Punjab."

FOOT ARTILLERY.

A GUN, *superscribed with* BENGAL ARTILLERY *surrounded by a* LAUREL WREATH, *and surmounted by a* CROWN: *the word* "UBIQUE" *below*.

1st battalion, head quarters, "Bhurtpore."
1st company, "Seringapatam." "Maharajpore." "Punjab." "Chillianwalla." "Guzerat."
2nd company, "Carnatic." "Allyghur." "Delhi." "Laswarrie." "Deig." "Bhurtpore."
3rd company, "Bhurtpore." "Punjab." "Chillianwalla." "Guzerat."
4th company, "Seringapatam." "Bhurtpore."

---

* The distinctions for the Mutiny of 1857-58 have not yet been published.

2nd battalion, 2nd company, "Carnatic." "Mysore." "Seringapatam." "Cabul, 1842." "Ferozeshuhur." "Subraon." "Punjab." "Mooltan." "Guzerat."
3rd company, "Arracan." "Cabul, 1842." "Ghuznee, 1842."
4th company, "Arracan." "Affghanistan." "Candahar." "Kelat-i-Ghilzie."
3rd battalion, head quarters, "Bhurtpore."
1st company, "Mysore." "Allyghur." "Delhi." "Laswarrie." "Deig." "Java." "Bhurtpore."
2nd company, "Bhurtpore."
3rd company, "Subraon." "Punjab." "Mooltan." "Guzerat."
4th company, "Java." "Bhurtpore." "Subraon." "Punjab." "Mooltan." "Guzerat."
4th battalion, head quarters, "Bhurtpore." "Ferozeshuhur." "Subraon." "Punjab." "Chillianwalla." "Guzerat."
1st company, "Plassey." "Buxar." "Allyghur." "Delhi." "Laswarrie." "Deig." "Maharajpore." "Subraon." "Punjab." "Chillianwalla." "Guzerat."
2nd company, "Carnatic." "Mysore." "Bhurtpore." "Ferozeshuhur." "Subraon." "Punjab." "Chillianwalla." "Guzerat."
3rd company, "Bhurtpore." "Moodkee." "Ferozeshuhur." "Subraon."
4th company, "Arracan." "Ferozeshuhur." "Subraon." "Punjab." Detachment "Chillianwalla." Detachment "Guzerat."
5th battalion, 1st company, "Punjab."
2nd company, "Seringapatam." "Allyghur." "Delhi." "Laswarrie." "Deig." "Pegu."
3rd company, "Ava." "Pegu."
4th company, "Ava."
6th battalion, head quarters, "Subraon." "Punjab."
1st company, "Subraon." "Punjab."
2nd company, "Moodkee." "Ferozeshuhur." "Subraon."
3rd company, "Subraon." "Punjab."
4th company, "Ferozeshuhur." "Subraon." "Punjab."

ROLL OF ALL OFFICERS
WHO HAVE
PERIODS OF ADDISCOMBE SERVICE
TO
RECKON TOWARDS PENSION AND RETIREMENT.

ENGINEERS.

	Y.	M.	D.			Y.	M.	D.
C. F. Adey	1	10	3	E. S. Garstin	...	0	8	30
John Staples Alexander	1	8	8	T. G. Glover	...	1	10	6
G. E. Anderson	0	11	16	H. T. Gordon	...	1	10	4
G. F. Atkinson	1	10	10	W. W. H. Greathed	...	1	10	8
J. P. Beadle	1	4	10	F. C. Grindall	...	1	10	6
John Reid Becher	1	10	6	H. W. Gulliver	...	1	10	3
J. Birney	1	10	7	W. R. Y. Haig	...	1	10	10
H. F. Blair	1	10	12	E. Haines	...	1	10	1
G. W. Boileau	1	10	1	J. C. Harris	...	1	9	4
A. M. Brandreth	1	10	6	G. P. Hebbert	...	1	10	9
A. Cadell	1	9	25	T. Herschel	...	1	10	11
J. D. Campbell	1	10	10	J. F. Heywood	...	1	10	12
H. A. L. Carnegie	1	9	25	G. S. Hills	...	1	10	7
J. P. Clarkson	1	10	1	C. J. Hodgson	...	1	4	27
J. Crofton	1	10	6	W. B. Holmes	...	1	10	12
W. A. Crommelin	1	10	9	C. W. Hutchinson	...	1	10	0
R. C. Danbuz	1	10	11	G. Hutchinson	...	1	10	2
J. T. Donovan	1	10	12	H. Hyde	...	1	10	6
H. Drummond	1	10	4	A. Impey	...	1	5	23
J. H. Dyas	1	10	4	C. D. Innes	...	1	10	12
A. C. Eatwell	1	8	1	T. S. Irwin	...	1	10	10
J. Eckford	1	10	6	F. A. Jackson	...	1	4	19
W. R. Eliott	1	10	1	C. N. Judge	...	1	10	7
J. G. Forbes	1	3	20	E. J. Lake	...	0	11	22
A. Forsyth	1	10	7	P. Lambert	...	1	10	6
A. Fraser	1	10	7	R. Larkins	...	1	9	20
E. Fraser	1	4	10	E. B. Litchford	...	1	10	1
G. W. W. Fulton	1	6	16	G. Livinton	...	1	10	7
P. Garforth	1	6	14	C. H. Luard	...	1	10	7
H. G. Garnault	1	10	6	R. Maclagan	...	1	10	1
A. W. Garnett	1	0	11	J. M. McNeile	...	1	10	12

Vide G. G. O. No. 234 of '40, 204 of '48, 725 of '57, 856 of '59, and 725 and 803 of '60.

ENGINEERS.—(Continued.)

Name	Y.	M.	D.	Name	Y.	M.	D.
H. Macsween	1	10	11	F. Scrivener	1	9	24
F. R. Maunsell	1	9	8	W. D. A. R. Short	1	10	10
J. H. Maxwell	1	10	1	G. Sim	1	8	15
C. C. S. Moncrieff	1	10	12	R. G. Smyth	1	10	6
W. E. Morton	1	9	10	J. P. Steel	1	10	6
C. D. Newmarch	0	10	9	C. T. Stewart	1	4	11
J. E. T. Nicholls	0	6	1	A. Taylor	1	4	13
G. E. Norton	1	10	10	E. T. Thackeray	1	9	25
W. S. Oliphant	1	0	22	A. N. Thompson	0	1	7
W. H. Oliver	1	10	12	E. Tulloch	1	1	22
A. C. Padday	1	10	11	R. Vincent	0	4	21
C. S. Paton	1	10	27	F. Wale	1	10	10
W. D. Playfair	1	10	1	T. P. Westmorland	1	10	11
C. Pollard	1	10	10	G. R. Weston	0	7	1
T. Rattray	1	10	1	F. Whiting	1	10	10
G. Robertson	0	11	20	R. Young	1	10	2
D. G. Robinson	1	3	1	Henry Yule	1	10	8

ARTILLERY.

Name	Y.	M.	D.	Name	Y.	M.	D.
P. A. Agnew	0	1	25	H. R. Brownlow	1	0	5
R. Aislabie	1	9	26	R. R. Bruce	1	1	12
D. C. Alexander	1	10	4	J. H. Bryce	1	10	11
J. Alexander	1	10	9	A. Bunny	1	9	13
J. H. Alexander	1	10	10	F. R. Butt	1	10	11
E. Allen	1	10	1	H. M. Cadell	1	10	11
P. C. Anderson	1	10	9	K. W. S. M. Cameron	1	10	10
J. A. Angelo	1	4	5	De. V. F. Carey	1	6	4
C. V. Arbuckle	1	10	13	H. Chichester	1	10	13
C. E. Armstrong	1	9	28	A. Christie	1	8	7
B. Ashburner	1	7	24	P. Christie	1	3	11
St. G. Ashe	1	10	7	W. Clephane	1	0	24
A. G. Austen	1	4	4	F. Coddington	1	10	11
C. H. Barnes	1	10	9	J. A. S. Colquhoun	1	10	4
C. A. Bayley	1	7	2	C. H. Cookes	1	8	9
H. P. Bishop	1	5	6	W. D. Couchman	1	10	8
G. F. Blackwood	1	10	10	C. V. Cox	1	10	10
H. M. Boddam	1	10	3	W. F. Cox	1	2	22
A. H. Bogle	1	10	8	G. Cracklow	1	10	12
J. Bonham	1	10	9	W. R. Croster	1	10	10
T. H. Bosworth	1	5	4	W. B. Cumberland	1	10	11
G. Bourchier	1	2	11	R. Currie	1	10	8
C. V. Bowie	1	1	25	A. H. Davidson	1	10	8
G. R. Brown	1	3	11	E. W. Day	0	4	10
W. Brown	1	10	7	F. R. DeBudé	1	10	12
W. C. Brown	1	9	27	C. E. Delafosse	1	10	10
W. T. Brown	1	10	11	C. Dempster	1	10	6

ARTILLERY.—(Continued.)

	Y.	M.	D.		Y.	M.	D.
E. A. C. D'Oyly ...	1	10	9	E. Harrison ...	1	10	6
G. C. Depree ...	1	10	9	T. N. Harward ...	1	10	8
C. H. Dickens ...	0	4	5	J. G. Hathorn ...	1	10	12
T. E. Dickins ...	1	10	9	E. L. Hawkins ...	1	10	12
T. A. Dirom ...	1	10	3	A. H. Heath ...	1	10	6
A. Dixon ...	1	10	11	F. H. Hebbert ...	1	9	15
G. M. Dobbin ...	1	10	9	E. H. Hildebrand ...	1	5	7
A. Donie ...	1	10	7	J. Hills ...	1	10	3
W. Dowell ...	0	10	3	H. O. Hitchins ...	1	8	13
E. H. Dyke ...	1	10	11	T. E Hughes ...	1	10	7
E. L. Earle ...	1	10	14	E. T. Hume ...	1	10	12
J. A. H. Eckford ...	1	10	11	C. Hunter ...	1	10	7
E. D. Elliott ...	1	10	3	W. C. Hutchinson ...	1	1	0
M. Elliot ...	1	10	11	H. D. Jackson ...	1	10	9
H. J. Evans ...	1	10	6	E. B. Johnson ...	0	11	6
F. V. Eyre ...	1	10	8	H. L. Jones ...	1	9	24
R. C. H. B. Fagan ...	1	0	28	The Hon'ble F. Kennedy ...	1	10	3
W. R. Fitzgerald ...	1	10	6	J. H. Lamb ...	1	6	11
M. M. FitzGerald ...	1	10	9	P. C. Lambert ...	1	3	6
F. FitzRoy ...	1	10	3	C. S. Lemarchand ...	1	10	9
W. K. Fooks ...	0	3	17	C. E. Lewes ...	1	10	13
H. T. Forbes ...	1	10	11	F. E. Lewes ...	1	10	8
W. E. Forbes ...	1	10	7	E. P. Lewin ...	1	10	12
R. R. Franks ...	1	10	8	A. H. Lindsay ...	1	10	11
A. Fraser ...	1	10	3	R. F. Lowis ...	1	10	10
E. Fraser ...	1	10	8	D. MacFarlan ...	1	10	11
J. McK. Fraser ...	1	10	13	J. R. Mackay ...	1	10	11
J. W. Fraser ...	1	9	17	K. J. L. Mackenzie ...	1	10	10
F. E. Gammell ...	1	10	4	W. A. Mackinnon ...	1	10	3
R. Le. L. St. George ...	1	10	13	H. D. Macsween ...	1	10	9
J. S. Gibb ...	0	5	16	H. A. Mallock ...	1	10	8
A. Gillespie ...	1	10	4	R. J. Mallock ...	1	10	3
J. F. Gilmore ...	1	10	4	G. R. Manderson ...	1	3	25
R. S. Gilmore ...	1	10	10	J. A. Manson ...	1	7	2
H. Girardot ...	1	10	12	W. B. Marshall ...	1	2	21
D. W. Gordon ...	1	9	22	J. R. Martin ...	1	9	9
G. G. Gordon ...	1	10	3	H. H. Maxwell ...	1	10	3
W. M. Gowan ...	1	4	5	C. W. Maynard ...	1	10	3
W. J. Gray ...	1	10	7	A. O. Mayne ...	0	10	19
E. C. Griffin ...	1	9	24	F. H. McLeod ...	1	10	8
J. C. Griffith ...	1	10	2	D. McNeill ...	1	10	3
J. H. Grant ...	1	10	2	C. J. Mead ...	1	10	9
W. Gully ...	1	10	7	J. A. R. Mead ...	1	10	8
G. F. Hamilton ...	1	10	10	J. F. Meiklejohn ...	1	10	7
W. Hamilton ...	1	10	8	C. McW. Mercer ...	1	10	3
H. Hammond ...	1	7	16	W. Miller ...	1	10	6
R. T. Hare ...	1	10	7	G. Moir ...	1	4	7
H. E. Harington ...	1	10	11	J. Money ...	1	8	21

ARTILLERY.—(Continued.)

	Y.	M.	D.			Y.	M.	D.
H. Murray	1	10	7	H. Smithett	...	1	10	8
H. Munro	1	10	5	W. P. Somerville	...	1	10	3
W. A. Mylne	1	10	6	J. Stewart	...	1	10	12
C. E. Nairne	1	10	7	W. Stewart	...	1	0	2
D. J. F. Newall	1	10	7	W. J. Stewart	...	1	10	11
T. Nicholl	1	10	2	S. W. Stokes	...	0	3	10
				F. W. Stubbs	...	1	4	5
W. O'Brien	1	10	12	F. W. Swinhoe	...	1	10	10
J. Oldfield	0	4	18	A. Swinton	...	1	10	11
H. A. Olpherts	1	10	4					
W. Olpherts	1	1	21	C. S. S. Taylor	...	1	10	3
M. W. Ommanney	1	8	14	J. W. Taylor	...	1	10	4
R. M. Paton	1	2	28	H. P. de Teissier	...	1	5	25
A. Pearson	1	10	4	D. Thomson	...	1	10	11
J. B. Pearson	1	10	11	J. Thompson	...	0	10	13
D. S. Pemberton	1	10	13	P. Thompson	...	1	10	7
J. Percivall	1	10	9	E. Tierney	...	1	10	11
H. G. Perkins	0	8	12	C. W. Timbrell	...	1	10	9
R. H. Pitt	1	6	6	H. V. Timbrell	...	1	10	2
R. H. Pollock	1	7	9	H. Tombs	...	Nil.		
J. C. G. Price	1	10	11	S. E. Townsend	...	1	10	3
T. W. Pulman	1	5	19	G. B. Traill	...	1	8	24
				J. S. Tulloh	...	0	.5	0
W. F. Quazle	1	10	4	F. H Turnbull	...	1	10	8
P. B. Raikes	1	10	10					
J. F. Raper	0	2	2	F. D. Urquhart	...	1	10	12
E. C. W. Raynsford	1	8	29	D. C. Vanrenen	...	1	6	9
G. A. Renny	1	10	6	M. J. Vibart	...	1	3	8
F. S. Roberts	1	10	12	G. E. Voyle	...	0	8	15
A. Robertson	1	10	8					
C. G. Robinson	1	10	3	W. P. Waddy	...	1	10	3
R. S. Robinson	1	10	11	A. J. Wake	...	1	9	24
A. Rotton	1	10	14	A. Walker	...	1	9	23
G. A. Russell	1	10	10	E. W. E. Walker	...	1	10	6
E. H. Ryan	1	10	11	F. W. Ward	...	1	8	5
T. Ryan	1	10	11	C. A. M. Warde	...	1	9	27
				H. De G. Warter	...	1	10	11
E. Salwey	1	8	19	J. E. Watson	...	1	9	18
M. C. Sankey	1	1	5	D. J. Welsh	...	1	10	13
J. Sconce	1	8	8	C. A. Wheelwright	...	1	10	1
P. Sellow, formerly Smith	1	2	14	E. H. Willoughby	...	1	10	14
E. Sharpe	1	9	26	G. D. Willoughby	...	1	10	4
J. H. Shuldham	1	9	24	W. Willson	...	1	6	26
A. P. Simons	1	2	15	A. Wintle	...	1	10	2
F. C. Simons	1	5	8	S. C. Woodcock	...	1	0	23
F. E. Smalpage	1	10	3	J. Y. Worthington	...	1	10	10
H. M. Smith	1	0	7					
R. A. Smith	1	10	11	C. M. Young	...	1	2	4
T. P. Smith	1	10	11	J. Young	...	0	8	18

xvii

INFANTRY.

	Y.	M.	D.			Y.	M.	D.
R. J. Abbott	... 1	10	11	W. B. Castle	...	1	10	3
G. P. B. Alcock	... 1	10	10	G. N. Cave	...	1	1	22
A. Allen	... 1	10	3	S. Chalmers	...	1	10	9
A. J. Anderson	... 1	10	12	W. A. Chalmers	...	1	10	8
C. J. Anderson	... 1	9	24	R. Y. Chambers	...	1	4	11
R. E. Anderson	... 1	10	10	J. U. Champaign	...	1	10	11
F. C. Angelo	... 1	10	6	W. Champion	...	0	9	14
R. M. S. Annesley	... 1	0	18	G. T. Chesney	...	1	10	8
C. Baddeley	... 1	10	3	C. Clark	...	1	5	23
F. J. S. Bagshaw	... 1	9	22	P. C. Clark	...	1	3	29
W. Baillie	... 0	2	12	W. C. S. Clarke	...	1	10	13
G. A. A. Baker	... 1	9	23	M. G. Clerk	...	1	9	28
W. T. Baker	... 1	6	29	H. A. Cockburn	...	1	10	13
G. D. Barbor	... 1	10	3	H. Collett	...	1	10	8
G. H. Basevi	... 1	5	23	F. W. Collis	...	1	10	4
J. P. Basevi	... 1	10	12	A. K. Comber	...	1	4	12
J. M. Bayley	... 0	1	2	E. Cookson	...	1	3	1
C. C. Bean	... 0	9	5	H. C. A. Cooper	...	1	8	13
C. J. Bean	... 1	7	18	E. B. Cox	...	1	10	10
H. S. Belli	... 1	10	2	J. B. Cox	...	1	4	29
W. F. Belli	... 1	10	11	A. W. Craigie	...	1	10	4
J. P. Bennet	... 1	7	12	F. J. Craigie	...	1	10	8
H. L. C. Bernard	... 1	10	11	G. A. Craster	...	1	10	8
W. T. Birch	... 1	2	24	R. Creighton	...	1	10	3
G. A. Bishop	... 1	6	19	P. K. Croly	...	1	9	22
J. Bleaymire	... 1	10	3	G. A. Crommelin	...	0	2	3
W. W. Boddam	... 1	10	5	G. W. Cunninghame	...	1	10	6
E. J. Boileau	... 1	4	2	H. L. Darrah	...	1	10	7
S. S. Boulderson	... 1	10	4	E. Davidson	...	1	10	11
Raoul de Bourbel	... 1	9	15	C. F. Davis	...	1	10	10
P. Bourchier	... 1	10	4	M. Davis	...	0	11	28
H. R. Bradford	... 1	10	8	J. Dawson, 1st	...	1	10	9
J. A. Brereton	... 1	10	3	J. Dawson, 2nd	...	1	1	9
O. S. Bridges	... 1	10	8	C. L. Dayrell	...	1	9	24
D. Briggs	... 1	1	22	H. G. Delafosse	...	1	9	24
H. M. Bromley	... 1	9	30	J. W. Delamain	...	1	10	9
W. E. D. Broughton	... 1	10	13	F. V. Demole	...	1	9	28
R. Brown	... 1	9	28	E. L. Dennys	...	1	10	8
E. P. Brownlow	... 1	10	12	C. W. D'Oyly (absent sick,				
H. A. Brownlow	... 1	10	11	one term)	...	1	10	0
G. Buch	... 1	10	3	G. F. D'Oyly	...	1	5	2
J. Burn	... 0	10	24	T. C. H. D'Oyly	...	0	7	25
J. P. Burton	... 1	10	11	E. N. Dickenson	...	1	6	8
A. D. Butler	... 1	10	12	F. A. Dickins (absent 4				
W. J. D. Cairnes	... 1	9	24	months)	...	1	6	11
W. Campbell	... 1	10	10	R. Dougall	...	1	10	8
W. C. D. Campbell	... 1	10	13	W. L. P. Drummond	...	1	10	8
H. Campbeill	... 1	10	11	J. M. Earle	...	1	0	14
W. Carnell	... 1	5	10	J. J. Eckford	...	1	9	11

INFANTRY.—(Continued.)

	Y. M. D.		Y. M. D.
R. J. Edgell	1 2 21	H. L. Hawkins	1 10 4
M. F. Edwards	1 9 14	W. W. F. Hay	1 10 7
R. A. F. W. Ellis	1 4 7	W. Hichens	1 10 9
H. P. Evans	1 10 11	R. J. F. Hickey	1 10 9
R. Fergusson	1 10 8	T. R. Higginson	1 10 3
W. P. Fisher	1 10 13	T. W. Holland	0 7 10
J. H. FitzGerald	1 10 7	C. Holroyd	0 7 26
A. FitzHugh	1 10 7	D. C. Home	1 10 11
F. B. Foote	1 10 11	R. Home	1 10 11
F. M. H. Forbes (absent 7 months and 20 days)	1 0 20	J. St. J. Hovenden	1 10 9
		W. R. H. T. Howell	1 10 12
E. S. Fox	1 10 0	R. H. Hudleston	1 10 7
A. Francis	1 10 10	M. A. Humphrey	1 10 9
G. W. Fraser	0 4 20	E. W. Humphry	1 10 11
J. E. Fraser	1 10 10	A. Hunter (absent sick, one term)	1 3 22
W. M. Fraser	1 10 11		
F. P. W. Freeman	1 10 7	E. Hyndman	1 3 27
W. F. Fulford	1 2 22	H. F. M. Hyslop	1 10 3
A. Fytche	1 10 10	J. J. McL. Innes	1 10 8
W. A. Garden	1 10 11	C. Irvine	1 10 4
N. D. Garrett	1 9 18	C. Jackson	0 4 0
E. C. Garstin	1 10 13	G. O. Jacob	1 10 6
T. J. Geldart	1 8 30	M. James	1 10 7
M. G. Geneste	1 10 14	W. Jeffreys	1 10 3
P. O. Gibbes	1 10 3	S. C. Jervis	1 10 9
W. M. Gibbon	1 10 13	C. C. Johnson	0 5 18
C. J. Godby	1 9 19	W. L. Jones	1 10 9
F. T. Goldsworthy	1 10 3	S. A. T. Judge	1 10 3
H. Goodwyn	1 10 13	E. A. C. Lambert	1 10 12
W. Gordon	1 4 1	F. W. Lambert	1 10 3
W. R. Gordon	1 10 11	J. Lambert	0 5 27
J. A. H. Gorges	1 10 10	F. Lance	1 10 13
J. M. Graham	1 10 10	A. M. Lang	1 10 11
J. H. Graves	1 10 4	D. M. C. D. Law	1 10 0
J. Graydon	1 10 6	F. L'Estrange	1 7 18
C. J. Griffiths	1 10 4	J. E. Lee	1 10 13
G. H. Griffiths	1 9 26	E. Leeds	1 10 6
F. J. Gully	0 8 13	H. G. Leslie	0 6 0
C. V. Hamilton	1 9 17	T. H. Lewin	1 10 11
G. M. Hand	1 9 30*	E. D. F. Lewis	1 10 8
G. C. Hankin	1 6 8	G. A. H. Lillie	0 3 18
F. H. Hanmer	1 10 6	D. Limond	1 7 14
G. Henderson	1 10 7	J. Liston	1 10 7
W. Henderson	1 10 11	J. M. Lockett	1 8 26
A. F. P. Harcourt	1 10 8	C. M. Longmore	1 7 24
J. P. Harris	1 10 3	W. L. Louis	1 10 3

* Sic in the *Gazette*.

INFANTRY.—(Continued.)

	Y.	M.	D.			Y.	M.	D.
B. M. Loveday	1	4	6	W. C. Parsons	...	1	5	18
P. S. Lumsden	1	10	4	J. S. Paton	...	0	3	9
W. H. Lumsden	1	10	11	H. B. Pearson	...	1	10	3
J. Macdonald	1	7	0	W. S. Pearson	...	1	10	7
D. Macintyre	1	10	14	F. W. Peile	...	1	10	5
A. M. Mackenzie	1	8	29	R. C. B. Pemberton	...	1	10	11
D. Macleod	1	6	7	J. O. Penson	...	1	10	7
R. B. Macleod	0	9	21	A. E. Perkins	...	1	6	24
J. K. McCausland	1	10	10	J. Pickard	...	1	10	11
C. A. McDougall	1	8	8	E. R. Pogson	...	I	10	11
A. McNeill	1	10	8	T. E. Powell	...	1	10	3
J. C. McNeill	1	10	9	M. G. Prole	...	1	10	3
F. C. Maisey	1	3	12	H. T. A. Raikes	...	1	10	14
R. J. Mallock (absent sick, one term)	1	6	12	W. E. M. B. Ramsay	...	1	6	18
				W. L. Randall	...	1	10	14
D. G. Manning	1	10	11	G. J. Reeves	...	1	0	21
H. D. Manning	0	2	24	D. Reid	...	1	10	11
G. W. Manson	1	10	11	H. P. Repton	...	1	10	6
W. E. Marshall	1	10	6	R. Reynolds	...	1	9	5
H. D. Maunsell	1	1	25	G. R. Roberts	...	1	3	30
H. Maxwell	1	10	3	C. A. Robertson	...	2	10	12
J. G. Medley	1	10	4	H. L. Robertson	...	0	8	29
C. F. Middleton	1	9	14	B. Rogers	...	1	10	3
F. N. Miles	1	10	10	J. Ruggles	...	1	10	9
J. Miller	1	7	19	L. Russell	...	1	10	5
J. C. Miller	1	10	13	P. C. Rynd	...	1	10	11
D. Mocatta	1	8	23					
J. R. Monckton	1	10	11	P. Salkeld	...	1	7	28
T. G. Montgomerie	1	10	7	E. W. Salusbury	...	0	10	20
J. A. H. Moore	1	10	4	F. O. Salusbury	...	1	10	8
T. Morland	1	10	11	P. G. Scot	...	1	10	3
B. W. D. Morton	1	10	3	W. A. Scott	...	1	10	4
P. Murray	1	10	8	A. Shaw	...	1	10	12
G. Newmarch	1	10	3	C. R. Shaw	...	1	10	4
C. Newton	0	6	10	W. F. Shaw	...	1	10	12
L. Nicholson	1	3	29	W. B. Shawe	...	1	10	7
H. N. Noble	1	8	9	J. F. Sherer	...	1	10	4
F. B. Norman	1	10	8	R. S. Simonds	...	1	8	30
J. M. Nuttall	1	10	3	C. B. C. Simpson	...	1	10	9
				E. H. C. Simpson	...	1	10	9
E. C. Oakes	1	0	22	J. R. Simpson	...	1	10	9
J. S. Ogilvie	1	10	9	R. M. Skinner	...	1	10	7
H. T. Oldfield	1	10	8	J. Smith	...	1	10	8
H. R. Osborn	1	10	9	J. D. Smith	...	0	9	24
R. Ouseley	1	10	10	J. W. Smith	...	1	5	22
C. F. Packe	1	7	2	M. C. Smith	...	1	10	10
E. Packe	1	10	10	W. Smith	...	1	10	3
C. H. Palliser	0	9	22	N. R. Sneyd	...	1	2	17
C. O. B. Palmer	1	5	14	O. McC. Span	...	1	10	10

INFANTRY.—(Continued.)

	Y.	M.	D.			Y.	M.	D.
H. G. W. Spens	1	10	11	E. D. Vanrenen		1	5	17
F. S. Stanton	1	10	9	J. A. Vanrenen		1	10	8
T. Staples	1	10	9	A. Vivian		1	9	24
R. Steuart	0	8	28	H. F. Waddington		0	1	28
H. B. Stevens	0	6	8	E. Walker		1	10	3
P. Stewart	1	10	14	R. J. Walker		1	10	11
R. Stewart	1	10	8	R. H. Wall		1	10	8
W. F. Stewart	1	2	6	N. H. Wallace		1	9	24
P. Story	1	10	3	W. F. N. Wallace		1	10	10
C. B. Stuart	0	9	2	J. S. Walters		1	10	8
S. S. Sutherland	1	10	13	D. Ward		1	10	3
J. D. Swayne	1	10	3	W. E. Warrand		1	4	8
F. L. Tandy	1	10	4	C. H. L. Warren		1	10	12
A. Taylor	1	10	10	D. C. Warren		1	9	29
F. S. Taylor	1	10	11	T. P. Waterman		1	6	25
G. F. Tennant	1	10	11	G. E. Watson		1	10	11
C. S. J. Terrot	0	9	10	J. L. Watts		1	10	3
C. S. Thomason	1	10	11	T. E. Webster		1	1	25
G. H. Thompson	1	1	13	E. G. Whish		1	10	8
R. Thompson	1	10	6	T. W. White		1	6	18
J. Thomson	1	10	12	E. A. Wilde		1	10	3
W. B. Thomson	1	9	13	H. D. A. D. Willan (absent sick, 6 months)		1	10	10
C. G. Thorp	0	6	24					
F. H. Tomkinson	1	1	19	A. Willes		1	7	0
J. Tovey	0	10	21	E. C. S. Williams		1	2	14
J. Trevenen	1	7	9	F. H. Wilson		1	10	4
S. T. Trevor	1	10	9	J. C. Wood		1	10	3
W. S. Trevor	1	10	11	J. Yorke		1	3	19
W. R. Tucker	1	10	13	G. G. Young		1	10	10
R. H. Tulloh	1	10	9	W. S. Young		1	10	13
R. H. D. Tulloh	1	10	6					
B. C. Urquhart	1	10	11					

CAVALRY.

C. M. S. Fairbrother ... 1 10 8

LIST OF OFFICERS

Attached to Turkish Contingent, who are permitted to reckon periods as service, during the time they were so employed.

No. 487 of 1857.—With reference to General Order No. 415, of the 4th April 1855, the Right Honorable the Governor-General of India in Council is pleased to direct the publication in General Orders of the following military letter from the Honorable the Court of Directors to the Government of India, No. 22, dated 28th January 1857, with returns of officers who have been employed under the orders of Her Majesty's Government during the recent war, and of officers whose merits and services are favorably noticed by Major General Sir H. K. Storks, K. C. B. :

MILITARY DEPARTMENT.

No. 22 of 1857.

OUR GOVERNOR-GENERAL OF INDIA IN COUNCIL.

1. Referring to the announcement made in our letter of the 7th February 1855, No. 26, we forward to you a return received from the War Department of the officers of your establishment who have been employed under the orders of Her Majesty's Government during the recent war, showing the dates of their appointment, and the dates on which their services terminated.

2. We also forwarded to you copy of a letter addressed to us by Major General Sir Henry K. Storks, K. C. B., expressing his sense of the merits and services of the undermentioned officers of your establishment, whilst attached as staff officers to the infantry depôt at Scutari : *viz.*

Dated 4th November 1856.

Captain George Henderson, 30th regiment Bengal native infantry. *(Since dead.)*

Lieutenant John Morland, 1st Bengal fusiliers.

We are, &c.,
(Signed) W. H. SYKES,
And Eleven other Directors.

London, 28th January 1857.

OFFICERS of the Bengal Establishment employed under Her Majesty's Government during the recent War with Russia, with the Turkish Contingent.

Name and Rank.	Date of Appointment.	When struck off the Force.
Richardson, R., Captain, 4th Light Cavalry	20th March 1855	1st May 1856.
Austen, A. G., Captain, Artillery	Ditto	28th May 1856.
Campbell, A. H., Lieutenant, 9th N. I.	Ditto	1st July 1856.
Thurburn, F. A. V., Lieutenant	Ditto	Resigned at Constantinople, 9th August 1855.
Francis, Henry, Lieutenant	Ditto	2nd June 1856.
McNeill, D., Lieutenant	Ditto	3rd June 1856.
Smyth, Edmd., Lieutenant	Ditto	31st August 1856.
Baillie, John, Lieutenant	Ditto	11th June 1856.
Lucas, C. P., Lieutenant	Ditto	1st May 1856.
Armstrong, Chas., Lieutenant	Ditto	13th July 1855.
Quin, C. W., Lieutenant	Ditto	1st May 1856.
Gammell, F. E., Lieutenant	Ditto	24th September 1855.
Low, H. J. R., Lieutenant	Ditto	6th October 1855, struck off for ill health.
Grierson, W. M., Lieutenant	Ditto	10th June 1856.
Hawkins, E. L., 2nd Lieutenant	Ditto	2nd June 1856.
Glanville, G. J., 2nd Lieutenant	Ditto	23rd June 1856.
Jackson, H. D., 2nd Lieutenant	Ditto	Resigned 30th September 1855.
Evans, D. F., Lieutenant-Colonel	27th March 1855	5th June 1856.
Bogle, A. H., Lieutenant	31st March 1855	29th May 1856.
Campbell, Edwd., Surgeon	17th April 1855	1st September 1855.
Ainger, Major, Assistant Surgeon	30th April 1855	24th June 1856.
Vaughan, J. S., Captain	17th July 1855	4th June 1856.
Speke, J. H., Lieutenant	1st Aug. 1855	4th June 1856.
Mackenzie, C. Fras., Lieutenant	Ditto	2nd June 1856.

Officers with the Turkish Contingent.—(Continued.)

Name and Rank.	Date of Appointment.	When struck off the Force.
Hind, Joseph, Lieutenant	12th Sept. 1855	6th June 1856.
Winniett, A. W., Lieutenant	1st Oct. 1855	28th May 1856.
Young, James, Captain	9th Oct. 1855	17th June 1856.
Toogood, A. D., Lieutenant	1st Nov. 1855	25th May 1856.
Evans, Thomas William, Lieutenant	18th Feby. 1856	15th May 1856.
Maxwell, Robert, Lieutenant	Ditto	25th May 1856.
With the Osmanli Irregular Cavalry.		
Beatson, W. F., Lieutenant-Colonel	26th April 1854	Resigned 17th October 1855.
Olpherts, William, Captain	15th Dec. 1854	Went home in charge of troops and reported himself at W. D. 25th July 1856.
With the Army under Omar Pasha.		
Hinde, C. F. E., Lieutenant	1st March 1854	26th July 1856, arrived in England August 1856.
Arbuckle, C. V., Lieutenant	6th March 1855	Removed from staff 9th March 1856, $\frac{89}{150}$.
With the Land Transport Corps.		
Larkins, Robertson, Captain	26th Jan. 1855	12th December 1855.
Hoste, W. D., Lieutenant	27th Jan. 1855	13th July 1855.
Under Lord Wm. Paulet on the "Bosphorus."		
Gordon, Chas., Captain		
Henderson, Geo., Captain		
Morland, John, Lieutenant		
Ryan, E. M. Captain		

xxiii

1, *St. James's Place, 4th November* 1856.

Sir,

The Officers of the Honorable East India Company's Service named in the margin, having served for a considerable time as Staff Officers attached to the Infantry Depôt at Scutari, I consider it an act of justice to them to request you to be good enough to bring their names to the notice of the Court of Directors.

<small>Captain G. Henderson, 30th Bengal native infantry (since dead).
Lieutenant J. Morland, 1st Bengal fusiliers.</small>

I had every reason to be satisfied with the zeal and efficiency with which they performed every duty required of them; and I am glad to have the opportunity afforded me of expressing the sense I entertained of their merits and services.

I beg respectfully to recommend them to the favor and protection of the Court of Directors.

I have the honor to be,
Sir,
Your most obedient, humble servant,
(Signed) H. K. Storks, *Major-General.*

Sir James Melvill, K. C. B.,
&c. &c. &c.

LIST OF OFFICERS

Who have been allowed to count one year's service, in consideration of their distinguished services in the memorable defence of the Residency of Lucknow—Vide G. G. O. No. 1407 of the 12th October 1858.

Major-Genl. J. C. C. Gray, 48th N. I.
Col. R. A. Master, C. B., 2nd En. L. C.
Col. H. Palmer, 48th N. I.
Lieut.-Colonel C. A. Barwell, 71st N. I.
Lieut.-Colonel E. Marriott, 57th N. I.
Major R. P. Anderson, 25th N. I.
Major H. L. Bird, 48th N. I.
Major T. T. Boileau, 2nd En. L. C.
Major J. W. Carnegie, C.B., 15th N. I.
Major H. Dinning, 71st N. I.
Major R. J. Edgell, 53rd N. I.
Major H. Forbes, 1st En. L. C.
Major R. C. Germon, 13th N. I.
Major G. Hutchinson, Engrs.
Major J. J. McL. Innes, V.C., Engrs.
Major T. James, 2nd N. I.
Major M. F. Kemble, 41st N. I.
Major J. W. Sanders, 41st N. I.
Major A. C. Warner, 2nd En. L. C.
Major G. R. Weston, 65th N. I.
Major T. F. Wilson, C. B., 13th N. I.
Captain T. Green, 48th N. I.
Captain W. H. Hawes, 63rd N. I.
Captain E. H. Langmore, 71st N. I.
Captain J. Ruggles, 41st N. I.
Captain G. Strangways, 71st N. I.
Captain C. B. Stuart, 4th En. Regt.
Captain J. A. Vanrenen, 54th N. I.
Captain T. P. Waterman, 13th N. I.
Captain J. T. Watson, 12th N. I.
Lieutenant R. H. M. Aitken, 13th N. I.
Lieutenant J. Alexander, Arty.
Lieutenant F. M. Birch, 71st N. I.
Lieutenant J. Bonham, Arty.

Lieutenant C. W. Campbell, 10th N. I.
Lieutenant W. Campbell, 71st N. I.
Lieutenant B. R. Chambers, 13th N. I.
Lieutenant C. D. S. Clarke, 73rd N. I.
Lieut. W. G. Cubitt, V. C., 13th N. I.
Lieutenant H. Z. Darrah, 41st N. I.
Lieut. J. H. T. Farquhar, 2nd En. L. C.
Lieutenant C. W. Fletcher, 48th N. I.
Lieutenant F. W. Graham, 11th N. I.
Lieutenant G. L. K. Hewett, 41st N. I.
Lieutenant G. C. Huxham, 48th N. I.
Lieutenant H. Inglis, 41st N. I.
Lieutenant G. L. Keir, 41st N. I.
Lieutenant A. R. Loughnan, 13th N. I.
Lieutenant D. MacFarlan, Arty.
Lieutenant R. Ouseley, 48th N. I.
Lieutenant R. M. Sewell, 71st N. I.
Lieutenant O. L. Smith, 48th N. I.
Lieutenant A S. Thain, 13th N. I.
Lieutenant A. Tulloch, 58th N. I.
Lieutenant E. B. Ward, 48th N. I.
Lieutenant J. H. Worsley, 71st N. I.
Surgeon J. Campbell, M. D. and C. B.
Surgeon J. Fayrer.
Surgeon H. M. Greenhow.
Surgeon S. B. Partridge.
Assistant Surgeon G. B. Hadow.
Hony. Asst. Surgeon R. F. Thompson.

FOR CAWNPORE.

Major Delafosse, 53rd N. I.
Major Thompson, 53rd N. I.

NOTE.—An order has been published, by which the Queen has granted one year's extra service to all members composing Havelock's Force. The list of Officers has not yet been prepared.

PERIODS OF LEAVE

Sanctioned by Government

TO OFFICERS PASSED IN AND OUT OF INDIA,

TO RECKON AS SERVICE FOR PENSION,

OCCASIONED BY

SICKNESS OR WOUNDS CONTRACTED ON, OR BY, SERVICE.

Months.

Aitken, R. H. M., Capt., 13th N. I.		1 year 2 months and 19 days; 10 Oct. 59 to 29 Dec. 60.
Alexander, J., Lt., Arty.	18	
Allgood, G., Capt., 49th N. I.		Time passed on voyage to India from England.
Amesbury, J. W. R., Asst. Surgn.	18	
Anderson, R. P., Bt.-Major, 25th N. I.	18	
Anderson, T., Asst. Surgeon	15	
Angus, J. A., Capt., 9th N. I.		2 months and 22 days passed on voyage to India.
Armstrong, C., Bt.-Capt., 10th N. I.	18	
Bacon, C. B. G., Capt., 3rd Eurns.	18	
Baker, G. A. A., Lt., 60th N. I.	15	
Bates, C. E., Lt., 36th N. I.	15	
Becher, A. M., Bt.-Col., c. b., 61st N.I.	15	
Beckett, S., Lt., 25th N. I.	6	
Birch, F. M., Lt., 71st N. I.	18	6 May 58 to 6 Nov. 59.
Birch, R. G., Lt., 1st L. C.	18	
Bird, H. L., Major, 48th N. I.	18	

xxvii

	Months.	
Boileau, F. W., Lt., 16th N. I.	2	and 16 months.
Boileau, T. T., Capt., 7th L. C.	36	
Bonham, J., Lt., Arty.	18	25 Jan. 58 to 25 July 59.
Boulderson, S., Lt., 5th L. C.	18	
Bromley, H. M., Lt., 52nd N. I.	15	
Broughton, W. E. D., Lt., 6th Eurns.	18	
Brown, J., Asst. Surgeon	15	10 Dec. 58 to 10 March 60.
Brown, J. B. S., Surgeon	15	13 Jan. 58 to 13 April 59.
Browne, S. J., Bt. Lt.-Col., 46th N. I.	18	10 Jan. 59 to 10 July 60.
Bush, R. Y. B., Lt.-Col., 32nd N. I.	36	To count under the old rules.
Butler, T. A., Lt., 1st Fusrs.	...	1 year 2 months and 23 days; 10 Jan. 59 to 2 April 60.
Cafe, W. M., Capt., 56th N. I.	18	
Campbell, J., Surgeon	18	
Cannon, H. M., Surgeon	15	6 May 59 to 6 Aug. 60.
Cantor, C. H., Lt., 2nd Fusrs.	18	10 Dec. 58 to 10 June 60.
Carleton, H. A., Lt.-Col., Arty.	18	
Cary, S., Lt., 37th N. I.	15	20 July 58 to 20 Oct. 59.
Cavenagh, O., Lt.-Col., from April 55 to 12 July 56	24	Service, entitling to promotion to Bt.-Colonel.
Chalmers, J., Lt., 39th N. I.	...	1 May to 1 Nov. 58.
Chalmers, O. J., Lt., 4th Eurns.	...	1 year 1 month and 10 days; 24 Nov. 58 to 3 Jan. 60.
Chalmers, R., Lt., 45th N. I.	18	10 Apl. 1860 to 10 July 61.
Chalmers, R. W., Bt.-Capt., 11th N. I.	15	
Chalmers, S., Capt., 53rd N. I.	15	
Chambers, B. R., Lt., 13th N. I.	18	11 Feb. 58 to 11 Aug. 59.
Christopher, L. R., Capt., 71st N. I.	15	
Clark, C., Lt., 2nd Eurns.	24	
Clark, W. F., Asst. Surgeon	18	6 May 58 to 6 Nov. 59.
Clarke, C. D. S., Lt., 73rd N. I.	36	

Months.

Clarke, C. M. L., Lt., 37th N. I.	18	
Clarke, J., Col., 25th N. I.		8 months and 16 days; 10 Jan. to 26 Sept. 59.
Cockburn, H. A., Capt., 53rd N. I.	15	
Coke, J., Col., C. B., 10th N. I.	15	10 Jan. 59 to 10 April 60.
Cubitt, W. G., Lt., 13th N. I.	12	
Daly, H. D., Lt.-Col., C. B., Bom. Fus.	15	
Davidson, A. H., Lieut., Arty.	4	17 July to 15 Nov. 57.
Delafosse, H. G., Lt., 53rd N I.	15	
Dinning, H., Capt., 71st N. I.	18	
Dunsford, H. F., Bt.-Col., 59th N. I.	15	10 Nov. 60 to 10 Feb. 62.
Eckford, A. H., Lt., 69th N. I.		20 May 58 to 1 Nov. 58.
Edgell, R. J., Bt.-Major, 53rd N. I.	15	
Elton, J. F., Lt., 73rd N. I.	18	
Etesen, A., Asst. Surgeon	2	
Fairlie, C. H., Lt., 1st Eur. Cavy.	18	
Farquhar, J. H. T., Lt., 3rd Eur. Cavy.	18	
Fayrer, J., Asst. Surgeon, M. D.	15	
Fellowes, C. M. N., Lt., 3rd Eurns.	36	
Finch, H., Bt.-Major, 31st N. I.	18	10 Feb. 59 to 10 Aug. 60.
Fletcher, C. W., Lt., 48th N. I.	18	
Forbes, H., Capt., 1st E. L. C.	15	
Forbes, H., Major, 1st L. C.	3	5 Sept. to 5 Dec. 59.
Forbes, H., Major, 1st L. C.	3	5 Sept. to Dec. 59.
Garden, H. R., Bt.-Major, 2nd N. I.	18	11 Feb. 58 to 11 May 59; and 11 May to 11 Aug. 59.
Germon, R. C., Capt., 13th N. I.	24	
Glubb, J. M., Lt., 38th N. I.	18	
Gordon, J., Major, 5th Eurns.		20 July 58 to 12 Dec. 59

xxix

	Months.	
Graham, T. C., Lt., 4th Eur. Cavy.	18	
Grant, J. A., Lt., 8th N. I.	18	
Graydon, W., Capt., 16th N. I.	14	
Green, T., Capt., 48th N. I.	18	21 May 58 to 21 Nov. 59.
Greenhow, H. M., Asst. Surgeon	18	
Gulliver, H. W., Bt.-Major, Engrs.		2 months and 10 days; 20 Sept. to 1 Dec. 57; and 6 months, from 11 April to 11 Oct. 58.
Harington, H. E., Lt., Arty.	18	10 Dec. 58 to 10 June 60.
Heath, A. H., Capt., Arty.		1 year 2 months and 19 days; 24 Dec. 58 to 11 March 60.
Hire, S. J., Major, 22nd N. I.	18	and 69 days passed in going to and from England in 1858.
Hockin, P. R., Capt., 48th N. I.		1 year 1 month and 8 days; 2 Feb. 59 to 11 March 60.
Hood, J., Bt.-Major, 49th N. I.		2 years; 20 July 58 to 20 July 60.
Huxham, E. C., Lt., 48th N. I.		1 year 5 months and 11 days; 25 April 58 to 6 Oct. 59.
Inglis, H., Lt., 41st N. I.	18	
Ireland, W. W., Surgeon	18	also from 27 March 60 to 27 Sept. 61.
Jackson, E. S., Lt., 12th N. I.	15	
James, T., Bt.-Major, 2nd N. I.		10 months and 19 days, from 11 Feb. 58 to 2 Jan. 60.
Jervis, F. V. R., Capt., 56th N I.		6 July to 30 Nov. 58.

		Months.	
Johnson, A. B., Bt.-Major, 5th Eurns.			1 year 2 months and 23 days; 10 Jan. 59 to 2 April 60.
Jones, H. T., Lt., 31st N. I.	...	15	18 May 58 to 18 Aug. 59.
Lambert, E. A. C., Lt., 1st Fusrs.	...	18	
Lambert, F. W., Bt.-Major, 56th N.I.		18	27 April 60 to 27 Oct. 61.
Lane, C. P., Major, 3rd E. L. C.	...		2 months and 26 days.
Law, C. P. St. J., Capt., 11th N. I.		18	25 Oct. 58 to 25 April 60.
Light, A., Bt.-Major, Arty.	...	18	
Lindsay, A. H., Lt., Ben. Arty.	...	18	
Loughnan, A. R., Lt., 13th N. I.	...	18	
Luard, F. P., Lt., 1st L. C.	...	18	
Macaulay, R. W., M. D.	...	15	also 3 months—Indian leave.
Mackenzie, A. M., Bt.-Capt., 56th N.I.	{	15 3	11 Oct. 58 to 11 Jan. 60; and 11 Jan. to 11 April 60.
May, J., Ens., 72nd N. I.	...	18	
McClelland, J., Surgeon		15	
McFarlan, D., Lt., Arty.	...	18	12 Jan. 58 to 12 July 59.
Mitchell, G., Lt., 2nd Fusrs.	...	18	
Money, G. N., Lt., 1st Eurns.	...	18	20 June 58 to 20 Dec. 59.
Moore, T., Bt. Lt.-Col., 8th Cavy.	...		12 Feb. 44 to 16 Oct. 46.
Mouat, F. J., Surgeon	...	2	10 April to 10 June 45.
Munro, C. A., Lt., 25th N. I.	...	15	
Nightingale, M. N., Capt., 2nd Eurns.			13 Feb. 49 to 14 Feb. 50; and from 14 Feb. 50 to 15 Nov. 52.
O'Brien, P., Asst. Surgeon	...	18	
O'Callaghan, D. J., Surgeon	...		11 months and 27 days; 17 Nov. 58 to 14 Nov. 59.
Ogilvie, G. M., Surgeon	...	18	
Osborn, D. H., Capt., 54th N. I.	...	18	

Months.

Packe, G. F., Lt., 4th N. I.	18	9 Feb. 58 to 9 Aug. 59.
Palliser, C. H., Lt., 63rd N. I.	15	
Parsons, W. T., Capt., 1st Fusrs.	24	
Partridge, S. B., Asst. Surgeon	18	
Pearson, J. R., Lt., Arty.	15	
Pemberton, D. S., Lt., Arty.	18	
Playfair, A. L., Lt., 7th N. I.	15	
Pollock, H. T., Capt., 35th N. I.	{ 4	1 Sept. 57 to 1 Jan. 58; and
	24	9 Feb. 58 to 9 Feb. 60.
Powell, F., Asst. Surgeon	18	
Prinsep, A. H., Lt., 4th L. C.	15	
Reid, J., Capt., 37th N. I.		1 year and 9 days; 11 Nov. 58 to 20 Nov. 59.
Richardes, C., Lt., 63rd N. I.	18	
Richardson, J. F., Major, Staff Corps	15	11 Nov. 58 to 11 Feb. 59.
Rickards, E. J., Major, 5th Eurns.		24 Aug. to 19 Sept. 57; and the time from Bombay to England, should he take remainder of unexpired furlough.
Ringer, T., Asst. Surgeon	15	
Roberts, F. S., Bt.-Major, Arty.	15	
Robertson, R. S., Lt., 6th Eurns.	15	
Ruggles, J., Capt., 41st N. I.	18	
Salusbury, F. O., Major, 1st Fusrs.		4 Oct. to 12 Nov. 57; and time from Calcutta to England in 59.
Sanders, J. W., Major, 41st N. I.	18	11 April 58 to 11 Oct. 59.
Scot, P. G., Capt., 12th N. I.	18	11 Aug. 58 to 11 Feb. 60.
Seaton, D., Lt.-Col., 1st Fusrs.	18	
Sewell, B. M., Lt., 71st N. I.	18	
Simpson, E. H. C., Lt., 39th N. I.	15	

xxxii

Months.

Simpson, G. B. C., Lt., 23rd N. I.	18
Sitwell, F. H. M., Lt., 31st N. I.	24
Smith, A. S., Bt.-Major, 24th N. I.	
Smith, C. M., Asst. Surgeon	18
Smith, W., Lt., 28th N. I.	
Smithett, H., Lt., Arty.	
Snow, T. R., Capt., 4th Cavy.	36
St. George, E., Capt., 1st Fusrs.	18
Stewart, P., Major, Engrs.	
Strangways, G., Capt., 71st N. I.	18
Syme, P. M., 2nd Capt., Arty.	

Smith, A. S.: 18 May to 15 Oct. 58.

Smith, W.: 11 months and 16 days; 25 Feb. 59 to 12 Feb. 60.

Smithett, H.: 1 year 1 month and 4 days; 24 Nov. 58 to 29 Dec. 59.

St. George, E.: 20 June 58 to 20 Dec. 59.

Stewart, P.: His furlough in 58.

Syme, P. M.: Leave to count from 24th September 1858, as having expired, instead of 14th December 1858, as on the former date he joined the Royal Arsenal, Woolwich.

Taylor, A., Bt. Lt.-Col., C. B., Engrs.	
Taylor, C. C., Lt., 56th N. I.	15
Thackeray, E. T., Lieut., Engrs.	12
Thain, G. G., Lt., 2nd N. I.	18
Thompson, M., Lt., 53rd N. I.	15
Thompson, R. L., Bt.-Major, 10th N. I.	18
Thring, E. B., Surgeon	18
Tombs, H., Capt., Arty.	15
Trail, G. B., Lieut., Arty.	6
Trench, H. LeP., Major, 35th N. I.	15
Tytler, J. M. B. F., Bt.-Col., C. B., 37th N. I.	18
Vanderguclit, T. E., Lt., 5th Eurns.	18

Taylor, A.: 1 year 8 months and 20 days; 9 Feb. 59 to 29 Oct. 60.

Thackeray, E. T.: 25 Sept. 61 to 25 Sept. 62.

Months.

Walker, T. N., Lt., 2nd Fusrs.	18	
Waller, H. E., Lt., 40th N. I.	18	
Walters, J. S., Lt., 28th N. I.	18	
Ward, G., Capt., 5th L. C.	18	18 March 58 to 18 Sept. 59.
Waterman, T. P., Capt., 13th N. I.	36	
Watson, J. T., Lieut., 12th N. I.	24	
Wauchope, R. A., Lt., 57th N. I.	15	9 Feb. 58 to 9 May 59.
Welchman, J., Bt.-Colonel, C. B.	18	18 March 58 to 18 Sept. 59.
Wells, W. W., Surgeon	18	
Wemyss, H. M., Lt., 1st Fusrs.	18	
Weston, C. S., Capt., 36th N. I.	18	
Weston, G. R., Major, 65th N. I.	18	
White, W., Surgeon, Medical Dept.		3 months and 3 days.
Wilkinson, O., Capt., 4th Cavy.	18	
Williams, G. A., Bt.-Capt., 26th N. I.		1 year 5 months & 17 days: 24 April 58 to 11 Oct. 59.
Wilson, T. F., Bt.-Major, 13th N. I.	15	
Wilson, W., Bt.-Major, Arty.	18	
Yorke, P. S., Lt., 12th N. I.	18	

MEMBERS

OF THE

MOST HONORABLE ORDER OF THE BATH.

KNIGHTS GRAND CROSS.

General.
Sir George Pollock, Artillery.

Major General.
Sir Patrick Grant, Infantry.

KNIGHTS COMMANDERS.

Generals.
Sir Robert Houstoun, Cavalry.
Sir William Richards, Infantry.

Lieutenant-Generals.
Sir John Cheape, Engineers.
Sir George Petre Wymer, Infantry.

Major Generals.
Sir R. J. H. Birch, Infantry (*Civil*).
Sir John Bennett Hearsey, Cavalry.
Sir Robert Napier, Engineers.
Sir Justin Sheil, Infantry (*Civil*).
Sir Archdale Wilson, *Bart.*, Artillery.

Colonel.
Sir H. B. Edwardes, Infantry (*Civil*).

COMPANIONS.

General.
Alexander Lindsay, Artlilery.

Lieutenant-Generals.
Thomas Monteath Douglas, Infantry.
James Eckford, Infantry.
George Edward Gowan, Artillery.
Henry Hall, Infantry.
George William Aylmer Lloyd, Infy.
William Pattle, Cavalry.
Abraham Roberts, Infantry.
John Tulloch, Infantry.
Edmund Frederick Waters, Infantry.

Major Generals.
Augustus Abbott, Artillery.
James Alexander, Artillery.
Arthur Mitford Becher, Infantry.
John Fowler Bradford, Cavalry.
George Brooke, Artillery.
Charles Montabin Carmichael, Cavalry.
Alexander Carnegy, Infantry.
Stuart Corbett, Infantry.
William John Gairdner, Infantry.
Christopher Godby, Infantry.
Charles Grant, Artillery.
Charles Hamilton, Infantry.
Andrew Hervey, Infantry.
George Hicks, Infantry.
John Hoggan, Infantry.
Edward Huthwaite, Artillery.
George Huyshe, Infantry.
Charles Richard William Lane, Infy.
John Theophilus Lane, Artillery.
Joseph Nash, Infantry.
James Parsons, Infantry.
Archibald Fullerton Richmond, Infy.
Henry Fisher Salter, Cavalry.
Philip Francis Story, Cavalry.
Christopher Dixon Wilkinson, Infy.

XXXV

Colonels.

James Brind, Artillery.
Neville Bowles Chamberlain, Infantry.
John Coke, Infantry,
R. Drought, Infantry.
H. F. Dunsford, Infantry.
Henry Marion Durand, Engineers.
Vincent Eyre, Artillery.
Henry Foster, Infantry.
Frederick Gaitskell, Artillery.
John Craigie Halkett, Infantry.
C. Hogge, Artillery.
G. St. P. Lawrence, Cavalry (*Civil*).
J. D. Macpherson, Infantry.
Robert Augustus Master, Cavalry.
J. K. McCausland, Infantry.
Charles Reid, Infantry.
William Riddell, Infantry.
Francis Rowcroft, Infantry.
Sir R. C. Shakespear, Kt., Artillery (*Civil*).
St. George Daniel Showers, Infantry.
Richard Baird Smith, Engineers.
W. B. Thomson, Infantry.
Henry Tombs, Artillery.
Colin Troup, Infantry.
Auchmuty Tucker, Cavalry.
Frank Turner, Artillery.
J. M. B. F. Tytler, Infantry.
John Welchman, Infantry.

Lieutenant-Colonels.

C. H. Blunt, Artillery.
G. Bourchier, Artillery.
Jeremiah Brasyer, Infantry.
Samuel James Browne, Infantry.
H. A. Carleton, Artillery.
C. Davidson, Infantry (*Civil*).
G. W. G. Green, Infantry.
E. B. Johnson, Artillery.
H. B. Lumsden, Infantry.

Lieutenant-Colonels.—(Continued.)

James Metcalfe, Infantry.
G. Moir, Artillery.
H. W. Norman, Infantry.
W. Olpherts, Artillery.
D. M. Probyn, Cavalry.
F. F. Remmington, Artillery.
John Hall Smyth, Artillery.
A. Taylor, Engineers.
K. Young, Infantry.

Majors.

C. H. Barchard, Infantry.
J. R. Becher, Engineers (*Civil*).
William Tod Brown, Artillery.
J. W. Carnegie, Infantry (*Civil*).
W. A. Crommelin, Engineers.
W. C. Erskine, Infantry (*Civil*).
W. W. H. Greathed, Engineers (*Civil*).
R. C. Lawrence, Infantry (*Civil*).
W. A. Mackinnon, Artillery.
H. Ramsay, Infantry (*Civil*).
J. F. Richardson, Infantry.
G. W. Williams, Infantry (*Civil*).
T. F. Wilson, Infantry.
Frederick Turner Wroughton, Infantry.

Captains.

B. Henderson, Infantry (*Civil*).
H. R. James, Infantry (*Civil*).

Inspector General of Hospitals.

C. Mackinnon, M. D.

Deputy Inspector-General of Hospitals.

John Campbell Brown.

Surgeon.

John Campbell.

BENGAL ARMY.

THE ORDER OF THE VICTORIA CROSS.

Lieut.-Col. S. J. Browne, c. b., 46th N. I.
,, Olpherts, c. b., Artillery.
,, Probyn, c. b., Cavalry.
,, Tombs, c. b., Artillery.
,, Travers, c. b., 2nd N. I.

Major Aikman, 4th N. I.
,, Cafe, 56th N. I.
,, C. J. S. Gough, 5th European Cavalry.
,, H. H. Gough, 1st European Cavalry.
,, Innes, Engineers.
,, G. A. Renny, Artillery.

Captain Forrest, Veteran Establishment.
,, Harrington, Artillery (since dead).
,, Raynor, Veteran Establishment.
,, Roberts, Artillery.
,, Tytler, 66th N. I.

Lieutenant F. Brown, 1st Fusiliers.
,, J. Buckley, Veteran Establishment.
,, Butler, 1st Fusiliers.
,, Cadell, 2nd Europeans.
,, Cattley, 62nd N. I.
,, Cubitt, 13th N. I.
,, J. C. Daunt, 70th N. I.
,, Hills, Artillery.
,, Jarrett, 26th N. I.
,, Lyster, 72nd N. I.
,, Roddy, Unattached.
,, J. Smith, Veteran Establishment.
,, Thackeray, Engineers.

Ensign P. Gill, Unattached.
,, Rosamond, Unattached.

DATES AND ACTS OF BRAVERY
OF THE
MEMBERS
OF
THE ORDER OF THE VICTORIA CROSS.

LIEUTENANT (NOW CAPTAIN) F. R. AIKMAN, *late 4th Regiment Native Infantry.*—Date of act of bravery, 1st March 1858. This Officer commanded the 3rd Sikh Cavalry on the advanced picket, with 100 of his men; having obtained information, just as the force marched on the morning of the 1st March last, of the proximity, three miles off on the high road, of a body of 500 rebel infantry, 200 horse, and 2 guns, under Moosahib Ali Chuckladar, attacked and utterly routed them, cutting up more than 100 men, capturing two guns, and driving the survivors into and over the Goomtee. This feat was performed under every disadvantage of broken ground, and partially under the flanking fire of an adjoining fort. Lieutenant Aikman received a severe sabre cut on the face in a personal encounter with several of the enemy.

LIEUTENANT F. D. M. BROWN, 1*st Fusiliers.*—Date of act of bravery, 16th November 1857. For great gallantry at Narrioul, on the 16th November 1857, in having, at the imminent risk of his own life, rushed to the assistance of a wounded Soldier of the 1st European Bengal Fusiliers, whom he carried off under a very heavy fire from the enemy, whose cavalry were within forty or fifty yards of him at the time.

COLONEL S. J. BROWNE, *C.B., late 46th Native Infantry.*—For having at Seerporah, in an engagement with the rebel forces under Khan Allie Khan, on 31st August 1858, whilst advancing upon the enemy's position at daybreak, pushed on with one Orderly Sowar upon a nine-pounder gun that was commanding one of the approaches to the enemy's position, and attacked the gunners, thereby preventing them from re-loading and firing upon the infantry, who were advancing to the attack. In doing this a personal conflict ensued, in which Captain (now Lieutenant-Colonel) Samuel James Browne, Commandant of the 2nd Punjab Cavalry, received a severe sword-cut wound on the left knee, and shortly afterwards another sword-cut wound, which severed the left arm at the shoulder, not, however, before Lieutenant-Colonel Browne had succeeded in cutting down one of his assailants. The gun was prevented from being re-loaded, and was eventually captured by the infantry, and the gunner slain.

DEPUTY ASSISTANT COMMISSARY OF ORDNANCE JOHN BUCKLEY. —Date of act of bravery, 11th May 1857. For gallant conduct in the defence of the Delhi Magazine on the 11th May 1857.

LIEUTENANT T. A. BUTLER, *1st Europeans*.—Date of act of bravery, 9th March 1858. " Of which success the skirmishers on the other side of the river were subsequently apprised by Lieutenant Butler, of the Bengal Fusiliers, who swam across the Goomtee, and, climbing up the parapet, remained in that position for a considerable time under a heavy fire, until the work was occupied." [General Sir J. Outram's Memorandum.]

LIEUTENANT THOMAS CADELL, *late 2nd European Bengal Fusiliers*.—For having, on the 12th June 1857, at the Flag Staff Picket at Delhi, when the whole of the picket of Her Majesty's 75th Regiment and 2nd European Bengal Fusiliers were driven in by a large body of the enemy, brought in from among the enemy a wounded bugler of his own regiment under a most severe fire, who would otherwise have been cut up by the rebels. Also, on the same day, when the Fusiliers were retiring, by order, on Metcalfe's house, on it being reported that there was a wounded man left behind, Lieutenant Cadell went back of his own accord towards the enemy, accompanied by three men, and brought in a man of the 75th Regiment, who was severely wounded, under a most heavy fire from the advancing enemy.

CAPTAIN (NOW MAJOR) W. M. CAFE, *late 56th Native Infantry*.— Date of act of bravery, 15th April 1858. For bearing away, under a heavy fire, with the assistance of Privates Thompson, Crowie, Spence, and Cook, the body of Lieutenant Willoughby, lying near the ditch of the Fort of Ruhya, and for running to the rescue of Private Spence, who had been severely wounded in the attempt.

LIEUTENANT H. C. CATTLEY, 62nd *Native Infantry*, has also received the Victoria Cross. (Date and act of valor not yet published).

LIEUTENANT W. G. CUBITT, 13th *Native Infantry*.—Date of act of bravery, 30th June 1857. For having, on the retreat from Chinhut, on the 30th June 1857, saved the lives of three men of the 32nd Regiment, at the risk of his own.

LIEUTENANT J. C. C. DAUNT, 10th (*late* 70th) *Native Infantry*.— Dates of acts of bravery, 2nd October and 2nd November 1857. Lieutenant Daunt, &c., are recommended for conspicuous gallantry in action on the 2nd October 1857, with the mutineers of the Ramgurh Battalion, at Chota Behar, in capturing two guns, particularly the last, when they rushed at and captured it by pistolling the gunners, who were mowing the detachment down with grape, one-third of which was *hors de combat* at the time.

CAPTAIN GEORGE FORREST, *Veteran Establishment*.—Date of act of bravery, 11th May 1857. For gallant conduct in the defence of the Delhi Magazine on the 11th May 1857.

SERGEANT-MAJOR (NOW ENSIGN) P. GILL, *Loodiana Regiment*.— Date of act of bravery, 4th June 1857. This Non-Commissioned Officer also conducted himself with gallantry at Benares on the night of the 4th June 1857. He volunteered with Sergeant-Major Rosamond, of the 37th N. I., to bring in Captain Brown, Pension Pay-master, and his family, from a detached bungalow to the barracks, and saved the life of the Quarter-Master Sergeant of the 25th N. I. in the early part of the evening, by cutting off the head of the Sepoy who had just bayonetted him. Sergeant-Major Gill states, that on the same night he faced a guard of twenty-seven men with only a Sergeant's sword; and it is also represented that he twice saved the life of Major Barett, 27th N. I., when attacked by the Sepoys of his own Regiment.

MAJOR C. J. S. GOUGH, *late 5th European Cavalry*.—Dates of acts of bravery, 15th and 18th August 1857 and 27th January and

23rd February 1858. *First.*—For gallantry in an affair at Khurkowdah, near Rhotuck, on the 15th August, in which he saved his brother, who was wounded, and killed two of the enemy. *Secondly.*—For gallantry on the 18th August, when he led a troop of the Guide Cavalry in a charge, and cut down two of the enemy's sowars, with one of whom he had a desperate hand to hand encounter. *Thirdly.*—For gallantry on the 27th of January 1858, at Shumshabad, where, in a charge, he attacked one of the enemy's leaders, pierced him with his sword, which was carried out of his hand in the mêlée. He defended himself with his revolver, and shot two of the enemy. *Fourthly.*—For gallantry, on the 23rd February, at Meangunge, where he came to the assistance of Brevet-Major O. H. St. G. Anson, and killed his opponent immediately, afterwards cutting down another of the enemy in the same gallant manner.

LIEUTENANT (NOW MAJOR) HUGH HENRY GOUGH, 1*st European Light Cavalry.*—Dates of acts of bravery, 12th November 1857 and 25th February 1858. Lieutenant Gough, when in command of a party of Hodson's Horse, near Alumbagh, on the 12th November 1857, particularly distinguished himself by his forward bearing in charging across a swamp, and capturing two guns, although defended by a vastly superior body of the enemy. On this occasion he had his horse wounded in two places, and his turban cut through by sword cuts, whilst engaged in combat with three Sepoys. Lieutenant Gough also particularly distinguished himself near Jellalabad, Lucknow, on the 25th February 1858, by showing a brilliant example to his Regiment, when ordered to charge the enemy's guns, and by his gallant and forward conduct he enabled them to effect their object; on this occasion he engaged himself in a series of single combats, until at length he was disabled by a musket ball through the leg, while charging two Sepoys with fixed bayonets. Lieutenant Gough on this day had two horses killed under him, a shot through his helmet, and another through his scabbard, besides being severely wounded.

LIEUTENANT HARRINGTON (with others), *Bengal Artillery* (since dead).—Dates of acts of bravery, from 14th to 22nd November

1857. Elected respectively under the 13th Clause of the Royal Warrant of the 29th January 1856, by the Officers and Non-Commissioned Officers generally, and by the private Soldiers of each troop and battery, for conspicuous gallantry at the relief of Lucknow, from the 14th to the 22nd November 1857.

LIEUTENANT (NOW MAJOR) J. J. McLEOD INNES, *Bengal Engineers.*—Date of act of bravery, 23rd February 1858. At the action of Sultanpore, Lieutenant Innes, far in advance of the leading skirmishers, was the first to secure a gun which the enemy were abandoning. Retiring from this, they rallied round another gun further back, from which the shot would, in another instant, have ploughed through our advancing columns, when Lieutenant Innes rode up, unsupported, shot the gunner who was about to apply the match, and, remaining undaunted at his post, the mark for a hundred matchlockmen, who were sheltered in some adjoining huts, kept the artillerymen at bay until assistance reached him. [Letter from Major-General Thomas Harte Franks, K.C.B., of the 12th March 1858.]

LIEUTENANT H. C. J. JARRETT, *late 26th Native Infantry.*—Date of act of bravery, 14th October 1858. For an act of daring bravery, at the village of Baroun, on the 14th October 1858, on an occasion when about 20 Sepoys were defending themselves in a brick building, the only approach to which was up a very narrow street; in having called on the men of his Regiment to follow him, when, backed by only some four men, he made a dash at the narrow entrance, where, though a shower of balls was poured upon him, he pushed his way up to the wall of the house, and, beating up the bayonets of the rebels with his sword, endeavored to get in.

LIEUTENANT H. H. LYSTER, *late 72nd Native Infantry.*—Date of act of bravery, 23rd May 1858. For gallantly charging and breaking, singly, a skirmishing square of the retreating rebel army from Calpee, and killing two or three Sepoys in the conflict. Major-General Sir Hugh Rose, G.C.B., reports that this act of bravery was witnessed by himself and Colonel Gall, C.B., of the 11th Light Dragoons.

CAPTAIN (NOW LIEUTENANT-COLONEL) W. OLPHERTS, *C.B.*— Date of act of bravery, 25th September 1857. For highly distinguished

f

conduct on the 25th September 1857, when the troops penetrated into the City of Lucknow, in having charged on horseback with H. M.'s 90th Regiment, when gallantly headed by Colonel Campbell, it captured two guns in the face of a very heavy fire of grape, and having afterwards returned under a severe fire of musketry, to bring up limbers and horses to carry off the captured ordnance, which he accomplished. [Extract from Field Force Orders of the late Major-General Havelock, dated 17th October 1857.]

CAPTAIN (NOW LIEUTENANT-COLONEL) D. M. PROBYN, *C.B.*, has been distinguished for gallantry and daring throughout this Campaign. At the battle of Agra, when his Squadron charged the rebel infantry, he was some time separated from his men, and surrounded by five or six Sepoys; he defended himself from the various cuts made at him, and before his own men had joined him, he had cut down two of his assailants. At another time, in single combat with a Sepoy, he was wounded in the wrist by the bayonet, and his horse also was slightly wounded; but, though the Sepoy fought desperately, he cut him down. The same day he singled out a standard-bearer, and, in presence of a number of the enemy, killed him, and captured the standard. These are only a few of the gallant deeds of this brave young Officer. [Despatch from Major-General Sir Hope Grant, K.C.B., dated 10th January 1858.]

CAPTAIN WILLIAM RAYNOR, *Veteran Establishment.*—Date of act of bravery, 11th May 1857. For gallant conduct in the defence of the Delhi Magazine on the 11th May 1857.

MAJOR G. A. RENNY, *Bengal Artillery.*—Date of act of bravery, 16th September 1857. Lieutenant-Colonel Farquhar, Commanding the 1st Belooch Regiment, reports that he was in command of the troops stationed in the Delhi Magazine after its capture on the 16th September 1857. Early in the forenoon of that day a vigorous attack was made on the post by the enemy, and was kept up with great violence for some time without the slightest chance of success. Under cover of a heavy cross fire from the high houses on the right flank of the magazine, and from Selimghur and the Palace, the enemy advanced to the high wall of the magazine, and endeavored to set fire to a thatched roof. The roof was partially set fire to, which was extinguished on the spot by a Sepoy of the Belooch Battalion, a Soldier of the 61st Regiment having in vain attempted to do so. The roof having again been set on fire, Captain Renny, with great gallantry, mounted to the top of the wall of the magazine, and flung several shells with lighted fuzes over into the midst of the enemy, which had an almost immediate effect, as the attack at once became feeble at that point, and soon after ceased there.

LIEUTENANT F. S. ROBERTS, *Bengal Artillery.*—Date of act of bravery, 2nd January 1858. Lieutenant Roberts's gallantry has, on every occasion, been most marked. On following up the retreating enemy on the 2nd January 1858, at Khodagunge, he saw in the distance two Sepoys going away with a standard. Lieutenant Roberts put spurs to his horse, and overtook them just as they were about to enter a village; they immediately turned round and presented their muskets at him, some of them pulled the trigger, but fortunately the caps snapped, and the standard-bearer was cut down by this gallant young Officer, and the standard taken possession of by him. He also, on the same day, cut down another Sepoy who was standing at bay, with musket and bayonet, keeping off a Sowar. Lieutenant Roberts rode to the assistance of the horseman, and, rushing at the Sepoy, with one blow of his sword cut him across the face, killing him on the spot.

ENSIGN (NOW LIEUTENANT) P. RODDY, *Unattached List.*—Date of act of bravery, 27th September 1858. Major-General Sir J. H. Grant, K.C.B., Commanding Oude Force, bears testimony to the gallant conduct of Lieutenant Roddy on several occasions. One instance is particularly mentioned. On the return from Kuthirga of the Kupperthulla Contingent, on the 27th September 1858, this Officer, when engaged with the enemy, charged a rebel (armed with a percussion musket), whom the cavalry were afraid to approach; as each time they attempted to do so, the rebel knelt and covered his assailant; this, however, did not deter Lieutenant Roddy, who went boldly in, and when within six yards the rebel fired, killing Lieutenant Roddy's horse, and before he could get disengaged from the horse, the rebel attempted to cut him down. Lieutenant Roddy seized the rebel until he could get at his sword, when he ran the man through the body. The rebel turned out to be a Subadar of the late 8th N. I., a powerful man, and a most determined character.

SERGEANT-MAJOR (NOW ENSIGN) M. ROSAMOND.—Date of act of bravery, 4th June 1857. This Non-Commissioned Officer volunteered to accompany Lieutenant-Colonel Spottiswoode, Commanding the 37th N. I., to the right of the lines, in order to set them on fire, with the view of driving out the Sepoys, on the occasion of the outbreak at Benares, on the evening of the 4th June 1857 ; and also volunteered, with Sergeant-Major Gill, of the Loodiana Regiment, to bring off Captain Brown and his wife and infant, and also some others, from a detached bungalow, into the barracks. His conduct was highly meritorious, and he has since been promoted.

SERGEANT-MAJOR (NOW ENSIGN) JOHN SMITH, *Unattached, Bengal Sappers and Miners.*—Date of act of bravery, 14th September 1857. For conspicuous gallantry, in conjunction with Lieutenants Home and Salkeld, (both of whom would have had the Cross had they lived), in the performance of the desperate duty of blowing in the Cashmere Gate of the fortress of Delhi in broad daylight, under a heavy and destructive fire of musketry, on the morning of the 14th September 1857, preparatory to the assault. [General Order of Major-General Sir A. Wilson, K.C.B., dated Head Quarters, Delhi City, 21st September 1857.]

LIEUTENANT EDWARD TALBOT THACKERAY, *Bengal Engineers.*—For cool intrepidity and characteristic daring in extinguishing a fire in the Delhi Magazine enclosures, on the 16th of September 1857, under a close and heavy musketry fire from the enemy, at the imminent risk of his life, from the explosion of combustible stores in the shed in which the fire occurred.

COLONEL TOMBS, *C.B.*, AND LIEUTENANT JAMES HILLS.—Date of act of bravery, 9th July 1857. For very gallant conduct on the part of Lieutenant Hills before Delhi in defending the position assigned to him in case of alarm, and for noble behaviour on the part of Lieutenant-Colonel Tombs in twice coming to his Subaltern's rescue, and on each occasion killing his man. [See Despatch of Lieutenant-Colonel Mackenzie, Commanding 1st Brigade, H. A., dated Camp near Delhi, 10th July 1857.]

COLONEL J. TRAVERS, *C.B.*, *late 2nd Native Infantry.*—For a daring act of bravery, in July 1857, when the Indore Residency was suddenly attacked by Holkar's troops, in having charged the guns with only five men to support him, and driven the gunners from the guns, thereby creating a favorable diversion, which saved the lives of many persons, fugitives to the Residency. It is stated that Officers who were present considered that the effect of the charge was to enable many Europeans to escape from actual slaughter, and time was gained which enabled the faithful Bhopal Artillery to man their guns. Colonel Travers's horse was shot in three places, and his accoutrements were shot through in various parts. He commanded the Bhopal Levy.

LIEUTENANT (NOW CAPTAIN) J. A. TYTLER, 66*th* (*Goorkha*) *Bengal Native Infantry.*—Date of act of bravery, 10th February 1858. On the attacking parties approaching the enemy's position, on the occasion of the action at Choopoorah, on the 10th February last, Lieutenant Tytler dashed on horseback ahead of all, and alone rode up to the enemy's guns, where he remained, engaged hand to hand, until they were carried by us; and where he was shot through the left arm, had a spear wound in his chest, and a ball through the right sleeve of his coat. [Letter from Captain C. C. G. Ross, Commanding 66th (Goorkha) Regiment, to Captain Brownlow, Major of Brigade, Kumaon Field Force.]

NOTE.—Captain Shebbeare, of the late 60th Native Infantry, was also decorated with the Order: he died in China. Many others, had they survived, would have had the Order, amongst whom would have been Howe, Salkeld, and the brothers Willoughby. Majors Thomson and Delafosse, the survivors of Cawnpore, are, I hear, to get this coveted decoration.

OFFICERS
WHO HAVE RECEIVED FOREIGN ORDERS.

Spanish—*San Fernando.*
Colonel W. F. Beatson, Infantry.

Affghan.	Dooranee.
Lieut.-General A. Roberts, C.B., Infantry	2nd Class.
Major-General J. Parsons, C.B., Infantry	ditto.
Lieut.-General T. M. Douglas, Infantry	ditto.
Major-General C. M. Carmichael, C.B., Cavalry	3rd Class.
Major-General G. Warren, Infantry	ditto.
Major-General H. F. Salter, C.B., Cavalry	ditto.
Major-General D. Birrell, Infantry	ditto.
Major-General A. Abbott, C. B., Artillery	ditto.
Colonel J. Christie, Cavalry	ditto.
Colonel F. Wheler, Cavalry	ditto.
Colonel G. St. P. Lawrence, C.B., Cavalry	ditto.
Colonel *Sir* R. C. Shakespear, C.B., Artillery	ditto.
Colonel C. Troup, Infantry	ditto.
Colonel B. Bygrave, Infantry	ditto.
Colonel J. Abbott, Artillery	ditto.
J. Forsyth, Medical Department	ditto.

Lieut. Cattley, 5th Class Legion of Honor.

THE BENGAL STAFF CORPS.

The following List, alpahabetically arranged, may prove useful. It is compiled from the Official List, and arranged so as to afford a ready reference. All Officers rank in it from the 18th February 1861. The Rules constituting the Staff Corps will be found in G. G. O. No. 332 of 1861, dated 10th April 1861.

A.

LIEUTENANT-COLONEL.

Atkinson, F. D., Controller of Military Finance.

MAJORS.

Adams, R. R., 2nd Class Deputy Commissioner, Punjab, Shahpore.
Adlam, H. C., Commanding Behar Irregular Horse.
Agnew, W., Judicial Commissioner of Assam.
Alexander, F., 1st Class Executive Engineer, Department Public Works, 1st Circle, North-Western Provinces.
Alexander, W. R. E., Officiating Commandant, 3rd Bengal Cavalry.

CAPTAINS.

Aikman, F. R., v. c., Europe, Medical Certificate, 4 years.
Aitken, R. H. M., Deputy Inspector-General of Police, Oude.
Allan, A. S., Cantonment Joint-Magistrate, Cawnpore.
Allen, A., 1st Class Executive Engineer, Department Public Works, North-Western Provinces, Superintendent, Roorkee Work-shops.
Allgood, G., Europe, Private Affairs, 2 years.
Anderson, F. C., Revenue Surveyor, Baiswarrah, Oude.
Anderson, H. C., Officiating Assistant Adjutant-General, Peshawur.
Annesley, R. M. S., Commandant, Meywar Bheel Corps, and Superintendent, Hill Tracts, Meywar.
Austen, H. H. G., 2nd Assistant, Great Trigonometrical Survey of India, Cashmere Series.

LIEUTENANTS.

Alexander, G., Doing duty, 2nd Battalion, Her Majesty's Rifle Brigade.
Allen, F., Second in Command, 18th Native Infantry.
Andrew, A., Assistant Commissioner in the Cossyah and Jynteeah Hills.
Angelo, J., Interpreter and Quarter-Master, 8th Native Infantry.
Armstrong, R. G., Officiating Second in Command, 15th Native Infantry.

B.

LIEUTENANT-COLONEL.

Brooke, J. C., Political Agent, Jeypore.

MAJORS.

Bacon, B. E., 1st Assistant Secretary to Government of India, Military Department.
Baird, A. F., 3rd Class Executive Engineer, Department Public Works, Bengal.
Bartlett, H. T., Europe, Private Affairs, 2 years.
Becher, A. M., C. B., Quarter-Master General of the Army.
Becher, S. H., Finance Department.
Bivar, H. S., 1st Class Deputy Commissioner, Assam, Luckimpore.
Black, G. A., Second in Command, Erinpoorah Irregular Force.
Blackwood, A., Commanding 35th Native Infantry.
Briggs, D., 2nd Class Executive Engineer, Department Public Works, Bengal.
Briggs, J. P., 2nd Class Deputy Commissioner, British Burmah, Martaban.
Bristow, J. W., Second Class Deputy Commissioner, Punjab, Jhelum.
Bouverie, P. A. P., Political Agent, Bhurtpore.
Browne, S. J., C. B. and V. C., Commanding 2nd Punjab Cavalry.

CAPTAINS.

Babbage, H. P., 2nd Class Assistant Commissioner, Punjab, Attock.
Bacon, F. K., Acting 1st Class Barrack-Master, Allahabad.
Baillie, J.
Baker, W. T., Commanding 4th Goorkha Regiment.
Baldwin, C., Assistant Commissioner, Central Provinces.
Bamfield, A. H., Personal Assistant to the Inspector-General of Police, Punjab.

CAPTAINS.—*(Continued.)*

Barlow, W. J. P., Station Staff, Landour.
Barter, R., Commanding 15th Native Infantry.
Barwell, C. A., Deputy Assistant Adjutant-General, Oude.
Basevi, G. H., Deputy Assistant Quarter-Master General of the Army, Gwalior.
Battye, H. D., Assistant Pay-master, Rawul Pindee.
Battye, J. M., Post-Master General, North-Western Provinces.
Baugh, B. H., Cantonment Joint-Magistrate, Barrackpore.
Bayly, A. R., 3rd Class Executive Engineer, Department Public Works, Lahore and Peshawur.
Bean, J. W. F., Cantonment Joint-Magistrate, Rawul Pindee.
Bernard, H. L. C., Doing duty, 5th Goorkha Regiment.
Binny, W. H.
Birch, R. C., 1st Class Deputy Commissioner, Lohardugga.
Black, S., Secretary to Government, Punjab, Military Department.
Blunt, A., Commanding 8th Bengal Police Battalion.
Boileau, N. E., Deputy Judge Advocate-General, Peshawur.
Boisragon, H. F. M., Commanding 4th Sikh Infantry.
Boisragon, T. W. R., Commanding 30th Native Infantry.
Boulderson, S. S.
Bracken, R. D'O. C., Second in Command, 2nd Sikh Infantry.
Briggs, W., 1st Class Sub-Assistant Commissary-General.
Brown, C. L., Pay-master and Superintendent, Native Pensioners, Dinapore.
Browne, C. F., Deputy Judge Advocate-General, Meerut.
Brownlow, C. H., Commanding, 20th Native Infantry.
Bruce, A. H. B., Doing duty, Meerut.
Burn, J., Resident Councillor, Malacca.
Burne, H. K., Deputy Secretary to Government of India, Military Department.
Byers, C. H., Officiating Adjutant, 11th Native Infantry.

LIEUTENANTS.

Badgley, W. F., Adjutant, 26th Native Infantry.
Barwell, W. B., Adjutant, 16th Bengal Cavalry.

LIEUTENANTS.—*(Continued.)*

Bates, C. E., Second in Command, 23rd Native Infantry.
Battye, C. F., Adjutant, 22nd Native Infantry.
Beckett, S., Doing duty, 1st Sikh Infantry.
Beddy, E., Adjutant, 29th Native Infantry.
Bertie, F. A., Adjutant, Lahore Light Horse.
Bewsher, F. C., 3rd Class Assistant Commissioner, Punjab, Dehra Gazee Khan.
Birch, F. M., 3rd Class Assistant Commissioner, Punjab, Rawul Pindee.
Blair, J. J., Adjutant, 1st Regiment, Central India Horse.
Boddam, W. W., District Superintendent of Police, Punjab, Lahore.
Boileau, F. W., Second in Command, 12th Bengal Cavalry.
Bond, E. E. B., Adjutant, Corps of Guides, Officiating Commandant of Cavalry, Corps of Guides.
Boswell, J. J., District Superintendent of Police, Punjab.
Bruce, A. A., Adjutant, 17th Native Infantry.
Browne, S. J., Adjutant, 6th Punjab Infantry.
Burlton, N. R., 2nd Class Sub-Assistant Commissary-General, Meerut.
Bushby, J. T., 2nd Class Assistant Commissioner, Hyderabad.

C.

MAJORS.

Campbell, A. H., Officiating Deputy Assistant Adjutant-General, Oude.
Campbell, R., Commanding 43rd Native Infantry.
Caulfeild, J. P., Commanding 9th Bengal Cavalry.
Cave, G. N., Commanding 24th Native Infantry.
Cavenagh, O., Governor of Prince of Wales' Island, Singapore and Malacca.
Chamberlain, C. T., Commanding 1st Bengal Cavalry.
Chambers, R. W., Doing duty, Meerut.
Christopher, L. R., Officiating 1st Class Assistant Commissary-General, Meerut.
Cookson, G. R., Cantonment Joint-Magistrate, Meerut.
Cripps, J. M., 2nd Class Deputy Commissioner, Punjab, Ferozepore.
Curtis, J. C., Commanding 4th Bengal Cavalry.

CAPTAINS.

Cadell, R., District Superintendent of Police, 2nd Grade, Furruckabad.
Callander, A., Brigade-Major, Mooltan.
Campbell, H. L., Europe, Medical Certificate, 2 years.
Campbell, J. P. W., Commanding 1st Sikh Infantry.
Carnegie, G. F., Cantonment Joint-Magistrate, Futteygurh.
Carnell, W., District Superintendent of Police, 3rd Grade, Ajmere.
Chalmers, H. B., Officiating Assistant Commissary-General, 2nd Class, Presidency.
Chalmers, R., Second in Command, 14th Bengal Cavalry.
Chamberlain, T. H., Assistant to the General Superintendent of Operations for the Suppression of Thuggee and Dacoitee, Lucknow.
Chambers, R. Y., Doing duty, 43rd Native Infantry.
Clark, E. G.
Clay, E. B., District Superintendent of Police, Central Provinces.
Cockburn, H. A., Assistant, Military Finance Department.
Comber, A. K., 1st Class Deputy Commissioner, Assam, Luckimpore.
Conolly, W. P., Second in Command, 3rd Regiment, Central India Horse.
Cookson, S. B., Brigade Major, Sind Saugor, Rawul Pindee.
Cooper, J. K., Civil Architect, Calcutta.
Corbett, A. F., Officiating Deputy Commissioner, Lullutpore.
Corbett, T. A., Officiating 2nd Class Deputy Commissioner, Lullutpore.
Coxe, H. W. H., 1st Class Deputy Commissioner, Punjab, Peshawur.
Cracroft, J. E., 1st Class Deputy Commissioner, Punjab, Rawul Pindee.
Cunliffe, G. G., Doing duty, Moradabad.
Cureton, C., Commanding 15th Bengal Cavalry.

LIEUTENANTS.

Cadell, T., Deputy Bheel Agent and Second in Command, Malwah Bheel Corps.
Campbell, H., Europe, Medical Certificate, 3 years.
Campbell, R. B. P. P., Adjutant, 2nd Punjab Cavalry.
Campbell, R. D., Adjutant, 89th Native Infantry.
Case, C., Doing duty, 18th Bengal Cavalry.
Cattley, H. C., Second in Command, 19th Bengal Cavalry.
Chalmers, J., 3rd Class Assistant Commissioner, Punjab, Mooltan.

LIEUTENANTS.—*(Continued.)*

Chalmers, O. T., Doing duty, 5th Punjab Cavalry.
Chalmers, W. G., Adjutant, 23rd Native Infantry.
Chambers, B. R., Second in Command, 3rd Sikh Infantry.
Chapman, A. R., Doing duty, 15th Bengal Cavalry.
Chapman, H., Doing duty, Her Majesty's 8th Hussars.
Chester, C. W. R., Second in Command, 4th Goorkha Regiment.
Chester, H. D. E. W., Adjutant, 5th Bengal Cavalry.
Clifford, R., Adjutant, 1st Punjab Cavalry.
Codrington, E. C., Adjutant, 5th Goorkha Regiment.
Coghill, K. J. W., Brigade-Major, Cawnpore.
Collett, H., Second in Command, 21st Native Infantry.
Conolly, F. H., Doing duty, 5th Punjab Infantry.
Copland, A., Officiating Second in Command, 19th Native Infantry.
Cox, J. B., Doing duty, Cawnpore.
Cripps, A. W., Europe and Cape of Good Hope, Medical Certificate, 22 months.
Cross, R. C., Second in Command, Bhopal Levy.

D.

MAJORS.

Dalton, E. T., Commissioner of Chota Nagpore.
Davies, J. S., Judicial Commissioner, South-Western Frontier Agency, Chota Nagpore.
Davies, S. H. J., 2nd Class Executive Engineer, Department Public Works, 1st Circle, Punjab.
Dawson, J., 4th Class Executive Engineer, Department Public Works, Bengal.
Dennis, E. S., District Superintendent of Police, Punjab, Kangra.
Dennys, E. L., Second in Command, 35th Native Infantry.
Dennys, J. B., 2nd Class Deputy Commissioner, Central Provinces, Rajpore.
Dunbar, J. S., Officiating 1st Class Sub-Assistant Commissary General, Dacca.
Dwyer, H. A., 1st Class Assistant Commissioner, Punjab, Rawul Pindee.

liii

CAPTAINS.

Dandridge, C. C., Second in Command, 34th Native Infantry.
Dandridge, E., Commanding 40th Native Infantry.
Darwell, T. C., Cantonment Joint-Magistrate, Ferozepore.
Davidson, R., 1st Class Deputy Assistant Commissary-General.
Davies, H. N., Secretary to the Chief Commissioner, British Burmah.
Davies, W. G., Assistant Commissioner, Punjab, Loodianah.
Davis, W., Deputy Inspector-General of Police, Jhansi.
Delane, G., Commanding the Governor-General's Body Guard.
D'Oyly, C. W., Deputy Superintendent of Studs, North-Western Provinces, Haupper.
Dickens, A. D., 2nd Class Assistant Commissary-General.
Doran, J., Commanding 27th Native Infantry.
Drew, H. R., Commanding Kamroop Police Regiment.
Dunbar, J. S., Officiating 1st Class Sub-Assistant Commissary-General, Dacca.

LIEUTENANTS.

Darrah, H. Z., 4th Class Executive Engineer, Department Public Works, 2nd Circle, North-Western Provinces.
Davidson, J. P., Second in Command, 1st Punjab Infantry.
Davidson, T. R., Second in Command, 18th Bengal Cavalry.
Dayrell, T., Second in Command, 9th Bengal Cavalry.
DeKantzow, C. A., 3rd Class Assistant Commissioner, Delhi.
Dennehy, T., Deputy Inspector-General of Police, Allahabad.
Dick, A. A., Adjutant, 11th Bengal Cavalry.
Dodd, C. A., District Superintendent of Police, 3rd Grade, North-Western Provinces.
Drummond, W. L. P., Europe, Medical Certificate, 15 months.
Dunbar, F. W., District Superintendent of Police, 4th Grade, Meerut.

E.

LIEUTENANT-COLONEL.

Elliot, E. K., Chief Commissioner, Central Provinces.

MAJORS.

Edwardes, Sir H. B., K. C. B., Commissioner and Agent to the Lieutenant-Governor of the Punjab, Cis-Sutlej States.

MAJORS.—*(Continued.)*

Eliott, W. R., 2nd Class Deputy Commissioner, Punjab, Kurnaul.

CAPTAINS.

Earle, W. H. S., District Superintendent of Police, Bareilly.
Eckford, J. J., Deputy Inspector-General of Police, North-Western Provinces, Agra.
Ekins, C. C., Doing duty, Bareilly.
Elderton, A., Pay-master, Meerut.
Elphinstone, N. W., 3rd Class Deputy Commissioner of Punjab, Jullundur.
Elwyn, W., Cantonment Joint-Magistrate, Peshawur.
Emerson, J., Cantonment Joint-Magistrate, Dinapore.
Evans, J. M., Superintendent of Studs, Meerut.
Evatt, M. F., District Superintendent of Police, Etawah.

LIEUTENANT.

Eckford, A. H., 3rd Class Assistant Commissioner, Oude, Baraitch.

F.

MAJORS.

Faithfull, G., 2nd Class Deputy Commissioner, British Burmah.
Farrington, O. J. McL., 1st Class Deputy Commissioner, Punjab, Umritsur.
Fooks, G. A. St. P., Europe, Private Affairs, 2 years.
Fraser, J. E., Brigade-Major, Fyzabad.
Fytche, A., Commissioner of Tenasserim.

CAPTAINS.

Fagan, W. T., Commanding 4th Bengal Police Battalion.
Fendall, J., 3rd Class Deputy Commissioner, Punjab, Bunnoo.
Ferris, R. J. D., 1st Class Assistant Commissioner, Punjab, Bunnoo.
Fisher, J. F. L., Junior Assistant Commissioner, Kumaon.
Fitzgerald, C. M., Deputy Commissary-General, Umballah.
Forbes, F. M. H., Inspector of Schools, Punjab, Rawul Pindee.
Forbes, H., Commanding Bhopal Levy.
Forster, T. F., 1st Class Assistant Commissioner, Punjab, Mozuffergurh.
Forsyth, A. G., Second in Command, 42nd Native Infantry.

CAPTAINS.—*(Continued.)*

Fraser, G. L., Officiating Adjutant-General of the Army.
Fraser, G. W., Doing duty, 4th Native Infantry.
Fraser, The Honorable W. M., District Superintendent of Police, 1st Grade, Agra.
Fullerton, W., Acting Aide-de-Camp to Major-General J. MacDuff, c. b., Oude.

LIEUTENANTS.

Fagan, H. C., Doing duty, 27th Native Infantry.
Fellowes, H., Adjutant, 2nd Native Infantry.
Fisher, H. S. V., 3rd Class Assistant Commissioner, Oude, Luckimpore.
FitzGerald, J., Doing duty, 4th Punjab Cavalry.
Fitzhugh, A., Officiating Second in Command, 2nd Sikh Infantry.
Fletcher, C. W., Aide-de-Camp to the Lieutenant-Governor, North-Western Provinces.
Foote, F. B., District Superintendent of Police, Central Provinces.
Forbes, R. O. H., Doing duty, Gondah, Oude.
Forbes, W. E., 3rd Class Assistant Commissioner, Oude, Oonao.
Forlong, W. J., Doing duty, Corps of Guides.
Forsyth, J., Assistant to the Superintendent of Forests, Jubbulpore.
Freeman, F. P. W., Doing duty, Her Majesty's 8th Hussars.

G.

MAJORS.

Gardiner, P. F., Officiating Brigade-Major, Jullunder.
Gastrell, J. E., Revenue Surveyor, Backergunge.
Gibbs, J. T., Cantonment Joint-Magistrate, Shahjehanpore.
Gordon, W., Instructor of Musketry, Umballah.
Graham, S. F., 2nd Class Deputy Commissioner, Punjab, Thanessur District.
Green, G. W. G., c. b., Commanding 2nd Punjab Infantry.

CAPTAINS.

Garden, H. R., Assistant Quarter-Master General of the Army, Presidency.
Garstin, H. M., Commanding 42nd Native Infantry.
Gilbert, E. K. O., Brigade-Major, Dinapore.

CAPTAINS.—*(Continued.)*

Gill, P. H. P., Cantonment Joint-Magistrate, Benares.
Glasse, R. W., Second in Command, 15th Native Infantry.
Godby, C. J., Commanding 4th Punjab Cavalry.
Godby, R. F., Officiating Commandant, 15th Bengal Cavalry.
Gowan, J. Y., Doing duty, Saugor.
Graham, F. W., Doing duty, Presidency.
Graham, J., Officiating Deputy Assistant Commissary-General, 2nd Class, Bareilly.
Graham, J. M., Commanding 5th Bengal Police Battalion.
Grant, J. H., Officiating Revenue Surveyor, Nagpore.
Gully, F. J. S., Brigade-Major, Saugor.

LIEUTENANTS.

Garstin, C. J., Adjutant, 4th Goorkha Regiment.
Garstin, E. C., 2nd Class Assistant Engineer, Department Public Works, Irrigation Department, Punjab.
Garton, W. H., District Superintendent of Police, 5th Grade, Jounpore.
Gellie, F., Officiating Commandant, 39th Native Infantry.
Gibbon, W. M., Officiating Adjutant, Mhairwarra Local Battalion.
Gillespie, J., Second in Command, 1st Punjab Cavalry.
Glascock, T. B. M., Doing duty, 17th Bengal Cavalry.
Gordon, H. W., Adjutant, 20th Native Infantry.
Graham, G. F. T., Inspector-General of Police, Agra.
Graham, O. M., Officiating 1st Class Sub-Assistant Commissary-General, Jhansi.
Graham, R. B., District Superintendent of Police, 4th Grade, Etah.
Grey, L. J. H., Doing duty, 1st Punjab Cavalry.
Griffiths, C. J.
Gurdon, E. P., Assistant Commissioner, Punjab, Hosheyarpore.
Gustavinski, L., T. K., Adjutant, 2nd Punjab Infantry.

H.

LIEUTENANT-COLONELS.

Hamilton, G. W., Commissioner and Superintendent, Mooltan.
Hill, G. M., Military Accountant.

MAJORS.

Hall, G. W. M., Commanding 3rd Bengal Cavalry.
Hamilton, J. J., Junior Assistant to Commissioner of Mysore.
Hamilton, O., Pay-master and Superintendent of Native Pensioners, Haupper Circle.
Hatch, G. C., Deputy Judge Advocate-General of the Army.
Haughton, J. C., Superintendent of Port Blair, Andaman Islands.
Herbert, C., Superintendent of Mysore Princes and Ex-Ameers of Scinde, and Governor-General's Agent with the King of Oude.
Hire, S. J., Doing duty, Meerut.
Hockin, P. R., Commanding 12th Bengal Cavalry.
Holmes, G. E., Brigade-Major, Jullunder.
Holroyd, C., 1st Class Deputy Commissioner, Seebsaugor, Assam.
Hopkinson, H., Commissioner of Assam and Governor-General's Agent, North-Eastern Frontier.
Hunter, A., Deputy Pay-master, Allahabad.

CAPTAINS.

Haig, A. S., Europe, Private Affairs, 3 years.
Hall, C. H., 1st Class Assistant Commissioner, Punjab, Lahore.
Hallett, C. T., District Superintendent of Police, 1st Grade, Allygurh.
Hamilton, G., Assistant in Rajpootana Agency.
Hamilton, T. C., Europe, Medical Certificate, 20 months.
Hankin, G. C., Second in Command, 4th Bengal Cavalry.
Harrison, T. B., 1st Examiner, Pay Department.
Hawes, H. J., 2nd Class Deputy Commissioner, Rhotuck, Punjab.
Hay, G. J. D., Pay-master, Trans-Ravee, Rawul Pindee.
Hayley, H., Europe, Medical Certificate, 27 months.
Hildebrand, C. P., 1st Class Assistant Commissioner, British Burmah.
Hitchins, C. T., Instructor of Musketry, East India Regiment.
Hoggan, J. W., Second in Command, 25th Native Infantry.
Horne, J. C., 1st Class Assistant Commissioner, Rhotuck, Punjab.
Houchen, G. A. F., Superintendent of Roads, Department Public Works, Punjab, Simla.
Howard, E. W. E., Cantonment Joint-Magistrate, Delhi.
Hudson, J., Deputy Assistant Adjutant-General, Lahore.
Hughes, W. T., Commanding 1st Punjab Cavalry.

CAPTAINS.—*(Continued.)*

Hume, J. J., 1st Class Executive Engineer, Department Public Works, 2nd Circle, North-Western Provinces.
Hutchinson, A. R. E., Political Agent, Bhopal.
Hutchinson, G., Inspector General, Punjab Organized Constabulary.

LIEUTENANTS.

Hamilton, W., District Superintendent of Police, Ferozepore, Punjab.
Hammond, F., Adjutant, 4th Punjab Cavalry.
Hare, The Honorable H. H., Adjutant, 16th Native Infantry.
Harris, P. H. F., District Superintendent of Police, Punjab.
Hawes, C. W., Commandant, Cavalry, Corps of Guides.
Hawkins, F. D., Second in Command, 4th Punjab Cavalry.
Hawkins, F. K., 1st Class Assistant Commissioner, Oonao, Oude.
Hawkins, H. L., Doing duty, 7th Bengal Cavalry.
Heathcote, M. H., Deputy Assistant Quarter-Master General of the Army, 2nd Class, Meerut.
Hennessy, A. C., Adjutant, 14th Bengal Cavalry.
Hennessy, G. R., Doing duty, 2nd Goorkha Regiment.
Hewett, J. N. B., 3rd Class Assistant Commissioner, Oude.
Hewitt, G. L. K., Adjutant, 2nd Bengal Cavalry.
Hill, R. S., Adjutant, 1st Goorkha Regiment.
Hodgson, H. N., Second in Command, 31st Native Infantry.
Hoggan, G. H. W., Adjutant, 17th Bengal Cavalry.
Holroyd, W. R. M., Inspector of Schools, Umballah.
Horsford, N. M. T., Assistant Inspector-General of Police, Agra.
Hudleston, R. H., 3rd Class Assistant Commissioner, Peshawur, Punjab.
Hunt, J. V., 2nd Class (Officiating 1st Class) Sub-Assistant Commissary-General, Lucknow.
Hunter, C. P., Acting Adjutant, European Invalid Battalion, Chunar.
Hunter, M., Deputy Assistant Quarter-Master General of the Army, Oude.

I.

MAJORS.

Impey, H. B., 2nd Class Deputy Commissioner, South-Western Frontier Agency, Sumbulpore.
Irwin, W. B., Sub-Assistant, Stud Department, Ghazeepore.

CAPTAINS.

Ingram, J. S., Special Assistant Engineer, Department Public Works, Punjab.
Irvine, C., Second in Command, 27th Native Infantry.

LIEUTENANT.

Impey, E. C., Political Agent, Ulwar.

J.

MAJORS.

Jackson, G., Commanding 2nd Bengal Cavalry.
James, H. C., 4th Class Executive Engineer, Department Public Works, Bengal.
James, H. R., c. b., Commissioner and Superintendent of Peshawur.
Johnstone, H. C., Revenue Surveyor, Delhi.

CAPTAINS.

James, T., Examiner of the Commissariat, Barrack, Stud, and Clothing Departments.
Johnson, A. B., 2nd Class Assistant Secretary to Government of India, Military Department.
Jones, L. B., Commanding 3rd Punjab Cavalry.

LIEUTENANTS.

Jackson, E. S., 2nd Class Assistant, Stud Department, Saharunpore.
Jackson, W., 2nd Class Assistant Engineer, Department Public Works, North-Western Provinces.
Jarrett, H. C. T., v. c., Adjutant, 28th Native Infantry.
Jenkins, C. V., 3rd Class Assistant Commissioner, Punjab, Huzara.
Jenkins, F. H., Officiating Second in Command, Corps of Guides.
Johnstone, J. W. H., 3rd Class Assistant Commissioner, Punjab, Shahpore.

K.

CAPTAINS.

Keer, J., Officiating 1st Class Deputy Assistant Commissary-General, Kussowlie.

LIEUTENANTS.

Keen, F. J., Second in Command, 3rd Punjab Infantry.
Keir, G. L., Officiating 1st Class Sub-Assistant Commissary-General, Mooltan.
Kennedy, T. G., Second in Command, Corps of Guides.
Knyvett, F. A. C., District Superintendent of Police, 3rd Grade, Boolundshuhur.

L.

LIEUTENANT-COLONEL.

Lawrence, G. St. P., c. b., Agent to the Governor-General for the States of Rajpootana, and Commissioner for the Neemuch District.

MAJORS.

Lamb, C. F. G., Commanding Raneegunge Depôt.
Lawrence, R. C., c. b., Deputy Commissioner 1st Class, and Superintendent of Hill States, Simlah.
Layard, F. P., 2nd Class Superintending Engineer, Department Public Works, Bengal.
Leigh, R. T., 1st Class Assistant Commissioner, British Burmah.
Lloyd, B. P., Deputy Commissioner of Ajmere and Mhairwarrah.
Lumsden, H. B., c. b., Brigadier, Commanding Hyderabad Contingent.

CAPTAINS.

Lamb, T., Assistant Commissioner, Assam.
Lane, C. S., 1st Class Sub-Assistant Commissary-General.
Langmore, E. H., Commanding 33rd Native Infantry.
Leeds, E., 3rd Class Executive Engineer, Department Public Works, Pegu.
LeGallais, A., District Superintendent of Police, Sealkote.
Leicester, W. F., Officiating Second in Command, 35th Native Infantry.
Lind, J. B., Europe, Private Affairs, 2 years.
Lloyd, E. P., 2nd Class Deputy Commissioner, Assam, Kamroop.
Longmore, C. M.
Lowe, J. R. A. S., 1st Class Deputy Assistant Commissary-General, Benares.
Lumsden, P. S., Assistant Quarter-Master General of the Army, Peshawur.

LIEUTENANTS.

Lance, F., Second in Command, 2nd Punjab Cavalry.
Lowes, H. A., Adjutant, 30th Native Infantry.
Lightfoot, E., Adjutant, 44th Native Infantry.
Lindsay, A. F., Placed at disposal of Home Department.
Liston, J., Doing duty, 36th Native Infantry.
Loughnan, A. R., Adjutant, 18th Native Infantry.

M.

MAJORS.

MacDonald, J. D., Commanding Deolee Irregular Force.
Macpherson, R. D., 1st Class Assistant Commissary-General, Allahabad.
Marquis, J., Second in Command, 17th Native Infantry.
Matheson, J. B. Y., Leave on Private Affairs to Nynee Tal.
Mayne, R. G., Doing duty, Moradabad.
McAndrew, G., Deputy Inspector-General, Lahore Police.
McMullin, A. L., 1st Assistant to the Governor-General's Agent for Central India.
McMullin, J. R., Doing duty, Umballah.
McNeile, W., 1st Class Deputy Commissioner, Punjab, Loodianah.
Meade, R. J., Temporary Charge, Gwalior Political Agency.
Mills, H., 1st Class Sub-Assistant Commissary-General.
Moffat, A. K., 3rd Class Executive Engineer, Department Public Works, 2nd Circle, Punjab.
Morgan, W. D., Commanding 32nd Native Infantry.
Moxon, G. G., Deputy Inspector-General of Police, Central Provinces.
Mulcaster, W. E., Commanding 5th Bengal Cavalry.
Mundy, C. F. M., Presidency Pay-master and Pay-master to the Queen's Troops.

CAPTAINS.

MacAndrew, T. F., 1st Class Assistant Commissioner, Oude.
Macdonald, J., Revenue Surveyor, Scinde.
MacDougall, W. C., 1st Class Assistant, Stud Department, Haupper.
Mackenzie, A. M., Officiating Commandant, Deolee Irregular Force.

CAPTAINS.—*(Continued.)*

Mackenzie, H., Secretary to the Chief Commissioner, Central Provinces.
Mackenzie, J. M., Doing duty, Murree Convalescent Depôt.
MacLean, G. S., Officiating 1st Class Assistant Commissary-General, Saugor.
Macpherson, H. T., v. c., Commanding 3rd Goorkha Regiment, Acting Commandant, 2nd Goorkha Regiment.
Macqueen, A., Officiating 1st Class Sub-Assistant Commissary-General, Delhi.
Maisey, F. C., Deputy Judge Advocate-General, Sirhind District.
Malleson, G. B., Secretary, Military Finance Department.
Manning, H. D., Commandant, Azimgurh District Police.
Marshall, W. E., 1st Class Assistant Engineer, Department Public Works, Punjab.
Martin, D. W., Deputy Assistant Quarter-Master General of the Army, Rohilcund.
Martin, J. P., Second in Command, 41st Native Infantry, and Officiating Station Interpreter, Morar, Gwalior.
Martineau, E. M., 1st Class Sub-Assistant Commissary-General, Allahabad.
Maxwell, H., Deputy Assistant Quarter-Master General of the Army, Presidency Division.
Mayne, C. T. O., Assistant Commissioner, Central Provinces, Jubbulpore.
McDougall, C. A.
McGrigor, W. T.
McNair, G. A., Acting Commandant, 20th Native Infantry.
Mercer, T. W., 1st Class Assistant Commissioner, Punjab, Kangra.
Merrick, T. C., 1st Class Executive Engineer, Department Public Works, Irrigation Department, North-Western Provinces.
Miles, C. W., Europe, Private Affairs, 3 years.
Millar, J. C., Cantonment Joint-Magistrate, Jullunder.
Millett, A. H., Placed at disposal of Punjab Government.
Millett, H. L., Second in Command, 5th Punjab Cavalry.
Mocatta, D., District Superintendent of Police, Rawul Pindee.
Moncrieff, A. P. S., Assistant Commissioner, Chota Nagpore.
Montagu, A. W., Officiating Brigade-Major, Scalkote.

lxiii

CAPTAINS.—*(Continued.)*

Moore, J. A. H., Europe, Medical Certificate, 15 months.
Morton, B. W. D., 2nd Class Deputy Commissioner, Assam, Gowalparah.
Moseley, R. S., Officiating District Superintendent of Police, Hissar.
Munro, A. A., Officiating Deputy Commissioner, Kohat.
Murray, C., Commanding Sebundy Sappers and Miners.
Murray, J. T., Commanding 14th Bengal Cavalry.
Mylne, W. C. R., Officiating 1st Class Deputy Assistant Commissary-General, Umballah.

LIEUTENANTS.

MacFarlane, C., Officiating Cantonment Joint-Magistrate, Mooltan.
Macintyre, D., Second in Command, 2nd Goorkha Regiment.
Mackenzie, F. J. N., Staff Officer, Punjab Irregular Force.
Maclean, C. S., Officiating Adjutant, 5th Punjab Cavalry.
Maidman, G. E. J., Adjutant, East India Regiment and Quarter-Master.
Manson, G. W., District Superintendent of Police, Punjab, Derajat.
Mathias, H. V., Commanding Nagode Divisional Police.
McQueen, J. W., Second in Command, 4th Punjab Infantry, Officiating Commandant.
Melville, A. B., 2nd Assistant, Grand Topographical Survey of India, Cashmere Series.
Menzies, O., District Superintendent of Police, Punjab, Shahpore.
Miles, F. N., Europe, Medical Certificate, 3 years.
Miller, J. C., Adjutant, 12th Native Infantry.
Mitchell, W. C., Doing duty, Delhi.
Morton, H., Second in Command, 40th Native Infantry.
Munro, C. A., District Superintendent of Police, Arracan.
Murray, W. G., Assistant Surveyor, Topographical Survey, Gwalior and Central India.
Musgrave, W., Second in Command, 15th Bengal Cavalry.

N.

MAJORS.

Nation, J. L., Commanding 9th Bengal Police Battalion.
Nedham, A. G., Doing duty, Benares.

MAJORS.—(Continued.)

Nelson, F. J., Brigade-Major, Benares.
Nicoll, H., Brigade-Major, Delhi.

CAPTAINS.

Nembhard, W., 1st Class Deputy Commissioner, Central Provinces, Jubbulpore.
Nicholson, C. J., Europe, Medical Certificate, 4 years.
Nightingale, C. W., 2nd Class Executive Engineer, Department Public Works, Punjab.
Nightingale, M. R., Fort Adjutant, Fort William, and Superintendent of Gentlemen Cadets.
Norman, F. B., 2nd Class Deputy Assistant Quarter-Master General of the Army, Lahore.
Norman, H. W., C. B., Secretary to Government of India, Military Department.

LIEUTENANTS.

Newmarch, O. R., 1st Class Sub-Assistant Commissary-General, Lucknow.
Noble, H. N., Officiating District Superintendent of Police, Moradabad.
Norgate, J. T., Second in Command, 14th Native Infantry.
Nowell, R. A., Europe, Private Affairs, 2 years.

O.

MAJORS.

Oakes, G. N., 1st Class Deputy Commissioner, South-Western Frontier Agency, Maunbhoom.
Ouseley, R., Cantonment Joint-Magistrate, Saugor.

CAPTAINS.

Obbard, H. S., Commanding 41st Native Infantry.
Ogilvie, C. S. W., 1st Class Deputy Assistant Commissary-General, Presidency.
Ogilvie, J. S., 2nd Class Deputy Assistant Commissary-General, Meean Meer.
Oldfield, H. T., Europe, Private Affairs, 3 years.
Ouseley, R., Officiating Assistant Commissioner, 1st Class, and City Magistrate, Lucknow.

CAPTAINS.—*(Continued.)*

Owen, A. W., 1st Class Assistant Engineer, Department Public Works, North-Western Provinces.
Owen, S. R. J., 2nd Class Assistant Engineer, Department Public Works, North-Western Provinces.

LIEUTENANTS.

Oakes, R. E., Revenue Surveyor, Saugor and Nerbudda.
O'Donel, C., Adjutant, 41st Native Infantry.
O'Dowda, J. W., Officiating Assistant Inspector-General of Police, Rohilcund.
Ollivant, A., District Superintendent of Police, 4th Grade, Jhansi.
Ommanney, E. L., 3rd Class Assistant Commissioner, Punjab, Dehra Ishmael Khan.
Orman, C. E., Cantonment Joint-Magistrate, Roorkee.
Osborn, H. R., Second in Command, 5th Bengal Cavalry.
Osborn, R. D., Adjutant, 12th Bengal Cavalry.
Owen, A. G., Second in Command, 16th Bengal Cavalry.

P.

LIEUTENANT-COLONEL.

Phayre, A. P., Chief Commissioner of British Burmah.

MAJORS.

Parrott, B., Second Class Assistant, Stud Department, Kurruntadhee.
Paterson, A. H., 1st Class District Superintendent of Police, Patna.
Paton, J. S., Deputy Quarter-Master General of the Army.
Plowden, A. C., Europe, Medical Certificate, 18 months.
Pughe, J. R., 1st Class Deputy Inspector-General of Police, Burdwan.

CAPTAINS.

Packe, C. F., Second in Command, 3rd Bengal Cavalry.
Paget, W. H., Commanding 5th Punjab Cavalry.
Palliser, C. H., Commanding 10th Bengal Cavalry.
Parsons, J. E. B., 1st Class Assistant Commissioner, Loodianah, Punjab.
Paske, E. H., 3rd Class Deputy Commissioner, Goojerat, Punjab.
Paske, W., 1st Class Assistant Commissioner, Punjab, Delhi.

CAPTAINS.—*(Continued.)*

Perkins, J., 2nd Class Deputy Commissioner, Sutlanpore, Oude.
Peter, C. W., Officiating Interpreter and Quarter-Master, 5th Native Infantry.
Pierce, T., 2nd Assistant to Commissioner, Ajmere.
Pierson, W. S., Europe, Medical Certificate, 30 months.
Pollock, F. R., 1st Class Deputy Commissioner, Dehra Ghazee Khan, Punjab.
Poulton, H. B. A., Deputy Judge Advocate-General, Presidency Division.
Price, G., Civil Architect, Calcutta, Officiating Superintending Engineer, Department Public Works, 1st Circle, Bengal.
Priestley, A. G., 2nd Class Executive Engineer, Department Public Works, 2nd Circle, North-Western Provinces.

LIEUTENANTS.

Parker, Sir G. L. M., *Bart.*, Doing duty, 3rd Goorkha Regiment, Officiating Second in Command.
Parlby, B. S. B., Officiating Fort Adjutant, Fort William, and Superintendent of Cadets.
Parsons, Q. D., Placed at disposal of Punjab Government for Police employment.
Pasley, G. J., Adjutant, Bhaugulpore Hill Rangers (Police.)
Peacock, H. P., Second in Command, Governor-General's Body Guard.
Pennington, C. R., Adjutant, 13th Bengal Cavalry, Officiating Second in Command.
Phillips, G. F. M., Adjutant, Ajmere and Mhairwarrah Police Corps.
Pitcher, H. W., Adjutant, 4th Punjab Infantry.
Powlett, P. W., 3rd Class Assistant Commissioner, Goojranwallah, Punjab.
Pratt, H. M., Doing duty, 5th Punjab Infantry.
Procter, M. M., Cantonment Joint-Magistrate, Fyzabad.
Pullan, A., Doing duty, 14th Bengal Cavalry, and Officiating Cantonment Joint-Magistrate, Morar, Gwalior.

Q.

CAPTAINS.

Quin, H. E., 2nd Class Assistant Engineer, Department Public Works, 1st Circle, Punjab.
Quin, T., Second in Command, 6th Punjab Infantry.

R.

LIEUTENANT-COLONELS.

Ramsay, G., Resident at Nepal.
Ramsay, H., c. b., Commissioner of Kumaon.
Richardson, W., Commanding 44th Native Infantry.
Ryves, W. H., Commanding 8th Bengal Cavalry.

MAJORS.

Raban, H., 1st Class Deputy Inspector of Police, Patna.
Rattray, T., Inspector of Police, Lower Provinces.
Reid, B. T.
Reid, C., c. b., Commanding 2nd Goorkha Regiment.
Renny, R., Commanding 3rd Sikh Infantry.
Richards, E. J., Commanding Ajmere and Mhairwarrah Police Corps.
Richards, S., Deputy Assistant Adjutant-General, Presidency.
Richardson, J. F., c. b., Commanding 6th Bengal Cavalry.
Roberts, C. J., Commanding 17th Bengal Cavalry.
Ross, J., Brigade-Major, Sealkote.
Rothney, O. E., Commanding 5th Goorkha.
Rowlatt, E. A., Deputy Commissioner, Assam.
Ryan, E. M., 4th Class Deputy Commissioner, Burmah.

CAPTAINS.

Rawlins, J. S., District Superintendent of Police, Saharunpore.
Reeves, G. J.
Reid, J., 1st Class Deputy Commissioner, Oude.
Reveley, W., District Superintendent of Police, Tirhoot.
Roberts, G. R., 2nd Class Deputy Assistant Commissary-General.
Robinson, A., Second in Command, 28th Native Infantry.
Rose, H., 1st Class Executive Engineer, Department Public Works.
Ross, E. D. R., 4th Class Executive Engineer.
Rowcroft, G. C., Officiating Second in Command, 35th Native Infantry.
Ryall, B., District Superintendent of Police, Oude.
Ryder, S. C. D., Station Interpreter, Jubbulpore.

LIEUTENANTS.

Ramsay, M. H., District Superintendent of Police, Jullundur.
Repton, H. M., Placed at disposal, North-Western Provinces.

LIEUTENANTS.—*(Continued.)*

Rice, H. C. P., Officiating Second in Command, 1st Sikh Infantry.
Ricketts, M. P., Assistant Commissioner, Nursingpore.
Ripley, F. J., Adjutant, 11th Native Infantry.
Rogers, B., Adjutant, 15th Native Infantry.
Rogers, R. G., Officiating Second in Command, 20th Native Infantry.
Ross, A. G., Doing duty, 6th Punjab Infantry.
Ross, D., Adjutant, 42nd Native Infantry.
Rutherfurd, T. W., Doing duty, 14th Native Infantry.
Ryan, W., c. B. Adjutant, 3rd Punjab Cavalry.
Rynd, P. C., Doing duty, 19th Native Infantry.

S.

LIEUTENANT-COLONELS.

Scott, J. C., Deputy Commissary-General, 3rd Circle.
Shakespear, J. T., Europe, Private Affairs, 3 years.
Sherwill, W. S., Revenue Surveyor, Dinagepore.

MAJORS.

Sherwill, J. L., Officiating Revenue Surveyor, Maunbhoom.
Simeon, R. G., Assistant Adjutant-General, Meerut.
Simpson, E. J., Assistant Commissary-General.
Smith, E. F., Superintendent, Elephant Keddahs, Dacca.
Smith, F. H., Commanding 18th Bengal Cavalry.
Smith, J., Commanding Sebundy Levy, Sumbulpore.
Sneyd, N. R., Second in Command, 16th Native Infantry.
Spence, J. K., Commissioner, Nagpore, Central Provinces.
Stafford, W. J. F., Commanding 22nd Native Infantry.
Stainforth, F. G., 1st Class Assistant Engineer, Department Public Works, Lahore and Peshawur Roads.
Stewart, D. M., 2nd Assistant Adjutant-General of the Army.
Stuart, C. B., 3rd Class Executive Engineer, Department Public Works, 2nd Circle, North-Western Provinces.

CAPTAINS.

Sandilands, E. N., 3rd Class Executive Engineer, Department Public Works, Lahore and Peshawur Roads.

CAPTAINS.—*(Continued.)*

Scott, C. H. S., Brigade-Major, Gwalior.
Scott, E. H., Second in Command, 24th Native Infantry.
Scott, T. F. O., Second in Command, 44th Native Infantry.
Shaw, C., Second in Command, 2nd Bengal Cavalry.
Shaw, C. R., 1st Class Assistant Commissioner, Fyzabad, Oude.
Sheffield, W., 2nd Class Barrack-Master, Umritsur.
Sherer, J. F., Commanding the Kooky Levy, and Assistant to the Superintendent of Cachar.
Sibley, T. H., 2nd Class Assistant Commissary-General.
Smith, C. F., District Superintendent of Police, Punjab, Goorgaon.
Smith, O. L., District Superintendent of Police, Oude.
Smith, W., Cantonment Joint-Magistrate, Allahabad.
Smyly, J. B., 1st Class Assistant Commissioner, Punjab.
Somerville, M. R., Second in Command, 5th Punjab Infantry.
Sparke, J. G.
Spilsbury, E. J., 3rd Class Deputy Commissioner, Bristish Burmah, Myan-oung.
Stafford, J. F., Commanding 19th Native Infantry.
Staples, T., District Superintendent of Police, Punjab, Hissar.
Steel, J. A., 2nd Class Deputy Commissioner, Baraitch, Oude.
Stephenson, F. J., Interpreter and Quarter-Master, 3rd Bengal European Infantry.
Stewart, R., Superintendent of Cachar.
Stewart, W. F.
Stone, E. G., Europe, Medical Certificate, 2 years.
Stubbs, W. H., Officiating Garrison Quarter-Master, Fort William.
Swayne, J. D., 3rd Class Executive Engineer, Department Public Works, Burdwan Circle, Bengal.
Swiney, G., District Superintendent of Police, 2nd Grade, Jaloun.
Sykes, J., 1st Class Sub-Assistant Commissary-General.

LIEUTENANTS.

Sadler, E. T., Doing duty, 28th Native Infantry.
Sampson, D. T. H., Adjutant, 9th Bengal Cavalry.
Sandeman, R. G., 3rd Class Assistant Commissioner, Punjab, Peshawur District.

LIEUTENANTS.—*(Continued.)*

Sanderson, H. B., Doing duty, 21st Native Infantry.
Sconce, H., 2nd Class (Officiating 1st Class) Deputy Commissioner in Assam, Nowgong.
Sharpe, C. F., District Superintendent of Police, 2nd Grade, Oude.
Simpson, E. H. C., Doing duty, 4th Bengal Cavalry.
Simpson, G. B. C., Doing duty, 14th Bengal Cavalry.
Sitwell, F. H. M., District Superintendent of Police, 3rd Grade, Azimgurh.
Skinner, R. M., Assistant Superintendent of Police, 1st Grade, Bengal, Sarun.
Smith, B. N., Doing duty, Her Majesty's 8th Hussars.
Smith, M. G., Adjutant, 8th Native Infantry.
Snow, W., Adjutant, 1st Punjab Infantry.
Stafford, B. T., Second in Command, 22nd Native Infantry.
Stainforth, G. B., Adjutant, 4th Sikh Infantry.
Stainforth, R., District Superintendent of Police, 4th Grade, Oude, Baraitch.
Stewart, A., Cantonment Joint-Magistrate, Meean Meer, and Officiating Station Interpreter.
Stewart, C. E., Adjutant, 5th Punjab Infantry.
Stewart, G., Doing duty, 11th Bengal Cavalry.
Sutherland, S. S., District Superintendent of Police, Central Provinces.
Swetenham, E., 4th Class Executive Engineer, Department Public Works 2nd Circle, North-Western Provinces.
Szczopanski, H. C. A., 3rd Class Assistant Commissioner, Punjab, Kohat.

T.

MAJORS.

Taylor, R. G., Commissioner of the Derajat District.
Ternan, A. H., 1st Class Deputy Commissioner, North-Western Provinces, Jhansi.
Thomson, R. L., 2nd Class Deputy Inspector-General of Police, Bhaugulpore.
Thurburn, F. A. V., 2nd Class Deputy Commissioner, Oude.
Tickell, J., Cantonment Joint-Magistrate, Umballah.

lxxi

MAJORS.—(Continued.)

Tickell, S. R., 1st Class Deputy Commissioner, Burmah.
Tronson, R. N., Deputy Inspector-General, Mooltan Police.
Trower, C. P., Deputy Judge Advocate-General, Saugor and Gwalior.
Tulloh, J. S. D.
Turnbull, M. T., Army Clothing Agent, Fort William.
Turner, A., Deputy Judge Advocate-General, Benares.
Tytler, J. M. B. F., C. B., Europe, Medical Certificate, 18 months.

CAPTAINS.

Taylor, H. A., 1st Class Sub-Assistant Commissary-General, Gwalior.
Taylor, T., Second in Command, 13th Native Infantry.
Thelwal, J. B., C. B., Commanding 21st Native Infantry.
Thompson, E., 2nd Class Deputy Commissioner, Seetapore, Oude.
Thompson, G. H., Revenue Surveyor, 6th Division, Hazareebagh.
Thomson, J. E., Officiating 1st Class Sub-Assistant Commissary-General, Darjeeling.
Thomson, W. B., Assistant Commissioner, Central Provinces, Jubbulpore.
Tovey, J. T., 4th Class Executive Engineer, Department Public Works, Lahore and Peshawur Roads.
Tulloch, A., District Superintendent of Police, Punjab.
Twynam, E. J. L., 3rd Class Executive Engineer, Department Public Works, British Burmah.
Tyler, W. G. B., 2nd Class Deputy Commissioner, Lullutpore.
Tyrwhitt, E., Divisional Superintendent of Police, Meerut.
Tytler, J. A., V. C.

LIEUTENANTS.

Temple, A. B., Adjutant, 3rd Goorkha Regiment.
Temple, E., Adjutant, Bhopal Levy.
Thain, A. S., District Superintendent of Police, 3rd Grade, Lullutpore.
Thompson, H., Adjutant, 39th Native Infantry.
Thomson, G. C., Second in Command, 1st Bengal Cavalry.
Trevenen, J., Europe, Private Affairs, 2 years.
Tulloch, A., Quarter-Master, 22nd Native infantry.
Turner, F. R., Adjutant, 4th Native Infantry.

LIEUTENANTS.—*(Continued.)*

Tweedie, W., Officiating 3rd Class Assistant Commissioner, Hyderabad Commission.
Tyndall, H., Second in Command, 2nd Punjab Infantry.

U.

CAPTAINS.

Urmston, H. B., 3rd Class Deputy Commissioner, Punjab, Rhotuck.

LIEUTENANTS.

Upperton, J., Doing duty, 19th Bengal Cavalry.
Urquhart, B. C., Europe, Private Affairs, 2 years.

V.

LIEUTENANT-COLONEL.

Voyle, F. E., 1st Class Deputy Commissioner, Mooltan, Punjab.

MAJORS.

Vaughan, J. L., Commanding 5th Punjab Cavalry.
Verner, G., Commissioner of Arracan.

CAPTAINS.

Vanrenen, A. D., Revenue Surveyor, Jhansi and Bundlecund.
Von Andlan, The Baron F., Second in Command, 3rd Goorkha Regiment, Officiating Commandant.

LIEUTENANTS.

Vander-Gucht, T. E., Doing duty, Benares.
Vivian, A., Second in Command, 3rd Punjab Cavalry.

W.

MAJORS.

Whish, G. P., Brigade Major, Meerut.
Wilson, H. M., Commanding Bhaugulpore Hill Rangers.
Wilson, T. F., C. B., Commanding 7th Bengal Cavalry.
Wright, J. A., Cantonment Joint-Magistrate, Morar, Gwalior.

lxxiii

MAJORS.—(Continued.)

Wright, T., Assistant Adjutant-General of the Army, Peshawur.
Wroughton, R. C., Officiating Deputy Commissary-General, Presidency.

CAPTAINS.

Waddington, H. F., 3rd Class Deputy Commissioner, Central Provinces, Dumoh.
Warde, C., Cantonment Joint-Magistrate, Agra.
Watson, J. T., District Superintendent of Police, 2nd Grade, Benares.
Weld, G., Fort Adjutant, Chunar.
Wemyss, H. M., Brigade Major, Lucknow.
Wheeler, G., Cantonment Joint-Magistrate, Jhansi.
Whish, H. E., 3rd Class Executive Engineer, Department of Public Works, Irrigation Department, North-Western Provinces.
Willes, J. T., 1st Class Assistant Commissary-General, Benares.
Williams, G. A., Second in Command, 4th Sikh Infantry.
Williams, H. P., Pay-master, Lahore, Meean Meer.
Williamson, Commanding 26th Native Infantry.
Wintle, E. H. C., Cantonment Joint-Magistrate, Dum-Dum.
Wroughton, H. R., 1st Class Sub-Assistant Commissary-General, Fyzabad.
Wynch, H. P. W., Europe, Private Affairs, 30 months.

LIEUTENANTS.

Walker, R. J., Doing duty, 17th Native Infantry.
Walter, C. K. M., Assistant to Governor-General's Agent, Rajpootana.
Ward, W. J., Second in Command, 7th Bengal Cavalry.
Waterfield, W. G., 3rd Class Assistant Commissioner, Punjab, Delhi.
Watson, T. J., Second in Command, 17th Bengal Cavalry.
Wavell, L., Doing duty, 22nd Native Infantry.
Way, G. A., Doing duty, 1st Native Infantry.
Westmacott, G. K., Second in Command, 1st Cavalry Hyderabad Contingent.
Williams, B., Officiating Adjutant, 8th Bengal Cavalry.
Wimberley, E. B., Officiating Assistant to the Agent of the Governor-General for the States of Rajpootana.

LIEUTENANTS.—*(Continued.)*

Winson, W., Commanding 18th Native Infantry.
Wroughton, W., Doing duty, 4th Punjab Cavalry.

Y.

LIEUTENANT-COLONEL.

Young, K., C. B., Judge Advocate-General.

LIEUTENANT.

Young, G. G., 3rd Class Assistant Commissioner, Punjab, Goordaspore.

www.ingramcontent.com/pod-product-compliance
Lightning Source LLC
Chambersburg PA
CBHW020831020526
44114CB00040B/461